*Number Eighteen: Centennial Series of
The Association of Former Students,
Texas A&M University*

Los Mesteños

Los Mesteños

Spanish Ranching in Texas,
1721–1821

by

JACK JACKSON

Illustrated by the Author

Texas A&M University Press   COLLEGE STATION

Copyright © 1986 by Jack Jackson
All rights reserved

Library of Congress Cataloging-in-Publication Data
Jackson, Jack, 1941–2006
  Los mestenos.
  (Centennial series of the Association of Former
Students, Texas A&M University; no. 18)
  Bibliography: p.
  Includes index.
  1. Ranch life—Texas—History—18th century.
2. Ranch life—Texas—History—19th century.
3. Cattle trade—Texas—History—18th century.
4. Cattle trade—Texas—History—19th century.
5. Spaniards—Texas—History—18th century.
6. Spaniards—Texas—History—19th century.
7. Texas—History—To 1846. I. Title. II. Series.
F389.J25   1986   976.4'04   84-40561
ISBN 0-89096-230-8
ISBN 13: 978-1-58544-558-5 (pbk.)
ISBN 10: 1-58544-558-4 (pbk.)

Maufactured in the United States of America
Third printing, 2006

*For my Aunt Mattie,
who thought our folks brought the
idea of ranching to Texas,
and for Jim Jaeggli,
who gave me a glimpse of what was already here*

CONTENTS

Figures	xiii
Tables	xv
Preface	xvii
Abbreviations Used in Notes	xxi
Introduction	3
1. The Coming of the Cattle: *Entradas* and Conflicts	8
2. The Missions at Their Zenith: *La Cruz y Las Espuelas*	32
3. A Stirring in the Cradle: Raisers or Thieves?	50
4. "A Great Number of Cattle": For the Taking...	86
5. "We Are Enraged": Rustling and the Law	124
6. "La Luiciana": Up the Trail	172
7. "They Persist in Their Unjust Claims": Taxation without Representation	222
8. "Could They but Be Restored": Protests Abounding	278
9. "Damaged and Troubled Men": The First Big Roundup	320
10. "Released from Their Obligation": Slaughters and Secularization	376
11. "As Many Horses as Circumstances Permit": Neighboring Markets, Bold Smugglers	424
12. "By Risking Their Hides a Little": At Revolution's Threshold	462
13. "Hopelessly Lost in Their Misery": Disruptions of a Decade	524
14. A Look beyond 1821: The Legacy's Impact	584

APPENDICES

A. Cattle, Branded and *Orejano*, Exported from Texas under Governor Domingo Cabello, 1779–86	620
B. List of "Restored" Ranchers, Sent to Commandant General Ugarte by Governor Martínez Pacheco, October 14, 1787, with Letter No. 21	622
C. List of Those "Legitimately Engaged in the Business of Raising Cattle," July 18, 1795	623

D. "Notizia de los Ranchos . . ." (Notice of Ranches . . .),
Written at "Santa Cruz y Paso de las Mujeres" by
Gavino Delgado, November 13, 1809   624
E. "Relación de los Extrangeros . . . de la Jurisdicción de
Nacogdoches situados en Bayupier" (Account of the
Foreigners . . . of the Jurisdiction of Nacogdoches Living
in Bayou Pierre), by José María Guadiana, April 14, 1810   625
F. "Relación de los Extrangeros . . . en esta Jurisdicción de
Nacogdoches" (Account of the Foreigners . . . in This
Jurisdiction of Nacogdoches), by José María Guadiana,
May 8–12, 1810   626
G. "Noticia de los Ranchos . . . , Jurisdicción de Nacogdoches,
el nombre del praxe, el de el dueño, y la distancia . . ."
(Notice of the Ranches . . . , Jurisdiction of Nacogdoches,
the Name of the Place, That of the Owner, and the Distance
. . .), by José María Guadiana, April 14, 1810   627
H. "Lista de los Vecinos que pueden ser nombrano síndicos de
Ranchos . . ." (List of Citizens Who Can Be Designated
Commissioners of Ranches) by José María Guadiana,
June 14, 1810   629
I. *Síndico* Reports of the Béxar Jurisdiction, Taken in the
Year 1810   630
J. "Síndicos de Ranchos" (Commissioners of Ranches),
August (?), 1812   634
K. "Lista varios Ranchos y Haciendas g. sitan en este
Jurisdicción [Villa del Refugio] y sus dueños" (List of the
Various Ranches and Haciendas That Are Situated in this
Jurisdiction [Villa of Refugio] and Their Owners), by Felipe
Roque de la Portilla, December 22, 1814   635
L. "Noticia de los vecinos en este ciudad [Béxar] que tienan
ganado mayor y menor, caballos y mulas . . . sin expresar el
número" (Notice of the Citizens of This City [Béxar] Who
Have Cattle, Sheep, Horses, and Mules . . . without Showing
Their Numbers), by Francisco Flores and José Manuel
Granados, June 26, 1817   637
M. Partial List of Nueces Strip Ranches, Showing Acres in the
Survey and Amount of Land Confirmed by the Texas
Legislature, 1850–52   638
N. Brands
Brand Section A. Some of the First Brands Found Recorded

Contents

xi

    in the Bexar Archives; Lieutenant General Simón de
      Arocha's Export License Book Entry dated May 19, 1778   644
    Brand Section B. Brand Book for Opelousas-Attakapas
      Districts, 1739–1888 (Louisiana): A Selection of Marks
      Used in Saint Martin Parish and Saint Landry Parish   645
    Brand Section C. Register of the Marks Used by the
      Inhabitants of This District [San Estéban Tombecbe] to
      Mark Their Animals, 1795   648
    Brand Section D. Northern List for the Recognition of
      Brands (Undated)   649
    Brand Section E. Brands and Marks, Nacogdoches-Trinidad
      (Undated)   652
    Brand Section F. List of Cattle Confiscated from the
      Insurgents Who Have Left This Capital [Béxar], Their
      Number and Brands, February 28, 1814   656
    Brand Section G. List of Recaptured Animals Formed for
      the Commandant General, Showing Brands with a
      Description, February 8, 1820   657
    Brand Section H. List in Which Are Noted Brands of Stray
      Animals (*bestias mostrencal*) Kept at Béxar for the Free
      State of Coahuila y Texas, 1827–34   658
Bibliography   661
Index   677

FIGURES

Figure 1. Title page of the New Regulations of 1772 — 111
Figure 2. Signature page of Ranchers' Power of Attorney — 329
Figure 3. Roundup Report of Raphael Martínez Pacheco — 351

MAPS

"El Norte," Provinces Bordering Texas, Late Eighteenth Century — 7
Missions of Béxar, Showing Their Irrigated Fields and
  Agostaderos (Summer Pastures) — 39
Ranchos of the San Antonio River Valley, 1794 — 92
San Antonio de Béxar — 151
Lands Assigned by the 1787 Roundup Agreement — 324
Ranchos of the Nueces Strip — 445
Ranchos of Nacogdoches, 1810 — 492
Texas and the Eastern Provincias Internas, under Brigadier
  General Joaquín de Arredondo, 1813 — 536

TABLES

1. Livestock at Béxar Missions, 1762 — 36
2. Cattle at La Bahía Missions, 1758–83 — 37
3. Report of Roundup, December 2, 1780 — 220
4. Cattle-Export Permits Issued in 1781 — 227
5. Report of Roundup, February 26, 1782, Pertaining to 1781 — 230
6. Report of Roundup, December 20, 1782 — 245
7. Report of Roundup, December 28, 1783 — 259
8. Major Cattle Exporters, 1779–86 — 312
9. Governor Gayoso's Count of Herds in Natchez, 1792 and 1794 — 433

PREFACE

I have written this book out of a love for the story of ranching in Texas and a curiosity about the Spanish tradition that stands behind it. The project has been accomplished without generous endowments, institutional recognition, direction, or assistance, or the usual amenities associated with prolonged efforts of scholarship. In this undertaking I have been sustained by only a small circle of friends and fellow researchers, all as amazed as I at the richness of the historical record and the dearth of published information about it.

My interest in the subject comes from a background of ranching itself. I was born on the Ecleto Creek, in Wilson County, squarely amid the pasturelands contested by missionaries and private cattlemen of the eighteenth century. My family entered the contest when great-great-grandfather Solomon B. Jackson registered his brand at Béxar in 1850. Better late than never, as the saying goes. When Sol died of cholera several years later, his orphans were sheltered by that worthy old Texian patriot and stockman Creed Taylor.

These three boys were schooled in the rough-and-tumble variety of frontier stock raising practiced in South Texas when the term "maverick" first came into being. Soon one son married into the Wests, a family involved in the Regulator-Moderator War, and my roots were further entangled in the venerable tradition of fussin' and feudin', Texas style. Brothers, cousins, and nephews later went "up the trail"; one branch of the family relocated in Oklahoma and New Mexico as a result of the experience. Others stayed on the "Clayto," and there they remain. Long before the Jacksons and Wests reached Texas, another of my forefathers, named Trammell, cut a little one-horse trace into the Spanish province that men like Austin and Houston traveled to reach their destiny. I am as Texan as they come, and proud of it.

This pride in the accomplishments of my ancestors, however, does not keep a surge of appreciation from rising when I read of what other Texans were doing a century before them. Nor is this pride diminished in any way by knowing about the stock-raising exploits of these Spanish-Mexican rancheros and realizing how much their legacy influenced my own people. Pride is an infectious thing and can join people as much as divide them. When nothing else could prompt early Texans of diverse ethnic origins to work together, it was a fierce pride in their stock that did it. Ranching, more than anything else, forged a new society in this ancient land, and its imprint can still be felt, fading though it is.

Although I have labored outside the academic circle to piece together missing chapters of this sprawling saga, much work has preceded me. My debt and dependence on these groundbreaking studies will become evident soon enough. Special mention should go to Sandra L. Myres, one of the first to awaken us to the Spanish era that foreshadows our present ranching heritage. Charles Ramsdell, Odie Faulk, and Robert Thonhoff have also made notable contributions to this awareness. Tidbits can be sifted from a number of secondary sources, not to mention the largely unused Spanish archives themselves, but I have tried here to assemble everything into one coherent package. In so doing, I hope to present not the end but the beginning of inquiry.

This is not meant to be an "elitist" book. I have retained the Spanish documentation's view of Indians—whether the commentator was illiterate cowman or educated priest—rather than attempting to reconcile this harsh view with contemporary understanding of the Indian's culture and plight in face of white encroachment. I handle my footnotes in a casual fashion, generally placing them at the end of a paragraph or section, rather than attempting to account for every sentence and citation therein.

Because many of us still lack a thorough grasp of Spanish, I direct the reader when possible to available translations. Slowly but surely this body of information has been growing, and now many archival documents are accessible to English readers. A number are found at the University of Texas and other such centers of learning. John Wheat, the current translator of the Béxar Archives, in the University of Texas Archives, has been generous with help in deciphering terms related to early Texas stock raising. G. Douglas Inglis, during his recent work with the Nacogdoches Archives, offered much good advice on the historical overview and supplied me with items gleaned from the archives in Seville. John Ogden Leal, Spanish archivist at the Clerk's Office, Bexar County Courthouse, has aided considerably with his extensive knowledge of San Antonio's first families, land records, and so on, as has Richard C. Garay, another colonial scholar working without the support and recognition due him.

The staffs of the Eugene C. Barker Texas History Center (University of Texas Archives), the Texas State Library, the Catholic Archives of Texas (Chancery Office, Austin), and the General Land Office have done everything possible to assist, as have those at the Daughters of the Republic of Texas Alamo Library, San Antonio; Our Lady of the Lake University, San Antonio; and elsewhere. I would be remiss if I did not mention the years of accumulated research, freely shared, of J. T. Jaeggli, Jr., former chairman of the Wilson County Historical Commission; the Reverend Marion A. Habig, O.F.M., Saint Augustine Friary, Chicago; and Robert H. Thonhoff, resident historian of Karnes County. Donald E. Worcester, of Texas Christian University, read the manuscript and suggested ways to improve it, some of which I have hardheadedly ignored. I trust that the influence of fellow artist José Cisneros shows in my illustrations, for no other has come as close as he to accurately depicting the "Riders of the Borderlands" in pen and ink. Jo Mora might have been another, but California was his consuming passion (would that he had been dazzled instead by the Lone Star). Their drawings have been my inspiration. Thanks also to Vicki Bell, who typed and retyped my scribbled pages with keen eye and amazing faithfulness. My wife, Christina, encouraged me in this project and helped me immensely during the final, tedious phases of editing.

Last (but perhaps foremost) comes J. Frank Dobie, whose writings opened up to me a side of Texas that, as I was growing up, I sensed but dimly understood. I like to think that we could have had a lively "discussion" about what is in this book.

ABBREVIATIONS USED IN NOTES

See Bibliography for full citations.

ACZ   Archivo del Convento de Guadalupe (Zacatecas), Old Spanish Missions Research Library, Our Lady of the Lake University, San Antonio
AGI   Archivo General de Indias, University of Texas Archives, Austin
AGN   Archivo General y Público de la Nación, University of Texas Archives, Austin
ASFG Archivo San Francisco el Grande, University of Texas Archives, Austin
BA   Béxar Archives, University of Texas Archives, Austin
BAM   Béxar Archives, Microfilm Collection, University of Texas Archives, Austin
BAT   Béxar Archives, Translations, University of Texas Archives, Austin
BCSA Bexar County Spanish Archives, Bexar County Courthouse, County Clerk's Office, San Antonio
CA   Catholic Archives of Texas, Chancery Office, Austin
GLO   General Land Office of Texas, Spanish Archives, Austin
LA   Laredo Archives, Saint Mary's University, San Antonio
MA   Matamoros Archives, University of Texas Archives
NA   Nacogdoches Archives, Texas State Archives, Austin
SA   Saltillo Archives, University of Texas Archives, Austin

Los Mesteños

It is deeply to be regretted that those venerable [Spanish] archives could not have been preserved and protected, alike from ignorant, wanton vandalism, and the marauding speculator. The loss from these sources of destruction to the early history of our State will never be fully appreciated. The fragments left serve only to admonish us that it has been great and irreparable.
—Abner S. Lipscomb, Texas
   Supreme Court justice,
   writing in *Lewis* v. *San Antonio*, 1851

INTRODUCTION

In his classic of 1931, *The Great Plains*, Walter Prescott Webb issued a call for a history of the beginnings of the range and ranch cattle industry in southern Texas. Mentioning J. Frank Dobie's *A Vaquero of the Brush Country*, Webb observed that while it explored conditions following the Civil War it did not treat the early period. Although this task has continued to "defy" writers since, one suspects that if so inclined either of these giants could have written such a history. They were not so inclined, preferring instead to chronicle the struggle between the Anglo and Hispanic cultures in Texas for rule over the cattle kingdom. It was this quest, in which "Mexican cattle came into the presence of the mounted Texan armed with rope and six-shooter—the cowboy," as Webb rather dramatically phrased it, that occupied their attention.

Both men, though they were emotionally wed to ascendancy of the Anglo ranching tradition, still freely acknowledged the many advantages derived from cultural infusions that took place during the contest. Dobie especially, his roots planted in the Nueces country, was cognizant of the tremendous influence that the Spanish heritage exercised on the ranching practices and life-style of English-speaking people around him. He captured this legacy as no one else has in Texas, and it is to Dobie's writings that we of a later time must look for the flavor of an era. But though liberally sprinkled with spicy Spanish ingredients, his work only hints at the "early period." We come away with the feeling that a great conflict was raging, but for exactly what we are not sure. Likewise, we know who emerged the winner, but the prize is never clearly delineated, nor are the boundaries of the bequest adequately described. This ambiguity applies to the conceptual basis of ranching as much as to its tangible manifestations.

Perhaps the constraints and demands of the time made it so. Texas was then approaching its centennial celebration and had need of a wide lens with which to view the epic of its first century's accomplishments. These men certainly provided one, melding the intellectual and symbolic needs of their generation into one sweeping panorama. Now we find ourselves facing another birthday in Texas, and still no one has answered Webb's call for a study of the dynamic, formative period upon which our ranching institutions took root and flourished. Nor, in all likelihood, will the passing of this occasion be marked by much fanfare; its basis today remains little known or understood.

In 1787 the First Big Roundup was held in Texas, an event which dwarfed every corrida (roundup) conducted in the vast land until that time and every one for many years beyond. Thus the year 1987 will witness two centuries of ranching history for our people, but the fact is that the roundup held in 1787 represented a culmination of activities begun many years before in Texas. Even so, one would think such an anniversary worthy of note to a civilization founded largely upon the benefits of stock raising. In this spirit, then, *Los Mesteños* is a tribute to those beginnings, to those brave rancheros who pioneered an institution synonymous with this land and things Texan. They rode through our section of the world and left it forever changed, forever richer for the experience.

In our hectic modern era we tend to idealize the past, especially its pastoral simplicity and the quiet dignity of the rustic herdsman's life. Often the historical record reveals that such idyllic interludes were as rare then as now. If the problems were different from those that plague us today, they were nonetheless real, just as challenging and exasperating. A good example is afforded by the last quarter of the eighteenth century, particularly the decade of the 1780s. This was a difficult time for the cattlemen of Texas. Yet for some of these *ganaderos* and *criadores* it was a time of unprecedented expansion, consolidation, and prosperity. It saw the decline of the missions as the province's most powerful cattle raisers and the rise of individual, privately owned ranches to take their place. It saw the first serious attempt by the Spanish colonial administration to regulate the cattle industry and manage its growth. The trailing of cattle out of Texas to markets in Louisiana and those below the Río Grande began on a systematic basis during these years, providing the stimulating jingle of silver reales and opening new vistas to enterprising individuals. Most important, it was during this period that the major techniques of open-range stock handling were tried, tested, and proved for coming generations of ranchers from the Spanish borderlands northward to Canada.

Simply put, ranching as we now know it is the result of improvements derived from these Spanish antecedents in the Old Southwest. The truth of this is made manifest time and again as one studies the records which have survived and come down to us over the past two centuries, particularly those known as the Béxar Archives. Still, it was only during the nineteenth century, after stock raising had passed into the hands of Anglo colonists, that the institution gained widespread recognition as a distinctively Texan contribution to the frontier experience. By then, of course, it was perceived as the Anglo way of doing things and had attained mythic proportions. These myths have endured, often obscuring the antecedents. The reasons for this distortion are complex, interwoven with the exigencies of Manifest Destiny and mostly beyond the scope of this book. But the fact remains that Spanish Texans and their Indian helpers were wrestling with the identical problems their later Anglo counterparts would face, a long time before knowledge of such things was finally acquired by English-speaking Americans. The literature, or rather the official documentation, to prove this has existed from the beginning, as will be seen. The Spaniards wrote copiously about their ranching experience in Texas; it was just that we could not or did not read their accounts and therefore assumed that they had nothing to say on the subject.

They said a great deal, and most of it is very familiar to anyone who has ever chased cows on the broad pastures of Texas—be they amid thorn-infested thickets in the south, on wide-open plains along the coast, among overshadowing piney woods in the north, or through moss-draped bayous and bottomlands in the northeast. The reader should understand that because stock raising was so fundamentally a part of life in Spanish Texas it is difficult to extract information about ranching without bringing along the entire era. My aim here has been primarily to set the stage for the enactment of Commandant General Teodoro de Croix's earth-shaking cattle law of 1778 and then trace a few of its developments and complications in the San Antonio River valley. When possible I let the cattlemen speak for themselves, which tends toward longwindedness but at least exemplifies the human side of ranching. This personal dimension, after all, is what has given ranching its special significance to generations of Texans—not stale stuff like receipt books or industry statistics, but the interactions of land, men, and beasts as the rousing spectacle unfolds.

I hope that such a detailed study of Croix's controversial attempt to regulate what was an uncontrolled industry will also reveal much about how stock raising was conducted at the time. This in turn might help with an evaluation and better understanding of subsequent contributions to the legacy left us by the first ranchers of Texas, the Spanish *ganaderos* of the eighteenth century.

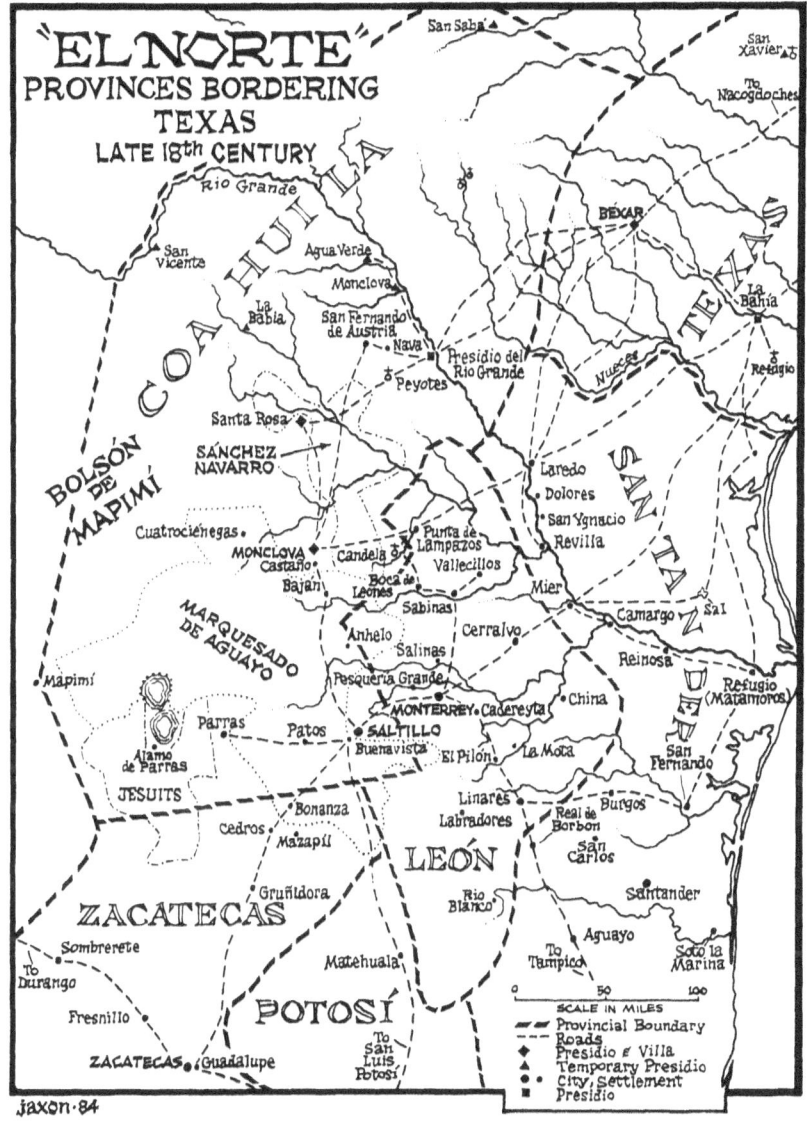

1
THE COMING OF THE CATTLE

Entradas and Conflicts

By 1775, Texas was teeming with cattle and horses, most of which were unbranded and roaming in a semiwild state. To avoid confusion, Spanish stockmen used several different terms to distinguish the animals according to their relative states of wildness. *Manso* or *ganado vacuno* (bovine animal) referred to gentle or tame stock, animals that were manageable and under control. *Alzado* referred to domestic stock that had strayed, run off, "gone wild," and was living in a wild state. *Orejano* meant stock without a mark on the ear (*oreja*) or anywhere else, hence unmarked and unbranded. *Mostrenco* was used to describe cattle with no known owner, property either abandoned or lost. When found, it had to be exhibited so that the rightful owner would have an opportunity to claim it legally. In this sense *mostrenco* stock was different from "vacant" property, or that which was totally wild and ownerless. It was the type of stray that later Texas stockmen called "maverick." The term *cimarrón* was given to stock that had run off and returned to nature. Practically speaking, it meant stock that was too wild ever to be effectively tamed and handled; the term was also used to describe runaway slaves. *Cimarrones* were the incorrigibles, in a class with bison and other beasts of the field. J. Frank Dobie's writings sometimes refer to these sly outlaws as *ladinos*.

To encompass all these fine distinctions, the Spaniards often used the term *me·teño*, from which is derived the English "mustang." It was a broad expression meaning wild and without owner, that is, ownerless. True to its later usage, the Spaniards often had equine stock in mind when speaking of mesteños, whereas *orejanos* indicated bovine stock; yet one occasionally finds the terms used interchangeably. Thus *alzado, orejano y mostrenco* meant "stray, unbranded, and ownerless," but *mesteño* implied all three. It was these mesteños, equine and bovine, that proved to be so troublesome in eighteenth-century Texas.[1]

Livestock accompanied almost every early entrada that ventured north from Coahuila and Nuevo León, of both the *ganado de mayor*, the "large" variety (cattle, horses, and mules) and the *ganado de menor*, the "small" animals (sheep, goats, and swine). As Dobie says, to enumerate the stock brought by each expedition would be a tedious chore. Enough work has been done on the subject to establish nonetheless that the Frenchman Louis Juchereau de St. Denis was not exaggerating when he wrote in 1715: ". . . The cattle left behind by the Spaniards has increased until they count now by the thousands, cattle as well as horses, and the land is overrun with them."[2] That did not prevent entradas aimed at permanent settlement from bringing more livestock with them. For example, when Fray Antonio Olivares submitted a requisition of items consid-

---

[1] For a discussion of the terms used by Spanish cattlemen to describe wild or stray stock, see Carlos Rincón Gallardo y Romero de Terreros, *El Libro del Charro Mexicano*, pp. 326–27; J. Frank Dobie, *The Longhorns*, pp. 8–12; J. Frank Dobie, *The Mustangs*, pp. 93–96; Wayne Gard, *The Chisholm Trail*, p. 6; Sandra L. Myres, *The Ranch in Spanish Texas, 1691–1800*, pp. 34, 37.

[2] Grazing Papers ("History of Grazing in Texas"), vol. 1 (University of Texas Archives). For the "Declaración de D. Luis de San Denis . . . , Junio 22 de 1715," see Charles Wilson Hackett et al., eds. and trans., *Pichardo's Treatise on the Limits of Louisiana and Texas*, 2:526.

ered necessary and essential for the establishment of a mission on the San Antonio River, he wanted 18 yoke of oxen, 30 breeding cows, 3 bulls, 17 steers, 100 ewes, and 100 nanny goats, with the due number of rams and billy goats. The Querétaran minister, founder of the first mission at Béxar (San Antonio de Valero—the Alamo), even specified that the 17 steers would be killed "to feed the Indians while the work is going on."[3]

As new entradas brought additional stock, they noted the survival of earlier animals abandoned because of unfitness, lost through stampedes and other accidents, or left on purpose to multiply. When Domingo Ramón reached East Texas in 1716, he found the Indians there trading horses and cattle to the French, indicating that St. Denis already had a source of supply although perhaps not as reliable as that hoped for under Spanish management. In 1718, Fray Francisco Céliz mentioned that the trails crisscrossed by the expedition of Martín de Alarcón were made by the increase of cattle that Alonso de León had left exhausted on his expedition of 1690. Besides these, they brought enough tame stock for Alarcón to proclaim that the new way station at Béxar was supplied with "all necessary livestock . . . without lacking anything whatsoever."[4]

The Marqués de Aguayo's entrada three years later brought large amounts of stock—4,800 cattle, 6,400 sheep and goats, and 2,800 horses. In 1722 he ordered 300 more cattle and 400 more sheep driven from Nuevo León to Los Adaes, yet Fray Juan Antonio de la Peña's account of the Aguayo Expedition describes "Castilian cattle" already roaming wild as far west from the Adaes region as the Guadalupe River. The stock brought on this expedition suffered terribly, doubtless owing to the fact that it was Aguayo who consolidated the province, placing it

---

[3] "Requisition of Father Olivares to the Viceroy, Duke of Linares, November 30, 1716," Grazing Papers, vol. 1; Marion A. Habig, *The Alamo Mission: San Antonio de Valero, 1718–1793*, pp. 20–23.

[4] Fray Francisco Céliz, *Diary of the Alarcón Expedition into Texas, 1718–1719*, trans. Fritz L. Hoffman, pp. 86–87. Other surveys of livestock brought on the early entradas are found in Gard, *Chisholm Trail*, pp. 5–6; Robert M. Denhardt, *The Horse of the Americas*, pp. 105–106; Gerald Ashford, *Spanish Texas, Yesterday and Today*, pp. 49, 54, 81, 110, 114, 126, 132; and Dan Kilgore, "Texas Cattle Origins," *Cattleman* 69, no. 8 (January, 1983): 111–20.

firmly under Spanish control. Although he ordered a fresh supply of 800 horses sent to Adaes, by the time he returned to Béxar, only 50 of the original 5,000 mounts and about 100 of 800 mules were still alive. Even so, Father Peña noted the beautiful expanses of land near La Bahía (Goliad), declaring that horses and all other kinds of stock could be raised there. Nor did the Marqués de Aguayo, a rancher of considerable wealth in Coahuila, fail to notice the rich pasturelands his expedition passed through—"the most fertile in all America, suitable for all manner of crops and animal husbandry"—and he soon was promoting stock raising for the province of Texas.[5]

In the first half of the eighteenth century the missions of Texas—not the military or civilian elements of colonial society—conducted most of the stock raising carried out in the new land. One of the many reasons why the Franciscan missionaries and their Indian herdsmen were initially involved with this frontier institution has to do with the nature of Spain's presence in Texas. The Spaniards came because the French in Louisiana were threatening their proprietary interests in Texas, and if they did not establish some sort of solid claim to the region, they stood to lose it. Thus the Spaniards marched northward and planted a few log bastions opposite the French in distant "Nuevas Philipinas" (an early name for Texas) essentially as a military maneuver. These expeditions were invariably accompanied by priests, if not instigated by them. The missionaries ventured into this uncharted wilderness seeking new converts for the Holy Church, and their missions sprang up beside the seedy presidios. In the years to come, when all other reasons for penetrating and remaining in Texas failed, it was always the French menace that set things in motion. Once the entradas clanked to a halt, the Franciscan padres were the ones who made sure that the animals that were brought along received care and multiplied.[6]

[5] Peter P. Forrestal, trans., *Peña's Diary of the Aguayo Expedition*, pp. 10–11, 57, 60, 65. For Aguayo's own report of this expedition, dated June 13, 1722, see AGI, Sevilla: Audiencia de Guadalajara, 67-3-11.

[6] Myres, *Ranch in Spanish Texas*, pp. 11–12; Charles [William] Ramsdell, [Jr.], "Spanish Goliad" (typescript, University of Texas Archives), p. 15.

San Antonio de Béxar was established only because it was a strategically situated resting place between San Juan Bautista, on the Río del Norte, and the East Texas "presence." Ironically, Béxar became the center of the padres' stock-raising endeavors—not the far-removed East Texas missions and presidios it was created to serve. The people who settled this outpost, it will be seen, were mostly young soldiers, many still in their teens, holdovers from one expedition to another. In time they either brought or acquired wives, many of them of the mestizo (Spanish-Indian) or *coyote* (mestizo-Indian) class. Alarcón found ten such families already living on the river when he arrived to establish a villa (town) in April, 1718.[7]

Who were these youths? Not stockmen by any means, but at least they came from frontier regions where such activities were commonplace. Many of the young men who accompanied the various entradas and stayed to man garrisons in Texas hailed from such northern provinces as Nuevo León, Nuevo Estremadura (Coahuila), and Nueva Vizcaya and were no strangers to the fundamentals of open-range ranching. They were given the tasks of handling and guarding livestock, not only the military caballada (horse herd) but also the animals brought by the aspiring priests. Still, apart from keeping a few milk cows, goats, pigs, and chickens for their families, these *presidiales* had little time, opportunity, or inclination to challenge seriously the mission fathers as stockmen of substance. A few retired soldiers might later become prosperous ranchers in Texas, but even then in terms of estancias—large ranching establishments— only the missions possessed the elements necessary to conduct operations successfully on such a scale: extensive grants of land, visionary leadership, and cheap labor.[8]

The early situation was not materially altered by the arrival in 1731 of sixteen families at crown expense from the Canary Islands, the only such group of Spanish colonists transplanted to

---

[7] For a muster roll of these soldiers, see Frederick C. Chabot, *San Antonio and Its Beginnings*, pp. 89–90.

[8] Fray Juan Agustín de Morfi, *The History of Texas, 1673–1779*, trans. Carlos E. Castañeda, 1:192–227, recounts the various duties which founding soldiers were expected to perform on Aguayo's expedition.

Texas soil. They were mostly peasant folk—farmers, fishermen, laborers—unaccustomed to stock raising from horseback on a New World scale. Upon their departure overland from Cuatitlán, each of the fifty-six immigrants was issued two horses, a saddle, bridle, spurs, and other accouterments, and the group was alloted six men (at one peso a day) to care for these animals, including the saddling and unsaddling. Despite such precautions the Isleños made a poor showing with the horseflesh His Majesty had bestowed upon them. A report filed on March 12, 1731 (three days after their arrival at Béxar), by Captain Juan Antonio Pérez de Almazán states that they reached their destination with 128 horses, 77 *mulas cargadas* (pack mules), and 32 oxen. This, it was noted, was fewer than the 142 caballos they had started with, not to mention those issued at Saltillo by Matías Aguirre and obtained at other places along the way. Altogether, 125 horses perished from "fatigue" on the journey. Like other observers, the captain at San Antonio commented unfavorably on the immigrants' equestrian skills and said that they were totally ignorant of horse gear, useless in mounted warfare as it had evolved on the frontier. Presumably this also applied to the tending of livestock from horseback.

Almost broken down by the trip, the surviving horses were put out to pasture under a light guard. One of the Islanders' first spats developed because Francisco Dubal, the *conductor* entrusted with their safe passage, would not allow them use of these animals for saddle horses, doubtless because his contract with the king specified otherwise. Although the horses were repeatedly designated crown property—for which Dubal was responsible—by the time the Canary Island settlers reached Béxar they probably thought of them as theirs. Captain Almazán would have none of it. When he refused the request of Juan Leal Goraz, spokesman for the group, to distribute the animals, he did nothing to endear Béxar's military presence to the struggling hidalgos.[9]

---

[9] Garay Transcripts, documents 54 and 175, made available to the author by Richard C. Garay, of San Antonio. Documents relating to the Isleños' overland journey are also found in the Louis Lenz Collection (Box 3J326, University of Texas Archives). Garay believes it unlikely that the settlers were not allowed to use these animals after their arrival.

Not only were these greenhorns afoot at Béxar, but, as noted, they had little livestock to tend. Before their departure the viceroy had promised them seed stock: 10 ewes and a ram, 10 goat does and a buck, 5 sows and a boar, 5 mares and a stallion, and 5 cows and a bull per family. At sixteen families this works out to a total of 640 animals. Isleño descendants later claimed that the 5 mares and a stallion were included, and the viceroy's orders so specified, but it seems likely that Captain Almazán had sufficient reason for withholding the jaded saddle horses from the allotment. Once he had the new settlers situated, efforts were made to secure their seed stock. By the end of 1731 it was delivered, having been obtained from surrounding missions, soldiers at the presidio, or ranches below the Río Grande. Sixty-one horses that Dubal had left at San Juan Bautista were obtained by Leal early in 1732 through an appeal to Viceroy Casafuerte, even though Visitador General Pedro de Rivera deemed the Isleños' petition "impertinent." Despite the colonists' protestations that the quotas were slow in being filled, it was soon necessary for Almazán to invoke civil authority to compel some of the settlers to give their livestock proper care and attention.[10]

Even if the settlers had wanted to venture into the prime cattle country around their new home, Apache hostilities, which intensified in the year of their arrival, would not have allowed it. The hostilities commenced soon after the Marqués de Aguayo built the adobe presidio at Béxar in 1722, keeping forty Indians continually at work until the job was finished. He left it in the hands of Captain Nicolás Flores de Valdés, confident that the fort was no longer "exposed to the insults of the In-

[10] Béxar Archives Translations (BAT), 2:4–12; Samuel M. Buck, *Yanaguana's Successors: The Story of the Canary Islanders' Immigration into Texas in the Eighteenth Century*, presents a highly readable account of the Isleños but does not give documentation. Chabot, *San Antonio and Its Beginnings*, pp. 83–84, lists the sixteen Canary Island families. Other accounts of the establishment of the colony are found in Carlos E. Castañeda, *Our Catholic Heritage in Texas*, 2:268–309; I. J. Cox, "The Early Settlers of San Fernando," Texas State Historical Association *Quarterly* 5 (July, 1901–April, 1902): 142–59; and Mattie Alice Austin, "The Municipal Government of San Fernando de Béxar, 1730–1800," Texas State Historical Association *Quarterly* 8 (April, 1905): 277–352. Cox and Buck claim that the settlers were not promised horses, but Castañeda (p. 299) cites the viceroy's instructions of November 28, 1730, saying that they were.

dians." But the Apaches, either drawn to Béxar by the presence of so many of their old enemies at the two missions or pushed there by inroads being made on their High Plains hunting grounds by the fierce Comanches, soon began to menace the place. They approached the tiny villa with its curious walled central plaza, preying upon livestock, supply trains, and citizens careless enough to wander too far from the settlement. Eventually the Indians grew bolder and raided the horse herd at midday, a distressing turn of events which resulted in a decision to pasture the military mounts 16 leagues away on Cibolo Creek. This measure likewise proved futile; after the loss of more than four hundred horses Captain Joseph de Urrutia ordered what was left of the caballada moved back near the presidio.[11]

These horses, and other livestock belonging to the residents of the presidio, became the basis for much disagreement between their owners and the Canary Islanders. Mostly farmers at this point, the Isleños planted their crops in fields bordered by the San Antonio River and San Pedro Creek. It was not long before the soldiers' stock, accustomed to grazing pretty much where it pleased, discovered the cornfields. Damage to crops became an unending source of bickering between the older military families and the new colonists. When the Islanders complained that the soldiers' roaming stock was destroying their corn, the soldiers in turn charged that the *vecinos* (citizens) killed or abused stock which wandered into the cultivated area. The *presidiales* were unwilling to watch their animals constantly or pen them at night, just as the farmers were unwilling to bear the cost of building and maintaining fences. Such quarrels soon spread beyond the horseshoe bend of the river to the stock grazing on mission pastures, involving their custodians as well.

Evidence that the settlement was suffering from a shortage of *manso* cattle in the mid-1730s is contained in a proclamation

---

[11] William Edward Dunn, "Apache Relations in Texas, 1718–1750," *Texas State Historical Association Quarterly* 14 (January, 1911): 233–44; Herbert E. Bolton, *Texas in the Middle Eighteenth Century*, p. 29; Robert H. Thonhoff, "The First Ranch in Texas," *West Texas Historical Association Yearbook* 40 (October, 1964): 91; Elizabeth A. H. John, *Storms Brewed in Other Men's Worlds: The Confrontation of Indians, Spanish, and French in the Southwest, 1540–1795*, pp. 263–74.

of Governor Carlos Franquis de Lugo. Noting that the population was starving, Franquis ordered the alcalde (chief magistrate) to organize hunting parties of six men each to exploit the abundance of Castilian livestock as well as buffalo, which could be had with "little labor and effort." Each hunting squad was to be protected by four soldiers, and the *carneadores* (meat hunters) were enjoined from killing more than they could carry home for the relief of their families. Franquis deplored the customary waste of such hunting expeditions, in which "they have often left the meat lying on the ground taking advantage only of the tongue." Placing little faith in his admonitions about conservation, the missionaries charged him with permitting and encouraging the settlers to take cattle regardless of its ownership. Implied was their view that all stock found in the pastures, branded or unbranded, was mission property. It was a view that they steadfastly maintained and led to serious consequences and decades of disunity.[12]

Although some of the residents of the villa obtained goats and other animals from the surrounding missions, worshiped in their chapels in preference to attending services at the presidio, and so on, the Canary Islanders and the Franciscans soon locked horns over the issue of cattle slaughters. The missionaries suspected the settlers of entering their pastures at night and "wantonly" killing calves and sheep to feed their families. Aware of the Isleños' destitute condition, the friars at first ignored this thievery, but when mission cattle were subjected to daylight raids, their protests began. The *vecinos* were charged with selling the surplus meat from such kills to their neighbors in town. After satisfying this market, they supposedly arranged for meat to be dried and carried to the fort at San Juan Bautista, where it was sold for cash or bartered for goods.

The industrious padres had no market themselves, and this was the crux of the problem. Except for the few residents of the presidio there was no place where they could easily sell either the increase of their seed herds or the produce of their irrigated

---

[12] Governor Carlos Franquis de Lugo, October 14, 1736, Grazing Papers, vol. 1, pt. 2, pp. 16–19; Castañeda, *Catholic Heritage*, 3:104–105. Morfi, *History*, 2:285, characterizes Governor Franquis as "rash, stormy and petulant" and is very unforgiving of his conduct toward the missionaries.

fields. Consequently the mission animals multiplied rapidly, and the herds were soon beyond their Indian vaqueros' limited ability to tend them. In an amazingly short time the surrounding country was overrun with semiwild mission cattle. As long as all the cattle belonged to the missionaries—and no viable markets existed anyway—disputes were minor. When roundups were held between the various missions, unmarked animals were simply divided in some equitable manner, and brands were applied.

But "since this is land with the enemy constantly in sight," any attempt at systematic ranching was precarious; the result was that tame livestock became a scarce commodity. Prices soared to an unheard-of 25 pesos a head in the villa, so difficult and dangerous was it to maintain livestock in a gentle state. Indiscriminate slaughtering was an oft-cited reason for the scarcity. Officials were usually reluctant to specify exactly who was committing these wasteful forays, but one suspects that the Apaches had some help from local *carneadores*, particularly the disgruntled Islanders. Certainly the appearance of meat hunters in mission pastures signaled an end to the padres' idyllic situation, and Governor Franquis's casual attitude on the taking of wild cattle brought their difficulties into sharp focus.

To return to the subject of crop damage, in the spring of 1735, Alcalde Juan Leal Goraz issued a decree giving farmers fifteen days to repair their fences, built, it would appear, some time after the trouble began. Owners of cattle, horses, and sheep were charged to place them in pastures well guarded in the daytime and to shut them up at night in the yards of their farms or in house enclosures. Fines for noncompliance on either side were set forth, yet the problem continued as before.[13] By September, 1737, the situation of settlers versus stockraisers had come to a head. In that year a new governor, Don Joseph Antonio Fernández de Jáuregui y Urrutia, determined to put an end to the constant strife. He ordered that all cattle belonging to the missions, soldiers, and residents of the presidio were to be removed from the cultivated fields; a guard was to be placed over them to prevent future damage. Likewise he commanded

---

[13] Juan Leal Goras, April 14, 1735, Béxar Archives, Barker Texas History Center, University of Texas at Austin (hereafter cited as BA).

the residents of the villa to fence their fields and maintain them, as provided by royal instructions, forbidding anyone to kill or spear (*rejonear*) livestock. Stiff penalties were set forth for violators who ignored the governor's pleas for fairness, Christian behavior, and the common good.

Rather than mollifying the villa's farmers, Governor Jáuregui y Urrutia's decree of 1737 spawned more paperwork. The farmers protested that they were too poor to bear the burden of fencing their fields; that, if the soldiers "had no herds there, we should not have to put up fences"; and that the soldiers earned 380 pesos a year while they had no source of livelihood other than the small farms which they worked themselves. Even so, the well-heeled soldiers pastured their cattle abroad without a caretaker, refusing to accept this modest expense. As for the charge that they "beat up" animals caught in the fields, the petitioners stated that it was absolutely impossible to get them out of the cornfields except at the point of a *garrocha* (an iron-tipped staff used in working cattle). They claimed that the goaded cattle sometimes viciously killed horses used in an attempt to clear the fields.

On the subject of horses more complaints were aired. The settlers protested the soldiers' constant use of their animals, pastured along with the presidial herd, saying they were useless even when they were left with the herd for four or five months. Warming to the controversy, the farmers asked that trespassers be kept out of their fields "by day or by night, because they steal from us" and "call us Jews if we try to protect our crops." Claiming that livestock owners had caused them the loss of over 400 fanegas of corn (1 fanega equaled about 1½ bushels), the citizens threatened to abandon their cornfields and even the settlement because "His Majesty, may God guard him, did not send us here to perish in this remote land."

This petition, submitted by the villa's cabildo (town council), or *ayuntamiento* (corporation), in what Visitador Jáuregui y Urrutia termed a "dissonant voice," gives us some insight into the scrappy nature of the Canary Islanders. The governor replied that their complaints were little justified and advised them in the future to use reflection and due maturity, not threats. Nevertheless, he called the contestants together, and they came to an understanding of sorts. Admitting that they had killed four head of cattle caught in their fields, the settlers agreed to accept damages of only 15 fanegas of corn during Jáuregui y Urrutia's term, the 400-fanega loss having supposedly occurred in the time of his predecessor, Franquis de Lugo. The governor then made the officers of Béxar Presidio agree that they would "do everything possible" to keep their animals out of the farms.[14]

The situation persisted because nothing changed. Four years later it was necessary for the presidio captain, Don Toribio de Urrutia, to address once again the subject of damage to cornfields. Stock owners were ordered to place caretakers over their animals, and the farmers to fence their plots. If guards for the herds could not be furnished "because of the scarcity of people in this jurisdiction," owners were advised to withdraw their stock a reasonable distance from the cultivated fields. Considering that Apache raids against the settlement were rife in the

[14] "Translations of Béxar Archives Fencing Documents" (Jáuregui y Urrutia, decree, September 28, 1737, Cabildo's reply [undated], Jáuregui y Urrutia to Cabildo, October 3 and 7, 1737) in Grazing Papers, vol. 1.

1730s and 1740s, one would surmise that stock owners did not dare graze their offending animals too far from the tempting corn patches.[15]

In the dispute between the settlers and the missionaries higher authority eventually had to be invoked. According to Fray Juan Agustín de Morfi, in 1745 it was necessary for the viceroy to repeat to the captain of Béxar Presidio that if he allowed any of the soldiers, settlers, or Canary Islanders to hunt wild cattle without first advising the priests so that they could round up and protect their stock he would be fined 500 pesos. Lengthy proceedings stood behind this ruling, some of which are detailed in Father Benito Fernández de Santa Ana's memorial of 1741. At issue was not only the killing of mission stock but also such questions as who should enjoy Indian labor and the right to sell provisions to the presidio. Following the viceroy's decision, Father Benito and the settlers reached an agreement which seems to have had a salutary effect on stock raising. A priest at Béxar declared that by this time the missions already had over 5,000 head of cattle browsing on surrounding pastures.[16]

It was not until 1749, when, in a grand ceremony, the Apaches and the Spanish at Béxar buried the hatchet, that beleaguered citizens and missionaries alike were able to turn their attention to the large herds wandering loose in the province. Only then did the colonists "breathe freely," "stack arms," and begin rebuilding, as a memorial later recounted. During the relatively peaceful interlude of fifteen years between the end of the Apache war and the beginning of hostilities with the Comanches and *los norteños* (the "Nations of the North," comprising the Caddo, Hasinai, Tonkawa, and Wichita tribes but usually referring to hostile subgroups of the latter, such as the Taovaya and the Tawakoni), raisers "often had four hundred breeding mares or jennets"; at Espada "more than six hundred" were

---

[15] Thoribio de Urrutia to citizens, May 20, 1741, in Grazing Papers. See also Frederick C. Chabot, *With the Makers of San Antonio*, p. 148, for an account (drawn from Morfi, *History*, 2:292) of similar problems in the mid-1740s.

[16] Morfi, *History*, 2:291–93; Castañeda, *Catholic Heritage*, 3:104–107; Fr. Benedict Leutenegger, trans., "Memorial of Father Benito Fernández Concerning the Canary Islanders, 1741," *Southwestern Historical Quarterly* 82, no. 3 (January, 1979): 265–96.

kept. Owing to this plentifulness the price went down to 6 pesos each for gentle horses and 5 pesos or less for cattle. These prices were low compared with those of former days, when a gentle cow could not be obtained locally for less than 30 pesos and a soldier named José Pérez traded a 30-vara (1 vara is slightly less than 1 yard) lot near the church for two horses needed for military service—an "actual value" of 75 pesos per horse. But, the memorialists sadly observed, because they were sinners, such prosperity was too good to last.[17]

Even so, peace with the Apaches provided a welcome respite, as evidenced by the issuance in 1751 of a regulation for the slaughtering of stock. Alcalde Joseph Padrón noted that there had been many irregularities in the hunting and slaughtering of cattle perpetrated by those who were "neither breeders nor owners." Because people saw the actual owners bringing in two or three carcasses, they did the same, saying that they had once owned a few head themselves. Because there was no law granting the right to hunt and kill even wild cattle, but mostly because another hunting expedition was in the offing and he had received complaints, the alcalde laid down four requirements. No outsider, newcomer, or resident who was not an owner could hunt any head of stock within 30 leagues of Béxar. No one, even an owner, could hunt "all kinds of cattle" within this radius ("all kinds of cattle" meant breeding cows, a provision designed to assure future increase of the herds). Punishments for violators were set forth: for a Spaniard, a fine of 25 pesos in gold, to be applied to public works; for a mestizo or mulatto ("faded or dark complexion"), 200 lashes and banishment. The fourth provision leads one to suspect who the "owners" were—the ones doing the complaining to alcalde Padrón. It specified that those who went with mission stewards on cattle

---

[17] "Memorial, Explanation, and Defense Presented by the Citizens of the Villa of San Fernando and the Royal Presidio of San Antonio de Béxar to Rafael Martínez Pacheco, 1787," trans. John Wheat, BAT, vol. 150, item 23 (hereafter cited throughout as "San Fernando Memorial"); also in University of Texas Archives, box 2Q245, vol. 821, trans. Mattie Austin Hatcher; portions in Grazing Papers, vol. 1, pt. 2, pp. 64–134. As Myres puts it, "This document traces the development of the livestock industry at San Antonio from 1718–1787" (*Ranch in Spanish Texas*, p. 60n.49a); thus its importance is readily apparent.

hunts must have a written license from the minister or face the same fines.[18] Certainly regulations of this nature would be necessary only during a time when men who were neither breeders nor owners felt safe enough to go out and take mesteño stock. Considering that the only substantial owners at the time were the various missions, it is not difficult to imagine whom this measure was intended to protect.

At the same time that peace with the Apaches came in Texas, Don José de Escandón was planting settlements on the Río Grande in a whirlwind of activity. In 1749, Camargo and Reynosa were settled; in 1750, Dolores and Revilla; in 1752, Mier; and finally, in 1755, Laredo. That these colonists were very active in ranching is revealed by a census taken in 1757, at which time the six settlements together had 1,800 inhabitants (twice that of the province of Texas) and over 200,000 head of livestock. Inspector José Tienda de Cuervo estimated that altogether the newly settled coastal province contained 80,000 head of cattle, horses, and mules and more than 300,000 sheep and goats.[19]

Even before Escandón received his royal commission to colonize Nuevo Santander, several bold ranchers had pushed their ranching operations from Monterrey up to locations near the Río Grande. Nicolás de la Garza arrived about 1745, followed by Antonio Tabares and Vicente Guerra; Guerra received permission to establish Revilla. Many of Escandón's captains and founders of villas became ranchers under his authority. Among them were a pioneer rancher from Coahuila, Captain José Vásquez Borrego, and the founder of Laredo, Captain Tomás Sánchez. No hacendados of their magnitude made it as far north as Béxar. They found plenty of room to locate their sprawling ranches near towns established by Escandón along the Río Grande del Norte, and there they stayed. In the coming years

---

[18] Alcalde Joseph Padrón, "Edict against Butchers of Cattle," January 5, 1751, in Grazing Papers, vol. 1, and BAT, 23:152. For other ordinances during this period, see BAT 30:3–4, 34: 35–38.

[19] Myres, *Ranch in Spanish Texas*, p. 60n.48, gives a breakdown of Cuervo's report by town, showing Camargo to be the most prosperous with 678 citizens and 81,963 head of livestock—almost twice that of Revilla, its closest competitor.

many attempts were made to extend colonization northward and plant towns on the Río Nueces, but none succeeded. Apart from the activities of a few bold Camargo-based ranching clans, the rugged *brasada* (brush) country above the Río Grande formed a natural barrier between stock raising conducted in Nuevo Santander and that in the province of Texas, centered around La Bahía and San Antonio de Béxar.

Don José Vásquez Borrego and Escandón are said to have been close friends. Vásquez Borrego possessed lands in Coahuila, midway between Monclova and San Juan Bautista, called Hacienda San Juan del Alamo, but upon hearing of the great expansion northward, he asked for another 50 *sitios de ganado mayor* and 25 *sitios de ganado menor*, a total of more than 270,000 acres.[20] Riding to present-day Zapata County, he selected the site for his new ranch and sent his son Juan José with a letter of authorization to close the deal. A nephew, Bartolomé, soon arrived with the first families and seed herds to start operations at Hacienda de Dolores, the first villa on the north bank of the Río Grande. Really more of a ranch than a town, it nevertheless was to remain an important base for further expansion in the coming years. In 1753 two more haciendas were added to the Borrego holdings: (1) Corralitos, 6 miles down from Dolores, assigned to José Fernando Vidaurri, a grandson of old Captain José Vásquez Borrego and the husband of Alejandra Sánchez (who was the daughter of Captain Tomás Sánchez), and (2) San Ygnacio, at the extreme southwest corner of the original grant. This settlement was entrusted to Captain José's son José Fernando.[21]

It should not be supposed that Escandón's colonists at the northern limits of Nuevo Santander moved into territory com-

---

[20] *Sitio* (site) was used interchangably with *legua* (league). A *sitio* for large stock was 4,428.4 acres; for small stock, 1,985.9 acres.

[21] An excellent picture of ranching in Coahuila as it pushed northward toward the Río Grande and the major families involved is found in Charles H. Harris, "A Mexican Latifundio: The Economic Empire of the Sánchez Navarro Family, 1765–1821" (Ph.D. diss., University of Texas, 1968). For information on Dolores and the Vásquez-Borrego family see Virgil N. Lott and Mercurio Martínez, *Kingdom of Zapata*, pp. 127–41; Jerry Thompson, *Sabers on the Rio Grande*, pp. 8–19; Robert S. Weddle and Robert H. Thonhoff, *Drama and Conflict: The Texas Saga of 1776*, pp. 161–65.

pletely unknown to Spanish livestock. Eighty miles upriver from Laredo were Presidio del Río Grande and Mission San Juan Bautista, the gateway to Texas since 1699. Nearby was Mission San Francisco Solano (which became Valero in 1718, when Fray Antonio Olivares moved it to the San Antonio River), and a third, San Bernardo. The last establishment soon became the richest mission in Coahuila, in terms of converts, fertile pastures, and livestock. As in other places along the exposed frontier, the padres had difficulty riding herd on all their wealth. By 1753 cattle had so increased in the region that it was a source of dispute among the various raisers, and particularly between those sacred and secular. This situation foreshadowed later events in the province of Texas and set a significant precedent for dealing with the similar conflict around Béxar.[22]

Escandón submitted a report in which he set forth information relative to the area's large number of stray cattle (*alzados*) and expressed his opinion that it was now impossible to ascertain their rightful owners. The missionaries at San Juan had raised objections to the exploitation of such stock by other ranchers on the assumption that "the first seed of the present propagation belonged to them." Thus they resisted and impeded capture or enjoyment of the contested herds. Escandón asked the viceroy to give him a resolution on the matter "because many people, and other missions, are insistently requesting permission to catch and drive to other sections of the country some heads of stray cattle for their use and to cover their human needs." Future developments indicate that the Borrego-Vidaurri clan and other large rancheros of Coahuila were the ones desiring such a resolution.

The *auditor general* of war, Don Domingo Valcárcel, responded that even if it were a positive fact that stray and wild (*alzado y mesteño*) cattle were progeny of gentle (*manso*) stock owned at one time by certain settlers, that even if the owners were still living and were known,

---

[22] Documentation on this dispute between the ranchers and the Río Grande missionaries is taken from Grazing Papers, vol. 1; also found in BAT, 26:1–19. The prosperity of these missions as early as 1737 is evident from their determined opposition to paying tithes on their herds of livestock (Castañeda, *Catholic Heritage*, 3:108–10, drawn from documents in AGN, Provincias Internas, Bolton Transcripts, vol. 32).

since they permitted their cattle to stray away and later made no effort whatever to round them up and domesticate them on their ranges and watering places, and instead allowed them to run wild and wander about without caretakers in someone else's land, without marks or brands to indicate any particular herd, they may be said to be wholly abandoned.[23]

The *auditor* noted that as the products of "that vast territory" became the property of the first person who because of his industry, work, and risks took possession of it, so should animals classed as strays owing to the carelessness of their owners and the wooded aspect of the country. This principle of the clever and energetic hunter, said the *auditor*, was firmly rooted in common law, especially so in these untamed lands. Never, he maintained, had any lawsuit been instituted against former owners of wild (*cimarrón*) stock, nor had such owners attempted to deny the use of these animals to those brave and resourceful enough to attempt it. If the owners had not tried to round up their stray cattle and utilize them, then it was "extraordinary" for them to prevent others from doing so. In practical fashion he observed that, once domesticated, the cattle would supply the needs of humanity, rather than damage crops and become a nuisance to settlers by their unlimited increase.

Thus Escandón was advised that as long as the cattle were truly stray and wild (*alzado y cimarrón*) he might permit anyone to catch and use them in a manner consistent with the overall effort to tame the wilderness. As a concession to those who considered themselves former owners, especially was he to grant them such permission—with the admonition that they could not kill any cattle for their hides and tallow alone, leaving the meat to rot and pollute surrounding districts. Confidence was expressed that once the missionaries at San Juan Bautista were informed of this resolution they would "desist in their opposition and cooperate in maintaining and preserving harmony and friendship with all the new settlements and the leader of the new colony," this to be expected from their well-known reli-

---

[23] Valcárcel to Gorraez, July 17, 1753, Grazing Papers, vol. 1.

gious character and ecclesiastic zeal. Such was not to be, for the padres, just like padres elsewhere, staunchly defended—in the name of their converts and God's holy work—prerogatives they believed theirs. The viceroy, Conde de Revillagigedo, approved his *auditor*'s opinion and forwarded it to Escandón. He in turn commissioned none other than Don Juan Antonio de Vidaurri, a settler of the province of Coahuila (and the son-in-law of Captain José Vásquez Borrego) to notify the reverend fathers at San Juan of the decision.

When Don Juan Antonio read and gave notice of the viceroy's dispatch to Reverend Father Alonzo Giraldo de Terreros, *presidente* of the Río Grande missions, and to Father Félix Gutiérrez Barona, *ministro* at Mission San Juan Bautista, they told him that the matter would have to be reported to the college "because of its noxious effects to their converts." Further, they would be obligated to point out how such a decision would result in loss to the Royal Treasury and the Catholic zeal of His Majesty and the waste of their own missionary efforts. A copy of the proceedings was left with Vicente de Alderete, military *alférez* ("sub-lieutenant") of Santa Rosa Presidio and temporarily in command at San Juan Bautista. Certain settlers, including Don Tomás Gonzáles de Cosio and Don Manuel de Santa Ana, asked for this copy to be made, perhaps feeling that it might come in handy when they went out in pursuit of the missions' *alzado* stock.[24]

They were entirely justified in taking such a precaution, as events soon showed. Shortly before this conflict arose, the Querétarans decided to secularize the missions of San Juan Bautista and San Bernardo, utilizing the opportunity to better support their endeavors on the San Xavier River in Texas. The Discretorio (senior council) of the college was aware that the two missions on the Río Grande had a reputation for excessive wealth, a factor which might help the offer of secularization win prompt acceptance with the viceroy. To sustain the three San Xavier establishments, Father President Terreros was ordered to

---

[24] Guevara to Vidaurri, May 18, 1754; Vidaurri, notification, August 16, 1754; Alderete, certification, November 7, 1758, all in ibid.

extract from the old missions 1,000 head of female goats before the contemplated secularization could affect such property. The flock would be conducted to Texas in such a manner as not to set tongues wagging, in other words, in secrecy.[25]

Two priests involved in the shifting of emphasis to the new Texas missions were the Pinilla brothers, José and Miguel. Fray José Pinilla apparently made an attempt to thwart the provisions of the *auditor*'s ruling by asking the governor of Texas, Ángel Martos y Navarrete, to issue an order prohibiting the capture of wild cattle claimed by his fellow Río Grande missionaries. Martos, unaware of the viceroy's ruling of 1754 on the subject, complied with Fray Pinilla's request, issuing a writ in favor of Mission San Juan for the purpose of preventing hunting expeditions. Such roundabout methods of obtaining any kind of "temporary restraining order" soon came to typify the nagging question of stray-cattle ownership.

---

[25] Bolton, *Texas in the Middle Eighteenth Century*, p. 239. Despite their planned secularization, the missions on the Río Grande lasted another twenty years.

Coming of the Cattle

The settlers around San Juan Bautista were not long in countering this subterfuge. In November, 1758, they also appealed to Governor Martos, declaring that their forefathers had been cattlemen of the presidio and that, over the years, some of their cattle had strayed. Now they were not permitted to capture any of the wild cattle descended from them because the priests at San Juan said that they belonged to the mission Indians. They pointed out that the writ obtained by Fray Pinilla directly conflicted with the provisions of the viceroy's superior dispatch, and they asked for justice.[26]

Governor Martos was quick to realize that the reverend fathers had put one over on him. Reviewing the hand-carried decision bearing the viceroy's rubric, he ruled that, since no new development had occurred to annul this superior order (such as the protest which Father Terreros stated he would make to his college), it would stand. He declared his concession to Fray Pinilla null and void and ordered the priests at San Juan to be advised that they "may not obstruct or impede the settlers of the aforementioned presidio who seek, and have the right to seek, the stray cattle to be found in the places mentioned, their capture and enjoyment of the meat, suet and fat for food for themselves and their families and servants."[27]

When Alférez Vicente de Alderete carried word of this reversal to Fray Pinilla the following month, the priest stated that he would appeal, a tactic used often, apparently to blunt opposition. Since both Governor Martos and their nearest prelate, Fray Mariano Francisco de los Dolores, were at Béxar Presidio, Pinilla requested that a full copy of the proceedings be sent there. So informed, Fray Dolores might then attempt to prevent and obstruct hunting expeditions on behalf of Mission San Juan. Alférez Alderete told him that in the meantime *carneadas* (meat hunts) would be allowed, provided they were not conducted on

---

[26] Ranchers' petition of November 28, 1758, signed by Don Tomás Gonzáles de Cosios, Don Manuel de Santayana, Don Tomás de Lombrana, Thadeo Flores, Joseph Minchaca, Juachín Sánches, Martín Sánches, Thadeo Montalvo, Diego Ximénes, and Xavier Montalvo, Grazing Papers, vol. 1.

[27] Martos y Navarrete, decree, November 28, 1758, ibid.

lands belonging to San Juan and that the cattle hunted were strays, having no guard whatever and completely wild.[28]

So ends the documentation relative to this instance of missionaries trying to stave off the inevitable: preventing ambitious individuals from taking advantage of livestock found around church establishments that were no longer able to handle the natural increase of their semiwild herds. In the minds of the churchmen there was no doubt that the *alzado* and mesteño stock belonged to them. If it was unmarked or strayed a little beyond their lands, that was understandable, considering the many arduous duties facing God's work on the exposed frontier. Perhaps it was Indian trouble, sickness, drought, floods, or a thousand other demands on their time which kept them from performing the annual roundup and branding. Regardless of the circumstances, the ministers truly believed that His Catholic Majesty's officials should view such technicalities with leniency and grant them the benefit of all doubt, owing to the spiritual nature of their work among the pagan tribes.

The settlers were also convinced of their right to the wild stock. Although at times greed would seem to motivate their claims, they were sincere in believing—as did their Anglo counterparts who were beginning to push inland from the Atlantic seaboard—that nature's bounty belonged to those bold enough to seize it. They were men of action and saw languor reigning over the wealth constituted by the wild herds. To them the padres could not utilize the mesteños even if they so desired. Consequently, there was no harm in seeking to exploit the situation and put the widespread herds to good use.

Escandón no doubt favored the individual rancher's point of view, being one himself. He also believed that isolated bastions, scattered in the vast land and maintained at crown expense, were not the answer to frontier defense. It was the citizenry, not the military, that he envisioned as the ultimate means whereby the land, like its Indians, would be "reduced." Thus he welcomed the northward march of ranchers seeking new places to pasture their stock, realizing that men will fight to protect

---

[28]Alderete, notification, December 4, 1758; decree, December 16, 1758, ibid.

such things. It is difficult to imagine Don José de Escandón accepting the viceroy's ruling on *alzado* stock around Mission San Juan with anything but favor, offering, as it did, rewards to militant and aggressive stockmen.[29]

It was not long before the implications of this landmark case were felt around San Antonio de Béxar. The only herds of any size belonged to the missions between Béxar and the coast. The Apache war and a host of other difficulties had left the padres there in a condition similar to that on the Río Grande. For the most part their cattle were scattered and unbranded. Now that peace had come, the reverend fathers could expect the hardscrabble settlers to increase their molestation of stock falling into the same *alzado*-mesteño category as that just ruled fair game around San Juan Bautista. It was a situation that the Texas missionaries had good reason to view with alarm.

---

[29] *Reducciónes* was the term often used to describe Indians who had submitted to mission life (Ashford, *Spanish Texas*, p. 86). It also referred to the system of missions used for conversion.

2

THE MISSIONS AT THEIR ZENITH

La Cruz y Las Espuelas

W<small>HILE</small> it is not my purpose to follow systematically the evolution of mission ranching in Texas, it is necessary to note the various establishments principally engaged in stock raising and scan their accomplishments. In the immediate area of Béxar during the colonial period there were five missions: San Antonio de Valero, founded in 1718; San José, founded in 1720; and the three along the river relocated from East Texas in 1731, Concepción, San Juan Capistrano, and Espada. The missions in Texas were administered by the Order of Saint Francis under both the College of Zacatecas and the College of Querétaro until 1773, when the College of Querétaro surrendered its missions to Zacatecas. Until this time San José was under the authority of

Zacatecas; the other Béxar missions, under Querétaro. A number of accounts of the founding, development, and eventual demise of these frontier institutions are available.[1]

Fifty leagues downriver at La Bahía were two more missions, Espíritu Santo and Rosario (both under the authority of the College of Zacatecas), founded in 1722 and 1754, respectively. Actually Espíritu Santo had been moved twice before being situated on the San Antonio River, first on the Garcitas (1722–26), near the former site of Sieur de La Salle's fort, and next on the Guadalupe (1726–49), before Escandón suggested moving it again. At its final location La Bahía still maintained vaquero huts and ranching operations on the Guadalupe at "Rancho Viejo," with the result that its cattle roamed the entire stretch of land between the Guadalupe and San Antonio rivers. Several works have established these downriver missions as owning the largest ranches, in both land and herds, in eighteenth-century Texas.[2]

Exactly how large these mission herds were, however, is mostly a matter of guesswork. Even the scant statistics left us by the various mission inspectors leave much to be desired, because they generally reflect branding tallies made under trying conditions, such as a shortage of help or Apache hostilities. For example, when Francisco Xavier Ortiz inspected the Querétaran missions for the first time in 1745, he recorded that Valero had about 2,300 head of cattle, 1,317 sheep, and 304 goats. An actual count was conducted during his visit (yielding 2,002 bovine head), but owing to the "nearness of the Apaches" the remainder went uncounted. Such work, he noted, was done by mission Indian vaqueros who kept 40 saddle horses for the purpose. This roundup, referred to variously in Spanish documents

---

[1] In addition to Castañeda's *Our Catholic Heritage in Texas*, there are a number of outstanding contributions by Fr. Marion A. Habig and Fr. Benedict Leutenegger. See the excellent bibliography in Robert S. Weddle and Robert H. Thonhoff, *Drama and Conflict*, chap. 7; and Malcolm D. McLean, "Our Spanish Heritage in Texas," *Sobretiro de Humanitas* 17 (1976). The definitive study on these missions' ranching activities is yet to be made.

[2] For accounts of the lower San Antonio River missions see Charles [William] Ramsdell, [Jr.], "Spanish Goliad" (typescript, University of Texas Archives); and Kathryn Stoner O'Connor, *The Presidio La Bahía del Espíritu Santo de Zúñiga, 1721 to 1846.*

as a *rodeo* or *corrida*, was an annual affair. Ortiz mentioned that for the branding which took place Valero had its own special iron. Overall, he said, the Béxar missions owned 5,115 head of cattle, 2,661 sheep, 664 goats, and 257 horses, indicating that Valero was by far the most prosperous Querétaran establishment at that time.[3]

Such enumerations do not hint at the unbranded stock hiding in the thickets or on the plains beyond the hurried sweeps made by mission vaqueros fearing Indian attack. Even more serious is the possible objection that the figures were understated to downplay the wealth of the missions. Certainly the priests were sensitive to the oft-made charge that their establishments were opulent, and they tried to refute such notions whenever possible. At the risk of presenting figures that may be misleading, if not meaningless, table 1 gives a summary of mission livestock submitted in 1762 by Father President Mariano de los Dolores to Fray Ortiz.

Figures on the Zacatecan Mission San José come from an inspection of 1758 by Governor Jacinto de Barrios y Jáuregui, who noted that all stock was branded and that San José had lost over 2,000 head of cattle in recent years ("since the peace treaty") to the Apaches. These losses, confirmed by other documentation, were suffered because San José's pastures, lying west of the villa, were near the villages that the Apaches had established to be safe from the Comanches, who had driven them out of their traditional hunting grounds. Although the missionaries protested the inroads that the hungry Apaches made on their herds, preserving the peace was judged more important than antagonizing Spain's new allies. Thus the mission protests were largely ignored. Six or seven bulls were slaughtered weekly to feed the neophytes, who, when they were sick, were fed chicken broth and lamb chops. Perhaps such special treatment

---

[3] Habig, *The Alamo Mission: San Antonio de Valero, 1718–1793*, p. 57, taken from Fray Ortiz, "Visita de las misiones . . . , 1745" (transcript, University of Texas Archives; parts in Grazing Papers, vol. 1, pt. 2, p. 20, University of Texas Archives). Castañeda, *Catholic Heritage*, 3:110–24, covers the Querétaran report of 1745, also citing figures of 2,000 cattle and 1,000 sheep for San José, given in 1749 by Father Guardián Ciprián. Ortiz also made another inspection trip in 1756 (Habig, *Alamo Mission*, p. 62).

TABLE 1. Livestock at Béxar Missions, 1762.

Mission	Cattle	Saddle Horses	Goats, Sheep	Mares	Donkeys, Mules
Valero	1,115	115	2,300	200	33
Concepción*	610	120	2,200	200	—
Espada	1,262	145	4,000	"11 droves"	9
San Juan	1,000	100	3,500	400†	—
San José	1,500‡	100	3,200	80	—
TOTAL	5,487	560	15,200	1,280 (?)	?

SOURCE: Carlos E. Castañeda, *Our Catholic Heritage in Texas*, 4:4–13. Castañeda's source was the report submitted by Fray Dolores and companions to Fray Ortiz dated March 6, 1762 (AGN: Historia, 28:162–83). A very similar report from the Archivo San Francisco el Grande (ASFG), 27:38–84 (Box 2Q256, University of Texas Archives), is found in the Grazing Papers, 1(2):33–36; its totals for livestock, however, differ somewhat from those given by Castañeda. See also Sandra L. Myres, *The Ranch in Spanish Texas*, p. 13; and Marion A. Habig, *The Alamo Chain of Missions: A History of San Antonio's Five Old Missions*, which treats these reports in detail; and compare with stock figures given in Hubert Howe Bancroft, *History of the North Mexican States and Texas*, vol. 15 in *Works*, pp. 632–33.

*A variation of this report has the following totals: 1,000 cows, 3,500 sheep and goats, and 400 mares in 11 "separate herds" (remudas).

†Pastured in 11 droves.

‡Fray Ildefonso Joseph Marmolejo's estimate of 1755 was 3,000 head.

accounts for the padres' frequent complaints that their Indians were in a perpetual state of ill health.[4]

Downriver at La Bahía the numbers of cattle in the same general period have been given as shown in table 2. Charles Ramsdell notes, "The total number of unbranded cattle that grazed on the mission pastures is not known, but they were at all times far more numerous than the branded ones." He estimates that during the best years as many as 40,000 head, both branded and unbranded, ranged the lower coastal plains around La Bahía. Other "conservative" estimates place the figure at

[4] Fr. Marion A. Habig, *The Alamo Chain of Missions*, pp. 91–93; Castañeda, *Catholic Heritage*, 4:11–15. For other accounts of stock owned by Mission San José at midcentury, see Fr. Benedict Leutenegger and Fr. Marion A. Habig, comps. and trans., *The San José Papers, 1719–1791*, pt. 1, pp. 98, 117, 125–26, 130.

TABLE 2. Cattle at La Bahía Missions, 1758–83.

Year	Espíritu Santo	Rosario
1758*	3,000+	700+ (branded)
1759	4,000+	1,000+ (branded)
1767–68	16,000	4,000+ (branded)
1774	15,000+	—
1780	—	10,000+ (branded)
1783	—	30,000 (including unbranded)

SOURCE: Charles [William] Ramsdell, [Jr]. "Spanish Goliad" (typescript), pp. 16, 40.
*On May 28, 1758, Fray Francisco Xavier de Salazar reported to the governor of Texas that Espíritu Santo owned 3,220 cows, 1,600 sheep, and 120 horses (ASFG, 12:62).

100,000, while some, not so conservative, suggest that "possibly even millions" of wild cattle and horses roamed the province at midcentury. The true figures were doubtless substantial, considering the sparse population relative to the abundance of cattle.[5]

At the beginning, before the missions were able to establish ranches in the outlying areas, stock was kept near the mission walls. The cattle, sheep, goats, and other animals necessary to the survival of the priests and their neophytes were closely tended. The stock was the means used to attract and hold Indians to the establishments for the obvious reason that it represented a dependable food supply. "In this manner are consumed whatever additions they [the missions] are able to make to their herds of large stock," wrote one priest, adding that temporal as well as spiritual aid went hand in hand with personal labor. The latter concept the missionaries strived mightily to impress upon their Indians by setting an example. Of course, it was considerably beyond the means of the small mission Indian population to consume the natural increase of the herds, especially under

[5] Ramsdell, "Spanish Goliad," pp. 15–16, 40. In 1811, Ramos Arizpe wrote that Texas was formerly covered with "millions of wild cattle and horses or mustangs, as they are called there." Other writers have repeated his extravagant claim.

the watchful eye of their frugal ministers. In addition to stock tending, the Indians were put to work planting crops, irrigating and weeding fields, gathering seeds and nuts, building houses, and doing a thousand other chores; but because they were "so slow and careless, it is always necessary for a Spaniard to watch over them." Despite such rigorous supervision, horses—and presumably other stock—were lost and were stolen by enemy Indians or by those who took them when they fled from the mission. The priests depended on empty stomachs to bring some of these runaways back.[6]

As the Texas missions took hold and began to grow, so did their herds. No longer able to contain their numbers in the immediate vicinity of the villa, the San Antonio missions began to pasture them on broad ranges granted by the king to expedite their proselytizing work among the Indians. It is possible to indicate the general location of these large grants, although the exact boundary lines are difficult to draw. The areas were so large and empty that it mattered little anyway, at least until private ranchers began to enter the picture.

Mission Valero's lands were generally north and northeast of the horseshoe bend of the river where the mission stood, extending to the Cíbolo. Its lower boundary lay along Martínez Creek, and its upper boundary followed the Salado back to the northwest. Included was *el monte*, the woods where cattle took refuge (later called Monte Galván). After peace was made with the Apaches, ranching operations were also conducted downriver at a place known as La Mora (the Mulberry Tree). This area lay on the right bank of the San Antonio River, roughly bounded by Arroyo de Espanta Perros (Scared Dog Creek) and Arroyo Escondida (Hidden Creek).

Concepción received 15 square leagues, "considered adequate for this mission to raise its cattle without conflicts," running from the east bank of the river to the Arroyo del Cíbolo. This mission, in the vicinity of modern-day La Vernia and

---

[6] Grazing Papers, cited as being from ASFG, "1756–1770, BNM" [Biblioteca Nacional de México], probably submitted as part of the report of 1762 by Dolores and his companions.

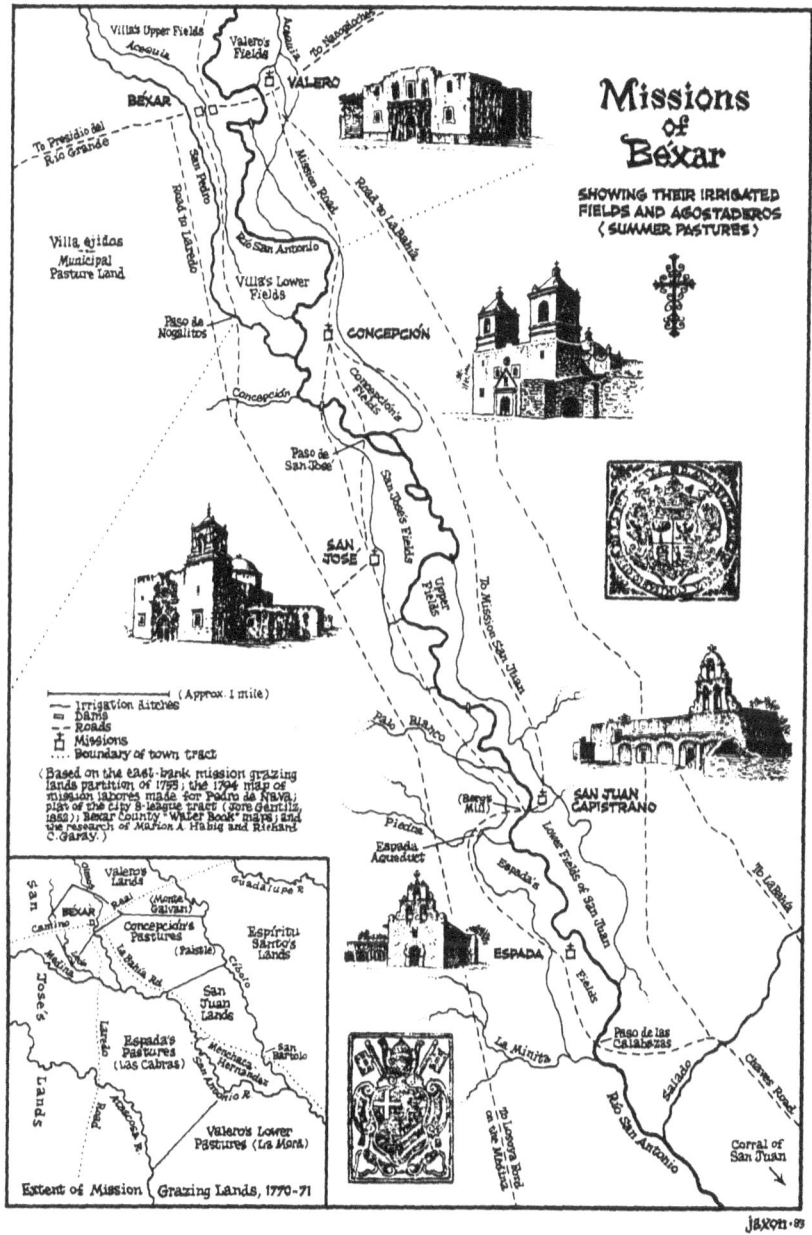

Sutherland Springs, had its Rancho del Paistle (Moss Ranch), doubtless named for the long, trailing moss once common on the majestic live oaks which still grace the river bottom (alas, the moss has long since been hauled off to serve as festive decoration and mattress stuffing). A branding report of 1782 notes "El Pastle" as being near the confluence of Santa Clara Creek with the Cíbolo, which would put it above La Vernia, but land claims filed after secularization place it closer to Sutherland Springs.

San Juan Capistrano, the other mission situated on the east bank of the river, had lands adjoining those of Concepción on the north. The grant extended 5 leagues east of El Águila (Eagle Creek) and Chayopine, on the Bahía Road going down by Lake Pataguilla, making it 10 leagues wide. The eastern boundary started at the place known as San Bartolomé, in El Rincón, the "corner," or wedge, of land lying between the San Antonio River and the Cíbolo. From there its grant went 7 leagues up the Cíbolo to the boundary of Concepción's lands—specified as the *manantials* (healing springs) of the Netro, no doubt the sulfur *ojos* at Sutherland Springs—and thence back to San Juan, providing this mission with (in the words of Captain Toribio de Urrutia) "more and better lands and waters for its cattle," consisting of 15 leagues, "if not more."

Some writers have suggested that La Mora, lying across the river opposite El Rincón, once belonged to Mission San Juan. This theory seems to be based on Fray Gaspar José de Solís's diary entries of 1768, in which certain confusion is evidenced about the ranches he was passing through. More likely San Juan's stock raising was centered high in El Rincón, at the laguna where their Pataguilla Indians pastured sheep (the present site of Floresville) and up near the mission itself, for Solís mentioned arriving at the Corral de San Juan Capistrano on March 17. According to Father José María Salas, Mission Valero started ranching operations at La Mora in 1757, a decade before Solís visited Texas.

On the west (right) bank of the San Antonio River, Mission San José had extensive holdings west and southwest of the villa. Its ranch, called El Atascoso (the Barrier), lay on both sides of the river of the same name between modern Pleasanton and Poteet. Stock ranged far afield of this location, however, especially along the Medina River at the place called San Lucas.

The pastures of Espada were also west of the San Antonio River, extending to the Laredo Road, which divided their land from that of San José. Ranch headquarters were at Las Cabras (the Goats), just below present Floresville. This site is presently being explored by archaeologists and may reveal information about the operation of a typical outlying mission ranch of the period.

At La Bahía were the missions with by far the most extensive pastures. In 1759 the minister at Espíritu Santo applied for and received all the land lying between the Guadalupe and San Antonio rivers. The upper limit was named as half a league beyond El Cleto (modern Ecleto Creek), at which point began the ranch of Don Bernabé Carvajal. Generally speaking, Espíritu Santo's pastures extended from the mouth of the Ecleto up to modern day Seguin and all the way down to the coast, taking in everything between the rivers.

Rosario, across the river from Espíritu Santo, led a troubled, on-again, off-again existence from its founding in 1754. Because it enjoyed vast grazing lands lying just below Espíritu Santo's, its herds prospered largely on their own. Like Espíritu Santo, Rosario was primarily a cattle ranch, and by the year following its founding, its herds were already the size of those owned by the Béxar missions. Soon it was second only to Espíritu Santo as a cattle owner, which was perhaps some consolation to the ministers who saw their hopes for Indian converts perpetually dashed.˜

While no detailed descriptions of how the padres worked their cows have survived, enough fragments exist to give us a hint. For example, instructions on conducting the affairs of Mission Concepción outline the following procedures for procure-

---

˜For a discussion of mission lands see Weddle and Thonhoff, *Drama and Conflict*, chap. 8; and Virginia H. Taylor, *The Spanish Archives of the General Land Office of Texas*, p. 26. "Missions of Texas," vol. 50, in GLO, contains the original documents relative to mission land titles, disputes, boundaries, etc., and is a virtual gold mine of information on ranching. See also the definition of east-bank mission pastures of 1755 by Captain Toribio de Urrutia, ACZ, roll 2, frames 2801–2802.

ment of weekly beef rations and other essential tasks. The *caporal* (foreman) was reminded early in the week to bring in horses "so that he with the cowboys, four or six in number, may go on Thursday and be back with the cattle on Saturday." Horses for this purpose were generally used for a month and then returned to the pastures to graze, a new caballada being brought in. It was the foreman's responsibility to take care of the mission's saddle horses, making sure that they had hay and were corralled at night if necessary. Cattle were slaughtered on Sunday morning, 4 to 6 head when the natives were few, and distributed among mission residents. The *fiscal* (supervisor chosen by the missionary) was responsible for such things as cooking the meat in the summertime, "so that it will not spoil," collecting tallow and fat from the butchered animals, frying and putting it in storage, and so forth. Doubtless Sunday was the high point of the week for mission dwellers because, after mass, along with beef was distributed tobacco.

Unlike hats, cloth, shoes, and so on, vaquero equipment was not rationed out. Rather, the missionary issued spurs, bridles, saddles, and other horse trappings as needed. A *mayordomo* (superintendent) appointed the cowboys needed each week to assist the foreman in such duties as bringing in the ration of beef and seeing that the mission oxen "as well as the cows that are kept at the mission are herded together every evening into the corral and led out in the morning to pasture."

During March or April sheep were sheared, either "on the ranch where they pasture or in another place which seems fitting." It was considered inadvisable to bring sheep to the mission for shearing owing to the risk of losing some by theft because of the nearby settlements. Shepherds were responsible for keeping count of the sheep, ewes, and lambs in their charge. They were also responsible for doing the castrating and advising the missionary of their number so that these animals could be sent in the annual shipment that in later years went to the Río Grande. A flock of 568 sheep sold by Mission San José in 1793 brought almost 2 pesos a head, the income being used to settle accounts with the college for merchandise supplied. Cowhides brought the same price, while buffalo hides sold at 4 pesos each.

The month of October or November was occupied with the annual branding: "All who can go are sent to herd the cattle in the mission pasture and brand the unbranded cattle." It was customary to inform other missions and residents of the presidio so that they could separate their cattle from the rest, and Concepción's missionaries cooperated in similar fashion when it was their turn to brand. This, at least, was the way it was supposed to work.

Saddlemaking was carried on at Mission Concepción, an activity that, according to the instructions, was reserved to "non-Indians": "The work of making saddles in all the missions is always done by a Spaniard (when I say Spaniard I mean a non-Indian); this is the usage here." This task, like some others that the Indians "cannot perform or are not able to perform with fidelity and with the necessary requirements," made the presence of a few Spanish servants or non-Indians very necessary at the mission. They were also preferred as shepherds, but since so few Spaniards were available, the priest was forced to appoint Indians. Saddlemakers were given a certain amount of corn and meat each month, suggesting that the *sillas* (saddles) ridden by mission vaqueros were not of the best quality. Unfortunately, no specimens survive, except for several crudely executed saddletrees of undetermined vintage.

Besides the horse gear produced locally, some was obtained through the supply system of the religious colleges. An invoice from the final decade of the century lists the following articles destined for the San Antonio and Bahía missions, "at wholesale prices": 24 pairs of leather saddlebags (*coxinillos*) at 14 reales each; 8 leather riggings (?) and saddletrees (*aderezos con su fustes*) at 7 pesos each; 6 leather saddle coverings and rump housings (*corazas con angueras*) at 4 pesos each; 12 pairs of protective leather skirts (*armas*) at 4 pesos each; 3 dozen saddle pads (*guruperas*) at 18 reales each; 44 dozen lassos (*lazos*) at 2 reales each; and 49 ropes (*reatas*)— probably woven rawhide—at 2 pesos each. The single bit (*freno*) with silver-adorned bridle in the shipment cost a staggering

15 pesos. Thus it can be seen that properly outfitting a vaquero, even on a mission Indian scale, was a fairly expensive proposition.[8]

Descriptions of other functions likely carried on at the Texas missions—curing hides for leather, packing suet and tallow, drying meat, and so on—are harder to come by. Ranchers at Béxar later stated that their herds were scattered because of the many hunting expeditions carried on to take fat, suet, and hides, indicating that such activities were widely pursued. The cattle fled hunting parties and turned even wilder, becoming more widely scattered than before. The more slaughters, the smarter the herds became at evading them. The meat taken in hunts was dried, and all these products were carried to distant markets, since before 1774 "it was not considered profitable to make cattle drives to other provinces."[9] If the two mission ranches near the coast conducted a hide-and-tallow trade—as the California missions did in the early nineteenth century—its extent is presently only guessed at. Records from the Papeles de Cuba or account books kept by the missionaries which were eventually housed in their respective college *conventos* may reveal something on the subject.[10]

We know a little more about how the mission ranches looked, at least some of them. They were obviously a source of pride to inspectors who visited them and resident *ministros* who were called on from time to time to report their progress. The most detailed physical descriptions are those of Mission Valero's and Mission Espada's ranches, both of which featured stone buildings. While the ruins of the latter structure still survive and are being explored, Valero's has perished entirely,

---

[8] The account of mission activities outlined here is taken from Fr. Benedict Leutenegger, trans., *Guidelines for a Texas Mission* . . . , pp. 17, 19, 30–34. Although the date of this *methodo* was tentatively set at 1760, material contained in Fr. Benedict Leutenegger, trans., *Management of the Missions in Texas* . . . , suggests that it was written almost thirty years later, ca. 1788. See also Leutenegger and Habig, *San José Papers, August, 1791–June, 1809*, pt. 2, pp. 20–21, 55.

[9] "San Fernando Memorial," BAT, vol. 150, item 28.

[10] Many of the Zacatecan-Queréteran *convento* records are now available on microfilm at Our Lady of the Lake University, San Antonio, along with a calendar of their contents.

though its location has been tentatively identified. The reader will remember that in 1758, when Governor Martos confirmed the viceroy's superior dispatch about mesteño stock around Mission San Juan Bautista, in the process voiding the respite obtained from him by Fray Pinilla, the reverend father declared his intention to appeal to Father Mariano de los Dolores, who was then at Béxar. In the following years Dolores and his companions compiled a detailed report on the Querétaran missions in Texas—including the livestock statistics already noted—submitting it in 1762 to Father Ortiz, *guardián* (dean) of the college. It is possible that this report was intended to serve as a defense of the missions, or at least as documentation, in case the college determined that an appeal was necessary to counter the adverse ruling on the Río Grande and keep it from being applied to mission herds in Texas.

This report of 1762—or rather collection of reports, one from each resident minister—provides us our best glimpse of the mission ranchos. Valero's was "some distance" from the mission compound, presumably down at La Mora by that time. Thus for protection it had a stone house and a stone chapel to accommodate the cowboys, shepherds, and possibly their families who lived on the site. The ranch house had three rooms with an arched portal. The structure was 24 varas (about 67 feet) long, and the chapel was 11 varas (about 30 feet) long. Inside the chapel was an altar with a stone cross 5½ feet tall, along with two sets of vestments for the celebration of mass. Most likely the chapel, like the one upriver at Las Cabras, was visited irregularly by priests traveling along the river road from Béxar to La Bahía. The road originally lay below the river, but in 1755 Captain Manuel Ramírez de la Piscina scouted a new one on the north side to connect La Bahía Presidio more directly to Béxar. Both of these early mission ranches, however, were below the river.

Mission Espada's ranch—doubtless the Goat Ranch, Las Cabras—had a good stone house with all necessary furniture and equipment to enable the cowboys and shepherds to live comfortably. It, like Valero's ranch, possessed a distinctive branding iron; these *hierros* (irons) were also noted by Fray

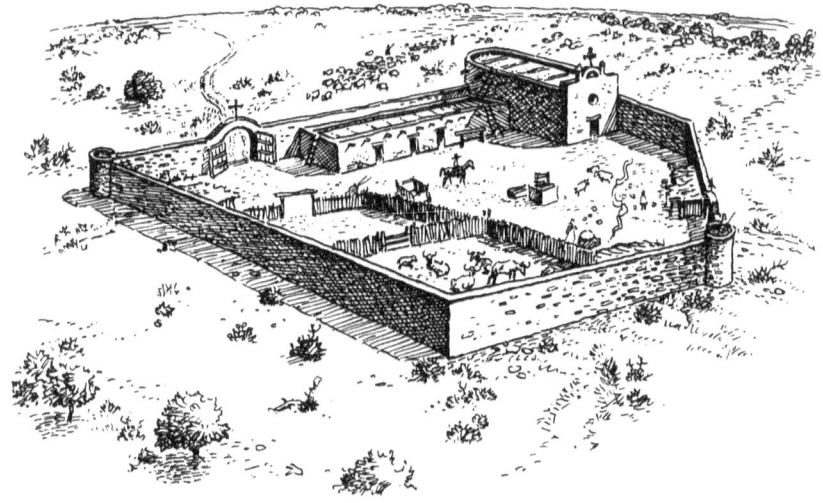

Ortiz in his report of 1745. Unfortunately, the other ranches are not described in any detail. Concepción's had "all accommodations needed." To judge from the report of 1745, it was distant from the mission compound and farm, for which reason the stock could not be counted in Fray Ortiz's presence. He said that the mission had its own brand. Most likely the several houses occupied by ranch hands were mere jacales (thatched huts) standing near the west bank of the Cíbolo at the place called Paistle. Very little is known about San Juan's ranch, only that its flock of sheep skyrocketed from 300 in 1745 to 4,000 by 1756, while its cattle remained at around 900 head (these figures depending on which archive the report is drawn from). By 1762, Mission San Juan Capistrano's lands were not considered extensive enough to support all its cattle and horses, despite Captain Urrutia's statement seven years earlier that it enjoyed more and better pastures than those of neighboring establishments. A branding iron is not mentioned in the report.[11]

Because Mission San José was a Zacatecan establishment, it was not a stop on Fray Ortiz's visits of 1745 and 1756, nor was

---

[11] See the version found in Grazing Papers, cited as March 6, 1762. It should be noted that this report ended with a request that the burden of temporal administration be removed from the missionaries at the six establishments under the College of Santa Cruz (Querétaro), a subject more fully treated in chapter 4.

information given about it by the Querétaran ministers in 1762. According to Fray Marmolejo's "progress report" of 1755, San José's rancho had a strongly constructed corral measuring 174 by 107 varas with a separate pen for bulls. Governor Barrios's report of 1758 mentions 1,500 "branded cattle," indicating that the mission likely possessed its own *fierro y marca* (brand and mark). In 1767, however, the Zacatecan college sent Fray Gaspar José de Solís to inspect its seven Texas missions, and he left a glowing account of San José's ranch, El Atascoso. It contained approximately 10 droves of mares, 4 droves of asses, 30 harnesses (*aparejadas*), 1,500 cattle, 5,000 head of sheep and goats, oxen for tilling the soil, and all necessary implements. White overseers or administrators were not needed, for the Indians had complete charge of the ranch. "They are industrious and diligent, and are skilled in all kinds of labor," Solís reported. "They act as mule drivers, masons, cowboys, shepherds, etc., there being no need to employ anyone who does not belong to the mission."[12]

Not much is known about the appearance of the Bahía mission ranches. At Espíritu Santo's second location (on the Guadalupe) near present Victoria and Mission Valley, are a number of rock ruins—walls, dams, and so on—associated with this site, but we have little definite information about it. Fray Solís described the mission after its relocation on the San Antonio River as being in better condition than Rosario. In 1768 it had 8 herds of animals and 30 harnesses: "Of the former there are about 100 tame horses, about 70 tame mules, 4 droves of asses used for breeding mules, which are raised in great numbers, 1,500 head of sheep and goats and 200 yoke of oxen."[13] Although Solís does not specify a figure for cattle, Ramsdell cites 16,000 from another source, unnamed (see table 2).

Rosario evidently had a ranch some distance from the mission. Solís mentions it several times, saying that it had good

---

[12] Paul J. Foik and Peter P. Forrestal, eds. and trans., *The Solís Diary of 1767*, p. 20; Leutenegger, *San José Papers*, pt. 1, pp. 129, 146, 158.

[13] Foik and Forrestal, *Solís Diary*, p. 16. See also O'Connor, *Presidio La Bahía*, pp. 25–32; John L. Jarratt, "Locations of 18th Century Spanish Presidios, Missions and Rancho Sites, Victoria County, Texas" (typescript list of eight ruin locations prepared in 1968 for the Victoria County Historical Society).

water and that several *puertos* (mountain passes), "one of which is called El Guardián," lay between the ranch and Mission Rosario. Describing Rosario as in a flourishing condition, temporally speaking, he said that it possessed 2 droves of asses, 40 tame horses, 30 tame mules, 12 harnesses, 5,000 cattle, 200 milk cows, and 700 sheep. From such figures it is easy to see that the Bahía missions far surpassed their upriver counterparts in stock raising.

Of all these long-since-crumbled mission ranches it may well be that the site at Mission Espada's Las Cabras offers the best possibilities for learning something about the architecture, construction, and activities of a removed ranch headquarters of the eighteenth century. A program of archaeological survey and testing was begun there during the summer of 1980 by the University of Texas at San Antonio for the Texas Parks and Wildlife Department, and certain preliminary findings are available. The compound measured 197 feet on its north wall, 98½ feet on its south wall, and 131 feet on both its east and west walls. Construction was of native red sandstone, and portions of the wall still stand 5 and 6 feet high in places. Small *torreón*-type (tower) bastions were placed on the compound's northwest and southeast angles, and the north wall sheltered three or four rooms, one of which is believed to have been a chapel. The rooms and the wall were built in one continuous operation, sharing one roof (likely flat) of lime and clay over log supports, whereas the "chapel" shows evidence of having been added to the compound later, along with the two guard towers. More rooms, either adobes or jacales, may have stood along other walls.

While the preliminary study estimates that construction began about 1760, my guess would be the decade of the 1750s following the Apache peace, at the same time the other ranchers began turning their attention to the wandering herds. Father Marion A. Habig thinks that it could have been established as early as 1745. If this is the structure described for Espada's ranch in 1762 as "a good stone house where the cowboys and shepherds could live comfortably," then 1750s vintage is certainly reasonable. Another interesting finding is that, although the structure indicates that a large expenditure of time and money was required to build it, the debris uncovered does not reveal that people of any great wealth lived there. This, of course, is consistent with occupation by Indian cowboys or shepherds—and that on a none-too-permanent basis—as opposed to the theory that the site was the residence of a well-to-do ranchero family.

The report concludes that the structure must have served as the headquarters of a ranch, adding that the nature of the work conducted at the site linked the people living at Las Cabras to the entire colonial network of the cattle business— trail drives out of the province, the rendering of cattle into tallow and hides, shipment of these products out of the area, and so on. Thus this strong-walled compound was "almost certainly in close contact with life in San Antonio, the rest of Texas, and northern Mexico, and should not be considered as a tiny rural village outside of the main currents of the culture of Frontier Texas."[14] Quite so, but it must also be remembered that this "culture"—especially the type enjoyed at Las Cabras by its newly converted Indian vaqueros—was essentially rustic, if not downright primitive. Such a life-style was not too drastically different from that of their neighbors in this remote province at the end of His Majesty's realm, the "half-savage" Spaniards of Béxar.

---

[14] James Ivey and Anne Fox, *Archaeological Survey and Testing at Rancho de las Cabras, Wilson County, Texas*, pp. 40–44. Since this writing, two more reports (nos. 121 and 123) for subsequent digs at Las Cabras have been released by the Center of Archaeological Research, University of Texas at San Antonio.

3

A STIRRING IN THE CRADLE

Raisers or Thieves?

As the British philosopher Bertrand Russell noted in his *Understanding History and Other Essays*, there is history in the large and history in the small. The first helps us understand how the world developed into what it is (the Big Picture), while the second helps us know interesting men and women and promotes a knowledge of human nature. He suggests that the two kinds of history should be learned concurrently, possibly so that we, in studying the grand design of things, do not lose sight of humanity and overlook the fact that "mere people" constitute the makings of history. It is this second, more intimate side of life that has always been important to an understanding of ranching in Texas, but never more so than in that era when the main characters were Spanish. Theirs was a society in which the family unit occupied a conspicuous place. "Clustered" with other such units, the resulting mergers formed dynasties of a sort, around which the entire fabric of the community was woven. Some of these expanded families were virtually synonymous with the cattle culture of their time and remained so through marriages with other prominent ranchero clans. This is not to say that early Tejano ranching families were royalty who put on high-flown airs or were fundamentally different from their later Anglo-Celtic counterparts, merely that a knowledge of genealogy is essential to an understanding of the way ranching developed in the San Antonio River valley.

This valley, of course, *was* Texas in the eighteenth century. The settlements of the time along the Río Grande, though their story is closely linked to the development farther north, cannot properly be considered "Texas." They were organized under and remained a part of the jurisdiction of Nuevo Santander (later Tamaulipas) until the Mexican War decided otherwise. While there were a few scattered ranches in the northeast as a result of settlement around Los Adaes and later at Nacogdoches, that area never rivaled the Béxar-Bahía complex as a stock-raising center. The rich grazing lands lying between the San Antonio and the Guadalupe must therefore be considered the cradle of Texas ranching. Correspondingly, the families who lived in this area, who developed its ranches, are the key figures in this small historical drama, and a study of their interrelationships is needed to follow the development itself. Seen in such a way, the sweeping saga of early ranching in Texas becomes something of a humanistic study, the lack of which has perhaps contributed to our long-standing disregard for the Hispanic role. When these one-dimensional, historically shrouded characters are permitted to step out of the past and are confirmed as living, breathing beings who faced many of the same problems, challenges, and triumphs as the subsequent Anglo culture, we will at last begin to appreciate the Spanish era and sense its influence on the present legacy that is western ranching. As with so much else in life, only by a careful scrutiny of the differences do we see the similarities in these two peoples, both of whom built their lives around stock raising in Texas.

Fortunately, considerable documentation—wills, deeds, land disputes, petitions, church records, census reports, and so on—has survived that enables us to make such an observation and establish many of these kinships. Much of this documentation is lively and tells our generation that these were indeed people of flesh and blood, with distinct personalities and recognizably human characteristics. Some sedate descendants will no doubt tremble with disbelief upon learning what the historical record reveals about their rambunctious progenitors. Apart from showing that a study of unvarnished history is not for the fainthearted, it only demonstrates that these people were very much like us—perhaps too much so for our own liking. Such are the perils of digging around in search of roots.

Providing a framework for this study is the monumental compilation of early San Antonio de Béxar genealogies by Frederick C. Chabot, a collection indispensable to anyone who would know how the province got its start. He, however, acknowledges that his material is drawn from many *relaciones*, *noticias*, and family histories, all set down by men and women who were very conscious of their place in the march of time. Apart from secondary sources like Chabot, the archives themselves reveal that family clusters existed and that various governors acknowledged as much in such matters as how roundups were organized, drives conducted, and disputes settled. Later when the ownership of mesteño stock became a hotly contested subject, certain leaders—troublemakers, from the government's point of view—emerged to press the stockmen's rights. These leaders were often founders of or heirs to ranching clans whose importance continued into the era of Mexican independence from Spain and the Texas Revolution. Thus it is of extreme importance to trace the founding and perpetuation of these eighteenth-century ranching "dynasties." Otherwise quite a few later events will seem to be devoid of significance.

First, it should be remembered that secular ranching in Texas followed the established pattern as the frontier of Nueva España advanced; that is, it was largely the prerogative of military men. In the northern provinces soldiering and ranching went hand in hand. The reasons for this become clear when one considers that ranching in virgin territories meant fighting Indians to protect stock, a function of the military establishment. Also, it was customary for the king to reward loyal soldiers for their work in the conquest of the frontier with large grants of land, grants which usually became the bases for ranching operations. It will be seen that many factors worked to the advantage of enterprising military men—especially presidio captains, active or retired—who wished to become large stock raisers.

At Béxar, as noted, the first settlers were soldiers, followed a decade later by the Canary Island families. In 1787 descendants of both groups, attempting to establish their mutual claims to mesteño stock, outlined the early history of Texas. The province, they said, was settled in 1715 and in the years 1721–22 by their forefathers, "brave souls" from Nuevo León (Monterrey) and Nueva Estremadura (Monclova). Although memory of them was already growing dim, among the foremost were Mateo Carabajal, Cristóbal Carabajal, and Francisco Hernández. Fifty soldiers under Captain Matías García joined this first group. On the muster rolls of these early entradas names begin to appear which took root in Texas and became closely associated with ranching—names like Ximénez, Urrutia, Barrera, Guerra, Castro, Menchaca, Flores, Galván, Pérez, de la Garza, Maldonado, and Chirino. From the Canary Island families who established a civilian colony near the small presidio came other names that would figure prominently in the ranching epic—Travieso, Arocha, Leal, Curbelo, Rodríguez, Delgado, and so on. It was the offspring of stock brought or tended by these first settlers that the memorialists of a generation later claimed as "our only patrimony, our only inheritance, our only wealth, and our only subsistence."[1]

Of course, the Béxar missionaries claimed otherwise; they believed that the stock propagated in the wild belonged to them. At Béxar, as at San Juan Bautista, their argument was that the wild herds sprang from their "first seed," even though in their time it was fairly well established that the wild herds noted by early chroniclers had descended from stock brought in by the various entradas of captains like de León, Domingo

---

[1] "San Fernando Memorial," BAT, vol. 150, items 2–3, 29.

Terán de los Ríos, Diego and Domingo Ramón (father and son), Alarcón, and Aguayo. Father José Antonio Pichardo relates that a church scholar, perhaps with a touch of sarcasm, attributed the first seed to Mother María de Jesús de Agreda's spiritual visitations, saying that she had brought from Spain the "numberless horses, the *pesos fuertes* [hard cash], spoons, clothing, etc." found by the Frenchman Sieur de La Salle when he arrived. Pichardo himself believed that the wild herds in Texas came from stock acquired "little by little" (by trade, theft, or both) in Nuevo León by Indians and brought north, or from Spanish stock that had strayed away. The last explanation has been strongly advanced by modern writers like Dan Kilgore, who view the upper coastal plains of Tamaulipas as the "great breeding ground" for Texas' mesteño stock, forerunners of the Longhorns.

Ignoring the account of 1718 of Fray Céliz, who attributed the wild cattle to those left by de León, Pichardo cited Father Solís's explanation, which says virtually the same thing, noting that this was where Father Juan Agustín de Morfi got the information for his *Historia*. Thus most early observers agreed that the wild herds sprang from Spanish "first seed." Whose it was and how it got there continued to be disputed by everyone concerned. Since the business of fighting Indians occupied the attention of military men in Texas until midcentury and stock raising during this formative period fell to the priests and their "reduced" Indian charges, quite possibly this was why they later felt that all natural increase belonged to them: because at the outset they were the principal *criadores*.[2]

That the military elite of Béxar could not initially afford the time or energy to indulge in the occupation of ranching, as did the soldier-captains of the Río Grande settlements, is evidenced in the story of Don Joseph de Urrutia. In 1734 he was appointed commandant of Béxar Presidio. Forty years of experience in

---

[2] Charles Wilson Hackett et al., eds. and trans., *Pichardo's Treatise on the Limits of Louisiana and Texas*, 2:525. The argument about who owned the feral increase of the "first seed" was critical—in the ranchers' minds at least—to the later decision to impose a royal tax on use of such stock. Dan Kilgore, "Texas Cattle Origins," *Cattleman* 19, no. 8 (January, 1983): 112.

dealing with troublesome Indians already lay behind him. So serious was the Apache menace around Béxar at the time that the new captain was obliged to report to his superiors that the *vecinos* lived in constant fear, afraid to tend their stock, afraid even to venture far from the presidio walls. Urrutia claimed that the Apaches were able to enter the presidio by night, creep to the center of the plaza without detection, and take horses from their corrals—even animals tied to the doors of houses—without as much as being heard. Such enemies, the old expert dryly noted, were to be feared, "for he who is not warned by the ill-fortune of others must be considered rather foolish."[3]

Captain Urrutia died in 1741, leaving behind a sad account of his personal affairs. "I am a poor man," he had written, "burdened with many years, many children, and family without having been able to accumulate anything in so many years of service." It was service such as Urrutia's that led the king to bestow honors and large grants of land to the heirs of soldiers, although this particular family stayed in military circles rather than choosing to become ranchers. Joseph's wife was the daughter of Captain Diego Ramón, one of the early soldier-explorers in charge of Presidio San Juan Bautista until his death in 1723. Joseph's son Toribio succeeded him as captain of Béxar Presidio after the father's death in 1741. One of Joseph's daughters married a soldier, José Antonio Menchaca (also called Francisco), a member of another family active in the military, and their son Luis Antonio grew up to follow his uncle Toribio as captain in 1763.[4]

---

[3] Frederick C. Chabot, *With the Makers of San Antonio*, pp. 15–21; Samuel M. Buck, *Yanaguana's Successors: The Story of the Canary Islanders' Immigration into Texas in the Eighteenth Century*, pp. 156, 206; Frederick C. Chabot, *San Antonio and Its Beginnings*, pp. 28–29. Also see Elizabeth A. H. John, *Storms Brewed in Other Men's Worlds: The Confrontation of Indians, Spanish, and French in the Southwest, 1540–1795*, pp. 192–94, 205, for a good account of Captain Joseph de Urrutia's early military career in Texas.

[4] Fr. Benedict Leutenegger, trans., *The San José Papers, 1719–1791*, pt. 1, pp. 74–91, for Toribio's report on taking command in November, 1740, at which time he speaks of "my deceased father." His commission from the king was dated April 28, 1741. Francisco Flores claimed that before moving to Las Mulas (his father-in-law's ranch) in 1762 he worked at Toribio de Urrutia's ranch, starting in 1753. This suggests that the captain owned a ranch, though perhaps not a very large one.

Stirring in the Cradle

It was in Luis Antonio Menchaca's time that the traditional affinity for soldiering and raising cattle appeared around Béxar, the Menchaca clan forming one of the most powerful cattle dynasties of the era. Two of Don Luis's brothers were also army men, as was his first cousin, Manuel de Urrutia, another grandson of Joseph's. Then, following Captain Luis Antonio Menchaca's retirement, his son José kept the tradition going, being a first lieutenant of the Béxar presidial company and later having charge of various installations on the Río Grande.

From a variety of sources we begin to see that ranching was little practiced by the residents of the presidios at San Antonio de Béxar and La Bahía until the decade of the 1750s, that is, until peace with the Apaches came. Toribio de Urrutia's report of 1740 said of the Islanders: "Most of them strive to better the little they have, be it with cattle or in other ways." But even after the treaty there was considerable peril in stock raising (as shown by San José's herd losses), lending support to the hypothesis that the first privately owned ranches established in the San Antonio River valley were not occupied full time, except possibly by a few hired cowboys and shepherds. Like the ranch owners along the Río Grande, owners lived in town and went out to the ranches only when certain duties required their presence. In time, however, ranch houses were built in outlying compounds which eventually grew into small settlements as families expanded, intermarried, and continued to live close together for mutual protection. It is because of these tight-knit establishments that the family "cluster" approach is so useful. Such places as Rancho de San Bartolo soon came to have clear connotations, insofar as ranching history is concerned, distinct from neighboring ranches like Las Mulas.

As might be expected from the above, when secular ranching began in the river valley, soldiers were responsible for the initial endeavors. Captain Manuel Ramírez de la Piscina, placed in charge of the Presidio La Bahía immediately after it was relocated on the San Antonio River, observed that on the southeast and southwest were vast plains, "well suited to livestock grazing."[5] From 1749 until his death in 1767 he had a cattle ranch upriver from La Bahía, situated on the west bank. This, along with the fringe benefits of a presidio commander—such as running the commissary store for men under his command—allowed him to amass a respectable fortune. Doubtless many of Captain Piscina's soldiers were detailed to work on his ranch in addition to carrying out military duties like guarding the presidial horse herd, which was pastured downstream. Since cattle were plentiful, the presidio did not lack meat, and in 1755 the captain reported that five or six bulls a week were being consumed by the people living there. It was only a matter of the soldiers and Indians driving a number of the abundant wild cattle into stoutly built pens. Ramsdell says, "It seems likely that the first ones branded at Espíritu Santo were wild stock rounded up on the immense ranges that had been assigned to the mission when it was on the Guadalupe."[6]

Upriver from La Bahía different soldiers under Captain Piscina's command were granted land. One of these was Alférez Bernabé Carvajal, who received land, called Rancho de Cleto or Rancho de los Corralitos, at the upper limits of Mission Espíritu Santo's pastures in the vicinity known as Ojo de Agua Martínez. When Carvajal was granted possession in November, 1755, by Captain Piscina, the tract was called Corralitos (Little Pens). Carvajal, in a sworn statement made six years later, when he deeded the ranch to the Indians of Mission Espíritu Santo, claimed that he had settled it around 1741, "twenty years previously." At that time the mission was accustomed to pasturing its cattle in the region from El Capote to the Arroyo de Cleto (the

---

[5] Robert S. Weddle and Robert H. Thonhoff, *Drama and Conflict: The Texas Saga of 1776*, pp. 156–59; Kathryn Stoner O'Connor, *The Presidio La Bahía del Espíritu Santo de Zúñiga*, pp. 22–32; Carlos E. Castañeda, *Our Catholic Heritage in Texas*, 3:178–79.

[6] Charles [William] Ramsdell, [Jr.], "Spanish Goliad" (typescript, University of Texas Archives), pp. 15–16.

eastern portion of present-day Wilson County). If this statement is accurate, the *alférez* must have been at Bahía Presidio while it was situated on the Guadalupe (1726–49), and it is unlikely that he actually resided on his ranch.*

The exact boundaries (*linderos*) of Los Corralitos are difficult to pinpoint from the original grant of 1755 but are clarified by other documents. It was bounded on the south by Martínez Spring Branch (Ojo de Agua Martínez, a place-name that seems to have survived as Ojo de Agua Creek, near Runge, in Karnes County); extended west up the San Antonio River to the junction of the Cíbolo and up that stream to La Laja (now known as Rocky Ford Crossing); ran east to the headwaters of the Cleto (modern Ecleto Creek); was bounded on the north by the road to some military post on the Guadalupe (most likely the overland road between Béxar and Espíritu Santo Presidio when it stood on the Guadalupe, perhaps the route described by Father Solís in his diary entries of April 11–17); and then extended back to the mouth of Martínez Branch in the San Antonio River.

These *linderos* shifted somewhat with the Edict of Possession of 1759, in which Mission Espíritu Santo's lands were confirmed by Governor Martos y Navarrete. They extended upriver as far as the Cleto and *half a league beyond it*, "which shall be the limit to divide the lands from the ranch of Don Bernabé Carvajal." From this description Los Corralitos was situated, more or less, between present Ecleto and Cibolo creeks, bounded on the bottom by the San Antonio River and on the top by the pastures of Mission Espíritu Santo. Father Juaquín Garzía del Santísimo Rosario, pastor at Espíritu Santo, in his petition for the mission's pasturelands, asked for the cove near the mouth of the Ecleto, "for it is obvious that . . . a great distance is necessary because the lands are without any shelters and open." Thus it would appear that Don Bernabé had in fact erected some little corrals and that their value was recognized by the reverend father. None of these technicalities were all that im-

---

*The documents associated with Bernabé Carvajal's ranch are found in GLO, 50:149–55, under "Año de 1778: Expediente [no. 59] promovido por el vezinos de la villa San Fernando Sobre periencias tierras y Ganados." Ramsdell, "Spanish Goliad," p. 24, mentions Carvajal's bequest to Espíritu Santo dated June 6, 1761.

portant because two years later Carvajal deeded "el Rancho San Visente llamado los Coralitos," along with its sheltering cove and cattle pens, to Mission Espíritu Santo, with the exception of small ranches (*sitio de ganado menor*) in the area belonging to Juan José Flores, Miguel Guerra, and Martín Lorenzo de Armas. He supposedly deeded the land because the Bahía Indian converts needed more room to pasture their stock.[8]

Thus after Don Bernabé's conveyance the missionaries owned all the land bounded by the Guadalupe and San Antonio rivers, up the latter to the Cíbolo junction, and up the Cíbolo's east bank 7 leagues to Paso de Laja. From the Rocky Ford the line ran northeast to the headwaters of the Cleto and from there up to El Capote (modern-day Capote Hills) and down the Guadalupe River to its junction with the San Antonio. The lands north of the Guadalupe were always regarded as *realengas*, the king's unappropriated lands; neither the private ranchers nor the mission raisers had rights to wild stock found there.

As mentioned above, a few brave souls were attempting to ranch east of the Cíbolo when Carvajal deeded Los Corralitos to the padres at La Bahía. But even Carvajal acknowledged that when he first began raising cattle up around Ecleto Creek the only other rancher in the area was Andrés Hernández. That Hernández owned and operated what may be termed the oldest known private ranch in Texas is established by documents on record in the General Land Office. From the beginning they

---

[8] Sandra L. Myres, *The Ranch in Spanish Texas, 1691–1800*, p. 12, confuses the Cleto (modern Ecleto Creek) with the Coleto; Ramsdell is correct in giving this southwestern boundary line as the Ecleto. The best description of the boundaries of Corralitos is found in the May 24, 1765, approval of the grant by Francisco Antonio de Echavarri, the *juez privativo* of royal lands—approval obtained after it had been deeded to the mission. See also Weddle and Thonhoff, *Drama and Conflict*, p. 156; and O'Connor, *Presidio La Bahía*, pp. 59–64, for Malcolm D. McLean's translations of Espíritu Santo's titles (originals in GLO, 50:149–55, 198–210). The Edict of Possession states that the upper boundary was defined as those lands "whereupon their cattle are located," a definition subject to considerable flux and one which would later give the missionaries headaches when it was challenged by the ranchers. It must be noted that Mission Rosario also contested Carvajal's deed, claiming that it should have gone to them. Indeed, Carvajal seems to have originally intended these lands to benefit Rosario, but possession was nonetheless given to Espíritu Santo (GLO, 50:198–215). Various ranchers swore that the deed was fake, for reasons of their own.

have formed the basis of considerable litigation, an unhappy development but one which perhaps contributed to their preservation.

Hernández settled his ranch, San Bartolomé, or San Bartolo, as it was later known, in El Rincón, the fork, or "corner," of the San Antonio and the Cíbolo. His father, Francisco Hernández, a soldier in the Alarcón Expedition, had received permission to establish such a ranch, a claim that was ratified and made official in 1737 by Governor Carlos Franquis de Lugo. In December of that year Corporal Andrés Hernández was ordered to take nine soldiers to the "paraje del Zíbolo," where the presidial caballada was pastured, and recover what was left of it after severe Apache raids. When the minister at San Juan Capistrano learned of this, he petitioned Governor Prudencio de Orobio y Bazterra (Franquis's successor) to have Hernández return any of the mission's fugitive Indians that he found, since he was going "where the Zayopines live." They and several other tribes had left the missionary's care so as "not to be subjected to the political and social aims of their *reducción*." Evidently Andrés or his father before him had seen duty at the downriver horse pasture, and it was this spot that they chose for their own.[9]

The little huts and pens that Andrés Hernández finally erected on the west bank of the Cíbolo in the early 1750s for the purpose of raising horses, mules, cattle, sheep, and goats could not have been very impressive, as later accounts attest. Yet his modest San Bartolo must stand as a symbol of something greater in the new and wild land, for the Hernández family had come to stay. Unlike Don Bernabé Carvajal's Los Corralitos, the ranch they established in El Rincón was intended to be lived upon—at least for long enough periods to classify it as an occupied place. Eventually the thatched-roofed jacales were replaced with more solid structures built to withstand the constant Indian menace. If the ancient specimen that once stood near Czestochowa is any indication, some were partly underground, resembling dugouts used by buffalo hunters on the plains. Doubtless the rock-walled compound being erected at

[9] Lamar Papers, folders 2823–24 (Texas State Archives).

nearby Las Cabras was envied by every other aspiring rancher, although few could ever come close to its grandness. Native sandstone, adobes, mesquite posts, or massive logs hewn from the oak and cottonwood trees of the area were their building materials. Typical was the *chamacuero*, described by Berlandier as a stout log structure covered with straw or earth. The houses were perhaps not *casas fuertes* of the type built by the Río Grande ranchers at outlying places like Dolores Viejo, Capitaneño, and San Ygnacio, but they were solid nonetheless.[10]

The most prosperous ranchers built their houses with flat roofs, either sod or pebbles, the kind that did not catch fire easily, the kind that a man could climb atop and fight from, crouching low behind its parapets. Instead of windows the houses had gun slits (*troneras*) or small ventilation openings covered with wooden grilles. Always they were surrounded by a strong fence or brush palisade, the first line of defense for livestock and loved ones. Such a rancho, built by a third-generation descendant of one of Béxar's early ranching families, was described by a contemporary visitor: "They have made a species of fortification as a precaution against the Indians. It consists of a square, palisadoed round, with the houses of the families residing there forming the sides of the square." For the less prosperous establishments, however, "picket houses" (jacales), adobe huts, lean-tos, and dugouts continued to be the most frequently used shelters.[11]

---

[10] Jean Louis Berlandier, *Journey to Mexico during the Years 1826 to 1834*, trans. Sheila M. Ohlendorf, 1:264. For a photographic treatment of some representative old stone ranch houses in the Río Grande settlements, many of them now submerged, see Eugene George, *Historic Architecture of Texas: The Falcón Reservoir*. Few eighteenth-century ranch structures in the Béxar-Bahía region have survived, even those originally built of stone.

[11] William Kennedy, *Texas: The Rise, Progress, and Prospects of the Republic of Texas*, p. 404. The description given is of Don Erasmo Seguín's Casa Blanca taken from Beales's journal entry of February 1-2, 1834. This rancho, called San Juan de Nepomuceno, was also described by Berlandier (*Journey to Mexico*, 2:553) as "arranged around a square, intimately connected without exterior doors or windows, but with an entrance into the courtyard which can be barricaded." The place was not Seguín's La Mora Ranch but one upriver on the Arocha grant, doubtless on the league conferred to him by Ignacio de Arocha on June 30, 1831 (Bexar County Deed Book C, p. 261, BCSA). Another of the Arocha leagues was bought by Erasmo from the heirs of Anna María de

In testimony taken by Captain Piscina in 1758, Hernández stated that he was presently living at the ranch and had been living there for more than five years, which would place occupation of the site at 1753. This habitation was made "by virtue of a grant which the governor, Don Carlos de Franquis, made to his late father, being four leagues and eight *caballerías*[12] of land in the said place called San Bartolo more than twenty-two years ago." Andrés's memory and/or paper work was correct because Franquis was governor in 1736–37, during which time he seriously offended Captain Joseph de Urrutia by taking over his quarters in the royal presidio, known thenceforth as the Governor's Palace.

It is something of an odd coincidence, then, that the man to challenge the grant issued by Governor Franquis to the Hernández family was none other than Captain Urrutia's grandson, Luis Antonio Menchaca. Luis's father, Francisco, like Andrés Hernández's father, had been a soldier on Alarcón's founding trek of 1718, and the son brought suit to have San Bartolomé's lands included in the 15-league, 12-*caballería* grant received with the help of his "intimate friend," Alcalde Manuel Carvajal. Although Hernández claimed that he and his kin had occupied and improved the contested lands before Menchaca made his claim, when the court proceedings were carried to Mexico City, a special judge ruled against him. As Chabot has noted, the old pioneers sometimes suffered at the hands of "new politicians," a situation that was to repeat itself throughout the coming years.

In a compromise agreement dated April 12, 1758, the dispute was settled. Andrés Hernández held legitimate the final sale of 15 leagues, 12 *caballerías*, made to Luis Antonio Menchaca, who in turn transferred 4 leagues, 8 *caballerías*, to Hernández, including the "place called San Bartolomé, where he has his ranch, and the pasture ground adjoining the corner [El Rincón]." Hernández's land was now to lie along the west bank

---

Arocha de Leal on January 8, 1836, shortly before the fall of the Alamo, for 125 pesos (Bexar County Land Grant Survey, no. 640, BCSA; and Cassiano-Pérez Collection, folder 89, Daughters of the Republic of Texas Library at the Alamo, San Antonio).

[12] A *caballería* was a measure of land considered necessary to keep one horse fit for service to the king; in Texas, 105.7 acres.

of the Cíbolo, starting at its mouth and running upstream in a swath 1 league wide until the 4 leagues, 8 *caballerías*, were filled. As it finally worked out, the Hernández grant came to almost 20,000 acres in present Wilson and Karnes counties, while Menchaca's remainder (11 leagues, 4 *caballerías*) came to 50,000 acres.[13]

The compromise was reached because "this is a war territory, in which in order to live all must help each other resist the enemy raids." Long and costly court delays were also cited as a reason for the agreement, and provision was made for a small area adjoining that of the two contestants: "As the Mission of San Juan Capistrano needs the Pataguiya Lake for its small stock [sheep and goats] they have grazed there, and a ranch being at said place, in the same manner Luis Menchaca grants possession to said Indians."[14] Thus began the legal existence of two of the first privately owned ranches in Texas. As the illiterate Andrés Hernández learned from the experience, doubtless much to his sorrow, legality was at times more important than achievement.

In May, 1763, five years after becoming undisputed owner of the largest private ranch in Texas, Luis Antonio Menchaca took his uncle Toribio de Urrutia's place as captain of Béxar Presidio. Upon taking command, he wrote a long report on the

---

[13] Chabot, *Makers of San Antonio*, pp. 35–36. Details of this historic lawsuit are found in Robert H. Thonhoff, "The First Ranch in Texas," *West Texas Historical Association Yearbook* 40 (October, 1964); and Weddle and Thonhoff, *Drama and Conflict*, pp. 145–46. The Compromise Agreement of 1758 is found in GLO, 50:161–64, attached to a petition submitted by Menchaca (see also ibid., 42:98). BAT, 32:70–87, contains the resulting grant to Hernández of four *sitios*, eight *caballerías*, dated September 1, 1759. Reference was also made to a Wilson-Karnes county land abstract for the "Las Mulas League" (in author's possession, courtesy of J. T. Jaeggli, Jr.), which confirms the above, including the original grant to Francisco Hernández dated March 26, 1737; also Cassiano-Pérez Collection, folders 18, 21. The 1785 will of Juana de "Oca" (Ollos), Andrés Hernández's widow, claimed that San Bartolomé Rancho contained 6 leagues, a figure also mentioned in Andrés's will.

[14] Although Weddle and Thonhoff (*Drama and Conflict*, p. 147) suggest that Rancho de Pataguilla lay "wedged between" Menchaca and Hernández, a survey made by Louis Giraud in 1876 distinctly shows "Laguna de Patahuilla" situated between the townsite of Floresville and the San Antonio River (Cassiano-Pérez Collection, folder 386, brought to my attention by Richard C. Garay). Therefore, it lay just above Menchaca's ranch, separated from him by Pajaritos Creek.

wretched state of affairs in the province and listed the ranches in operation below Béxar, five in all. Although he modestly did not list himself among them, Menchaca later claimed the honor of being "first settler of all the ranchos in this province," giving 1751 as his date of occupation.

Vicente Álvarez Travieso, a member of the city council, lived most of the time at his ranch, Las Mulas, about 20 leagues from San Antonio. Andrés Hernández, "another old-timer," lived at his ranch on the Cíbolo, contradicting Carvajal's bequest statement that he was then deceased. Also on the Cíbolo were the ranches of Juan José Flores, "one of the first, started in 1756," and Miguel Guerra. They, along with Martín Lorenzo de Armas, were the three men mentioned in Don Bernabé's deed as having ranches east of the Cíbolo whose rights he wanted Espíritu Santo to uphold. Captain Menchaca's report said that Martín Lorenzo lived at Las Mulas as a neighbor of Travieso's and that he was not one of the original Canary Islanders but a later arrival.[15]

Both Martín Lorenzo de Armas and his brother Ignacio were in fact born in the Canary Islands, and both arrived at Béxar with the other colonists, having joined the migration along the way. They were single men and, along with the Pérez brothers, were counted as a founding family, the sixteenth and final unit so recognized. This in itself was an important distinction. They were *hijos dalgo*, or hidalgos, "sons of something," meaning something important, and besides the title, certain privileges went with being a don. One of them, as mentioned, was free seed stock from His Majesty.

Martín, born in 1710, married María Robaina de Bethencourt, the widow of Juan Rodríguez Granado, who had died on the trek at Veracruz. Their ranch was called San Antonio del Cíbolo, and it is unlikely that the proud Don Martín would have appreciated being called a later arrival. Doña María subsequently made the astounding charge that their houses and corrals east of the Cíbolo had been set afire by Bernabé Carvajal

---

[15] Castañeda, *Catholic Heritage*, 4:19–21. Statements from the ranchers themselves concerning the occupation of their establishments are found in GLO, 50: 159–95.

and troops from La Bahía, perhaps accounting for Captain Menchaca's statement that this family lived at neighboring Las Mulas.¹⁶

Most reports on the situation around Béxar at this time reflect great concern that the settlement could not defend itself in case of Indian attack. In 1762, Fray Mariano de los Dolores complained to Governor Martos that the peace with the Apaches had become a farce. The Indians killed, stole, and destroyed property with impunity, especially the herds of cattle, which were being decimated and threatened with annihilation. Fray Pedro Ramírez said that if the Apaches were pacified Mission San José could gather 4,000 head of cattle but that as things stood only 400 head were available. These had to be kept close to the pueblo walls. He maintained that his Indian neophytes were hungry and miserable and that the beef allotment had dropped from 6 head slaughtered a week to only 2. Depredations also occurred at La Bahía but were seemingly not as bad as those at Béxar, where it was dangerous to cultivate the fields and to establish or maintain ranches "beyond the city limits," a description similar to Captain Urrutia's of thirty years earlier. The following month a petition of like tenor was presented to the governor by the cabildo, including Luis Antonio Menchaca, Andrés Ramón, Francisco Delgado, and Vicente Álvarez Travieso.¹⁷

Yet at this very time a noteworthy event in the history of Texas ranching took place. On July 1, 1762, Governor Martos

---

¹⁶ Buck, *Yanaguana's Successors*, pp. 134–36, has Ignacio as the brother marrying the wealthy, beautiful widow; Chabot (*Makers of San Antonio*) gives it correctly as Martín.

¹⁷ Fray Pedro Ramírez, June 6, 1762, ASFG, 13:71 (University of Texas Archives). See also Fray Dolores to the Viceroy, January 16, 1760, for a similar complaint (Grazing Papers, vol. 1, pt. 2, p. 35, University of Texas Archives).

issued a cattle brand to Juan Joseph (or José) Flores, the first such brand on record.[18] An earlier brand is mentioned in the Béxar Archives, one granted to Nicolás Saez on October 4, 1742. Saez was a resident of the Real Santiago de las Sabinas, and his *fierro* was issued by Pedro del Barrio Junco y Espriella as governor of Nuevo León, so it hardly qualifies as Texas' first. A brand that is a legitimate contender for the honor, however, is the one granted by Governor Francisco García Larios to Francisco Joseph de Estrada on January 16, 1748. Governor García Larios issued it while on an inspection tour as a reward for Estrada's devotion and long service to the king in the presidios of Los Adaes, Río Grande del Norte, and "this of San Antonio." He instructed Estrada to separate a third of his mares for the breeding of mules and to assist in the recovery and return of stray animals without having to resort to a sale, "as is the practice when royal justice intervenes." This brand was confirmed by Barrio Junco on June 16, 1749, after he succeeded García Larios as governor of Texas. Estrada was up in years by this time and does not appear to have been among the group of early private ranchers like Flores and Hernández who gave the institution its actual start in the San Antonio River valley.[19]

Thus Captain Menchaca was not entirely amiss in recognizing Juan José Flores as one of the first ranchers of Texas. He certainly was in the running, and his brand predates that of the Hernández family by two and a half years. In a petition of 1778 Don Juan José wrote that he had been the *diezmero* (tithe collector) for six years, during which time he had collected a little over 600 head of cattle. These he kept at his Cíbolo ranch, a practice he started in 1756 when he originally bought the tithes of the province. Flores observed that he had paid the bishopric 540 pesos for stock comprising the tithe at a time when the going price was 300 pesos, this arising from the numerous head

---

[18] Martos y Navarrete to Flores, July 1, 1762, BAT, 36:189–90. This historic brand with slight variations is shown in several studies. See, for example, Gus L. Ford, ed., *Texas Cattle Brands: A Catalog of the Texas Centennial Exposition Exhibit*, p. 1; and Hortense W. Ward, *Cattlebrands and Cowhides*, p. 180. Ward states (p. 178) that the Flores brand is "the oldest known record of a brand registered within what is now known as Texas."

[19] BAT, 15:1; ibid., 19:12–15. For these and other early brands see brand section A.

kept by growers during these years. His occupation in 1756 was later acknowledged by no less a personage than Commandant General Teodoro de Croix, who noted that Flores claimed all unbranded cattle in the vicinity of his Arroyo del Cíbolo Ranch and that other cattlemen arrived later, including Don Bernabé Carvajal. Juan José Flores de Abrego y Valdés and his brother Francisco continued to play leading roles as *criadores* in the coming years, as would their sons after them.[20]

Students of ranching history should exercise extreme care in identifying members of the Flores family. Of all the genealogies of clans who ranched in El Rincón, theirs is the most complex and difficult to sort out. Besides the line mentioned above, there were other Floreses in the area who ranched at the same time. For instance, Miguel Guerra—the stockman Menchaca listed as one of the earliest—married María Josefa Quiñones y Flores de Abrego. She was the daughter of Joseph, an old soldier who died at Béxar in 1752 leaving many descendants. Then there was the Flores de Valdés family, of which Nicolás was the first in Texas, already mentioned as being appointed captain of Béxar Presidio when it was first built in 1722. Another family, also including prominent soldiers, used the surname Flores only: Antonio, Domingo, and Miguel came to Béxar on the expedition of 1716. Ranching documents reveal that a Flores y Galán line was present in the area as well.

Last of all is the Flores de Abrego family, descended from Francisco Flores de Abrego, of Saltillo, who married María Saucedo. They had a son, Francisco (d. 1757), who married Rosa Hernández. Their son Joseph Joaquín married Teodora Móntes de Oca, and they had Joseph Antonio. He was the father of four sons, all active in the struggle for Texas Independence, and his daughter Gertrudis married Juan N. Seguín, for whom the town Seguin is named. Floresville, the Wilson County seat, honors this particular family as well because one of the four brothers mentioned above, José María (who was married to Juan Seguín's sister Leonidas), owned land on the spot selected for the town.

---

[20] Croix to Governor of Texas, May 14, 1778, BAT, 69:29, 31. Flores's own statement of his occupation, dated May 6, 1778, is in GLO, 50:171–72.

Their daughter Josefa (who married the sheriff Sam Barker) donated the site, hence Floresville. Trying to follow accurately the activities of the illustrious Flores "family" can prove very frustrating.[21]

Perhaps no ranching dynasty in the San Antonio River valley had as interesting and colorful a character as the man who founded Las Mulas, Don Vicente Álvarez Travieso. Because his daughters also married men active in stock raising, the cluster of extended families at the Mules became a power to be reckoned with. This clan was very energetic both in catching mesteños and in defending its right to them, traits which did nothing to popularize the Traviesos with either the missionaries or the governors who tried to keep them west of the Cíbolo, that is, out of mission pastures.

From an examination of the archives one might conclude that Don Vicente, appointed *alguacil mayor* (chief constable) of Béxar for life, was something of a troublemaker. He was a close friend of Francisco de Arocha, founder of another important ranching family, and they married sisters, daughters of Juan Curbelo. Soon after arriving in Béxar, Travieso filed a formal complaint because he had been refused permission to seek medical attention in Saltillo. When other settlers became disillusioned with their new home, Travieso served as their appointed champion. More than once he was entrusted by his fellow citizens with the task of traveling to Mexico City to seek redress for grievances or deliver petitions that irritated the provincial governing establishment.[22]

One such instance was the "very expensive" appeal initiated by Travieso in 1756 on the subject of land and water rights. Although details are sketchy and widely scattered, it appears that the *alguacil* was attempting, on behalf of others who

---

[21] Chabot, *Makers of San Antonio*, pp. 56–64; J. T. Jaeggli, Jr., *The Court House Story*. For information on the site of Floresville, see Bexar County Deed Book B (Red), p. 204, partition of the lower Arocha grant; Wilson County Deed Book C, pp. 74–75, deed to the townsite; Wilson County Plat Book 1, p. 87, map of the 1840 partition of the Arocha 8-league grant; Bexar County Deed Book G–I, p. 401; Spanish Deed Book 3, p. 294.

[22] Buck, *Yanaguana's Successors*, has several interesting examples of the sheriff's activities in early Béxar; also see Chabot, *Makers of San Antonio*, pp. 163–68.

wished to limit the Béxar missions' expansion plans, to save this option for the settlers themselves. According to area ranchers, the suit was brought because the missions, "looking out for their Indians, protected by the King's laws for that purpose, sought to extend their lands all over the province. We sought a similar expansion as first settlers." In a petition directed to Captain Toribio de Urrutia, the missionaries were charged with oppressing the villa through attempts at land monopoly. Upon learning that various citizens wished to apply for grants, the padres "viciously built jacales and set up a ranch on these lands to keep the *vecinos* from getting them." While this is an oversimplification of the dispute between the mission and private cattlemen, Vicente Álvarez Travieso was certainly at the forefront of the controversy and remained so until his death in 1779. His sons, sons-in-law, and grandchildren perpetuated this noteworthy tradition of protest and rebellion into the following century, as will be seen.[23]

The authority under which Don Vicente settled Las Mulas was also the subject of much dispute. There is no doubt, however, that the Travieso clan regarded it as theirs. It lay on the west bank of the Cíbolo, just above and contiguous with the Hernández ranch. Travieso claimed that he had settled it in 1758 and that various governors had refused to give him title for fear of a dispute with the missionaries. He suggested that Concepción's Rancho de "Paste" (Paistle) was subsequently located on lands he desired, which was perhaps the basis for his latest quarrel. Governor Martos stated that Vicente had helped Andrés Hernández in the defense of his title to San Bartolomé, going to Mexico City, paying legal costs, and so forth. This statement confirmed that Jacobo Hernández had sold his part of Rancho San Bartolo to the Traviesos in 1755 for two horses which he needed for the royal service, although the deed was later contested on the grounds that it failed to specify northern

---

[23] "San Fernando Memorial," BAT, vol. 150, item 26; Cabildo to Urrutia, August 25, 1756, signed by Francisco Delgado, Vicente Álvarez Travieso, Martín Flores, Joseph Curbelo, Luis Antonio Menchaca, Joseph Padrón, and Andrés Ramón, BAT, 30:54–61. See chap. 4 for later developments in this lawsuit.

and southern boundaries.[24] Still other documents indicate that Las Mulas reached from "Paraje de Puten" (or "Reten," reserve, or reservoir), down the Cíbolo to the Hernández lands; surveys made during the Republic locate Travieso's ranch just above the present Wilson-Karnes County line. Because the Bahía (Goliad) Road crossed the Cíbolo near where Las Mulas and San Bartolo adjoined, this property became very valuable—and troublesome to those who would defend its title.[25]

Don Vicente Álvarez Travieso's brother-in-law Francisco de Arocha served for many years as the secretary of the cabildo, supposedly being the only one of the Islanders who could write a legible hand (though that was not so). He was obliged to resign as the town's *escribano de consejo y público* (city clerk and notary) in 1757 because the job did not "yield enough to support his family." This was no doubt true, because he and his wife had fifteen children. One of them, Simón, became El Rincón's most prosperous rancher, related to almost every powerful cluster in the river valley. Simón was also a military man, serving as commandant of the Béxar militia and lieutenant general of the province. He was the nephew of Vicente Álvarez Travieso, and his wife was Luis Antonio Menchaca's first cousin. Moreover, his wife's mother (the wife of Joaquín de Urrutia) was a sister of Andrés Hernández, and Arocha was tied by marriage to that ranching dynasty as well. Don Simón and his brothers established their Rancho de San Rafael on the east bank of the San Antonio River, directly above Captain Menchaca's spread. The 1756 suit over lands mentions this ranch as another which Father Dolores and his Querétaran brethren opposed. Its lower

---

[24] See proceedings in BAT, vol. 140, in which Francisco Xavier Rodríguez protested the "sale" (i.e., control) of Las Mulas to his brother-in-law Tomás Travieso. Cited was the *auto* of Governor Martos dated August 12, 1762, concerning Don Vicente's help to Hernández, and Jacobo's "bill of sale," dated June 2, 1755.

[25] The "Las Mulas League" abstract of title contains all the pertinent documentation, including records drawn from deed books of both Bexar County and Wilson County (formed in 1860). Maps of the Hernández–Las Mulas grant include a survey by John C. Hays of October 1, 1841, recorded in Bexar County Survey Book F-1, p. 12; and a partition of 1884 of Las Mulas from Bexar County Survey Book M, p. 195. See also folders 113, 114, 120, and 238 of the Cassiano-Pérez Collection for plat maps, survey notes, etc., associated with this grant. The litigation on Las Mulas has been voluminous.

portion included the place where Mission San Juan had formerly had its Indians tending sheep and goats, perhaps accounting for Arocha's eventually adding "de Pataguiya" to "San Rafael."

Several other clans were intermarried with Don Simón de Arocha's, a circumstance which figured in his rise to prominence (for example, as the leading exporter of cattle to other provinces). Among them were the Delgado, Leal, and Móntes de Oca families, whose names appear frequently in ranching documents. Simón's brother Juan married María Manuela Móntes de Oca, and she was shown as a cattle raiser many years after her husband's death in 1788. Simón's sister Anna María Arocha married Joaquín Leal, and their ranch of eleven sitios adjoined Simón's on the north, separated by the Arroyo Calaveras. Other Arocha girls married ranchers Ignacio Calvillo and Manuel Delgado, and most of the Arocha boys married into ranching families.[26]

Others, like the Carvajal, de la Garza, Seguín, Rodríguez, and Sambrano families will be mentioned in due course because they were important eighteenth-century ranchers in the Béxar jurisdiction. A careful study of all these clusters immediately reveals one important point: practically everyone in El Rincón was related to everyone else within two generations or less. Being "kin," they behaved like all other such close-knit groups living in a relatively isolated frontier environment. They stuck together and worked out their problems among themselves. This is not to say that they did not quarrel among themselves; yet when they were threatened from outside, they invariably closed ranks against the intruder. This attitude was lamented by more than one official who was attempting to use their petty differences against them in enforcing unpopular cattle laws. It did not take the first commandant general, Teodoro de Croix,

---

[26] Chabot, *Makers of San Antonio*, pp. 167–70, supplemented by the unpublished work of John Ogden Leal, Bexar County archivist, who has compiled extensive records on many Canary Islanders, taken from the records kept at San Fernando Church, the Spanish Archives still at San Antonio, etc. Bexar Survey Book F-1, pp. 48–49, contains a copy of a partition of 1845 of the Joaquín Leal grant, the original of which is missing.

long to learn this. Soon after taking control of the Interior Provinces, he complained, "The Officers of San Fernando form a most ridiculous *cabildo*, because of the ignorance of all, and do many absurd and shameful things due to the difficulty of appeal to distant superiors." Other observers were even less kind to this hardy band of pioneers who had dared set up ranching operations in El Rincón. But these founding folk called their rich river valley La Joya (the Jewel), and they meant to keep both it and the cattle that grazed on its broad pastures.[27]

Oddly enough, it is to a Frenchman, Pierre Marie François de Pagès, that we owe our best description of the environment, appearance, and practices of these early *ganaderos* and their vaquero herdsmen. Perhaps Spanish chroniclers neglected to provide such a description because it was taken for granted that Texans raised cattle as everyone else did in Nueva España; that is, it was common knowledge, and it was not worth describing what everyone already knew. Not so with Monsieur de Pagès; to him it was all new and quite remarkable.

Arriving at Los Adaes in 1767, Pagès carefully noted the appearance of the "species of cavalry" which occupied the dismal post. He said that for pleasure they related the perils and hardships they regularly faced, boasted about their exploits in battle, or mounted their horses, "visiting and taming their cattle." The common soldier's dress consisted of a large hood and short cloak, adorned around the neck with broad stripes of gold lace. Beneath this was worn a "sort of under-waistcoat and breeches without a seam, but pieced together with buttons of gold and silver and commonly ornamented with lace." To protect himself from arrows, the soldier also wore a greatcoat made from three or four folds of deerskin quilted with cotton, a garment that the stockman no doubt wore as well. His stockings

---

[27] Myres, *Ranch in Spanish Texas*, p. 39, citing I. J. Cox, "The Early Settlers of San Fernando," Texas State Historical Association *Quarterly* 5 (July, 1901–April, 1902): 155. Aurelia Flores Deuvall and Peggy A. Rodríguez, *Our Family Heritage*, contains a compilation of El Rincón ranchero family genealogies beginning at about the point Chabot leaves off. This collection, as the name implies, was an outgrowth of family reunions held in Wilson County at the old Yndo Ranch, now a park.

were made of skin, and a pair of "enormous spurs about 5 or 6 inches in length" armed his heels.

Pagès also was fascinated by the soldiers' neatly dressed and stamped saddle leathers, describing them as garnished along the edges with trinkets of steel which, like little bells, were kept perpetually ringing by the horse's motion. "Ponderous stirrups" composed of massy bars of iron arranged in the shape of a cross and weighing at least 50 pounds were used to keep the rider steady in his seat, lending to a style the Spaniards considered most graceful. For Pagès, however, they caused a swelling of the legs and near dislocation of his joints. "In fine, the half-savage Spaniard, with all this singular extravagance, is an excellent rider, and when completely equipped and mounted never failed to revive in my mind all the ideas of ancient chivalry." [28]

Since Pagès did not alter this image on his subsequent journey into the interior of Mexico, it is reasonable to assume that he believed that it was representative of the "species of cavalry" encountered throughout the country, except for possible refinements on its Adaesaño rusticity. His description and others by military inspectors of the period establish that mounted soldiers, militiamen, and ranchers of the province all dressed in a similar fashion, for the same men were often engaged in these activities. According to the Marqués de Rubí, who entered Texas on a tour of inspection from below the Río Grande at the same time that Pagès crossed over from Louisiana, the uniforms at Béxar were "highly individualized" in style and color, shades of red being the most popular. They were dirty and ragged but still bedecked with costly silk handkerchiefs, lace, and silver buttons, each garb vying with the others in makeshift gaudiness, while weapons were either nonexistent or unserviceable. Horses were bought in Coahuila or from the Béxar missions at 8 or 10 pesos each, but the soldiers had to pay 16 to 25 pesos for them.

---

[28] Pierre Marie François de Pagès, *Travels round the World in the Years 1767, 1768, 1769, 1770, 1771*, 1:50–56. Marilyn McAdams Sibley, *Travelers in Texas, 1761–1860*, pp. 8–9, 48, 69–71; and Gerald Ashford, *Spanish Texas, Yesterday and Today*, pp. 169–71, provide interesting background material on this early tourist and place his visit in historical context.

Saddles were imported from Pénjamo (a district in the present state of Guanajuato) at a cost of 12 pesos each and sold locally for 28, a state of affairs typical of the way *presidiales* were exploited by their commanders and post purveyors. These conditions, which Rubí termed deplorable, were found to exist virtually throughout Texas, and he formed a set of recommendations designed to change things on the frontier.[29]

When Pagès reached the Brazos River, "in the province of Tegas," he began to see "traces of horned cattle, which were originally tame, but have long since become wild, and now roam in large herds all over the plains." He described a cow hunt—one hundred years before post–Civil War Anglo cowboys "invented" the activity—just as he later left a detailed account of a roundup in the vicinity of San Luis Potosí. On both occasions fatigue was a key feature of working cows on the open range, the cattle being chased until they dropped.[30]

Arriving at Béxar in late November, one month after leaving Nacogdoches, the French visitor noted that the principal employment in the area was raising horses, mules, cattle, and sheep. Roaming cows were rounded up every two months and driven into fields near the houses, where they were confined, starved, and rendered tame and tractable by various means. Then the animals were turned out, and a new bunch was brought in. He commented, "Such of the inhabitants as are at pains to prevent their herds from running entirely wild, are found to possess five or six thousand head of cattle." While this may be something of an exaggeration, at least for the private *ganaderos* in 1767, wild stock was indeed plentiful around

---

[29] Castañeda, *Catholic Heritage*, 4:235–42, summarizes Rubí's inspection tour; also see Herbert Eugene Bolton, *Texas in the Middle Eighteenth Century*, pp. 377–84; Ashford, *Spanish Texas*, chap. 14.

[30] Pagès, *Travels round the World*, 1:79, 82–83, 132. Wayne Gard, *The Chisholm Trail*, p. 13. admits that Anglo cowboys learned much from their vaquero counterparts but seems to imply that the "recognized system" that resulted was original, or greater than the sum of its Spanish-derived parts. This, of course, reflects the way Anglo stockmen have traditionally viewed their accomplishments. Glenn R. Vernam, *Man on Horseback*, gives a more detailed (and accurate) account of the debt Anglo ranchers owe their Spanish predecessors, in terms of equipment, methods, etc., as do authorities like Jo Mora, Robert M. Denhardt, and Richard E. Ahlborn.

Béxar. Pagès said that the people milked their tame cows or took fat (tallow) and dried beef. Once horses and mules were broken, they were sold. Unlike Rubí, he claimed that prices were low, mentioning that he traded a pair of shoes for a good horse. What he perhaps failed to realize was that Texas abounded with wild horses but custom-made French shoes were in extremely short supply.

Although poles were used in provincial Texas—witness the early complaints about stock being speared (*rejoneado, garrocheado*) to eject them from cultivated fields—one suspects that the *lazo* (lasso) gradually replaced them as the ultimate tool for working cattle. *Picas* (lances), however, remained in use as a weapon of horsemen, military and civilian alike, as late as the Texas Revolution and the Mexican War (for that matter, so did ropes). No doubt the *picas* were used to poke cows from time to time.

Pagès mentions use of the lasso in a spirited narrative, saying, "The inhabitants of San Antonio are excellent horsemen, and particularly fond of hunting or *lacing* [sic] their wild animals." He observed that hunters seldom failed to catch their targets around the neck or horns with a cast of the loop. On a roundup in the interior of Mexico he witnessed another technique used to stun cattle taken on the run that sounds much like a practice later used in Texas. It was called *coleada del toro* ("tailing the bull") and was accomplished by coming alongside a fleeing animal and seizing and jerking the tail upward, thus upsetting its stride and dumping the animal on its nose. Vaqueros would then dismount and tie its feet with a short rope known as a *peal*.

Owing to the shortage of herdsmen around Béxar (there were only one or two, according to Pagès), even domestic stock was accustomed to run day and night in the woods. This practice presented no problem because "the keen eye which the habit of close and minute attention has bestowed on these people is truly surprising." In other words, they were good trackers, "nor do they despair of finding him [a bull] before they have gone fifteen perhaps twenty leagues from home." To accomplish such feats without becoming lost in the wilderness, the Spaniards had devised some ingenious methods, a system of recognized landmarks and wood lore, which allowed them to range far afield in search of their livestock.[31]

Some scholars have concluded that the rodeo, or organized cattle roundup, was inspired by a form of "Indian hunt." The conqueror of Nuevo León, Don Luis de Carvajal, actively engaged in slaving operations against the Indians before he and his colonists turned their attention to founding villas and developing large ranches north of the Pánuco River. He was not the only conquistador so occupied. Pagès mentions that soldiers at Béxar roped not only cows but Indians, carrying them to the missions bound in carts. There is little doubt that Indians were hunted, either as slaves or as neophytes for the missionaries. Priests in Texas were constantly complaining that the various governors would not give them sufficient soldiers to preserve order or help bring runaways back to the fold. At other times they denounced expeditions against the Indians as little more than slave-catching operations, perhaps executed in corrida (roundup) fashion.[32]

Working from sixteenth-century documents, François Chevalier describes the way such roundups were conducted by the hacendados of Mexico. Cowboys mounted on horseback fanned out in a circle and drove cattle toward the estancias; or the herds were converged at a prearranged place, where vaqueros would sort them with the aid of long, iron-tipped *garrochas*. After cattle moved into the virgin territories of the northern provinces, great roundups were held. Hundreds of horsemen, spread out in an immense circle, drove the cattle toward a center designated by provincial law officers. There the cattle were sorted according to owners. Unbranded animals (*orejanos*) were divided up among the stockmen, while strays bearing unfamiliar brands were handed over to the king's representatives as *mostrencos*. These practices, with modification, soon made their way on a smaller scale north to Texas, to be practiced by

---

[31] Pagès, *Travels round the World*, 1:96–99, 132.

[32] Ibid., pp. 101–102. Myres, *Ranch in Spanish Texas*, p. 26, cites the work of François Chevalier as a basis for comparison of Indian hunts with cattle roundups; also see Bolton, *Texas in the Middle Eighteenth Century*, p. 31; Kilgore, "Texas Cattle Origins," p. 112.

the up-and-coming *ganaderos*, who were threatening the missions' dominance of stock raising.[33]

Forty years after Pagès visited and recorded glimpses of Texas ranching culture, Zebulon Montgomery Pike passed through the province and left another account.[34] Things changed slowly on the frontier, and many of Pike's observations round out the picture of inhabitants "always ready to mount their horses," on which he said they spent half the day. Pike's "Map of the Internal Provinces of New Spain" of 1807 shows "Immense Herds of wild Horses" ranging between the Río Colorado de Natchitoches (Red River) and the Río del Norte, and his journals are replete with lavish descriptions of thundering wild-horse herds and the manner in which they were captured and broken to the saddle, for which business he assumed there was "no nation in the world superior to the Spaniards of Texas." Further, he touched on manners, morals, government, commerce, military, and other aspects of New Spain. His account, taken with that of his contemporary Ramón de Murillo, also offers us the best description of the saddles in use at the close of the eighteenth century. Because frontier cattlemen and *soldados de cuera* ("leather-jacket soldiers") used similar saddles and because so much debate continues about how these prototypes of the modern American western stock saddle both looked and functioned, it is worth examining their accounts.[35]

---

[33] François Chevalier, *Land and Society in Colonial Mexico—The Great Hacienda*, p. 111. Findings on stock raising since Chevalier's work are discussed in Colin M. MacLachlan and Jaime E. Rodríguez O., *The Forging of the Cosmic Race: A Reinterpretation of Colonial Mexico*, pp. 150–65.

[34] All quotations on Pike's journey are from Donald Jackson, ed., *The Journals of Zebulon Montgomery Pike*, hereafter cited throughout as *Pike's Journals*. Volume 1 contains the diary of his trip through Texas; vol. 2 contains his report on the province, its morals, manners, customs, etc.

[35] Map no. 1438, Texas State Archives. The bibliography in Russel H. Beatie, *Saddles*, pp. 365–80, offers a good survey of the sources on the evolution of the western stock saddle. Unfortunately, he advances the unprovable notions that New World saddles did not have horns until "between 1820 and 1835" and that vaquero saddles had a "much lowered fork with no horn" (pp. 48–50), making these statements several times. He even goes so far as to imply that Pike did not see the horned saddle he described, while at the same time reproducing several examples of eighteenth-century saddles with horns (pp. 48, 59, 266).

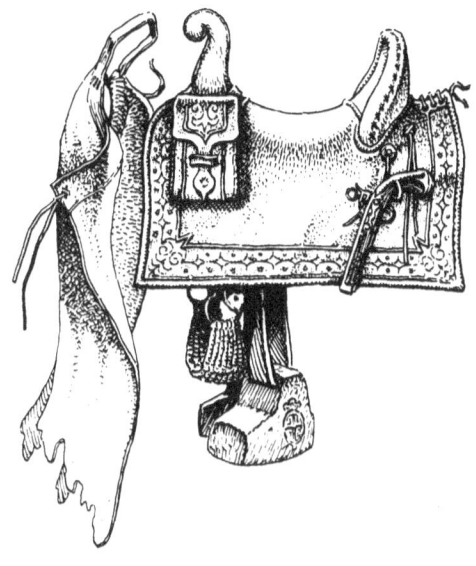

First, a bit of background is in order. Briefly it can be said that Spanish saddles brought to the New World were primarily war saddles. They had a high rear cantle to keep the rider from being pushed out the back and a high projecting piece to protect him in the front; he was literally encased in the seat. These war saddles proved to be impractical for working cattle and were considerably streamlined, but the basic component parts remained the same: a wooden saddletree (*fuste*) composed of two sidebars (*tablas*); a front piece, or fork (*fuste delantero*); and a rear piece, or cantle (*fuste trasero*). These pieces were joined firmly together by stretching and sewing pieces of wet rawhide over them. When dry, these layers contracted, forming the tree into one solid unit.

The *tablas* were covered with pads (*lomillos*) to protect the horse's flanks, and skirts (*bastos*) were added for more protection. This was the basic skeleton, which rested on a saddle blanket or sweat pad (*sudadero*). Straps, or stirrup leathers (*arciones*), hung from the bars and supported foot stirrups, which could be of numerous kinds. Some were made of metal in a cruciform design (*estribos de cruz*); others were carved from a single block of wood (*estribos de baúl, de palo, de madera,* and so on), either open or closed; and still others were made of metal and box-shaped, with open or closed ends. Elaborate forms of leather toe fenders or stirrup covers (*tapaderas*) were created further to protect the rider's foot.

Spanish horsemen wore buckskin *botas* (leggings) on their lower legs, but as an additional protection from thorns and brush they used *armas*, or *defensas*, large rawhide covers that hung from the saddlehorn. These could be pulled up over the thigh and secured behind the saddle. If they were waterproof, they were called *armas para agua*. In time the *armas* evolved into *armitas*, smaller rectangular slabs of leather tied back over the leg from a belt attachment. They are credited with being the forerunner of closed-leg *chaparreras*, from which term came the word "chaps."

The framework of the vaquero saddle was covered with a removable housing, or *mochila*, which had openings for the fork and cantle. Saddlebags (*coginillos*) were attached to the fork; Pagès called them "two little leathern boxes." Other coverings (*corazas, coronas,* and so on), some fancy, some very functional, were also in use. The saddle was secured with a front rigging, or assembly, which later became known simply as "Spanish rigging." It was composed of pieces of leather (*reata y contra reata*) which encircled the fork on each side or reached from behind the cantle, connecting to a rigging ring (*argolla del enrreatado*). The cinch (*cincha*) which went under the horse's belly was tightened by use of a strap called a *latigo*, connected to the rings. In the early days an elaborate housing (*anquera*) was sometimes attached to the rear of the saddle. It must originally have served a defensive purpose but evolved into an ornamental piece called a *cola de pato* ("duck's tail"), used to protect a fancy blanket or a lady riding double from the animal's sweat.[36]

---

[36] For more information on the evolution of the saddle see Sidney B. Brinckerhoff and Odie B. Faulk, *Lancers for the King: A Study of the Frontier Military System of Northern New Spain, with a Translation of the Royal Regulations of 1772*, pp. vii, 23; Odie B. Faulk, *The Leather Jacket Soldier: Spanish Military Equipment and Institutions of the Late 18th Century*, pp. 62, 72, 77; Lee M. Rice and Glenn R. Vernam, *They Saddled the West*, pp. 2–14. The best study so far is Richard E. Ahlborn, ed., *Man Made Mobile: Early Saddles of Western North America*.

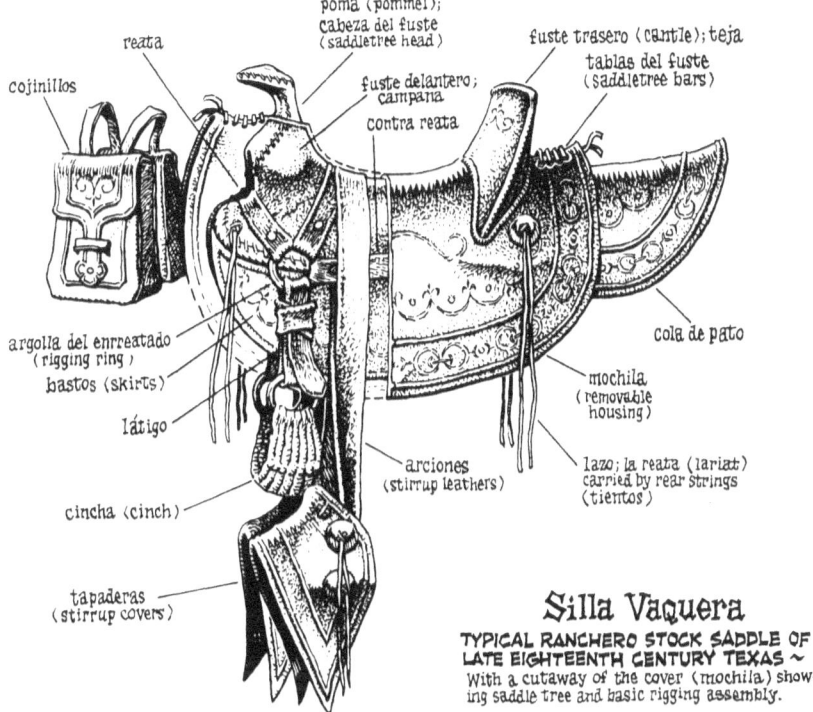

Silla Vaquera

TYPICAL RANCHERO STOCK SADDLE OF LATE EIGHTEENTH CENTURY TEXAS ~
With a cutaway of the cover (mochila) showing saddle tree and basic rigging assembly.

This was the basic design of the vaquero's rig, little changed for two hundred years. Certain modifications were made, however, to meet the demands of working cattle and long hours spent in the saddle. Stirrup leathers were lengthened, and the cantle was redesigned and slanted to provide a more comfortable ride. The head of the saddletree (*cabeza del fuste*) was whittled down into a pommel (*poma*) and then strengthened and capped with an "apple" (*manzana*) to provide a post for securing a rope. Pike described the need that gave rise to the saddle horn: "They will catch another horse with a noose and hair rope, when both are running nearly full speed, with which they will soon choke down the beast of which they are in pursuit." After he cast his loop, it became the vaquero's practice to take a turn of rope (*da le vuelta*, a term later corrupted by Anglo cowboys to "dally") around the saddle horn or pommel, thus securing the catch and allowing the saddle, not the roper's arm, to receive the jolt of the captured animal. Doubtless many a cap was broken from its horn before this design and technique became refined.

George Vancouver observed the practice in Alta California fifteen years before Pike's trip through the Interior Provinces. At Santa Clara, down the bay peninsula from San Francisco, in November, 1792, he was treated to a roundup by local soldiers. Each man had a lasso of either braided horsehair or rawhide with a long running noose: ". . . this is thrown with great dexterity whilst at full speed, and nearly with a certainty, over the horns of the animals, by two men, one on each side of the ox, at the same instant of time; and having a *strong high-peaked pummel to their saddles*, each takes a turn round it with the end of the line" (italics added).

On this subject Richard E. Ahlborn, of the Smithsonian Institution, has observed: "It may turn out, that the roping horn was a northern or northwest Mexican development, rather than a south-central (Zacatecas to Mexico) one." Specimens from this critical transition period are virtually nonexistent, and it remains to be established exactly how, when, and where the transition took place. As José Cisneros, another student of saddle evolution, says, it is a "very complicated business," because several different northward routes were followed, and the prototypes themselves varied between the heavy, European war saddle (*estradiota*) and a lighter, Moorish rig (*jineta*). Consequently, says Cisneros, saddles in Mexico acquired all sorts of shapes, "especially the horn—with and without." Such detailed accounts of roping activities as Captain Vancouver recorded are harder to come by in eighteenth-century Texas, but it can be safely assumed until proved otherwise that saddles there conformed to the horned type found elsewhere in northern New Spain.[37]

The Royal Regulations of 1772, adopted as a result of Rubí's recommendations, required such a vaquero-style saddle (*la silla ha de ser vaquera*) with a corresponding cover (*mochila*),

---

[37]Jackson, *Pike's Journals*, 2:88; Marguerite Eyer Wilber, ed., *Vancouver in California, 1792–1794*, pp. 44–46; private correspondence with José Cisneros and Richard E. Ahlborn.

Stirring in the Cradle 83

a saddle pad (*coraza*), leather leg guards (*armas*), front-mounted saddlebags (*coginillos*), and enclosed wooden stirrups. The use of large stirrups such as those noted by Pagès was henceforth prohibited since they were deemed unsuitable and dangerous. In 1776 Commandant Inspector Hugo Oconor gave an account of how these regulations were being enforced, saying that the mounted soldier's gear consisted of a vaquero saddle with "matching leather covers called *mochila* and *coraza*, leather side skirts to protect the legs from thorny brush, a cushion and wooden stirrups." This vaquero saddle became the standard riding gear for the mounted troops of New Spain. Likely it saw use before the 1770s in Texas, where stock handling was a way of life for many provincial soldiers and militiamen.[38]

In 1804, just a few years before Pike passed through the Provincias Internas, a report was presented to King Charles IV's

---

[38] Brinckerhoff and Faulk, *Lancers for the King*, pp. 22–23; Weddle and Thonhoff, *Drama and Conflict*, p. 92.

minister of state by one Ramón de Murillo which discussed frontier conditions and then made certain proposals. Some of them outlined the equipment still used by the leather-jacket soldiers that Murillo wanted changed because it was such *despreciable mueble* ("contemptible furniture"). On the subject of *silla de la montura* (saddle trappings), he said that they resembled a jousting seat with large front and back mounts. He noted that the stirrups were of wood and "cut like a bucket so the foot is better guarded in the rough country." No breast leathers or cruppers were used, and the master cinch was made from horsehair. "The cover is of strong cowhide [*baquera fuerte*] and a notable defect is the lack of holsters [*canoneras*]. They have in their place great bags [*mas bolsas grandes*] in which to put the water and provisions, carrying the pistols below the back *fuste* hanging from rings in the cover." In terms of changes in this horse furniture Murillo suggested only using saddle blankets (*mantillas*), moving the pistol holsters forward to the *fuste delantero*, and switching the large saddlebags to the rear, developments which become standard in the early nineteenth century. As an afterthought he recommended breast leathers, cruppers, medium boots, and regulation spurs, since the spurs being used made it "impossible to walk when the need arises."[39]

Pike's report, made at virtually the same time, is interesting because it comes from a military man trained in the Anglo, not the Hispanic, tradition. Yet his observations on the Spanish soldiers' saddle trappings are much the same. In 1807, Pike said that pistols were still mounted behind the rider, on each side of the saddle, while a "carabine" was slung in a case on the front. The saddle was made "after the Persian mode," with a high, projecting pommel and likewise raised behind. It was covered with two or three leather housings of embroidered workmanship, some with gold and silver in a superb manner. Stirrups

---

[39] Ramón de Murillo, "Plan demostrativo que manifiesta el estado en que se hallan las Provincias Ynternas del Reyno de Nueva España . . . ," AGI, Sevilla, Mapas y Planos, México, nos. 57, 81, 89, copy provided the author by G. Douglas Inglis. One of Murillo's watercolors—which should prove that these saddles had horns—is in Editors of Time-Life Books, *The Spanish West*, p. 68.

were of wood and closed in front, generally carved into the head of a lion or some other beast. These stirrups were heavy and "to us present a very clumsy appearance." Captain Pike went so far as to deem the Spanish horse equipment superior to the English, for all its awkward appearance, adding, "They have the advantage over us as to the skill of the rider, as well as in the quality of the beast." He noted that their bridles had a strong curb and that when riders were seated in the saddle it was impossible for the most vicious horse to dismount them. "In short, they are probably the most expert horsemen in the world"— not bad for a group of people some of whom had arrived in Texas a generation earlier barely able to ride.[40]

---

[40] Jackson, *Pike's Journals*, 2:88.

4

"A GREAT NUMBER OF CATTLE"

For the Taking...

Less than three years after Juan José Flores registered what can be considered the first cattle brand of a Texas *ganadero*, another such *marca* was issued to a prominent El Rincón ranching clan. On January 28, 1765, Alcalde Bernabé Carvajal (the same Carvajal who had formerly owned Los Corralitos) issued two marks to Don Andrés Hernández and his wife, Juana de Oyos, "on behalf of their son, Joseph Miguel Hernández, for his herd of twenty-four mares that are bred with jacks."[1]

Such an event may seem mundane, but it is noteworthy for two reasons: first, because so few early Texas cattle brands have survived, and both of these on record belonged to important ranching families; and, second, because it was in the mid-1760s that raids began to be directed against Béxar by the powerful Comanches and their allies, and it took some courage to think of raising mules under those conditions. Stockmen had grown somewhat accustomed to Lipan Apache thievery, but the appearance of *los norteños* in the area was a frightening new complication.

[1] BAT, 42:77.

According to an alarmist report given on April 9, 1763, by Fray Joseph Ignacio María Alegre y Capetillo, the *procurador* (agent) of the Querétaran establishments in Texas, the situation was pretty rough. He said that the numerous "Nations of the North," enemies of the Spaniards since 1758, had destroyed the herds—"las manadas, Ganados maiores y menores"—and had depopulated the seventeen ranches which the missions and citizens had established along the banks of the San Antonio River, as well as those of the Arroyo del Cíbolo and Salado. These hostile Indians had killed many people, both Spaniards and mission Indians, not only in the surrounding area but in their homes as well. Belongings had been captured and carried away and were now scattered far and near, all the way to the sea. No one was willing to venture even one league from the villa, so grave was the danger. Father Alegre said that the vecinos were terrorized and that many wanted to leave—"Some have already." He ended with an appeal that the citizens be permitted to abandon San Antonio unless they had a military obligations requiring them to stay. As noted earlier, other missionaries were writing glum reports of the Indian situation at the same time, blaming the Apaches for stock depredations.[2]

Nonetheless, the 1760s carried forward the momentum started in the previous decade. New families moved downriver into El Rincón, possibly from the little settlement known as Las Islitas which was situated opposite Paso de las Borregas, the ford where mission sheep were moved across the river to new pastures.[3] Father Solís's diary, kept when he visited Texas in early 1768, allows us a fair idea of the ranches which existed in the San Antonio River valley at the time. From his diary and that of Nicolás de la Fora, a talented member of Rubí's inspection tour, and Pagès's account, more details emerge.

---

[2] Genaro García Collection, folders 138 and 197 (Benson Latin American Center, University of Texas).

[3] John Odgen Leal has done considerable research on the location of Las Islitas, placing it on the right bank of the San Antonio River in the Mariana (Mariano) Seguín grant above Graytown and the present Bexar-Wilson county line. Paso de las Borregas Road was later called Elmendorf Road, as old maps show (John Rullmann, June 7, 1887, Map of Bexar County, no. 1788, Texas State Archives).

In mid-March Solís left Rosario's rancho near La Bahía and headed upriver toward Béxar, traveling on the west bank. He went through a ranch called San Joseph "belonging to the captain of La Bahía" (Captain Piscina).⁴ This was no doubt the ranch described the year before by Nicolás de la Fora as El Capitán. Leaving La Bahía en route to Laredo, Rubí's party traveled 10 leagues west over gentle hills with abundant pasture and some clumps of trees. "[The hills] are covered with cattle, some of the herds belonging to the missions, some to the deceased captain, some to the settlers," La Fora commented. At 2 leagues the military inspectors passed the mission of El Rosario and 2 leagues farther a small rancho dependent on this mission. Going 6 leagues more they camped near the Arroyo Cunillo. On the right was El Capitán, situated on the bank of the San Antonio River, 10 leagues from the presidio.⁵

On March 16, above the Escondida, Solís wrote: "I passed La Parrita, the Capote ranch, located on the banks of the San Antonio River, went through the Mora Ranch, the property of San Juan Capistrano mission and located on the banks of the same river, and finally arrived at the Padre Cárdenas ranch, also on the banks of the river."⁶ La Parrita (the Grapevine) would be difficult to place except that Solís identifies it as the "Capote ranch." The Capote Hills were far north of Solís's route, up near the Guadalupe, and while El Capote (the Cape) was a familiar landmark, it is highly unlikely that any ranch existed there, especially that early. It was usually cited as the limit of Mission

⁴This ranch was subsequently claimed by Carlos Martínez, a soldier at La Bahía and a well-known rancher in the last quarter of the century. It was settled by Carlos's father, Joseph, in the area known as Ojo de Agua Martínez (Martínez's Spring), according to a declaration made in 1778 (GLO, 50:180), and lay just above Captain Piscina's ranch (Robert S. Weddle and Robert H. Thonhoff, *Drama and Conflict: The Texas Saga of 1776*, pp. 158–59; Virginia H. Taylor, *The Spanish Archives of the General Land Office of Texas*, pp. 27–28).

⁵Lawrence Kinnaird, ed., *The Frontiers of New Spain: Nicolás de la Fora's Description, 1766–1768*, pp. 178–79.

⁶References to Solís's visit are taken from Paul J. Foik and Peter P. Forrestal, eds. and trans., *The Solís Diary of 1767*, pp. 9, 15–18, 20–23, 30–32, 39, parts of which can be found in Kathryn Stoner O'Connor, *The Presidio La Bahía del Espíritu Santo de Zúñiga, 1721–1846*, pp. 40–50. Although Solís started out from Zacatecas in November, 1767, he did not cross the Río Grande until February of the next year.

Espíritu Santo's pastures, beyond which lay the king's lands. The ranch referred to by Solís was probably San Simón del Capote, a ranch described as "empty and abandoned" when Joachín de la Garza and his son asked for possession of it in 1773. It was bounded on the north by the river, on the south by royal lands and the Arroyo Escondida, and on the east by the junction of that arroyo with the San Antonio River. This places it squarely between La Mora and El Capitán, consistent with Solís's description.[7]

As mentioned, at this time La Mora most probably belonged to Valero, not San Juan Capistrano. Likewise it is difficult to say with certainty what the "Padre Cárdenas ranch" was. At first glance one is tempted to associate this place with Fray José Luis Mariano de Cárdenas, who was in charge of San Juan Capistrano during the next decade. According to Marion A. Habig, Cárdenas was not in Texas until 1772 or later, and the ranch of Padre Cárdenas was recognized earlier than this date. For example, when the Delgados settled along Arroyo Espanta Perros in 1766, they acknowledged Cárdenas's prior occupation, saying that Manuel de la Fuente had claim to lands in the area because they bordered on the padre's. The answer seems to be that this rancho was owned or operated by the *bachiller* Reverend Juan Ygnacio de Cárdenas, pastor of the Villa de San Fernando in 1758, not the Franciscan brotherhood. It will be recalled from the Menchaca-Hernández compromise, however, that a decade earlier Mission San Juan did have stock in this general area (across and upriver) at the place called Pataguilla.[8]

The next day a goat ranch (doubtless Las Cabras) was

---

[7] Joachín and Martín de la Garza to Gov. Ripperdá, September 19, 1773, Daughters of the Republic of Texas Library at the Alamo. This petition for land was accompanied by Simón de Arocha's approval.

[8] Fr. Marion A. Habig, "Biographical Dictionary," in Fr. Benedict Leutenegger, trans., *The Zacatecan Missionaries in Texas, 1716–1834: Excerpts from the Libros de los Decretos of the Missionary College of Zacatecas, 1707–1828*, p. 114; letter no. 35, Documentary no. 7 (letters of Fray Mariano de los Dolores y Viana), unpublished, made available to the author by Father Habig. He adds in private correspondence that the fact that Solís was of the Zacatecan college probably accounts for his confusion about the establishments administered by the Querétarans. For more information on the Padre Cárdenas Ranch, see the lawsuit of 1770 between Manuel de la Fuente and Manuel Delgado, box 2Q236, University of Texas Archives.

passed through, several creeks were noted, and then Solís crossed the river to the east side, arriving at the "Corral de San Juan Capistrano." To judge from the following day's journey, this corral was near the road that led up to the mission from the San Antonio River but below the Salado junction.

After several weeks in Béxar, visiting the various missions and writing his report of Mission San José and its ranch, El Atascoso, Solís resumed his journey, heading for East Texas. The route he followed took him into El Rincón, east of the San Antonio River. Later that summer on his return trip from La Bahía to Béxar he passed over to the east bank, above Agua Escondida, through the same area.[9] The ranches that he noted were as follows:

1. Chayopines, described as below Las Calaveras, on the road "leading from the river," probably the Bahía Road scouted by Captain Piscina in 1755. Later Solís referred to it as a ranch belonging to the priest of the "Chayopines presidio," a rather puzzling description. It is known that the Chayopines, Zayopines, or Sayopines were a tribe or band of Indians used to found Mission San Juan (Morfi) and that Don Simón de Arocha's Rancho de San Rafael was in this vicinity. Since Arocha became head of the Béxar militia, and since he later claimed that he and his brother Juan had occupied their ranch from 1766, perhaps Solís meant the Arochas' little settlement.

Other evidence suggests that the Peña family was early associated with the place-name Chayopines, Challopines, and so on, but usually on the opposite (right) bank of the river. Ignacio Peña claimed in 1778 that he had been at the "Challopin Rancho" since 1768, staying even through the worst of the Indian wars. Francisco Flores, the grandson of the pioneer rancher Juan José Flores, received title to the place named Chayopines on the west bank in 1827, claiming occupation since his father's time.[10]

Apparently the name switched to the west bank of the

---

[9] Foik and Forrestal, *Solís Diary*, pp. 21–22, 39.

[10] While some early documentation identifies Francisco Flores de Abrego y Valdés and his son Vizente with Rancho Chayopines, it appears that the Francisco who obtained title was descended from old Francisco's brother, Juan José. See Chabot, *Makers of San Antonio*, p. 62, for grantee Francisco (shown as III, 2) and his will, dated November 17, 1858 (Probate Records, estate no. 556, BCSA); this grant is in GLO, 31:99.

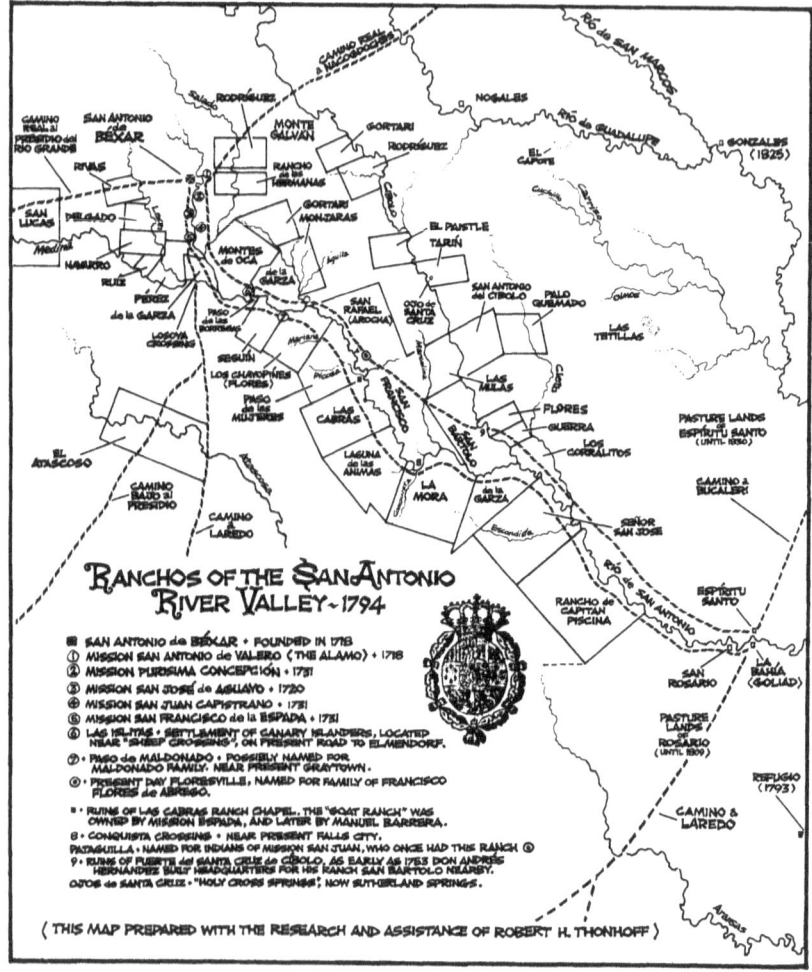

river. Another fragmented copy of Solís's diary clarifies the matter somewhat. On April 9 he "went past the Calaveras and . . . arrived at the Chayopines, a tributary of the San Antonio River." Returning upriver on July 31, "We arrived at the place where the Chayopines live, at the ranch of the resident priest of the said presidio." A search of the archives reveals that this priest was José Antonio Yldefonso de la Peña, perhaps related to Ignacio. At any rate, Father Solís noted that the place contained enough inhabitants to merit saying mass and erecting a cross. La Fora's diary has "Los Chayopines" as 4 leagues below the Las

Calaveras crossing in Aguila Creek; from there to the Marcelino (Marcelinas Creek), 7 leagues.[11]

2. San Francisco, which Solís bypassed on his first outing, going directly through the place where the Patauyas (or Pantayas) and Pajaritos (Little Birds) Indians lived and over the Marcelino. But on his final trip upriver he mentions arriving at a ranch "belonging to a man named San Francisco, captain of the presidio de Béxar." Father Benedict Leutenegger's translation has it "of San Antonio de Béxar which is called San Francisco." According to the diary, it was midway between the Escondida crossing and Chayopines. This, of course, was the ranch of Captain Luis Antonio Menchaca, the land he received despite the prior claims of Andrés Hernández.[12]

3. San Bartolo, Guerra, and Amoladeras, the ranches on the lower Cíbolo, the earliest establishments in El Rincón. Rancho Amoladeras (Grindstones) was owned by Miguel Guerra and his wife, Doña Josefa Quiñones; San Bartolo still belonged to the Hernández family. La Fora wrote: "Two leagues below [the Marcelino] was El Cíbolo, on whose banks are the *rancho* San Bartolo and several others belonging to the settlers of San Antonio. Some seasonal corn is sown and they raise some horses and mules."[13]

4. Los Corralitos de Reyes, which, according to Solís, belonged to Espíritu Santo Mission and was stocked with cattle and horses. This was the Little Pens Ranch formerly owned by Don Bernabé Carvajal.

These, then, are the river ranches mentioned by Fray Solís and engineer-cartographer La Fora. As stated, there is evidence that a few others existed along the fringes of the river valley and up the Cíbolo. In 1758, Vicente Álvarez Travieso settled Las Mulas, where he was soon joined by members of his numerous clan. Opposite San Bartolo was the widow of Martín Lorenzo de Armas, Doña María Robaina de Bethencourt, at the place called

---

[11] Carlos E. Casteñeda, *Our Catholic Heritage in Texas*, 4:228, traces the Rubí–La Fora route from San Antonio to East Texas, giving modern reference points. For the recent translation of Solís's diary fragments (from ACZ) see Fr. Benedict Leutenegger and Fr. Marion A. Habig, comps. and trans., *The San José Papers*, pt. 1, pp. 151–52.

[12] Foik and Forrestal, *Solís Diary*, p. 22; Leutenegger and Habig, *San José Papers*.

[13] Foik and Forrestal, *Solís Diary*; Kinnaird, *Frontiers of New Spain*, pp. 160–62.

San Antonio del Cíbolo. When this ranch, which was settled as early as 1756, was burned to the ground by soldiers from La Bahía led by Bernabé Carvajal—perhaps to protect his own interests—Don Martín asked the governor for land between La Laja Pass and the confluence of the Cíbolo with the San Antonio. The family stayed until 1769, when the Indians cleaned them out. Carlos Martínez was another rancher who claimed that his rights had been trampled by Carvajal's Corralitos deed. Although Martínez fled to Béxar for safety, he never relinquished his claim to lands around the Ojo de Agua Martínez.

Apart from these scattered ranches there were only the mission establishments, such as San José's rancho on the Atascosa River and Concepción's Paistle on the upper Cíbolo. It is likely that the place known as Monte Galván, even higher, was occupied at this time. In fact, a rather detailed agreement had been reached the preceding year concerning the manner in which Valero, Concepción, and San Juan would have access to these woods. In the agreement were specified the exact entrances and areas to be used by each, as well as procedures for roundups, slaughters, and sharing of *orejanos*. Monte Galván (near present Randolph Air Force Base) was prosperous by 1772, supplying all three east-bank Béxar missions with beef rations.[14]

But surrounding pastures were full of cattle, even if the ranch headquarters clung to the riverbanks. When Solís went downriver in April, 1768, after passing Los Corralitos, he left the river road and headed northeast cross-country. It would appear that he followed a well-worn path to the Guadalupe, for Inspector General Rubí and his captain of engineers, Nicolás de la Fora, took the same route in 1767, both parties bound for East Texas. Thus it is interesting to compare their travel entries.[15]

Solís wrote: "We passed by a place called Sinfonía and after-

---

[14] GLO, 50:180, 183, 185; ACZ, roll 2, frames 2802–2804, called to my attention by Isabel de Pedro.

[15] The foldout maps in Herbert Eugene Bolton, *Texas in the Middle Eighteenth Century*, and Castañeda, *Catholic Heritage*, vol. 4, show approximately these routes. Also see J. W. Williams, *Old Texas Trails*, ed. and comp. Kenneth F. Neighbors, pp. 166–68, which labels this route the "Southern Loop" and suggests that it crossed the Guadalupe south of, or near, the site of Cuero.

wards came to a large brook, in which we found good water and a large supply of fish. The brook, which is called Deto, supplies water for the livestock of the Bahía mission." Sinfonía (Symphony), or Encinas de la Sinfonía, is often mentioned in the Béxar Archives. Perhaps this landmark was a grove of live oaks particularly noted for pleasing harmonies made by the wind playing among its leaves. While it is difficult to establish with precision this and other old place-names, Robert H. Thonhoff has made an attempt, locating Sinfonía just north of present Runge.[16] Testimony given in 1777 places it near the headwaters of Arroyo Alonso, where the ranchers had built several corrals. The "Deto," as a reading of Rafael Cervantes's edition of Solís's diary will show, is the Cleto (modern Ecleto Creek). La Fora noted it as being 6 leagues beyond the San Bartolo ranches; it was there that Rubí's entourage camped. They found the creek almost dry (it was in late August) except for stagnant pools. El Cuchillo Arroyo (Knife Creek) was the next campsite of both Solís and Rubí. La Fora said that it was principally northeast from the Cleto stopping place, "formed by three small streams [which] unite a short distance from where we crossed." At the Cuchillo, Fray Solís was met by a party of La Bahía Indians, who had come to accompany him on his journey.

Between Cuchillo and the Guadalupe, Solís wrote, "On the pastures throughout this territory also we found a great number of cattle and mules belonging to the Bahía del Espíritu Santo mission." La Fora's diary says that it was 8 leagues from Cuchillo to the Guadalupe and that the crossing was made at the place called Vado del Governador. Carlos E. Castañeda suggests that this site was near modern Hochheim, possibly where Governor Alarcón came near drowning. If so, "Knife Creek" must have been modern-day Sandies Creek, which is fed by at least three tributaries.[17]

---

[16] Weddle and Thonhoff, *Drama and Conflict*, pp. 155–56.

[17] Rafael Cervantes, intro. and annot., *Diario del padre fray Gaspar José de Solís en su visita a las misiones de Texas 1768*, p. 58. Stephen F. Austin's "Mapa original de Texas" (1829) shows the Cuchillo, the Carrizo, and the Olmos to be what is now known as Sandies Creek and its related tributaries, all of which enter the Guadalupe River near Cuero (Robert S. Martin, "Maps of an Empresario: Austin's Contribution to the Cartography of Texas," *Southwestern Historical Quarterly* 85, no. 4 [April, 1982]: 391–95). In

Solís and La Fora mention many of the same reference points beyond the Guadalupe—Arroyo El Cuervo (La Fora), or Cuero (Solís); El Rosal; La Mota del Padre Campa; Los Ramitos; La Vaca; Breviario, and so on—moving toward the Navidad River. It was between the Colorado and Brazos rivers that Father Solís, like Pagès, remarked on the wild herds and their origin, remarks thought by some to be the source of Fray Juan Agustín de Morfi's subsequent account. Noting the many deer, turkeys, quail, bison, and bears and several droves of horses and cattle of Castilian breed that ran about wild and without any owner, Solís wrote, "These animals are very plentiful for the reason that Captain León (of happy memory), who was the first to discover and conquer these lands, left on the riverbanks a bull and a cow, a stallion and a mare."[18]

Both of these reports, along with that of Pagès, also speak of the modest enclave of ranches near the Louisiana border. Fray Solís, after crossing the "Atollaque" and several brooks, came to Aís Mission, at a distance La Fora gave as 5 leagues beyond the "Arroyo Atoyaque." Two leagues past Los Aís was Palo Gacho, a spring or creek; and 2 leagues beyond was what Solís called the Lobanillo de Gil Ranch, where he took dinner. La Fora termed it El Lobanillo (the Wart) Arroyo, "where the missionaries of Aís had a rancho which they themselves are believed to have ordered burned." If so, apparently the Gil y Barbo family had already occupied the place and begun ranching there. Antonio, born in 1729, the son of Matheo Antonio Ybarbo (as it is often written) and Juana Lasgarda Hernández, started this ranch soon after his marriage, along with seven brothers. (Gil was a sur-

---

the tracing of early routes, streams, and place-names between Béxar and La Bahía, it is helpful to consult Jean Louis Berlandier's *Journey to Mexico during the Years 1826 to 1834*. He describes various *parajes* (resting places) along the way, such as Las Calaveras, Encinal de la Candelaría, and Pajaritos, as well as San Bartolo, where there "formerly existed a rancho." San Bartolo was also the name given to the lower Cíbolo (pp. 372–73, 552–56).

[18] Foik and Forrestal, *Solís Diary*, p. 24; Fray [Juan] Agustín [de] Morfi, *Excerpts from the Memorias for the History of the Province of Texas*, trans. and ed. Frederick C. Chabot, pp. 58–59; Fray Juan Agustín de Morfi, *The History of Texas, 1693–1779*, trans. and ed. Carlos E. Castañeda, p. 151n.80, which establishes his source as Solís's diary entry of "April 23rd" (should be April 22).

name, not a given name; Ybarbo's name was thus a combination of two family names, Gil and Barbo.) It lay on the King's Highway just east of Los Aís, near present Geneva, and was described in 1772 as "already a pueblo." Under the energetic Antonio, whose father was a soldier-rancher at Adaes Presidio, El Lobanillo soon became the largest—and the most notorious—ranch in East Texas.

Thirteen leagues beyond the Sabine, just before the old settlement of Los Adaes, was Rancho de los Tres Llanos (Three Plains Ranch).[19] That there were other ranches is suggested by Fray Solís's remark that the ministers looked after the spiritual needs of the whites at the presidio and "some of the ranches." Robert S. Weddle and Thonhoff mention one called Rancho de Vallesillo (Little Valley Ranch), placing it midway between the Sabine and Los Adaes, also along the Camino Real, while Louis R. Nardini locates it near present-day Pleasant Hill, Louisiana. Other sources, including Solís, mention a ranch belonging to the Adaes Mission called El Baño, which was half a league away. Other than these ranches between Los Aís (San Augustine) and Los Adaes (Robeline) only the "small *rancho* at a place called El Atascoso" is referred to by La Fora. It was situated on the lower Trinity, near the presidio known as Orcoquisac, 50 leagues south of Nacogdoches.[20]

Spanish stock raising in the region opposite Natchitoches was not on a scale to compare with that in the Béxar-Bahía region, as is evidenced by all observers in the mid-eighteenth century. Ranching was attempted, however. According to Solís, Aís Mission had fewer than one hundred head of livestock, while the one at Nacogdoches had approximately "eighty sheep and asses, thirty oxen, fifty cows, bulls and calves, twenty-five tame horses, twenty tame mules, . . . and two droves of mares, each

---

[19] In the Neutral Ground land claims registered in 1824, Los Tres Llanos, or La Nana de los Río Pedro, was filed on by the son of Manuel Sánchez, who was originally granted the 3 square leagues in 1730 (Louis Rafael Nardini, *My Historic Natchitoches, Louisiana, and Its Environment*, p. 151).

[20] Ibid., pp. 31, 114, 120; La Fora as cited in Weddle and Thonhoff, *Drama and Conflict*, pp. 159–61. Foik and Forrestal, *Solís Diary*, pp. 29–37, speaks of the sojourn in East Texas.

drove with its stallion." La Fora said that no Indians were living at either mission. From Pagès's account cattle were also pastured around Adaes Presidio, an observation sustained by archival sources. On October 31, 1764, Governor Martos issued the garrison orders to tend the "registered cattle on our inventories," since it was impossible to find citizens to shoulder this burden. Twelve horses were allotted for this duty, to be delivered to soldier Juan Joseph Córdova. Like most presidio captains, Martos himself owned a ranch, although its exact location is unknown. Nardini gives a version of how stock raising and trade with the neighboring French got its start at Los Adaes, crediting "Lieutenant Governor" José González with laying the groundwork around 1735. Nardini also touches on the situation at Natchitoches, regarding its stock-raising efforts. A Natchitoches post census of 1766 lists 914 "oxen"; 580 horses, mares, and mules; 597 hogs; and 157 sheep. When he passed through the settlement, Pagès saw hunters and cattle herders in the nearby woods, but—as at Adaes—it is difficult to guess the number of wild cows roaming the Red River vicinity.[21]

Also of interest because it was mentioned by another fact-finding expedition conducted the previous year is the Rancho Real de Santa Petronilla (or Petronila). Owned by Captain Blás María de la Garza Falcón (II), the founder of Camargo, the ranch was situated 5 leagues southwest of the bay at the mouth of the Nueces, near present Chapman Ranch, due south of Corpus Christi. Blás María and his brother Miguel, both military captains, were sons of the former governor of Coahuila, who had served from 1723 to 1728 and again from 1733 to 1737. When Escandón arrived to plant his first villa on the Río Grande, he found Captain Blás María II already camped there with forty families and made him alcalde of Camargo on March 3, 1749. Founded as a way station between the lower Río Grande towns and La Bahía, on the San Antonio River, Santa Petronilla was garrisoned with a detail of royal soldiers, who used it as a base

---

[21] Grazing Papers, vol. 1 (University of Texas Archives); Nardini, *Historic Natchitoches*, pp. 60–61, 80–81; Genaro García Collection, folder 138; Pagès, *Travels round the World*, 1:43.

from which to patrol the coastline for foreign intruders and to keep an eye on Indian activities. It consisted of a number of settlers who planted some corn and tended their herds of cattle and sheep. Although isolated from frequent contact, the settlement was destined to grow into a small center for ranching as more stock raisers pushed upward from the Río Grande, seeking new pastures for their sizable herds.[22]

Just as the success of the reverend fathers at the two missions near San Juan Bautista aroused the cupidity of their ranching neighbors on the Río Grande, so was the case at Béxar. Time after time the missionaries protested incursions made on their herds, but such protests did little more than cause the scruffy Canary Islanders and the wretched families of the presidio to resent their prosperity even more. As early as 1759 the situation had deteriorated so much that Fray Mariano de los Dolores made a formal offer to resign, an offer which was repeated in the report of 1762. Speaking on behalf of his Querétaran brethren, the veteran missionary expressed a willingness to turn over temporal administration of their missions to some secular au-

---

[22]Castañeda, *Catholic Heritage*, 4:215–19; Dan Kilgore, *Nueces County, Texas, 1750–1800: A Bicentennial Memoir*, pp. 5–7; Nueces County Historical Society, comp., *The History of Nueces County*, p. 29.

thority. Involved was all property owned by the four missions in San Antonio and the two at San Juan Bautista—seat of the recent dispute over stray mission stock—including herds of cattle, flocks of sheep and goats, droves of horses and mules, farms, implements, and so on.

Also contained in Fray Mariano's offer to abdicate control over temporal affairs was an indictment against the civil and military officials of the province. They had been slow to assume their respective responsibilities, he said, forcing the churchmen into areas not suited to their ministry. Thus what should have been an undertaking of love had spawned hatreds. Although peace and union were desired, unmerited criticism and abuse had been their reward. Why? For protecting the Indians, their lands, livestock, and the products of their labor against the "sordid ambitions of unscrupulous Spaniards," duties that more properly belonged to the king's administrators (such as the governor and his military officers). So now the priests were accused of being more interested in the accumulation of temporal goods than in the salvation of souls, of forgetting their vows of poverty for the ease and comfort of worldly luxuries. Doubtless he echoed the sentiments of every harried servant of God when he stated that it was desirable to eradicate completely the problems of temporal administration—litigation over lands and protection of the cattle from thieves and marauders—efforts which only gave the churchman a "bad name."[23]

While Fray Mariano was correct in realizing that the missions' troubles were rooted in their considerable possessions, which incited greed in the less prosperous, it is questionable that he really expected his offer of resignation to be accepted.

---

[23] Castañeda, *Catholic Heritage*, 4:259–72, gives a detailed account of the Queréteran withdrawal from Texas. Fray Mariano's complaints resemble those made in his report of 1762: "One blushes with shame to report that missionaries are constantly called upon to explain away, as far as possible, all manner of vexations and wrongs committed against the poor Indians by their neighbors and by persons from the presidios, not only upon their lands and cattle but even their persons; and the result has been that members of the church have been unjustly given the reputation of being cruel, avaricious, usurers, underhanded, profiteering, and what not" (Grazing Papers, vol. 1). Castañeda gives the date of the father president's offer to resign temporal authority as of February 6, 1769; the year should be 1759 (perhaps a typographical error).

One suspects that he knew that Martos, Barrios, and the other dignitaries assembled at Béxar could not undertake such responsibilities on their own initiative. In case they *were* tempted, the father president warned of the grave responsibilities implied in temporal administration of the helpless neophytes' worldly possessions and of the concomitant duty to increase their prosperity in this realm. Freed from such onerous tasks, living on the charity of the king, the missionaries could then pursue their divine calling, instructing the natives in the True Faith. Somehow the offer sounds too simplistic, as though Fray Mariano was playing a card he knew could not be trumped. The response, coming on the very same day, justifies this suspicion: such a proposed change was so sweeping that the viceroy himself must first be consulted. So nothing was done on the subject for another decade.

In the meantime several citizens of Béxar lodged a protest against the missions Valero, Concepción, San Juan, and Espada, likely an outgrowth of the movement to limit mission expansion that had begun in 1756. The current appeal (1771) was directed to Don Diego Antonio Cornide y Saavedra, a member of the royal council and special judge over land sales and distribution. The missions were attempting to lay claim to extensive lands, said to total 116 *sitios* for large stock, near the town. Hearing of their effort, the citizens formed an opposition led by Vicente Álvarez Travieso (*alguacil mayor*) and his son Juan Andrés (*regidor*), just as the chief constable had led them in similar complaints against the missionaries all the way back to 1739. Their opposition was founded on the damage which would result to the entire province if the missionaries' request was granted. Travieso pointed out that originally the missions had not been supposed to locate close to town and had clustered together contrary to the king's intention, severely impinging on lands intended for the development of a colony. Even now the available lands were so restricted that settlers had "absolutely no place to expand or even a location in which to establish their ranches."

Aided by an attorney, Travieso deftly picked apart the missions' application for additional lands, in the process depicting them as a greedy colossus bent on devouring all the choice acreage in Texas without leaving a single spot where a private citizen could locate. Whenever an individual wanted to establish a ranch, he was invariably opposed by the missions, who wished to become "masters of the whole river and of all the watering places." Travieso claimed that the Béxar missions had more land than they needed, considering their small Indian populations. The smallest establishment presently owned twenty-three *sitios* for cattle and horses, while Concepción's grant embraced forty-two. He argued that the missions' application distorted the true state of affairs, such as claiming that stock was on existing lands when in fact they had none. Challenged, the fathers could only weakly amend their statements to read that in time they *hoped* to use the desired lands.

According to Travieso, it was evident that the padres did not need what they already had, much less any additional lands. He said that they neglected their extensive holdings, using only a cultivated strip between the river and mission walls. Therefore, a suspension of their new grant would cause them no injury, whereas its approval would be to the settlement's great detriment. It was pointed out that most of the province was worthless for haciendas because of a lack of dependable water and an abundance of hostile Indians, whose insults and injuries had forced the abandonment of existing ranches. The lands desired by the missions were, of course, the best, ranging from the head of the San Antonio River to its mouth, including lands along the Medina and the León. Added to this was the charge that the first local judge in the matter of land distribution (apparently Simón de Arocha) acted as a tool of the father president and now owned a ranch in the desirable zone. Emphasizing that their settlement would be destroyed if the missions were allowed to claim all the good lands, Travieso's petition closed by asking that such grants be postponed.

Curiously, the Bexareños' localized demand that further mission land acquisition be curtailed and current tenure patterns redefined to meet private needs was timed perfectly with larger events then astir in New Spain. That very year King Carlos III called upon the church hierarchy to consider reforms, not the least of which pertained to a division between spiritual and temporal matters. Certain crown advisers suggested that expropriation might be necessary to correct the prevailing imbalance of church-owned property, held (in the reformers' view) without economic benefit to secular society. Pressure was applied to the clergy from various quarters, aimed at eventual reduction of their control over temporal affairs. When the church demonstrated reluctance to yield its wealth and privileges, it became the target of much criticism, some of which undoubtedly struck exposed nerve endings, like those exhibited by Father Mariano.[24]

In any event, when Travieso's suit reached Mexico City, it received surprisingly quick attention. The mission proponents were instructed in June, 1771, to offer their arguments in the matter of awarding lands. The Audiencia, however, rejected this appeal on July 12 and soon afterward ordered Juez Cornide to return its decision to Texas so that the citizens' claims could be fully developed and their rights to the lands in question honored. Advised of this propitious turn of events, Travieso and members of the Béxar cabildo asked the governor to comply in the division of lands between settlers and missions. This explosive matter was skirted by the governor of the province, Juan María, Barón de Ripperdá. On February 20, 1772, he suspended execution of the measure until such time as he was ordered by the viceroy to proceed, claiming that he lacked the necessary instruction and knowledge to attend to such things and that other, "more important business of the royal service" required his attention. There the important question of who should be the province's landed ranchers, private citizens or the missions, lapsed for the remainder of Ripperdá's administration. His decision not to decide was one the baron would come to regret, for it contributed in no small way to his difficulties with Tejano cattlemen.[25]

---

[24] For mention of the movement toward clerical reforms initiated in 1771, see Colin M. MacLachlan and Jaime E. Rodríguez O., *The Forging of the Cosmic Race: A Reinterpretation of Colonial Mexico*, pp. 274–78.

[25] Fragments of this lawsuit—believed by some to have been the basis for the eventual occupation of mission lands by private ranchers on a "lease-purchase" arrangement—are found in BCSA, preserved in a folder designated "Miscellaneous Spanish

An interesting document, apparently related to this question of mission versus private land tenure, is found in the Archivo del Convento de Guadalupe in Zacatecas, even though the *diligencias* (proceedings) were initiated by the College of Santa Cruz in Querétaro. It is the result of fifteen questions posed by Father President Acisclos Valverde touching on the justness of mission claims and seemingly directed toward their vindication. In it were even specified the witnesses whom Fray Valverde wished Captain Luis Antonio Menchaca to call. The answers of the witnesses are almost identical, suggesting some strong coaching, to say the least.

Among the things Valverde wanted the captain to ascertain from these old-time residents was whether the settlers had built ranchos on lands contiguous to those desired by the missions. Yes, they replied, the Móntes de Oca, Peña, Delgado, and Granados families had ranches next to mission lands, but their claims did not overlap and were not under dispute. The deponents stated that, except for the Peña rancho and that of Mission Espada, all had been ravaged by the Indian wars, settler and mission ranches alike. The other question pertaining to ranching was number 8, which asked whether it was true that the lands desired by the missions were on the banks of the San Antonio and Medina rivers. The answers provide a spatial delineation of the area's ranches, some of them being noted for the first time.

The San Antonio de Valero, Concepción, and San Juan Capistrano missions (on the left bank) occupied the riverbanks "from the source [*ojo de agua*] to the Arroyo Arenoso," but from there, 4 leagues distant to the Mojoneras (Landmark

---

Records." Mattie Austin Hatcher translated these documents (box 2Q236, University of Texas Archives), parts of which are also in Grazing Papers, vol. 1, pt. 2, pp. 47–51. See also box 3J326 of the Louis Lenz Collection, University of Texas Archives. The final item in this incomplete *expediente* is a summation by the *asesor* Pedro Galindo Navarro dated January 29, 1783. Until that time nothing had been accomplished, no petition had been presented on behalf of the missions, etc., and therefore the matter was "dropped entirely." No further decision was considered required by the superior government other than to send these documents back to the governor of Texas, notifying him that in 1779 jurisdiction in land matters had been moved from the Audiencia de México to that of Guadalajara. Sale and/or distribution of royal and vacant lands was now subject to the decision of the latter court, said the *asesor*.

or Heap of Rocks)—where Captain Menchaca's lands commenced—they did not occupy the riverbanks. Menchaca owned the banks from Arroyo de las Mojoneras to the Pass of San Francisco and then shared them with Hernández to the mouth of the Cíbolo. Likewise, they shared the stretch up the Cíbolo to the Real de Joaquín, inside the *potrero* (pasture) formed by the junction. Another piece of land onward from the fork was noted as occupied by Miguel Guerra, Juan Joseph Flores, and Martín Lorenzo up to the boundary of Concepción's lands.

On the right bank Mission Espada occupied the Medina riverbank from the crossing of the camino headed to the Río Grande down to Paso de Costales. From there the Medina banks were occupied by Martín de Peña and Juan Joseph Móntes (going toward the junction with the San Antonio and down its banks). From the corner of Peña's field toward Arroyo de la Parrita, the riverbanks were owned by the ranch of Espada, called Las Cabras. From Parrita up to the little bridge of Espanta Perros were the Delgados, and from the *puentecito* down to Arroyo Blanco the riverbanks were occupied by Mission Valero (La Mora). Of all these lands only two arroyos, the Salado and the Cíbolo, were said to have dependable, "rapid-running" waters. Each witness was careful to note that the padres wanted more land for their Indians, not for themselves, and also that the missions would have more converts (and hence the need for extra lands) were it not for the hostile Indians that scared them off. Many, however, said that they did not know by what right Vicente Travieso and his son Juan Andrés held their land along the Cíbolo. Nor would they venture a guess whether Travieso had legitimate grounds to dispute the missions' claims.[26]

As it turned out, distant circumstances and viceregal decisions were required to achieve the goal fervently sought by both Fray Mariano de los Dolores and Vicente Álvarez Travieso. Needed in Pimería Alta because of the banishment of the Jesuits from New Spain, the College of Querétaro was relieved of du-

---

[26] "Testimonio de las Diligencias . . . ," March 9–16, 1772, ACZ, roll 3, frames 3600–31. Named to give testimony were Balthazar Pérez, his brothers Joseph and Luis, Martínez de la Zerda, Gerónimo Flores, Juan de Arocha, Miguel de la Garza, and Juan Joseph Padrón.

ties to its six missions in Texas and Coahuila by a decree dated July 28, 1772. But when the transfer of the Texas establishments took place the next year, it was not to seculars but to the authority of the Zacatecan college, because the Indian neophytes were not yet deemed ready to function, either spiritually or temporally in a "civilized" existence. It is doubtful that overall secularization was even seriously considered at this time, according to Habig.[27] Consequently, the "root of all their troubles" between the opposing cattlemen, sacred and profane, did not disappear; it merely shifted from one religious college to another. From the standpoint of the individual rancher like Travieso, the resulting inequity was even more awesome, for it meant that all church possessions and prerogatives in the province were now consolidated under one authority, the Zacatecans. Rather than "peace and union" resulting from this change, quite the opposite occurred.

San Juan Bautista was the first mission to be affected by the viceroy's order. It was handed over to the Franciscan representatives from the Province of Santiago de Jalisco (Guadalajara) in November, 1772, after the protests of nearby settlers were satisfactorily answered. This mission's cattle ranch, 6 or 7 leagues southeast, had a good stone-and-mortar house and the necessary corrals, saddles, and accessories. A roundup revealed 672 branded cattle; 698 horses, mules, and donkeys; more than 5,300 sheep; and 657 goats. The transfer of San Bernardo took place the following month, and the inventory showed it to be even more prosperous than its neighboring mission: 1,204 cattle, 6,900 sheep, more than 900 goats, 835 mares, 212 horses, and 100 mules. All of this considerable wealth was still in the custody of churchmen, presided over on behalf of their 350 Indian converts, a fact which perhaps needled certain ambitious stockmen in the vicinity of old San Juan Bautista.[28]

Before we take up the transfer of the four Querétaran missions at Béxar—Valero, San Juan, Espada, and Concepción—

---

[27] In personal correspondence on this subject, Fr. Habig writes, "There was no question of secularizing the Querétaro missions at this time—not till 1793."

[28] Castañeda, *Catholic Heritage*, 4:259–72; Leutenegger, *San José Papers*, pt. 1, p. 191.

a review of intervening events is in order. It will be recalled that ranchers were hard hit in the 1760s, that between the desperate thefts of the starving Lipans and the new incursions by Comanches serious losses were sustained to herds pastured in the area. Once the presidio at San Sabá was abandoned in the spring of 1768, following Parilla's crushing defeat on the Red River a decade earlier, the Comanches and their *norteño* allies struck closer to Béxar. So many outrages swept outlying ranches that the town cabildo appealed to the interim governor, Oconor, for protection, echoing Captain Menchaca's claim that not one road or place in all of Texas was safe from hostile Indians.[29]

Although Oconor moved his headquarters from Los Adaes to Béxar to facilitate defense of the area, there is little evidence that the move made much difference. Unable to secure support for an offensive campaign from his superior, the Marqués de Croix, Oconor ordered the ranchers to leave their exposed houses and awaited the arrival of his successor. The ranchers later claimed that when the governor moved to Béxar and it became the capital, they thought that this change would bring protection. Such was not the case; rather, they had to leave their ranches and abandon all. The Indians "stole everything" and killed the rest; only a few cattle hiding in the woods were spared.[30]

No sooner did the new governor, Ripperdá, enter Béxar than his problems commenced. Attempting to put the villa's proud hidalgos to work renovating the Casa Real for his official use, the aristocrat's decrees were met with a barrage of hostility and protest from the citizens, led by Captain Menchaca. In a *representación* dated July 7, 1770, the cabildo reminded the new governor that increasing Indian hostility had forced the abandonment of many ranches between the Cíbolo and the San Antonio River. Knowing that Ripperdá was expecting a relief

---

[29] Elizabeth A. H. John, *Storms Brewed in Other Men's Worlds: The Confrontation of Indians, Spanish, and French in the Southwest, 1540–1795*, pp. 380–82, cites this protest (Menchaca to Oconor, August 18, 1768) and speaks of the stockmen's woes. See further the petition of the cabildo dated February 27, 1769; and also Luis Menchaca to Viceroy Croix, March 2, 1769, which describes the "deplorable state" to which they had been reduced (Genaro García Collection, folders 138, 197).

[30] "San Fernando Memorial," BAT, vol. 150, item 24.

column of twenty-one men from San Sabá, the citizens urged him to establish a post midway between La Bahía and San Antonio, using the new squad. Under such protection and safeguard, argued the cabildo, ranchers could return to their abandoned estancias, "without which this settlement cannot subsist, and . . . gather the scattered remnants of their herds."[31]

Although nothing was accomplished at the time, the seed was planted and would soon germinate. When troops from Los Adaes and Orcoquisac were recalled the following winter, Ripperdá decided to use them for the defense of El Rincón stockmen. In February, 1771, he ordered the citizens to plant crops and tend their cattle, extending assurances that their safety would be provided for. He wrote to the viceroy of his plans for a post but made the mistake of calling a public meeting to decide where best to locate it. What Ripperdá wanted appears to have been something like Rancho Santa Petronilla, near the Nueces,

[31] Castañeda, *Catholic Heritage*, 4:275, 279.

an establishment to be operated in common by area cattlemen under the protection of soldiers stationed there, all for the benefit of Béxar's residents. Once the Indian trouble subsided, each ranching clan could then reoccupy its own estate.[32]

The governor's proposal was greeted with little enthusiasm or agreement on a site for the proposed fort. Considering the known aversion of stockmen to having soldiers pasture horses on their land and hunt their cattle for meat, this reluctance is understandable. As a group they recognized the need for a fort to protect their ranches, but no individual wanted it situated on his spread. Ripperdá, now committed to the idea of an outlying garrison, was forced to make his own choice. He picked Tawakoni Crossing, on the Cíbolo, 18 leagues east of Béxar, just off the Bahía Road on the right. In April he reported that fifty men were at the new post and a fort was being built, including a good stockade. Such a measure, Ripperdá told the viceroy, was indispensable for the protection of the citizens who occupied "numerous ranches" in its vicinity. By June the fort and stockade of Santa Cruz were almost finished, and Ripperdá again begged the viceroy's blessing for the establishment. Near desperation over his inability to win the inhabitants' cooperation or to improve the defensive posture of his province, the governor even asked permission to burn the fort he had erected without authorization unless the viceroy would recognize it. Finally formal approval for Santa Cruz was granted by the viceroy on November 2, 1771.[33]

Two petitions submitted by the citizens in October, 1772, indicate that conditions in the province were almost as deplorable as noted in their previous appeal to the captain general. While their primary reason for submitting the new protests was Ripperda's attempt to coerce them to work on the barracks and jail, a number of references indicate that resettlement of the ranches did not take place as the governor had assured them it would. Thus they deeply resented their conscription for public

---

[32] Ripperdá to citizens of Béxar, February 10, 1771, Grazing Papers, vol. 1.
[33] For the founding of the Cíbolo fort, see Castañeda, *Catholic Heritage*, 4: 279–80; Bolton, *Texas in the Middle Eighteenth Century*, pp. 386, 392ff.

works: "The least of the calamities that could happen to these citizens if they are forced to yield on this matter is that they will abandon . . . the roundup of the few heads of cattle they have left." The first petition was signed by sixteen prominent ranchers, headed by Francisco Xavier Rodríguez and Joseph Phéliz (Félix) Menchaca; the second, by only six. Viceroy Antonio María de Bucareli wrote Rodríguez and Menchaca in February of the new year, ordering them to get the citizens to help with the construction and cease aggravating Ripperdá. He told the governor not to press the matter, however.[34]

Ironically, at the same time the Barón de Ripperdá was worrying over the fate of his fort on the Arroyo del Cíbolo, the establishment of just such a garrison was being considered in Spain. It was one of the recommendations made by Rubí as a result of his inspection of 1767 and was soon adopted as part of the Nuevo Reglamento (New Regulations) of 1772, a sweeping set of orders designed to modernize the entire cordon, or "line," of presidios on the northern frontier (see figure 1). The Béxar company was increased to eighty men, twenty of whom were to be detached and stationed permanently on the Cíbolo "to guard the ranches belonging to various inhabitants of San Antonio and to make less vulnerable the intervening area of almost fifty leagues" between Béxar and La Bahía. Scouting companies were to range between the new post and Bahía Presidio, impeding the penetrations of hostile Indians into the district. Las Tetillas (the Nipples, several small hills near Mound Creek, just east of present-day Gillett) eventually became their rendezvous. The detachment at the Cíbolo post was placed under the command of a lieutenant, who proved to be José Menchaca, son of Captain Luis Antonio Menchaca, owner of the nearby Rancho de San Francisco.[35]

---

[34] Citizens' petitions, October 3 and October 16, 1772, BAT, 53:47–50, 60.
[35] Stanley B. Brinckerhoff and Odie B. Faulk, *Lancers for the King: A Study of the Frontier Military System of Northern New Spain, with a Translation of the Royal Regulations of 1772*, p. 61. The role of another military inspector, José de Gálvez, in the adoption of the New Regulations of 1772 and other sweeping changes made in 1776 should not be omitted. See Herbert I. Priestley, *José de Gálvez, Visitor-General of New Spain, 1765–1771*, pp. 293–95.

INSTRUCCION
PARA FORMAR UNA LINEA Ó CORDON
DE QUINCE PRESIDIOS
Sobre las Fronteras de las Provincias Internas de este Reino de Nueva-España,
Y
NUEVO REGLAMENTO
Del número y calidad de Oficiales y Soldados que estos y los demas han de tener, Sueldos que gozarán desde el dia primero de Enero del año próximo de mil setecientos setenta y dos, y servicio que deben hacer sus Guarniciones.

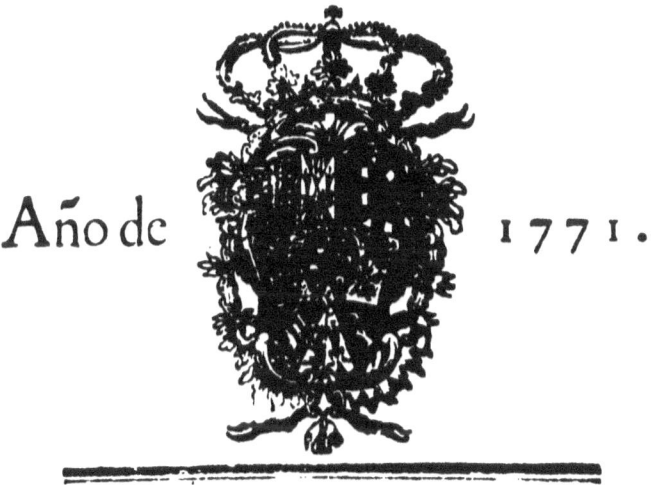

Año de 1771.

DE ORDEN DE SU EXCELENCIA
En Mexico en la Imprenta del Br. D. Joseph Antonio de Hogal,
Calle de Tiburcio.

Fig. 1. Title page of the New Regulations of 1772. Although the king did not sign the royal *cédula* for these regulations until September 10, 1772, news of the radical changes was "leaked" and the document printed in Mexico in 1771 by order of the viceroy, Marqués de Croix (copy provided by G. Douglas Inglis).

Apart from legitimizing the little fort on the Cíbolo, Carlos III's *cédula* of September 10, 1772, called for a withdrawal of all Spanish settlement above the Béxar-Bahía line, that is, all of Texas as far east as Natchitoches. The relocation of Los Adaesaños and their halfhearted attempts to begin life anew around Béxar caused a multitude of problems until some of these refugees eventually returned to Nacogdoches at the close of the decade. As one might expect, many of these problems revolved around ranches and stock that the settlers were forced to leave behind. It was at this juncture that the four Querétaran missions of Béxar were transferred to Zacatecan authority. Rubí's report referred to them as the "opulent missions of San Antonio," an appellation that persisted in government circles until secularization. This description, as Rafael Martínez Pacheco informed the viceroy, referred to their prosperity as contrasted to the wretchedness of the Spanish settlements around them. He described the farms, ranches, and irrigation ditches of the missions as the best and most successfully operated in the province. Also, their herds of cattle, flocks of sheep, and other stock were the most numerous, with the exception of horses, which had been stolen by Indian enemies in recent years.

Martínez Pacheco, formerly captain of the presidio at Orcoquisac, argued that it was the apostolic zeal of the missionaries which had led to the spiritual and temporal welfare of the missions, a condition that Rubí mistakenly perceived as opulent. Martínez Pacheco attributed their success to hard work and declared that the methods used by the missionaries could not be improved upon. He blamed the incompetency of various governors and military commanders for the troubles of the province, not any fault of the padres. Still, the mission system continued to be denounced by critics, and its wealth, especially its lands and herds, remained a source of contention as long as the missions remained a vital force on the frontier. Placing their administration under a different religious convent did not alter this basic fact.[36]

Despite Martínez Pacheco's rosy picture of mission life, the

---

[36] Martínez Pacheco to the Viceroy, November 8, 1772, Castañeda, *Catholic Heritage*, 4:267; Leutenegger, *San José Papers*, pt. 1, pp. 189–91.

1772 *inventarios* of the Querétaran establishments at Béxar reveal without a doubt that their outside ranching activities at this time were faring poorly, mostly because of repeated attacks by hostile Indians. Only one place was still occupied, the ranch called Monte Galván, 3 or 4 leagues east-northeast of Mission Valero, where a "large number" of cattle were pastured, supplying the mission's weekly beef ration. La Mora was uninhabited owing to the "unjust hostility of the pagans," as was the ranch of San Juan Capistrano and Concepción's "El Pasthle" (El Paistle, abandoned since 1767). It would seem that Monte Galván, situated fairly close to the east-bank missions, was supplying meat to all three of them, for San Juan and Concepción claimed to have as much right to the ranch and its cattle as Mission Valero (doubtless by virtue of the concord of 1767).

A "fair estimate" of cattle in La Mora's pastures was placed at 4,000 to 5,000 head, and Espada's Las Cabras still had large herds, although its rock-walled compound was evidently abandoned like the others. Listed was a wide selection of stock, including 281 mares, 1,100 sheep, 1,621 goats, 150 milk cows, and 1,050 gentle head of cattle plus an estimated 3,000 head running loose in Espada's pastures. Mission San Juan's inventory showed that a November roundup had netted 461 branded animals and listed as owned 1,400 head of cattle, 2,117 goats, and 140 tame horses. Unfortunately, with the ranchos overrun by *los norteños* little of this wealth could be properly administered or enjoyed. These difficulties, taken with those presented by a diminishing population of Indian converts, indicate that by 1772 the San Antonio missions were feeling the palsied hand of decline creeping over them.[37]

Shortly after Governor Ripperdá witnessed the transfer of these "opulent" Querétaran missions to the College of Zacatecas, he began carrying out instructions issued by the new *comandante inspector*, Hugo Oconor, for the withdrawal from East Texas. In mid-May he sent orders to the settlements at Los

[37] Fr. Benedict Leutenegger, trans. and ed., *Inventory of the Mission San Antonio de Valero, 1772*, pp. 33–37. I am indebted to Fr. Marion A. Habig for calling attention to the *inventarios* of 1772 and sharing information on those not yet published. The Espada and San Juan Capistrano documents are found in ACZ, roll 3; Valero and Concepción, ACZ, roll 4.

Adaes and Orcoquisac, telling the inhabitants to stop all work on their crops and commence gathering cattle and other possessions for the evacuation. It was at this time of crisis that Antonio Gil Ybarbo, owner of El Lobanillo, stepped forward as the leading spokesman for Los Adaesaños. His establishment, near the old Aís Mission, 30 leagues west of Los Adaes, was perhaps the most prosperous of its kind. It contained fourteen families composed of sixty-five persons, none of whom wanted to leave. The evidence is strong that, in addition to being a stock-raising operation, the Wart Ranch was a center for contraband goods from Louisiana, a trade which was almost synonymous with living opposite the former French possession.

Ripperdá went to Los Adaes, arriving during the first week of June, 1773. He assembled the area's almost five hundred residents and told them that they must begin their march to Béxar no later than June 12. The furor and panic can be imagined. Their painful exodus has been chronicled by other writers and will not be described in detail here. Suffice it to say that, after pleading for time, offering a thousand excuses, and begging to remain without the garrison and missions, the humble pioneers began their trek. They left behind fields of corn not yet ripe and numerous herds of cattle scattered over the countryside. Some Adaesaños fled to avoid the march, staying with the Indians or with French friends in Natchitoches until the convoy had departed and it was "safe" to return. El Lobanillo was never totally abandoned. It was the first resting stop on the journey, and Gil Ybarbo's mother and other relatives remained there because they were too sick to travel. The twenty-four persons left behind were later joined by stragglers who dropped out of the march and crept back, as well as the estimated thirty-five who remained at the presidio. It is to be assumed that they tended the rancho's stock and lived as best they could, smuggling liquor to the Indians or plying the time-honored contraband trade in other ways.[38]

It is questionable that the Adaesaños ever really intended

---

[38] Nardini, *Historic Natchitoches*, pp. 85–89, suggests that the wholesale evacuation of East Texas has been greatly exaggerated and that more inhabitants—especially those active in the Indian trade, in business or intermarried with the French at Natchitoches—stayed than has been supposed. See also Herbert E. Bolton, "The Spanish Aban-

to give up their East Texas (now Louisiana) homes. Three months after beginning their march, they trudged into Béxar, footsore, weary, and demoralized. Those too weak to finish the last leg of the trip lingered around the new post on the Cíbolo, where a few of them remained. Although Governor Ripperdá instructed these dispossessed people to set about selecting new homes for themselves, "taking care not to interfere in any way with property already owned or occupied by citizens of the villa or the missions," the Adaesaños were not reconciled to the idea of remaining at Béxar. On October 4, 1773, they submitted a petition to Ripperdá asking for permission to go back to Los Aís and found a settlement. They said that such a move would allow them to recover much of their abandoned property and that it was impossible to find suitable vacant lands in the jurisdiction of Béxar without encroaching upon the rights of others. From town to the Guadalupe the country was already "infested" with livestock, missions, and men, noted the seventy-six petitioners, and they even agreed to bear all the expense of their return.[39] On their way to see the viceroy (with Ripperdá's blessing), agents Gil Ybarbo and Gil Flores stopped in Coahuila and penned a petition to Oconor in Chihuahua, who was absent. The petition emphasized that the region from San Antonio to the Guadalupe River was overrun with cattle belonging either to missions or to settlers and that their relocation there would inevitably lead to quarrels and complaints. Out of these protests developed the long ordeal which resulted in the founding of a new settlement, Nuestra Señora del Pilar de Bucareli, on the Trinity River a year later.[40]

Upon learning of the Adaesaños' attempt to return to their former homes and ranches, Comandante Inspector Oconor opposed it vigorously. He said that there were ample and sufficient lands for them in the vicinity of San Antonio, downriver to

---

donment and Re-Occupation of East Texas, 1773–1779," Texas State Historical Association *Quarterly* 9, no. 2 (October, 1905): 88–89; Nyal C. King, "Captain Antonio Gil Y'Barbo, Founder of Modern Nacogdoches, 1729–1809" (Master's thesis, Stephen F. Austin University, 1949), pp. 17–18.

[39] Castañeda, *Catholic Heritage*, 4:304.

[40] Charles Wilson Hackett et al., eds. and trans., *Pichardo's Treatise on the Limits of Louisiana and Texas*, 4:197.

La Bahía, and ordered Ripperdá to proceed with the intent of the royal order. Writing to the viceroy, Oconor expressed a belief that Gil Ybarbo and his companions wished to return to Los Adaes and environs so that they might engage in the illicit trade for which the area was notorious. That, he stressed, was the real reason for their petitions and trip to Mexico City. Moreover, Oconor implied that Governor Ripperdá was in on the profitable smuggling operations because of his sympathy for their plight.

Regardless of Oconor's efforts to stop the move back toward East Texas, Ripperdá pushed the measure through. Interestingly enough, when Gil Ybarbo's band of exiles set out to establish Bucareli, they were escorted by Lieutenant Simón de Arocha and four soldiers. Arocha, who had staked out for himself Rancho San Rafael in El Rincón—the area in which the Adaesaños maintained they could not find lands without causing conflicts—was entrusted by the governor to put Gil Ybarbo and his fifty to seventy men, plus their families, in possession of the site on the Trinity River. This Arocha did in the fall of 1774, reporting that the area was fertile but that steep riverbanks made irrigation impractical. If Oconor's suspicions were correct, this drawback would have been of little consequence to the happy returnees.[41]

Gil Ybarbo, whom Ripperdá had appointed captain of militia and chief justice before he left Béxar, wasted no time getting his new settlement on firm footing. He immediately went to Los Adaes and returned with supplies, borne on his own mules. Stopping at his ranch, El Lobanillo, the headstrong Gil Ybarbo doubtless gathered more stock and recruits for Bucareli. The colonists there were joined by some of those left at Béxar as circumstances permitted, but during its five-year existence Bucareli continued under a cloud of suspicion. Oconor never ceased to oppose it as a refuge for contrabandists providing pelts, hides, horses, and so on, to the Louisiana market and trade goods to the various Texas tribes in the vicinity of the Trinity. Gil Ybarbo's elevated status on the frontier was aggravating.

---

[41] Bolton, *Texas in the Middle Eighteenth Century*, pp. 413–17; Castañeda, *Catholic Heritage*, 4:313–14.

Oconor once arrested him on contraband charges; he remained in jail for several months until Ripperdá came to Texas and released him, an act which the former governor seems to have resented and viewed with suspicion. As if that were not enough, the place, noted Oconor, could not have been better chosen to enable its occupants to engage in illicit trade and to encourage the northern Indians in stealing droves of horses from the Béxar and La Bahía presidios, and even as far as Laredo, "as lately has been done." It goes without saying that he suspected that Gil Ybarbo was deeply involved in such activities.

The trade with Louisiana was one that Spanish officials had long tried to stop, with very little success. Not so with those who lived on the frontier. According to Nardini, one of Adaes Presidio's earliest spokesmen, a man named La Lima, recognized that the market for cattle and horses was with the neighboring French and not Mexico City, declaring that the "French Market and the French supply of goods" made the Spanish settlement possible. He suggested that the inhabitants receive grants of land and commence stock raising, an idea welcomed by St. Denis, the commander at Natchitoches. Captain José González at Los Adaes was also receptive to La Lima's plan to carry on trade furtively with the French post fifteen miles distant. In 1735 he called a group of cattlemen together, notified them they would be awarded lands, and suggested a trip beyond the Sabine, where, under the protection of troops, they would round up wild horses and cattle to increase their herds. "Once the process of obtaining livestock by this method is perfected it will be continued," said González, adding that perhaps people would be found in the Nacogdoches area "who will gather such stock in advance, so that our merchandise"—obtained from the French—"will be traded to them for the stock." One soldier of Los Adaes who took the captain's proposition seriously (if Nardini's uncited source can be credited) was Juan Antonio Moraín, who became a ranchero and adopted the "Anchor Brand," said to be one of the oldest marks in Texas.[42]

---

[42] Nardini, *Historic Natchitoches*, pp. 60–61. Concerning Moraín's (or Amoraín's) "anchor" brand, documents in BAT, 29:1–20, establish this mark as belonging to the Béxar notary, Francisco de Arocha. Miguel de Córdova, a vaquero for the priests at Adaes, testified that the mission brand was in the shape of a heart.

If such trade thrived, soon being conducted on the Spaniards' terms, "especially concerning livestock," it was being done contrary to the government's wishes. Yet both a viceregal ban on trade as early as 1730 and another in 1740 had to be rescinded because of their impracticality. The distances involved were simply too vast to allow the East Texas outposts to be sustained by Mexico-based supply lines. The French agitation for a livestock trade, dating back to St. Denis's entry into Spanish domains, intensified during the administration of Jacinto de Barrios y Jáuregui, who is remembered as the governor of Texas "most criticized for contraband trade"—and the one who made the most money at it. In 1752 Barrios was advised by the commandant of the Natchitoches post that an expedition was en route to purchase 500 head of cattle from the missions at Nacogdoches and Los Aís. Commandant Césaire de Blanc asked that this purchase be allowed, in view of the famine and sickness raging at New Orleans. The governor, while admitting that there was an abundance of cattle in the province under his command, replied that unfortunately it would not be possible to grant permission for the export of such a large number from Texas without the viceroy's permission. But Barrios, in his letter to Viceroy Revillagigedo, pressed approval for the transaction, both because it was the Christian thing to do and because his French neighbors were constantly bothering him about it.[43]

In response to another such request, made by Governor Louis de Kerlérec on September 6, 1755, Barrios received a short-lived permission from the *fiscal* in February, 1756, for the sale of "surplus" cattle to Louisiana. The reason given was that in the past the French had helped sustain Los Adaes with needed supplies. In due course the matter came to the attention of the king. Writing to the viceroy on May 4, 1760, His Majesty referred to a complaint made by the French in regard to certain cattle which they had asked of the governor of Texas for their subsistence and which had been denied them. The king noted that the viceroy had subsequently allowed some cattle to cross the border, judging that it would not create a lack in Texas, having satisfied the owners as to the value of their livestock. These orders, in view of recent developments with France, the king wanted revoked. Concerning the commandant of Natchitoches and his requests for cattle, "let all communication and trade in those regions with the French be thwarted completely. To this end you will issue the most strict instructions that none of the effects for which they ask may be sent them."[44]

---

[43] Bolton, *Texas in the Middle Eighteenth Century*, pp. 38–39; *Handbook of Texas*, 1:115; Grazing Papers, vol. 1, pt. 2. p. 32; Blanc to Barrios, April 28, 1752, Barrios to Blanc, July 17, 1752, Barrios to Viceroy Revillagigedo, July 18, 1752 (AGN, Provincias Internas, Bolton Transcripts, 34:81–85).

[44] Hackett et al., *Pichardo's Treatise*, 2:202–207; see Bolton, *Texas in the Middle Eighteenth Century*, pp. 9, 63–76, 359–64, for an account of French activities which were viewed as threatening Spain's interests at this time and were factors in the king's ban; see also Sandra L. Myres, *The Ranch in Spanish Texas, 1691–1800*, pp. 44–48, and Sandra Lynn Myres, "The Development of the Ranch as a Frontier Institution in the Spanish Province of Texas, 1691–1800" (Ph.D. diss., Texas Christian University), pp. 130–34; Nardini, *Historic Natchitoches*, pp. 60–61, 78–79, explores the trade associations formed among the inhabitants which nullified any distant policy decisions, practically speaking.

Thus the door was slammed shut on any legitimate trade whereby the remote settlers of Texas could have exchanged their most abundant resource for the much-needed trade goods that entered the province of Louisiana through the port of New Orleans. Not that this meant that the back door to Louisiana was not constantly being used, of course. Herbert E. Bolton tells the story of a prosperous rancher of the Attakapas region, one M. Masse, "evidently well known to Governor Barrios," who asked for permission to settle at Orcoquisac, bringing his many slaves and large herds of stock, including 700 head of cattle and 100 horses. Noting Masse's subsequent reputation as a contrabandist and Barrios's rewarding involvement in such illicit trade, Bolton dryly observes that there was likely "something besides generosity" in the governor's support for his confederate's proposed relocation on the lower Trinity.

Martos y Navarrete, Barrios's successor, was even less discreet in his pursuit of the forbidden trade. Rubí charged that this official lived like an Indian instead of a Spaniard, buying goods at Natchitoches and selling them to the Adaes garrison at 1000 percent profit. Luxury items that Martos was accustomed to handling (silk shawls, braid, ribbon, etc.) cost less at Los Adaes than in other presidios because they were imported from New Orleans, and once-scarce items like nails became plentiful on the frontier. Citizens of Béxar charged the governor with refusing to pay them a fair price for their horses, keeping them from selling supplies to the garrisons, and even preventing them from hiring on as drovers to Adaes "when cattle are scarce on your ranch" and had to be obtained at San Antonio. Despite such complaints and Rubí's harsh opinion of Martos y Navarrete, the settlers at Adaes seem to have prospered more under his tenure than under any governor before him.[45]

To understand these developments, it should be remembered that Louisiana, while incorporated into the Spanish Empire in 1762, was joined to the captaincy general of Cuba, a separate jurisdiction from the Interior Provinces. Therefore, it was not subject to all the normal mainland taxes, and the

---

[45] Bolton, *Texas in the Middle Eighteenth Century*, pp. 359–64.

French inhabitants managed to secure a wider selection of goods than could their Spanish neighbors, goods that could be obtained more cheaply from New Orleans than by way of the overland route to Texas from Veracruz, the only Gulf-side open port in Mexico. The original price of merchandise in Spain was swollen by a multitude of duties, *alcabalas* (excise taxes), freight charges, interest rates, and other fees at every step of the journey, from its departure from Cádiz to its eventual arrival in the Saltillo marketplace. In later years this unwieldy commercial system was described as "the most terrible and the most merciless whip from which the Americas have suffered." As Odie Faulk aptly notes, such a situation was conducive to smuggling.[46]

As mentioned above, Hugo Oconor suspected Governor Ripperdá of complicity in this proscribed commerce and saw his espousal of Bucareli as a way to revive it. Oconor's suspicions of foul play were no doubt intensified when the Spanish governor of Louisiana, Luis de Unzaga y Amézaga, suggested to Ripperdá a limited trade in livestock. Asking for permission to send agents to Texas, "as many citizens of this province wish to buy horses from that one," Unzaga even proposed a way to keep smugglers from exploiting the proposed trade. He suggested that a special brand be designated with which the citizens of Louisiana could countermark horses or mules to indicate that they had been acquired legitimately. Persons who introduced animals without this brand would be punished, and the thievery of Indians would be checked, "for if they found no one to buy them, they would desist."[47]

While such a scheme might have worked for a while, Governor Unzaga clearly underestimated the ingenuity of those people to whom the contraband trade was a way of life. The

---

[46] Nettie Lee Benson, trans. and ed., *Report That Dr. Miguel Ramos de Arizpe . . . Presents to the August Congress on the Natural, Political, and Civil Condition of the Provinces of Coahuila, Nuevo León, Nuevo Santander, and Texas*, p. 41; hereafter cited throughout as *Report of Ramos Arizpe*; Odie B. Faulk, *A Successful Failure*, pp. 100, 157.

[47] Unzaga y Amézaga to Ripperdá, September 13, 1774, Hackett et al., *Pichardo's Treatise*, 3:463.

issue was further pressed when El Cabellero de Clouet, Unzaga's lieutenant governor of the posts in Opelousas and Attakapas, took it upon himself to send a captain of militia (Agustín de Grevembert) and four soldiers to Texas, laden with trade goods, to secure the "mules, horses, asses, etc., so much needed in the capital of this province which, by his Majesty's orders, must supply each year for Havana a quantity of lumber and 80,000 sugar casks." Clouet repeated the governor's plan to have Ripperdá order the counterbranding of all animals sent from the jurisdiction of Texas, the absence of such a mark on stock in Louisiana being "sufficient to indicate them as stolen."[48]

Actually, Governor Unzaga came close to getting his "much-needed" mules and other livestock, even with the king's prohibitive decree in force. Ripperdá sent these requests to *bailío* Bucareli at the end of June, 1775—after having confiscated the emissaries' trade goods—and suggested that, while at present there was a shortage in Texas of horses and mules, Nuevo Santander abounded in them: "Many wild horses could be taken in that vicinity, and as that province [Louisiana] is now in need of cattle also, of which there is an abundance here, the inhabitants and the missions might profitably send them some of the said animals." Bucareli replied that it was not possible to comply with the Louisiana requests since trade between individuals of those colonies was entirely prohibited, "notwithstanding the fact that they are vassals of his Majesty." Several days later, however, *fiscal* José Antonio de Areche ruled that because the trade goods had been introduced in good faith they could be sold or traded for horses or mules equal to their value. He stressed that this was an exception and "shall not serve as a precedent for any subsequent similar case." But the *asesor general* agreed with Bucareli on the grounds that peninsular commerce would suffer if the door was opened to trade goods coming in from New Orleans. This ruling reaffirmed the status of Texas as a colonial appendage subservient to the prosperity of Cádiz-based Spanish

---

[48] Clouet to Ripperdá, November 10, 1774, ibid., pp. 466–67. For an account of this and the Attakapas post in their early days see Winston De Ville, *Opelousas: The History of a French and Spanish Military Post in America, 1716–1803*.

mercantile interests. On January 10, 1776, he ordered the goods returned in the hope that "preventing this sale will serve as a precedent for closing the door more firmly."

Informed of these proceedings, the king approved, and Minister-General of the Indies José de Gálvez so notified the viceroy in June. But in terms of the future, it was deemed "less inconvenient" to His Majesty's interests that the inhabitants of Louisiana obtain livestock from Texas than through a contraband trade with their English neighbors, so near, to the east of the Mississippi. *Asesor* Galindo Navarro later characterized the king's decision as tantamount to permission to open the cattle trails between Louisiana and Texas. Even so, it would be several years before this interpretation was applied and exploited. Governor Ripperdá, aware of the benefits his province would enjoy from legalized trade, would not see it materialize during his term. Further, his support of the idea earned him nothing but censure from his superiors, even to the point where Viceroy Bucareli forbade him to communicate with Spanish officials in Louisiana. All things considered, it is easy to see why Oconor was apprehensive about what was going on at Bucareli, knowing that Texas and Nuevo Santander abounded in horses, cattle, and men willing to smuggle them to satisfy demands in Louisiana.[49]

[49] Hackett et al., *Pichardo's Treatise*, 3:463–69; Grace A. Edman, trans. and ed., "A Compilation of Royal Decrees Relating to Texas and Other Northern Provinces of New Spain, 1719–1799," pp. 348–49; Elizabeth A. H. John, *Storms Brewed in Other Men's Worlds*, pp. 447–56; AGN: Provincias Internas, Hackett Transcripts, 182:46.

5

"WE ARE ENRAGED"

Rustling and the Law

Ripperdá was having his own problems at Béxar, with both hostile Indians and hostile Spaniards. Increasing Comanche raids around the villa frightened the Apaches so badly that they left the area in 1773. Luis Antonio Menchaca retired as captain of the Béxar presidio that year with an annual pension of 270 pesos. In March, 1774, he filed a written charge against the governor, claiming that Ripperdá allowed the *norteños* to come and go freely under the guise of peace and ignored their crimes. Even more damning, both Menchaca and Rafael Martínez Pacheco hinted that the baron was personally involved in the Indian trade, information that Inspector General Oconor used to advantage in his running feud with Ripperdá. Any effectiveness that the governor might have had in containing *los bárbaros* was neutralized by the opposition of both Oconor and Viceroy Bucareli to his policies. As a result, ranching in the river valley suffered; provincial soldiers and militiamen were constantly in the saddle as raids intensified.

That ranching continued in a desultory fashion even in the worst of times is demonstrated by the story of Carlos Martínez, a son of one of the first soldiers in Béxar Presidio and himself a soldier at La Bahía. From a land petition of 1778 we learn that Martínez served for twelve years under Captain Piscina, who died in 1767. Then he served another four years, from 1768 to 1772, under Captain Francisco Tovar and thus had a total of sixteen years in the royal service when he retired. In 1773 this veteran soldier settled his Rancho del Señor San José just above the ranch previously held by Captain Piscina, which had reverted upon his death to Mission Rosario. Carlos's ranch was bounded by the Escondido and Hondo creeks and, like the captain's, lay on the west bank of the San Antonio River. Carlos Martínez is important to this discussion because years later his fellow ranchers remembered him as having been involved in one of the first skirmishes with Ripperdá on the subject of who owned the region's mesteño stock.

The incident took place in 1774, just a year after Martínez settled his Señor San José. He took a number of branded and *orejano* (unmarked) stock from his own pastures to Béxar for the purpose of selling them. He considered this to be his right; yet because the Barón de Ripperdá was possessed with "some unfounded and tenacious idea, which he got from the ministers," that they (the missions) owned all stray stock, the governor ordered Martínez's cattle seized and the proceeds applied to the work of the church. The basis for the order was that in the past the missions had owned more stock than anyone else, and their argument ran that the greater absorbed the lesser. In effect, all loose, unbranded stock belonged to the mission herds with which it commingled, which meant that in time it became impossible to distinguish the cattle's true owners and sort them out of the mass. Though Martínez would later appeal this decision and win, for the time being Ripperdá's action was law. It effectively established the rights of missionaries over the private ranchers to unbranded stock found in pastures contested by both parties. Ripperdá was to pursue this line of reasoning until the end of his administration, destroying his working relationship with the ranchers of the province as other policies had with his superiors.[1]

---

[1] "San Fernando Memorial," BAT, vol. 150, item 9.

Apparently in 1774 and 1775, Ripperdá granted certain settlers permission to hunt cattle on the fringes of La Bahía's mission pastures for sustenance. A party under Antonio Leal set out with a permit to kill cows "on the other side" of the Guadalupe, that is, in the king's unappropriated lands. However, when hunters under Miguel de la Garza killed "on this side" of the Guadalupe, in Espíritu Santo's pastures, they were fined 11 pesos each by the governor. It appears that abuses of this privilege soon caused Ripperdá to revoke his "ill-advised" decision to allow unbranded stock to be killed for eating purposes. He not only revoked permission to hunt below the Guadalupe River but prosecuted a number of men "que carnearon" ("who took meat") in the months of January and February, 1775, charging them with killing stock belonging to Missions Espíritu Santo and Concepción.[2] Since ranchers later recalled that it was not considered profitable to make drives to other provinces *before 1774*, perhaps they were doing more with the *orejanos* caught in outlying areas than simply converting them into *charqui* and *fajitas* for home consumption. Subsequent testimony speaks of drives conducted to markets below the Río del Norte soon after such incidents began occurring in or near mission pastures.[3]

Despite this friction, Ripperdá allowed Francisco Xavier Rodríguez and other ranchers to go into the summer pastures of La Bahía in 1775 to extract cattle which had wandered there because of drought. A petition filed by fourteen ranchers in November of that year indicates that their grievances against the mission raisers were far from being settled. As customary, the petitioners' preface stated that they had abandoned their ranches because of Indian hostilities. Many of their cows were

---

[2] The eight individuals fined and tossed in prison were Marcos Zepeda, Miguel de la Garza, Antonio Leal, Francisco de los Santos, Guillermo Casanoba, Salas de la Zerda, Bentura Rico, and Joseph Martín Delgado. Later, on January 6, 1778, they filed a petition saying that they had gone with a permit from the governor to take stock, and on May 23, 1778, the *asesor* reversed Ripperdá's sentence, saying that he could not proceed with the case because of "muchas nulidades." Their fines were restored to the vindicated cattlemen, and Father President Ramírez was awarded 100 pesos' damages, all of which took until August, 1782. For the relevant documents see *expediente* no. 270, "Año de 1775, no. 111: Causas formadas . . . contra dos cuadrillas de vecinos del . . . Villa San Fernando . . . ," SA, 3:135–279.

[3] "San Fernando Memorial," BAT, vol. 150, item 10.

leaving, especially during the current and previous year, because of drought. Even with the severe local shortage of grass, the presidial horse herd was still put on their pastures to graze.

Getting to the heart of the matter, the ranchers noted that Ripperdá had forbidden them to look for their stock farther than one league beyond the Cíbolo. This order complicated their task because the only place where they could sort cattle was on mission lands, yet various missions would not allow it. They charged that, when the missions gathered, they took all the cattle, including those belonging to the private ranchers: "These limitations have moved us to seek justice; to round up our cattle wherever they may be found, as well as *orejanos* which we might recognize as ours." If not individually, then the ranchers sought the right to conduct roundups collectively, along with mission Indians, proposing to split costs in fair fashion. But the key to their argument rests in the following assertion: "Since our rights of possession are the same [as the missions'], it seems we should have equal rights to gather our cattle wherever we find them."

Ramsdell characterizes this petition as a denial that Espíritu Santo held any title to the immense ranges said to extend "from the sea to the sources of the Guadalupe," that is, the Comal, at modern New Braunfels. The ranchers believed that these pastures were rightfully theirs, and they also maintained that unbranded cattle found on property claimed by the mission in reality belonged to their own herds, scattered because of Indian raids. In other words, the position of the private cattlemen was directly opposed to that of the mission caretakers, and by 1775 the two groups had come into open confrontation. Governor Ripperdá, in a note dated November 28, said that the petition was based on lies and that he did not want any more such items unless they were founded on "truth, solidity, and good faith." But the protests were only beginning.[4]

---

[4] Ripperdá, summation, December 4, 1777, BAT, vol. 64; petition of Béxar citizens (undated) and reply of Ripperdá, November 28, 1775, GLO, vol. 50, under no. 59, "Año de 1778, Expediente promovido par el vezinos de la villa San Fernando Sobre . . . criadores de Ganados."); Charles [William] Ramsdell [Jr.], "Spanish Goliad" (typescript, University of Texas Archives), p. 25. Signing the petition were Vicente Álvarez Travieso, Miguel de Gortari, José Félix Menchaca, Marcos de Castro, Juan José Flores, Juan Andrés

The year 1776 brought promising changes to the northern frontier of New Spain, just as it did to the rebellious thirteen colonies on the American seaboard. The Provincias Internas were taken out of the viceroy's control and given to a commandant general who would report directly to the king. He would maintain headquarters near the sprawling frontier and exercise both civil and military jurisdiction. The first man to occupy the new position was Teodoro de Croix, a nephew of the former viceroy Carlos Francisco de Croix, Marqués de Croix. In a short time Texas ranchers would have reason to curse his name.

For the struggling colony at Bucareli, 1776 was a year of promise as well. A prominent French trader and associate of Gil Ybarbo's, Nicolás de la Mathe, built them a fine church, and they hoped eventually to secure the services of a priest. La Mathe was a merchant based on the Mississippi River at Pointe Coupée, and even before the abandonment of East Texas he and the owner of El Lobanillo Rancho engaged in a profitable trade with the Indians, exchanging goods and trinkets for horses and furs. These the Frenchman no doubt transported back to Louisiana at considerable profit. Also, a contract was arranged with a Béxar merchant named Juan de Ysurieta whereby the Trinity River residents would supply products of that country, intended for sale at the Béxar and Bahía presidios or in exchange for necessary goods. The area offered fine prospects for the raising of horses, cattle, sheep, and goats, being situated well above the raiding patterns of the Indians who plagued *criadores* around Béxar. Large herds of buffalo and wild cattle roamed a day's journey west of Bucareli, and it was hoped that fat could be processed in sufficient quantity to justify the manufacture of soap. If so, it could be sold to the soldiers stationed in Texas installations, who were presently dependent on Saltillo for this "luxury item," as Rubí said it was regarded.[5]

Travieso, Jacinto Delgado, Francisco Flores, Joaquín Leal, Simón de Arocha, José Marcario Sambrano, Juana de Ollos, Francisco Xavier Rodríguez and Manuel Delgado—names that soon become integral to the cattle controversy.

[5] Ripperdá to Bucareli, January 25, 1776, Charles Wilson Hackett et al., eds. and trans., *Pichardo's Treatise*, 4:207–209; Nyal C. King, "Captain Antonio Gil Y'Barbo, Founder of Modern Nacogdoches, 1729–1809" (Master's thesis, Stephen F. Austin University, 1949), p. 11.

The importance of Saltillo to Béxar and the rest of Texas as a trading center and source of merchandise in the eighteenth century is not generally recognized. Yet it was this city more than any other which provided Tejanos with many of their goods from the outside world. Presidio captains maintained purchasing agents there, and through these individuals were obtained most of the articles eventually used by the soldiers of the province, not to mention items which were destined for the Indian trade or made their way into private hands.[6]

Nor should it be supposed that trade on the route between Saltillo and San Antonio headed only northward. Many prominent families of Béxar were linked to Saltillo by kinship ties, still maintained houses there, educated their children there, and identified strongly with that prosperous city in the mountains of Coahuila–Nuevo León. Because Saltillo was used as a recruiting ground for *presidiales*, who often were *de color quebrado* ("of broken color"), it was home to other, less prominent Bexareños as well. But the focus of all this cultural and economic exchange was the annual fair held in Saltillo. Pagès visited "Sartille," and years later Pike mentioned its importance for provincial Coahuila, which received all its merchandise from Mexico by land, giving in return horses, mules, wines, gold, and silver: "There is an annual fair held at Saltelo, in New Leon, where there is an immense quantity of merchandise disposed of, and where merchants of very large capitals reside."[7]

Political and social reformer Miguel Ramos Arizpe, however, describes the yearly marketplace and its economic impact on the surrounding underdeveloped regions in more brutal fashion. Because Saltillo was situated near the only practicable pass through the great mountain range of the eastern Sierra Madre, it was the natural theater of commerce for the provinces of Coahuila, Nuevo León, Nuevo Santander, and Texas. Ramos Arizpe writes:

There in September of each year the inhabitants of these four provinces gather at a great fair to pay tribute to their miserable bondage. They are forced to sell their products for a half of the amount that they

---

[6] Herbert Eugene Bolton, *Texas in the Middle Eighteenth Century*, pp. 6, 9, 345.
[7] Donald Jackson, ed., *The Journals of Zebulon Montgomery Pike*, p. 74.

need to supply clothing and so forth for their families; therefore, they are forced to buy the rest of the goods on credit with the obligation of paying for them with their future earnings. This account is renewed annually and comes to be a writ of perpetual bondage.

Frequently it happened that the honest laborer or the innocent shepherd was not able to pay his standing debt. He was ruined at a single blow, being deprived of his scanty possessions and placed in a condition of peonage. In the opinion of Ramos Arizpe such a system of commerce, blighting what would otherwise be fertile and productive provinces, deserved the name of "horrible and barbarous slavery rather than that of purely passive servitude."[8]

Thus not only did heavily loaded packtrains ply the trail north on a systematic basis, but citizens of Béxar made yearly excursions southward, carrying hides, dried meat, fat, suet, and other products of the frontier for trade in the big marketplace. The trip was made in August, and the "fiestas" lasted until the end of September, during which time the Bexareños attempted "to make something for a whole year's work." Until it became profitable to export animals on the hoof (and afterward as well), this was how the citizens supported themselves, taking advantage of one of the few sources of income available.[9]

Insight into how this trade worked can be gained through a bizarre incident which took place in 1776–77. Tomás Travieso, the son of Béxar's sheriff, regularly ran packtrains between Saltillo and San Antonio. He maintained a six-room house in Saltillo, which, with its "small yard," doubled as a residence and a depot for his merchandise. Because his father owned and ran Las Mulas Ranch, one suspects that these beasts of burden were the key to Don Tomás's operation. On the trip down from Béxar he would carry a drove of mules loaded with raw materials also for sale, such as hides, pelts, beef jerky, and bags of tallow. No doubt some of what he took belonged to his neighbors and was carried on commission. Once in Saltillo he would keep enough

---

[8] Benson, *Report of Ramos Arizpe*, p. 24. For stating these and other "notorious truths," Ramos Arizpe spent six years in a Spanish dungeon.

[9] R. B. Blake, Research Collection, Supplement ser., 2:244–71, University of Texas Archives.

animals to form his return packtrain north, this time taking manufactured goods purchased with the income from his Texas produce. Loads, or *cargas*, of items kept in his home suggest that this merchandise included blankets, flour, soap, pots, pans, jugs, salt, *piloncillos* (raw-sugar candy), and *aguardiente* (rum distilled from sugarcane). In his yard were all the tools of the trade needed by *arrieros*, the men who drove the mule trains (*muladas*): twenty-three mules (seventeen female, six male), nineteen pack riggings (*aparejos aperados*), coarse cloth blankets (*jergas* and *guangoches*), handbells (*esquilas*), collars (*collares*), headstalls, saddles (one with iron stirrups, one with wooden stirrups), and so forth.

Apparently Tomás Travieso's packtrain operation was successful enough to arouse the avarice of certain residents of Saltillo, including the city's alcalde. When a mulatto named Juan de Escamilla, who was working as a *cargador* (cargo handler) for Tomás, failed to come back to his wife, Juana, she charged Travieso with murder, basing her charge on the testimony of several witnesses who said that they had seen a man in a ravine—thought to be her Juan—dead of stab wounds. The hearsay charges were sufficient for the mayor of Saltillo to place Travieso in shackles, attach his goods, and put him to work in a "lumber shop." Travieso claimed that the alcalde's real motive in thus denying him justice was the confiscation of his goods, including three dozen pairs of shoes, three loads of *piloncillo*, and 100 pesos cash.

At considerable cost to himself Tomás obtained the services of a lawyer, who established that the dead man in the ditch was not a short mulatto but a tall, blond fellow. A lieutenant stationed at a post below the Río Grande near where the body was found, testified to that effect. Two other men declared that Escamilla had left the packtrain one night and that no one had been able to find him thereafter. Another witness, José Antonio de la Garza, said that he heard that the mulatto was in "Peyotea" (in Coahuila), shearing sheep, while others swore that they had seen him as far north as La Bahía. After all the evidence was in, Travieso was absolved of guilt because Juana's husband had obviously deserted her and was alive and well somewhere on the frontier, a verdict which perhaps offered some small measure of comfort to the poor woman. Some time after this distasteful affair Tomás quit the road, moved his family to Béxar, and became a full-time rancher at Las Mulas.[10]

That the trip between Béxar and markets in the south could be perilous in other ways is without doubt. Yet brave souls continued to make the journey, traveling with mule teams or driving "oversized" herds of cattle which Governor Ripperdá suspected them of taking from mission pastures. For example, in 1776, Francisco Xavier Rodríguez, a son-in-law of Don Vicente Álvarez Travieso (Tomás's father), went to Saltillo with stock gathered under a cloud of suspicion because "in the establishment of Santa Cruz [the Cíbolo fort] there were no cattle." Also making him suspect in the governor's eyes was that his ranch was immediately adjacent to his father-in-law's ranch (Las Mulas), meaning that it fronted on pastures belonging to Espíritu Santo. Another son of Don Vicente, Nepomuceno Travieso, accompanied his brother-in-law Rodríguez on the Saltillo drive, but they also took other herds to Camargo, Laredo, and other settlements—all the cattle being unbranded and gathered from the mission's summer pastures, according to Ripperdá.[11]

The grim realities that lurked beneath each of these bold endeavors became apparent the following year in the fate of Nepomuceno Travieso, one of the most daring of El Rincón's second-generation *ganaderos* and frontiersmen. On September 7, 1777, Nepomuceno departed from Presidio del Río Grande (San Juan Bautista) for the trip home, driving a *mulada* laden with goods. With him were Francisco Casanoba, Joseph Sánches, Ignacio Peña, Pedro de los Santos, Miguel Péres, Xavier Cortina, Bentura Rico, and María Josefa de Flores, all of Béxar. On the night of the eleventh, a full moon, Apaches attacked the party at La Cochina (the Sow) a spot just below present Cotulla near the Dimmit–La Salle county line. Travieso and Casanoba offered resistance and were speared; the others took refuge in the darkness. After scalping Travieso, the Apaches left, taking all the

[10] BAT, vol. 66, contains these proceedings.
[11] Summary of Ripperdá, December 4, 1777, BAT, vol. 64.

mules and merchandise. The Flores woman then crept out of hiding to attend the wounded, but Travieso died later that night. His scalp eventually turned up among the Taovayas and was recognized by the Indian agent Athanase de Mézières because it had almost no hair. It was Nepomuceno's habit to shave his head frequently, which made it easy to identify the grisly trophy that Mézières saw hanging in a *norteño* lodge.[12]

It was perhaps the constant threat of death in obscure places at the hands of *los indios bárbaros* that made the Spanish ranchers of Texas feel exonerated as they pursued their quasilegal means of livelihood. Living and working under such conditions, they may have found fine distinctions of ownership superfluous, caught up as they were in the greater struggle to tame the frontier and snatch from it some measure of subsistence. When survival itself was always in the balance, it was meaningless to quibble about who owned the only potential wealth of the province, its mesteño stock. To the pragmatic ranchers the person who "owned" this wealth was the person bold enough, skilled enough, and fortunate enough to ride out and take it. If the mission raisers, the padres and their Indian

---

[12] Nepomuceno Travieso's death is described in BAT, vol. 79, and is alluded to during the rustling trial, (BAT, vol. 64). Elizabeth A. H. John, *Storms Brewed in Other Men's Worlds: The Confrontation of Indians, Spanish, and French in the Southwest, 1540–1795*, p. 517, identifies this scalp as belonging to Nepomuceno "Trujillo," based on Mézières's account.

vaqueros, could not or would not exploit stock running wild in the pastures, then rugged individuals like Nepomuceno Travieso saw no reason why they should not, even at the risk of death. This was the fundamental issue—not esoteric questions of "first seed," not formalized extent of pastures, not technical points of Castilian law relating to the *mesta*—but simply whether or not a man had the right to seek out, use, and profit from wild animals that were there for the taking. As far as the ranchers were concerned, they had such a right, and no governor or churchman could convince them otherwise.

Word reached Ripperdá in late 1776 that he was to be transferred to another job, a post in Honduras that could be regarded as a promotion but he knew was otherwise. Viceroy Bucareli, convinced of Ripperdá's involvement in the contraband trade, his mistaken Indian policy, and his general incompetence, had worked to have him removed, even though no charges could be proved. Domingo Cabello y Robles received a commission from the king to take over the governorship as early as September, 1775. He was unable to fill this position for another three years, so Ripperdá was forced to continue in the post. One is tempted to speculate, therefore, on the lame-duck governor's motives for using what remained of his administration to launch a bitter attack on the stock raisers of the province. It may be termed the first big rustling trial in Texas, although the ranchers clearly considered it outright persecution.[13]

The case began innocuously enough in March, 1777, when Ripperdá noticed some branding irregularities on stock which the residents of El Rincón were bringing to the presidio. Stating that at various times he had suspected local cattlemen of seizing herds of unbranded cattle from summer pastures that belonged to "all other breeders," the governor observed that he had confiscated stock brought to the presidio for sale or slaughter. All cattle without brands were extracted from these droves and given to charitable funds or establishments as punishment for

[13] Care must be taken not to confuse the rustling proceedings of 1777, contained in BAT, vol. 64, with those of 1778, which are found in BAT, vols. 72–75. The first trial began in March and ran into December, 1777; the second was held in September and October, 1778.

the "neglect and excesses [of recent branding] that I had discovered in the corrals of said breeders." Particularly irregular were cattle that the citizen Marcos de Castro and the sons of Miguel Guerra had brought in from their ranches and that were found to be either without brands or with brands freshly put on. Ripperdá ordered a fine of 5 pesos a head and took sworn statements from those involved, with the result that Castro, Guerra, and Guerra's son Francisco were put in prison. It was noted that since there was no public jail the presidio's *cuerpo de guardia* (barracks for single men, which also contained the guardhouse) was used to hold the prisoners.[14]

The governor then began a long-drawn-out process of taking testimony to establish exactly where the ranchers gathered stock exhibiting the branding "excesses" he had observed. In the early phases of this testimony the ranchers, their sons, and their hired vaqueros obviously could not perceive his intent. Thus they often incriminated themselves and others in the governor's growing web of evidence spun to show that they in fact were going into Mission Espíritu Santo's summer pastures and rustling cattle. This mesteño stock, it will be remembered from Carlos Martínez's sad experience in 1774, Ripperdá considered to belong to the missionaries. Since mere confiscation of the unbranded cattle did not seem to stop the practice, the governor now decided to apply penalties as a way to keep the private raisers out of "other breeders'" pastures. But as the testimony mounted, it became obvious that the violations were too serious and widespread to be ignored. Ripperdá soon became convinced—if he was not of the opinion before initiating the proceedings—that he had a full-blown criminal conspiracy on his hands.

It was during the deposition of Francisco Guerra, Miguel's oldest son (aged nineteen), that the investigation widened and took on its conspiratorial aspect. Francisco said that after he and his brother Mariano found some missing *chichiguas paridas*

---

[14] *Expediente* no. 74, "Year of 1778" (but actually for the 1777 trial), under proceedings begun by Governor Ripperdá against Marcos de Castro, Miguel Guerra, Francisco Xavier Rodríguez, Juan José Flores, and Nepomuceno Travieso, "concerning the exportation of unbranded cattle, March 7, 1777–November 10, 1786," BAT, vol. 64.

(wet mares) they stopped to fish. Meeting Marcos de Castro, they were asked to help with a roundup that Castro and three other men had begun; any *orejanos* that were caught would be divided. The boys agreed and rode off with Castro's *partida*, going on both sides of the Arroyo Cleto, veering off one league on the other side and going up beyond the Juntas del Arenoso (Junctions of the Sandy). This was the crossing of the military road that soldiers of the Fuerte de Santa Cruz regularly used to meet those scouting from Presidio La Bahía. They caught thirty head, claimed young Francisco, most of them large animals.

After the catch was divided, Francisco Flores and Francisco Xavier Rodríguez arrived, saying that it was three days since the people from Las Mulas had left the ranch with a herd and they had not yet arrived. Don Francisco's brother, Juan José Flores, was left stranded at a corral waiting to receive the cattle, an enclosure that Juan José had erected three leagues east of the Cleto. Asked about this corral, Miguel Guerra replied that it was built to keep the cattle gathered from a place at least three leagues farther on, and the herd held there contained many unbranded animals. He added that after the Fuerte de Santa Cruz was reinforced stock raisers from the Cíbolo vicinity became encouraged and again began branding all their cattle, which they brought from the other side of the Cleto.

It was for this straightforward testimony that the three men were put in prison, their fines to be held on deposit until the rightful owner of the unbranded stock was determined. Knowing that Juan José Flores had taken the cattle mentioned in the proceedings to the presidios of the line (those along the Río del Norte), Ripperdá then ordered more testimony to determine exactly where Flores's herd had been taken and how many of them were unbranded. Thus as a succession of witnesses was called, these were the questions: Where from? and How many? Cañada Verde, Arroyo Arenoso, Corral of Los Granados, El Cuchillo, El Carrizo—all east of the Cleto—were frequently mentioned, establishing that the forays extended well into Espíritu Santo's summer pastures. The response that Ripperdá elicited in each deposition strengthened his case that the ranchers were gathering stock that they knew did not belong to them.

The testimony of thirty-three-year-old Francisco Xavier Rodríguez also landed him in jail, Ripperdá vowing that he would remain there until the proceedings were concluded. Rodríguez had delivered to Juan José Flores's herd forty head (most of which were unbranded), taken in three roundups at Arroyo Arenoso, Cañada Verde, and El Cacaste. Rodríguez stated that he and Juan José Flores had a 50-50 agreement since their herds ran together. This, in the governor's eyes, was the damning admission: "For in their summer pastures the resident ranchers of El Cíbolo do not permit the unbranded cattle that they catch among their own cattle to be divided." Hence the assumption that, since they did divide this catch, they knew that they were taking someone else's stock.

Noting that some of the trail drivers had returned from Presidio del Río Grande, Ripperdá summoned a number of them, including Joaquín Flores, Sebastián Monjarás, Amador Delgado, Joaquín Leal, Francisco de la Garza, Blás de Avila, and José de Arocha. Their testimony was as guileless as that previously given, leading to the possibility that they were proud of all the unbranded stock they had been able to catch and sell outside the province, as if this was a measure of their prowess in the saddle and certainly nothing to hide. Indeed, one senses that at times these vaqueros were almost boasting, perhaps feeling a bit self-important at being called to help out the baron with his survey of ranching conditions in Texas. It is difficult to pinpoint exactly when these witnesses realized that Ripperdá was deadly serious, out to nail their hides to the wall. By the same token it is hard to say when the governor became convinced that the ranchers were running an organized rustling ring whose purpose was methodically to clean mission pastures of cattle, but in time he did. By summer words like "instigator," "ringleader," "cover-up," and "the accused" began making their way into *expediente* 74 as the sheaf of documents grew.

On June 3, Ripperdá ordered a confession to be taken from Rodríguez because of "the long delay which the coming of Juan José Flores may occasion." Rodríguez stated that he had divided his cattle with Flores because he had more in the east, transferring them at 20 reales (2½ pesos) a head to pay for provisions needed for the Fiesta of La Purísima Concepción. He professed not to know that to do so was a crime. This "confession" must have pleased the governor because he allowed Jacinto Delgado, Simón de Arocha's brother-in-law, to post bond for Rodríguez and let him go free.

Five days later Juan José Flores, "the accused," appeared before Ripperdá and gave a statement. He listed his age as sixty-four and stated that he had just returned from Presidio Monclova, where he had taken a herd of 650 cattle. From the testimony it is difficult to determine whether this place was the new presidio established on the San Rodrigo River opposite present Quemado, Texas, or old Santiago de la Monclova, the colonial capital of Coahuila. Flores said that he gave Francisco Xavier Rodríguez "for his fiestas" many items: a barrel of *aguardiente*, a bolt and a half of *manta vareada* and of *villalta*, a cut of serge with ornaments, 6 varas of Querétaro cloth, 1 arroba of chocolate, 10 or 12 pesos' worth of soap, *piloncillo*, half an arroba of wine, and so on, offering to receive cattle as payment provided he and Rodríguez shared *orejanos* caught on the Cleto. Then Flores listed the various other people who brought cattle to form his herd, 150 head of which were delivered to Monclova Presidio for a price of only 1 peso, 2 reales, each. Nepomuceno Travieso took 100 head to San Bernardo and got 3 to 3½ pesos each. At the end of this testimony, Ripperdá confined the old cattleman to house arrest and commenced gathering more evidence.

Juan José Flores did not stay under house arrest very long. On August 11, Governor Ripperdá noted that Flores had petitioned for permission to go to the annual Saltillo fiestas and, not waiting for an answer, had taken flight from the *cuerpo de guardia*. Flores later swore that after ten days (another deposition had it two months) in the guardhouse he fled from Ripperdá to become a fugitive, going to Saltillo, where he became ill and was confined to bed.[15] Ripperdá was outraged by Flores's audacity and lack of respect, regardless of the circumstances. He ordered Simón de Arocha, as lieutenant general of the prov-

---

[15] Flores to Croix, petition, January 4, 1778, ibid.

ince, to seize all property belonging to Flores. Arocha duly drew up an inventory of goods confiscated and gave a receipt to Doña Leonor Delgado, listing her as Flores's "close friend" (she was his second wife).

Ripperdá noted that he had deferred doing anything more with the proceedings, partly because of his "accidents," but mainly because he wanted to do the right thing for the royal service, a standard excuse for procrastination. Nonetheless, when information leaked out during the questioning of one Joseph Antonio del Toro that Francisco Flores was the instigator of a prearranged story concerning the roundups and that he had also manipulated a cover-up, the governor's interest perked up. He called Don Francisco, who listed himself as aged sixty-two and *regidor de cano* (senior councilman), to the witness stand. When questioned about his involvement in the roundup and the kind of deal Francisco Xavier Rodríguez had with his brother, Flores admitted only to going into the Cuchillo-Carrizo region. Finding thirty head, they put them in the corral of Martín Lorenzo de Armas, described as being near Rancho Las Mulas. Then one night Nepomuceno Travieso arrived with more cattle, which were also placed in the corral (other testimony had the corral so packed with animals that they kicked out and ran off). The dignified brother of the fugitive closed by saying that he knew nothing of a "deal" except that one man was to supply *aguardiente* and chocolate for the fiestas of the Virgin and the other was to pay for these refreshments with unbranded cattle.

The baron accelerated his proceedings in the month of November, possibly because he knew that the new commandant general was coming to Béxar soon on an inspection tour and wanted to have the case concluded. On the second he wrote into the record that Miguel Guerra had departed this life after his last deposition. The fine (30 pesos) assessed Castro had been received, and he ordered the heirs of Guerra to come up with their 25-peso fine—certainly not a very tactful way to deal with a family in mourning. A week later Ripperdá noted the death of Nepomuceno Travieso "last September" as he was returning from the presidios of the line and the Mission of San

Bernardo; he noted also that the Guerras had paid their fine. He stated that the flight of Juan José Flores had implicated him as having principal guilt, along with Francisco Flores and Francisco Xavier Rodríguez, and gave them all four days to appear. Since Nepomuceno was regrettably deceased, the governor ordered his father to appear instead.

The fireworks started when the old *alguacil mayor* walked into the baron's courtroom. He stated that if Nepomuceno gathered cattle it was without his license because he had been ill for three years and his son, a grown man, was acting on his own. Brushing aside Ripperdá's feints, Don Vicente came briskly to the point. Since the year 1731, His Majesty had given them cattle, "from which I never received the tithe," that is, the increase. Further, he said, he considered that he had "as much right as those who have gathered exceeding numbers of unbranded cattle, to which no one has objected since it is publicly known that all the cattle is spread all over the land." The old Isleño boldly claimed innocence of all charges.

The next day Francisco Xavier Rodríguez's bail was revoked, and Travieso's son-in-law was put back in the guardhouse, accused of resisting obedience to Ripperdá's former decrees. When he appeared to defend himself, he was in leg-irons but spoke eloquently nonetheless. He said that the summer pastures, "which Your Lordship says are others', have been known as free land ever since having use of my reason." Rodríguez claimed never to have seen proof of possession by Espíritu Santo, only cattle which grazed on these lands bearing Cíbolo ranchers' brands or unbranded cattle. He reminded Ripperdá that, when Bernabé Carvajal "sold" his ranch along the Arroyo Cleto to the Bahía mission he would not yield up the rights of the Cíbolo ranchers who grazed in those summer pastures. Sounding a bit as though he had been tutored, Francisco brought up the matter of Ripperdá's prior decrees, which allowed the taking of unbranded cattle four leagues from the Cíbolo ranches, in a westerly direction through the arroyos, mentioning that in fact a license had been issued for a roundup at Los Olmos. He said, "If I see that he who does it now is held criminally liable by Your Lordship, and if he be a cattleman or settler dedicated to

all that has been done in defense of the homeland and its possessions, we would be greatly distressed and unconsoled."

Rising to the attack (and at the risk of rancher solidarity), Rodríguez accused the governor of playing favorites and of allowing other cattlemen a military escort for making corrals, holding roundups, branding cattle, and so on, and ended by waving his family credentials in the aristocrat's face. His father was a soldier and first settler of Béxar, he said, and was among those who had lost—as he himself was now losing—stock. Sharing these losses was his father-in-law, Vicente Travieso, "who is respected as the foremost *criador* and knows how to round up cattle better than anyone else in this villa and mission." Their herds were very widespread because of a multitude of troubles. Unable to retrieve the strays, they now saw them being given to charities which served neither cattlemen nor settlers.

Alarmed that charges of favoritism were being read into the record, Ripperdá ordered the culprits to be more specific. He wanted the names of the people who supposedly enjoyed certain privileges at crown expense. Rodríguez's reply was a virtual indictment of Béxar's entire clerical and military ranching elite. Mission Concepción got help, he said, even though it was not branding time, and extracted unbranded herds from the contested lands. Félix Menchaca and Amador Delgado, he stated, carried unbranded cattle to the presidio for Lieutenant General Simón de Arocha. Those that were not sold to the closer missions they branded for themselves and released. Mission Valero had an *apartadero* (separating area) where cattle were killed or branded and sold, yet Rodríguez had not seen any attempt made to cut out unmarked stock for the ranchers until this year. Others, like the Delgados, were "enjoying privileges we do not." For example, they were permitted to brand cattle on a mission ranch (Valero's La Mora). They were also allowed to take herds in groves along the Guadalupe—up to 500 head, the most branded being 15 or 20. "And since it is probable that the missions have no limitations on summer pastures, nor that Your Lordship prohibits them from branding unbranded cattle as you prohibit us, we are enraged. Are not the missions and the resident public equal? Since all are cattlemen, we too have a right to all unbranded cattle. Señor, I do not know how Your Lordship does not know that the settlers of this villa were the first cattlemen."

After this outburst, Ripperdá moved briskly along, calling only the three accused for final statements before sentencing. Vicente Álvarez Travieso reiterated that he was not responsible for his deceased son's doings. In terms of "favoritism," or the subject of who extracted unbranded herds without dividing them, he mentioned only three instances involving Sebastián Monjarás, Juan José Flores, Manuel Delgado, Félix Menchaca, and Simón de Arocha, all of whom took herds to the frontier presidios. Marcos de Castro had nothing to say, and the widow of Miguel Guerra, Doña Josefa Quiñones, pleaded extenuating circumstances. Her ranch, she said, was next to the Arroyo Cleto, one of the places protected by Carvajal's bequest. It was irritating to see cattle which crossed the arroyo lost to them simply because pastures on the other side belonged to the mission. Besides, Castro and her son had not taken many head, and what they took was merely to compensate for all the stock lost to La Bahía because ranchers were forbidden to cross the creek. She asked the governor to arrange for Espíritu Santo to round up its cattle for annual branding and to require them to surrender "those which appear to be another's, as is customary among the local residents."

Thus ended the proceedings. On December 4, 1777, Ripperdá ordered all records collected, and he marked the flyleaf "for fraud against the cattle industry," naming the accused as Marcos de Castro, Miguel Guerra, Francisco Xavier Rodríguez, Juan José Flores, and Nepomuceno Travieso—two of whom were dead and a third a fugitive. Then he wrote a long summation, discussing the case point by point. It began with the following statement: "Considering their guilt and the punishment which the culprits deserve, I should and do indict them. Let the penalty which they have incurred for robbery be imposed."

Ripperdá's summation, true to his tactics in conducting the case, shows little sympathy for the ranchers of the Cíbolo Valley. The testimony, in his view, clearly indicated that they ranged as close as 16 leagues from La Bahía, penetrating into pastures granted to the mission for its Jaraname and Tamique Indians. He noted that, when Governor Martos delineated the upper border in 1759, "places where their cattle are concentrated" were reserved for the mission's use. In 1770 the borders of the Béxar missions were measured, and unappropriated lands, from Concepción's to the northern boundary of Valero, were added to those of the deponent. Thus Espíritu Santo's pastures bordered those of Concepción "from the cited boat crossing over the Cíbolo and from the one across the headsprings of the Cleto, as far as the Guadalupe River." Concepción's lands adjoined those of San Juan and Valero on the south, meaning in effect that the entire region was mission-owned. There was no doubt about it: the ranchers were taking stock from other owners' pastures.

Having established this crucial point, Ripperdá then set about demolishing the objections raised by the defendants. He maintained that their roundups and branding had taken place not only at the appointed times but constantly ever since the establishment of Fort Santa Cruz in 1771. They had committed these abuses because their own cattle did not suffice for such frequent and oversized extractions. That was where all the exports were coming from, the herds taken to the line presidios by Rodríguez, Flores, and others. And why were the herds scattered? Because the cattle they branded were taken illegally from beyond the Cleto, it was only natural that they should wander back to their home ground. If Cíbolo ranchers' brands were to be found in these pastures at all, it was because they had "continuously branded and marked cattle of all ages belonging to the mission." He admitted that letting the ranchers go into this region during the drought was a mistake, even though he had specified that only branded cows and suckling calves could be taken and had sent two mission representatives along so that the mission's unbranded stock could be separated. The ranchers had refused to perform this separation on equitable terms. Also, the idea of allowing meat hunts was quickly dropped, and the protests of the father president had prompted him to prohibit the killing of stock below the Guadalupe altogether.

Addressing the subject of favoritism, Ripperdá noted that even before the founding of the Cíbolo fort a detachment had been established for escort and security duty on all the ranches except Concepción's. This mission's pastures were vast, and since its Indian vaqueros could not venture far from the Bahía Road because of the ever-present Comanche danger, escorts had been allowed them. The governor felt justified in this, although he admitted that the work was never done well owing to the threat of attacks. Likewise the Comanche hostilities had kept the Jaranames of La Bahía from tending their stock, doing their branding, and so on. Perhaps the roundup of San Antonio de Valero's La Mora had not always been to the satisfaction of residents, but the mission had tried. In fact, Mission Valero bent over backward to accommodate the claims of ranchers. It allowed them entry to look for their cattle and remove those found with private brands, along with following calves. The mission lost in this process, not the other way around. The ranchers could not find one suckling calf with a mission brand; it was always the opposite. Nor could the settlement's meat ration be faulted for extractions which compromised the ranchers: "The missions stay on their own pastures, the ownership of which is proved, despite Francisco Xavier Rodríguez's perverse allegations" (evidently the missions supplied beef to the presidios at this time, although not on an "exclusive" basis, as evidenced by Simón de Arocha's deliveries).

It was not likely, the baron continued, that the ranchers antedated the missions as cattlemen. La Bahía had had many cattle before the ranches of the Béxar vicinity were established, Andrés Hernández's ranch being the first and others congregating afterward with "the few head the Apaches left for them in the neighborhood of this presidio." Nor was it true that the governor's charities gouged the private *ganaderos*, because a mere eight head had been given for the cemetery building. The residents, not the missions, disobeyed orders repeatedly. They brought in cattle of all ages, some unbranded and others "with blood gushing from their marks," for slaughter and sale. Unfortunately, it was not practical to try to prove the rightful owner, so Ripperdá closed his *expediente* by implying a lack of legality and an insufficiency of all that had been said by the defendants.

This was the state of affairs as the year 1777 came to a close, and San Antonio de Béxar stood on the threshold of the most momentous decision ever to affect the stock raisers of Texas. Why Ripperdá found it necessary to consider the most prominent citizens of the province as little better than criminals is a matter open to speculation. Father Morfi said that the baron tried to establish good relations between various factions at Béxar and that this was the reason why the settlers "conspire against him, causing him many headaches."[16] Writers of more

---

[16] Fray Juan Agustín de Morfi, *The History of Texas, 1693–1779*, trans. and ed. Carlos E. Castañeda, pp. 417, 427.

distance have not been so generous, terming Ripperdá straitlaced, legalistic, and self-righteous. Certain it is that he had proceeded to get off on the wrong foot with his subjects almost as soon as he took office in 1770. "One look at the villagers and their surroundings convinced him they stood in need of correction—in their works, in their manners, and in their morals," is how Weddle and Thonhoff describe his attitude.[17]

So proceeded the confrontation until it assumed the proportions of a full-scale war on vice, the Barón de Ripperdá versus the entire province. Most of the men from whom he confiscated liquor and whom he prosecuted for gambling, bootlegging, cock fighting, smuggling, horse racing, and other dissolute practices were the same men involved in raising stock. Thus by the time they were brought in for irregularities in mission pastures, the ranchers were no strangers to the governor's fine-tuned sense of propriety, being long since alienated by his efforts to save them from themselves. A clash of personalities doubtless fed the dispute, the slothful, vice-prone frontiersmen arraying themselves against the haughty son of Madrid nobility. In short, "there was no bridging the gap between them."[18]

When Commandant General Teodoro de Croix rode north to inspect his Provincias Internas, he took with him a future historian of Texas, Fray Juan Agustín de Morfi. Evidence exists that Morfi did not particularly want to accompany the nephew of the former viceroy, who had arrived from Spain nine months previously to take over his new duties. Croix first expressly requested, then begged, and finally threatened to make Morfi come with him under an "oath of obedience" if the priest would not otherwise consent to volunteer. This suggests that Croix had definite ideas about the kind of spiritual adviser he wanted on his grand tour and that Fray Morfi was that individual.[19]

Morfi recorded impressions of the trip in a diary, later ex-

---

[17] Robert S. Weddle and Robert H. Thonhoff, *Drama and Conflict: The Texas Saga of 1776*, pp. 59–61, gives an assessment of Ripperdá and his difficulties with the Bexareños.

[18] Ibid., pp. 10, 134; Morfi is quoted as saying that many complaints and gossip were voiced about Ripperdá whom "these people abhor because of his zeal and good conduct," a remark found in the priest's diary entry of January 6.

[19] Castañeda, "Biographical Introduction," in Morfi, *History of Texas*, p. 18.

panded into his *Memorias* and used to compile *The History of Texas, 1673–1779*. None of these works saw publication until after his death in 1783, and it is safe to assume that the five handwritten copies of his *Historia* known to be still extant had a very limited circulation in their time. But his ideas about what was rotten in Nueva España were more widespread, at least among the progressive of Morfi's contemporaries. It is these ideas that perhaps influenced Croix as they moved about the northern provinces trying to determine whether conditions were really as bad as local officials continually claimed. To judge from the caustic comments in Morfi's *Memorias*, they were indeed, both temporally and spiritually.

Before reaching Texas, the reverend father had already seen enough to horrify him. He did not like big haciendas, with their absentee landlords and oppressed *peones*; he was dismayed by all the different racial categories on the frontier and the mutual hatred and suspicion that these various *castas* were caught up in. Especially did he lash out at those who exploited the natives. A noted Mexican historian later called Morfi's diary "a revelation of the deep-rooted, age-old causes that have retarded the agricultural development of Mexico to this day."[20]

Nor was Fray Morfi impressed by the cluster of ranches that he saw along the banks of the San Antonio River, viewed in the stark clutches of winter. They were of such little consideration and so shabby, all the way to Santa Cruz and the Cíbolo, that, he said, he almost avoided mentioning them entirely. The ranch called Chayopa contained only eight persons; Pataguilla, three; Cabras, twenty-six; Francisco, seventeen; Mora, twenty-six; Las Mulas, five—a total of eighty-five souls "who live in such dread and emminent risk of loss of life, even within their miserable huts, that not a single one of these ranches deserves the name of 'establishment.'"[21] He acknowledged in his *Historia* that seventeen ranches had formerly been established along the banks of

---

[20] Ibid., p. 20. The authority cited there is Vito Alessio Robles, "Notes on the Diary of Morfi."

[21] Fray [Juan] Agustín [de] Morfi, *Excerpts from the Memorias for the History of the Province of Texas*, trans. and ed. Frederick C. Chabot, p. 67. These six ranches are also listed in Morfi, *History*, p. 102. The numbers of inhabitants are the same, but the

the San Antonio River. At Béxar he found Governor Ripperdá still living in the *cárcel* (military prison) and noted that Ripperdá's wife had chosen the *calabozo* (lockup) for her bedroom because it was the most comfortable room and the best shelter. As for the barracks, they were "uninhabitable, even as stables." The king had spent over 80,000 pesos, said Morfi, and after "forty-six years" (actually fifty-seven) there was nothing to show for the investment but a miserable settlement made up of dilapidated houses and streets that became quagmires after every rain.

If the future historian was unduly critical of the little settlement, he was even less kind to its inhabitants, saying that they aspired only to independence and not to have anyone witness their conduct. They called themselves proprietors of extensive possessions, from none of which they received any benefit. "This is their character, this is their passion; and in order to indulge it, they disregard all danger." Lest there be any doubt about the kinds of colonists His Majesty had sent at great expense to the distant province of Texas, Morfi went on to excoriate these "gentlemen" (caballeros) who were too proud to dirty their hands in cultivating a land whose fertility constantly reprimanded their laziness:

Their cattle, and that which has multiplied in the province from the time of Captain León, is their greatest refuge. They live from it clandestinely killing it in the country, and already taking part of it to sell to the presidios and settlements of Coahuila and Nuevo León. This, such an easy means of support, is the base of their laziness.

Noting that they were in perpetual controversy with the missionaries and governors, Morfi suggested that they should work, raise cattle, and avail themselves of the advantages offered by the rich country. But accustomed to receiving the necessities of life without an effort to procure them, they looked upon orderly administration as tyranny and prosecution as persecution. "Finally, I repeat that in New Spain, there is no better country,

spellings of the ranches vary slightly, i.e., "Chayopin," "La Patoguilla." Seven persons were then living at the "wretched fort of Santa Cruz." Evidently the priest was working from census reports associated with Croix's visit, such as the list prepared by Simón de Arocha on February 3, 1777 (ASFG, box 2Q257, University of Texas Archives).

but on the other hand, no worse people." As if this were not bad enough, the old captain's son, Lieutenant José Menchaca, smoked stinking cigars.[22]

If Fray Morfi had leisure to contemplate reasons for the seedy conditions at Béxar, Croix did not. From the moment his entourage entered the villa, he was swamped with petitions, many of them having to do with Ripperdá's rustling trial. Arriving at three o'clock on the afternoon of January 1, 1778, he and Morfi repaired to the parish church to give thanks to the Lord for their safe passage. The company was formed in the plaza and saluted them, whereupon they entered the church. There the commandant was received by the curate and town cabildo, "a band of nondescript, ill-clad citizens" (*una cuadrilla de trapiendos de todos colores*).

From the church they passed to their lodging, the habitation of the old captains of the presidio, so small and badly constructed that not all of the party could be lodged there, nor was there one comfortable room (this building was doubtless the *comandancia* on the west side of the Plaza de Armas described by Captain Menchaca in 1762 as a very strong edifice built of stone, or "pebbles," and mortar, one of the few structures in the Quartel that was not in ruins). While the commandant received the inhabitants of the place, other members of the party went out to see the town, or at least started out. They were caught in such a storm and downpour that they could hardly leave the houses on horseback. The new dignitary was immediately met by so many requests that he could not even take a rest, and within two hours enough work for many days had accumulated.[23]

Juan José Flores was there, seeking restitution for two barrels of confiscated *aguardiente* and the 11-peso fine levied against him back in 1774. Carlos Martínez wanted the cattle that Ripperdá had confiscated and given to charities the same year. Vicente Álvarez Travieso came to present the Audiencia's dispatch of 1771 regarding the division of lands between the missions and the private ranchers—which Ripperdá had chosen to

---

[22] Morfi, *Excerpts from the Memorias*, pp. 58–59.
[23] Ibid., p. xx.

ignore—asking Croix to carry out its intent. Others petitioned that the lands of Mission Valero be given to the homeless Adaesaños, since so few Indians were living there. If this was impossible, a number of other locations were suggested, including the area around the fort on the Cíbolo, a proposal which elicited little support from members of the cabildo, who argued that lands available near their ranches were insufficient.[24]

While most of the petitions were from individuals, one containing twenty-six signatures (all ranchers) was soon brought to the attention of the assessor general, Pedro Galindo Navarro, Croix's "able and legal-minded advisor," a member of the commandant general's party.[25] The petition focused on the boundary dispute with Mission Espíritu Santo and rehashed many of the points made during the trial concluded just the month before. The ranchers accused Ripperdá of unfairness—of treating them as though they were liars. They noted that this situation had been going on since 1775, when conditions had reached the point where they had been obliged to lodge a written protest. The governor had ignored their petition despite a serious loss in cattle since that time; for example: ". . . he who branded ten, did not brand this year even five." They claimed that branding had been done at customary times, except in the year 1775, when the cattle had left their usual grazing pastures owing to the drought.

This, of course, led to the heart of the matter: who was

---

[24] Agustín Rodrígues to the Governor and the Commandant General, January 4, 1778, cited in Castañeda, *Our Catholic Heritage in Texas*, 4:345–48. For the proceedings that Carlos Martínez brought against the governor, see *expediente* no. 337, "Año de 1778 . . . por haberle injustamente quitado algunas bacas, y puesto en prisones," presented to Croix on January 4, 1778, and answered by the *asesor* Galindo Navarro from Chihuahua on April 21, SA, 4:99–105. For the petition presented by the men Ripperdá found guilty of killing mission cattle in 1775, see SA, 3:214.

[25] The description of Pedro Galindo Navarro is Castañeda's, *Catholic Heritage*, 4:322. Most authorities do not acknowledge the *asesor*'s presence in Croix's party, but documents contained in GLO, vol. 50, bear his notations with dates to indicate that he was on this historic tour. Castañeda suggests as much (*Catholic Heritage*, p. 345), but proof that he was in the entourage is found in Eugenio del Hoyo and Malcolm D. McLean, eds., *Diario y Derrotero (1777–1781) por Fray Juan Agustín de Morfi*, pp. 99–106, and in Fr. Benedict Leutenegger, trans., *Journal of a Texas Missionary, 1767–1802: The Diario Histórico of Fr. Cosme Lozano Narvais, Pen Name of Fr. Mariano Antonio de Vasconcelos*, p. 14.

entitled to use pastures in the Cleto vicinity. The ranchers maintained that Ripperdá had deprived them of roundups far afield, limiting their activities to the area west of the Arroyo Cleto, a mere "one league" beyond the Cíbolo. If their cows crossed the Cleto, the ranchers were not supposed to catch *orejanos*; yet cattle of missions grazed openly "from where the Guadalupe flows into the sea, up to its beginning." The missions were deemed to have a right to *orejanos* and mesteños resulting from the herds of both parties. Ignoring the fact that they, the ranchers, were the first settlers, the missionaries had used the ranchers' cattle to build up mission herds—an amazing assertion. "Yes," the ranchers complained, "it is true that the missions are strongest in cattle, but this is because they have freedom to round up and brand *orejanos* without limit to territory or time."

They defended themselves for having built corrals on the lands of Espíritu Santo, claiming they had been erected "at the order of the former [mission] for export," not clandestinely. Moreover, they charged, the governor had wanted them to work for the priests, rounding up their branded cattle and all *orejanos* without ordering the missions to pay the costs. They mentioned the killing of two citizens by Indians on the Cleto as they were coming with a herd from Mission La Bahía and said that the governor had kept the presidio's horse herd in their midst since 1775, "despite the fact that elsewhere were pastures, well watered." For these and other reasons too numerous to set forth, they said, Ripperdá's orders fell heavily on them. They ended their petition by urging Croix to set limits on the pastures of La Bahía and Mission Concepción so that all raisers could take equal advantage of *orejanos*. The *asesor*, Galindo Navarro, apparently passed this petition on to the missions' spokesman and in a marginal note dated January 7 asked them to produce their titles. Likewise he required the ranchers to submit their titles, proof of rights, and so on, a process that took months.[26]

---

[26]"Sundry Representations of the Inhabitants of Béxar, Praying for Special Grant of the Same Tract as Settlers, Year of 1778, no. 59" (GLO, vol. 50). It bears the date January 5, 1778, and is apparently the same document referred to in Weddle and Thonhoff, *Drama and Conflict*, p. 149, as dated October 5, 1778, listing the identical twenty-six signatories.

But for those individuals whom the governor had recently pronounced guilty of fraud, the visitation of the new commandant general provided an ideal avenue of appeal, and they were quick to use it. Juan José Flores produced a piece of paper dated June 20 to prove that the previous summer he had asked the governor to state the charges against him, that he was a "prisoner in the guardhouse" and needed to make a defense. He included Ripperdá's reply, which stated that he would tell Flores why he was a prisoner when his (Ripperdá's) occupations permitted and when in his judgment the time was suitable. In his appeal to Croix, Flores said that after two months in prison without response he had left as a fugitive to seek justice in another court, noting that his possessions had been confiscated that very day. He pictured himself as "driven from my house to suffer dangers of the road" and ended his appeal by asking for the justice his ensuing illness had made it impossible to obtain.

Francisco Xavier Rodríguez's petition was much the same as the others'. He opened with a list of his family's services and loyalty to the king, stating that misfortunes at the hands of Governor Ripperdá had made him weary. He said that he had been held in the guardhouse for two months without food, thirty-five days of that time in leg-irons (Bartolomé Seguín had been permitted to make bail for him on December 25, "since it was the Paschal season"). The origin of his case was in "some unbranded cows I took for my tithe." Rodríguez noted that he had not profited from the source of his woes. The cattle had been offered up to the Holy Mother, given to demands of the *fiestas juradas* (as pledges for the Feast of the Immaculate Conception), of which he was in charge. He said, "Because my father lost cattle at the first founding of this establishment without anything ever returned to him, I believe the lost cattle to be those which I took." The young rancher added that he had been denied the right to give facts relative to the true situation, and he begged Croix's court to clarify the summer pastures which the governor called another's but which he, Rodríguez, called his own.[27]

---

[27] The petitions of Flores and Rodríguez, dated January 4, 1778, and January 5, 1778, respectively, are in BAT, vol. 64.

On each petition that came across his desk, Croix scribbled a note ordering Governor Ripperdá to reply to the supplicant, perhaps annoyed that so much of his time was being spent on trivial matters. The commandant general was in Béxar to talk about sweeping issues like Indian policy, not stray cattle and other such petty grievances.[28] A proposed feature of this new Indian policy would call for war on the Apaches and an alliance with the Comanches and *los norteños*, if possible. Presents and gifts would be necessary to keep the *norteños* happy, and funds would be needed to buy them. Unfortunately, Croix's budget was already strained, and it was therefore imperative to come up with some new source of revenue. It did not take the commandant general long to realize that the vast herds of wild stock roaming the province were just such a source; less than a week elapsed before he claimed them, in the name of the king, for the Royal Treasury.

The bombshell was dropped on January 11, 1778, posted as a proclamation of "good government." This document must be closely examined because it is the cornerstone of all future attempts to regulate the cattle industry in Spanish Texas. Croix stated that, since it was his duty to oversee upright administration of justice in affairs civil and criminal, public and private, he was making a personal review of the province to determine the cause of its backwardness and the reason it had not progressed since its founding.

He charged that the Indian hostilities in the province were caused by the *vecinos*' laxity of conduct, including theft, dissoluteness, concubinage, indulgence in prohibited games, drinking, and "the ease with which vagabonds have established themselves and live." These vagabonds had no purpose in life other than propagating their perverse habits, contaminating the children of decent folk, and preying upon the goods, wealth, and cattle of honorable men. On the pretext that the cattle were wild and without brand or owner, they ran them, took them, and destroyed them at will. The ranchers seemed to think that

---

[28] John, *Storms*, pp. 500–506, contains a discussion of Croix's primary objectives in holding juntas at Monclova and Béxar.

they could go out, build corrals, and commit these kinds of excesses, but Croix had news for them: "Now these animals, both the cattle and the horses, belong to the Real Cámara y Fisco de Su Magestad [Royal Chamber and Exchequer], first because they are strays and have no known owner, and also because they are born and raised in his unappropriated lands, not given in grants."[29]

To prevent the destruction of these wild herds and to protect individual growers, the new commandant general outlined a five-part program that was guaranteed to injure the "false pride" that Fray Morfi had observed in local rancheros who fancied themselves owners of extensive properties. Part of what they imagined they owned were the wild herds, but now, with one stroke of the pen, they belonged to the king. Croix's decree prohibited anyone from going out, rounding up, killing, or taking wild, unmarked cattle or horses in the entire province. Penalties for the first offense were a loss of the animals and a fine of 4 pesos a cow, 2 pesos a horse, and eight days in the public jail. For second offenders the fine and the jail sentence were double, and for a third offense the fine would again double along with a sentence of four years' exile at hard labor.

He decreed that no one could export cows without first obtaining a license (free except for paper cost), which would contain information about the number of head, their kind, and the respective gathering places. Magistrates were designated to keep a license book so that exports could be monitored. Penalties for failure to comply were, for the first offense, loss of animal; for the second offense, loss of animal and a fine of 4 pesos a cow and 2 pesos a horse; for the third offense, the same fines plus two years' hard labor.

Since roundups were held to protect legitimate owners, they would be permitted only at times designated as suitable by judges and were to be attended by a *juez* commissioned for that purpose. Each year roundup information would be required, this to be kept in a book along with export information. But to help "honorable men," the governor was empowered to grant

---

[29] See BAT, 68:3–14, for Croix's decree.

roundup licenses as needed. For each horse taken, a fee was set at 6 reales; for each cow taken, 4 reales—to be paid into a chest with three locks and keys (one held by the governor, one by the first-ranking alcalde, and one by the oldest *regidor*). Finally, it was forbidden to sell guns to "pagan" Indians.

Thus was begun the Fondo de Mesteñas, or Mustang Fund, one of the most controversial taxation experiments attempted in Texas under Spanish rule. While the *caja* (cash box) was kept at Béxar, monies were also collected at Nacogdoches and La Bahía and forwarded to the capital. Few officials who handled these funds escaped charges of malfeasance—charges usually leveled by those being taxed. The Fondo, or Ramo (Bureau), did raise some revenue, most of which was devoted to pacifying the hostile Indians and buying freedom for their captives, but it never equaled Croix's fond expectations. Worse than this failure, however, was the great unrest that the decree's provisions caused in Texas, embracing all factions of the nascent livestock industry. In time, as the administration of the Mustang Fund became ensnarled by a succession of unpopular interpretations and tax increases, more than one crown authority would regard it as a curse, hardly justifying the revenue produced.

The following day Morfi wrote in his diary: "Today the Commandant General published the *bando* on good government [in] which among other things there were rules on the killing, capturing, and export of wild cattle; it was not very well liked by the *vecinos*, who abhor all subordination and good government, accustomed as they are to living on their own laws, like the Apaches their neighbors."[30] This proclamation dovetailed nicely with the interests of at least three of the men present when it was formulated: for Croix it provided needed tax revenue, for Ripperdá it simplified the vexatious question of who owned mesteño stock, and for Morfi it embodied his ideas on frontier moral decay and the work ethic. Indeed, it is tempting to attribute the moral thrust of Croix's decree to his spiritual adviser. In Morfi's view the great ease with which the vagabonds

---

[30] Fray Juan Agustín de Morfi, *Viaje de Indios y Diario del Nuevo México*, ed. Vito Alessio Robles, p. 229.

lived off free cattle was the "base of their laziness." They were insolent wretches, imagining themselves to be caballeros, hidalgos, while cowering fearfully in their miserable huts. Morfi wanted these provincial Spaniards to straighten up, stop begging from the industrious mission Indians, shed their false pride, and go to work, instead of living clandestinely off nature's bounty, the wild herds. Perhaps an "orderly administration" would prove uplifting to the citizens' well-known laxity of conduct; certainly it could not hurt.

The fatal flaw, of course, in such a surmise was that the commandant general's measures not only injured the "vagabonds" who stood in need of chastising but crippled the very raisers they were supposedly promulgated to help, the "honorable men" of the province, Father Morfi's fellow missionaries. They were the "strongest in cattle," as the ranchers' petition admitted. But the truth was—and everybody in Texas knew it— that the mission communities had long since given up the effort to brand all increase of the vast herds, their principal wealth. Yet the first section of Croix's *bando* also clearly prohibited the priests from taking mesteño stock, stripping them of this wealth just as surely as it deprived those who pretended to own it. How could the learned padre have missed the significance of this ruling and the impact it would have on the Indian converts? It was, after all, for their temporal welfare that the mission herds were being tended by diligent priests.[31]

If Fray Morfi's trip did anything, it convinced him of the missionaries' unselfish labors and filled him with admiration for their heroic virtues. Consequently, when he sat down to write his *Historia*, vindicating his brethren in Texas was a main objective. Casteñeda characterizes him thus: "Injustice and unfairness aroused in him the deepest emotions; and, accustomed to crush

---

[31] John, *Storms*, pp. 506–507, touches on Croix's decision to claim the wild herds for the king. Odie B. Faulk, *The Last Years of Spanish Texas, 1778–1821*, p. 85, says that it was inspired by a need for tax revenue, as he does in his "Ranching in Spanish Texas," *Hispanic American Historical Review* 44 (May, 1965): 258. See also Castañeda, *Catholic Heritage*, 4:27; Weddle and Thonhoff, *Drama and Conflict*, pp. 131, 169–70; Myres, *Ranch in Spanish Texas*, pp. 17, 37 of which the last presents the most useful and orderly summary.

his opponents with cold, unanswerable logic, he set out to prove not only the innocence of the missionaries, but the guilt of those who accused them, proclaiming at the same time the profound injustice of the accusation." Certainly Morfi, regardless of his low opinion of the Texas ranchers, does not sound like a man who would advocate enacting a law which would reduce the upright missionaries and their Indian neophytes to penury.[32]

Nor does it appear that Governor Ripperdá would have recommended a decision of this nature. On the contrary, his actions in prosecuting the Cíbolo ranchers were predicated on the conviction that the missions owned all loose, unmarked cattle found in "summer pastures." Practically speaking, this designation covered almost all the land between Béxar and La Bahía, a situation about which the ranchers were very unhappy and which they were continually agitating to change. Certain it is that Ripperdá was fond of attempting to legislate the morality of his subjects, posting notices on everything from the "infamous act" of climbing fences or gathering roasting ears to the exact number of lashes to be meted out at the presidio corral's "ring of shame" for stealing 10 pesos or more. Perhaps he saw Croix's decree as a way to bring order out of chaos, a consideration which has been known more than once to override nit-picking distinctions like those the ranchers were trying to press with their mesteño-ownership claims. Bound for another post as soon as his successor, Domingo Cabello y Robles, arrived, Ripperdá was no doubt glad that all this petty bickering would soon be behind him.[33]

However it came to pass, one suspects that the complex

---

[32] Castañeda, "Biographical Introduction," in Morfi, *History*, p. 26. Ramsdell, "Spanish Goliad," p. 27, suggests that Croix's order "may have been designed to embarrass the clergy and reduce their power," although recognizing that it could just as well have been done to impress the king.

[33] Ramsdell, "Spanish Goliad," p. 25, describes Ripperdá's actions against the ranchers as part of his "lively feud" with them and says that their arrests were a result of the governor's having sided with the priests. He depicts Ripperdá's successor, Cabello, as "not so friendly" to the missionaries' interests. Weddle and Thonhoff, *Drama and Conflict*, pp. 61–65, present a very amusing account of Ripperdá's efforts to control his subjects' moral conduct.

problems, the burdensome administrative complications, that this regulation would spawn were little guessed at in January, 1778. On its face the decree seemed simple, almost a stroke of genius. There were those countless animals, most of them unbranded, grazing on the open grasslands of the province. They were the natural increase of livestock introduced largely at crown expense. It must have seemed perfectly fair to Croix to claim all mesteño stock for the Royal Treasury and to collect a modest fee for animals subsequently appropriated to private ownership. Orderly roundups, the export-license book, and the brand register would allow a measure of control which the industry needed if it was to flourish. Thus it is easy to imagine the commandant general riding away from Béxar in mid-January thinking that he had set the cattle business on a firm footing, completely unaware of the "bitterness and economic dislocation he had wrought." It should perhaps be noted that in one sense the Tejanos were fortunate because Croix devised no less than fifteen different duties whereby the citizens of neighboring Coahuila would contribute after 1780 toward the raising of a special militia for their protection. Included were a tax of 2 reales each on "young animals" and 4 reales on each beef, as well as taxes on wheat, pulque, wine, and so on. The entire package was protested by the Marqués de Aguayo as ruinous to the province.[34]

A few days after the first commandant general left to continue his inspection of the presidios in Coahuila and Nueva Vizcaya, en route to his headquarters at Chihuahua, Governor Ripperdá responded to Croix's order to answer the supplicants from Béxar. Smarting from the howl of discontent about his administration embodied in the stack of grievances that had confronted Croix, Ripperdá told his superior, "I fear not your evaluation." He professed amazement at how Francisco Xavier Rodríguez could have encountered the judge and collected parts of his record, indicating that Rodríguez's statement that he

---

[34] John, *Storms*, p. 507; Francis de Burgos, "The Administration of Teodoro de Croix, Commander General of the Provincias Internas de Mexico, 1776–83" (Master's thesis, University of Texas, 1927), pp. 336–37, 366–76.

had been "denied the right to give facts," that is, his side of the story, was not far from the truth. Turning to Juan José Flores's petition, the governor allowed a bit of exasperation to creep into his reply. Mentioning that he had pressed these charges because of the ranchers' repeated abuses in other raisers' summer pastures, as Croix was aware, Ripperdá displayed some resentment about the leniency shown Flores: "I suppose you have thought it well to pardon the supplicant for the escape he made from the guardhouse, so I have not prosecuted for his imprisonment and punishment." In other words, the case was dropped. All the relevant papers were forwarded to Croix, however, and on April 24, 1778, he sent them over to the *asesor* Pedro Galindo Navarro, and eventually they were combined with a subsequent *expediente*.[35]

On February 9, 1778, Ripperdá issued a proclamation extending the commandant general's decision to La Bahía, saying that it would have the same effect there that it had at Béxar. Until further orders, no one was to gather *orejanos* for six

---

[35] Ripperdá's closing remarks on both these petitions are dated January 20, 1778, BAT, vol. 64.

months in the area two leagues beyond the Guadalupe. Don Luis Cazorla, the captain of Bahía Presidio, was empowered to designate "places he knows of" at the same distance below the junction of the San Marcos. Above the junction and past the Guadalupe (north), however, unbranded animals could be taken. During this six months Mission Espíritu Santo was to be permitted to gather and drive off any cattle it had above the Guadalupe. This is the first mention of a period of grace during which a raiser would have the right to gather stock before the decree took effect. Demands for similar extension periods soon proliferated. In effect the order gave the missionaries a little breathing room, a head start on their private ranching competition, doubtless because the area was large and their herds were scattered. Ripperdá was quick to note that after this six-month period Espíritu Santo, just like everyone else, would be allowed to gather only at times specified by the captain. In regard to wild horses, however, Captain Cazorla could issue roundup licenses for any place and time he deemed fit, and he was delegated the authority to maintain all records called for by the decree. Fees for captured cattle and horses were to be collected at the designated rates.

Captain Cazorla published this instruction in the Bahía Presidio on February 16, 1778, and Fray Escobar published it at Espíritu Santo and at Rosario on March 17 and 26, respectively. Its main feature proved to be the provision allowing a "grace period" during which unbranded stock could be gathered and branded before Croix's regulations and the accompanying taxes went into force. The notion that all raisers were entitled to such a time consideration quickly took hold and was exploited to its fullest.[36]

Concerning the dispute over pasturelands between the twenty-six ranchers and Espíritu Santo, it will be recalled that the *asesor* Galindo Navarro asked both parties to submit their titles, deeds, and other documents so that a determination could be reached. The mission's father president, PedroRamí-

---

[36] Ripperdá's proclamation of February 9, 1778, along with its publication notices, is found in *expediente* no. 88, BAT, vol. 68.

rez, soon submitted a petition on this subject. It contained copies of Fray Joseph Juaquín Garzía's original request for Espíritu Santo's lands and Governor Martos's Edict of Possession, which stated clearly the mission's rights to the pastures in question. It also contained a detailed account of the ranches below Béxar and their activities, most of which were considered prejudicial to the interests of the Indians under Ramírez's care.

Fray Ramírez's assessment of the various men "who want to designate themselves as raisers" is scathing. He admitted that four ranches had the right to operate (Rancho de San Francisco; Rancho de Las Mulas; Rancho de San Bartolo, recently "annexed" by José Macario Sambrano; and Rancho de Su Cuñado, Ignacio Calvillo's small-time pasturing operation at his brother-in-law's place) but spoke none too kindly of the men who ran them. He answered their complaints against the missions one by one, maintaining that few of the signatories had any right to gripe. Sebastián Monjarás, for example, had been a tailor until two years before, when he had received the *diezmo* of the area from one of his brothers, who had never owned any cattle. Since Monjarás could not pay even the first year's tithe, he hardly qualified as a *criador*. Carlos Martínez had fled from Captain Tovar at Bahía Presidio, arriving at Béxar with the horse he rode and not much else. Now he had a cattle brand and a *señal* (earmark) and vigorously maintained his right to *orejano* stock. Although he claimed to be open-minded on the subject, it is obvious that the father president believed that few of these men's pretensions were justified.[37]

Receipt of this petition led to a *bando* dated April 18 requiring all raisers and residents of ranches in the province to present their "papeles, títulos, mersedes o derechos que alas tiera tienen" (papers, titles, royal favors, or rights to their land). This order, and Galindo Navarro's recommendation to Croix that Espíritu Santo should be required to show its grant papers, titles, and so on, prompted a flood of response from the Béxar

---

[37] GLO, 50:140–44, contains the April 13, 1778, petition of Father President Ramírez and related documents. Ramsdell, "Spanish Goliad," p. 25, describes the gist of the priests' complaints as saying that the ranchmen "were really no better than rustlers."

ranchers, who perhaps scented a change of official policy in the wind. The area's most prominent cattleman, Don Luis Antonio Menchaca, and his brother Joseph Félix led the procession on May 3, followed closely by twenty others. These rancher "title documents," are little more than statements about the date on which they situated themselves on the land, their good-faith occupancy, and their devotion to the king. However, they do contain a wealth of information about where they were situated, the extent of their range, the conditions under which they maintained their livestock, and their relationships with the various mission ranches and other private establishments. In short, they present an excellent profile of the earliest ranches in El Rincón from their founding until 1778. Menchaca's petition, as one might expect, contains the most impressive legalistic jargon, though he too admitted that his title was incomplete.[38]

While the documents pertaining to the questions of pasture and *orejano* ownership were assembled, attempts were being made to comply with Croix's regulation. Lieutenant General Simón de Arocha, whom Ripperdá entrusted with the record-keeping chore, began what was termed a "book recording licenses issued to residents and missions of this jurisdiction for cattle exportation." The only substantial roundup shown in this "book" took place on May 19 at Las Cabras, where Don Simón issued a license, intended "for sale at the presidios of the line." It covered 250 head for Tomás Travieso, of his father and brothers' brand; 40 head for Vizente Flores, of his father's brand; 150 head for Sebastián Monjarás (100 of his brand, 50 belong-

---

[38] BAT, 69:26–28. For Galindo Navarro to Croix, May 9, 1778, recommending that the governor of Texas further investigate Mission Espíritu Santo's titles to such extensive pastures, see BAT 69:26–28. BAM, roll 12, frames 276–77, and BAT, 69: 29–31, contain the statement of Juan José Flores maintaining that he settled his Cíbolo ranch in 1756 and that others followed in 1760—a claim also mentioned in the *asesor* Galindo Navarro's opinion written from Arizpe, dated October 25, 1782. GLO, 50: 159–95, contains the rancher "title documents" of Luis Antonio Menchaca, Joseph Félix Menchaca, Jacinto Delgado, Miguel de Gortari, Joachín Leal, Juan Joseph Flores, Francisco Flores, Macario Sambrano, Francisco Xavier Rodríguez, Joseph Antonio Curbelo, Joaquín Menchaca, Joseph Ygnacio de la Peña, Juan Francisco Granado (at the request of his mother, the widow of Martín Lorenzo de Armas), Marcos de Castro, Joseph Joaquín Flores, Joaquín de la Garza, Juana de Ollos (widow of Andrés Hernández), Leonardo de la Garza, Carlos Martínez, Sebastián Monjarás, Vicente Álvarez Travieso, and Ygnacio Calbillo.

ing to various others); 312 head for Francisco X. Rodríguez (200 belonging to Espada, 100 to Luis Menchaca, and 12 of his own); 13 head for Guillermo Casanoba, of his father's brand (Joseph Antonio Péres); and 14 head for Martín de la Garza, of his own brand—a total of 779 head. The brands were shown in the margin opposite these notations, but it is difficult to link them with exactness to the owners intended. It would appear that the listing shown in brand section A, at the end of this book, is the correct one.

Added to this (but showing no cattle brands) was a long list of individuals who branded *orejanos* taken "in surrounding areas and on unappropriated summer pastures," the roundups covering the period February 18 to May 25 and totaling 353 head. Then in October licenses were issued to Jacinto Delgado for 311 head, the inspection being conducted at La Mora; and to Francisco X. Rodríguez for 100 head, both of these herds evidently for export. Altogether it was reported that for the year 1778, the first year in which an attempt was made to regulate the cattle "industry," export licenses were issued for a total of 1,290 head.[39]

Before leaving office in 1778, Governor Ripperdá made one more attempt to chastise the Béxar-Cíbolo ranchers for their cattle forays into mission pastures east of the Cleto. He began taking testimony on September 23 as *juez receptor* (delegate judge) and by the next day had his old nemesis Juan José Flores back in jail, along with Josef Andrés Hernández, the son of the founder of Rancho San Bartolo. The charges were the same, taking cattle from Las Tetillas, Arroyo Alonzo, and other pastures of Espíritu Santo, but now the governor had some teeth in his charges: the stiff fines set forth in the commandant general's decree for those who violated roundup procedures and failed to pay the stipulated fees. Consequently, the new proceeding had much more serious implications than those of the "trial run" conducted the previous year.

It must be admitted that there is something puzzling here.

---

[39] BAT, 68:58–67. See also Frederick C. Chabot, *With the Makers of San Antonio*, p. 164, and opposite p. 15, for a facsimile of Arocha's manuscript containing the brands, the original of which is in BA, box 4C434.

On May 23, *asesor* Galindo Navarro rendered an opinion reversing Ripperdá's sentence passed on the men who had conducted *carneadas* below the Guadalupe River during January and February, 1775. Croix, basing his action on this opinion, ordered restitution of their fines a week later. Since the proceedings of Ripperdá's first rustling trial (in 1777) were also being considered at this time—and fines were also involved—it is possible that the reversal included both cases. This is difficult to ascertain, but the complex "refund vouchers" do not indicate that the slate was wiped clean of the fines of 1777. In any case, what it all meant was that Governor Ripperdá chose to prosecute a second and final rustling trial, knowing that an earlier attempt at criminal proceedings had not been sustained by his superiors. Therein lies the puzzle.[40]

By the time Ripperdá called the imprisoned men forward for more questioning, other testimony had established that they had gone farther into the mission pastures than they had admitted. Josef Andrés Hernández said that he "forgot" to mention going up to the Alonzo corral, but when asked why he had gone there, knowing that the Cleto was the boundary line, old Flores defiantly replied, "To get what belonged to me." In coming days the testimony mounted, with each new bit of evidence incriminating a growing number of individuals, just as it had during the first big trial. Melchor Ximénez was put in chains for admitting his part in roundups east of the Cleto, while Juan José Flores begged to be removed from his cell owing to his advanced age (he was now sixty-five), old shoulder wounds, and "bad urine."

On October 10, Ripperdá took a break from his function as

---

[40] As noted, the testimony covering this second trial is found in BAT, vols. 72–75, most of the volumes being devoted entirely to the subject; for a brief treatment see Wilson E. Dolman, "Mission Cattle Rustling," *Texas Parks and Wildlife* 33, no. 3 (March, 1975): 22–25. Herbert Eugene Bolton, *Guide to Materials for the United States in the Principal Archives of Mexico*, p. 427, citing SA, *expediente* no. 270, says that Ripperdá's proceedings against the various citizens of Béxar for killing the missions' cattle, "1775–1778," were reversed by the commandant general, who fined Ripperdá—the latter having fined the citizens. Weddle and Thonhoff, *Drama and Conflict*, p. 170, say that Croix ordered restitution of their fines "later in 1778," charging Ripperdá for the money; Myres, *Ranch in Spanish Texas*, p. 41 says the same thing. See note 2 above.

juez receptor to order the citizens to separate their horses from those belonging to the soldiers. He noted that the presidio had over 1,100 head, and the large number was causing accidents at the corrals and much shifting from pen to pen. Breeding mares with colts under three years old were also complicating matters. Giving owners fifteen days to remove their horses, Ripperdá stated that those not separated would be put in the local public corral, where they could be claimed. If any returned to the presidio's caballada, the mares and colts would again be taken out, and the stallions would be gelded.[41]

Returning to his cattle proceedings three days later, the governor sent shock waves through the villa by arresting twelve of San Antonio's leading citizens. Since Juan Andrés Travieso was a *regidor* (councilman), he was confined to house arrest, rather than being put in prison with the others. Witnesses called to testify in the case represented the broad spectrum of life at Béxar: Carlos Riojas—born in Coahuila, age thirty-one, journeyman, tailor; Josef María Móntes, "Indian"—born in El Monte, thirty, servant of Vicente Travieso; Francisco Antonio Flores—born in Béxar Presidio, twenty-two, fieldworker and vaquero; Vizente Flores—born in "this presidio," twenty-two, laborer; Santiago Seguín—born in "this presidio," twenty-four, "cares for harvests"; Francisco Flores de Abrego—born in Saltillo, sixty plus, laborer; Joaquín Flores—born in Saltillo, thirty-six, "no employment except his intelligence" (signed "Flores y Zendeja"); Juan Andrés Travieso—born "here," forty, "occupies in cultivation the little property he owns"; Manuel Granado—born on the Isle of San Zarote,[42] fifty, laborer; and Josef Padrón—forty-five, *creditor* of the Martín Lorenzo de Armas Rancho.[43]

By October 18, Ripperdá had named those principally guilty as Juan José Flores, Josef Andrés Hernández, Mariano Guerra, Vizente Flores, Francisco Travieso, Juan Andrés Travieso, Francisco Flores de Abrego, and Josef Padrón. He said that

---

[41] Ripperdá to citizens, October 10, 1778, Grazing Papers, vol. 1 (University of Texas Archives).

[42] Lanzarote, the island in the Canaries that most Bexareños hailed from, according to an Isleño descendant, John Ogden Leal.

[43] BAT, vol. 72, contains the proceedings through the jailing of October 13, 1778.

"they were leaders of the last two instances of the eight cattle runnings, which they have made since last May." Specifically the charge was that they took more than four hundred head of cattle belonging to the Tamique and Jaraname Indians of Mission Espíritu Santo from pastures already established as belonging to them, mainly those east and northeast of the Cíbolo from its mouth and more than 7 leagues upstream to La Laja Pass and beyond.

The governor stated his position thus: "I was excessively tolerant with the Cíbolo ranchers so that they could round up in the four leagues which is the least distance between it and the Arroyo Cleto (even though it belongs to Espíritu Santo with one exception); yet greed has compelled them to penetrate six, eight, and more leagues beyond the Cleto in early hours." He charged all the named ranchers with the crime of taking another's property and for the falsity with which they maintained their rights to cattle in mission pastures. A week later he ordered the accused released except for five men, whom he refused bond because they had perjured themselves during testimony. However, because of his "deplorable health," the old rancher, *diezmero*, and trail driver Flores was kept under house arrest, as was Travieso because of his councilman status. Thus three men remained in jail, and writs were drawn up not only for larceny but for perjury as well.

Notified of the charges against them before their release, each answered in a separate petition which became a part of Ripperdá's *expediente*. Flores, still passing blood in his urine and with little time left to live, gave a spirited reply, although he must have been weary of the self-righteous baron and his endless examinations. Flores said that he understood this lawsuit to be against those who had gone to get their cows in the Arroyo Los Olmos, toward the upper part, up to Las Tetillas and the Arroyo Alonzo, and that this area was claimed by Espíritu Santo. He admitted to having built with his own labor three corrals: one at Las Tetillas, one on the Arroyo Alonzo, and one on the Cleto. He claimed to be "responsible" for these lands. Although Espíritu Santo grazed its cows in the vicinity, the old frontiersman felt that he held them better because of what he had constructed there. Furthermore, Flores maintained, Bernabé Carvajal's sale of Los Corralitos to Espíritu Santo was invalid for three reasons: Carvajal did not have a good title, he did not complete the minimum limit of one year's settlement, and he did not cite the parts and supplements of the ranch, even if he had the right to sell. This was a restatement of the position that Flores, Martínez, the widow of Martín Lorenzo de Armas, and other ranchers had taken in their title claims of May. He ended by saying that he was angry because "no one has a right to what is mine."

Josef Andrés Hernández was brief, and so was Juan Andrés Travieso, who also admitted to having built corrals in the contested area, one in the Arroyo Los Olmos, two in the Arroyo Carrizo (one for cattle and one for horses), one in the Arroyo Cuchillo, and one at the headwaters of Arroyo Alonzo. His family, therefore, was operating above the corrals built by Flores, closer to the Guadalupe. Travieso said that they did not technically own their lands but in fact "possessed" them—possession in his mind weighing heavily, as it did on most frontiers. Juan said that, since Travieso's kin were near the eastern part of what his father claimed (Las Mulas) and had large families, they were going to ask for an extension of their lands. East was the only way they could go, Concepción's ranch, El Paistle, being on the north, the ranches of the Cíbolo on the south, and those of the San Antonio River on the west. Santiago Seguín said only that his grandfather, the deceased Don Pedro "Oconitrillo," had been a cattle breeder for thirty years and that they kept their cows in the Arroyo Cíbolo.

Born around 1723 and a widower when he married Francisca Travieso (daughter of Vicente Álvarez Travieso), Francisco Flores de Abrego y Valdés claimed to have been a breeder since 1753, adding that he had settled at Las Mulas in 1762 and had lost most of his cows in the neighborhood. But when Ripperdá made known on October 28 his intention to close the case and inquired whether anyone had something to add, Don Francisco made known his feelings. Through them we catch a glimpse of the resentment Spanish ranchers harbored toward their Indian counterparts—especially when the rights enjoyed by mission vaqueros were held superior to their own. Don Francisco said the Espíritu Santo Indians butchered more cattle than did the ranchers, "for they are the enemies of every good, living thing." The Indians built corrals and took and branded cattle without regard to ownership. He maintained that the greater part of Bahía Mission's stock was outside the sites in question—Las Tetillas, Los Olmos, Los Nogales, El Carrizo, El Capote, and others—since all of these were 30 leagues from Espíritu Santo. Since their own ranches were only 8 leagues from these pastures, Flores reasoned that the cattle found there belonged not to the mission but to men like himself.[44]

Following the receipt of this response and noting that the others sustained their previous statements, on October 31, 1778, Governor Ripperdá wrote a summary of the entire trial. It was to be his last effort to "restrain and punish" offenders of Croix's cattle regulations. In the process he penned a little history lesson, the object of which was to deflate the self-importance of the ranchers and their claims to stray cattle which rightfully belonged to the mission establishments. As in most other polemics, strong elements of sarcasm are present in his essay on how ranching really evolved in El Rincón. Many of his points merely repeat the reasoning found in his first rustling proceedings; a few touch on Croix's decree and the new situation it embodied. At the core, however, is Ripperdá's conviction that the men opposite his bar of justice would say and do anything to defeat his purpose. "Supposing themselves to have equal rights" to Mission Espíritu Santo's pastures, "they make themselves unaware of its true ownership." How these upstart ranchers had acquired their cattle was obvious to the governor: they had stolen them from mission pastures. He ended his summation of the case by charging that the accused ranchers took cattle in defiance of several laws and royal ordinances, without licenses and without payment of the required fees, and treated all stock encountered on other people's land as their own. This

---

[44] Ripperdá's review of the case, his indictment of those "principally guilty," and the defendants' statements of October 22 are found in BAT, vol. 73. For the Ocón y Trillo–Seguín kinship see Chabot, *Makers of San Antonio*, p. 136.

"We Are Enraged" 171

was forbidden, even on unappropriated lands, the governor added, finding the defendants guilty of thievery.[45]

Thus ended the nine-year administration of Juan María, Barón de Ripperdá, governor of Texas. He exited as he entered, at odds with the citizens of the province, in a storm of indignation and protest. Without a doubt the legacy of bitterness engendered by his cattle trials of 1777 and 1778 placed his successor in a difficult position from the outset. The resentment that Ripperdá's zealous prosecutions created among the leading citizens of Béxar ran too deep for the new governor not to be touched by its swirling undercurrent. When the baron handed over the symbols of office to Domingo Cabello on November 1, 1778, he also handed over a stack of criminal indictments and a province full of ranchers livid with anger.[46]

---

[45] Final statements and Ripperdá's summary fill BAT, vol. 74.

[46] BAT, vol. 75, contains the actual lawsuit against the ranchers, listed as *expediente* no. 39. Documents relating to the disposition of this case, including Ripperdá's *auto* of October 31, 1778, in which he declared the offenders guilty of larceny, are found in BAT, vol. 113.

6
"LA LUICIANA"
Up the Trail

COLONEL Domingo Cabello y Robles reached Texas with a long, unblemished record in His Majesty's royal service. He was a thirty-seven-year veteran, having seen service in Havana during the Seven Years' War, as well as in Florida and Nicaragua, where he was a governor. Indian problems occupied Cabello's attention from the early days of his term and continued to dominate both his time and his energy until they became all-consuming. Maintaining a delicate balance between the numerous and diverse tribes of Texas, playing one off against the other, gradually moving toward a reconciliation with the powerful Comanches and their *norteño* allies while keeping the Lipan Apaches placated—these were the challenges of Cabello's era, and he took to them with a relish. Indeed, one comes away with the feeling that this capable administrator regarded his many accomplishments in Indian diplomacy as the apogee of his tenure in Texas, especially his peace efforts with the Comanches, a goal which Cabello came to believe would more than compensate for the years he spent in the wretched province.[1]

As with most other heads of government who find their energy directed, either by external exigencies or by internal

---

[1] Cabello to Rengel, May 20, 1785, BA (also found in R. B. Blake, Research Collection, Supplement ser., 2:160), leaves little doubt that Cabello viewed his dealings with the Comanches as the high point of his service in Texas. For a discussion of his initiation into the complexities of Indian policy, see Elizabeth A. H. John, *Storms Brewed in Other Men's Worlds: The Confrontation of Indians, Spanish, and French in the Southwest, 1540–1795*, pp. 531–56. One of the best studies available of his term is Odie B. Faulk, "Texas during the Administration of Governor Domingo Cabello y Robles, 1778–1786" (Master's thesis, Texas Technological College, 1960).

inclinations, to the Big Picture, Cabello's term of office was not noted for its accomplishments on the home front. This is not to say that he purposely ignored the cattle industry or that it suffered serious abuses owing to mismanagement, negligence, or excesses on his part. On the contrary, Cabello was always "correct," careful to be above suspicion, and was a conscientious bureaucrat when it came to threading his way between administering Croix's cattle regulation and refereeing the ongoing conflict between mission and private raisers. But the Comanches struck Bucareli the same month this well-meaning official arrived, and they continued to batter at the gates of the province for years afterward, threatening the very existence of Spain's outposts in Texas. Thus it is hard to fault Domingo Cabello if his mind was on more serious issues than the dubious ownership of mesteño stock at a time when the *norteño* menace made life itself a contested possession.

Like it or not, he was forced to deal with Ripperdá's leavings on the rustling and *bando*-violation case. The outgoing governor was very specific as he transferred to Cabello the writs against Juan José Flores et al. for their "habitual thefts of unbranded cattle in the summer pastures of Espíritu Santo." He wanted Juan Andrés Travieso and Flores to remain under house arrest, and he wanted the other three men kept in chains because they had perjured themselves. Then he handed over vouchers totaling 51 pesos, 7 reales, the amount due the Mustang Fund, and recorded in the book of strays gathered (at 6 reales per horse, 4 reales per cow) since the inception of Croix's regulation. As a fund-raising device the cattle law had proved rather disappointing in its first year: only 10 pesos, 2 reales, of the total was in cash money, the remainder being still owed.[2]

Cabello reviewed the stack of writs and on November 7, a week after taking office, noted that those charging perjury were not sufficiently proved. Since the matter was now before the commandant general, the men must remain in prison until a decision was reached, said the new governor. He relented, however, and at the end of the month those imprisoned were allowed to post bond and go free. This act of generosity also

[2] BAT, 75:171.

prompted the *regidor*, Juan Andrés Travieso, to petition for "release," even though he was only under house arrest. He claimed that the charges against him were not exact because he had taken the offspring of his own cattle, not those of others, as Ripperdá had accused. As for defying the order of the commandant general in branding and marking cattle taken, Travieso said that, since the missions were accustomed to selling stock either unbranded or recently marked to the general public in the Plaza de Armas, he figured that this was permissible for individuals. Such a line of reasoning harkened back to the argument "If the missions do it, why can't we?" These arguments never seemed to work with Ripperdá, whom Travieso politely termed "predecessor of Your Excellency." But Cabello was a new man, with few prejudices on the cattle question, and in the coming months the ranchers advanced to him many of their old ideas on who really owned the mesteño stock in Texas. Travieso ended his appeal by saying that Croix's *bando* called for a first-offense sentence of eight days in prison, a sentence his term had far exceeded. He was set at liberty on December 6.[3]

Like so many other thorny cases which would arise from the cattle dispute, Ripperdá's rustling-trial proceedings were sent to the commandant general's office. They were shuffled, attached to related items, and forwarded to the lord assessor's office for legal disposition. Once there they underwent another round of examination and reclassification by Galindo Navarro in a painstaking process to assemble laws, rulings, and precedents and pronounce an opinion, which was then forwarded to Croix, who in turn ordered it enforced on the provincial level. Often it took years for a particular case to reach a decision, and then it would reappear attached to an *expediente* completely different from the one originally submitted. This had the affect of putting most crucial cases in suspension, leaving them unresolved, while additional complications arose to burden further the efficient administration of Croix's regulation. It also made it very difficult for Governor Cabello to keep tabs on the various files he compiled and sent to Chihuahua, each one containing yet another kink, another twist in an increasingly complex puzzle.

[3] Ibid., pp. 128–33.

In the last full-scale rustling trial conducted by Ripperdá, the ranchers did eventually win a vindication of sorts. The reversal was based on *asesor* Galindo Navarro's opinion dated October 25, 1782, in which he said that Ripperdá's verdict of larceny was premature and thus suffered the "notorious defect of invalidity." The governor, in his haste to conclude the case, had ignored certain technicalities. For instance, a verdict "must await the final sentencing and not come before." Also, the defendants were due a transcript of the proceedings for preparation of their defense, and this had not been permitted. In other words, it was obvious to Croix's legal adviser that behind Ripperdá's shoddy prosecution of the case was a heavy-handed attempt to railroad the ranchers. Thus Galindo Navarro ordered all the original *autos, causas, sumarias* and other items that composed the *expediente* sent back to Texas so that Cabello could proceed according to the proper methods, a legally correct way of saying, "Put it in the dead file."[4]

Governor Cabello had scarcely disposed of his predecessor's criminal proceedings against the ranchers when another dispute arose, this one among the ranchers themselves. The new case, more than any other, would affect the way in which Texas's cattle laws were conceived, interpreted, and enforced over the coming years. Out of it came temporary methods of dealing with cattle taken in the contested pastures, as well as a long-range set of practices for the entire industry. It was, therefore, a pivotal case which took years to evolve and which can be seen as a continuous thread in the mysterious interweavings of Croix's original cattle ordinance.

It began as a protest designed to stop the missionaries from gathering herds from the contested pastures until their true ownership could be determined. That it was intended as a test

---

[4]See BAT, 113:64, for the fragment of *asesor* Galindo Navarro's opinion of October 25, 1782, which tossed out Ripperdá's guilty verdict in the last trial (1778) for "larceny," i.e., cattle rustling. Because Ripperdá was charged for the fines (208 pesos) restored in the case of 1775, it has been said that he was pursued by his woes after leaving Texas. That may be, but the baron was not long troubled by his "distasteful" experiences with the Tejano cattlemen. He died in October, 1780 (only a year later), leaving a widow and two surviving children; four of his six Texas-born children had died in infancy. Robert S. Weddle and Robert H. Thonhoff, *Drama and Conflict: The Texas Saga of 1776*, pp. 170, 182.

case, an attempt to gain a temporary restraining order of sorts, is fairly obvious, because the three men named in the suit were kinsmen, friends, neighbors, and fellow ranchers of those who lodged the protest. The defendants, however, were only drovers of the herd in question; behind them loomed the ultimate defendant—Mission Espíritu Santo—and the issue was whether the missionaries enjoyed rights that the private raisers did not, that is, the right to extract herds from the lands in question.[5]

The unfortunate cattlemen caught up in this particular episode of the ongoing controversy were Sebastián Monjarás, José Padrón, and Joaquín Flores. Monjarás was an active cattleman and trail driver, though Father Ramírez had styled him a tailor. As we have seen, he was also one of the province's *diezmeros*, or tithe collectors, who the year before had raised a storm of protest at Bucareli by collecting dues from parishioners who did not even have the services of a priest. This had led to an exemption from both civil and ecclesiastical taxes for the struggling settlement just before Cabello took office.[6] Being partly responsible for collecting the church's "tenth," Monjarás took advantage of the ranching facilities owned by the various missions whenever possible. In testimony given in 1777, for instance, he called Concepción's "Pastle" (Paistle) *his* ranch because he stopped there while transporting cattle to the mission.

José Padrón, in his mid-forties, listed himself as a creditor of Martín Lorenzo de Armas's ranch, San Antonio del Cíbolo. Martín, whose wife was the widow Granados (María Robaina de Bethencourt), had died in 1769, and their daughter Antonia was Padrón's wife. Thus he, with other "creditors," now owned and ran the estate. Joaquín Flores likely was the Joseph Joaquín, age

---

[5] For these proceedings see *expediente* no. 89, December 14, 1778–November 21, 1786, in BAT, vol. 76.

[6] Odie B. Faulk, *The Last Years of Spanish Texas, 1778–1821*, p. 105, says that the government collected the "ever-present tithe . . . since church and state were one." The activities of Sebastián Monjarás, Juan José Flores, and Flores's successor, Juan Barrera, suggest that these tithe collectors took their orders from the bishop; worked closely with the local, secular clergy; and were on occasion at odds with both the king's administrators and the missionaries. For one such instance see Carlos E. Castañeda, *Our Catholic Heritage in Texas*, 5:27–28; see also ibid., 4:322–23, for the Trinity River settlement of Bucareli's protest of the tithe, where the commandant general "requested" the bishop of Guadalajara to grant an exemption.

thirty-six, born in Saltillo, who signed his name "Flores y Zendeja." If so, his mother was Rosa Hermenegilda Hernández (sister of Andrés), and his father was Francisco Flores de Abrego.[7] Their intention to gather a herd of approximately three hundred head from Las Tetillas, Nogales, and the Olmos headwaters first came to Cabello's attention in a long petition (*instancia*) from fifteen ranchers, submitted in December, 1778.

The petitioners claimed that the extraction, made because Mission Espíritu Santo wanted to sell a herd to the presidios of the line, was unjust because the ranchers had made petitions claiming the stock in those places. The commandant general had ordered the mission to present its titles; therefore, until Croix decided the question, these herds were to remain unmolested. Since the ranchers had been "indicted and publicly castigated by being put in jail" for having run stock in this area as a violation of Croix's *bando* of January, 1778, it was not just that the missions should be exempt from the same provisions. Further, the *bando* made it illegal for inhabitants to run, kill, mark, or brand *orejanos*, not just in the summer pastures of another but on *realengas* (royal lands) as well. The ranchers claimed that the gathering spots cited were more king's lands than missions'.

Boldly the ranchers maintained that the documents giving title to Espíritu Santo were void "owing to irregularity"— namely, that the *linderos* (boundaries) on all four compass points were not specified. Such a grant was "contrary to royal and natural law." Although the mission claimed all land as far as the sea in a circle of more than one hundred leagues, there were no landmarks. Where was the northern boundary? asked the ranchers, pointing out that wandering livestock cannot serve as a boundary. Thus, because of pending litigation, the mission should not be allowed to gather so large a herd on *realengas*, certainly not on private ranchers' pastures.[8]

[7] Frederick C. Chabot lists Juan José Flores de Abrego y Valdés as also having a son named Joaquín (*With the Makers of San Antonio*, pp. 57, 62), confirmed by Flores's will and other documentation.

[8] This petition was signed by Vicente Álvarez Travieso; Francisco Flores de Abrego; Miguel de Gortaris; Tomás Travieso; Juan Andrés Travieso; Juan José Flores; Domingo Hernández; José Joaquín Flores, "at request of" José Plácido Hernández; Man-

Cabello wasted no time acting on the ranchers' petition. On December 14, 1778, he issued a decree noting that a roundup permit had been issued to Monjarás, Padrón, and Flores and that the sale was considered legal and proper according to article 2 of Croix's *bando*. Then he proceeded to specify the requirements which prospective exporters must observe: no animal could be driven out of the province—not even if *manso*—unless it was marked with the brand of its proper owner; a signed statement of owners must be obtained before cattle bearing their brands could be sold to the presidios of the line; exporters must maintain a record of the number of head and their brands for each herd taken out, to expedite issuance of an export license; and, finally, if drovers planned to export *orejanos*, a separate record must be kept of the number and species *unless the buyers posted security* for an amount equal to the value of the *orejanos* at the time of purchase, so that upon return from their journey the value thus secured could be deposited. This sum would remain in escrow until the commandant general decided to whom it belonged, a state of affairs euphemistically described as the *orejanos* being "restored to their rightful pasturelands."

Félix Menchaca (the old captain's brother), acting as first alcalde, notified the three drivers of this decree the same day it was issued. José Padrón said that he was holding the herd for inspection at great expense and asked for an export license so that he could move them out without delay. He stated that the herd contained four hundred head, mostly unbranded, bought from Father Escobar and delivered by Espíritu Santo's agent, Joaquín de los Santos. Padrón declared his willingness to post bond for 22 reales a head, the price agreed upon with Father Escobar.

On December 20, Menchaca went to inspect the herd where it was being held on the Cíbolo. He found a total of 574 head, 348 of which were *orejanos*. Four days later Simón de Arocha and two other men made bond for the *orejanos*, and Cabello issued an export license based on this security. Then on

uel Muñoz, "at request of" José Pérez Casanova; José Francisco Flores, "at request of" Carlos Martínez; Juana de "Hoyos" (Ollos); Francisco X. Rodríguez; Joaquín Leal; Domingo Hernández, "at request of" Josefa Flores; and Marcos de Castro, "at request of" Josef Andrés Hernández.

January 21, 1779, Cabello wrote that after the father president had responded to the ranchers' petition the entire *expediente* would be forwarded to the commandant general. When he was notified of this, Father President Ramírez advised Cabello that his reply would be "extensive" and begged a transcript for reference. The governor answered that there was no cause for him to provide Father Ramírez with a copy and sent the proceedings, *expediente* 89, to Croix on February 12.

In his cover letter to the commandant general, designated number 18 of the same date, Cabello outlined both his apprehensions and his intended modus operandi. With little change these procedures were to last until mid-1783, when *asesor* Galindo Navarro's reply to the Monjarás-Padrón cattle drive was finally activated by Cabello, therefore necessitating modifications. The governor explained that some ranchers on the Cíbolo had asked him to stop an export of *orejanos* which Mission Espíritu Santo was planning to send to the presidios on the Río Grande and at Santa Rosa. This, he noted, was the reason he had taken the precaution to obtain security until a decision was reached. Cabello asked for a quick decision because "these disputes [between settlers and missions] take up so much time that they hinder my ability to dispose of matters of greater import for which I am responsible."[9]

To make things worse, another dispute had arisen. A roundup had been conducted by local residents "as provided by Your Excellency," but among the cattle gathered in their summer pastures were 120 *orejanos* claimed by Mission Concepción. The ranchers, of course, denied this, saying that the *orejanos* were on their pastures and with their *manso* livestock. Further they claimed that when the situation was the reverse they did not protest the mission's right to sell *orejanos*—a claim not supported by their suit against Monjarás et al., on which the ink was not dry. Cabello ended his appeal for fast action in deciding these worrisome questions by saying, "Therefore I have ruled their value [that of the 120 head] be pledged until you render a decision. It will serve as a general rule."[10]

[9] Cabello to Croix, no. 18, February 12, 1779, BAT, 78:98.
[10] Ibid.

"La Luiciana"

The matters of greater import to which Governor Cabello referred in his cover letter were without doubt Indian problems, mainly those which, at the time he wrote, were forcing the abandonment of Bucareli. Attacks against this exposed settlement began in October, 1778, with the driving off of approximately 250 horses and as many, if not more, head of cattle. Most of the stolen horses belonged to Nicolás de la Mathe, the former Louisiana Indian trader who had provided Bucareli with its church and presently enjoyed the confidence of those in high places. All signs pointed to a widespread renewal of hostilities not just on the Trinity but at Béxar as well. Late in January, 1779, a party of four hundred "friendly" Indians visited San Antonio, causing the governor considerable anxiety. At the time he had twenty of his troops stationed at the post on the Cíbolo, ten out on scouting duty, twenty detailed to form Ripperdá's departure escort, and twenty-four guarding the horse herd, which numbered 1,232 animals, being pastured some distance south of the villa. This left him with "one gunsmith and two sick soldiers" at the presidio, a fact which his unwelcome visitors would be hard pressed not to notice.

At least at the beginning of his term Cabello did not trust Indians and told the commandant general as much. He recommended various ways to increase revenue in the province and wanted every real used to improve the frontier military posture until "all the Indians were brought under subjection or exterminated." He believed that there was no such thing as a friendly Indian, including Indians reared in the missions who from time to time reverted to the "original type." Contrary to the ideas held by Ripperdá, Mézières and other Indian experts, Cabello thought that the Comanches and their *norteño* friends were little better than the Apaches—this in spite of the recent high-level policy shift to befriend the former and isolate the latter. When presented with the abandonment of Bucareli as an accomplished fact owing to Comanche hostilities, Cabello had little difficulty accepting both the plight of the unfortunate settlers and the new home that Antonio Gil Ybarbo and his Adaesaños chose for themselves, Nacogdoches.[11]

By bold, direct action Gil Ybarbo was thus able to end the tortured exodus of some of his people and bring them back close to their former homes, in the process defeating the Marqués de Rubí's recommendations as incorporated in the Royal Regulations of 1772. Associated with the return is a document executed by Gil Ybarbo at Nacogdoches on April 6, 1779, soon after the old Adaesaño families began settling in. He declared that he had taken possession of a place named Attoyac, 10 leagues from Nacogdoches, on which to pasture stock. The "nearest neighbor," he said, was 5 leagues distant on the east, north, and south and half a league on the west—a quaint way of defining the limits of his pastures. This, of course, was in the neighborhood of Gil Ybarbo's old Lobanillo Ranch, which lay east of Los Aís, where the stock raisers had been petitioning to return since their ejection back in 1773. The ranch was now being run by Gil Ybarbo's son-in-law, Juan Ignacio Guerrero, who was a smith and the husband of Antonio's firstborn daughter, María Antonia "Ibarro y Panto." Gil Ybarbo asked that title to the Attoyac establishment be confirmed to this couple, since he had agreed for them to own it. The captain's livestock from El Lobanillo was apparently transferred at this time to the new

---

[11] For the abandonment of Bucareli see Castañeda, *Catholic Heritage*, 4:326–35; Herbert Eugene Bolton, *Texas in the Middle Eighteenth Century*, pp. 432–38; John, *Storms*, pp. 523–26, 532.

location, being closer to Nacogdoches. Later evidence reveals that this tract lay mostly on the east bank of the Attoyac, reaching almost to Los Aís, on both sides of the Camino Real. A house was built at the crossing, and nearby on an island formed by the river was eventually established a farm called La Lunaca (the Crescent).

Other old residents proceeded in like fashion to reoccupy their abandoned ranches or start new ones, using stock that had survived the trek from Bucareli or what remained of herds left in the area years before. According to one writer, these lands were dispensed by Gil Ybarbo after the fashion of a "medieval conqueror," but it seems that many ranches were awarded on the basis of earlier occupancy. Pedro Padilla, for instance, went back to his Santo Domingo, one of the first ranches in the area. He was the captain's father-in-law, and his rancho was 4 or 5 miles north of Nacogdoches. Above him, on La Nana Arroyo, was Joaquín Córdova's ranch, another old one. Sons later asked for 3½ leagues which their father had "without document but with permission from Captain Gil Ibarbo and thus kept it." These lands, along with the old Arriola place a mile or so northeast of town and the "former home" of the Gil Flores family near Black Jack, were among the first ranches populated by the returnees. As Nyal C. King has noted, it may be supposed that much contraband passed through the hands of Gil Ybarbo and his fellow ranchers at these locations.[12]

Even though 1779 saw Antonio Gil Ybarbo reestablish a settlement near the old environs, many of the Adaesaños were still scratching out an existence at Béxar, awaiting some decision on the lands promised them when they were uprooted from Los Adaes. It will be recalled that among the petitioners who made Commandant General Croix's arrival at the villa hectic was a group of these refugees, led by one Agustín Rodrígues. In a petition dated January 4, 1778, and signed by sixty-three heads of families, they formally requested a place to settle and

---

[12] BAT, vol. 80; Nyal C. King, "Captain Antonio Gil Y'Barbo, Founder of Modern Nacogdoches, 1729–1809" (Master's thesis, Stephen F. Austin University, 1949), pp. 76, 87–88, 90, 112, 117.

the necessary aid to start life anew. Four years of waiting had reduced them to the status of beggars, despised by the Bexareños for their wretchedness.

Croix referred the matter to his *asesor general*, who rendered an opinion only four days later. Galindo Navarro said that since the Adaesaños were not needed to defend Béxar there was no reason for insisting that they stay if they desired to move elsewhere. The insufficiency of lands suitable for irrigation in the vicinity had been already emphasized by all parties concerned. Then came the matter of where to relocate them. Governor Ripperdá, in keeping with his affection for Bucareli, suggested sending them there to strengthen the colony that Gil Ybarbo and some of their more aggressive brethren had already planted. The Béxar cabildo supported a settlement on the San Marcos River, justifying the considerable expense by the rich pasturelands between the San Marcos and the Guadalupe rivers on which prosperous ranches could be developed.

Captain Cazorla, of La Bahía, wanted them established on the Cíbolo at the site of the fort near which some still remained, never having completed the trip to Béxar. This, argued Cazorla, would permit the troops there to move to another locality on the Cíbolo to "protect more efficiently the ranches between the San Marcos and the Guadalupe." Since these were unappropriated lands belonging to the king, perhaps Cazorla was thinking ahead. It should be noted, however, that Ripperdá had suggested placing a fort at this location in 1772, saying that it was "well stocked with cattle." If it was, the herds were likely unbranded and wild, having strayed there from mission pastures. As might be expected, the councilmen opposed giving the Adaesaños lands in the midst of their Cíbolo Valley ranches and praised instead the virtues of other sites: the Guadalupe Springs (present New Braunfels), El Capote (near present Seguin), and especially the lands held by Mission Valero.

This was the spot most ardently advanced by the cabildo, and it had many advantages. Only forty-two Indians lived at Valero, yet its lands were extensive and its irrigation ditches superior to all others. Secularizing the mission, and distributing its lands to Indian families and the Adaesaños, was deemed "unquestionably the best ... solution to the problem." Father Ramírez expressed his willingness to help the unfortunate people in some temporary fashion, by letting them farm mission lands as renters, hiring them as field hands, and so on, but when they were notified of his generosity, the Adaesaños respectfully declined. They feared that too many problems would result from consigning themselves to a sharecropper existence, noting that Father Ramírez had cast a slur on their character by suggesting that in the name of distress and misfortune they perhaps desired to "live and dress without sufficiently exerting themselves."

The situation dragged on until June, 1779, while the former citizens of Los Adaes continued to fall ever lower in their new neighbors' esteem. Reviewing the case, Galindo Navarro concluded that the villa of San Fernando and the five missions on the river possessed valid claims to all available lands suitable for cultivation. To keep these people from leaving the frontier altogether out of desperation, some immediate relief was essential. His solution was to establish them on the site of the near-defunct Mission Valero, as the cabildo had recommended. Out of this decision grew a detailed plan for secularization which the commandant general, aware of the acute suffering caused by the relocation process, enthusiastically approved on June 8, 1779. Despite this, Cabello failed to implement secularization procedures at Valero, and the travail of this pitiful remnant continued until they eventually lost their identity at Béxar as a distinct cultural subgroup.[13]

San Antonio lost several of its most prominent ranchers during 1778–79 with the deaths of Andrés Hernández, Juan José Flores, and the old *alguacil* Vicente Álvarez Travieso. Flores's will, dated January 13, 1779, is a lengthy affair which itemizes all his worldly possessions and gives some idea of their value. Among these was a ranch "in the area named San Bartolo, with its pasture and all cattle within bearing my mark and brand."

---

[13] Castañeda, *Catholic Heritage*, 4:345–56; Herbert Eugene Bolton, ed., *Athanase de Mézières and the Louisiana-Texas Frontier, 1768–1780*, 1:335. There seems to have been considerable contact between Béxar and Nacogdoches despite the distance and difficulties of travel.

The old pioneer, his failing health without doubt affected by the recent deliberations of Governor Ripperdá, specified certain bequests to his sons. To Joachín he left a mule and two tame horses; to Pedro, a pair of oxen and two cows; and to Juan José, a tame mule and a horse. To José Francisco (the son of his second wife, Leonor Delgado), he left his gun, sword, shaft bearings, saddle, and a bridle with silver ornaments. From the valuation set on his livestock can be surmised prices then current at Béxar: cows, 5 pesos each; horses, 6 pesos; mares, 3 pesos; mules, 15 pesos; and a "saddle with ropes and brands," 3 pesos. The fact that mules were three times the price of horses explains why many Texas ranches, like Travieso's Las Mulas, specialized in breeding them.[14] On March 7, 1779, Cabello advised Croix of Travieso's death, noting that the post of chief constable was left vacant. Two days later he forwarded information that the death of Juan Nepomuceno Travieso, Don Vicente's son, had indeed been at the hands of Lipan Apaches, not Comanches, even though his scalp had turned up far north among enemies of the Lipans.[15]

As mentioned earlier, it is difficult to say with certainty when Andrés Hernández died. Fray Ramírez's petition of April 13, 1778, noted that San Bartolo was owned by his widow, Doña Juana de Ollos, and had been "annexed" by José Macario Sambrano. Ripperdá's trial summation of 1778 confirms this, but Hernández's will is not dated until March 20, 1779. In it he gave his son Francisco three horses, a vaquero saddle with all its accouterments, an *escopeta* (rifle similar to a shotgun) with its cover, a pair of spurs, a bit, some cushions, and a shield. Sons Joseph Plázido and Joseph Miguel received the same, but his

---

[14] Juan José Flores's will, dated January 13, 1779, is found in BAT, vol. 82. Weddle and Thonhoff, *Drama and Conflict*, p. 67, mention this instrument (including its execution) as being 145 pages long; and while their account says that one of Flores's slaves, Juan Rosali, was "to remain with his wife, Francisca Travieso," BAT has the mulatto remaining with Flores's wife for her future service. Don Juan José was noted as a "great drunk at several festivals"; he died on January 19.

[15] The account that follows is based on Cabello to Croix, March 7, 1779, and March 9, 1779 (*exp*. no. 74), BAT, vol. 81. The account of Nepomuceno's death is in BAT, vol. 79. Travieso's will, dated January 16, 1779, fills BAT, vol. 29a—most of the ensuing paperwork being devoted to the questionable title of Las Mulas and the number of livestock in its pastures. Don Vicente's cattle brand is shown in these documents.

livestock was apparently awarded to Joseph Andrés and Joseph Joaquín, who had worked ("more than the others") to make the rural property a success. Mentioned were four *manadas* (herds of mares), by color, and 260 head of cattle branded two years previously, no general herding having occurred since then owing to Indian troubles. Hernández listed among his possessions 6 leagues of land at San Bartolo and a ranch which he had been compelled to move in January of the previous year (1778) "on account of the ravages of the Indians." According to Ripperdá's trial summation, two sons of Don Andrés had been killed by Indians below the Cleto, and it was after this that San Bartolo "moved to the San Antonio River." A debt to Father President Ramírez of 100 pesos was acknowledged and Hernández claimed that he was owed 72 pesos by Luis Menchaca.[16]

[16] Folders 21 and 22, Cassiano-Pérez Collection, Daughters of the Republic of Texas Library at the Alamo. Sambrano's agreement with Juana de Ollos is dated August 4, 1776, indicating that Don Andrés was inactive several years before his death.

With the passing of these three old frontiersmen ended a chapter in the history of ranching in El Rincón, and in the history of Texas itself. It is to the memory of such men that imposing statues are erected, but their monument is the wind playing lost symphonies through moss-shrouded oak groves of the river valley where they rode, chasing cows that governors said belonged to someone else. They knew better and had the grit to say so. That is their only memorial, but it is a lasting claim to the eternal Cowboy Hall of Fame and should be recognized as such in the earthly realm by those who cherish this heritage.

On April 4, Cabello again wrote his superior, this time about a possible reduction in the fee for catching wild horses. Taking notice that the sum in the Mustang Fund was too small even to allow for the construction of a chest with three locks and keys, the governor suspected that the six-real fee was responsible. At this steep rate no one wanted to catch them simply because it took a good, fast horse to catch mesteños, a horse which might get hurt, and it was not considered worth it. Also, unbroken horses sold for only 3 reales, half of what it cost for the privilege of catching them, risking life, limb, and good horseflesh in the process. If the fee was reduced to 2 reales, the increase in people going out on mustang hunts would more than make up the difference, suggested Cabello. The duty on bovines he felt was reasonable and presented no difficulties. He asked Croix to describe the missions' situation in reference to his recent number 18 and added that at present they were not catching cows. Returning to the subject of the strongbox specified by Croix's *bando*, Cabello stated that it would cost 22 pesos to have one constructed. He had turned the delinquent mesteño accounts over to Alcalde José Antonio Curbelo the month before, but collecting from citizens and soldiers was a slow process. Since Ripperdá had only submitted 14 pesos cash, Cabello had provided out of his own pocket the extra 8 pesos required, paying also for a register book.[17]

Hints of a possible rift between Cabello and some of Béxar's leading families—the sort of thing that had plagued Rip-

---

[17] Cabello to Croix, April 4, 1779, BAT, vol. 80.

perdá's administration—emerge in a letter written soon afterward. The retired captain, Don Luis Antonio Menchaca, wanted the commandant general to make his son Miguel Jorge a cavalry cadet, in keeping with the family's military tradition. In 1777 both Luis and his brother José Félix were accorded military honors and use of the official uniform, a distinction granted to old soldiers which also had the happy result of making New Spain's defenses seem stronger to its enemies than they really were. At the same time another of the old captain's sons, Lieutenant José Menchaca, was in charge of the twenty troops stationed at Fuerte de Santa Cruz, and José's cousin Manuel de Urrutia was serving as a sergeant. It must have rankled Don Luis considerably when he learned that in a letter to Croix the governor opposed Miguel's appointment: "The father plays cards just as much as do the sons, from which Your Lordship can infer the poor upbringing and lack of modesty and respect."[18]

This was not a very courteous way for Cabello to treat the province's most affluent citizen, for a census taken by the governor in July, 1779, proved Luis Antonio Menchaca to be just that. Menchaca owned two houses, two irrigated *suertes* (farm tracts), and 2,444 head of livestock. According to Max Moorhead's analysis, 194 *vecinos* of Béxar (65.3 percent of the population) owned a total of 7,434 head, while 79 *soldados* (98.8 percent of the garrison forces) owned a mere 1,067 animals, most of them no doubt horses kept for military service. Moorhead notes that many civilians at Béxar (such as Don Luis) were actually retired military personnel and suggests that such service may have been related to their subsequent prosperity. Certainly most soldiers did not enjoy such exalted pecuniary status, even if they were routinely shown as *españoles* on census reports. In reality, many of them were men of mixed blood or "broken color," who typically garrisoned other presidios on the frontier. Regardless of Menchaca's wealth, it would seem that the gover-

---

[18] Cabello to Croix, April 12, 1779, BA; see also Weddle and Thonhoff, *Drama and Conflict*, p. 62. Captain Luis Antonio's *mother* was the daughter of Captain Joseph de Urrutia; thus Toribio de Urrutia was Luis's uncle, not his brother-in-law, as they state. For the correct Menchaca kinships see Chabot, *Makers of San Antonio*, p. 103.

nor held neither him nor his family in any great esteem. This, of course, meant that things would soon be heating up for Domingo Cabello, because the old captain's clan was not one to cross.[19]

Developments afoot in the summer of 1779 gave the stranded Adaesaños reason to turn their eyes toward East Texas and think of life as it had once been on the French frontier, for it was at this time that cattle exports to Louisiana were finally permitted. As noted, the intercolonial trade was a long-standing practice—carried on even before Louisiana was ceded to Spain in 1762—more than one governor sharing in its illegal profits and more than one resident drawing livelihood from its forbidden rewards. The transfer of Louisiana, however, did little to drop the formal barriers on free trade between the two ethnically diverse provinces. When the East Texas settlements were suppressed, most of the well-beaten contraband stock trails fell into disuse. Still, officials like Oconor could never believe that the trade had died entirely and became obsessed with the idea that men like Gil Ybarbo might make it flourish anew.

Fortunately, the situation underwent a number of changes in the 1770s, all of which were conducive to a relaxation of prohibitions on interprovincial livestock trade. First in significance came the promotion of José de Gálvez to the Ministry of the Indies, resulting in the immediate creation of the *Comandancia General*. That same year, 1776, Oconor was replaced by Croix as head of the Interior Provinces. Then Bernardo de Gálvez, a close friend of the new commandant general (and the nephew of Don José) was appointed governor of Louisiana. Soon afterward Cabello replaced Ripperdá as governor of Texas, so the baron's suspect motives relative to opening the trade were no longer an issue. Last but not least in this shuffle of personalities on the northern frontier was the decision to transfer the capable Athanase de Mézières from Natchitoches to Croix's service in Texas. Mézières, whose vast experience and knowledge of the Indians was respected by both young Gálvez and

---

[19] Max L. Moorhead, *The Presidio: Bastion of the Spanish Borderlands*, pp. 183, 241–42; AGI, Audiencia de Guadalajara, Dunn Transcripts, 53:71, box 2Q142 (University of Texas Archives).

Croix, played a key role in the promotion of a mutually beneficial livestock trade between Louisiana and Texas until his untimely death in November, 1779. Because his influence so profoundly affected his superiors and lingered after him, it is proper to examine the background of this remarkable Frenchman in the service of Spain.

Mézières spent most of his life in Louisiana, arriving there as a soldier in 1733. He was a Parisian, born of high station, and had two uncles who were generals in the French army. In 1746 he married a daughter of Louis Juchereau de St. Denis, the man who by coming to Texas in 1714 (ostensibly to purchase cattle, horses, and grain) had precipitated Spanish reoccupation of the province. Thus Athanase was related to a premier family of Louisiana, one that directed affairs from the western part of the province for many years. Promoted to captain in 1756, he retired from military service at the time of the French cession to devote his energies to private interests, such as planting and trading. When the Spaniards actually took control of the territory in 1769, Governor Alejandro O'Reilly chose him to serve as lieutenant governor of the Natchitoches District, where he enjoyed a position of influence with the various Indian tribes comparable to that of his distinguished father-in-law, by then deceased. He was still in that post when Croix selected him to take Ripperdá's place as interim governor until Cabello arrived or to serve in some other capacity "commensurate with his rank, merit and services."[20]

Croix had great hopes for the development of Texas when he took office as commandant general, hopes that he worked diligently over the years to achieve. Mézières shared and encouraged this vision of economic prosperity. In his travels among the Indians, Mézières had not failed to notice the potential wealth of wild herds that roamed Texas. Crossing the Guadalupe, Colorado, and Brazos valleys in 1778, he reported seeing "an incredible number of Castilian cattle and herds of mustangs that never leave the banks of those places."[21]

While he was at Béxar in February of that year, he made a

---

[20] John, *Storms*, p. 522.
[21] Bolton, *Athanase de Mézières*, 2:187.

detailed listing of livestock prices prevalent in the area, a report he submitted to Governor Gálvez on March 17, 1779: fat cows, 4 pesos each; sheep three and a half years old, 6 pesos; breeding ewes, 3 pesos; goats, 3 pesos; half-broke horses, 6 pesos; mares (in droves), 1 peso or less; wild mules, 8 pesos. He told Don Bernardo that to conduct droves of cattle, sheep, horses, and mules servants were needed and could be secured at reasonable prices. Saddles, bridles, lassos, and halters were also cheap. The best season was autumn, when the rivers were fordable and the pasturage good. It usually took fifteen days to go from Béxar to the Trinity and an equal time from that pueblo (Bucareli) to "Los Opeluzas." On account of the very great difficulty of conducting stock and the danger of stampedes, he considered it impossible to take large droves. He also noted that Mission Espíritu Santo owned the most cattle at the lowest prices and assured Governor Gálvez of prompt delivery, all of which suggests that his visit to Béxar had produced an understanding in the right places.[22]

Back in New Orleans, a reluctant Mézières found that Governor Gálvez considered his transfer to Texas vital to Croix's solution of the Indian problems in that province. Further, once in Texas the Indian expert would provide Gálvez with a much-needed agent through whom livestock could be obtained for Louisiana. After Spain declared war on England (July, 1779), thereby becoming allied with the insurgent American colonies, the demand for beef to feed troops would require still more herds. But even before this need became manifest, Mézières was a firm believer in the prospect offered by such a trade and remained so until his death. Writing Croix in October, 1779, just a month before he died, he extolled the benefits of expanded commerce:

I ask again, what is the cause of so little progress? The indolence of its inhabitants. And from what does this originate? From the lack of emulation. And this? From the lack of trade. O, what an abuse! . . . Deign to permit the exportation of meats, hides, lard, tallow, wool, . . . and other goods peculiar to rural economy, in which this province [Texas]

---

[22] Ibid., 2:242; John, *Storms*, pp. 526n.47, cites this item, also found in Grazing Papers, vol. 1 (University of Texas Archives).

abounds to so little profit. . . . What competition will not result? What progress will not be made in agriculture and stockraising?[23]

Commandant General Croix was receptive to the idea of reciprocal trade, seeing it also as another source of possible revenue for the Royal Treasury and a way to defray the costs of improved Indian relations and frontier defenses. Therefore, when Governor Gálvez sent an emissary, one Francisco García, to Texas in June, 1779, requesting permission to buy 1,500 or 2,000 head of cattle, it was no surprise that his friend and former comrade Teodoro de Croix expedited the transaction. In such a manner was the decision of January 10, 1776, by the *asesor general*, Baltazar Ladrón de Guevara, annulled and the door opened to intercolonial livestock trade, a door that the viceroy's legal counsel had hoped would remain firmly closed.[24]

Governor Cabello advised the commandant general of the emissary's arrival on June 20, and Croix replied several weeks later. He expressed satisfaction that Cabello had waited for his approval of the requested export, but because "the king's service requires it," he instructed the governor to proceed immediately with Gálvez's requirements, giving preference to his needs. Cabello was to ask Father President Ramírez for his assistance, and sufficient bulls for breeding were to be included in the herd. Cabello was given immediate authority to permit removal of livestock as he saw fit—the first formal authorization for cattle exports from the province of Texas. As an afterthought the revenue-conscious commandant general asked Cabello whether it might be convenient to impose some moderate duty on the cattle, "to defray cost of the military."[25]

In connection with these deliberations, of interest is a

[23] Bolton, *Athanase de Mézières*, 2:292; see also Sandra Lynn Myres, "The Development of the Ranch as a Frontier Institution in the Spanish Province of Texas, 1691–1800" (Ph.D. diss., Texas Christian University, 1967), p. 69.

[24] Croix's efforts on behalf of liberalized trade are mentioned in J. Villasana Haggard, "Neutral Ground between Louisiana and Texas," *Louisiana Historical Quarterly* 28, no. 4 (October, 1945): 1075–78, although Haggard cites several of the documents incorrectly as to their authorship and other details.

[25] Cabello to Croix, June 20, 1779, BAT, 83:18–21; Croix to Cabello, August 16, 1779, BAT, 85:112. Robert H. Thonhoff, *The Texas Connection with the American Revolution*, explores the military campaigns of Governor Bernardo de Gálvez and his need for Texas beef.

letter written to the viceroy by José de Gálvez, young Bernardo's influential uncle, who supported Croix's ideas on trade. On August 29, 1779, he wrote, "Get in touch with the governors of Havana and Louisiana, send to the latter as much help as he may need in troops, funds, war supplies, and food supplies." The granting of such broad powers of procurement by one so close to the king doubtless did much to put Texas cattle on the trail to Louisiana.[26] That this new, relaxed policy was not limited to the needs of Bernardo de Gálvez and the war effort but in fact intended for broader exportation is evidenced by another authorization given by Croix the next day. It concerned three hundred head of cattle that Doña María de St. Denis, a resident of Natchitoches (possibly St. Denis's daughter, who was the wife of Antonio Manuel Bermúdez y Soto), had acquired in Béxar. She wanted her agent and relative, Félix Menchaca, to conduct the herd eastward; Croix instructed Cabello to grant her request.[27]

Before the end of August yet another drive was sanctioned and in progress, this one for Nicolás de la Mathe and Francisco Rosé, both prominent traders with extensive frontier connections on whom Gálvez could depend to effect delivery of Louisiana-bound cattle. In this particular instance La Mathe obtained a passport for 800 head, making an arrangement with Béxar businessman Juan de Ysurieta to secure the herd. Ysurieta was related by marriage to the Menchacas, and Félix, the old captain's brother, was put in charge of both assembling and driving the herd to "La Sapilusa," "Los Opeluzas," or "El Apiluza," as the district of Opelousas, Louisiana, was variously called. José Félix Menchaca, who became a key figure in the family ranching operations and a leading trail driver at this time, had been unfortunate in his early attempts at stock raising. Suffering from Indian raids in El Rincón, he had tried to ranch at a location on the Nueces River until *los norteños* drove him to the Río Grande in 1769. The Apaches inflicted even greater losses on him there, and he returned to the San Antonio River valley. On his first

---

[26] Grace A. Edman, trans. and ed., "A Compilation of Royal Decrees Relating to Texas and Other Northern Provinces of New Spain, 1719–1799" (Master's thesis, University of Texas, 1930), pp. 377–82.

[27] Croix to Cabello, August 17, 1779, BAT, 86:1; Cabello to Croix, September 15, 1779, BAT, 87:38; Thonhoff, *Texas Connection*, p. 54.

drive to Louisiana, Menchaca also ran into one of the crippling snags of the business, litigation.[28]

Félix assembled La Mathe's herd at Rancho de San Francisco. While he was there, he was visited by the Frenchman, who asked him to receive—in addition to the 800 head specified by the passport—another 100 head sold to him by Mission Valero and "those belonging to Pacheco." This, as it turned out, amounted to 40 bulls owned by Juan José Pacheco and supposedly covered by a passport. Pacheco was eager to find a larger herd heading out so that he could mix in his bulls and take advantage of the new market. Added to these were another 30 head, included to cover possible losses along the way. Menchaca's herd was therefore considerably over its authorized size by the time it reached Nacogdoches and was inspected by Antonio Gil Ybarbo on August 30, 1779.[29]

Gil Ybarbo, after years of running his affairs on a shoestring, was on the verge of being awarded an annual salary of 500 pesos along with the impressive title "Captain of the Militia and Lieutenant Governor of the Pueblo of Nacogdoches." Following swiftly on the heels of this recognition of Gil Ybarbo's personal worth on the frontier came the opinion of *asesor* Galindo Navarro that paved the way, at long last, for the recognition of Nacogdoches as a permanent settlement for the former inhabitants of Los Adaes. La Mathe, en route to Béxar in June to see about the cattle drive, had stopped in Nacogdoches to visit his friends. When he left, he took a train of mules, horses, and cattle, part of which belonged to Gil Ybarbo and the settlers. Many of these animals were lost, and Alférez Juan de la Mora was killed in a Tawakoni attack not far away, possibly leaving a bad taste in the captain's mouth about La Mathe's venture. Mora was one of Gil Ybarbo's compatriots, and, by some accounts, a son-in-law.[30]

---

[28] GLO, 50:165. José Félix Menchaca—also called "Josef Félis" and "Joseph Félix"—is not to be confused with his nephew Lieutenant José Menchaca, who at that time manned the Cíbolo fort along with other local ranchers' soldiering sons.

[29] *Expediente* no. 83, covering the proceedings of this troubled export, is found in BAT, vol. 97. See also Thonhoff, *Texas Connection*, pp. 50–53.

[30] John, *Storms*, pp. 536–37; Castañeda, *Catholic Heritage*, 4:339. Testimony in the Las Ormigas land grant reveals that Juan de Mora was Gil Ybarbo's son-in-law (Louis Nardini, *My Historic Natchitoches, Louisiana, and Its Environment*, p. 112), although

Croix's authorization for exports to Louisiana specified that Cabello could arrange for "the necessary escort service, to be composed of residents and troops" so that prompt delivery of stock could be facilitated. The result was that several soldiers were detached from duty to accompany each herd, and local guides and other "boys" were hired to manage the cows. Such was the case with Menchaca's drive. Accompanying him were Francisco Pérez, Francisco Flores Galán, Agustín Ruíz, Julián de Orosco, Lorenzo Reñe, Félix Guerrero, Alberto Ximénez, and Miguel Menchaca, the last apparently the same young man whom Cabello had opposed as a cadet. Thonhoff, citing a troop-strength report of October 19, 1779, which notes that Lieutenant José Menchaca and twenty-one men were absent on a journey, suggests that this was a reference to the Louisiana trail drive. This "journey" was, in fact, escort duty for a Tonkawa delegation to the Colorado River. But if José did not accompany his uncle José Félix to "La Sapilusa," his brother Miguel was along, one of the boys receiving daily wages of 6 reales.[31]

In any event, when Menchaca and his *partida* brought La Mathe's herd through Gil Ybarbo's new settlement, the captain was not inclined to overlook the herd's excessive size. He confiscated Pacheco's forty bulls because they had no passport, giving three head to Joaquín Córdova "for permit"—perhaps for his work in inspecting the herd. Menchaca continued on with the cattle and sold them at Opelousas for 11 pesos a head, a tremendous profit considering that a fat cow brought only 4 pesos at Béxar. When Pacheco approached Félix about payment for his 40 bulls, Menchaca told him to collect from Gil Ybarbo, who had confiscated his animals. This prompted a long, bitter lawsuit between Pacheco and Menchaca, demonstrating the legal perils associated with early Texas trail drives; the suit was not settled until 1785.

As summer lengthened into fall, planning began for other

---

this individual was apparently alive in 1795. Blake, Research Collection, Supplement ser., 3:146, notes that the captain had a grandson named Gregorio Mora, no doubt the same man who was a tithe collector in the Neutral Ground (1794–95), as his uncle Jacinto had been before him.

[31] Thonhoff, *Texas Connection*, pp. 50–53; John, *Storms*, pp. 349–50.

drives and the procedures to implement them. On September 16, Croix responded favorably to Cabello's suggestion that the fee for catching wild horses should be lowered to 2 reales, especially since the 6-real charge had not produced enough income to repay Cabello for the 8 pesos he spent to construct a special chest. Governor Cabello put this change into effect with a decree dated October 27, 1779, noting that the fee for cattle remained 4 reales each. Penalties for ignoring the provisions of this law were forfeiture of the mesteños, which would then be sold and the proceeds applied to court costs; the offender still had to pay the 2-real fee on top of this. Alcaldes were responsible for imposing penalties and keeping the books.[32]

Since the commandant general's letter mentioned that the *asesor* was still considering the matter "concerning ownership of livestock by missions and residents," Cabello gave him a progress report on the herds intended for Louisiana. The order for 2,000 head for Governor Gálvez, wrote Cabello on September 20, would be filled by Father President Ramírez. However there were difficulties. Francisco García, Gálvez's agent sent to take the herd, had returned to New Orleans. More critically, most of the stock would be *orejano*, and there was some question whether this type could be exported. Cabello said he would ask Fray Escobar at Espíritu Santo whether he had enough cattle. If

---

[32] Croix to Cabello, September 16, 1779, BAT, vol. 87; Cabello to Croix, October 8, 1779, Cabello, decree, October 27, 1779, BAT, vol. 88. The governor notified Croix on October 8 that he had published his decision, although the decree is dated October 27. Odie B. Faulk, "Ranching in Spanish Texas," *Hispanic American Historical Review* 44 (May, 1965):259, says that this reduction was made because wild horses were "twice as difficult to catch" as wild cattle, but Dobie tells us otherwise.

not, perhaps the residents could make up the difference, although they might not want to because the market and payment at the line presidios of Río Grande and Santa Rosa (Agua Verde) were better than "the delays to be expected in a contract between Gálvez and the Father President."[33] The governor also reviewed the particulars of the Monjarás-Padrón export, noting that the same basis for contention could apply if Espíritu Santo attempted to fill Gálvez's order from disputed pastures. He admitted that the ranchers' petition was correct "in that the cattle are gathered from where their own graze."

If, however, the *orejanos* were gathered 50 leagues from the villa—between La Bahía and the seacoast—the citizens' protests should not matter, since these were clearly pastures containing no private stock. Cabello notified the commandant general that it was his intention to specify such terms for the roundup. He would write to García at "El Apelusan" that his permit was granted, and, if García could not be found, Gálvez would be asked to arrange for someone else to receive the herd there. Croix replied to this letter on November 24, giving formal approval for 2,000 head.[34]

Two other items in the Béxar Archives suggest that further export operations were being conducted late in 1779. One is a reference made by Cabello in his *expediente* 94 about a protest likely related to an export of Simón de Arocha's consisting of two herds taken out in the month of August. The first *guía* (license) was issued on August 1 to Francisco de Arocha for 281 head, obtained from the missions of Espíritu Santo and Rosario; the next came eight days later to brother Julián for 441 head belonging to him, to various citizens, and to the missions of Espíritu Santo and Rosario.[35] The other reference is merely a

---

[33] Mézières told Governor Gálvez that he would have no problem getting prompt delivery of Texas cattle "under the condition that they be paid for in money." Just as acceptable as cash were sight drafts on Mexico City, Veracruz, San Luis Potosí, or Saltillo. Chabot, *Makers of San Antonio*, p. 165.

[34] Cabello to Croix, September 20, 1779, BAT, 87:86; Croix to Cabello, November 24, 1779, BAT, 90:35.

[35] *Expediente* no. 94 is found in BAT, vol. 108; "Notice of the Number of Bovine Cattle, Branded and *Orejano*, Which the Citizens of This Royal Presidio of San Antonio de Béxar and Villa of San Fernando Have Gathered and Driven to Various Provinces . . . ," November 29, 1786 (hereafter cited as "Record of Exports"), BAT, 142:130–38.

notation in an inventory of papers, number 51, mentioning proceedings "concerning the exportation of a herd of *orejana* cattle from the mission of El Rosario." Clearly exploitation of wild stock in the province was causing some headaches.[36]

Early in November, Governor Cabello announced that it was branding time. Thus began *expediente* 80, a file on the yearly roundup and branding operation that he kept until the end of his administration. The first item, dated November 7, expressed the governor's desire to curtail previous irregularities, that is, the taking of *orejanos* belonging to the missions, especially Espíritu Santo. Wanting to make sure that "one stock owner does not take advantage of another," Cabello advised the citizens that he was notifying Padre Ramírez so that he could appoint an agent to look after his interests. This agent was to be present at the roundup, thus assuring that the mission's livestock would be cut out before any private branding took place.[37]

Father President Ramírez replied at length to this notification, expressing an idea (as the governor observed) which had led to disputes in the past, namely, that all *orejanos* were mission property. He began by reminding Cabello that the commandant general "has prohibited every citizen from entering pasturelands not his." Therefore, it stood to reason that any *orejano* cattle found in a man's pastures must belong to him and not another. This, maintained Ramírez, was the common opinion of all theologians and jurists: that the lesser part which mixes with the greater belongs to the greater.

Having dispensed with technicalities, he pointed to the practical considerations of how citizens' roundups differed from his missions' efforts. The citizens, said the father president, cut out each other's cows but not those of Espíritu Santo. The mission normally did not cut out citizens' cows from its own.[38] Lest this sound uncharitable, he was quick to point out that

---

[36] "Inventory of Papers, 1778–1779," December 20, 1779, BAT, 90:83; Thonhoff, *Texas Connection*, p. 57.

[37] *Expediente* no. 80, "Concerning Branding by Ranches on the Cíbolo and San Antonio River, November 7, 1779–November 29, 1786" (hereafter cited as "Concerning Branding"), BAT, vol. 89.

[38] In their memorial of 1787, the ranchers claimed to have an agreement with the missions that whatever one party found in its pastures without a mark belonged to the *finder* and all others had to be kept under guard.

Espíritu Santo could not be blamed for the practice since it had not recently been able to conduct roundups at all. Most of the establishment's Jaraname converts had run away eighteen years ago, only returning the past year. Those remaining behind had died, some of them at the hands of the Comanches, during whose raids no help was forthcoming from the presidio. These circumstances, Ramírez wrote, should not excuse the citizens, for they had only a few cattle and small pastures, protected by a fort and twenty men. He nonetheless admitted that the citizens' clamors had justness. He suggested that general permission might be granted to all citizens to go anywhere and gather stock on condition that a mission agent was present. He would prevent Espíritu Santo's *orejanos* from being driven out. Such an arrangement would have greatly benefited the mission, of course, amounting to having private *ganaderos* doing its roundup for them, something the ranchers had complained of bitterly on previous occasions. Fray Ramírez further suggested that the citizens should be ordered to scour their own pastures first. Then, when they were ready to enter Espíritu Santo's lands, he would send his agent. This procedure would save them money since the mission's agent was being paid one peso a day.[39]

Cabello, no doubt impressed by the fiscal austerity of the Zacatecan brotherhood, issued a *decreto* stating that the several appeals prompted by the missionaries' attitude had as yet brought no reply from Croix and that the branding must proceed; it could be postponed no longer. He appointed Tomás Travieso to oversee the citizens' roundup as *juez de campo* (field judge). The citizens could keep all branded cattle found in their pastures, including calves following marked mothers. Cabello stressed that the decree of January 11, 1778, forbidding seizure of *orejanos* must be observed. Also, in compliance with the third article of the decree, a tally of branding done must be submitted. In a *despacho* written the following day, he specified that possession of *orejanos* would be the only proof of violation needed.[40]

Thus began a cat-and-mouse game between the governor,

---

[39] Ramírez to Cabello, November 10, 1779, BAT, vol. 89.

[40] Cabello, *decreto*, November 10, 1779; Cabello, *despacho*, November 11, 1779, ibid.

eager to impress the commandant general with his diligent stewardship over the stock industry, and the rancher chosen to oversee branding of the annual harvest of calves. The irony was supreme because not only were the judges rounding up on their own behalf but they were supposed to keep an eye on their friends and kinsmen as well, none of whom considered Espíritu Santo's rights of much importance. It is doubtful that Cabello really expected these men to report and prosecute violations committed by their fellow ranchers. Yet results were expected. Entries had to be made in the book, and the figures were supposed to look good, that is, to reflect progress over preceding years.

It was the job of Cabello's *juez* to conduct the annual fall roundup smoothly, settling all disputes on the spot and seeing that as many calves as possible were caught and branded. Apparently the governor, on this first roundup, did not want the ranchers to gather *orejanos*, that is, full-grown stock without marks, until the commandant general decided their ownership. In later years, however, taking such animals and branding them were considered a primary function of the roundup—as long as the Royal Treasury got its 4-real head fee. Hence it became the judge's task to report just enough *orejanos* to appease the governor but not so many as to damage his friends' pocketbooks, a delicate undertaking.[41] Later indications are that Tomás Travieso, who had been running Las Mulas since his father's death, did not fulfill Cabello's expectations. But a combination of factors may have mitigated the governor's response to Don Tomás's initial poor showing: Indian visitors were in town, Mézières had died of the pox, word of war with England reached Béxar, and Cabello dislocated his left shoulder.[42]

---

[41] Sandra L. Myres, *The Ranch in Spanish Texas, 1691–1800*, pp. 32–36, presents a survey of how the *mesta* worked in Texas, the activities of *jueces*, etc. These practices appear to have been a watered-down version of the *mesta* elsewhere in New Spain.

[42] Thonhoff, *Texas Connection*, pp. 54–57, mentions news of war with England and Cabello's shoulder problems; see John, *Storms*, pp. 551–56, for the "dizzying succession of crises" that the governor faced at year's end. Word of Mézières's deteriorating health ("diarrea y Gonorrea") is found in Cabello to Croix, October 20, 1779, BA, twelve days before he died. His condition was apparently worsened by a fall from horseback en route to Béxar, and he was buried on November 3. John Ogden Leal, "Burials of San Fernando," vol. 2, entry no. 704 (1779).

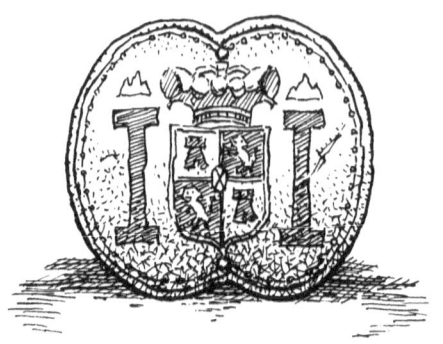

In January, 1780, Governor Cabello was in the Presidio La Bahía on an inspection tour that was to last nine months. It was anticipated that the Gulf of Mexico would become an important war front, and many duties—not the least being to provide Gálvez and his troops with a reliable supply of beef—required the governor's presence at the presidio founded to guard the coast. Before leaving Béxar, Cabello had placed the old captain's son, Lieutenant José Menchaca, in charge of the military garrison and had named Joseph Antonio Curbelo as lieutenant governor to oversee affairs of the political realm.[43]

High on Cabello's list of things to do at La Bahía were reviewing and reorganizing the cavalry company. Light troops (*tropa ligera*) were essential to effective coastal reconnaissance and rapid response when Indians reported sightings of foreign intruders. In the first week of January a report was made on the stock owned by the troops of the garrison:

Yeguas (breeding mares): 124
Cavallos (saddle and work horses): 554
Mulas (mules): 69
Yuntas (yokes of oxen at two): 75
Bacas viente (milk cows): 225
Obezas y cabras (sheep and goats): 12

[43] Thonhoff, *Texas Connection*, p. 57, says that Cabello left Joseph Félix in charge, but the document cited (BAT, 80:85–88), states that it was First Lieutenant Joseph (José) Menchaca, Don Luis's son. José's commission from the king promoting him to first lieutenant is dated October 19, 1775. Edman, "A Compilation of Royal Decrees," p. 339.

Burros y burras (he and she donkeys): 2,3
Toros y nobillos (bulls and bullocks): 114[44]

On January 24 the acting commander, Lieutenant Eugenio Fernández, filed a report on the cavalry company, which had thirty men in the *tropa de cuera* (leather-jacket outfit) and eleven in the *tropa ligera* (light troop), a total of forty-one counting the drummer and the armorer. Other muster rolls indicate that the light troop was as big as the *cuera* troop, around thirty each. (Most ranking military authorities objected to the use of the *cuera* as bulky, stiff, and impeding rather than helping, but these padded-leather jackets continued to see service on the frontier well into the nineteenth century.) Altogether the presidio's strength was ninety-five men, including thirty-three "with the horse herd," twenty "at Cíbolo fort" and twelve "in the cattle crew for the paymaster," all carrying out duties which left Fernández shorthanded.[45]

All the troops stationed at La Bahía were cavalry, practically speaking, because it was unthinkable to venture far afield unless one was mounted. Thus the 554 saddle horses at the presidio were those kept in obedience to the Royal Regulations of 1772, which required each soldier to have six "serviceable" horses, a colt, and a mule. As at Béxar, Bahía Presidio pastured a considerable number of horses a distance away from the fort, and if indeed thirty-three men were needed to guard the herd, it must have been considerable. Cabello, in a detailed report on La Bahía dated January 12, 1780, noted that cattle raising in the area was not profitable to the populace because the missions Espíritu Santo and Rosario owned the best pasturelands, the

---

[44] Cabello, "Report on Stock of Presidio La Bahía Troops," January 3–5, 1780, Grazing Papers, vol. 1. See also the detailed report dated August 10, 1780, AGI, Audiencia de Guadalajara, Dunn Transcripts, 53:2–25, box 2Q142, University of Texas Archives.

[45] Thonhoff, *Texas Connection*, pp. 79–84; Eugenio Fernández, "Royal Presidio de la Bahía del Espíritu Santo: Report of Articles of Raiment Owned by the Individuals in Cavalry Company . . . ," no. 14, January 24, 1780, BA. Cabello's report (cited below) shows 59 soldiers at La Bahía; troop strength at this fort fluctuated considerably. See Moorhead, *Presidio*, pp. 185–200, for a discussion of Croix's military innovations, especially the *tropa ligera*, which was an extension of the "flying company" concept initiated for the frontier provinces in 1713 by the viceroy, Duque de Linares.

best watering places, and the most land. Thus, "Not even in this pursuit [cattle raising] could the populace achieve great success, their efforts to improve themselves being frustrated."[46]

Since most of the large-scale cattle raising in the province centered around and radiated out from the missions of La Bahía, affairs touching the business soon occupied the governor's attention. Disputes among soldiers, citizens, and the missionaries were frequent, with results that were almost as damaging to an orderly working relationship as they were at Béxar. These problems would have to be addressed if the numerous herds requested in Louisiana were to be gathered and sent on their way. On March 6, Cabello reviewed the archives of La Bahía and found that Croix's decree of January 11, 1778, in reference to the separation of mission cattle from those declared the property of His Majesty, had not been circulated properly to the reverend fathers. He blamed Ripperdá for this and implied that if the former governor had done his job properly all the mission protests would have been unnecessary. "Wanting to exterminate them" (the protests), he then ordered Ripperdá's proclamation of February 9, 1778, applying the provisions of Croix's *bando* to La Bahía, reissued.[47]

During the following month much of the governor's time was devoted to a smuggling case which arose when Félix Menchaca's vaqueros returned from the fleshpots of Louisiana, bringing with them a considerable quantity of contraband goods purchased with their new wealth. Lieutenant Fernández found the articles, including twenty-two bundles of tobacco and some bolts of cloth, hidden in a ditch outside town. Realizing that the governor was aware of their scheme, Menchaca and Ysurieta turned themselves in several days later and surrendered several loads of clothes that they had introduced into the

[46] Cabello, "Real Presidio de la Bahía de la Espíritu Santo: Extracto General de la Tropa . . . en que se comprende el Padrón de sus Familias, Armamento, Ganados . . . ," January 12, 1780, BAT, 90:50–51. An interesting examination of Cabello's census of January, 1780, at La Bahía is found in Alicia V. Tjarks, "Comparative Demographic Analysis of Texas, 1777–1793," *Southwestern Historical Quarterly* 77 (January, 1974): 322, 328–34.

[47] *Expediente* no. 88, which includes Croix's proclamation of "good government" of January 11, 1778, BAT, 68:1–21.

province without paying the required taxes. More were discovered in a subsequent search, whereupon Cabello indicted the most prominent members of the cattle drive—mainly Menchaca, his kinsman Juan de Ysurieta, and Francisco Flores Galán—for smuggling contraband goods. Unable to make the charges stick, the governor had to settle for a division of the spoils, valued at 519 pesos. As judge, Cabello received one-third of the confiscated items; Julián de Orosco, as informer, received a third; and the remainder went to Lieutenant Fernández and his men. The case was not concluded until November, 1782, when Cabello absolved Flores Galán and Agustín Ruíz from payment of double the value of the confiscated tobacco plus costs, because of their insolvency and the commandant general's indisposition to "inflict further detriment" on them. It was noted that both were glad to be released from the guardhouse, feeling lucky that only their tobacco and time were lost.[48]

Another cattle case developed in April, 1780, this one also concerning a herd that a local rancher wanted to drive to the Río Grande. This incident, contained in *expediente* 91, involved Juan José Flores, the son of old Juan José, so persecuted by Ripperdá. Juan José the younger was employed by Don Francisco de Yermo, termed a resident and trader of the Presidio del Río Grande. In 1779, Flores petitioned the governor for 904 pesos to satisfy his father's debt to Yermo, owed by the estate. Apparently Yermo was involved with the collection of tithes in Coahuila, held a contract to supply beef to the presidios of the line, and had been doing business with Juan José the elder before his death. This no doubt involved the cattle and other livestock that Flores acquired in his function as *diezmero*, stock for which he then had to find a market to maintain his job. Now Juan José wanted permission to take another herd to the presidios of Coahuila, in accordance with his deceased father's obligation as a beef supplier, and had already made arrangements with Fray Escobar of Espíritu Santo. Flores stated that a roundup

---

[48] Cabello, "Proceedings . . . for the Smuggling of Tobacco," October, 1782–February, 1783, BAT, 113:68–74, BAT, 96:14–20; Thonhoff, *Texas Connection*, pp. 59–60.

of only branded cattle was troublesome, involving a loss of time and the need to cut out *orejanos*. He implored permission to round up both kinds, agreeing to pay the proper value.[49]

Cabello, eager not to expose himself to censure on the future repercussions of such exports, said that Flores could proceed once he guaranteed completion of the exportation, meaning as soon as he posted security for the value of his *orejano* cattle. Inspecting Flores's herd, Lieutenant Governor Joseph Antonio Curbelo found that there were 440 head, 240 branded and 200 unbranded. The latter were further broken down into 167 cows valued at 26 reales each and 33 others valued at 20 reales each. Although the mathematics on this figures out to 625 pesos (8 reales = 1 peso), Cabello stated, "Value assessed, 500 pesos." Reaching some figure was necessary because the cattle were gathered in Tetias, Mesquite, and Arroyo del Tajillo, lands that were "involved in lawsuits between citizenry of this region and the missions at La Bahía." Should the commandant general finally decide that, for instance, heirs of Andrés Hernández owned these *orejanos*, Cabello wanted to make sure that someone besides himself would be obligated to come up with the money. Thus the reason for his precautions in the Monjarás-Padrón export—this one and others yet to come—all based on the final article of his decree dated December 14, 1778.

The ranchers of El Rincón soon got wind of Flores's cattle drive. They submitted a protest to the lieutenant governor, just as they had when the first herd was trailed out. They were "gravely insulted" by Flores's roundup on lands between the Cleto and the Guadalupe. Since the time of Ripperdá, noted the petitioners, they had defended unbranded cattle as their own, and the commandant general had not decided otherwise. All stock raisers, they maintained, should benefit from the export of *orejano* stock, since all claimed ownership of it. The ranchers, apparently unhappy that he was about to make some money and they were not, expressed their willingness to export contested stock on the same terms as young Flores.

[49] The proceedings of this export—almost as important as the one conducted by Monjarás-Padrón in December, 1778—are contained in *expediente* no. 91, BAT, 95: 69–86; see also Moorhead, *Presidio*, p. 215.

This objection had some legitimate grounds, as future interpretations would prove. The ranchers argued that, if Flores was allowed to export, then missionaries and citizens of Coahuila would send people up to exploit the region's *orejanos*— "their" *orejanos*—on the same basis. Flores's employer (Don Francisco Yermo, of Coahuila), and by implication others like him, would benefit—to their own detriment. This, of course, would violate the spirit of the commandant general's decree, which he had specifically stated was being enacted to protect the individual growers of Texas. Having thrown this new twist on things, the *criadores*, seventeen in all, then begged "suspension of exportation of said cattle." Nine days later Cabello ruled this petition inadmissible, and *expediente* 91 went into limbo while the cattle went under their claimants' protest to feed soldiers stationed at presidios on the line.[50]

In June, Juan José Pacheco began his lawsuit against José Félix Menchaca for the bulls lost on their Louisiana drive. Cabello was fresh from his experience with the smuggling charges against Menchaca, and there is little doubt where his sympathies lay; his feud with the Menchaca clan was taking shape. Even after acknowledging that Pacheco had not obtained a license for his forty bulls—as Pacheco steadfastly claimed he had—the governor still ordered his interim appointee at Béxar, Curbelo, to pursue the investigation. The Menchacas could only regard such a decision as thinly veiled intimidation.[51]

Shortly thereafter, Cabello decided to begin charging an export duty of 2 reales a head on herds trailed to Louisiana. He felt that this was a reasonable and moderate fee, which might help cover some "militiaman expenses." Croix, it will be remembered, had asked Cabello what he thought of such an imposition

---

[50] BAT, 95:80. This petition, dated May 13, 1780, was signed by Juan Joseph Móntes de Oca; Marcos de Castro; Miguel de Gortari; Juan Andrés Travieso; Ygnacio Calbillo; Juan Francisco Granado; Francisco X. Rodríguez; Luis Menchaca; Joachín Menchaca; Manuel Delgado; Simón de Arocha; at request of Doña Mariana Curbelo (by Clemente de Arocha); at request of Teresa Flores (by Juan Navarro); at request of Josef Pérez Casanoba (by Clemente de Arocha); at request of Juana de Oyos (by José Guadalupe de Agreda); at request of Manuel Granado (by Ygnacio Calbillo); and Joseph Macario Sambrano.

[51] *Expediente* no. 83, June 2, 1780—November 22, 1786, BAT, 97:30–160.

in his first formal authorization for Louisiana exports. The governor now expressed the opinion that this new fee—along with the duties on mesteños—would soon begin to add up, making an annual report in order.[52]

This decision was reached in context with a herd of 1,500 cattle, purchased from Mission Espíritu Santo, that Marcos Hernández wanted to drive to "the *pueblo* of La Apeluza." Hernández was a resident of La Bahía, likely related to the ranching clan at San Bartolo, on the Cíbolo. It is known that in 1778 he attempted to acquire a ranch near "Las Moras" and was opposed by the missionaries at Valero. They claimed that the land in question was legally theirs and that their cattle were accustomed to grazing beyond the area; they no doubt feared that Hernández might be tempted to add a few of them to his own herd.[53]

Cabello granted an export permit to Hernández since the gathering places indicated were "not among those mentioned by the residents . . . in certain petitions that they have presented." However, he imposed three conditions: Hernández must pay the 2-real head duty to His Majesty, no cattle were to be driven from the contested lands, and he must allow an inspection and count. The herd was to be gathered at the Arroyo El Osso and the Arroyo de los Nogales, away from disputed pastures, and inspected by Felipe (often spelled Phelipe) Flores. Since Felipe was also commissioned to oversee the roundup and was the son of Juan José the elder, it is safe to assume that Hernández carried no cattle to Louisiana bearing brands of or suspected of belonging to the ranchers of El Rincón. When the tally was made, 1,234 head were found milling and bawling in

---

[52] Cabello to Croix, letter no. 239, June 11, 1780, BAT, 98:64.

[53] For the arguments relative to Marcos Hernández's petition for lands near La Mora, see *expediente* no. 301, "Año de 1778 . . . sobre unas tierras que sirven de abrigo a los ganados del rancho de la Mora pertenecientes a la misión San Antonio de Balero . . . ," SA, 4:164–75. Father President Salas's statements concerning the lands between Arroyo Hondo and Arroyo Escondida (in Karnes County, just below present Kenedy and Runge), Rancho San José, Rancho de Capitán Piscina, the ranch of Mission Rosario, Lipan Apache attacks, and how the cattle of La Mora grazed all the way down to the Nueces are found on pp. 166–69. A number of Texas land-grant files became part of the Saltillo Archives; others were registered at San Luis Potosí (after 1786), but appear to have been lost.

the corral, meaning that Marcos Hernández had to pay His Majesty 308 pesos, 4 reales, before he could point them north. In this case a warrant against José Félis Rámos, chaplain at La Bahía Presidio, was accepted by the governor.[54]

That conducting drives to Louisiana at this time was a hazardous proposition is established by the fate of another herd, also put together in June. Comanches had recently come forth from the region between the Colorado and Guadalupe rivers to menace the exposed ranches lying below. First they hit Las Mulas and San Bartolo at night, driving off some horses. Pursued by nine soldiers from Fuerte de Santa Cruz and citizen Tomás Travieso, the Indians massed on the north bank of the Guadalupe, presenting an array which terrified the Spaniards and put them to precipitous flight. Other strong parties which later arrived to challenge the marauders left with the same impression: it was madness to cross the Guadalupe and dangerous to remain anywhere in the vicinity.

Learning this the hard way was the cattle crew under Don Cristóbal de Córdova,[55] camped on the Arroyo de los Nogales with a herd of over 1,000 head, ready for the trail. The export had been arranged by Governor Gálvez's secretary, José Foucher, and the *padre presidente* of the Texas missions, Fray Pedro Ramírez. Espíritu Santo was to provide two herds of 1,000 each, and after delivering the first to Nacogdoches, Córdova was to return to La Bahía for the second. When his cow camp was struck by the Comanches late in June, it contained twenty men, some of them Bexareños hired to deliver the herd by authority of Father Ramírez. One of the vaqueros was killed, two others were wounded, and the entire herd was lost, for after the attack no one would dare try to reassemble the dispersed stock. A courier riding for help found soldiers, militiamen, and citizens under Alférez Marcelo Valdés and Lieutenant José Menchaca still near their fortified mustang corral on the south bank of the

---

[54] *Expediente* no. 90, BAT, 96:49–62; Thonhoff, *Texas Connection*, p. 63.

[55] Blake, Research Collection, 53:234, says that Córdova (a retired veteran of the Béxar presidio who was placed in command at Nacogdoches in 1792 after Captain Gil Ybarbo's arrest) had his sixty-second birthday on May 14, 1792, making him fifty years old at the time of this drive.

Guadalupe. But pursuit offered little reward, either at Nogales or up the wide trail opposite the corral on the Guadalupe. The Comanches had long since vanished into the wind.[56]

Depredations worsened as the raiders became emboldened by these early successes. A supply train was attacked on the Bahía Road, and Rancho de San Bartolo was hit again, this time resulting in the death of two vaqueros caught at the morning milking. The warriors then proceeded to smash the ranch house and carry off all the calves, acts of "wanton destruction" which old Indian experts at Béxar were at a loss to comprehend.[57]

One thing, however, was certain: cattle exports to Louisi-

---

[56] The combined force of 110 men followed the Comanches across the Guadalupe as far as Gerónimo Flores's spring, later known as Tío Gerónimo's Spring, which survives as the name of a community just north of present Seguin. José Antonio Navarro had a much-noted ranch there beginning in the 1830s.

[57] For an account of these Comanche raids which "speedily undid all that Cabello had accomplished toward shipping the livestock that Gálvez needed for Spanish and American forces," see John, *Storms*, pp. 615–19; Thonhoff, *Texas Connection*, pp. 63–65; and Cabello to Croix, October 20, 1780, BAT, 104:40–51.

ana were at a standstill. Cabello wrote Croix that incursions from above the Guadalupe had so intimidated residents of the province that no amount of money was considered sufficient pay for the dangers faced by the herdsmen. The priests were reluctant to place their cattle in such perilous circumstances, much less expose the lives of drovers. Even corralling animals was considered risky, lest these prizes invite attack. Writing again a week later, the governor sounded desperate: "Not a moment passes in which news of rapacities and catastrophes does not reach me. All these ranchos find themselves completely helpless and abandoned. And from this will result the total destruction and loss of this province."[58]

If he had known of the royal *cédula* at that moment crossing the ocean on its way to him, Croix would have perhaps been afflicted with a sense of irony as he sat at Arizpe, reading reports of how the stream of beef at last flowing to Gálvez's forces in Louisiana was being dammed up and choked off by Indian hostilities. For on May 1, 1780, the royal secretary wrote, by way of the viceroy, a response to Croix's request for permission to sell cattle to Gálvez's agents: "The king has approved your action in ordering the governor of Texas to send 1,500 head of cattle to Louisiana immediately to replenish the notable want in that territory. . . . It is his will that Your Lordship order that stock continue to be sent to Louisiana whenever its governor requests it."[59] Thus the export of cattle from Texas to Louisiana had acquired its long-sought royal sanction, only to be effectively stymied by the fierce Comanches. But the traffic would continue, despite the dangers of the drive, and this royal authority would, in the words of Castañeda, "let down the floodgate" to

[58] Cabello to Croix, letter no. 254, July 10, 1780, and letter no. 257, July 17, 1780, BAT, 100:16–20, 37–49. A translation of letter no. 254, listed as "July 12," is found in Grazing Papers, vol. 1.

[59] Castañeda, *Catholic Heritage*, 5:225; Myres, *Ranch in Spanish Texas*, p. 48. This is perhaps the "Royal *cédula*," June 14, 1780, mentioned in J. B. Wilkinson, *Laredo and the Rio Grande Frontier*, p. 76, as being promulgated in Nuevo Santander, although his description of it sounds more like a version of Croix's decree of 1778 on wild cattle, with its "50 centavos," i.e., 4 reales, head tax. I am uncertain to what extent Croix's *bando* was applied to neighboring provinces, but one of the fifteen *arbitrios* (taxes) imposed at Parras in 1780 called for a 4-real duty on beef cattle (Francis de Burgos, "The Administration of Teodoro de Croix, Commander General of the Provincias Internas de Mexico, 1776–83" (Master's thesis, University of Texas, 1927).

foreign traders desiring to exploit the wild herds of Texas—and beyond to those of distant Coahuila and Nuevo Santander.

By mid-August the situation was little improved. Cabello had to send an *escolta* (escort)[60] to the villas of the Río Grande to buy seventy or eighty horses and some mules to replace mounts stolen by the Comanches. The governor regretted to inform Croix that he could not reinforce the Cíbolo fort with another twenty to thirty men because his forces were already spread too thin. Consequently the adjacent ranches could expect little protection from further Indian assaults.[61]

An acknowledgment that Indians were raiding and running off stock not just in Texas but throughout the Interior Provinces is found in Commandant General Croix's *bando* on the subject of animals recaptured from the hostile tribes. It was intended to both protect the original owner and reward those bold enough to "harass and fight with stubbornness the savage Indians," in the process recovering stock stolen from Spanish owners. The *bando* contains eight provisions, setting forth a rather complex system of rates which owners were obliged to pay captors for returning their animals. Depending on how far away from the presidio tracking parties had to ride in pursuing raiders, the recovery fees ranged from 2 to 8 pesos for mules and 1 to 5 pesos for horses. How long the animals were held by the Indians was also a factor. To prevent fraud (such as stealing someone's stock and then pretending to rescue it), the *bando* contained a clause calling for a document which would serve as a receipt for the captor, entitling him to claim "the reward assigned by the law as a prize for his merit and courage."

Lists of recovered animals, their brands, and so forth, were to be compiled and posted in each province. This enabled the owner to learn how and when to reclaim his stock and pay the appropriate amount. Four months were allowed, but if the owner or his agent had not come forward by the end of this period, the animal or animals became the property of the captor. A special brand was devised to be applied to animals reverting to their

---

[60] Usually a *cabo* (corporal) and five soldiers; on this occasion two sergeants and six soldiers.

[61] Cabello to Croix, letter no. 261, August 10, 1780, BAT, 100:73–76.

captors, this serving as proof of legitimate ownership. Further, to avoid disputes, upon recovery total value of the booty was to be appraised, from which would be deducted the cost of damages "that the enemy have caused to the property." After the prizes were distributed among the captors, any remainder was to be divided equally—whether soldiers, citizens, or Indians—among those present at the time of the engagement. Cowards, however, received nothing.

Cabello published this decree at Béxar on November 4, 1780, and sent it on to Nacogdoches the following January 28, 1781. First he made a slight revision based on frontier realities. Experience had proved, he said, that when an Indian got his hands on stolen property "he runs away at such a rate of speed that it takes but a very short time for him to reach his own land." Accordingly, such an Indian was never captured within the distance limit of 8 leagues after eight days' possession. To reward those who acted quickly, with the extra diligence required to recapture stock before eight days elapsed and before the enemy left the vicinity (since that was the only way it could be realistically accomplished), the governor decreed a reduced set of fees ranging from 4 to 12 reales. If the stolen stock was recovered in twenty-four hours, however, the captor received only "damages," as provided in Croix's third provision.

Thus some measure of incentive was at work for all the different situations likely to be encountered when stock was retaken from "the enemy who pillages in these provinces under my command," as Croix phrased it. The proposed system offered the greatest rewards to those whose pursuit was the most stubborn and long-range, attempting also to relieve breeders, drovers, muleteers, and livestock dealers of the heavy burden involved in collecting and driving home stolen stock. In one form or another, rewards for the return of such animals were to remain in effect throughout the colonial period, indicating that the problem was a persistent one.[62] Soon afterward the com-

---

[62] *Expediente* no. 75, "Relating to Rewards for Recapture of Stock from Indians," BAT, 101:10–22. See also Grazing Papers, vol. 1, for a translation made in 1940 by Raquel Welch; and Faulk, "Ranching in Spanish Texas," p. 259, who mentions Croix's decree of August 16, 1780 (citing it, however, dated August 15, repeating this in *Last Years*, p. 88).

mandant general gave approval to Cabello's export duty of 2 reales—this in reference to the Marcos Hernández drive—as sufficient to defray military expenses, which was its purpose. He told the governor of Texas to continue this charge on all Louisiana-bound cattle.⁶³

But in truth no herds could go up the trail as long as the Comanches menaced the route, and Cabello's primary task thus lay in making peace with these fierce Mongols of the Plains. Realizing that his presence was required in the capital, he traveled there in September, inspecting the Cíbolo fort on the way. He condemned the site selected by Ripperdá as "the most inappropriate, strange, and unusual place that could be chosen." Such an evaluation would have caused the baron considerable pain. Ripperdá's rustling-trial summation indicates that he was proud of his part in founding the Fuerte de Santa Cruz, believing that it afforded considerable benefit to ranches in the vicinity. Cabello wrote Croix that he proposed to relocate the fort where it could protect the ranches on the San Antonio River, as well as those on the Cíbolo. To that end he went to Rancho San Bartolo, met with area ranchers, and agreed with them on a new site.

Although the governor promised to draw a map of the region for the *comandante*, perhaps to illustrate the advantages of his new location, it is uncertain whether he ever did so. Comanche attacks in the Cíbolo Valley continued, particularly against the fort, where three soldiers were killed and some horses stolen on September 18. Troops were put to work strengthening the stockade, but there was little Cabello could do for the post in the way of reinforcements, especially since it took so many men from the presidio just to guard the horse herd.⁶⁴

To make things worse, Cabello found that his long absence from Béxar had created a backlog of problems, not the least of which was the chain of command at the presidio. When the governor arrested Lieutenant José Menchaca for acts committed during his tenure and sent him in disgrace to the Presidio San

---

⁶³ Croix to Cabello, September 10, 1780, BAT, 102:10.

⁶⁴ Cabello to Croix, September 14, 1780, ibid., pp. 15–19; John, *Storms*, p. 621; Thonhoff, *Texas Connection*, p. 67.

Juan Bautista, his long-simmering feud with the Menchaca clan reached the boiling point. Cabello charged the old captain's son with six abuses of his official capacity, concluding that "his bad conduct makes him unworthy of consideration of anything." José had (1) failed to make reports, (2) ordered his men to conceal the contraband of his uncle Félix and cousin "Yzurietta," (3) done nothing about the animals his father had sold to the soldiers but failed to deliver, (4) bullied troops into electing him paymaster (a position traditionally open to lucrative abuse), (5) lived openly with his servant's wife, and (6) smeared the governor's name, with help from his father, the retired captain.[65] A month after taking this bold step, Cabello wrote Croix that he expected problems with the Menchacas owing to the old captain's disposition and intrepidity. He suspected the entire family of complicity in the recent smuggling episode, saying that brother Joaquín's testimony proved that Luis Antonio had hidden the contraband brought in by Félix and was therefore liable too. The following spring Don Luis's son Miguel Jorge ran off to the Indians for reasons unknown.[66]

That November another minor episode occurred in the ongoing struggle to tame the frontier: Felipe de Luna was killed by Indians near his sod house at Arroyo La Mora, where he ran a few cows. He had asked for lands there at the same time that the Garzas had petitioned for San Simón del Capote, but formal title was withheld owing to objections by the Valero missionaries. Since Luna died intestate, Marcos Zepeda was sent by the governor to round up his stock, a job which took a "boy" almost a month to accomplish at a wage of 4 reales a day. The paltry fifty-one head netted for the estate were appraised at values ranging from breeding cows at 4 pesos, 4 reales, a head; mature bulls at 2 pesos, 2 reales; and yearlings at 1 peso.[67]

Another legal case occupying Cabello's attention in the fall of 1780 gives us insight into the mechanics of a typical cattle drive made to satisfy the demands for Texas beef along the Río Grande. Like most other such endeavors, the details vary,

---

[65] Cabello to Croix, nos. 280 and 281, September 20, 1780, BAT, 103:1–12.
[66] Cabello to Croix, letter no. 298, October 18, 1780, ibid., pp. 34–38.
[67] "Estate left by Felipe de Luna . . . ," BAT, vol. 105.

depending on whose side of the story is credited, the plaintiff Manuel Gonzáles's or the defendant Sebastián Monjarás's. It all started in 1779, when Monjarás was putting together a herd to drive down to Presidio Santa Rosa, one of the new presidios of the line founded as a result of Rubí's tour and the New Regulations of 1772.[68] At Rancho de Las Cabras he was approached by Gonzáles, a native of the Isle of Tenerife who had lived in Béxar only a year or so. Gonzáles was trying to raise money for passage home (so he claimed), and Monjarás, feeling sorry for the wayfarer, agreed to let him bring along fifty head on the Santa Rosa drive. Gonzáles had only one "boy," Antonio Cadena, to assist him, hired at a peso a day. When the herd was ready to drive, Juan Andrés Travieso gave each party an accounting of his ownership interest, expressed in kernels of corn.

The drive proceeded with little incident. Reaching their destination, Monjarás quickly sold his part of the herd, for the one-time *diezmero* was a familiar face to the meat purveyor at the presidio. He received 5 pesos, 2 reales, a head, and, noting his success, the tenderfoot Gonzáles asked him to speak to the paymaster and arrange a sale for his cows. This Monjarás did, the paymaster agreeing to take Gonzáles's stock at 5 pesos a head, but only if he would agree to accept a sight draft, payable in Saltillo. At this point accounts of the transaction begin to vary.

Gonzáles maintained that he wanted cash, not a promissory note, but Monjarás talked him into agreeing to the arrangement. He advanced Gonzáles 25 pesos until they reached Saltillo, but apparently by the time the two arrived, they had decided to expand the venture into a little partnership, investing the proceeds of their drive in goods which they could bring back to the presidio and sell on the sly at considerable profit. This they did, but Monjarás became ill at Saltillo, and the affairs of the partnership fell to Gonzáles, who seems to have been a poor trader. Sebastián pursuaded Gonzáles, who by now had totally forgotten his original plan to go back to Tenerife, to stay in the cattle

---

[68] It is uncertain if the destination of this drive was the Valle de Santa Rosa (now Múzquiz, Coahuila), situated northwest of Monclova on the Río Sabinas, or the new Presidio de Agua Verde, founded in 1773 with the garrison from Santa Rosa.

business with him. Instead of paying Gonzáles anything on this drive, he told Gonzáles that once they returned to Béxar he would pay him his profits in cattle at the rate of 2½ pesos a head, most likely neglecting to mention that the payoff would be in wild cattle caught by Monjarás. Since Gonzáles was so pleased with their trail-driving arrangement and the "security" enjoyed by Monjarás's herds, by sending this new shipment of cattle south, he would soon double his profits.

At some point the dull-witted Gonzáles realized that he was being taken, perhaps back in El Rincón when Monjarás refused to pay him for his kernels of corn in money, goods, or the king's cattle. Sebastián, of course, maintained that Gonzáles was the crook, that on top of all the losses his carelessness had cost their partnership Gonzáles had also taken a saddle pad from his house, had gone off with some chocolate and *aguardiente*, and had stolen chickens from his neighbor Josef María Hernández. Still Gonzáles had the presence of mind to sue the one-time *diezmero* for nonfulfillment of contract with the testimony of various witnesses, drovers, and the corn he still had in his possession, each kernel representing a unit of ownership in the communal herd.

In October, 1780, Monjarás was found guilty and jailed, and all his possessions were attached to satisfy the 120-peso judgment rendered against him. Unfortunately, he was not yet finished with this ill-considered affair. Convinced that Alcalde Salvador Rodríguez was prejudiced against him, he appealed from jail, demanding another judge and saying that an idiot could see the justness of his side. Six months later he was released by a *bando* of His Majesty freeing private debtors, but eventually the sum he owed was set at a staggering 298 pesos, the value of Gonzáles's cows at the price they brought at Presidio Santa Rosa, not their "cost" in Texas. Needless to say, this resourceful trail driver would have been better off not contesting Alcalde Rodríguez's original 120-peso judgment. When his property was auctioned, Father Salas had trouble obtaining payment of a 56-peso priority debt he held against Monjarás on behalf of Mission Valero. The fact that poor Sebastián was required to execute a lien in favor of Gonzáles for the difference indicates that in the future he perhaps kept his assets out near

Rancho del Paistle very fluid—on the hoof, so to speak—so that his irate creditors could not easily attach them.[69]

On November 9, 1780, Governor Cabello issued a writ ordering the fall branding. He noted that despite all his good intentions it had not been possible to avoid problems the preceding year and wanted the present effort to go better. He suggested that, since failure to brand was harmful both to the population and to the church's tithe, a new procedure should be followed: Rancho de San Francisco, the Delgados, and La Mora were to brand together; Pataguilla would brand by itself; and the ranches on the Cíbolo—Marcos de Castro, Los Guerras, Las Mulas, and El Paistle (also spelled Pastle, Paste, and Pasthle)—would conduct a third rodeo. To eliminate confusion about gathering areas, he specified the following partition:

Ranchos of the San Antonio River: On La Bahía Road, turning at "Las Calaberas" (Calaveras Creek) down as far as its union with the San Antonio River and going through the pastures of San Francisco, La Mora, and the Delgados (this area lies mostly in present western Wilson County).

Ranchos of the Arroyo Cíbolo: To proceed from the union of Arroyo El Cleto with the San Antonio River, by the most di-

---

[69] For this interesting *expediente*, September 19, 1780–May 13, 1781, see BAT, vol. 102.

rect route to Arroyo Alonzo, then in a line to Las Tetillas and the *loma* (hill) El Capote, then upriver along the Guadalupe to the corral of Las Mesteñas, turning toward Santa Clara Creek, then to its confluence with the Cíbolo, ending at El Paistle (this area is in present eastern Wilson County and lower Guadalupe County).

Cabello believed that this division would give the best results. In regard to *orejanos*, legitimate owners were authorized to catch them provided they were lawfully entitled, did not conceal their take, gave a report to the commissioner, and paid the 4 reales each stipulated by Croix's decree. Fines for violation were 4 pesos a head and eight days in jail. Because of the many Comanche attacks since June, troops would be detailed to circle and patrol the branding areas. The governor ordered the priests at Espíritu Santo and Concepción notified of the roundup and once again appointed Tomás Travieso to preside.[70]

When Travieso received word of his duties, he was on his ranch, Las Mulas. Since Don Tomás convened all the ranchers at San Bartolo on November 23 to give them the governor's instructions, and his report of the roundup is dated December 2, the actual corrida must have taken place during the last week of November, 1780. Travieso's report is summarized in table 3.

Commissioner Travieso noted that the following ranches were unable to participate owing to extremely inclement weather: Rancho of Don Simón de Arocha, El Paistle, Las Mulas, Las Cabras, and Los "Challapines" (Chayopines). A total of sixty-three *orejanos* were reported taken, and the income from this second annual roundup, 31 pesos, 4 reales, in IOUs, could not have been very encouraging to Governor Cabello. As in the year before, more serious problems detracted from the poor showing. Epidemics ravaged Béxar and La Bahía, while Comanche raiders continued to hit outlying areas, especially Mission Concepción's Rancho del Paistle.[71]

In late December, Cabello bared to the commandant general his feelings on the new policy of free trade with Louisiana,

---

[70] Cabello, writ, November 9, 1780, BAT, 89:66–67.

[71] Ibid., pp. 106–109; for Travieso's report of *orejanos* taken, dated December 20, 1781, listing the various participants, see BAT, 108:156.

TABLE 3. Report of Roundup, December 2, 1780.

Ranch or Owner	No. Stock Branded	No. Stock Owned
La Mora (Mission Valero)	410	1,422
Rancho San Francisco (Luis Menchaca)	136	500
Delgado brothers	117	450
San Bartolo (Juana de Oyos, her sons and Joaquín Flores)	60	380
Macario Sambrano	99	377
Juan Flores (Juan José the younger)	74	225
Joaquín de la Garza	25	100
Total	921	3,454

SOURCE: BAT, 89:106–109.

his remarks prompted by the arrival of Francisco Rosé, a French trader whom Gálvez had sent to promote the idea. Acknowledging the receipt of His Majesty's royal order, which Croix had forwarded on October 6, Cabello expressed a readiness to expedite delivery of whatever number of cattle Governor Gálvez should require. But perhaps suspicious of the profiteering motives of Rosé and others like him, Cabello implied that the new trade would benefit neither Texas nor his own reputation. One senses that Cabello had already been in Texas long enough to get a feel for the bureaucratic complexities that would accompany formal trade relations and was trying to hedge a bit.

He predicted that the year free trade became established bovine and equine livestock would become so scarce in Texas that a horse would be worth 20 pesos and a cow twice as much. So great would be the rush to "La Luiciana" that it would soon become impossible to supply the presidios in Coahuila, as was already happening. Thus "cattle will become totally lacking, and none will be found even for our own sustenance." The madness would extend southward into Nuevo Santander and Nuevo León; not a head would be left—all because in Louisiana a head of beef would bring "four fancy linen kerchiefs and some *maritatas* (trinkets)." Contraband would flourish like the pernicious tobacco and packtrains would enter Texas covertly, blemishing Cabello's honor as His Majesty's administrator, not to mention causing a drastic drop in revenues.

Cattle were already very scarce in the province, argued the governor, because the Lipan Apaches consumed great numbers, and the herds had not multiplied plentifully, for the people, terrorized by the hostilities of the enemy, were unable to devote themselves to attending their stock. There was such a great decline, declared Cabello, that he had found himself in the position of having to publish a *bando* setting a fine of 10 pesos for each breeding cow taken to the province of Coahuila, allowing only bulls and yearlings to be exported. He promised the commandant general, nonetheless, that he would be able to fulfill any obligation "in which Your Lordship might find yourself with respect to the *cavallero* Don Bernardo de Gálvez, and in order that the supply of cattle he might need should not be limited."[72] Despite such assurances of delivery, Cabello must have known that *los norteños* would pronounce the final word on any cattle trade with Louisiana and that not even the king's long-awaited approval could keep them from blocking the trails east.

---

[72] Cabello to Croix (fragment), December 20, 1780, BAT, 106:61–68. Thonhoff, *Texas Connection*, pp. 69–70, quotes at length from this letter. It is interesting to note that Cabello had not changed his opinion on trade at the end of his term; see Cabello to the Viceroy, November 25, 1787, Haggard, "Neutral Ground between Louisiana and Texas," p. 1077.

7

"THEY PERSIST IN THEIR UNJUST CLAIMS"

Taxation without Representation

Concerning Indians, the year 1781 began much as 1780 ended, except perhaps worse. From Cabello's reports throughout the spring, Béxar was like a tiny island in a large Comanche sea. In February the governor filed a report on conditions at the presidio, from which we learn that horses and mules of the company wore a special brand and also a large R with crown above, which was intended to make it more difficult to trade or sell animals stolen from the military. A recent bloody incident at the Cíbolo fort was described in which Indians killed six men, mutilating them horribly. Alférez Valdés went the next day in "pursuit" to the Guadalupe crossing known as El Paso del Tío Gerónimo, which was above another pass, Los Chiflónes. Coming back the day after to the deserted ranch El Paistle, Valdés saw many tracks and returned to Santa Cruz.[1]

A glimpse of the wretched conditions under which the citizens labored comes from an undated fragment of 1781 in the

---

[1] Cabello, "Report on Conditions" at the Béxar Presidio, February (?), 1781, BAT, vol. 107.

Béxar Archives. The *ayuntamiento* complained to Cabello that the Indian menace had farmers and ranchers of the province living in constant danger. There was "not a scrap of meat left to eat," nor butter nor a candle—not so much as a stick of firewood, they claimed. If the war continued for another two months, even the survivors would perish of starvation. The citizens had abandoned their ranches, and the petitioners said that mission ranches were also being destroyed, mentioning that six or eight herdsmen had been killed at Las Cabras. They predicted that the villa would be next.[2]

Croix, in his "General Report of 1781," described the situation in Texas almost as grimly as the inhabitants did, dating their current troubles from July, 1780. If the Comanches continued their attacks, the desolation of the province would be "consequent, irremediable, and immediate." So horrible and bloody was the onslaught that very few of the king's vassals in Texas would remain to contemplate the misfortune:

The province is overrun by these Indians, now alone, or as allies of the Nations of the North; at the moment not one foot of land is free from hostility. Its fruits of the field are despoiled, cattle ranches and farms that the happy days of peace had built are rapidly being abandoned, and the settlers in terror [are] taking refuge in the settlements, nor do they venture to leave their neighborhood without a troop escort.[3]

Allowing for exaggeration, possibly designed to prompt the flow of pesos so that he could improve defenses on the frontier, this turn of events must have discouraged the commandant general. The plains Indians were the key to survival in Texas, as his ear-

---

[2] *Ayuntamiento* to Cabello, petition (fragment), 1781, BAT, 108:179, bearing the following twelve signatures: Francisco Flores, José de la Santa, Juan A. Travieso, Joachín Leal, Marcos Móntes de Oca, Manuel Flores y Valdés, Marcos de Zepeda, Miguel de Gortaris, Joseph Ignacio de la Peña, Francisco Móntes de Oca, Joaquín Flores, and Joseph Marcos de Aguilar.

[3] Croix, "General Report of 1781," cited in Odie B. Faulk, "Texas during the Administration of Domingo Cabello y Robles, 1778–1786" (Master's thesis, Texas Technological College, 1960), pp. 49–50. For an ongoing tally of the casualties suffered by vaqueros while hunting stock in 1781, see Fr. Benedict Leutenegger, trans., *Journal of a Texas Missionary, 1767–1802: The Diario Histórico of Fr. Cosme Lozano Narvais, Pen Name of Fr. Mariano Antonio de Vasconcelos*, p. 16; Croix's section on Texas is also detailed in this respect, AGI, Audiencia de Guadalajara, box 2Q142, University of Texas Archives.

lier *juntas* had recognized, but these fierce warriors were proving difficult to reconcile to the interests of Spain. Some way must be found to win their friendship, but there was no light at the end of the tunnel.

Apparently conditions at Béxar were such as to permit a meat hunt on April 21. Marcos Zepeda and thirty-three men went to Las Mulas and San Bartolo, bringing back twenty-six *orejanos* for beef to feed the township. Cabello, always alert on behalf of the Mustang Fund, billed the hunters 13 pesos, a sum he was still trying to collect at year's end.[4] More evidence that the settlers were accommodating to the constant *norteño* guerrilla mode of warfare is found in the governor's ban on horse racing in the streets on June 24, 1781, the Feast of Saint John. As on other such occasions—Saint Peter's Day, Saint James's Day, and Saint Anne's Day—it was the custom to race through the villa, which caused various mishaps, "breaches of good etiquette, and other disgraces," but which had offered the only safe site for the festivities. Henceforth horse racing would be permitted only in the country, not in the plaza of the government building (the main plaza), or the plaza of the guardhouse behind the church (the military plaza). The penalties were directed at those engaged in the sport. If the horse belonged to the parents of an offending boy, the horse would be seized; if not, the rider would receive twenty-five lashes (*azotes*). If the rider was eighteen or older, he would lose his horse and spend one month at hard labor. Ramsdell describes similar problems at La Bahía, where a priest arrested a girl, shut her up with other females, and made her pray a *salve* in the chapel of Espíritu Santo because she had participated in a horse race on Saint Anne's Day—"an old custom in these regions."[5]

Another meat-hunting party was authorized on July 11, this one composed of men under the supervision of Alcalde Fran-

---

[4] This list of 34 *carneadores* is found in BAT, vol. 107; Robert H. Thonhoff, *The Texas Connection with the American Revolution*, p. 17n.25.

[5] BAT, vol. 108; Odie B. Faulk, *A Successful Failure*, pp. 177–78; Charles [William] Ramsdell, [Jr.], "Spanish Goliad" (typescript, University of Texas Archives), pp. 57–58. For an enumeration of the various religious holidays observed by Hispanic Catholics see Arnoldo de León, *The Tejano Community, 1836–1900*, pp. 137–46.

cisco Flores. Flores was directed to make sure that his party did not round up cattle other than those in the pastures of their own ranchos. Further, pastures belonging to those not taking part in the hunt were off limits unless the owner or his representatives were present. Wild stock taken had to be reported so that the king's fees could be assessed and paid, a duty which Flores later discharged by saying that six men owed a total of 6 pesos, 3 reales.[6]

In 1780 Cabello issued only two *guías* (export permits) for herds going south. They were issued to Simón de Arocha (for 306 head belonging to Espíritu Santo and Rosario) and Juan José Flores (for 440 head belonging to various owners). The year 1781—especially the month of August—showed a dramatic improvement. Seven export permits were issued, as shown in table 4.[7]

These drives reflect several additional modifications of procedures for earlier Coahuila-bound herds trailed out under Cabello's watchful eye: a cash deposit of His Majesty's 4-real duty was required before issuance of an export permit; for the remaining value of cows taken from contested lands, a bond continued to be accepted; and to protect breeding cows and ensure the growth of herds, extractions of branded stock were required to be a one-third ratio of cows, bulls, and bullocks.

Most of the permits issued in August had been applied for in mid-July, indicating that most of a month elapsed from the time of the initial paperwork to the time a herd was ready for inspection and the drive south. In his petition for a permit the individual listed the reasons for needing to export, the place where he planned to gather, the number of head, and so on. Then the governor issued a license to gather, stating the conditions which the applicant was required to observe. After the herd was assembled, Cabello sent an inspector, upon whose report—and

---

[6] The following list of hunters, dated July 11, 1781, is in BAT, vol. 108 (also found in Grazing Papers, vol. 1, along with Cabello's authorization): Francisco Flores, Tomás Travieso, Juan Andrés Travieso, Francisco Travieso, Chico Travieso, Clemente Delgado, Torivio Durán, Pedro Granados, Marcos de Castro, Miguel Gortari, Pedro X. Salinas, Manuel Casanova, Joachín de la Garza, Martín de la Garza, and Francisco de la Zerda.

[7] "Report of Exports," BAT, 142:130–31.

TABLE 4. Cattle-Export Permits Issued in 1781.

Date Issued	Driver	No. Cattle
January 23	Simón de Arocha	423
August 11	Luis Mariano Menchaca and Macario Sambrano	300
August 11	Mission La Espada	208
August 14	Juan José Flores	120
August 11	Vizente Flores	200
August 14	Simón de Arocha	419
October 14	José Antonio Curbelo	414
Total		2,084

SOURCE: "Report of Exports," BAT. 142:130–31.

the payment or pledge of the appropriate valuation—an export permit was issued. The herd inspector was normally an alcalde or other local official, and his report specified both the place where the animals were taken and their kind, branded or *orejano*, for the king's duties applied only to the latter. It should be remembered that the export duty of 2 reales applied to Louisiana exports, not to those sold in Coahuila. If the stock driven to Louisiana was *orejano*, not caught in recognized pastures, then theoretically the exporter would owe His Majesty 6 reales each (4 for catching, 2 for exporting); a more sweeping ruling soon took the place of this ambiguity.

To illustrate the above, Juan José Flores declared that he wanted to round up the "tenth part of his livestock to satisfy his annual obligation to his *amo* [master] Don Francisco de Yermo, magistrate and collector of tithes for the province of Coahuila." In another instance Vizente Flores wanted to round up on his ranch as far as the *cañada* El Quatralbo, near the Arroyo Cleto. Vizente, son of Don Francisco Flores, claimed that these were their summer pastures but that recent Indian hostilities had made it perilous to enter them. He further mentioned the areas of El Cuchillo, La Laguna corral, and Los Olmos, assuring the governor that Alférez Valdés would substantiate his claim that only Las Mulas cattle were there. When Cabello denied him permission, owing to the conflict between the citizens and the missions over unbranded stock grazing in the region, Vizente suggested the area below Las Tetillas and agreed to abide by the commandant general's decision. Simón de Arocha's drive was necessary because for four years (from 1773 to 1776), he had purchased the *diezmos* of the province, the cattle that citizens annually rendered to the church. This, plus the stock that Arocha already owned on his growing San Rafael (each year from 1776 to 1781 he branded about 150 calves), made a sale desirable.

Flores, one of the first to petition, replied to Cabello's requirement that he was not to export cows by saying that he needed to take female cattle as well. Mature and young bulls exclusively were of no benefit because of the low price they brought and their reputed scarcity in the pastures. The governor informed Flores of the one-third ratio and required him to pay 4 reales cash on each unmarked animal taken in the contested pastures mentioned in his petition. This was the same area that most other exporters asked to gather in—the same area that Ripperdá had considered it a criminal offense for the ranchers to exploit. Now, by executing a binding instrument—that is, promising to pay the value of captured *orejanos* to whomever the commandant general should decide they belonged to and by forking over His Majesty's 4 reales, a person could take cattle from this area legitimately.

Part of the difficulty in the administration of this law during its transitional period was arriving at a value for extracted herds. This was the sum which exporters were required to secure, pending Croix's resolution of the sticky ownership dispute. It fluctuated from case to case, usually averaging around 22 reales. Even more difficult was controlling the roundup activities of prospective exporters after they walked out of Cabello's office with their permits. Vizente Flores, for example, might say that he would stay below Las Tetillas to placate the governor's high-flown sense of duty, but there would be little to stop him from then riding to places he had originally had in mind. Once the herd was gathered and held at La Espada corral for inspection, Vizente's father, Francisco, or his uncle Tomás

Travieso—both frequently employed by Cabello as herd inspectors—were not likely to list gathering places expressly forbidden on the roundup permit. Cabello at least had the required paperwork to prove that he sought compliance, whether or not he got it.[8]

On January 4, 1782, the governor issued orders to brand, saying that the citizens had been frustrated in their attempts to do so during the past two months because of the Comanches, "who have kept us with weapons in our hands." A successful action had recently been carried out against them, he said, and now the annual branding could take place.[9] He appointed Macario Sambrano to oversee the corrida and defined areas as in the previous year. Permission was given to brand *orejanos* less than three years old if they were caught in the owner's pastures, this extraordinary boon supposedly granted because it had not been possible to brand for two years. Perhaps Cabello considered the poor results turned in by former Juez Tomás Travieso as such. A tally was to be kept on *orejanos* three years old and older, and the king's duty of 4 reales paid on them. A tally was also required on wild horses caught and branded.[10]

A *bando* written the following day set forth Cabello's irritation with the citizens on the subject of His Majesty's Mustang Fund. He ordered them to cease neglecting payment of duties on mesteño horses and *orejano* cattle, noting that the revenues produced over the past two years had been pathetically small. The governor reminded his subjects that, in spite of their concealment of animals they caught, he had worked to lower the

---

[8] Juan José Flores, *expediente* no. 92, July 11, 1781–November 24, 1786 (i.e., the end of Cabello's term); Vizente Flores, *expediente* no. 93, July 13, 1781–end of term; Simón de Arocha, *expediente* no. 94, July 19, 1781–end of term; José Antonio Curbelo, *expediente* no. 95, September 17, 1781–end of term, all in BAT, vol. 108. Thonhoff, *Texas Connection*, pp. 71–72, mentions these drives.

[9] The reference is to the December action in which the *alférez* Valdés and 172 men inflicted a stinging defeat on Comanches camped on the Medina, collecting much booty (including ten mules and seventy-four horses) but also sad reminders of fallen companions from Béxar. Elizabeth A. H. John, *Storms Brewed in Other Men's Worlds: The Confrontation of Indians, Spanish, and French in the Southwest, 1540–1795*, pp. 631–32.

[10] *Expediente* no. 80, "Concerning Branding," January 4, 1782, BAT, vol. 89.

fee on mustangs from 6 reales to 2, accomplished by his *bando* of October 27, 1779. Nevertheless, catches were still hidden and the paltry 2 reales not paid. Cabello ordered that henceforth all residents, upon capturing a wild animal, were to pay immediately 2 reales per horse and 4 reales per cow. The penalty for violation of this order was set at forfeiture of the captured animal and a fine of 6 pesos.[11]

TABLE 5. Report of Roundup, February 26, 1782, Pertaining to 1781.

Ranch or Owner	No. Stock Branded	No. Stock Owned
Las Mulas (the Traviesos)	647	850
La Mora (Mission Valero)	256	820
San Francisco (Luis Menchaca)	260	500
Pataguia (Simón de Arocha, "military commander")	116	500
Macario Sambrano	154	380
San Bartolo (Juana de Oyos)	226	227
Los Chaopines (Peña family)	50	110
Flores and Guerra families	188	86
San Cristóbal (Delgados)	37	80
El Paso de las Mugeres (ranch of Ignacio Calvillo)	30	60
Total	1,964	3,613

SOURCE: "Report of Joseph Macario Sambrano," February 26, 1782, pertaining to 1781, BAT, 89:125–29.

Sambrano's report of the roundup was filed on February 26, 1782, and reveals that a total of 183 *orejanos* were taken (compared to 63 the previous year), for a total owed the king of 91 pesos, 4 reales. Concerning the accompanying report of stock owned and branded by the various ranches (see table 5), several observations can be made. Las Mulas surpassed all other establishments both in total stock owned and in total branded.

[11] Cabello, *bando*, January 5, 1782, BAT, 109:46.

Furthermore, they reported branding in this single rodeo stock equaling three-fourths of their total owned, indicating that their vaqueros were very busy. Luis Menchaca's ranch, by contrast, branded half the number of his total owned, while San Bartolo branded one new head for every one owned. It was noted that neither Mission Espada's ranch (Las Cabras) nor Concepción's (El Paistle) branded. Valero's La Mora, however, was still active and near the top in both owned and branded stock.[12]

Events occurred during this roundup which led Governor Cabello to launch a bitter lawsuit against his former *juez de campo*, Tomás Travieso. The owner of Las Mulas found himself charged with uttering defamatory remarks about Cabello and various soldiers of the royal service, no inconsequential offense in an era when slandering the king, the royal family, or the government carried the death penalty.[13] This latest incident was not the first brush between Travieso's cowboys and soldiers from the Cíbolo fort out foraging for beef, but it was the one that prompted the governor to take action. Las Mulas, it would seem, was getting out of line—a bit too self-important to suit Cabello—and he intended to teach its prominent owner to show proper respect.

Early testimony indicates that a possible basis for the ensuing dispute was Las Mulas Rancho's coveted role as beef supplier to the Cíbolo fort. Other Cíbolo ranchers also sold stock to the fort, but, being closest, Las Mulas sold most of the beef, a convenient source of income that Don Tomás zealously protected. When a rancher brought beef to the stockade, he was paid with a receipt, which he presented at the company paymaster's office to receive his 5 pesos per head; such was described as routine procedure. During periods of Indian trouble, however, when the ranches were abandoned—as in the preceding year during the Comanche raids—the soldiers were obliged to form their own meat-hunting parties. Like the residents, they caught *orejanos*, usually on the lands claimed by the ranchers, and this

---

[12] "Report of Joseph Macario Sambrano," February 26, 1782, BAT, 89:125–29.
[13] Robert S. Weddle and Robert H. Thonhoff, *Drama and Conflict: The Texas Saga of 1776*, p. 62.

rankled aggressive meat suppliers like Travieso.[14] Five pesos for delivering a wild cow to a market so close to home was a good price, and it is not difficult to understand why the ranchers resented *carneadores* from the fort cutting into their income by depriving them of possible sales. It was Travieso's misfortune to be reported for saying what his fellow ranchers held to be self-evident: that the king's men were "all a gang of thieves."

Sergeant Manuel de Urrutia's report, written four days after Juez Sambrano gathered the ranchers at Las Mulas, launched the investigation. Urrutia said that a corporal, five soldiers, and several residents were sent to get beef. They caught three *orejanos* in the region beyond the arroyo of El Cuchillo, tied them with *cabestros* (halters), and left them there while they continued to hunt, intending to pick them up on the way back. It was at this point that Travieso's crew, out on their roundup, came across the three unbranded animals tied at the horns. Don Tomás sent young Vizente Flores to scout the area. For this purpose Vizente disguised himself as an Indian, stripping the saddle from his horse, donning a fox-pelt headdress, and wielding a lance. Finding and recognizing the intruders as soldiers, "because one was wearing something red around his belly," Flores alerted his uncle, who let his temper get the best of him.

The Las Mulas vaqueros stormed down on the meat hunters, and Tomás Travieso scolded the corporal severely, asking who had given him permission to take his cows, why they were in his lands, and so forth. There were plenty of other places to take cattle besides the area where the ranchers were gathering theirs, such as on the Guadalupe or at El Capote (where the Indians were), and Travieso accused them of cow hunting so that they would not have to patrol as soldiers were paid to do. Don Tomás let it be known that he was sick and tired of "the Governor" taking their cattle, whereupon he ordered his men to seize the three *anejas* ("attached" yearlings) and notch their ears, presumably with the Las Mulas *señal* (mark). He taunted

---

[14] A curious sidelight of such military meat-hunting expeditions is that the paymaster had to be notified of the number of *orejanos* taken so that the king's duty of 4 reales per head could be deducted from their pay, "this being the procedure when cattle are caught on *realengas*" (BAT, vol. 110).

the hapless soldiers, refusing to return their halter ropes—asking for a fight, said one deponent—and bloodshed was narrowly averted. Before Travieso rode off in disgust, he called them all a gang of thieves, a remark which Sergeant Urrutia took to include "all the officers and men of Your Lordship's company."

In March, 1782, after gathering several versions of the incident, Governor Cabello ordered Chief Constable Marcos de Castro to arrest Tomás for slander. From jail Travieso petitioned for release, claiming that it was the corporal whom he had accused of stealing, not the king or his royal service. Furthermore, he said, Sergeant Urrutia was a drunk, owed him money, held a grudge against him, and so on, implying that the charges against him were strictly a personal matter.

Cabello refused to regard it as such, nor would he accept the seizure of the soldiers' *orejanos* as anything but an insult to His Majesty's representatives. In a back-and-forth exchange of written messages, Travieso worked himself deeper into trouble with the governor. First he maintained that he was within the proper limits of his ranch, acting justly since the governor had said that they could mark and brand calves less than three years old. He gave the usual reasons why so many Las Mulas animals were unbranded, apparently attempting to direct the governor's attention away from his slander charges. When Cabello replied that Travieso had no right to catch *orejanos* on crown lands and that his brother Nepomuceno was once jailed for these offenses, Tomás answered that his deceased brother had not knowingly violated His Majesty's wishes. He maintained that there was an honest difference of opinion about who owned these pastures and that the priests' complaints had resulted in his brother's imprisonment, implying that this alone was sufficient reason for a man to be faced with confinement. He dryly noted that now it was the king, not the missionaries of La Bahía, who must be paid.

The governor was not deterred by this circuitous reasoning. In April he stated that all lands between the Cleto and the Cuchillo were *realengas*, crown lands. Travieso had no title to them, and he called that family's twenty-three-year occupancy "fraudulent possession." He ordered Tomás to present his deed of title and accused him of stalling by claiming that the soldiers' calves were caught on his land. Recognizing the threatening turn the case had taken, Don Tomás admitted that he had no legal instruments. He refused to acknowledge Cabello's subsequent communications, stating he had nothing more to say.

Mid-May found Travieso still in jail, with shackles on his feet. He had some company: Joaquín Menchaca was there with him on smuggling charges. When he was taken to the public auction of his property to satisfy postage and certain legal fees, Tomás "instantly produced" 50 pesos to prevent an attachment. Finally he was granted bail to await the legal opinion of a magistrate in the Valley of San Francisco, which pronounced that Travieso owed a 50-peso fine and an apology. Protesting the second part of the verdict, Tomás finally gave in before the end of the year and apologized to all concerned. By the time the affair was concluded, the head of the Travieso clan had spent 229 pesos in total costs and, like the Menchacas, certainly had no great love for Domingo Cabello.[15]

---

[15] These long proceedings—a classic study of *gachupín* versus creole mentality clashes in the frontier setting—are found in BAT, vol. 110 (lawsuit no. 55).

"They Persist in Their Unjust Claims"   235

In mid-March, 1782, the governor decided to abandon the Cíbolo fort, without mentioning another to take its place. He ordered the installation reduced to ashes "so that at no time may it serve for the enemy to take shelter there and so that no vestige of the place of its location may remain." Two wagons were to be provided by the *ayuntamiento* for hauling back to Béxar the fort's two cannon, religious articles, and so forth. While exasperation over Travieso's quarrel with the Cíbolo soldiers may have been the final straw in his decision to pull the garrison out of the region, Cabello was not acting without the commandant general's authority. Croix had suggested the previous summer that he consolidate all his forces at Béxar, including those at La Bahía and Nacogdoches if he felt that it would save the province from a Comanche bloodbath. While Cabello did not take such drastic steps, the "ill-placed" outpost on the Cíbolo was nonetheless put to the torch. Tomás Travieso would sell no more *orejano* cattle at neighboring Fuerte de Santa Cruz del Cíbolo.[16]

[16] Cabello to *ayuntamiento*, March 11, 1782, BAT, vol. 111. For the fort's ignominious end, see John, *Storms*, p. 630; Robert H. Thonhoff, "The First Ranch in Texas," *West Texas Historical Association Yearbook* 40 (October, 1964):94; and Robert H. Thonhoff, "El Fuerte de Santa Cruz del Cíbolo" (a winner of the 1970 Presidio La Bahía

In May, 1782, Antonio le Blanc, a Frenchman, asked permission to drive 2,000 cattle to Louisiana. Several men of the Blanc name were prominent on the Texas-Louisiana frontier in the late eighteenth century. Besides the cattle agent Antonio le Blanc (called "Blanco" in the Spanish documentation) and Indian trader Louis Pierre Villenfre de Blanc, there was Louis Césaire de Blanc, who served as commandant of the Natchitoches post (1754–62) before his brother-in-law Athanase de Mézières took over (1769–79)—both men having married daughters of the original commander, Louis Juchereau de St. Denis. Césaire's son, Louis Charles, was the post commander from 1788 to 1795, exercising civil and military authority. Not related to these families was the early "cattle king of Southeast Texas," James Taylor White. Said by some to have been named "Le Blanc," White was born in Louisiana in 1789, a member of the numerous clan which relocated to Opelousas from Virginia around 1782. He stated that he brought his family to Texas in 1828. Some accounts have him there in 1819, while others claim that his clansmen were driving Texas herds up the Opelousas Trail as early as 1790. According to researcher Gifford White, the earlier dates are highly unlikely.[17]

Blanc's cattle were to be purchased from Mission Espíritu Santo and gathered from the mission's watering places and pastures on the seacoast. Blanc named José Antonio Curbelo as his representative, who would be responsible for paying duties and meeting other requirements. Cabello responded favorably to

---

Award which I regrettably have not seen). Governor Muñoz (1790–99) wrote the viceroy on February 9, 1791, asking permission to use 200 pesos still on deposit for a new Cíbolo fort for construction of a guardhouse at Béxar. Property toward this purpose had been ceded by Luis Antonio Menchaca, and some of the materials had already been gathered. Plans were drawn up by Pedro Huizar, but the *fiscal* Posada rejected them. A town jail was built, but despite occasional talk another fort was not (Faulk, "Domingo Cabello," p. 108; Carlos E. Castañeda, *Our Catholic Heritage in Texas*, 5:195–96).

[17] Charles Wilson Hackett et al., eds. and trans., *Pichardo's Treatise on the Limits of Louisiana and Texas*, 3:450; Gifford White, *James Taylor White of Virginia and Some of His Descendants into Texas*; R. B. Scherer, Jr., "James Taylor White" (Anahuac Historical Marker research paper, in possession of author); *A Visit to Texas: Being the Journal of a Traveller through Those Parts Most Interesting to American Settlers*, pp. 116–23; Grazing Papers, vol. 1, pt. 2, pp. 201–12, 270–75 (University of Texas Archives).

this petition on May 8, specifying that the gathering must not prejudice citizens of Béxar and their pending lawsuit. Cattle were to be taken from El Tulillo, Las Ánimas, and the pastures between Arroyo Los Nogales and the Guadalupe. He appointed Antonio de la Garza, a citizen of La Bahía, to tally the herd and collect in "hard cash" 2 reales for every head assembled, this being "the rate of duties ordered collected by the Lord Commandant General in these Interior Provinces."

At the end of July, Garza filed his report, stating that the roundup had taken place in one of Espíritu Santo's pastures near the Arroyo de los Yndios, between Los Nogales and the Guadalupe River. His inspection, he said, took place at the corral entrance in the presence of Francisco Hernández, superintendent of the mission, and 1,200 head were counted. Since Blanc had no money, he issued a sight draft for 300 pesos on his attorney Curbelo, who paid the sum on August 23. Upon receipt Cabello issued a permit, the only one on record for 1782 with "Luiciana" as its destination. Apparently this was the last Texas herd intended for Gálvez's army, which had successfully completed its Pensacola campaign and was considering an invasion of Jamaica (which never materialized).[18]

On June 20, 1782, Don Simón de Arocha petitioned Governor Cabello for formal possession to his Rancho de San Rafael. Although his job as lieutenant governor of the province had been given to Antonio Gil Ybarbo upon the founding of Nacogdoches, Arocha was still commandant of the militia at Béxar and a prosperous citizen.[19] Somehow he managed not to become embroiled in the petty controversies surrounding other powerful ranching clans, even though he was related to most of them, and Cabello proudly noted that both Simón and his brother were the legitimate sons of a Canary Island patriarch. In time, however, this family's success caused some resentment in El Rincón, and the fur flew. Simón claimed that since the year

---

[18] *Expediente* no. 98, BAT, 112:10–13. The Bahamas were conquered, however, with the help of an American privateer vessel (John Walton Caughey, *Bernardo de Gálvez in Louisiana, 1776–1783*, pp. 243–47).

[19] John, *Storms*, p. 613; Herbert Eugene Bolton, *Texas in the Middle Eighteenth Century*, pp. 444–46; Castañeda, *Catholic Heritage*, 4:340–43.

1766, "with the verbal permission of Captain Luis Antonio Menchaca, my brother Juan and I have had a little ranch on which to maintain our stock of cattle and horses in the vicinity of the creek called Patahuila." He asked for 8 leagues, bounded on the south by lands of the ranch called San Francisco, on the east by the cluster of trees at the headwaters of the creek called Real de Manuel,[20] on the north by the place called Arroyo del Águila, and on the west by the San Antonio River.

Cabello approved the grant and summoned the neighboring landowners to witness Arocha's claim: Luis Antonio Menchaca (on the south), Joaquín Leal Goras (on the north), and Tomás Travieso (on the east). Leal Goras was the son of Leonor Delgado (the widow of Juan José Flores) by her first marriage to Bernardo Leal. He was also Arocha's brother-in-law. Travieso, whose family's claim to Las Mulas Cabello had recently deemed "fraudulent possession," may have been mollified by this gesture by the governor. The retired captain, while making no objection to Arocha's claim, was careful to reiterate the lines of his Rancho de San Francisco. Menchaca stated that his lands reached from the "Paharitus" creek, which was the lower border of the applicants' ranch, in a straight course to the so-called Real de Joaquín, the limit of his lands. They comprised the Real de Manuel cited in the manuscript, with the exception of the lands granted to Hernández on the margins of the Cíbolo, lands that extended upward for a distance of 1 league in depth and with a river frontage of 4 leagues.[21]

Thus did Don Simón de Arocha and his brother Juan become official landowners with a legal instrument to prove it,

---

[20] Although in northern Mexico the word *real* was used to indicate a mining or military encampment, Bexar County Archivist John Ogden Leal believes that in this context it was a small trading post set up with the government's blessing to do business with Indians or outlying frontiersmen and stockmen. The Real de Manuel appears to have been situated on Marcelinas Creek.

[21] Documents relating to the Simón and Juan de Arocha 8-league grant are found in GLO, 31:47. Plat maps for this and a few other grants made in the San Antonio River valley are also in the General Land Office; many similar documents are to be found in the clerk's office of the county in question. For example, in Wilson County Plat Book 1, p. 87, there is a map of José Cassiano's partition of the Arocha grant in 1840, with field notes by John James, a noted surveyor, land agent, and cattleman who took a herd to California before the Civil War.

something that many of their neighbors in El Rincón apparently never got around to doing. As Virginia Taylor notes, the records for the period are few and fragmentary, most land titles in the San Antonio–Goliad (La Bahía) area being held by "presumed grants." Indeed, the entire collection of papers for this cradle of Texas ranching consists of one General Land Office volume, an assortment of miscellaneous records and incomplete grants, and six land concessions considered actual titles. Only three of the six are recognized as valid: the grant of 1731 to Concepción, San Juan, and Espada; the settlement of 1758 of Luis Menchaca and Andrés Hernández; and the grant of 1788 to Carlos Martínez. Taylor, however, was aware that numerous ranches existed and that many Spanish titles were doubtless issued, calling their conspicuous absence somewhat mysterious. The Simón and Juan Arocha grant for 8 leagues, approved in 1782, is one of the few eighteenth-century ranchos whose boundaries can still be seen on Texas land maps. Others, like Las Mulas—despite the fact that they were equally flourishing settlements—are not there, and even the traces of their perimeters are obscured by the loss of old place-names and the ravages of time.[22]

Commandant General Croix must have recognized the practicality of Cabello's suggestions about the speedy recapture of animals taken by hostile Indians. He revised his *bando* of August 16, 1780, incorporating the governor's provisions, even Cabello's statement that it was rarely possible to overtake enemies within limits of the presidio because they fled so fast with their booty. If recovery was made in twenty-four hours, the captors received only damages incurred; if later, they received 12 reales per mule, 6 per horse, and 4 each for other animals— just as Cabello had stipulated for the province of Texas.[23]

The year 1782 did not see an increase in cattle exports over the previous year: 1,994 head, as compared to 2,084 in 1781, with its Comanche disturbances. Antonio le Blanc's herd of 1,200 bound for Louisiana bolstered the year's figure to

---

[22] Virginia H. Taylor, *The Spanish Archives of the General Land Office of Texas*, pp. 22–28.

[23] Croix, *bando*, June 26, 1782, BAT, vol. 101.

3,194. Two of the eight drives conducted in 1782 give an idea of Cabello's ongoing attempt to administer the cattle laws so as not to expose himself to possible censure. In each instance the red tape became more complex.

In *expediente* 96, Luis Mariano Menchaca sought permission to take a herd of *orejanos* to Coahuila, the stock to be gathered from locations considered crown lands, that is, between the Cíbolo and the Guadalupe. Cabello issued him a roundup permit with the following conditions: he was to pay 4 reales for each *orejano* caught; guarantee the results of this exportation at the rate of 22 reales per head by making bond, putting up real property, and so on; and name a gathering place near the Béxar presidio so that an inspector would have access to the herd without undue difficulty. The taking of branded animals, along with *orejanos*, would be permitted on the sole condition that they were in categories (cows, bulls, bullocks) with a tally of each; Cabello did not want it said that he was permitting the province to be stripped of breeding cows. Altogether, Menchaca's herd contained 243 head (53 with his father's brand and 190 *orejanos*). After he had paid 95 pesos in cash and had received an export license for the entire 243 head, Macario Sambrano stepped forward to act as guarantor for the old captain's son, tendering his person and property to the amount of 522 pesos, 4 reales (22 reales each for 190 head). This was necessary because the unbranded animals in Luis Mariano's herd came from lands "in litigation between citizenry here and mission of Espíritu Santo," as Cabello put it.[24]

Yet another refinement was added to the paperwork soon afterward when a herd was taken by Francisco de Arocha. On this export a sliding valuation scale was applied to *orejanos* based on age. Thus *orejanos* not only must be tallied but must be listed by age to determine the amount of bond required. In addition there was the export ratio requirement on branded stock, not to mention a fee for catching *orejano* cattle, another for catching mesteño horses, and still another for the right to export stock to Louisiana. The cattle business was clearly be-

---

[24] *Expediente* no. 94, June 26, 1782–November 24, 1786, BAT, 112-61.

coming more complicated, no longer something that could be measured in kernels of corn.[25]

In October the *asesor* Pedro Galindo Navarro rendered two opinions which tied up some loose ends but at the same time created new knots and tangles in Croix's original cattle law. First, he threw out Ripperdá's larceny verdict against Juan José Flores (deceased), Jose Andrés Hernández, et al., as premature and invalid.[26] The second ruling was in response to the Monjarás-Padrón drive conducted just as Cabello was taking office in late 1778 and was much more important, for it was a defense of the cattle laws in Texas. Not only did it vindicate Croix's decision to claim the province's mesteño stock for Carlos III, citing precedents for this action elsewhere on the frontier of the Interior Provinces, but it laid down a new set of guidelines for enforcement. This, of course, eventually necessitated the issuance of another *bando*, further complicating the lives of Texas stockmen.

Galindo Navarro's opinion of October 30, 1782, began by providing details on the way New Spain's *mesta* worked. It was an organization of stock raisers, he said, formed in 1529 to regulate practices and resolve conflicts among themselves, as well as to serve their special interests in the society at large. In other words, the *mesta* was much like the modern-day cattlemen's protective associations, and Galindo Navarro seems to have been describing the organization as it functioned on the northern frontier. Two assemblies were held each year, one on January 16, the other on August 31, each lasting ten days. At these times each raiser was notified to bring all mesteños for proper identification of ownership. The Concejo de la Mesta (Council of the Mesta) decided all questions at these roundups. Each owner was required to have a unique mark or brand, but any *mostrenco* stock without a mark was ordered held in safekeep-

---

[25] *Expediente* no. 97, concerning an export of 125 *orejanos* by Francisco de Arocha, does not appear in Cabello's book of *guías*, indicating that more herds went out than those the record substantiates and that there were *at least* nine drives in 1782 (BAT, 112:84).

[26] This fragment of Galindo Navarro's opinion dated October 25, 1782, is found in BAT, 113:64.

ing and that fact publicized. If it was unclaimed by the next assembly, it became His Majesty's property. Thus, once certain technicalities were observed, stray animals and other *mostrenco* or ownerless stock reverted to the king; this was standard procedure.[27]

None of this mattered in Texas anyway, in the *asesor*'s view, because the commandant general's *bando* had claimed all *mostrencos* for the crown to stop the senseless slaughter of stock and other abuses. Since all livestock in Texas was runaway, unbranded, or mesteño, it properly belonged to the Real Hacienda—not only by virtue of being *mostrenco* but also because it was born and raised on the king's unappropriated lands. Croix's *bando* provided for an annual branding, lists (a branding book), and licenses to kill or drive out stock. The object of all this was to make the livestock industry a profitable business by introducing order instead of allowing the brood herds to be indiscriminately depleted.

A precedent for this *bando* existed in California, said the *asesor*. It had been dictated on September 30, 1774, by Viceroy Bucareli to guide Felipe de Neve, who was leaving to take charge of that province. Article 20 of those instructions advised the governor to publish a *bando* giving stock owners four months to mark their animals, after which time those without brands would be declared unowned or runaway. They could then be used to sustain seamen and troops of the district—in other words, revert to the crown. In the California case (decided July 4, 1780) it was ruled that, although runaways might originate from tame stock, if their owners ceased to gather and confine them by rodeo, all animals bred and produced in *realengas* should be declared ownerless and lawfully applied to the Royal Treasury.[28]

---

[27] William H. Dusenberry, *The Mexican Mesta: The Administration of Ranching in Colonial Mexico*; C. J. Bishko, "The Peninsular Background of Latin American Cattle Ranching," *Hispanic American Historical Review* 32 (November, 1952); and Julius Klein, *The Mesta: A Study in Spanish Economic History, 1273–1836*, are among the works on this subject cited by Myres in *Ranch in Spanish Texas*. There seems to be some disagreement as to exactly when the *mesta* was founded, Galindo Navarro's date being a decade earlier than most studies recognize.

[28] See W. Michael Mathes, comp. and ed., *Cattle Brands of Baja California Sur, 1809–1885*, p. 17, for reference to Governor Neve's order dated March 14, 1775,

This, observed the commandant general's legal adviser, was also the law in Texas, except that stockmen there had an advantage not enjoyed by those in California. For a small fee they could gather ownerless or mesteño stock and profit thereby. Galindo Navarro was at a loss to understand why the inhabitants of Texas were not satisfied with this arrangement; yet they obviously were not. They persisted in their unjust claim of ownership, even though the stock was clearly mesteño and unbranded. They argued that it was produced by their ancestors' livestock, even though the first animals in the province had been paid for by the king. But the *asesor* would not swerve from the precedent set in California, and he said that Texas raisers must abide by it.

Having dispensed with the legalities of the case, the *asesor* made some specific suggestions to remedy what was rapidly becoming an untenable situation at Béxar. He recommended that Croix keep the January 11, 1778, *bando* in effect but issue a new one giving the raisers four months to confine their stock by rodeo and do the branding. After this period any stock found without a mark would be considered *alzado*, unowned, and mesteño, therefore belonging to the crown. This rule applied even if such animals were found in the summer pastures of raisers, both mission and private. Two books were to be kept, one listing the number branded, the other showing licenses issued. Anyone who rustled cows was to be declared a thief and made to pay the penalty, including forfeiture of animals illegally taken. Wild cows caught and branded must be reported, and the king's duties on them must be paid. Finally, local stock raisers were to receive preference over strangers in the granting of permits to catch wild cows and horses.

Coming back to the incident which had prompted all this wrangling, Galindo Navarro calculated that Fray Escobar at Mission Espíritu Santo owed His Majesty's Mustang Fund 957 pesos, a duty based on the export of 348 *orejanos* at 22 reales per head. Furthermore, the missionary owed fines because he had violated Croix's decree by permitting 400 head of cattle to be

which implemented the viceroy's decision. Although not mentioned by the *asesor*, the decision to "confiscate" wild livestock in California and Texas was likely based on the 1772 edition of the *Recopilación*, which declared all unclaimed minerals or other resources found in the royal domain to be crown property.

gathered without first obtaining a permit. While the fines in this instance would be waived because of Escobar's poverty ("his state and profession"), the *asesor* wanted 957 pesos collected, if not from the mission then from those individuals who had bonded themselves in the transaction, and placed in the chest with three locks. Such firm action was necessary to prevent similar cases in the future, and offenders were to be warned that in the next instance they would not be dealt with so lightly.[29]

The commandant general forwarded this opinion to Governor Cabello with a cover letter marked number 630. The letter noted that several neighboring ranches had sent him an *instancia* in 1780 (probably the May 13, 1780, rancher protest on the export of Juan José Flores), that he was in receipt of the governor's letter number 418 asking for a disposition, and that the *asesor*'s opinion on these matters was enclosed. Croix wanted its provisions put into practice. But, as has been observed, it was one thing to order a law enforced and another, entirely different thing to accomplish the feat, especially when the people of an entire province stood shoulder to shoulder in opposition.[30]

Cabello did not rush to promulgate this decision; it would take him six months to do so. Doubtless other problems occupied his attention, such as deteriorating relations with the Lipan Apaches and reports that they were planning a huge parley with the Tonkawas to secure guns. Then there was the annual branding, which he announced on November 12, again appointing Macario Sambrano commissioner. The gathering areas were also the same, but only *orejanos* less than two years old were exempted from duties, "since such calves could have been frightened away in roundups that have been made." A tally was to be kept on *orejanos* two years and older.

Sambrano discharged his duties promptly. Gathering the ranchers at Las Mulas four days after Cabello declared it the opportune time for branding, he gave them instructions. A month later the roundup was finished and a report prepared. Oddly, it

---

[29] Galindo Navarro's important ruling of October 30, 1782, is found in *expediente* no. 89, covering the Monjarás-Padrón export case, BAT, 76:54–72.
[30] Croix to Cabello, decree, November 5, 1782 (no. 630), ibid.

shows the same number of *orejanos* that were taken during his first year as commissioner. In the report the gathering operation is grouped under four ranches, which provides information about the cluster of families associated with each establishment, by either marriage or proximity. They were Las Mulas, San Bartolo, San Francisco, and PataGuilla; Mission Valero's La Mora Ranch gathered in conjunction with the Menchaca sweep. The leaders, in both branded and owned stock, were as shown in table 6. Las Mulas remained at the top of the list. It will be noted that, while Mission Valero's Mulberry Tree Ranch gathered with the retired captain's crew, it branded more than any other establishment, indicating a certain vigor even when its sister missions were no longer taking part.[31]

TABLE 6. Report of Roundup, December 20, 1782.

Ranch	No. Stock Branded	No. Stock Owned
Las Mulas	346	1,050
San Bartolo	375	841
San Francisco	290	758
La Mora	473	633
PataGuilla	179	505
Totals	1,663	3,787

SOURCE: "Report of Macario Sambrano," December 20, 1782, BAT, 89:150–55.

Unfortunately, this is the last detailed report of branding activities found in the Béxar Archives, although Cabello's *expediente* 80 continues until the end of his term and contains

---

[31] *Expediente* no. 80, "Concerning Branding," November 12, 1782, and "Report of Macario Sambrano," December 20, 1782, BAT, 89:150–55. The "clusters" were as follows: Rancho de San Bartolo: José Macario Sambrano, Josef Andrés Hernández, Joachín de la Garza, Francisco Móntes de Oca, Santiago Seguín, Juan (José) Flores, Marcos de Castro, and Mariano Guerra; Rancho de Las Mulas: Francisco Travieso, Tomás Travieso, Francisco Xavier Rodríguez, Marcos de Zepeda, Vizente Flores, Joachín Flores, Juan Andrés Travieso, Francisco Rodríguez, Pedro Granados, Miguel Gortaris, and Clemente Delgado; Rancho de San Francisco: Captain Luis Antonio Menchaca and Rancho La Mora; Rancho de PataGuilla: Don Simón de Arocha, Julián de Arocha, and Joachín Leal.

a fragment for 1783. Three days after Alcalde Sambrano submitted the tally of 183 *orejanos* and 8 mesteños caught, Cabello reminded him of his responsibility to see that the duty of 93 pesos, 2 reales, was collected and put in the chest. Manuel Delgado had just been elected ranking alcalde, and the money could be delivered to him. The governor wanted no delays, figuring that since the residents had already realized income from the roundup His Majesty's interests must be pressed now, before the "profits" evaporated.[32]

Unable to prevent the Apache-Tonkawa meeting on the Guadalupe, Cabello sent his versatile interpreter, Andrés Courbiere, to spy on the parley, which finally broke up on Christmas Day, 1782. The able Frenchman managed to disguise himself, penetrate the gathering, and later report that the Apaches brought 3,000 horses to trade for guns, many with Spanish brands. He said that a great pile of bones marked the spot, reckoning that they ate more than 4,000 cows, branded and mesteño, while carrying on their trading and talks about a united war against the Spaniards. It was perhaps of some consolation to the governor that the Apaches had to herd several thousand ponies back home, firearms being in short supply.[33]

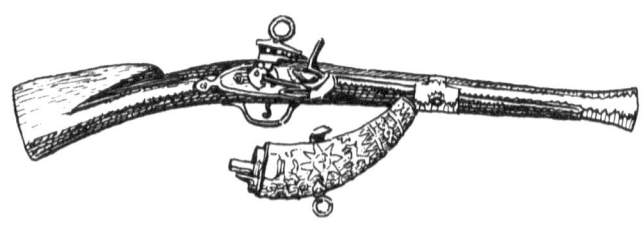

In January, 1783, José Antonio Curbelo left for Spain bearing gifts from Governor Cabello and the province of Texas to His Majesty, Carlos III. It has been surmised that Cabello wanted to ingratiate himself with the king by sending two bison bulls and four cows for the royal zoo, choosing Curbelo to conduct

---

[32] Cabello to Cabildo, December 23, 1782, BAT, 114:78.
[33] John, *Storms*, pp. 635–36.

this delicate mission. As it turned out, only two of the exotic animals (a bull and a cow) survived the ocean voyage, but the king was enthralled enough to appoint Curbelo a lieutenant in Béxar Presidio and allow him an astounding 10,000 reales (1,250 pesos) for his trip from Cádiz to Veracruz and another 300 pesos to get him home from there. In spite of His Majesty's pleasure at receiving the bison, the governor of Texas was instructed henceforth to refrain from sending any more animals abroad, not even a burro. This reprimand we can be certain diminished Curbelo's stature in the eyes of his fellow Bexareños not a whit, given their admiration for his grand achievement.[34]

By February, Cabello had become convinced that the policy of giving gifts to the hostiles was pernicious because it fostered greed rather than gratitude. He argued that it actually encouraged the Indians to steal livestock and invited other troubles associated with the contraband trade, but his protests did not fit well with Croix's plans for conciliating *los norteños*. Also, the old French trader Nicolás de la Mathe had convinced the commandant general that he was the man to utilize a system of trade and presents whereby the northern tribes could be kept quiet and attached to Spanish interests. For those services La Mathe would receive certain considerations, such as the right to export cattle to Louisiana at bargain prices and other trade concessions. Odie Faulk, in his study of Domingo Cabello's administration, credits La Mathe's work among *los norteños* for keeping the region relatively peaceful in 1782, indicating that the Frenchman perhaps earned the cattle concessions that Croix granted him.[35]

The year 1783 saw the arrival at Mission Espíritu Santo of the dynamic Fray José Mariano de Cárdenas, an appointment which he had received from the College of Zacatecas in August, 1782. In a report dated February 27, 1783, Cárdenas provides interesting insight into the stock-raising activities of his new mission. He blamed hostilities by the Lipan Apaches for much of Espíritu Santo's misfortunes, saying that they had begun to deci-

---

[34] Frederick C. Chabot, *With the Makers of San Antonio*, pp. 155–56.
[35] John, *Storms*, pp. 638–39; Faulk, "Domingo Cabello," p. 51.

mate the herds in 1781. Of the mission's *bueyada* (oxen) the Lipans had left only 20 yoke. Cattle suffered most since the Indians entered pastures at will, butchering freely "as if the cattle were theirs." Father Cárdenas was at a loss to explain why the governor did nothing about the situation, accusing Cabello of ignoring the settlers' problems by "protecting" the hostile Indians. In addition to Apache depredations, Cárdenas charged that the citizens of Béxar had rustled "many herds, and especially, in this year of 1783, they have stolen large numbers of *orejano* stock," presumably taking the stolen herds to Louisiana.

From August, 1782, until the following February 16, just before his arrival, the priest noted, 3,000 head had been collected by mission vaqueros, and another 6,000 branded head were estimated to be in the brush. The latter were hard to gather because of the open terrain—and the Lipans. Of *ganado menor* there were few more than 600 left. Despite his cattle figures, Cárdenas pronounced Espíritu Santo short of stock, saying that the "poor Indians barely have enough cattle to eat." The pastures were virtually "barren" owing to the rustling. Moreover, he complained, what the mission produced would go to the king, since at the end of the commandant general's prescribed term everything which remained *orejano* would become royal property. In this the Bahía priest recognized clearly the inherent threat posed to mission wealth by Croix's cattle law, a threat not mitigated by small concessions like branding extensions.[36]

In March, 1783, a dispute broke out which demonstrates that the families of El Rincón squabbled among themselves, not just with outsiders. Mariana Curbelo, the widow of the late Vicente Álvarez Travieso (and the aunt of José Antonio, who escorted the royal bison), charged her son-in-law Francisco Flores and his son Vizente with causing serious harm to her stock. They were gathering cattle from her ranch, Las Mulas, and "the crown pasture lands set aside for us to make roundups

---

[36] Cárdenas, "Report on Espíritu Santo," February 27, 1783, ACZ, roll 3, frame 3481. Since Cárdenas mentions the commandant general's four-month branding extension, saying that it expired at the end of December, it seems that this report either came in early 1784 (not 1783) or was subsequently revised.

at appointed times." Young Vizente, she maintained, probably had two hundred such head of *orejano* stock in a corral at the ranch "El Chayoin" (doubtless Rancho de Chayopines). In response Cabello cited Vizente for gathering in violation of Croix's *bando*, turning a family dispute to his own purpose. Vizente, not one to back off from a fight, countercharged his cousin Francisco Travieso with entering the pastures of Mission Espíritu Santo and taking cows at Los Olmos and *cañada* El Quatralbo.[37]

This affair dragged on for years without settlement, and another lawsuit launched in May, 1786, indicates that all was not well among the heirs of Travieso's Las Mulas Ranch, a situation which worsened after Doña Mariana's death in March, 1785. The old *alguacil*'s son-in-law Francisco Xavier Rodríguez protested the sale of Las Mulas to Tomás, son and executor of Don Vicente's estate. Rodríguez claimed that there were four documents which proved that the ranch belonged to all the heirs and not just to Tomás, who held title by virtue of having traded two horses to Jacobo Hernández for his share of the upper Hernández grant. Rodríguez maintained that the trade was illegal because no north–south boundaries were stipulated in the deed, which said only that the land was between the San Antonio River and the "Sívolo." The lands in question had been in litigation from 1755 to 1758 (the time of the trade) and thus could not be sold "free from encumbrances." Rodríguez's suit asked that the other heirs be granted access to Las Mulas, revealing what was really at stake: grazing rights and the *orejano* stock found on its vaguely defined pastures.[38]

Routine cattle affairs occupied Cabello's time during the first half of 1783. In June, Francisco Guerra was fined for catching and killing cattle without the king's license, even though the cattle killed were a paltry four head. Francisco, who at age nineteen had been a star witness in Ripperdá's first rustling trial, was charged 2 pesos, 4 reales, for each animal, plus a fine of 4 pesos each for violating the *bando*, plus the costs of the soldiers sent

---

[37] Proceedings ". . . for Branding against Provisions of the *Bando* . . . ," BAT, 116:1–16.
[38] BAT, 140:110–42; see also BAT, vol. 29a.

to catch him—three days' time at 1 peso a day for the *cabo* (corporal) and 4 reales a day each for the three privates. This came to 35 pesos, but since Guerra had no money, a portion of his salted meat, tallow, and fat was sold, bringing 36 pesos to satisfy the judgment. Francisco's woes were not over, however. Sometime later he was caught selling three *orejanos* for which he had not paid the fees. For second offenders the fines were more severe: 8 pesos plus forfeiture of the illegally captured animal (or its value). This time six horses and a mule were confiscated and sold at auction to pay the fine of the errant son of pioneer cattleman Miguel Guerra.[39]

Evidence began to emerge about this time that the concept of expanded trade with Louisiana—specifically the livestock trade—was in trouble. On May 24, 1783, the *asesor* advised Croix that although he lacked official documents prohibiting such commerce, some controls were necessary in view of the difficulties which had been experienced in the smuggling case of José Félix Menchaca, Juan de Ysurieta, and their companions—and in other suits of like nature. After reviewing the precedents which had been set during Ripperdá's administration, Galindo Navarro turned to the king's ruling of June 13, 1776, which had "virtually permitted" the traffic of cattle and horses between these two provinces, and on the basis of which instructions had been relayed to Cabello authorizing a trade in livestock and imposing a moderate tax of 2 reales a head to defray war expenses.

The problem, said the *asesor*, derived from the fact that there were no mines in Louisiana, and hence no source of coin. This meant that the Texans who exported cattle were obliged to accept "worthless" paper as payment or to barter their herds for goods and merchandise, all readily available in Louisiana. This the citizens gladly did because they had so few stores at home that could provide these items. But when they attempted to introduce these bartered goods into Texas, they violated His Majesty's trade laws, and the *asesor* believed it "indispensable that we designate the penalties which should be imposed in

[39] BAT, 119:17.

order to avoid this situation." Notwithstanding this serious obstacle, he believed that the future of Texas was in livestock and suggested that the industry be promoted.

It was pointless for the inhabitants to farm above the subsistence level because they could not profitably export agricultural produce, owing to the risk of Indian attacks, the great distances involved, and the small amount of revenue that grains generated when sold in Coahuila, Nuevo León, and Nuevo Santander. These considerations "leave only one solution," wrote Galindo Navarro: that Texas should concentrate on stock raising, for cattle were easier to transport. Because of the shortage in Louisiana, cattle sold at twice the price as in Coahuila, and Texas stockmen preferred the new market despite its greater distance and many risks. If only the bothersome matter of official trade policy infractions could be solved, an interprovincial livestock commerce would greatly benefit these regions. Otherwise, said the *asesor*, the punishments necessary to police such infractions would depopulate them.[40]

Ignoring his legal adviser's wry wit, Commandant General Croix wrote José de Gálvez the following month, lavishly depicting the prospects of trade. He cited Rubí's description of the "admirable fertility" of Texas, where "in the expansive grasslands you can see great multitudes of cattle and horses produced from the tame stock of the colonists." Athanase de Mézières's endorsement of a commerce in these animals with Louisiana was well known, said Croix, emphasizing that flour, tallow, lard, hides, and meat, "which are the products that are in abundance," could be sent to New Orleans by boat all the way from Bucareli on the Trinity River. This traffic would greatly develop Texas, as would cattle drives overland, having the additional benefit of thwarting the profits of foreigners "who by virtue of Louisiana's necessity provide them with such items." But contraband with the English could not be raised as an objection to trade between the Interior Provinces and Louisiana, argued Croix, because the English had been expelled from the banks of

---

[40] Galindo Navarro to Croix, May 24, 1783, AGN, Provincias Internas, Hackett Transcripts, 182:44–49.

the Mississippi. Thus some of the "just causes" that had led His Majesty to prohibit commerce in the past were no longer present.

The commandant general registered his determination to keep pressing this issue until he received a favorable ruling, even in view of the difficulties arising from a lack of hard cash in Louisiana, as noted by the *asesor*. He stated that he could find no royal regulations that specified penalties on the introduction of bartered goods and asked Gálvez—in advancing the idea of trade to the king—to consider all aspects of the case, whose merits outweighed such minor considerations. This Gálvez did, but Croix soon left the northern frontier for the viceregency of Peru, leaving his concerns with cattle on the Louisiana-Texas border far behind.[41]

Cabello may have been slow in issuing a *bando* in response to the *asesor*'s ruling of the previous October 30, but, as in all other things, he went through the motions of compliance. He acknowledged receipt of the commandant general's cover letter, and then in a decree he ordered a file set up, and on April 10 he issued a writ reminding himself to compose and publish a *bando*. Yet it was another three months before his *gobernador* (*bando* or decree) was released, which translated the lord assessor's ruling into law—four and a half years after the Monjarás-Padrón cattle drive to Coahuila had kicked up the dust.[42]

The new *bando*, dated July 10, 1783, and published in Presidio Béxar three days later, contained twelve articles for the regulation of ranching in Texas. If Croix's original *bando* was the foundation of Texas cattle-industry regulation, this document must be considered the ground floor. It consolidated Croix's initial concept and, because it represented a tightening of the screws, set the stage for another round of even more vehement protests. Ironically, it forced the mission and private raisers to put aside their infighting and speak in unison against the king's claim to "their" cattle. The assessor, Galindo Navarro, had much to learn about the cattlemen of Texas—in cassocks or

[41] Croix to José de Gálvez, June 2, 1783, ibid., pp. 36–42.
[42] *Expediente* no. 89, BAT, vol. 76.

buckskins—if he seriously believed they would yield their rights without a tenacious struggle.

Cabello's version of Galindo Navarro's approach, as delivered to the citizens of Texas, can be summarized as follows: All mesteños belonged to the king. The original *bando* called for fines of 2 pesos each for horses and 4 pesos each for cows caught without permission; but rather than everything flowing smoothly in the wake of this just ruling, citizens' claims to mesteño stock had caused problems. Although the *bando* of January 11, 1778, was still in full force, this new one would supplement it. Raisers had four months in which to round up and brand their stock. After such time all unbranded stock, regardless of where found, would belong to the king, and no person could catch it without permission. Once this term had expired, an accounting had to be given of all animals branded, along with the mark used; this information would form a permanent book. So that no problems would arise, each of the ranchers and missions was required to have a unique brand. A branded animal found in another's pastures must be returned to its owner; if it was appropriated, the man who did so was a thief and he would bear the penalties of such, besides paying the owner the value of his stock. Likewise, any man catching, killing, or driving out any unbranded animal, "even though it be in pastures, at watering places, or on lands that are his own property," would also be considered a thief, because the king was the rightful owner. A report must be given of this forbidden stock, after which the captor could do with it as he wished, provided he paid a royal duty of 2 reales for each mesteño horse, 4 reales for each head of *orejano* cattle (not to exceed fifty head). Violators were subject to the penalties set forth in the earlier *bando*.

To protect the wild herds and help raisers enjoy their benefits, the commandant general had authorized the governor to sell this *orejano* stock at the following modest prices: three years or older, 20 reales (2½ pesos); two to three years, 16 reales (2 pesos); and one to two years, 8 reales (1 peso). Calves and heifers were free with the price of the mother. Any person who wanted to buy *orejanos* was to specify in writing the number desired and the place where he planned to gather. His herd would then be inspected. If the buyer was a stranger, he would be furnished a guide for his drive out of the province; local raisers would receive preference in these exports. If all these provisions were observed, the catching of mesteños and *orejanos* was considered legal; otherwise, it was fraudulent, and the stock was considered stolen. Captured wild stock had to be taken to a convenient place for inspection and tally. Violation of this provision carried a fine of 25 pesos.

Holding that ignorance was no excuse, Governor Cabello ended his *bando* by ordering it proclaimed in the streets for three "holidays" in succession, accompanied by the beat of a drum. A copy was to be given to the father president of the Texas missions and to the Béxar city council "so as to make it possible for the cattle breeders and other citizens to read them whenever it may be most convenient for them to obtain full knowledge."[43]

It is difficult to judge the immediate response of the citizens to this *gobernador*, but there is little doubt that their resentment about it slowly turned into an obsession. It was perhaps only natural that they should blame Cabello for the hardships imposed on them, although the ranchers were not remiss in mentioning the contributions of Croix, Ripperdá, and even the *asesor general* to their ruination. Yet in the coming years it was Cabello whom they would hold primarily responsible for the restrictive *bando* of July 10, 1783. They considered him a "more dangerous enemy" than *los norteños* when it came time to collect their scattered stock. They accused him of regarding only the first and not the fourth provision of the commandant general's original proclamation, meaning that their legitimate rights as ranchers to round up their stock were ignored and violated. They blamed Cabello for taking away their unbranded stock and for making their lives miserable with permits, fines, and punishment, declaring that their battle with the governor was worse than the war with the pagan Indians.[44]

[43] Ibid., p. 82. The text of this *bando* was reissued by Governor Muñoz on July 20, 1793, BAM, roll 23, frames 650–58.

[44] "San Fernando Memorial," BAT, vol. 150, item 24.

What especially riled the ranchers was article 9 of Cabello's *bando*, the statement that even *orejano* stock found in their own pastures—"in our own corrals," as they were fond of saying—belonged to the king. They were never able to forgive anyone who pressed this concept, from the commandant general down. They later swore that if Cabello had attempted to control only the stock beyond the Guadalupe and had left them to enjoy their "ancient rights" below it, they could have lived with the usurpation of other prerogatives. It would not have been so bad, they said, if Cabello had construed Croix's decree to mean that wild stock found in remote regions was crown property and had issued permits to worthy citizens to seize it and pay the tax. But they chose to believe (or said they did) that Cabello wrongly informed the commandant general, who then had only the *asesor*'s misguided opinion to rely on. To their way of thinking, all the objectionable features of the *bando* of July 10—including the arbitrary four months' time limit on free branding—were concocted by Domingo Cabello simply to injure them. If the governor now had a simplified set of rules to administer the cattle business, the ranchers finally possessed a focus for determined resistance. That focus was the governor himself.[45]

One thing the *bando* solved was the question of who owned the *orejano* stock in Texas. It was not the missionaries or the first settlers, but the king. This meant that all the pending cases, with their guarantees for the value of unbranded stock taken out of the province, could now be closed, in theory at least. The king was due the money even if the cows were taken in contested pastures, a point made meaningless by the *asesor*'s ruling; if they were unbranded, they belonged to the king, and that was the end of it. Furthermore, in the future when stock was exported either to Louisiana or to markets to the south, the king's Mustang Fund would profit from the transaction—and not by a mere 2 reales but by a handsome 2½ pesos. This money, of course, would come out of the pockets of enterprising drovers and cut deeply into their profits. No longer would they be able to export cows to Coahuila for the 4-real capture duty or to

[45] Ibid., item 16.

Louisiana for 6 reales (4-real duty, 2-real export fee); now it would cost them 20 reales for the privilege. Thus economics as well as principle played a role in the stock raisers' opposition to Cabello's *bando*. They had received an answer to their petitions, but it was far from the one desired by the private cattlemen or prayed for by those in religious habits.

Expediente 91, concerning the export of Juan José Flores of 1780, was one of the long-standing cases which Cabello tried to close now that the ownership question was settled. In August he issued a decree saying that the commandant general had determined that all unbranded cattle and mustang horses living on the pastures of the province now belonged to His Majesty. He ordered that Flores was therefore to be notified that "he is to pay the value of *orejanos* he exported and be reminded of his obligation." Unfortunately, Juan José was out of town and could not be notified. The individual entrusted with this duty tried several times to notify both Flores and his wife, Manuela Aguilar, without success. Neighbors thought that he was at the Saltillo fair. Others merely shrugged; no one was sure when he would be back. So it went with others who knew that the governor, in his new capacity as bill collector for the Mustang Fund, would soon be looking for them.[46]

[46] Cabello, decree, August 9, 1783, in *expediente* no. 91, BAT, 95:69–86.

Father President Salas did not wait for Cabello to come collecting. On September 16 he protested that the branding limitation of four months was too short and argued that the missions should be exempt from the provisions of the *bando* anyway. His formal protest was followed by a petition from retired Captain Luis Menchaca, dated January 10, 1784, which echoed the complaint that four months was not enough time to accomplish branding. Cabello forwarded Fray Salas's protest to the commandant general two days after he received it, with his letter number 673 and a request from Nicolás de la Mathe to be allowed to export 1,000 head of cattle to Louisiana at the former fee of 4 reales.[47]

A disquieting event transpired in the fall of the year while Cabello was waiting to hear about the latest cattle petition. The old captain's son, Miguel Jorge Menchaca, appeared near the junction of the Medina and the San Antonio rivers dressed as an Indian. He accosted a convert from Mission Espada and asked where the king's horse herd was pastured. Miguel told the Jacame Indian that he had been living with the Comanches for more than two years. Then he left with some of his Indian friends, members of a tribe the mission neophyte could not identify. The same day, Gaspar Flores spotted Menchaca northeast of Béxar while he was out hunting horses. There was no doubt this time, for Gaspar had worked in the captain's household and knew Miguel. After chatting and inquiring about his family, the renegade rode off to rejoin his Indian companions. Cabello was convinced that young Menchaca had come to guide Comanche raiders to Spanish horses, but there was little he could do about it but fret. Part of his anxiety was attributable to a resumption of the Comanche attacks and instructions from above which ordered him to "overlook insults by the Indians."[48]

Frustration was evident in the governor's instructions for the annual branding. He again appointed Macario Sambrano to

---

[47]Salas to Cabello, petition, September 16, 1783, *expediente* no. 89; Cabello to Neve, letter no. 673, September 18, 1783, both in BAT, vol. 76.
[48]John, *Storms*, pp. 644–45. In a letter of April (?), 1784, Miguel Jorge Menchaca's appearance with the Indians was noted, along with the information that he had fled in April, 1781, and had a "big potbelly" (BAT, 125:57).

oversee the roundups and make sure that the ranchers did not enter *realengas* or catch any cattle other than those legitimately branded and their suckling calves. Cabello accused the owners of not complying with his *bando* of July 10 and its specified term: "Instead they have used all the period up to the present to wantonly drive and catch cattle, keeping them to the detriment of the royal income." The ranchers' excuse that they had many *alzado* cattle owing to lack of opportunity to gather them would no longer work. In every previous year the chance had been available, he noted. But should Sambrano think that there were branded cattle with unmarked calves in *realengas* or their watering places, he was authorized to let the owners go in to get them. They were not to overstep this generosity and catch nonsuckling *orejanos* because on these a tax was due.[49]

On November 28, in one of the wettest, coldest stretches of weather anyone could remember, Sambrano called his fellow ranchers together at San Bartolo and informed them of the governor's ill humor. Doubtless their disposition was not much better. The annual roundup's dismal totals certainly reflect it (see table 7). The branding commissioner's report tried to explain: "Totals between Cíbolo and San Antonio River only" and "totals do not include those impossible to round up owing to insufficient time."[50] But Cabello was not fooled; the old captain's ranch was in El Rincón, yet his vaqueros did not ride, nor did the vaqueros of some of the other ranchers. The governor wrote: "Despite the slowness and carelessness noticed—in that not all the ranch owners have done their brandings as they were supposed to—let these proceedings be entered." He noted that since no *orejanos* were caught no duties were involved.

By February of the new year Cabello was able to report to the new commandant general, Felipe de Neve, that the Mustang Fund was growing, slowly but surely: at the end of 1782 it had contained 2,499 pesos, and in 1783, including fines, it had

---

[49] *Expediente* no. 80, "Concerning Branding," Cabello to Cabildo, November 24, 1783, BAT, vol. 89.

[50] Sambrano, report, December 28, 1783, ibid., pp. 173–74.

TABLE 7. Report of Roundup, December 28, 1783.

Gathering Place and Rancher	No. Stock Branded	No. Stock Owned
San Bartolo		
José M. Sambrano	65	405
Josef A. Hernández	18	70
Francisco Móntes	6	40
Juan José Flores	40	90
PataGuilla		
Simón de Arocna	170	414
Total	299	1,019

SOURCE: "Roundup Report," December 28, 1783, BAT, 89:173–74.

grown by 976 pesos to a total by the end of the year of 3,475 pesos. Neve later replied, thanking the governor for the increase in the fund and lauding his zeal and efficiency. Neve was appointed interim commandant general in 1783 after Croix became viceroy of Peru, presiding over the Interior Provinces from Arizpe, Sonora, where Croix had established headquarters in November, 1779, after a long illness had kept him in Chihuahua. Neve's "Report on the Interior Provinces," dated December 1, 1783, mentions stock raising and how "mostrencos los Ganados mesteños sin fierro (without brands)" were applied to the Royal Treasury though not without giving rise to lawsuits, especially in Texas.[51]

Galindo Navarro was not long in overruling the protest of Father President Joseph María Salas. The *asesor* deemed the padre's arguments for exempting the missions from the provisions of Cabello's *bando* as without foundation. But in view of the difficulties which Salas said would be encountered—"as did

---

[51] Cabello to Neve, February 24, 1784, BAT, vol. 122; "Mustang Fund entry book for 1783" (fragment), which notes that charges were assessed at 4 reales per bovine head, 2 reales per equine head (BAT, 121:53); Neve to Cabello, May 14, 1784, BAT, vol. 125; John, *Storms*, p. 609; AGI, Audiencia de Guadalajara, 58:34 (Box 2Q142, University of Texas Archives); Max L. Moorhead, *The Presidio: Bastion of the Spanish Borderlands*, pp. 80, 93–94.

Menchaca in his petition of January 10"—by attempting to brand all wild stock in four months, Galindo Navarro agreed to extend the branding period another four months. The new extension was to be published by yet another *bando*, but he warned that after this time there would be no further extensions, nor would any more petitions be received on the matter. All animals found without a mark would then be considered *orejano*, mesteño, and *mostrenco* and belong to the Royal Treasury.

Concerning the proposed concession to Nicolás de la Mathe, the *asesor* granted permission for him to export at the "favorable rate" because of services rendered His Majesty among the Nations of the North. La Mathe could not recover expenses if he had to pay rates of 20, 16, and 8 reales a head as specified by the *bando* of July 10, 1783. Thus he was to pay only 4 reales a head for his export of 1,000 head to Louisiana. But for other individuals the fees specified in article 10 would apply. Galindo Navarro, by granting this exception, opened the door to a scramble by other would-be exporters who were seeking favorable trade concessions in return for their services to the king, real or imaginary.

The commandant general forwarded this decision to Cabello on April 3, 1784, so that its recommendations could be acted upon. Concerning the petition of the Father President Salas, Neve wrote: "It seems he is not only making an attempt for an extension of the four months' time determined by *bando* for livestock owners to proceed with the branding but also trying to have the *bando* itself overturned as it applies to missions."[52] After this perceptive observation, the new commandant general noted that Don Luis Antonio Menchaca had made a similar solicitation in behalf of his Rancho de San Francisco. The situation remained unchanged until the month of August because several other cattle-related problems demanded Cabello's attention—not to mention Neve's insistence that relations with the restless Comanches must be put on a better footing, a thing easier said than done.

---

[52] Galindo Navarro to Croix, March 29, 1784, and Neve to Cabello, April 3, 1784, in *expediente* no. 89, BAT, vol. 76; Commandant General Neve's letter is also found in BAT, 125:35.

The first of these annoyances came early in the year, when the new collector of tithes, Juan Barrera, seized on the idea of making the residents of Béxar pay the church a tenth portion of *orejanos* they caught. Barrera, it will be seen, was an aggressive tithe collector. He first appears in Cabello's "Record of Exports" in December, 1782, when a *guía* was issued to him for 84 head "belonging to the *diezmo*." Other ranchers later suggested that Barrera prospered (at their expense) because of his custodianship of the church's tenth part of their cattle. According to Castañeda, the revenues from tithes were farmed out to individuals like Barrera—that is, to the highest bidders—who paid a lump sum and then were authorized to collect monies from those who owed the church. One of the greatest estates of the northern provinces was built by José Miguel Sánchez Navarro, who started out as *administrador de diezmos*, or administrator of tithes, for Coahuila and Texas between 1762 and 1773. A study of church tithes in the north needs to be done and would doubtless shed much light on Texas stock raising.[53]

In answer to Barrera's petition of January 27, 1784, Fray Rafael José Verger, bishop of Nuevo León (a diocese that included Texas, Nuevo Santander, and Coahuila), issued a dispatch declaring that wild cattle that were now the king's property were subject to tithes. Also, the fees collected for catching, branding, and so on—those placed in the chest with three locks—were subject to the *diezmo*. Bishop Verger, who had assumed office the preceding December, ordered his decision read in the churches of the province so that it would be obeyed. Armed with the bishop's dispatch, Barrera went to the Reverend Pedro Fuentes, pastor of San Fernando, and requested the payment of tithes for the years 1780 to 1783 on all wild stock caught and branded, just as parishioners were duty-bound to pay the church for the yearly branding of their own herds. The curate agreed and went further: May 3 he issued an *exorto* to Governor Cabello asking him to take notice of the bishop's decision and assist Barrera in collecting tithes on His Majesty's du-

---

[53] Castañeda, *Catholic Heritage*, 5:27–28, has an account of this attempt to exact tithes. See also ibid., 3:108; and Charles H. Harris, "A Mexican Latifundio: The Economic Empire of the Sánchez Navarro Family, 1765–1821" (Ph.D. diss., University of Texas, 1968), pp. 23–26.

ties. Cabello politely but firmly answered that he did not consider Bishop Verger's opinion sufficient for charging tithes on such revenue and that he was referring the matter to the commandant general. Pending his decision, aid in collecting the tithe—both on the value of *orejanos* and on the fee for catching them—would be suspended. Cabello forwarded the proceedings to Neve, including a copy of the bishop's letter, stating that he would not comply unless Neve so ordered, and there the matter languished.[54]

Cabello was still trying to collect the 500 pesos that His Majesty was owed by Juan José Flores on his export of 200 *orejanos* in 1780. He was having little success. On May 3 he added a note to *expediente* 91 telling how Flores had left the villa "with power of the citizens, attempting to acquire ownership of *orejano* cattle even though the commandant general has already said that they are His Majesty's." Irritated that Flores would try to go over his head in bearing ranchers' petitions directly to Neve without permission, the governor swore that when Flores returned he would be held accountable. Thinking of all the ways he could punish him, Cabello jotted down the 500-peso action, adding 4 reales per head for catching and applying the new system of valuation retroactively at 20 reales each. Little better than a fugitive from justice, Flores was to be caught and returned to Béxar if he appeared at any of the frontier presidios. Like his father, Juan José the elder, Flores knew how to incur a governor's wrath on the subject of cattle. He wisely did not return to Texas until after Cabello's term of office expired, working for the interests of the stockmen of the province from afar.[55]

It is interesting to note that Cabello chose this particular time to promulgate a decree which stiffened his existing ban on travel. Although Faulk suggests that the governor's concern was probably prompted by the large number of robbers in the province, it would seem that preventing the unauthorized exit of troublemakers like Flores was also a consideration. Cabello decreed that no person, regardless of station in life, could leave his

---

[54] Verger, proclamation, April 19, 1784, BAT, 124:67, and SA, 5:7–11; Fuentes, *exorto*, May 3, 1784, and Cabello, decree, May 14, 1784, both in BAT, vol. 124; Cabello to Neve, letter no. 835, May 20, 1784, BAT, vol. 126, and SA, 5:18–21.

[55] Cabello, May 3, 1784, in *expediente* no. 91, BAT, vol. 95.

place of residence without first obtaining a written license, or pass, from the local justice. The pass had to give such information as the day of departure, the proposed route, and the destination. Mission Indians were to obtain passports from their father superiors, and all transients found without a license would be arrested and taken before the district magistrate, where their goods were subject to confiscation. The governor ordered owners of haciendas, ranches, and way stations not to allow any persons to stay overnight at their establishments without first showing a permit no matter what the pretext, thus attempting to involve the citizenry in the enforcement of his edict. In effect the decree lumped people who went to seek an appeal of Cabello's justice with "wicked malefactors, vagabonds, the vicious, and those who lead evil lives."[56]

Second only to Don Simón de Arocha as a cattle exporter during these years was the old captain's son, Luis Mariano Menchaca. With one brother "banished" to Presidio de Agua Verde[57] and the other a renegade among *los norteños*, Mariano devoted much time to his father's ranch in the decade of the 1780s. By 1783, although he and his wife, María Concepción de Estrada, were shopkeepers in the villa, Mariano was gathering and trailing more cows to Coahuila than anyone else in the province. His two best years were 1783 and 1784, when he exported at least four herds totaling 1,400 head.

One of these roundups took place in the summer of 1784, when Luis Mariano and twenty-five men hunting wild cattle were attacked by a party of Taovayas. The *norteños* took one Spanish horse, barbecued some of their cows, disrupted the roundup, and forced Menchaca's vaqueros to retreat toward La Bahía, where they camped for the night.[58] That was only the beginning of Mariano's troubles. By mid-June he had managed to assemble a herd of 612 animals, 202 branded head and 410 *orejanos*. By far the largest number of branded head (125) be-

---

[56] Cabello, decree, April 30, 1784, in Faulk, "Domingo Cabello," pp. 113–14.
[57] Agua Verde was one of the "line" presidios established by the Royal Regulations of 1772. Located on the San Diego River below present Ciudad Acuña, it was founded by troops pulled out of the Valle de Santa Rosa. José Menchaca became captain there in 1783 following his abrupt transfer by Governor Cabello, but by that time Croix had ordered the garrison moved to the town of San Fernando de Austria.
[58] John, *Storms*, p. 648.

longed to his father, Don Luis Antonio. Some came from Mission Espíritu Santo and Mission Valero, and the rest from various individuals.

After separating the unbranded cattle into four categories, each with different rates, Cabello issued a *guía* for 612 head, omitting 52 *teneros* (calves) but not the corresponding 26 pesos. On June 14 he collected 852 pesos, put the money in his chest, and sent Menchaca on his way to Coahuila. In July, however, Cabello was given a secret denunciation claiming that Menchaca had gathered—and branded—more *orejanos* than he had taken to Coahuila or paid dues on. Part of these *orejanos* he marked and kept at San Francisco, "pretending to own them and not paying fees." These were serious charges indeed, and Cabello knew that if the Menchacas could do such a thing and get away with it, every other rancher in the province would follow suit.

That summer Governor Cabello began gathering testimony on Mariano's activities. In a manner reminiscent of Ripperdá he paraded a series of witnesses before his court, accusing several of them of lying to protect the old captain's son. From Amador Delgado he learned that the branding had been done in shifts, morning and afternoon, and had lasted four or five days. The work had kept eighteen hands busy, along with a boy to keep the irons hot, and perhaps 300 to 400 head had been marked. Other witnesses were questioned, and José Antonio Saucedo's testimony, feigning ignorance, won him a musty corner in the presidio guardhouse. After fifteen days in jail, Saucedo (whose wife was kin to Luis's wife) begged to be released, claiming that he had "got his memory back." He said that two roundups took place: the first produced 600 to 700 head, and the second netted 400 to 500, from which the 410 *orejanos* trailed to Coahuila were cut out.[59]

When Mariano returned from the drive to find himself facing criminal charges, his defense was addressed directly to the commandant general. He gave the circumstances of the case: he had purchased 462 head from the governor, paying 852 pesos; he also paid 600 pesos to eighteen vaqueros at the rate of 1 peso

---

[59] *Expediente* no. 86, commencing May 17, 1784, BAT, vol. 126.

fuerte a day. "Hard cash" was necessary, he explained, because hostiles would not stay away from his roundup. His men shut the *orejanos* in corrals and hid at night, afraid of being attacked, whereupon the Indians came and turned the cattle loose. Then the vaqueros had to come back and round up the scattered stock a second time at extra cost. This was also the reason Mariano had added 202 branded cattle—so that the venture would not lose money. He claimed that the entire affair had nonetheless been conducted to his "great loss and detriment."

Worse, Menchaca told the commandant general, he had come back to find Cabello on his neck. He accused the governor of putting pressure on witnesses and of finding a hand named Tadeo Santos who made a false denunciation so as to "support himself without working." It was no secret that Cabello was much pleased by Santos's allegations; birds of a feather flock together, rashly observed Luis Mariano. "The governor has a grudge against my family," he flatly charged, adding that it was notorious that Cabello had been after the Menchacas ever since he came to Béxar. The governor, he said, had threatened to "pull teeth" of those put in jail, forcing them to change their testimony. "The only branding I did was of calves whose mothers I was taking and were already branded," Menchaca maintained.

Though aware of the impossibility of proving fraud, that is, of finding and proving the origin of animals Menchaca had hidden on his ranch two months before, the governor was still not inclined to let the matter drop. He issued an *auto*, noting that unfortunately he could not say exactly how many head Menchaca should pay the king for. Then he forwarded *expediente* 86 to Neve, accusing Luis Mariano of poaching. Cabello told the commandant general that Menchaca was a troublemaker and that he wanted to make an example of him, convinced that he had been guilty of such violations at other times. In spite of all diligence, he said, "the malice and collusion of these people with one another in such matters is such that they are capable of blinding the most keen-eyed Argus."[60] It was two

---

[60] Cabello to Neve, letter no. 859, August 9, 1784, BAT, 128:21; Neve to Cabello, March 4, 1785, BAT, 131:19–20, concerning concealment of *orejano* cattle belonging to His Majesty, and "surreptitious exportation."

years before Galindo Navarro ruled that this proceeding could not be finally determined. Carefully choosing his words, the *asesor* wrote, "One infers that Menchaca branded three hundred, intending to defraud the government." About all Galindo Navarro could suggest was that Cabello try to make him deposit duties for this number temporarily while the case was being tried: "Do as you see fit." It all came to nothing and was another of the many unfinished cases that Cabello turned over to his successor.

Around the time Governor Cabello was denouncing the old captain's son to Commandant General Neve, another case of *bando* violation was taking form, this one much more serious because Don Luis Cazorla, the captain of Bahía Presidio was thought to be implicated. It began in late July, when Fray Joseph Francisco Mariano de la Garza[61] advised the governor that a cash sale had been arranged of 1,000 head of Mission Espíritu Santo's cattle to Don Francisco de Yermo, official purveyor of supplies for the Coahuila presidios. Yermo was awarded a contract to provision the Coahuila companies of Monclova, San Juan Bautista (where he lived), Agua Verde, and La Babia for four years, starting January 1, 1784. This was part of Croix's attempt to reform the way in which presidios were supplied. By that date Presidio Monclova had been returned to the Villa de Monclova, Agua Verde to San Fernando de Austria (Zaragoza, Coahuila), and La Babia to Santa Rosa (Múzquiz, Coahuila), leaving only Presidio San Juan Bautista situated on the Río Grande. An agent of Yermo's, one Don Blás María de Eca y Múzquiz, had arrived from the Valley of Santa Rosa, and Father Garza asked Cabello to grant him a permit to withdraw the herd, a favor that would be greatly in the interest of the natives at the mission. Replying three days later, Cabello told the priest that the export was acceptable, "provided [the cattle] are of one or another of the brands belonging to the mission."[62] In the event that the

---

[61] Garza was father president in 1782 and 1783 but left Mission San José to return to the Zacatecan college, later returning to help found Mission Refugio (Fr. Marion A. Habig, *The Alamo Chain of Missions: A History of San Antonio's Five Missions*, p. 242).

[62] This statement implies that Espíritu Santo had at least two different cattle brands, one perhaps a road brand. Unfortunately, records in BA and NA apparently do not contain *fierros* used by the missions. Perhaps such marks will be found at the

cattle were unbranded, a permit could not be granted. The reason was supposedly a set of regulations in force between Lieutenant José Santosa (or Santoja), acting commander of the presidio, and the priest at Espíritu Santo, Fray Cárdenas, regarding the counting procedure for *orejanos* branded. But another letter written the same day, July 31, to Bahía Presidio indicates that a fear that *orejanos* would compose much of the herd was the actual reason for Cabello's caution—unless, of course, the exporter wanted to pay 2½ pesos a head for the right to take out *orejano* cattle, something that the reverend fathers at La Bahía assuredly did not want to do. In reply Captain Cazorla hinted that they might be willing to make such an arrangement should it prove impossible to complete the herd of 1,000 head from the branded stock.

In what appears to have been a devious way of setting up Cazorla, Cabello told him that Espíritu Santo should have no trouble filling the contract since he knew that sometime during the middle of the previous year they had branded no less than 2,800 head. Since Cabello could not grant any special favors, he told Cazorla that the fees prescribed in his *bando* of July, 1783, would have to apply but that bulls could be extracted for 12 reales each. The governor closed by urging the captain to keep a close eye on the gathering operation, in view of "misappropriations that have occurred in transactions of that kind."

If Captain Cazorla had any hint of what Cabello was getting at, he certainly did not show it. Perhaps his absence during the years when Croix's original *bando* was taking its toll on the cattle industry accounts for his "everything is under control" report to the governor, which meant, in Cabello's mind, that he had taken the baited hook.[63] Cazorla stated that Múzquiz had departed on August 22 with a herd of 1,000 head, all of them "property of the mission, having been earmarked and branded with their irons." Two sergeants of the garrison, Francisco

Zacatecan college *convento* or in one of the archival collections housed elsewhere, such as the fiscal records kept at San Luis Potosí. It is extremely odd that the brands of the province's most important *criadores* should have passed unnoticed by generations of Texas historians.

[64] Cazorla had just returned to La Bahía Presidio from seven years' duty (1778–84) as inspector of presidios in Texas and Coahuila during Croix's commandancy.

Vásquez and Antonio Treviño, checked everything while the herd was accessible, and it was ascertained that 530 were cows, the rest being bullocks.

Cabello wasted no words on this simplistic portrayal of what had happened at La Bahía. He knew that there was no way that Espíritu Santo could have sold 1,000 branded and marked cattle. When Carlos Martínez bought 50 head from the mission, it could only furnish him 32 branded; when Fray Cárdenas sold 300 head to Felipe Flores, he was unable to get together more than 25 or 30 branded animals. Also, Flores had turned over his herd—279 *orejanos* plus the few branded—to some Indian vaqueros of Espíritu Santo who showed up with an urgent plea from the padre. These were added to 500 others of the same kind that Múzquiz rounded up and was holding in mission corrals in the neighborhood of El Durasno and Las Ánimas.

It seems the governor had laid his groundwork well. Furthermore, in this case Béxar residents would talk, for Múzquiz was a stranger, as was Francisco de Yermo, the other man who was making money on this export. It is uncertain exactly who Don Blás was, but the Eca y Múzquiz name was prominent in the military affairs of Coahuila. Also a roster of the Béxar Presidio, dated December 31, 1787, shows a José Antonio de Eca y "Musques" as third in command. Múzquiz had apparently taken the place of the fugitive Juan José Flores as cattle agent for Yermo, perhaps a factor in the citizens' opposition to the drive. The profits on these *orejanos* headed down to the presidios in Coahuila could have been theirs, calculated the locals. People who met the herd on the trail provided Cabello with damning information, proof that Cazorla's story was far from accurate. Manuel Galbán said that he saw 1,300 head in the herd, at least 300 of them *orejanos*. Young Miguel Ygnacio Gortaris claimed that half of the cattle he saw on the Río Grande were *orejanos*, the other half having brands of Espíritu Santo and Béxar ranchers. Three *peones* who went with the herd said, without explaining their grasp of higher mathematics, that they counted it at the gate upon departure. The tally: 1,314 mature head and 294 yearlings, two-thirds unbranded and the calves totally unmarked. Many of these were later observed on the trail, old, tired-out

"They Persist in Their Unjust Claims" 269

animals, sucklings, or young bulls, none showing marks. The governor reasoned that if these pitiful specimens had not been marked it was altogether unlikely that wild animals in the herd had brands. If they did, it was because they were "freshly branded (as such is the custom at this mission)"—meaning fraudulently.

In mid-September, Cabello charged Captain Cazorla with conspiracy. He calculated that the fraud had resulted in damage to the Royal Treasury amounting to 1,000 pesos and advised Cazorla that he would be held responsible for failing to exact the proper duties. Múzquiz, termed Cazorla's "protégé," was, Cabello said, little better than a rustler. He added, perhaps a bit prematurely, that when the facts emerged and "fraud is revealed" the proceedings would be sent to the commandant general. The "facts" seemed to indicate that the herd was made up mostly of *orejano* cattle. So that they would not be counted as such, they had been branded after the gathering operation by Indian vaqueros and hired hands; thus the required duties could be avoided.

When questioned, the two sergeants testified that Múzquiz's herd was presented for inspection on a plain in front of Espíritu Santo. All 1,036 animals had mission brands and were "very tame." Cabello reprimanded the sergeants, asking how they could tell such a lie. Sergeant Vásquez shrugged his shoulders and suggested that perhaps Múzquiz had switched herds after the inspection—perhaps he obtained *orejanos* later, from a nearby corral. The sergeant noted that all cattle supplied to his company by Mission Espíritu Santo were of this type, that is, unbranded. The soldiers' testimony, given late in September, 1784, settled it for Cabello. Now more than ever he was convinced that all parties concerned had entered into a sinister pact to defraud the king of his rightful duties, swearing secrecy among themselves. Captain Cazorla was fully implicated, as were Blás Múzquiz and Fray Cárdenas, serious charges all.

Cabello forwarded his *sumaria* to the commandant general on December 28 with his letter 18, in which he tempered slightly his earlier condemnations. Cazorla was accused of showing favor to his "protégé" Múzquiz, permitting a sizable export of *orejano* cattle without collecting the appropriate fees. The padre was "led astray" by the captain, he claimed, perhaps realizing that it would not help his case to accuse Fray Cárdenas of criminal activities. This *expediente* also languished until the end of Cabello's administration with little result except possibly to make the governor's position among the mission cattlemen of Texas more untenable. Certainly it could not have helped his working relationship with Croix's hand-picked inspector, Luis Cazorla.[64]

These were not the only two cattle proceedings that made Cabello's life hectic during the latter part of 1784. In fact, it was a period of great activity for everyone connected with the business, from the governor down to the lowliest *muchacho* who kept the branding irons hot. It is reasonable to attribute this flurry of activity to the *asesor*'s March decision overruling the petitions of Father Salas and Luis Menchaca, the acknowledged leaders of both cattle-raising factions. Word had a way of trickling down, and ranching activities took on a sense of urgency. For example, during the period from June to September (always the peak period for cattle exports) at least ten herds totaling 1,839 head received permits, not counting the Múzquiz export.[65]

By this time Cabello had reduced the export procedure to a standardized routine. He even referred to a roundup report submitted to him by his commissioner as a "form letter." It con-

[64] These long proceedings are found in BAT, 127:45–112, under *expediente* no. 85. Selected passages, translated by Martin Henry with explanatory notes, are also in Grazing Papers, vol. 1. Odie B. Faulk, "Ranching in Spanish Texas," *Hispanic American Historical Review* 44 (May, 1965):259, cites Cabello to Rengel (no. 18), dated December 28, 1784, as evidence of "another fund-raising device" which specified a 2-peso-per-head export fee for cattle and horses. It should more properly be noted that the fees of which Faulk speaks had their origin in article 10 of Cabello's *gobernador* of July 10, 1783.

[65] "Record of Exports," BAT, 142:134–35.

tained six price breakdowns for the various types of *orejano* stock assembled at any inspection site. In one instance all commissioner Joaquín Menchaca had to do was fill in the proper blank spaces with his count of Juan José Pacheco's herd. Also, the old days of promising to pay by means of bonds, pledges, guarantees, and so on, were gone. Credit was no longer extended; Cabello wanted hard cash for his chest. The new procedures perhaps had an effect on the class of people who were now able to organize and conduct drives, which were no longer simply a matter of elementary cattle-working skills. Finance was working its way into the picture, a fact doubtless lamented by the crusty old-timers who could remember trailing cows to Coahuila with no strings attached.[66]

The only snag in this smooth-flowing uniformity—assuming that Cabello's bookkeeping and the reports it was based upon were correct—came with an occasional exception to the rule, such as the concession to Nicolás de la Mathe to export 1,000 head at special rates. Rather than exploit this concession themselves, receivers sometimes conferred their privilege on others, doubtless for a price. In September, 1784, Luis Mariano Menchaca (whom Cabello had labeled a troublemaker only the month before) asked the governor's authorization to sell 400 *orejano* cattle "from those which Don Nicoles de la Mate has permission to take from the province." This, claimed Menchaca, was because "Mate" had long ago granted him by contract the right to take a herd to the line presidios. He stated his intention to gather between the Guadalupe and the "Queleto" (Ecleto), where everyone caught *orejanos* with permission. As it happened, Menchaca took only 144 *orejanos* at the Indian agent's bargain price, but then Simón de Arocha became involved in the deal. He had 266 *orejanos* penned at Las Mulas, and the French trader agreed to let him export them for the 4-real fee. Cabello's bookkeeping became even more complicated when Vizente Flores put together a herd, charging off 155 *orejano*

[66] For a sample of drives conducted during this peak period of activity, see the Manuel de Arocha proceedings in BAT, vol. 126; the Santiago Seguín *expediente* in BAT, vol. 127; the Francisco Xavier Rodríguez *expediente* and the *guía* issued to Juan José Pacheco, both in BAT, vol. 128.

bulls purchased from La Mathe at the special duty and then filling in another 140 mixed head at the normal *bando* prices.[67]

On August 1, the beleaguered governor finally got around to the matter of the four months' extension of branding. He wrote Commandant General Neve of his intention to issue a new *bando*, noting that he would use caution "appropriate to my knowledge of the perversity of character of the citizenry here and their innate propensity to misappropriate as much *orejano* livestock as they can." The next day Cabello issued a scathing writ saying that the appeals of Father President Salas and retired Captain Menchaca for an extension of branding time were impertinent and entirely lacking in veracity. Unlike the other raisers, they had delayed doing their branding during the period specified by his *bando* for their own particular ends. Nevertheless, the months of November and December would be allowed for the missions and all other stock raisers to accomplish their branding.[68]

Two weeks later he sent a dispatch to Captain Cazorla ordering him to collect the 957 pesos which Galindo Navarro had ruled were due from Mission Espíritu Santo on the Monjarás-Padrón export. Unfortunately, Father President José Francisco Mariano de la Garza could not be reached by the Bahía captain because he had returned to Mission Espada. On October 21 the governor sent alcalde Francisco Xavier Rodríguez to Espada to inform him of Espíritu Santo's obligation to the king. Fray Garza sent word back that he would get the mission to comply, but there is little evidence that the father president intended this assurance as anything but a delaying tactic.[69]

On October 26, 1784, Cabello issued a *bando* containing five articles, officially granting the cattle raisers an extension for branding as recommended by the *asesor*'s opinion of March 29, the commandant general's order of April 3, and his own writ of

---

[67] BAT, 128:44. The "Queleto" mentioned by Menchaca was doubtless either the Cleto (modern Ecleto Creek) or the Coleto—from his description most likely the former.

[68] Cabello to Neve, August 1, 1784, BAT 128:1; Cabello, writ, August 2, 1784, *expediente* 89, BAT, vol. 76.

[69] For these feeble collection attempts made in the late summer of 1784 see BAT, vol. 76.

August 2. Mentioning that the new order had its origin in the protests lodged by the Most Reverend Father Salas, minister of Mission Valero and president of the Texas missions, and also the retired captain Don Luis Antonio Menchaca, Cabello emphasized that the commandant general in a decree of binding authority had ruled these protests out of order by sustaining his own *bando* of July 10, 1783. "However, in view of the before-mentioned petitions, and others that might be presented in the future, His Excellency has been pleased to grant a two months' extension to the time limit set for branding the before-mentioned wild cattle."

Since the governor was empowered to specify the time at his own discretion, he set forth the following conditions. From November 1 to December 31, 1784, a roundup would be held in accordance with article 5 of his previous *bando*. Exhibiting a disdain for cold weather and the annual religious festivities, Cabello wrote: "The months of the year best suited to undertake the before-mentioned branding of cattle are the months of November and December." Only property owners were permitted to brand. When the two months had expired, a list must be given of the number taken and the brand used by each owner; there was a 50-pesos fine for noncompliance. At the end of this extension no more branding could take place. Because a special period had been set aside for a suitable time of the year, that is, the annual fall roundup, branding at other times was strictly forbidden regardless of the established custom at some ranches. Cabello finished by saying that his *bando* of July, 1783, was still in full force except for the new extension of time.

In regard to article 2 it should be noted that owning property was now a condition of eligibility for participating in the branding operation. A person must be the rightful owner of the rancho or hacienda on which he gathered stock, "under strict interpretation of the law." According to Cabelló, this provision was necessary because it was a matter of well-attested knowledge that persons who were not themselves landowners engaged in plundering expeditions to the detriment of rightful owners of such properties. Although stiff penalties were provided for violators, the article was no doubt broadly interpreted by the ranchers themselves, regardless of the incompleteness of *papeles* and *títulos* under which they claimed ownership to their lands. Occupancy was considered sufficient to all, except possibly the governor and a few ranchers fortunate enough to have their papers in order. Certainly families like the Traviesos believed that their right to brand was unimpaired by such technicalities. Cabello's closing remarks made it clear to all missions, owners of ranchos, and cattle breeders that, while they had been granted this two-month extension, they had not been granted and would not be allowed, any further extension of time for the branding of wild cattle and horses found in their recognized pastures:

No further argument and pleading will be permitted upon the same subject, and the Government hereby officially classifies as wild all cattle and horses found unbranded and unmarked after the expiration of the before-mentioned period of grace, and this classification will apply regardless of whether or not the animals in question are found in pastures and at watering places that are the individual property of a mission, rancho, or hacienda belonging to any citizen whatever of this province, in view of the fact that all such cattle and horses are to be regarded as the property of the crown.[70]

Despite this emphatic statement on the subject of future petitions, Fray Garza submitted one the following week, attacking the governor's latest missive on a number of points. First the father president asked that the two-month period be moved to another, more favorable time, as from mid-August to mid-October of the next year—which would allow them to take advantage of finding "the beasts" in their summer pastures. Claiming the governor's ruling would despoil them, Fray Garza maintained that the commandant general's intention was to help the missions accomplish their rights. The months of November and December were the regular time for branding anyway, he argued, without the commandant general's approval. Therefore, the special dispensation should not be applied to this period but should go beyond it; otherwise it would be of no

---

[70] Cabello, *bando*, October 26, 1784, ibid.; Grazing Papers, vol. 1, contains Henry's annotated translation.

added benefit. By simply granting what was already theirs by right, the governor was violating the spirit of the commandant general's ruling.

Fray Garza chided Cabello for trying to force the cattle raisers into a rigid, inflexible program. The commandant general should be told that it was customary to grant breeders all the time necessary to do their branding, without a limit of one, two, or three months. Normally their roundups took place from August to October, and at some missions the branding required two months to finish and at others three. The time varied according to the situation, said the priest, and since the idea behind the commandant general's extension was to expedite rather than hinder the orderly management of the livestock of the province, Cabello's *bando* was not in accordance with his superior's wishes. To make things worse, the missions did not have enough horses, and the few they had were weak from drought. He asked that the missions receive another two-month period later while being allowed to go on their "regular" roundup at the present time. It must be admitted that this request had merit, for Galindo Navarro's opinion of March 29 authorized a *four*-month extension, which the governor then arbitrarily cut in half. He could have granted another two months, but he was not so inclined. Cabello returned Fray Garza's petition on the same day it was submitted, November 3, with the notation that there was no reason to grant what he solicited.[71]

There is no indication that a regular, scheduled branding took place either in this period or in the following year. When he left office in November, 1786, Cabello claimed that it was not possible to determine the number of cattle branded over the past two years but believed it certain that branding had taken place owing to the citizens' avarice, "with many *orejanos* taken as furtively as possible," and to avoid payment of duties.[72] There exists, however, a *cuaderno* (memorandum) of wild animals caught by citizens in the year ending 1784. It is a monthly recap

---

[71] Garza to Cabello, petition, November 3, 1784, and Cabello to Garza, November 3, 1784, BAT, vol. 76.

[72] *Expediente* no. 80, "Concerning Branding," entry of November 28, 1786, BAT, vol. 89.

listing many individuals and showing a total duty of 4,010 reales (501 pesos), which sum was noted as being in the chest. If the citizens were charged 4 reales a head, this figure would indicate that 1,000 *orejanos* were taken during the year, certainly a dramatic increase over the small number reported in the annual fall roundups through 1783. An accounting for the Mustang Fund also shows that the new export duties were beginning to produce some of the revenue hoped for by Croix when he launched his regulations for "good government" back in 1778: 4,253 pesos were raised in 1784 alone, enabling Cabello to pay Captain Antonio Gil Ybarbo three years' back salary and still show an increase of 2,656 pesos over the end of 1783.[73]

While the governor was involved in disputes over cattle with the private raisers, the mission fathers, and even his own captain at Bahía Presidio, the ambitious Neve died, in November, 1784, and his place as interim commandant general was taken by the more realistic Joseph Antonio Rengel.[74] Rengel, a former commandant inspector, was no stranger to the northern frontier. Knowing the difficulties faced by subordinates, he tended in his instructions to address what was attainable, rather than the lofty. For example, on December 9, 1784, he ordered all livestock recaptured from the Indian enemies returned to their owners without collection of the sums formerly charged under the name of removal fees. This eliminated the unwieldy system of rewards proposed by Croix in his ruling of August 16, 1780, which was impossible to administer fairly.

Further streamlining Croix's *bando* 75, Rengel provided that owners could appoint agents, with a power of attorney and a copy of their brands, to reclaim lost stock. To facilitate the process, lists would be made of recaptured animals, their brands, and so on, and posted for four months at certain places,

---

[73] For the *cuaderno*, see BAT, 129:82; the report of "*orejano* catching" for the year ended 1784 is in BAT, 130:18. The report of *orejanos* for the year January 1 to December 31, 1784, shows the balance at the end of 1783 as 3,475 pesos; the balance at the end of 1784 is shown as 6,131 pesos, less Gil Ybarbo's salary for 1782–83 of 1,097 pesos and his salary for 1784 of 500 pesos, leaving 4,534 "liquid" pesos in the box.

[74] John, *Storms*, p. 654; see also Moorhead's evaluation of these two men (*Presidio*, pp. 95–100).

including Monclova, Santa Rosa, and Béxar. The reward was simply this: if the animals went unclaimed at the end of the four-month period, they were forfeit and credited to their captors. To protect the ownership rights of these individuals, even if the previous owner appeared later and demanded them, the rewarded animals were to be given the same countermark that Croix had specified (a brand that later cattlemen might call an "AR connected"). Cabello soon issued a *bando* putting Rengel's changes into effect, noting that livestock recaptured from the Indians in campaigns was now to be returned to owners without collection of the fee formerly charged.[75]

Concerning Cabello's *bando* on a time extension for branding, the new commandant general acknowledged receipt of the governor's letter (no. 13) on the last day of 1784. Rengel approved the two-month period allowed, especially approving article 5 with its finality on the subject of no additional extensions. "Yet," he wrote, "if necessary you may extend more time to them."[76] The governor, already convinced that his liberality was being taken advantage of by the stockmen and that men in high places were conspiring to prevent a fair administration of the cattle laws, was not disposed to be more generous. He was becoming very weary of the ingratitude and insolence manifested by his subjects on the cattle question. Perhaps thinking that the worst of the protests were over, Cabello was about to have a rude awakening. The protests were only beginning.

[75] Rengel to Cabello, December 9, 1784, BAT, 129:53–54; Cabello, *bando*, February 14, 1785, BAT, 130:91.
[76] Rengel to Cabello, December 31, 1784, BAT, 129:113.

8
"COULD THEY BUT BE RESTORED"

Protests Abounding

In terms of Indian policy, the year 1785 was the most successful year of Domingo Cabello's administration, for he made substantial gains in achieving peaceful relations with the Nations of the North. After initial successes in the spring with Taovayas, Wichitas, and allied groups, his crowning achievement came in October, when a treaty was at last forged with the Comanches. It was a concord that the ranchers of Texas described as "unexpected" and "miraculous," ending for the most part a war that had raged spasmodically for twenty years. Cabello, who claimed that his stay in Texas had broken his health, consoled himself for reverses on the domestic front with such triumphs in Indian diplomacy. In May, 1785, believing his term of office almost over, the governor wrote Rengel that his Comanche peace overture was a vast and difficult project but one which "appears to me . . . the greatest service to God, to the King and to all these provinces."[1]

[1] Cabello to Rengel, May 20, 1785, BA. Elizabeth A. H. John, *Storms Brewed in Other Men's Worlds: The Confrontation of Indians, Spanish, and French in the Southwest, 1540–1795*, pp. 655–68, says that his Comanche peace negotiations were "the crowning triumph of the year, indeed of Cabello's whole term."

The year also saw churchmen zealously engaged in working toward a reversal of Croix's cattle law and all subsequent *bandos* based upon it. Their arguments, while containing much of value to the student of Texas ranching, must be regarded as a blending of wishful thinking and fervent prayers tempered by the grim realities they faced. Consequently, their writings on what ailed the mission system—including its ranching activities—tend to be one-sided, slightly bending the truth to fit the needs of God's holy work. The priests, entrusted with the temporal welfare of their converts, were no doubt sincere in their efforts to establish the missions' ownership of wild cattle. As Ramsdell says, "It is not always possible to tell, at this distance, what was true and what was false in the charges and countercharges that fill the Spanish Archives," a statement which certainly applies to the mesteño question.

Following the death of Don Matías de Gálvez, viceroy of New Spain, in early 1785, there resulted one of those power vacuums that invariably accompany the loss of such an important figure. Before the dynamic Bernardo de Gálvez arrived to take his late father's place, the reins of government were held by the royal Audiencia, of which Don Vizente de Herrera was the acting president. It was during this transitional period that Fray José Antonio García, son of the apostolic college of Nuestra Señora de Guadalupe de Zacatecas, acting as *procurador* (solicitor) for the missions of Texas, chose to deliver his thrust against the cattle laws. Even more remarkable is the fact that Herrera chose to answer it just three short weeks before the new viceroy landed at Veracruz to assume such sweeping responsibilities himself. His ruling was as close to a reversal of the universally detested cattle regulations as the zealous clergymen would ever come.[2]

Illustrating the bias with which mission advocates approached the cattle question, Fray García neglected to mention that the problem in Texas had its source with a decision at the commandant general's level. Instead, he led the acting president Herrera to believe that it was an irresponsible act by the gover-

---

[2]For Bernardo de Gálvez's succession to the viceregency of Nueva España see John Walton Caughey, *Bernardo de Gálvez in Louisiana, 1776–1783*, pp. 250–53; Odie B. Faulk, *The Last Years of Spanish Texas, 1778–1821*, p. 9; John, *Storms*, p. 600.

nor which took away the missions' unbranded stock and made it royal property. In so doing, the padre *procurador* was guilty of either surprising ignorance or calculated manipulation. But if his opening remarks were a bit misleading, García's construction of the facts adhered closely to the traditional views of cassocked frontier stockmen.

His arguments were not new. In fact, they were based on reports received from the minister at Espíritu Santo, Fray Mariano de Cárdenas. Ruin of Espíritu Santo's cattle was being experienced "because the greater part of them are without any brand or mark." The reason they were without brands—and thus subject to the governor's capricious edict—was because Texas was a wilderness, where customary stock-handling procedures did not work. It was not easy to "pin down" the roaming herds, and often their Christianized Indian caretakers ventured forth to gather and brand strayed stock at great peril to life and limb. Why? Because of frequent attacks by hostile savages, the oldest excuse in the book. If hostilities continued to be committed against the mission Indians and their cattle were killed, he feared "with sufficient reason" that the Texas missions would be lost.

Indeed, these fears were already being realized, Fray García added, especially since the governor's *bando* allowed the slaughter of mission stock which had wandered or been driven to crown lands, bringing the herds near the brink of annihilation. Breeding cows were being killed indiscriminately, an abuse which was encouraged by the *bando* and which would soon rebound to the "detriment of both Majesties." In other words, if the missions failed, the Royal Treasury would suffer in the long run because the king would be obliged to pay for things now covered by the Order of Saint Francis—a prospect gloomy enough to stir any conscientious royal administrator to action.[3]

The spokesman for the Zacatecan college then attacked the issue of who really owned the cattle, regardless of where found

[3] Confirmation that the missions' herds were dwindling comes in an inventory taken at San José by Father Salas in 1785. He said that 250 pesos were spent rounding up only 682 head of cattle, all of which were "very lean" and had to be turned loose. Many cattle had already died. The mission owned 51 horses and one lame mule. *Ganado menor*, however, was plentiful: 6,075 sheep and 92 goats (Fr. Benedict Leutenegger and Fr. Marion A. Habig, comps. and trans., *The San José Papers, 1719–1791*, pt. 1, p. 244).

or their unbranded condition. That they were property of the missions, he said, admitted no argument. When the missions were founded, there were no cattle in Texas. They were introduced for the encouragement and sustenance of the Indian converts, and it was spurious for the governor to reason that because the herds had since spread out on crown lands they now belonged to the king. Owing to the piety of His Catholic Majesty, it was the duty of those charged with ministering his kingdom to sustain the faithful and seek an increase of those newly attracted to the church. Since the Indian nations were exempt from many other laws, Fray García did not see why exemption from the cattle law should not apply to converts in the missions. The cattle belonged to them, as did the pastures whereon the cattle grazed (when not molested by others), and it was from such things that the poor Indians drew their worldly support. To undermine this economic foundation would be to weaken the spiritual gains built upon it, thereby subverting His Majesty's wishes. Seen from such a viewpoint, revocation of Cabello's *bando* was not only the logical but the moral thing to do.

Vizente de Herrera appears to have agreed. Perhaps ignorant of the inner workings of the distant northern frontier, he took Fray García at his word and ordered the present governor, as well as those who would succeed him, to cease and desist in the persecution of these "pitiful" Indians. In his dispatch dated April 30, 1785, he charged the administrator of Texas to show proof that he had complied, saying that steps must be taken to ensure the growth of the missions, their numbers of Indians, and the province's livestock industry. These purposes, noted Herrera, were superior to every other consideration that might have prompted the governor to issue his destructive *bando*. Consequently, the acting president of the royal Audiencia considered it appropriate to defer to the *procurador*'s request in its entirety: "Wherefore I order the governor of Texas to proceed to publish a *bando* contrary to the one he has ordered published, . . . making known to the entire public by means thereof that *any cattle found without a brand are to be considered [property] of those missions.*"[4]

[4]BAT, 131:141–53 (emphasis added).

By summer Herrera's ruling (number 65) was in the hands of Father President José Agustín Falcón Mariano at Mission San José. To him and his fellow missionaries, it must have represented the answer to all their prayers, better than anything they could have hoped for. Fray Mariano wasted no time presenting this dispatch, issued directly from the superior government of Mexico, to Governor Cabello. In a petition drafted in July he pointed out that the ruling required Cabello not only to revoke his *bando* imposing a time limit on the branding (after which all unbranded stock would have reverted to the king) but to publish a new one announcing that all *orejano* cattle without a mark or brand belonged to the missions. Father Mariano asked Cabello also to recall all licenses presently issued for the catching, assembling, or killing of unbranded stock—"especially to the supplier of this villa and presidio"—which would freeze all operations considered detrimental to the rights of the missions and their Indians. Finally, he requested that the original of this precious decree be returned, after the governor had made a copy, so that it might be preserved in the archives of the presidency.

Cabello was not one to concede a point easily. He pondered over the acting president's revocation order until he found a loophole and then moved decisively. He could not comply, he noted in a decree of July 16, because his *bando* was issued on the express orders of the commandant general, and thus it was impossible for him to countermand its contents without first informing his superior officer. These things had to pass through proper channels, and by going over the commandant general's head directly to the top, the missionaries had given Cabello the means to negate their victory. He returned Fray Mariano's petition along with the *procurador*'s windfall response, reproaching the priest for some imagined allusion to a breach of propriety in the way that beef was supplied to the town and presidio. Since a copy of this was going directly to the commandancy general, as Cabello informed the father president, he wanted to make it clear, for the record, that he had no personal interest in who did or did not go out and kill *orejanos* to supply the needs of the general public. The priest, by implying that he had an official supplier, had made a "great error" because none existed, just a faithful and legal man who brought some *orejano* cattle from time to time, a man who paid His Majesty's fees on such stock.[5]

When the governor sent his file to Rengel several days later, asking for a decision on this new order from Mexico City, his cover letter reflected a slightly accusatory air, almost a mild rebuke. Since his two *bandos* had met with approval, he wondered why this dispatch to the contrary had come. That he felt betrayed by the system is evident. He had followed orders to the best of his ability, knowing that such orders would not endear him to his subjects, and now he had to defend those orders against higher authority as well. Implied, of course, was the dutiful public servant's resentment that things were in such chaos at the top level. Herrera's dispatch had put the governor in an uncomfortable situation, and he did not appreciate it. Moreover, while the man who was responsible for this confusion, Croix, had won promotion to the viceregency of Peru, he, Cabello, was still trapped in Texas trying to administer it. As if things were not bad enough, here was the head of the royal Audiencia issuing orders that contradicted established policy, and Rengel, who also held his job on an interim basis, did not understand what was really going on. It was all very irritating.[6]

Cabello would have been even more annoyed had he known of Juan José Flores the younger's activities in Chihuahua at this very time. During the summer of 1785, Flores, styling himself "attorney for the residents and raisers of livestock in the province of Texas, or Nuevas Philipinas," submitted three petitions to the commandant general. The first came on May 6; in it he "attempted to have revoked . . . the provisions dictated by the Most Excellent Señor Caballero de Croix." Reviewing this petition later, the *asesor* noted that, although Flores did not express it clearly and definitively, in substance the lawyer was asking that *orejano* livestock be declared the property and possessions of the residents and raisers themselves.[7]

---

[5] Falcón Mariano to Cabello, petition (undated), and Cabello, decree, July 16, 1785, ibid.

[6] Cabello to Rengel, no. 101, July 20, 1785, BAT, 133:44.

[7] Flores, petition, May 6, 1785, referred to in Galindo Navarro to Commandant General, February 22, 1786, BAT, 136:145–56.

A fragment of Flores's second petition, dated June 1, indicates that, while his thoughts may not have been expressed coherently, they were nonetheless focused on the issues that were later incorporated into the most impressive of all rancher documents of protest, the San Fernando Memorial of 1787. Apparently the self-proclaimed attorney polished his first draft, because the paper that Galindo Navarro summarized was dated the next day. "He [Flores] argued," said the *asesor*, "that they should continue in possession of the lands they had held and defended until then in good faith, even though they lacked titles." The citizens were prepared to solicit them personally from the royal Audiencia of the district (at Guadalajara) if they were not otherwise recognized. Since the periods of time previously granted for branding had been ineffective, Flores asked that six months be extended to them anew, distributed in three parts: August and September, 1785; January and February, 1786; and July and August, 1786. The roundups were to be carried out not only on lands over which they had possession "but also on crown lands of the province to which the pursued cattle fled and took refuge."

Flores claimed that the ranchers had not made use of the time extensions granted because they were awaiting the reforms already solicited. He further charged that the governor had given insufficient notice of the roundups for hands and horses necessary for such a task to be assembled in time and that their operations were confined to a severely limited terrain. He maintained that the commandant general had left them free to round up not just on lands "owned in good faith since the beginning" but on crown lands as well. Countering Cabello's attempt to exclude all nonowners of property from the roundup, Flores asked that his fellow ranchers be allowed the quiet and peaceful possession of lands long since held and protected in good faith, "even though we may lack formal title." Flores also asked that, until steps were taken on his previous petition, he and the other residents receive mercy and justice.[8]

The "third and last" petition that Flores presented came

---

[8] Ibid. For Flores's "rough draft," dated Chihuahua, June 1, 1785, see BAT, 132: 85–88.

two months later. Galindo Navarro described the Béxar attorney as having materially altered his previous stance. Basically Flores proposed that in exchange for an unrestricted roundup lasting fourteen months the ranchers would no longer resist Croix's decree. This, it would seem, was an attempt to bargain for realistic gains as opposed to his initial position, which claimed all but could show nothing. Future petitions and clamors on behalf of the ranchers would continue this notion that in return for certain options they would yield their rights and comply with the wishes of the government. It was their prolonged and stubborn resistance to Croix's original *bando* that gave strength to Flores's bargaining position. The only question was exactly how much the king's men would forfeit to have peace and quiet in the province of Texas.[9]

Meanwhile, life continued as usual. Cabello, slated for the governorship of Nueva Vizcaya, hung on until word of his relief should come. Don Simón de Arocha once again regained his position as the top cattle exporter, taking out a herd of 760 head in late August. In his petition the militia captain stated that, in order to assist his poor family and send his son to the seminary in Mexico City, he needed to gather 300 *orejano* bulls. The governor restricted his gathering places to the arroyo Los Alamos or Las Mulas, on the far (east) side of the Cíbolo, and

---

[9] Galindo Navarro, opinion, February 22, 1786, BAT, 136:145–56.

issued an export permit after the receipt of 289 pesos, 4 reales. From July through September seven herds totaling over 2,000 head were trailed out. According to Cabello's book of *guías*, exports had been at this level since 1780.[10]

On August 17, Commandant General Rengel suggested that mustangs be caught and broken for use by soldiers, a plan necessitated by a scarcity of horses in Nuevo Santander and Nuevo León. Cabello was authorized to organize roundups, secure the services of tamers, and so on. When the horses were broken, the expenses incurred and a fair value for them could be deducted from the Mustang Fund.[11] It is not known to what extent Cabello utilized this plan, but no evidence exists to indicate that mesteño horses were as highly sought a prize as the province's *orejano* cattle. Even the lowering of the capture fee from 6 reales to 2, supposedly because wild horses were twice as difficult to catch as wild cattle, did not provide the incentive needed for Texas stockmen to exploit the wild *mestañadas* (herds of horses). Markets were another problem, for the provinces on the south specialized in raising horses, sheep, and goats rather than cattle, and the demands of Anglo-Americans pressing westward had not yet arisen. It would be another decade or more before men like Philip Nolan pressed into Texas seeking horses—among other things—and the export of equine stock came to rival the commercial prospects for bovine stock.

The governor's feud with the Menchaca clan continued in 1785. First came news that the case which he had drawn up against Luis Mariano for fraud, concealment of *orejano* cattle belonging to His Majesty, and "surreptitious exportation" was being forwarded to the *asesor*.[12] Also, the proceedings in the lawsuit in which Juan Jose Pacheco was suing José Félix for compensation for his forty bulls were sent to Saltillo for a deci-

---

[10] "Record of Exports," BAT, 142:135–36; *expediente* no. 105, BAT, 133:57–59. The son Don Simón spoke of was perhaps the *bachiller* José Clemente de Arocha, who later became curate at San Antonio after having established a chapel at Valero for soldiers stationed there, using articles from the secularized mission. Like his kinsmen he was a rancher of substance.
[11] Rengel to Cabello, August 17, 1785, BAT, 133:96.
[12] Previously noted as BAT, 131:19–20.

sion in August of that year. The decision, rendered on October 3 by the *licenciado* (attorney) José M. Bucheli, went heavily against Menchaca. It ruled that since the bulls confiscated by Gil Ybarbo at Nacogdoches did not bear the brands of Mission Valero they were not Pacheco's, meaning that Pacheco's bulls— minus three head cut out for costs—were in fact sold by Menchaca and that he was therefore responsible for them. The lawyer's opinion hinged on the fine point that Pacheco's stock were mixed in with Menchaca's herd at the same time Mission Valero's cattle were added, under the assumption that all such animals would be branded accordingly. This, of course, was a ridiculous assumption to make about one of the first cattle drives to Louisiana, conducted back in 1779, when branding was not considered necessary.

Regardless of this, Menchaca was held liable, and Pacheco billed him for 727 pesos. On November 24, Governor Cabello made a notation in *expediente* 83 that Menchaca had fled, taking with him a number of horses and mules to ensure the success of his flight. The fugitive had no doubt gone to appeal this decision to the commandant general, and Cabello ordered him apprehended and sent back in captivity, with his belongings. Menchaca's departure with so many animals, said the governor, was proof that he was headed to "distant places." In December he ordered Menchaca's possessions confiscated to satisfy Pacheco's judgment, but the old captain's son, Luis Mariano, said that he did not know anything about his uncle Félix's possessions except that he was completely supported by his father, Don Luis. Nonetheless, two town lots were auctioned for 300 pesos, and the following year Cabello gave Pacheco permission to enter the old captain's Rancho de San Francisco to look for cattle bearing Félix's brand. One can imagine the reception that Pacheco got there.[13]

Another dispute involving the Menchacas broke out in November, this one between them and the Arocha clan. The nature of the quarrel was trivial, but because it involved two promi-

---

[13] For the original lawsuit (no. 83) and its subsequent developments, see BAT, vol. 97; see also BAT, 135:94.

nent Canary Island families, the matter could not be dropped without legal formalities. Fernando de Arocha, a brother of Don Simón and Juan, went into Luis Mariano's store drunk and asked for another bottle. When he was refused, a scuffle ensued during which grave insults were uttered in the presence of many witnesses. Mariano's wife struck Fernando with a measuring stick when he would not leave, calling him a "worthless mulatto dog" like all his family. Arocha, who had already called Menchaca a skinflint, called him worse things, including "*cabrón cornudo*" (cuckold), as the melee spilled into the street.

When Juan de Arocha heard about the aspersions that Menchaca's wife had cast on his family's good name, he immediately went to his brother Fernando, who was a carbineer in the presidio's cavalry company, and got him released. Then he pressed charges against Luis Mariano, asking that the slanders about the Arochas be proved or else public satisfaction be given. Cabello, having long ago decided that Luis Mariano was a troublemaker, promptly threw him in jail. Wiser heads prevailed, however, and Fernando retracted what were described as words uttered in "imagined fevers in the heads of youths of which nothing should have been made." Charges were withdrawn. Since Fernando could not write, brother Simón signed his petition, indicating who was behind the move to quell this unsavory public display. Mariano, after ten days in the guardhouse, also apologized and offered to pay court costs, which amounted to 29 pesos.[14] Cabello, who lived in the Casa Real, presided over this case there because it was more comfortable than the presidio guardhouse, where the prisoners were held. Listening to this testimony he could not have been in the best of moods. He had just been notified by Viceroy Gálvez, without explanation, that his transfer to Nueva Vizcaya was canceled. He was to remain in Texas with no relief in sight.[15]

---

[14] BAT, vol. 135. Several instances of racial prejudice against mulattoes, or against those suspected of being mulattoes, are cited in Alicia V. Tjarks, "Comparative Demographic Analysis of Texas, 1777–1793," *Southwestern Historical Quarterly* 77 (January, 1974): 323–28. To be called a mulatto in colonial Texas was "an insult or sure defamation."

[15] John, *Storms*, p. 664.

If the citizens of Béxar had a self-tutored attorney representing their interests in the province's *orejano* stock, the mission fathers were not derelict in defending their own claims. As has been seen, solicitor Fray García managed to obtain a ruling which would have made all unbranded stock—including that claimed by private ranchers—mission property. If news of this attempt was spread abroad, it could have done nothing to ease the minds of secular raisers concerning their old dispute with the missionaries over ownership of the contested animals. It also indicates that until 1785 the "private quarrel" between mission and individual ranchers was still very much alive. If Cabello had even attempted to implement Herrera's dispatch, the furor raised by the residents of the province would doubtless have amounted to insurrection. But Fray García's petition, and the information from the minister of Espíritu Santo upon which it was based, was not the only such effort in the works. Another report, much more comprehensive in its scope, was being written by Fray José Francisco López.

López was in a position to know the situation in Texas, having been a missionary there for at least twenty-six years. He was at Espíritu Santo when Solís visited in 1768. From 1773 to 1783 he was the minister at Concepción, holding the office of interim *presidente* from 1781 when Fray Ramírez died, until Fray Garza was appointed the following year. In 1783 he moved to Valero and remained there even after he succeeded Fray Oliva as father president. It was at Valero during his tenure of 1786 as acting father president—before Oliva's appointment began—that he penned his report, the most eloquent of church protests on the cattle question and a piece of writing that approaches inspired propaganda.[16] It must stand with the ranchers' San Fernando Me-

---

[16] López was acting father president, December, 1785–October, 1786. His report was signed at Mission Valero on May 5, 1786, not 1789, as stated in J. Autry Dabbs, trans., *López's Report of the Texas Missions in 1785*, p. 24. Fr. Marion A. Habig, *The Alamo Chain of Missions: A History of San Antonio's Five Old Missions*, and Leutenegger and Habig, *San José Papers*, pt. 1, and others, relying on this misstatement, have written that Father López's report came in 1789, but in fact it describes conditions in Texas in 1785. See the copy, "Razón e Ynforme que el Padre Presidente de las Misiones de la Provincia de Texas o Nuevas Filipinas remite . . ." (Box 2Q237, University of Texas Archives). Another error in Dabbs's translation (p. 5) is the date on which the royal order was issued at El Pardo; it should be January 31, 1784, not 1781. This order was the

morial of 1787 as one of the two most significant historical documents dealing with Texas ranching in the eighteenth century. Both papers sought a common goal—the repeal of Croix's decree—but beyond that the two literary efforts went their separate ways.[17]

Conflicting reports, it seems, had reached His Majesty concerning the religious establishments of Texas, their wealth, and their ability to bring the heathen children of that land to Christianity. Thanks to the intercession of powerful churchmen at court, Carlos III wanted to know the true state of affairs in the province still sometimes called the New Philippines. A royal order to this effect, issued at El Pardo on January 31, 1784, eventually made its way to Fray Rafael José Verger, bishop of Nuevo León. Viceroy Bernardo de Gálvez sent it to him on August 4, 1785, and he forwarded the order to the father guardian of the College of Zacatecas, who in turn forwarded it to the father president of the Texas missions.

López, writing to the bishop (but ultimately for the king), touched on many aspects of the mission system in Texas: census figures; descriptions of the Indians—the way they talked, their habitual laziness, the diseases that afflicted them, and so on; and how the missions looked and how they were run. But always he returned to the subject of cattle: "The herds of cattle increase rapidly, and they constitute the principal wealth. All the missions had considerable property of this kind. With these herds they maintained themselves without enduring many hardships or privations; and could they but be restored, the missions would regain their former prosperity."[18]

Croix, by adding to the Royal Treasury all unbranded cattle, had taken away the wealth that by right belonged to the church, since Indian troubles prevented the missionaries from branding much of their stock. Consequently, almost all the cattle in the

---

basis for a long report, *Informe sobre las Misiones*, made in 1793 by the viceroy, the second Conde de Revillagigedo.

[17] Sandra L. Myres, *The Ranch in Spanish Texas, 1691–1800*, pp. 13–14, expresses the idea that Fray López's "polemic" of 1785 was in fact a well-written piece of propaganda and cites its influence on the thinking of Bancroft and Castañeda.

[18] Dabbs, *López's Report of the Texas Missions in 1785*, is the basis of this section, with corrections of dates as noted, pp. 5, 24.

province were unbranded, meaning that the missions—which had raised them in the first place—were now without beef. To obtain cattle for their own use, God's servants had to pay, like any stranger, the stipulated fee of 4 reales a head. As a result, said Fray López, their converts suffered and endured great sorrow, for they were reduced to poverty, their wealth stripped from them by fiat. Their plight he likened to the lamentations of the prophet Jeremiah: "Our inheritance is turned to aliens; our houses to strangers."

Had Croix's zealousness, "without being sufficiently well informed," as López put it, enriched the king's coffers? Not so, argued the padre; while the Ramo de Mesteñas (Bureau of Herds) should have produced over 25,000 pesos, rumor had it that the fund contained scarcely 6,000 or 7,000 pesos. It was doubtful that a single real had been taken out and sent to the Royal Treasury. Thus, while the missions no longer enjoyed this wealth, neither did the king. The herds themselves were scattered and severely depleted. He noted that twelve years before, in 1773, Espíritu Santo had branded more than 15,000 head of cattle counted at the corral gate, an "incomparably greater number" remaining unbranded in the woods. Yet today not 3,000 branded head could be gathered. They, plus those that survived unbranded, López did not think would amount to the branded group alone of twelve years previously. As for Mission Rosario, its wealth once consisted mainly of cattle and horses, the branded number of which exceeded 10,000 head. Of these the Lipan Apaches and coastal tribes had left not even a sign.

In López's mind the decimation of the Franciscans' herds had been brought about by the numberless irregularities attendant on Croix's proclamation. For example, the cattle were now being indiscriminately preyed upon by no less than five offenders. There were the Apaches, who killed for food, or simply because they felt like it. There were the *carneadores*, the Spanish meat hunters, who went into the pastures, killing great numbers on each expedition. There were also the purveyors for the presidio, who had contracts to bring in beef to feed the king's men. Fourth were the soldiers themselves, who, on patrols or engaged in various duties like guarding the horse herd, killed many cattle, certainly more than they needed. Last, there were the drovers, who rounded up large herds and trailed them out of the province, sometimes taking 1,000 head a drive, many of which were cows needed for breeding. López believed that during the past eight years 15,000 head lost in this manner would be a conservative estimate. Not as easy to ascertain was which of these various marauders were most responsible for the depleted condition of the once vast herds; all of them vied for the honor, all eagerly rushing in the "wide door" opened by Croix's unwise proclamation. While bemoaning that much of their herds' decline was due to large exports, López failed to mention that Espíritu Santo and Rosario had profited considerably from this trade because they supplied most of the cattle purchased and legally trailed out of Texas during the peak years—an understandable omission, considering his intent.

Fray López also had some harsh words for the governor and the way he conducted his office. He noted that this official would not help the missions stop their Indians from running away and that he would not help the missionaries round them up again once they were gone. He mentioned how renegade Indians lured the civilized Indians away or threatened them, and he expressed the hope that some punishment would be adopted to correct this problem.[19] Owing to the penury in which Croix's decree had placed them, said López, the fathers could not care for the Indians presently housed in the missions, much less afford to seek new converts. It was a vicious circle, enough to test the faith of their poor Indian converts. They saw the Comanches raid at will because the governor was unable to stop them. What horses the Comanches failed to steal the Apaches took. To add insult to injury, the converts saw the same Apaches allowed to enter the royal presidio in friendship. The next day the Apaches would be out again, taking their horses and cattle and killing herdsmen. Worse still, the soldiers themselves, who were supposed to protect the converts' interests, stole and slaughtered as much as the hostile Indians did, so poorly were they governed. With all this adversity it was no wonder that the priests' "poor orphans" deserted their missions.

In a final thrust Father López attacked the insensitive men who kept the situation from improving—from the revenue-conscious commandant general down to his foraging soldiers. Someone should have thought of the ruin Croix's decree would bring before allowing it to be enforced. The heads of the province should have kept in mind its potential abuses before adopting the resolution of applying to the Royal Treasury "that which, in all justice, belonged to the missions." By going beyond the limits of the laws concerning pastures and cattle, they had unquestionably acted against the royal will and intention, which looked primarily to the conservation and conversion of Indians into the ranks of the Holy Church. This goal, in López's view, had been frustrated by political maxims and ill-advised practices.

Alas for the devoted priest, the missions' days in Texas were numbered. Attacks on the system were becoming increasingly bitter and government administrators more impatient with a state of affairs which kept out of the Royal Treasury's reach the only possible source of revenue in the province, the wild herds claimed by the missions. Thus the idea, in the words of Castañeda, "grew and became a conviction firmly fixed in the mind

---

[19] The murder of one of the most notorious renegades, "El Mocho," was arranged by Spanish authorities in July, 1784; see John, *Storms*, p. 653.

of officials that the missions had served their purpose." Not even the eloquence of a Father López could stem the tide; secularization was the wave of the future, and all his pleadings on behalf of the poor, orphaned Indians of Texas amounted to nothing in the face of the settlers' envy and the government's greed.[20]

It will be remembered that in 1759 Fray Mariano de los Dolores had offered to abdicate the temporal administration of missions held under the Querétaran brotherhood, only to have them eventually handed over to the Zacatecan college. In January, 1780, the Discretorio of Zacatecas had petitioned Commandant General Croix on the same subject, begging to be relieved of the grave responsibility of temporal administration of the missions, a task alien to their ministry. Once essential, this practice now served only as a constant source of disagreement with royal officials and with the citizens, who were always trying to take advantage of the Indian neophytes. The Discretorio felt that an equitable secularization was the best approach, dividing each mission's worldly goods among its converts. The king, as has been observed, also wanted to formulate new regulations pertaining to the missions; Croix had referred the royal order to his *asesor general.* Galindo Navarro, in an opinion dated July 20, 1781, recommended that no hasty decision should be made on the temporal affairs of the missions until the matter had been fully discussed because it was of such vital interest to the future welfare of New Spain's northern provinces. There the question would remain throughout the 1780s, but Father López's report to Bishop Verger leaves little doubt about his feelings on the subject. His Indians, "moved more by gifts than by the strongest and clearest reasoning," were not ready to be thrust into the mainstream of Spanish society. Such a course would destroy them entirely.[21]

December was a month given over to festivals and rejoicing by the inhabitants of San Fernando de Béxar. Celebrations honoring the Virgin of Guadalupe ran into those of the Christmas season, followed by a high mass on New Year's Day. Feast days were accompanied by bullfights (días de toros) and fan-

---

[20] Carlos E. Castañeda, *Our Catholic Heritage in Texas,* 5:24.
[21] Ibid., pp. 25–26; see also pp. 50–51 for Fray Lava's offer to resign temporal administration, made to Croix while he was in Texas (1778).

dangos, starting in mid-December. It was at such a bullfight that a Comanche couple encountered Governor Cabello on December 15, greeting him as "Tata." They were one of many unexpected delegations that the astonished governor found himself entertaining after the peace treaty of three months before.[22]

Cabello's book of entries for the year 1785, entitled "Duties Paid by Those Who Have Caught *Orejano* Cattle and Mustangs," showed a total of 4,589 reales collected, or 573 pesos, 5 reales, in silver. This amount, it was noted, was figured at 4 reales per *orejano* and 2 reales per mesteño. As was customary, the accounting contained a list of individual forays by name. Fray Cárdenas, of Espíritu Santo, sent Cabello 140 pesos for the year, based on use of His Majesty's *orejanos*. Cárdenas said that the Lipans were putting an end to cattle raising at La Bahía and that little profit could henceforth be expected for the royal fund. "Now one finds nothing but bulls," was his comment, as unpropitious a prospect as was ever voiced by a cattleman.[23]

In February, 1786, Cabello directed a personal letter to Commandant General Rengel, warning him that the citizens of Béxar had an attorney, one Juan José Flores, of which Rengel was doubtless already aware. Flores had left the province to present a petition on *orejano* cattle, said Cabello, mentioning that he had written of this matter in greater detail in a letter of May 6, 1784, to which he had had no reply. "Knowing the unruly and quibbling nature of these people," he said, "it is felt and is evidently true that if Your Excellency travels to this location [Béxar] they will foment so many snarls that a lawyer will be needed to answer and satisfy [their complaints], and also the missions will raise a petition concerning the dispatch they obtained." The governor's reference was to his letter of July 20, 1785, in which he requested a decision on Herrera's dispatch, to which he also had no reply. Cabello protested his innocence of any wrongdoing but dreaded the problems he foresaw: "These incidents will bring about many bad times."[24]

[22] John, *Storms*, pp. 689, 690.
[23] "Duties Paid by Those Who Have Caught *Orejanos* and Mesteños, Year Ending 1785," BAT, 135:158–70; Cárdenas to Cabello, January 8, 1786, BAT, 137:19.
[24] Cabello to Rengel, February 20, 1786, BAT, 137:132.

Replies, however, were on the way. On February 22 Galindo Navarro issued his most detailed decision since that of October 30, 1782, in which he defended Croix's cattle law for Texas. He followed it a month later with a concise opinion relating to Herrera's dispatch. Pedro Galindo Navarro was the one constant on a rapidly shifting political stage. As legal adviser to a series of commandants, he had guided the implementation of Croix's decree since its inception. He was aware of the opposition in Texas, for it was across his desk that their cases passed for review and final disposition. Consequently, he had soon come to know the Tejano offenders by their first names; he knew which were the ringleaders and which were most perverse in their violations of the *bandos*. He was also wise enough, one suspects, to know that a province could not be effectively governed when its leading citizens were branded cattle thieves; at least his opinions on criminal cases so indicate. In any event, while it was one thing to pull the wool over the eyes of a pious, well-meaning member of the Audiencia in distant Mexico City it would not work with the king's seasoned legal expert at Arizpe. By the time Galindo Navarro got around to answering Cabello's pleas for guiding opinions in the early spring of 1786, he had finally realized that the stockmen in Texas were stalling, whether through citizen Flores's petitions to the commandancy general or through Fray Procurador García's petition to a member of the royal Audiencia. They were the same old delaying tactics, and the guardian of the king's coffers had had enough.

Addressing the "defects" of the system under which the Eastern Interior Provinces were governed, Ramos Arizpe later maintained that the position of *auditor de guerra* offered only the "slightest check" on the commandant general's power and said that reports submitted generally did nothing more than confirm the opinion which the general had already presented.[25] In the case of Galindo Navarro, however, it was sometimes the other way around—at least in such long protracted matters as the cattle issue. Year after year his judgments governed the ac-

---

[25] Nettie Lee Benson, trans. and ed., *Report of Ramos Arizpe*, pp. 26–27. The offices of *auditor de guerra* and *asesor* were combined in Galindo Navarro.

tions of a succession of different administrators. His opinion of February 22 is interesting because it traces the evolution of the Texas cattle law, following its principal milestones from 1778 to 1786. It starts by giving a summary of Juan José Flores's three petitions of 1785 and then rapidly moves into a recap of the *asesor*'s attempt to deal fairly with the ungrateful ranchers, who met every ruling with howls of protest. Noting that peace with the Comanches had finally come and that the "scant proceeds from the Mustang Fund do not cover the expenses occasioned by the gifts which are given to the Comanches annually for the purpose of maintaining the peace," he reproached the cattlemen for their tight-fisted claims to wild cattle, declaring that, even though they had some right to *orejano*, mesteño, and *alzado* stock, they ought to have declined to exercise it and gladly contributed the small impost designated for the Royal Treasury.

In other words, Galindo Navarro wanted the stockmen to pay the cost of buying peace with the Comanches, an arrangement that he felt would benefit them in the long run. Since Texas had been a constant drain upon the crown from the time of its first occupation, it did not seem overharsh to the *asesor* that the province should start paying a few of its own bills. He was not the only administrator of King Carlos who felt that way, as has been shown. Now the ranchers wanted another fourteen months on top of all the other extensions granted them. Such an attempt in his mind could have no other purpose than to allow them to round up, catch, and mark all the remaining *orejano* and *mesteño* livestock in the province in order to divest the Royal Treasury of its legitimate ownership. This action was "not just and should not be permitted."

However, to avoid more petitions and appeals on the matter, the *asesor general* suggested a new and final four-month period for branding. The ranchers must be reminded that their claims were inappropriate and warned that when the new time expired all livestock found without a mark or brand of a known owner would be classified as *orejano*, mustang, and wild and that they would be granted no additional time to mark them. This last extension should be administered in such a way that "there shall remain to them no excuse or pretext whatsoever to the contrary."[26] Five days after this opinion was issued, Commandant General Rengel wrote to Cabello, noting his refusal to comply with Herrera's dispatch, which would have revoked Croix's cattle laws and required the governor to issue a counter order. Neither an approval nor a rejection, Rengel's letter of February 27 was merely an acknowledgment, saying that Cabello's *expediente* 101 was being sent to the *asesor* and that he would "in view of his opinion advise Your Lordship of the resolution he makes."[27]

---

[26] The *asesor*'s opinions are found in BAT, 136:145–51, of which that dated February 22 is by far the most useful because it reviews attorney Flores's efforts in Chihuahua City to combat Croix's decree. Faulk seems confused here, citing this document as containing news of a "royal revocation" (Odie B. Faulk, "Ranching in Spanish Texas," *Hispanic American Historical Review* 49 [May, 1965]: 261), stating that the king "had revoked Croix's decree of 1778 and all subsequent orders qualifying or modifying it," an error also found in Faulk, *The Last Years of Spanish Texas, 1778–1821*, p. 88; and in Sandra L. Myres, "The Spanish Cattle Kingdom in the Province of Texas," *Texana* 4 (1966):245, citing Faulk as the authority. Myres, it should be acknowledged, does not repeat the mistaken idea that the king personally overturned Commandant General Croix's cattle decree of 1778 in her longer work, *Ranch in Spanish Texas* (p. 39); but David Dary, *Cowboy Culture: A Saga of Five Centuries*, perpetuates it in his chapter "Moving North."

[27] BAT, 136:156.

That opinion was not long in coming. The lord assessor said that Herrera's dispatch was issued by virtue of a report contrary to the truth of the facts, a comment that came very close to calling Father García, of the Zacatecan college, a liar. The dispatch was sent without knowledge of the precedents which had given rise to the just provisions of the cattle laws, in the mistaken concept that the governor of Texas had initiated these laws on his own authority. To put it bluntly, the acting president of the Audiencia had been duped by the church faction, and Galindo Navarro suggested that the dispatch obtained in the process be ignored. He advised Rengel to adhere to his opinion of February 22 in the matter of the wild herds of Texas, "or you may resolve all of this as you are most pleased to." Thus, in these two opinions the protests of the ranchers—both church and private—were overruled, and the ranchers were granted a new four-month period of grace.[28]

In May, Cabello did some bookkeeping, producing a "Statement of Mustang Fund." He juggled his figures in such a manner as to show the fund's ending balance of 1785 as 6,460 pesos, close to the amount that Father López had surmised it contained. It was noted that Mission Espíritu Santo still owed the fund 957 pesos from long before.[29] The truth of the matter was that Father President Garza's protest, made shortly after Cabello issued his extension *bando* of October 26, 1784, was slowly working its way up to the viceroy, even though the governor had ordered it returned to Garza. Until their appeal was answered by the king or someone above the commandant general's level—well known for hostility to their position—the missionaries were not about to pay for the 348 *orejanos* taken out by Sebastián Monjarás, José Padrón, and Joaquín Flores in December, 1778. Cabello finally suspended the debt in July until some decision was reached on Fray Garza's protest and

---

[28] Ibid., p. 151.

[29] "Statement of Mustang Fund," May 24, 1786, showed 4,532 pesos on hand at the end of 1784, plus 1,500 pesos "repaid" by Gil Ybarbo's salaries, and a yield by 1785 of 1,721 pesos, making a total of 7,753 pesos, less various expenses to be reimbursed by the Royal Treasury totaling 1,294 pesos, leaving a balance as of December 31, 1785, of 6,460 pesos (BAT, vol. 138).

ended by turning over to his successor an IOU for the entire amount.[30]

Another shakeup of the Provincias Internas took place in April, 1786, when Jacobo Ugarte y Loyola replaced Rengel as commandant general. Rengel reverted to commandant inspector, but under a new division of the frontier military command into three sectors he was given the central division (Nuevo México and Nueva Vizcaya). Ugarte himself had the western division (Sonora, Sinaloa, and Baja and Alta California), while Colonel Juan de Ugalde had the eastern sector, including Texas. Supreme command was now to be vested in the viceroy, Bernardo de Gálvez—who devised the new arrangement—rather than having the commandant general report directly to Spain. As Elizabeth John has written, "The result was an administrative monstrosity that virtually defied coordination and continuity of policy among its diverse elements."[31]

On June 30, 1786, Cabello filed a report on conditions in Texas, saying that it had been very dry during the first half of the year, as had the last third of the preceding year. In addition, a late freeze at the end of April had killed new grass. Cows were very thin, and horses were also suffering, but much rain had fallen during June, and prospects for the province now looked better. If so, Texas was fortunate because unusual weather conditions in 1785–86 destroyed many crops, causing Mexico to be devastated by famine.[32] Perhaps the rainfall and the peace with the Comanches were contributing factors in making the year 1786 the best year for cattle exports of Cabello's administration. *Guías* were issued for twelve herds totaling more than 3,000 head, most of them trailed out between August and September. Don Simón de Arocha topped all competitors with an export herd of 800 head.

---

[30] As noted, the proceedings of this pivotal case are found under *expediente* no. 89, December 14, 1778–November 21, 1786, BAT, vol. 76.

[31] John, *Storms*, p. 696; Max L. Moorhead, *The Presidio: Bastion of the Spanish Borderlands*, p. 100.

[32] Cabello, June 30, 1786, BAT, 138:137; Colin M. MacLachlan and Jaime E. Rodríguez O., *The Forging of the Cosmic Race: A Reinterpretation of Colonial Mexico*, p. 287.

With so much activity naturally there were abuses—probably more than the desk-ridden governor guessed at. Several verdicts, rendered on prior *bando*-violation cases and received by Cabello during the peak export period, could not have done much to encourage him in further prosecution. Two, given by Galindo Navarro in July but not reaching Cabello until early September, were the *expedientes* initiated against Blás Eca y Múzquiz and Luis Mariano Menchaca in the summer of 1784. Cabello had put a lot of work into both cases and hoped that they would stick, but they did not. Múzquiz, noted the *asesor*, had not confessed and had not been formally charged, nor had his defenses been heard. Thus a "final determination" could not be ascertained. The same was concluded about Menchaca, whose guilt could only be inferred. About all that Galindo Navarro could suggest was for Cabello to try to collect the fees he thought were due on each transaction while trying to put the formalities in order for another round of prosecution, in other words, "put it in the dead file."

Addressing a more easily solvable side issue, Don Pedro gave instructions on what was to be done in the future with *orejano* mission cattle which Espíritu Santo supplied to the Bahía Presidio. In case any surplus animals were branded and put to pasture by the mission, the governor was to determine the *exact* number branded in this manner beyond the appointed time. Then the mission could be charged His Majesty's duties at 4 reales a head. But Galindo Navarro wanted the missionaries warned against this practice, for it did not technically agree with the branding provisions set forth in existing *bandos*. The stipulation about obtaining an "exact" figure was a subtle reference to the fact that in neither the Múzquiz nor the Menchaca case had the governor been able to prove the exact size of the herds gathered or exported in violation of Croix's cattle law. Such technicalities were a bitter pill to Cabello, who saw the overriding question as being the guilt of the offenders, not the precise degree of their offense. Needless to say, these decisions made enforcement of the law well-nigh impossible and gave stockmen the distinct impression that if they held out long enough charges brought against them would eventually come to naught.[33]

A proceeding that Cabello began against Luis Mariano Menchaca for a new offense just before he received the *asesor general*'s verdict on the charges of 1784 is a case in point. Mariano approached the governor in July, declaring that he, a merchant of the villa, had to go to Saltillo in August to cover pending debts and take his brother some cows. José Menchaca, it seems, was down at San Fernando de Austria, although the presidio was still referred to as Agua Verde. Mariano asked for a license to take more than three hundred head, some with his brand and some with the brands of others who, he said, "are indebted to me and have nothing else with which to pay." Cabello told Menchaca on July 31 that he would grant such permission only on the following terms: that a commissioner in whom Cabello had confidence would monitor the operation; that proof of permission was obtained from owners of other brands taken; that all recent brands were subject to confiscation; that when the herd was complete a *guía* would be issued, based on the commissioner's report; and that the herd must leave as soon as the *guía* was issued. The commissioner would remain with the herd until it was certain that the number could not be secretly increased before its departure, a tactic that appears to have been common.

Menchaca left for Rancho de San Francisco and proceeded to gather his herd without waiting to hear Cabello's careful safeguards and without a commissioner to watch his activities. Such behavior, observed the governor, indicated that Menchaca had "no wish to legally make the acquisition of cattle to comprise the herd, which he wishes to export without the intervention, knowledge or presence of the commissioner." Cabello claimed that under such circumstances he had weighty reasons not to permit the export of cattle or the products from slaughters at the Menchaca ranch. He then denied permission for the drive and ordered Mariano to appear.

[33] Galindo Navarro to Ugarte, July 12, 1786, BAT, 127:45–112; *expediente* no. 86, BAT, vol. 126.

This the old captain's son did on August 11, protesting that his actions had not been taken in an "absolute" manner and that it was slander for the governor to say such a thing. He explained his reasons for haste and asked to take out some merchandise as well: six loads of wool, five loads of meat and "grease" (lard and tallow), three loads of empty barrels, one load of leather bags, and one load of bullion. Cabello granted permission for the drive and the merchandise export, in view of the small quantity, and by the time Galindo Navarro's previous verdict reached him on September 4 Menchaca was already gone; he was at the Saltillo fair, Cabello's *auto* noted, where he had gone the past August. Blás Eca y Múzquiz was also at the annual *feria*, but Cabello recorded his determination to wait until the cattle agent returned to Santa Rosa and issue an order having the governor of Coahuila extradite Captain Luis Cazorla's "protégé." Both projects remained unfinished business.[34]

Cabello, however, was not finished with the Menchacas. His feud with this powerful family reached its culmination in *expediente* no. 84, in which proceedings were initiated against *reformado* (retired) Captain Luis Antonio Menchaca for irregular branding procedures. Like his predecessor, the Barón de Ripperdá, Cabello seemed determined to end his administration with deep enmities with the leading cattlemen of the province. Perhaps such a state of affairs was inevitable, considering the ranchers' estimation of their rights—so directly opposed to the wishes of the government—but officials like Ripperdá and Cabello cannot be accused of avoiding confrontations or of failing to exacerbate the conflict once joined.[35]

At the same time that he was fuming about Mariano's Coahuila-bound herd Cabello issued an *auto* (writ) locking

---

[34] BAT, 139:112.

[35] Robert H. Thonhoff, *The Texas Connection with the American Revolution*, p. 78, sums up the Menchacas' feud with Ripperdá and Cabello as one of men bred to the frontier who "embodied ideas of rugged individualism and freedom that were both alien and irritating" to governors. Although he is incorrect in several of his Menchaca genealogical connections, Thonhoff is perhaps justified in viewing the fortunes of this noted ranching and military dynasty as a prime Texas example of the "*peninsular* vs. *criollo*" animosities that soon fanned the flames of revolt in Nueva España.

horns with Mariano's father, Don Luis, in no uncertain terms. He had news that Menchaca was continually rounding up and placing *orejano* stock in his corrals, branding the large animals and earmarking the small ones. "Thus he has acquired a considerable number of cattle, gotten as if he raised them." Every year son Luis Mariano exported many of these to Coahuila and Saltillo, like the herd of 300 for which permission had just been granted. In fact, charged the governor, the exported cattle were those his father had marked fraudulently, adding that both he and his brother José Félix branded every time they went to the ranch. In an attempt to investigate the number of *orejanos* taken in this illegal fashion, Cabello sent the *alférez* of the Béxar cavalry company, Francisco Amangual, to Rancho de San Francisco. He was also to question some soldiers under the command of Don Luis's son José from the San Fernando (Coahuila) company. These men, asserted Cabello, were at the ranch rounding up for export.

The taking of testimony moved swiftly along. Juan José Pacheco swore that he had witnessed branding violations when he went to San Francisco looking for some of José Félix's stock to satisfy his judgment. Private José Miguel Gámes, a fifty-four-year-old veteran, said that he saw fresh brands, perhaps 20 or 30. Rumor had it that the old captain marked and branded all year long, while saying that all cattle on his lands belonged to him—as did José Félix. For this reason theirs was the biggest ranch on the San Antonio River and the Cíbolo. Gámes, whose name was still carried on the presidio's muster roll as an *ymbalido* (invalid), said he thought that the Menchacas had a secret corral for such activities. The most damaging account was given by Francisco de la Cerda, a forty-year-old hired hand of the tithe collector, Juan Barrera. When he went to San Francisco to collect the ranch's *diezmo*, he saw 400 head, 300 of which bore Don Luis's and brother José Félix's brand. Another 100 head were strictly *orejano*, which the vaqueros were busy marking. They delivered to him as a tithe 20 head of those just branded, "bleeding and smoking," plus 30 with marks. As for the presence of son José's soldiers on the ranch, a carbineer in the Agua Verde cavalry company testified that he had been sent by his commander to get some mules loaded with corn and beans and to "take care of business" for José.

In September, Alférez Amangual filed his report. Of 400 head held in a corral, he observed 30 recently branded with the Menchacas' mark. He tried to check the pastures, but the herds were wild—so wild that during five days in the field his helpers could catch only 20 head. The *alférez* suspended operations after realizing that it was impossible to make the cattle already branded and marked enter the corrals, stating that the retired captain was unwilling to pay the wages of the four hands used. Apart from being ruffled by Amangual's errand, Don Luis probably did not consider these intruders worth a peso a day for five days' labor. On the other hand, considering that their efforts produced so few instances of misconduct with the Menchaca cattle, perhaps the 25-peso charge was well worth the results. Either way, the old captain was not inclined to underwrite Cabello's wild-cow chase.

Amangual's report, incidentally, sheds further light on how Texas stockmen of the eighteenth century regarded their *marcas y fierros* (marks and brands).[36] Noting that the cattle held in the Menchaca corral were earmarked with Félix's *marca* but branded with Luis's *fierro*, the *alférez* inquired why, since it was "the usage of the country to give preference to the mark over the brand." The captain replied that his brother's mark was used because it was less likely to attract blowflies. Elaborating in later testimony, Luis said that Félix used a "mark of the fork," the mark used by their parents, and that it caused less bleeding than his earmark; thus it was used by Menchaca hands during the worm season. Later he added his own brand "because among us brothers the brand takes precedence and not the mark."

When he was called before Cabello to confess, the seventy-year-old retired captain took an oath on the hilt of his sword. Then he refused to answer the governor's questions concerning year-round branding, saying only that he had appealed to the

---

[36] Earmarks, sometimes called *marcas*, were more specifically designated *señales* ("sign," or "signal"), while *hierro*, or *fierro*, as used in America, referred to the iron used in branding, as well as to the mark applied with such an iron. Brand books or registers were called *libros de marcas* or *planillas de fierros*.

commandant general on this matter. Nevertheless, in November he, "under compulsion," gave a statement. Considering that it came from the province's oldest and most influential living soldier-rancher, it is the classic defense of its kind, worthy of paraphrasing at length to catch the flavor of an era gone forever.

Don Luis said he had seen the deceitful, fraudulent, and ill-formed petition of Juan José Pacheco. He called Gámes Pacheco's "lying confederate," who for the past seven years had been testifying against the Menchacas before the governor. The old captain said that he told Pacheco when he came snooping around that the governor had already taken Félix's stock, asking him why he did not go out into the pastures and catch some with his brand. No, said Pacheco, they had to be at the corral. This, confessed Don Luis, made him angry: "I told him I was no servant of his, or of Félix, or anyone else." They lied, as Amangual would attest, claimed the captain, seemingly confident that he could rely upon a fellow officer to support his testimony. For Private Gámes he had especially bitter words. That this man was for some reason a thorn in the side of the Menchacas is fairly obvious. Luis said that he was a hostile witness and that he would not accept Gámes as an inspector. He was "hateful, suspect, tattling and deceitful" and enjoyed an invalid status he was not entitled to. He vomited fake blood, charged Menchaca, and after retirement had been catching cows on *realengas*. The old proverb "A liar is sooner caught than a cripple" fit these scum well, in his opinion.

Don Luis claimed that he had not been able to brand in 1784 or 1785 or pay his tithes, citing his son Luis Mariano's contingent imprisonment as the reason, and also because his brother Félix had gone to seek justice from the demands of Pacheco. Implying that the governor was behind both of these family misfortunes, he quoted from a written opinion on how Cabello had "directed his efforts" against the Menchacas, stating that the commandant general agreed with this assessment. Since he could not manage the branding thus impaired, he ordered his cows turned loose until August, when it became necessary to pay the tithe. After gathering, Don Luis summoned his neighbors to sort, as was the universal custom. Only after the roundup, he claimed, could he pay his tithe, for "it was necessary to brand in order to pay it." The soldiers from Agua Verde were rounding up mustangs in the vicinity, as were soldiers of Béxar Presidio, who did not need permission to do so. The old captain doubtless still harbored a grudge against Cabello for ousting his son José from the Béxar military installation over a few measly bundles of contraband goods found hidden in a ditch.

About the vicious charge of illegal branding, Menchaca denounced as liars those who said it. "I should charge them," he countered. His accusers built corrals on lands not theirs. They had rights "we raisers do not enjoy," such as catching cattle on the pretext of hunting mesteño horses. *They* should be prosecuted, not ranchers like himself. Don Luis pointed out that his corrals stood on his own property and that he was not a trespasser on crown lands, as were others. "I am gravely injured," he concluded, "and can find no one to take up the pen for me, so this is my defense." It was submitted late in November, only a few days before Cabello left office, passing this and many other headaches to his successor. The Menchaca clan was doubtless glad to see him go.[37]

Fortunately for Cabello, not all exports were as difficult to process as were those conducted from Rancho de San Francisco. But because of suspected frauds, by the end of his term the governor had evolved a set of rules, and all persons desiring to export stock had to abide by them. If stock was freshly branded, however, it was automatically subject to confiscation. The five steps were as follows: (1) a license to hunt was applied for; (2) a commissioner was appointed; (3) the herd was inspected by the commissioner, who then submitted a breakdown showing number, kind, and so on; (4) the fees were paid; and (5) the *guía* was issued. As for the fees exacted, cattle taken above the Guadalupe, that is, in the king's lands, were charged at only 4 reales each, the standard catching fee. But for all cattle taken below the river, that is, in contested pastures, the sliding scale as set forth in Cabello's *bando* of July, 1783, was applied,

---

[37] *Expediente* no. 84, BAT, vol. 140, contains the proceedings against the "Old Captain," Don Luis Antonio Menchaca.

ranging from 20 reales for a mature cow to 8 reales for a yearling. Cabello's five requirements remained the standard practice in future years, and other export *expedientes* vary only slightly.

Nowhere are the workings of this formula better illustrated than in the instances of the herd taken out of the province by Francisco Xavier Rodríguez in October, 1786, and other drives conducted at the same time. Julián de Arocha, for example, asked to hunt between the Guadalupe, San Marcos, and Colorado rivers at the rate of 4 reales a head but could not find enough wild stock to fill out the herd desired. He finished by hunting below the Guadalupe and paying the steeper fees. Juan and Manuel de Arocha and their brother-in-law Ignacio Calvillo also sought permission to export cattle in August, 1786, "having an urgent need for reales." When José Días went to inspect their herd at "Los Challopines," he found that most of them were branded but that 55 were *orejanos* of various ages. Thus, after 69 pesos, 4 reales, were deposited in Cabello's chest, these three entrepreneurs received a *guía* for all 208 head. The system worked like a charm as long as people were willing to abide by it.[38]

Some good news for the ranchers was transmitted to Béxar by Commandant General Ugarte on September 30, 1786. It was in reference to the collection of tithes on *orejano* stock, the issue initiated by Bishop Verger and pressed by Bachiller Pedro Fuentes. Basing his decision on Galindo Navarro's opinion, Ugarte upheld Cabello's refusal to comply: "Consequently, for the time being and until new instructions, you shall suspend the payment of *diezmos* on stray cattle which breed in lands and forests of that province. You shall do likewise with regard to income generated by the tax being charged for the license to round up and catch aforesaid cows."[39] Cabello notified the citizens of their good fortune on November 11, congratulating members of the cabildo (mostly ranchers) for having managed to defend this point to the benefit of all those who were granted licenses to round up mesteño and *orejano* cattle. He hoped they realized the credit due them, "though hardly repaid."[40] The governor could afford to be gracious: his successor, Rafael Martínez Pacheco, was on the way. In fact, Commandant General Ugarte's suspension of the collection of mesteño tithes was addressed to Martínez Pacheco in that capacity. Cabello informed Ugarte that the citizens had been advised that they no longer owed taxes—meaning the church's tithe—on wild stock captured. Bishop Verger protested the decision, but with little success.[41]

Cabello spent his remaining two weeks in office trying to

---

[38] BAT, 141:18, 47. A similar petition is found in Manuel de Arocha et al., *expediente* no. 112, BAT, 139:78.

[39] Ugarte to Martínez Pacheco, September 30, 1786, BAT, 141:114.

[40] Cabello to Cabildo, November 11, 1786, BAT, 142:102.

[41] Cabello to Ugarte, November 19, 1786, ibid., p. 110; Castañeda, *Catholic Heritage*, 5:27–28; Faulk, *Last Years*, p. 88; Myres, *Ranch in Spanish Texas*, p. 40.

tie up loose ends, a formidable task. Martínez Pacheco presented his credentials on November 30, and the next two days were spent in briefings, primarily on the coming formalization of peace with the Comanches. On December 3, 1786, Cabello formally turned the governorship over to Martínez Pacheco, along with inventories of the various documents—many of them pertaining to cattle—for which his successor would now be responsible. Yet Cabello lingered in Béxar another four months, putting his records in order, particularly the Mustang Fund accounts.[42]

One of the many pending cattle *expedientes* to which Cabello hurriedly added finishing flourishes was number 80, his branding file. The governor's frustration over the lack of branding done during the past two years has been noted. He also admitted that his rulings were inadequate, and that slowness and *descuido* (neglect), but mostly the attitudes of the citizens, had resulted in great loss. The problem could not be attributed to Indian hostilities because peace had been achieved in October, 1785. Nonetheless, concluded Cabello, this file was to be added to the record of exports and turned over to Rafael Martínez Pacheco, along with others on the subject.[43]

This "record of exports" was a long document listing *guías*, which Cabello finished on November 29, saying: "It appears that 18,449 head of branded and *orejano* cattle have been exported from this province to the surrounding ones between July 19 of the year 1779 and November 2 of 1786. This information has been derived from the *guías* which have been issued to the persons who have exported the aforementioned cattle."[44] The *guías* were listed by date of issue, the name of the applicant, and the number of stock covered, both branded and *orejano*. A running total was then extended in the margin. Although the shortcomings of Cabello's bookkeeping will be discussed later, it is appropriate to mention here that only two herds specifically destined for Louisiana were shown in this listing, one taken in October, 1780, by Marcos Hernández (1,234

[42] John, *Storms*, p. 723.
[43] "Concerning Branding," *expediente* no. 80, BAT, vol. 89.
[44] "Record of Exports," entry of November 29, 1786, BAT, 142:130–38.

head) and another taken in August, 1782, by Antonio le Blanc (1,200 head). To learn the intended destination of drives other than these, individual *expedientes* must be consulted. Many entries simply say "Coahuila or elsewhere," indicating that this information was not considered vital. The top ten exporters during Cabello's eight-year administration, as indicated by his *guía* information, are shown in table 8.

TABLE 8. Major Cattle Exporters, 1779–86.

Rancher	No. Head Exported
1. Simón de Arocha	3,226
2. Luis Mariano Menchaca	2,216
3. Felipe Flores	1,286
4. Vizente Flores	1,259
5. Juan José Flores (the younger)	897
6. Juan Barrera	731
7. Julián de Arocha	707
8. Santiago Seguín	581
9. Manuel de Arocha	542
10. José Antonio Curbelo	414

SOURCE: Cabello, "Record of Exports," November 19, 1786, BAT, 142:130–38. These totals do not count the two Louisiana exports mentioned, and Curbelo actually should rank higher in the list, since a herd taken out by Manuel Delgado contained 225 head belonging to him. A complete summary of Cabello's record of exports is shown in appendix A.

Many herds discussed in the foregoing chapters are not included in this list—as the ranchers would soon point out in their condemnations of Cabello—which makes one suspect that his grand total of 18,449 was too low. Father López's estimate of 15,000 for the period, "most of them cows," was still more conservative.[45] The ranchers themselves guessed that more than 13,000 head were legally trailed out under Cabello,

[45] Dabbs, *López's Report*, p. 13. Fray López did say "more than" 15,000 head, but since he listed five factors destroying the herds, perhaps he felt it best to understate the inroads made by exporters, especially since his missions were foremost.

an estimate that seems even further off.[46] Like the estimates given for the sizes of the herds owned by the missions of Texas during their zenith, export figures quoted by modern-day authorities vary considerably. For example, Faulk states that Texas cattle were driven to Louisiana after 1780 at the *annual* rate of 15,000 to 20,000 head.[47] Castañeda says only that from 1780 to 1788, "according to official records, over 24,000 were caught, killed, or driven to market in the adjoining provinces. The injudicious waste of this valuable asset was the forerunner of the economic ruin of the missions and the Spanish civil settlements of Texas."[48] Neither writer cites the records consulted.

While he leans heavily toward Father López's views on the demise of the missions, Castañeda has a clear-eyed view of the Béxar *vecinos*: "It is further to be kept in mind that the hunters of wild cattle were not particular about reporting accurately the number caught or killed because the more accurate the report was, the greater the amount that would be due the royal treasury." Applying this insight to the numbers exported, one can judge why Cabello fretted about additional *orejano* stock being added to taxed herds after they left the inspector's sight. Likewise, it can be deduced that attempts to calculate the true numbers exported are little more than exercises in futility. It is safe, however, to assume that the actual exports exceeded the official figures, just as wild stock always exceeded the number the cattlemen managed to brand and tally. In my opinion, Spanish ranching in the eighteenth century does not, in the final analysis, depend on impressive figures to reflect its impact on the Texas legacy, for its contribution transcended the numerical realm.

Perhaps it was the "injudicious waste" that Castañeda speaks of that led to a halt on the livestock trade begun with Louisiana in 1779. On many occasions during the 1780s, Croix extolled the advantages of interprovincial commerce to the

---

[46] Robert S. Weddle and Robert H. Thonhoff, *Drama and Conflict: The Texas Saga of 1776*, p. 171 (the authors' source not noted).

[47] Faulk, "Ranching in Spanish Texas," p. 264.

[48] Castañeda, *Catholic Heritage*, 5:31–32.

king, and Colonial Secretary José de Gálvez unfailingly pressed the issue, asking the viceroy to do the same. In 1783, the year that Croix was appointed viceroy of Peru, he wrote Gálvez a long letter suggesting the opening of a trade route between Béxar and New Orleans, a move which, he said, would cause the province of Texas to "flourish and grow rapidly." With Gálvez's endorsement the proposal was referred to the Sala del Consulado de México (Royal Consular Tribunal of Mexico) for study. In a decision dated September 7, 1786, this distinguished body handed down a ruling on Croix's suggestions that amounted to the kiss of death.

The ruling cited various statistics to demonstrate that New Spain was almost completely dependent on the Interior Provinces for its supply of livestock (to the extent of 30,000 head of cattle, 300,000 sheep, and 200,000 goats annually), as well as such products as leather, wool, and fats. Unfortunately, Indian troubles on the frontier had reduced the ability of these provinces to furnish their quotas, even to the point where Coahuila and Nuevo León were forced to draw heavily upon the Texas herds. It was feared that if Texas was allowed to export stock to Louisiana, Nueva España's reserve would be alarmingly diminished. Thus the tribunal of commerce, while recognizing the benefits of a livestock trade between Texas and Louisiana, opposed the opening of such trade until the Indian situation could be stabilized. José de Gálvez, ennobled as the Marqués de Sonora, had worked hard to obtain a favorable ruling and was no doubt severely disappointed. In any case, his death the next year silenced one of New Spain's strongest spokesmen for expanded commerce.[49]

---

[49] J. Villasana Haggard, "Neutral Ground between Louisiana and Texas," *Louisiana Historical Quarterly* 28, no. 4 (October, 1945): 1075–77 (drawn from documents in AGN, Provincias Internas, vol. 182 of the Hackett Transcripts, University of Texas Archives). In reference to Croix's and José de Gálvez's efforts to secure trade between Texas and Louisiana, see Gálvez to the Viceroy, May 5, 1784, and November 3, 1785, Grace A. Edman, trans. and ed., "A Compilation of Royal Decrees Relating to Texas and Other Provinces of New Spain, 1719–1799" (Master's thesis, University of Texas, 1930), pp. 404, 409. For a discussion of economic and trade reforms pushed by José de

The ban on exportation of stock was implemented in the decision rendered on June 2, 1787, on a petition of April 3, by Nicolás de la Mathe to take a small herd to Louisiana with the help of three *mozos* (servants). The *fiscal* decided not to honor the former commandant general's recommendations on La Mathe's petition, "much less allow him [La Mathe] to remove cows and other items covered by laws which should not be contravened." After leaving office, Cabello added his voice to the opposition, echoing opinions expressed at the beginning of his term. He told the viceroy that inhabitants of Louisiana were "greedily eager to enjoy the cattle of Texas, both the wild stock and the herds owned by the settlers," for which they exchanged merchandise instead of money. This, of course, led to much smuggling, the result being that the revenue on goods shipped from Mexico, and commerce itself, would diminish. Such opinions swayed official policy in both provinces, as indicated by the decree that Commandant Louis de Blanc posted in Natchitoches on June 4, 1788. By order of Governor Estévan Rodríguez Miró, he notified the inhabitants that trade with Texas was henceforth prohibited. So once again the border was sealed to herds of Texas cattle, and the trade was forced into clandestine routes.[50]

Domingo Cabello, stirring around his quarters in the Casa Real, struggling to balance his accounts and work through a tall stack of unfinished paperwork, most likely had other things on his mind than the exact number of cattle smuggled out of the province behind his back. Nor did he make claims to an exact count of the legal export, saying only that "it appears" that 18,449 head were taken. His efforts were merely a valiant attempt at satisfying appearances. Even though he was destined for a more comfortable post in Havana, he could not have felt confident about leaving his delicate Comanche negotiations in the hands of a man like Martínez Pacheco. His successor was not an administrator but a soldier, a grizzled old veteran of military

Gálvez, such as the intendancy system, see MacLachlan and Rodríguez O., *Forging of the Cosmic Race,* pp. 268–74.

[50] Genaro García Collection, folder 197; R. B. Blake, Research Collection, Supplement ser., 2:302 (University of Texas Archives); Haggard, "Neutral Ground."

in-fighting who was not likely to treat the Comanches or any other Indians with the restraint that Cabello felt was essential to a good working relationship. Also, he was old, in retirement from a controversial but undistinguished military career.

The stories about Martínez Pacheco were legend to everyone associated with the colonial affairs of New Spain. Twenty-odd years before, Captain Martínez Pacheco had singlehandedly resisted a force sent out by Governor Martos to strip him of his command at Orcoquisac—a force composed of twenty of Martínez Pacheco's own men who had deserted their post. When Lieutenant Marcos Ruíz read the governor's edict and then ordered his men forward to arrest the deposed captain, he boldly declared that he would not relinquish his command while he was alive. He fired into the soldiers and fought them off with his fists until he could bar the door of the fort. Finally Ruíz set fire to the fort, thereby forcing all of its occupants to come out—all but Martínez Pacheco, and an examination of the smoldering ruins revealed no charred corpse.

The captain had escaped through a secret passageway. Despite Ruíz's efforts to stop him, he eventually made his way to Mexico City. Pleading his case before the viceroy, Martínez Pacheco won vindication; all charges against him were dropped, and he returned to Texas to resume his command at Orcoquisac, by then called San Agustín de Ahumada. Neither Governor Martos nor Marcos Ruíz fared as well: both were arrested for burning a royal presidio, a very serious offense. Ruíz was dismissed from the king's service, and the governor's trial dragged on for fourteen years in the capital. Finally Martos was found guilty of complicity and fined heavily, his career ruined by a petty vendetta with the man who was now to be the new governor of the province.

Thus Rafael Martínez Pacheco had survived and kept his job on the frontier, but stubbornness was not necessarily a quality that would help him with the Comanches. It might, in fact, do just the opposite—imperil the fragile peace or destroy it altogether. He had a known dislike and distrust of all the Nations of the North. He had conspired with Oconor, who shared his views of the plains tribes, to undermine the administration of former governor Ripperdá (this, of course, could have been a point in his favor with the citizens of Texas). After Martínez Pacheco went "berserk," as John describes it, in East Texas, he wound up serving as a presidial captain at San Antonio de la Babia in Coahuila with about the same effectiveness. That he had even been considered fit to govern the province was a sad commentary on the quality of men available for frontier service in New Spain. But the matter was out of Cabello's hands.[51]

[51] Accounts of Martínez Pacheco's military background in Texas are found in Herbert Eugene Bolton, *Texas in the Middle Eighteenth Century*, pp. 367–72; Castañeda, *Catholic Heritage*, 4:87–94, 266–71; John, *Storms*, pp. 436–38, 448. John, it should be noted, portrays Martínez Pacheco in a less favorable light than that of the other authorities cited.

Just as Ripperdá had left him a legacy of bitter relations with the stockmen of the province, Cabello proceeded to turn over his accumulated woes to Martínez Pacheco. The *sumaria* on Blás Eca y Múzquiz's export of August, 1784, was one of them, as was José Félix Menchaca's flight from justice in 1785 and the new case against old Captain Menchaca—like a freshly applied brand, still "smoking and bleeding." As might be expected, Cabello wanted his successor to deal harshly with the ranchers who had given him the most trouble, Luis Mariano Menchaca and Juan José Flores. He wanted the troublemaker Menchaca held accountable for a value put on several herds after they were driven out, and Flores had also been retroactively assessed for two drives—one in early 1780 and another in 1781—both conducted when the exportation fee amounted to only 4 reales. While it is true that the governor had warned them that they might be responsible for the value of animals caught in contested pastures, there was possibly some vindictiveness in his disposition of these cases. In one, *expediente* 91, he had written that Flores had left the villa on behalf of its citizens in an attempt to acquire ownership of unbranded cattle for them, despite the commandant general's claims for the king. The economic reprisals outlined reflect considerable enmity toward this rebellious member of the ranchero society.

This view is further evidenced by the fact that Cabello turned over to Martínez Pacheco other proceedings from his "dead file," marking each as requiring further pursuit. Included were Ripperdá's final rustling trial—the one with strong criminal implications—involving primarily the elder Juan José Flores, and even the one held in 1777, long since put to rest. The *asesor* had returned this case, *expediente* 74, in October, 1782, so that "justice could be administered to the defendant," but by then the old rancher was deceased. Considering that the case had long since been closed for all practical purposes, it is difficult to say why Cabello still regarded it otherwise, except out of a predilection for bureaucratic niceties. In fairness to the governor, it should be mentioned that he also turned over other past-due *expedientes* for collection, such as those of Vizente Flores and José Antonio Curbelo. Perhaps he surrendered all these "un-

"*Could They but Be Restored*"   319

finished" documents to his successor not out of malice but merely because it was standard procedure in turning over archives. One thing, however, is definite: the ranchers of Béxar were as glad to be rid of Domingo Cabello as he was to be rid of them.[52]

In terms of ranching, his eight-year administration had witnessed the first legally sanctioned exportation of livestock to Louisiana, a trade now terminated. His period of office had been wracked by the implementation of Croix's cattle law and the many protests that had stemmed from this universally detested edict. These protests the lord assessor had firmly rejected in an array of opinions, all aimed at upholding His Majesty's claim to the wild herds in Texas. As the year 1786 ended, there seemed no alternative for the stock raisers of the province but to submit their ownership claims and yield to the demands of "good government." About all they could hope to gain, as Juan José Flores acknowledged in his last petition, was another roundup extension, during which they would ride forth and capture as many animals as possible before the hated tax was levied. Such a gloomy prospect might have discouraged ordinary men.

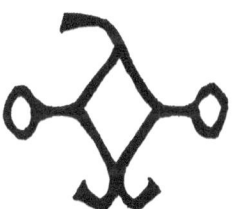

---

[52] See final entries in *expediente* no. 96, BAT, vol. 112; *expediente* no. 86, BAT, vol. 126; *expediente* no. 91, BAT, vol. 95; *expediente* no. 92, BAT, vol. 108. Among the files that Cabello transferred because "important business" had kept him from attending to them were the rustling proceedings of 1777, *expediente* no. 74, BAT, vol. 64; and the *expediente* of 1778 charging larceny, BAT, vol. 113, different from but related to lawsuit no. 39 drawn up against these same individuals for perjury, BAT, vol. 75.

9

"DAMAGED AND TROUBLED MEN"

The First Big Roundup

Perhaps no one was as glad to see Cabello go—or to see Rafael Martínez Pacheco take his place—as the retired captain Don Luis Antonio Menchaca. Both of them were old military men with much experience in Texas, and Menchaca had helped Martínez Pacheco when he was on the run from Orcoquisac. After fleeing the burning presidio, Martínez Pacheco made for La Bahía; there Captain Piscina gave him temporary refuge and a horse. Going on to Mission San José to seek sanctuary, Martínez Pacheco was nonetheless arrested there by Captain Menchaca upon receipt of a proclamation from Lieutenant Ruíz ordering him apprehended (the right of sanctuary in churches was usually withheld from the military). Menchaca, however, soon put him at liberty, and he lived for several months at San José, free to come and go. Castañeda describes the situation thus: "Governor Martos was indignant at the laxity of Menchaca and later reported that he had not only failed to keep Martínez Pacheco in prison but had gone with him to a bullfight in San Antonio. On another occasion Martínez Pacheco had attended a mask ball disguised in woman's apparel without being molested in the least."[1]

From this it can be seen that Governor Martínez Pacheco was somewhat indebted to Don Luis Menchaca and not likely to exact Cabello's pound of flesh from the old captain or his family. Other prominent ranchers welcomed the change of guard as well. A group of them addressed him several years later saying that they were "forty years disunited until you came to put us at peace," a fairly strong endorsement since the cattlemen of Béxar were not noted for their good relations with governors. Martínez Pacheco not only was sympathetic with the outraged cattle raisers and missionaries of the province but worked steadfastly for their interests throughout his term of office.[2]

A good example of the progress (from the ranchers' point of view) that took place under Martínez Pacheco is the roundup agreement dated January 8, 1787, one month after he assumed office. The agreement was headed "Agreement Celebrated by the Cabildo and Residents of This Presidio of San Antonio de Béxar of the Province of Texas with the Missions of the Province, Regarding the Rounding Up of Their Cattle, Bovine and Equine, Branded as Well as Unbranded, Stray, and Ownerless." None of the roundups of the past approached this rodeo in planning, scope, and execution, and it can be regarded as the First Big Roundup in Texas, the most important event of its kind in the eighteenth century.

The parties to the agreement represent a virtual who's who

---

[1] Carlos E. Castañeda, *Our Catholic Heritage in Texas*, 4:93. Martínez Pacheco's official appointment as provisional governor did not come through until February 27, 1787. He was granted a salary of 1,400 pesos besides his annual pension of 1,000 pesos (Grace A. Edman, trans. and ed., "A Compilation of Royal Decrees Relating to Texas and Other Provinces of New Spain, 1719–1799" [Master's thesis, University of Texas, 1930], p. 423).

[2] A citizens' petition "protesting an election of cabildo officers," March 1 and 2, 1790 (R. B. Blake, Research Collection, Supplement ser., 2:244–71), contains the quote about Martínez Pacheco's abilities as a peacemaker. Elizabeth A. H. John (*Storms Brewed in Other Men's Worlds: The Confrontation of Indians, Spanish, and French in the Southwest, 1540–1795*, p. 755) says that he "never earned or merited the confidence of . . . his Spanish constituents"—or anyone else, for that matter—but Castañeda praises Martínez Pacheco for his sympathy and support of the province's cattlemen (*Catholic Heritage*, 5:29), viewing his earlier actions in East Texas as somewhat justified.

of early Texas ranching. Representing the private raisers were Simón de Arocha, first alcalde; Luis Mariano Menchaca, second alcalde; Joaquín Menchaca, *regidor de cano* (senior councilman); Joaquín Leal, second *regidor*; Pedro Sambrano, third *regidor*; Mariano Delgado, fourth *regidor*; Joaquín Flores, fifth *regidor*; Santiago Seguín, sixth *regidor*; and Juan José Bueno, *procurador síndico general* (city attorney). Also present were Juan José Flores, in the capacity of "general agent" for the residents, and Macario Sambrano, acting in a similar role. Having returned to Béxar after self-imposed exile since mid-1784, Flores was no doubt glad to be home. His return so soon after Cabello's official stepdown must have galled the former governor, who was still in town and remained there until March 26.

Representing the missions in the agreement were Fray José Francisco López, of San Antonio de Valero; Fray Manuel de Villegra, of Concepción; Fray Manuel Gonzáles, of San Juan; Fray Pedro Noreña, of Espada; and, attending for Fray José Luis Mariano de Cárdenas, of Espíritu Santo, was the father *presidente*, Fray José Rafael de Oliva, of Mission San José. San José, it should be noted, was not a party to the roundup, since its lands were far removed from the contested ground. Also, San José mission had few cattle to protect by this time.[3]

All these dignitaries came before Governor Martínez Pacheco and stated that it was now fourteen years, "more or less," since they had been able to do their branding with the formality to which they had been accustomed in the past. This hiatus, they maintained, had been caused in part by the continuous and incessant Comanche war, only recently concluded. They asked to be allowed to do their branding in seven different parties, specifying an area in which each corrida would operate. The private cattlemen were divided into three groups: San Bartolo and the Guerras; Los Granados and Las Mulas; and the largest, composed of ranchers Hernández, Marcos de Castro, the Men-

---

[3] Fr. Marion A. Habig's *The Alamo Chain of Missions: A History of San Antonio's Five Old Missions*, pp. 234–56, contains a very helpful guide to the priests who served in eighteenth-century Texas, as does his "Biographical Dictionary" in Fr. Benedict Leutenegger, trans., *The Zacatecan Missionaries of Texas, 1716–1834: Excerpts from the Libros de los Decretos of the Missionary College of Zacatecas, 1707–1728*.

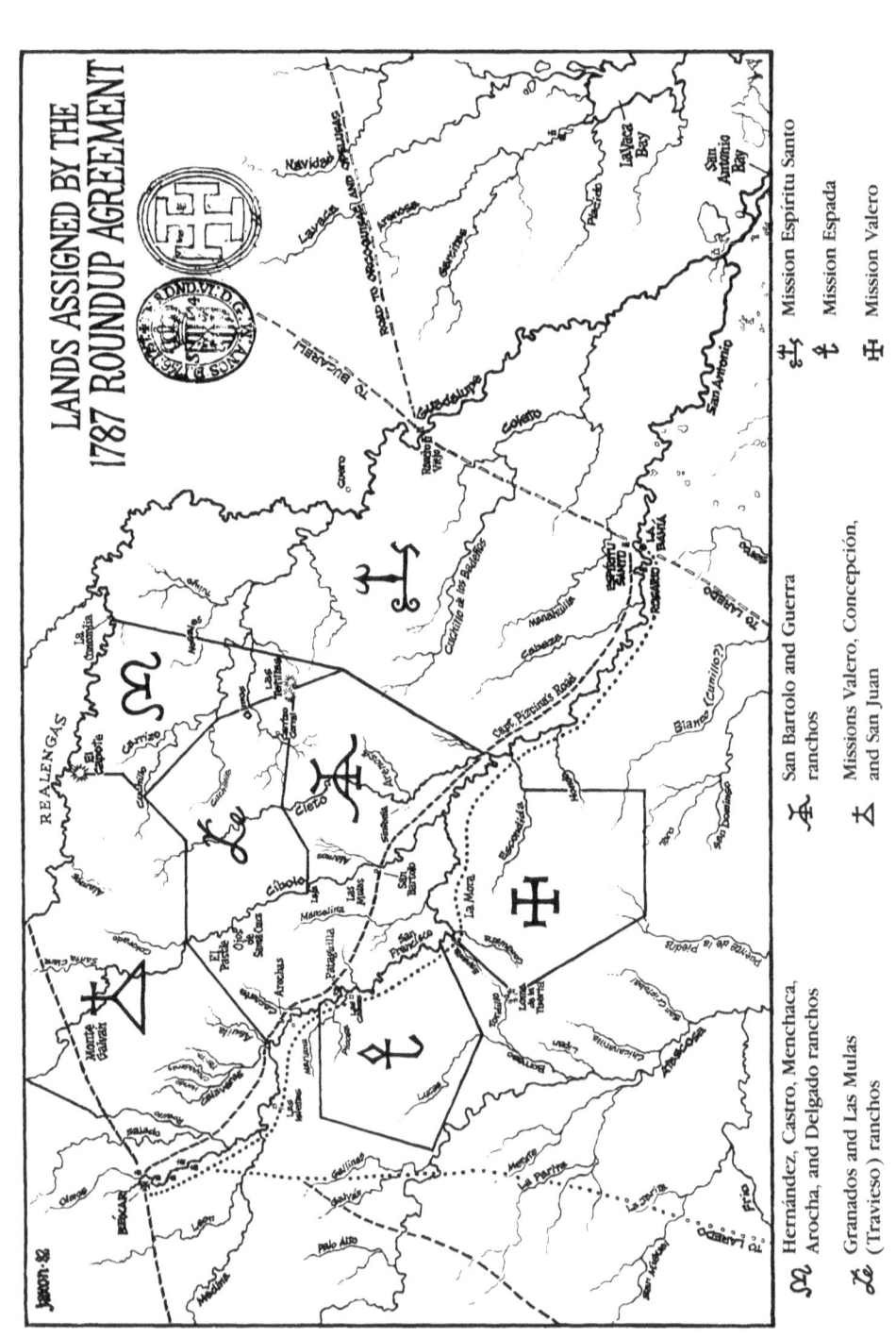

chacas, the Delgados, and the Arochas. The missions would ride in four groups: Espada; Valero; a group composed of Concepción and San Juan, including vaqueros from Valero; and Espíritu Santo. For the first group, its ranch, Las Cabras, was the designated area of operation. Valero would search the pastures of La Mora; and the joint *partida* would operate in grazing grounds shared by all three, i.e., those in the area where present Bexar, Wilson, and Guadalupe counties converge. Mission Espíritu Santo would gather by itself, ranging throughout its vast domain between the Guadalupe and the San Antonio rivers.

The designated area covered a triangular swath with its apex at Green Lake, above Tivoli, up the Guadalupe River as far as present McQueeney, and over to present Schertz-Cibolo. Its base line skirted San Antonio, running to the vicinity of present Pleasanton and Jourdanton, and then back down the coast. The triangle, pointing in an easterly direction, had bulges on the north line to present Gonzales and on the south to present Pawnee. It took in all of present Wilson and Karnes counties and half of Victoria, De Witt, Gonzales, Guadalupe, and Goliad counties, as well as portions of Bexar and Atascosa (see map "Lands Assigned by the 1787 Roundup Agreement"). The private ranchers, while wedged in between the hunting grounds of the missions, gained the right to hunt in lands formerly claimed by Espíritu Santo—lands from which it still cost them 20 reales each to take cows, according to the *bandos* Cabello had left in effect. Martínez Pacheco, in his authorization of the roundup provided for possible eventualities of this nature, requiring that, once the sweeps were complete, each raiser must present to him a list or sworn report of the number and types of whatever unbranded, stray, and ownerless stock which they took and branded, "so that whatever repercussions might develop in this matter, the raisers will be within their rights against any charges which might be brought against them."[4] Signing this historic

[4] The roundup agreement, trans. John Wheat, is in BAT, 144:10–19. Another translation made in 1940 by Martin Henry, is available in Grazing Papers, vol. 1 (University of Texas Archives), and includes a discussion of the various Spanish terms for wild cattle. See also Pacheco's correspondence with Fray Oliva, ACZ, roll 3, frame 2936, etc. The existence of this roundup agreement has been acknowledged by most authorities, but few have dwelt on its significance, i.e., Castañeda, *Catholic Heritage*, 5:29; Charles

agreement, aimed at achieving the "best union and peace" which had not been seen before between mission and private raisers, were the same individuals named above, except that Fray Joseph María García rather than Villegra signed for Mission Concepción and Francisco Travieso added his signature to the ranchers' number.

Other documents were soon added to the initial agreement, doubtless the result of serious bargaining. The dispute apparently was precipitated by the resurrection of Fray Lorenzo Medina's protest lodged back in 1759 against the possession of lands conveyed by the Bernabé Carvajal deed of 1761. In lengthy proceedings submitted by Fray Cárdenas to Captain Luis Cazorla at La Bahía under date of March 17, 1787, this dispute was rehashed, its central point being that the lands in question belonged to Mission Rosario. This snag soon came to the attention of the cattlemen at Béxar, who, it seems, were busily pursuing the gains won by their recent "treaty" with the padres. In mid-May they acknowledged receipt of four documents of possession filed with a petition from Father President Oliva and registered their dismay at this unforeseen complication.

Oliva's petition, however, was directed to the governor, not the Béxar cabildo. It acknowledged the compromise of "seven articles" signed in his presence on January 8 and noted that the missions had relinquished much in this document whereas the citizens had given little. Despite this—or perhaps because of it—the *presidente*'s remarks clearly reveal that private cattlemen believed that the agreement marked the end of the missions' power and were already abusing the conditions set forth. The agreement did not allow them to take lands belonging to the missions, reiterated Oliva, or to squat there and build houses, corrals, and so forth. The agreement was strictly for a once-only branding, not for future roundups or brandings. Many individuals, said Oliva, did not want to understand this and had assumed that the roundup areas and boundaries were perpetual. Because of their high-handedness, as well as to prevent future

---

[William] Ramsdell, [Jr.], "Spanish Goliad" (typescript, University of Texas Archives), p. 26; Sandra L. Myres, "The Spanish Cattle Kingdom in the Province of Texas," *Texana* 4 (1966): 240–41.

abuses and protect the mission Indians, it was necessary to address these points. Father Oliva asked the governor to restrain the citizens and remind them of the exact terms as specified by the agreement. He noted that the Indians under his care "suffered unceasingly" because some cattlemen had taken undue advantage of its provisions.

The cabildo's response was immediate, denying vigorously all charges made by the father president. It was not true, said Alcalde Simón de Arocha and associates, that the cattle of the missions had suffered grave harm from their community. In attempting to get at the facts, the cabildo had to observe that the missionaries were not being honest about such damages. Nor could the priests say that they had made allowances to the citizenry in lands, "something they can never prove." Arocha told Governor Martínez Pacheco that the citizens did not recognize any rights on the papers submitted because of the many nullities associated with Carvajal's deed. Not only was the date of possession lacking, but the missions did not populate those lands as required.

Furthermore, said Arocha, it was well known that the cattlemen had sent an agent to defend before the commandant general their rights to unbranded stock in the province, a defense conducted without cost to the missions. Both the first reprieve of four months and the "six-month extension" had been rejected by the ranchers' representative—with good reason, the cabildo added, because if it had been accepted it would have done them grave harm at the end of that branding period. The ranchers would have been placed in a condition of enforced idleness, "which the padres wish us in now." Rather than the missionaries having conceded anything to the citizens, Arocha claimed, it was the other way around—by virtue of the missions' inability to conduct roundups as ordered by the governor. Since the ranchers were able to do so, Arocha reasoned, in agreeing not to enter certain pastures they—not the missions—were granting the concessions.[5]

---

[5] See GLO, 50: 198–215, for the documents growing out of Fray Medina's protest of 1759 on behalf of Mission Rosario, even though it seems he was then a minister at neighboring Espíritu Santo. Contained are copies of (1) Carvajal's grant from Governor Barrios of November, 1755; (2) a Barrios–Father Garzía document dated February 4,

Out of this dispute came a power of attorney granted on May 20, 1787, to Juan José Flores, Simón de Arocha, and Joaquín Menchaca by twenty of their fellow ranchers (see fig. 2). No doubt Oliva's protest had some influence on this decision, but the focus was elsewhere, on matters of greater import. Stating that they wanted to end the feud with the missions (especially with Espíritu Santo) regarding limits of pastures and doubtful landmarks, the cattlemen put their heads together and appointed these spokesmen. Apparently the private raisers felt themselves to be in total command of the situation relative to the Béxar missions, for this liaison was formed strictly to deal with Fray Cárdenas at La Bahía. These were the pastures rich in *orejanos* where the aspiring *ganaderos* faced competition when it came to gathering them. If any problems arose over the January partition, Flores, Arocha, and Menchaca were entrusted to iron things out.

On June 20 the three representatives reached an accord with Fray Cárdenas, removing all obstacles from the long-sought roundup. It specified a new, slightly different line between the ranchers and Espíritu Santo and set severe penalties for those who encroached upon territories assigned to others: a 100-peso fine and transfer of cattle taken to the offended party. Anyone who was unhappy with the arrangement had to put up 500 pesos to contest it, a deposit so exorbitant that it virtually guaranteed satisfaction. The Bernabé Carvajal deed was upheld, and ranchers ceased their claim to these lands, but only if the mission maintained its control. Strangely, most of the Carvajal bequest lay above the line—in the ranchers' assigned hunting area—so perhaps this was a future concession. In any case, the heirs of Juan José Flores, Martín Lorenzo de Armas, and Miguel Guerra were allowed to seek their own agreements with the padres at Espíritu Santo. Finally, while both branded and unbranded stock could be taken on the roundup, a sworn report was to be given the governor.

1759 (which mentions Fray Medina's "contradiction"); (3) Carvajal's deed of Corralitos to the Indians of Espíritu Santo dated June 6, 1761; and (4) Francisco Antonio de Echavarri's confirmation of Carvajal's title, dated at Mexico City, May 24, 1765. These were no doubt the four documents of possession rejected by the Béxar cabildo (GLO, 50:214).

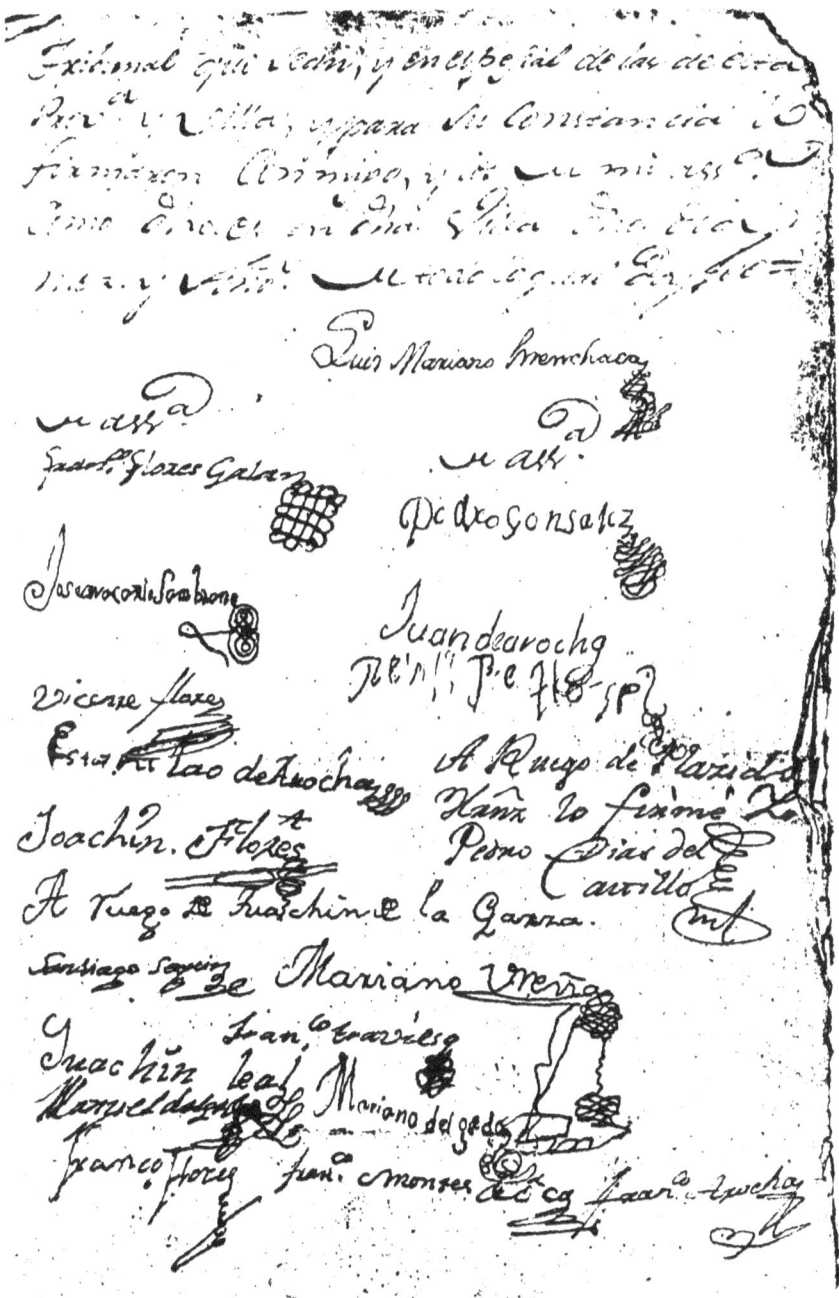

Fig. 2. Signature page of ranchers' power of attorney, May 20, 1787.

The new northern boundary between Espíritu Santo and the ranchers was defined as follows: from the place where the Alonzo emptied into the Cleto; to the headwaters of "said arroyo" (the Alonzo), on the banks of an *encinal* (oak grove); to the corral of Juan Flores; then in a straight line north to La Tetilla ("where the mine was"), on to the second hill, and then to the third; then east across an arroyo of Rosario; from there in same direction between the arroyos of Nogales and Tuliyo, to the Nogales; and from there *east* to the Río Guadalupe at its watering place, where a small stream entered. In honor of the agreement, this spot was dubbed "La Concordia." This creek, since lost, seems to have been in the general vicinity of present Gonzales, around the junction of the San Marcos and the Guadalupe rivers, although it could be argued that it was as far downriver as Fulcher Creek, near the Gonzales–De Witt county line. Either way, it represented substantial gains for the private ranchers.[6]

Having reached agreement with Espíritu Santo, the principal mission cattle owner, the Béxar ranchers then set about to organize their roundup among themselves so as to avoid any misunderstandings. The cabildo and the agents for the citizens worked out a schedule of how many vaqueros would be allowed in each *partida*, summarized as follows:

The Arochas and affiliates	10
Menchaca and affiliates	16
The Delgados and affiliates	16
Hernández, Sambrano, and affiliates	16
The Floreses and affiliates	16
The Guerras	6
Las Mulas and affiliates	16
The Granados and affiliates	16
Total allowed	112

[6] NA, Transcripts, 6:90–101. See figure 2 for a facsimile of the following signatures from the power of attorney of May 20: Francisco Flores Galán, José Macario Sambrano, Vizente Flores, Estanislao de Arocha, Joaquín Flores "at request of" Joachín de la Garza, Santiago Seguín, Mariano Ureña, Francisco Travieso, Joachín Leal, Manuel Delgado, Francisco Flores, Mariano Delgado, Francisco Móntes de Oca, Francisco de Arocha, Luis Mariano Menchaca, Pedro Gonzáles, Juan de Arocha, Phelipe [?] Flores, Pedro Días del Castillo "at request of" Plácido Hernández.

All parties agreed to limit their roundup to the lands assigned in the January agreement. Especially they would respect the boundaries indicated in the latest adjustment made with the mission of Espíritu Santo on the south, as well as with the missions on the north. This list was presented to Governor Martínez Pacheco on July 4, 1787, so that the ranchers might "undertake their roundup of *orejano* cattle in the same terms cited in the clauses of the agreement celebrated on the eighth day of the month of January of the year 1787, except that all the woods of Galván are made free by the mission of San Antonio Balero." The Monte Galván (near present Randolph Air Force Base) was part of Valero's lands, but since these woods were traditionally full of mission cattle, it is unlikely that Concepción, San Juan, and especially Valero under Fray López's guidance, would open them to general exploitation. Possibly this area was designated "free" in the sense of being set aside as a reserve, to be used as a gathering grounds at some future date but not on this particular roundup (the corrida authorized by Governor Muñoz in 1795 specified such a use for these woods).

Concerning the demarcation of boundaries, it is interesting to note a discovery reported by an archaeological team working on the Walker Ranch. This area lies on Salado Creek just west of Randolph Field, between Loop 410 and Ranch Road 1604, north of San Antonio but still in Bexar County. Two limestone pillars were found, each about a yard and a half tall; both display what appear to be cattle brands, and one bears the date 1786. Since Mission Valero's traditional western boundary extended up the Salado, and the roundup agreement specified its gathering area as coming down from the Cíbolo to "Corral de Barrancas," thence to the Rosillo (a tributary just east of the Salado), it is tempting to associate the cross-shaped brand motif with this mission. Further, the date suggests that perhaps these pylons were erected in anticipation of the celebrated agreement, suggesting also that others yet undiscovered were set up to mark various specified *linderos*. Indeed, it seems possible that the stone ruins on Walker Ranch may date from colonial times and could well have been the corral mentioned or another used by Mission Valero in conjunction with its Monte Galván Rancho. The discovery of similar pillars would do much to support such a view, but, as Father Morfi tells us, it was customary for the missions to mark the limits of their lands. In the instance of Espada, *mojoneras* (boundary stones) "painted with crosses" were used.

Also attached to the governor's acknowledgment of July 4 of the ratio of hands were what appear to be additional concessions granted by Espíritu Santo to the three families mentioned in Bernabé Carvajal's bequest of 1761. Las Mulas was grouped with "Los Granados," the heirs of the first marriage of María Robaina Bethencourt de Granados and those of her union with Martín Lorenzo de Armas. These areas, it would seem, lay beyond Ecleto Creek, in the eastern portions of Wilson and Karnes counties, slightly overlapping into the western portions of De Witt and Gonzales counties. This, of course, was the contested ground between Espíritu Santo and the ranchers of El Rincón, the same area for which the Cíbolo stockmen were punished for entering in Ripperdá's two rustling trials. It was in those rich, open grasslands, that old Juan José Flores, the sons of Andrés Hernández, and those of Vicente Álvarez Travieso had built their cattle pens and exploited the wild herds grazing there. Carrying the hard-fought struggle of their fathers to a successful end must have been sweet for the sons of those old pioneers. Juan José Flores the younger wasted little time capitalizing on the victory: late that summer he and his brothers were in Saltillo negotiating a contract to sell 1,000 bulls and bullocks at a price of 6 pesos each, receiving 4,000 pesos in advance, the balance to be paid on delivery.[7]

In August, Martínez Pacheco sent the contents of the strongbox from Cabello's administration, 7,627 pesos. The remainder of a total of 13,446 pesos (5,819 pesos) he noted as "engaged in assorted transactions"—probably used to meet

---

[7] Attached to the roundup agreement of January 8, 1787 (BAT, 144:17–19); William R. Hudson, Jr., et al., *Walker Ranch: An Archaeological Reconnaissance and Excavations in Northern Bexar County, Texas*, pp. 19, 22; Fr. Juan Agustín de Morfi, *Viaje de Indios y Diario del Nuevo México*, p. 219; Cattle Transactions, September 20 and October 6, 1787, Protocolos, Archivo Municipal, Saltillo, transcript provided by Adán Benavides, Jr.

various expenses the Mustang Fund was intended to cover. It was not until the following year, however, that Martínez Pacheco received the money due for 1786 from the other two locations where fees were collected, La Bahía and Nacogdoches. The former sent 114 pesos, 3 reales, and the latter sent 27 pesos, 4 reales, a total of 141 pesos, 7 reales. Adding this to the above gave Martínez Pacheco a starting figure for his administration of 7,769 pesos, although it took a while to get it.[8] Nor did exports stop with the change of governors. Captain Cazorla wrote in September about a resident of El Cantaro who planned to drive out a herd, gathered partly from Espíritu Santo and partly from Sergeant Antonio Treviño, of the Bahía Company. A *guía* was issued for 112 head, including 34 *orejanos*. Other similar extractions were made at La Bahía that September.[9]

Sometime during the late summer the ranchers submitted their "long and confused paper," or, as it was formally titled, "Memorial, Explanation and Defense, Presented by the Citizens of the Villa of San Fernando and the Royal Presidio of San An-

[8] BAT, 146:18; see also "Reports on Mesteños, 1786–1788," SA, 5:49–53, 56–62.
[9] BAT, 146–67; BAM, roll 18, frames 128–29, 172–73, 247–51.

tonio de Béxar to Rafael Martínez Pacheco, 1787."[10] Their stated purpose was to prevent the commandant general from issuing decrees which might work against their rights to *orejano* and mesteño stock. This stock, claimed the memorialists, had been seized for the Royal Treasury because of the unjust statements made by former Governor Cabello to the commandant general. Like many other assertions in the jumbled document, this one was not entirely correct, but it suited the purposes of the ranchers. Yet if it was not entirely true, it was at least half true, for Cabello had been their nemesis and was responsible, they believed, for the unpopular law he had so painstakingly enforced. It could not have mattered much to these men whether or not it was his creation; he was the one who shoved it down their throats.[11]

In consideration of their rights, "we the citizens" were joined by attorney Juan José Flores (as might be expected) and an associate, Macario Sambrano. Flores, however, was most likely instrumental in the planning and execution of the memorial, having submitted earlier a number of more modest efforts, all similar in their aim and all lacking in stylistic clarity and definition, as was the longer paper of 1787. Besides denouncing Cabello, the ranchers had two purposes in mind: to prove their legal right to the wild stock and to show why the former governor had taken them away. Unable to restrain themselves, the memorialists then gave the reason immediately: his self-interest, "concealed beneath superior orders." Cabello had never showed them any of the commandant general's original orders, despite their requests, and had greatly damaged their interests to wild stock by his unfair decrees over the past seven years. It was Cabello's fault, for surely no one so kind, wise, exalted, and so forth, as the commandant general would have taken "such hasty and intemperate action." Thus from the beginning Cabello was to be the scapegoat for all their afflictions.

The ranchers were not long in dangling the carrot, the con-

---

[10] This restatement of their case was being made "in spite of your [Martínez Pacheco's] kind letter of August 28, 1787," which dates the document after that time.

[11] "San Fernando Memorial," BAT, vol. 150. Other locations are cited in chap. 1, n.17 above.

cession they were willing to make if their rights were upheld. Wishing to clear away the confusion between livestock within their limits and that found beyond the Guadalupe River, on lands "we have never considered ours, but as unappropriated public domain," they freely ceded to the king all wild stock found in the latter places. This they did because of his "expenses," a ploy possibly inspired by the *asesor*'s scathing remarks of February 22, 1786. The stock beyond the Guadalupe was admittedly on royal lands and now wild, but "descended from ours," claimed the ranchers, and only their loyalty and appreciation to the king motivated such a sacrifice. Even so, they felt obliged to point out that it was a terrible thing for the lord assessor to say—"that even if we had a right to the stock we should renounce it." After all the hardships endured in twenty years of Indian warfare, to be deprived of what little they had left was not right, and he had no business asking it.

Flores had not been idle during his exile. He had obviously searched diligently for everything he could find with a bearing on the situation in Texas, going all the way back to various "ancient laws of Spain." He enlisted the help of counselors as well, like Doctor Don Antonio Bustamante, described as "governor of the vacant See of this bishopric."[12] It is very likely that the paper was conceptualized over a period of time, with new details added as he came upon them. Briefly scanning the early history of Béxar, the San Fernando Memorial moved quickly to the point: there was no livestock in the province until the first settlers brought it. Sweeping by the early attempts to introduce stock into East Texas, the paper stated that neither the settlers at Adaes nor the missions there started cattle breeding. Their efforts had gone unrewarded, and when the area was abandoned in 1773, it was "deserted as in the beginning." Although Antonio Gil Ybarbo could possibly have refuted this statement, the memorial went on to maintain steadfastly that the Canary

---

[12] Texas was administered under the bishopric of Guadalajara until 1777. Carlos E. Castañeda, *Our Catholic Heritage in Texas*, 5:27, mentions the "newly erected bishopric of Nuevo León" and says that Bishop Verger was responsible for Nuevo León, Nuevo Santander, Coahuila, and Texas. The bishop resided at Linares until the seat was moved to Monterrey in 1779; Verger served from 1783 until his death in 1790.

Islanders were responsible for stock raising in the province. It all started when each of the fourteen families received "five cows and a bull, five mares and a horse," and so on, secured from Coahuila at royal expense as part of their colonization benefits. Cabello, they maintained, spread the lies that the early captains left stock at crossings and so forth. The first explorers ate buffalo, not cattle. An animal on an expedition that gave out would have been slaughtered for meat—"the purpose of bringing it"—not left to breed. The truth was, said the memorialists, that the first entradas never intended to leave any stock to become wild. If these "crazy notions" were true, then their ancestors would have found a lot of cattle or traces of them. But that was not the case—"we ourselves saw it," with various eyewitnesses named to prove it. These men said that there was only a handful of stock in the beginning, and it had to be secured in Coahuila at great cost. The king never had any cattle ranches in Texas: "Thus they are ours."

The next section of the memorial was devoted to proving that unmarked animals in Texas had never been recognized as belonging to His Majesty. Why were duties not paid on slaughters conducted in the early 1770s? Because the cattle were recognized as belonging to individuals or the missions. The only dispute of ownership was between the ranchers and the missionaries—a "private quarrel"—until it was seized upon by the commandant general. How could stock belonging to *three* owners possibly be kept in the same pastures? they asked. It was difficult enough with only two. Yet until Croix's ruling the king had never been an owner of cattle, and it was this usurpation of their stock that the ranchers addressed next.[13]

The legal definition of a "stray," as defined in the proclamation of January 11, 1778, was the basis of attack. Strays in their pastures could not be included under the provisions of Croix's decree because they were not *mostrenco* as the law defined such. The Laws of Castile said that a stray found without an

---

[13] The above points are covered in "San Fernando Memorial," art. 1, items 1–12. Also mentioned are specific forays into the contested lands during Ripperdá's administration, none of which were taxed.

owner must be turned over to a justice and kept for "one year." If no owner appeared to claim it, *then* it could revert to the treasury. Thus, they claimed, Croix's proclamation contradicted ancient law. Not only that, but the law specifying advertisement of strays was not followed. The fact that no waiting period was observed made the decree "null on its face." Let the commandant general and the *asesor* prove otherwise; the ranchers were not convinced. "Natural right has been outraged, the office of justice has been flouted, our personal rights have been trampled, God dishonored, the King treated with disrespect, and we injured as to our honor and property."

The memorialists then began a round of emotional lamentations, rivaling Father López in their depiction of the woes wrought by Croix's decree. Had their plight reached the commandant general's ears, they said, his heart would have melted. But they did not go to him at first. They were negligent, divided among themselves, everyone—including the missions—"astounded at the blow to our wealth." No one knew how to protest; they did not want to insult Governor Cabello, new in office. Then Cabello began to declare their stock the king's property, even though it was within their own pastures, their own corrals, and so on. All of this, just one of a thousand contradictions, had promoted frauds and made the ranchers "damaged and troubled men." Who could stand guard so that their unbranded stock would not be stolen, surrounded as they were by countless enemies? The idea of a four-month respite for branding before all mesteño and *orejano* stock reverted to the king was no help; no one had ever asked for such a thing. None of their many protests had been heeded. Directing their remarks to Martínez Pacheco, they said: "We hope for a remedy under you. If not, this province is at a standstill, and we will be ruined in service of God and King."[14]

In case the "ancient laws" of Castile did not impress Governor Rafael Martínez Pacheco—and others who might read the petition farther up the line—Cabello's *bando* of July 10, 1783, was attacked, the ranchers citing more recent precedents. A law

[14] Art. 1, items 13–16, ibid.

from the Revised Recopilación of the Indies was cited as saying that wild stock without known owners was to be placed in the care of an honest person and advertised in that jurisdiction. If after consultations the owners remained unknown, such stock became property of the Royal Treasury. Also cited was another law which stated that if the owners of strays did not appear *after the required measures were taken* the stock reverted to the king. In ignoring these wise safeguards, the *bando* of July 10 was rendered null and void. The reason it had taken the ranchers so long to form a defense was because they were all "in shock." Finally they had regained their senses, but the damage had already been done.[15]

Believing that they had established firmly their right to the stock in the province, particularly to that between Béxar and the Guadalupe River—"and especially in our immediate vicinity"—the ranchers repeated their desire to give the king everything beyond the river. Then they set out to establish why their stock was so scattered and why they were not to blame for that condition. Three reasons were given: warfare with hostile Indians, disputes with the missions over boundaries of pasturelands, and continuous slaughter of the herds, which left them scared and driven to seek refuge in distant pastures. Added to these was a fourth: the decrees of the commandant general and his *asesor*. Such were founded solely upon the idea that their animals were strays, born and raised on royal lands, with no known owners. This, declared the San Fernando Memorial, was an error. But it was necessary for the stockmen to portray themselves as blameless for a very important reason: because *culpable neglect* on the part of the owners had to be established before the king, under the law, could appropriate stock found in a wild condition. If no neglect was involved, then they were not "strays," that is, subject to the king's treasury without observation of the safeguards protecting *mostrencos*. Since Croix's decree ignored these legal precautions, it was again null and void because the stock confiscated was not stray, it was not without known owners ("us"), and it was not raised on royal lands but had merely wandered there for the foregoing reasons.

---

[15] Item 17, restated in item 30, ibid., addresses legal precedents that the ranchers claimed Cabello's *bando* of July 10, 1783, violated.

Even the Barón de Ripperdá had recognized their ownership to stock below the Guadalupe, claimed the ranchers: "Neither before or after the proclamation did he give permits to us or the missions for strays there. Those caught were severely punished." The baron was said to have had three good reasons for acting as he had: the suit between ranchers and missions was pending, the stock was on lands with titles good for more than sixty years (although in a contested state), and the stock had known owners or had been produced from same (although in dispute between missions and private ranchers). If Croix's decree referred to stock *beyond* the Guadalupe, which was how the ranchers thought it should have been construed, they still owned the stock there, even though they now freely ceded it. It was theirs because the laws applying to strays were not applied or observed, and everything done contrary to the law should be held void—meaning Croix's decree.

Croix's proclamation claimed that the unbranded stock was *mostrenco*; this was not so. Wild animals (such as lions, bears, and bison), had never been considered strays because "natural law forbids it." They belonged to the good hunter. But even natural law differentiated *mostrencos* from *cimarrones*, stray animals that had served men but were now totally wild. Such stock should go the public welfare, granted the memorial, and the king was right to appropriate them as he saw fit. This had been pointed out by Fiscal "Caleazar" in 1753, in document 10, his ruling that *culpable neglect* had caused stock in the vicinity of San Juan Bautista del Río Grande to revert to the wild.[16] Such stock should, after proper advertisement, go to the Royal Treasury if the rightful owners did not appear. But in Texas neglect was not a factor. There it was war, not laziness, that had caused the cattle to stray.[17]

---

[16] This is perhaps a reference to Auditor Don Domingo Valcárcel and his opinion of July 17, 1753, or instructions associated with it; see chap. 1.

[17] In the "San Fernando Memorial," items 18–32 contain interesting observations on the suffering of the province (from a stockman's viewpoint), commencing with such profound observations as, "War is a terrible thing; it was bad for King David and worse for us." The many complaints lodged by the ranchers are outlined in item 26, offered as proof that the abandonment of outlying ranches was forced by Indian hostilities. As noted, such proof was central to their claims that the herds were scattered through no fault of their own.

Then began a brief recapitulation of some very important points. The abandonment of the Béxar ranches was forced, not willing. Several documents proved this. There were no known owners, said Croix's decree; yet "here we are," the residents of Béxar and La Bahía and the mission Indians. We will protest, said the ranchers, a "hundred thousand protests" if necessary. The unbranded cattle was theirs, not the king's; they had brought the stock into the province and had taken care of it. They would not rest until it was acknowledged as such. The lands were not royal lands but were owned by the cattlemen. Their titles dated back many years and certainly were theirs by peaceable possession for four years, "as the law requires." Also cited was a statute whereby a possessor could sell land he had occupied for a ten-year period. The stock, although *orejano*, was on their land, said the memorialists; therefore it belonged to them. It was not possible to construe these lands as *realengas* or *yermas* (wilderness) because their houses, corrals, pens, *mangas*, folds, and so on, proved otherwise. The stock was possessed by the same title as that for these other improvements—based on occupancy.

Even if their lands were "royal lands," they declared, the stock born and raised there would still belong to them for good reasons: land can produce trees, grass, and so forth, but not cows; offspring belongs to its parent and the owner thereof; offspring is not branded when it is born; offspring calls and seeks its true owner; and just because the land is the king's, it cannot be inferred that the cows are. "We put them there; thus they are ours." Several more legal rules governing the ownership of lost articles were given. For example, if a man found a treasure on his land and someone else could prove that it was his—where he had hidden it, its value, size, and so on—did the finder have a right to it, just because he found it on his land? No, stated the attorney for the ranchers, because "everything, wherever found, can be claimed by its owner." This was deemed a natural right. The finder could only advertise for the true owner and claim the treasure if no one appeared. So it was with the ranchers' cows. Then a second, "even more compelling," example was offered, this one for property lost by accident. It was intended to show that even if the ranchers' cattle had turned up on the king's land it still belonged to them. What did the commandant general expect of them, they wondered, "to ruin us entirely?" They had kept a lawyer for two years to defend their rights, and seven documents had been submitted, so far without tangible results: "Someday the King will hear of our plight," they promised.[18]

The memorialists ended by giving an enumeration of Cabello's shortcomings, including charges that he personally profited by taking their stock under the pretext of defending royal property. Claiming that their charges were motivated not by malice but in defense of their stock, the ranchers then proceeded to lay bare the former governor's black heart. He did not take Communion and confess once a year; he set a bad example by failing to attend mass and by cursing and blaspheming; he said that God did not have the power to change things because so-and-so had happened to him; he did not let the cattlemen pay church tithes on *orejanos*, telling them that they should pay the king instead; he drove families to the brink by his gossip and sex-related insinuations, and so on. But the heart of their attack was that Cabello had profited by defrauding His Majesty, a charge that governors of Texas had historically been subject to, some rightly so. Specifically, they said, he manipulated export *guías* and the Mustang Fund for his own enrichment, his bookkeeping contained numerous errors, he made up accounts from memory, and entire herds were taken out which he did not enter in his master ledger. Several herds were mentioned as being larger than the numbers reflected in his books, an implication that he put the fees for the difference in his pocket. The early exports in which a flat 20 reales per animal was charged "without distinction as to age or kind" were fraud-ridden. As far as the raisers were concerned, Cabello had made money by declaring their stock royal property.

All told, the ranchers calculated that he owed the chest 20 reales each on 10,901 head, or 27,254 pesos. This was stock

---

[18] Ibid. The arguments in items 33–41 on the "natural right" of an owner to property lost or unintentionally abandoned, will strike familiar chords to those with legal training. Yet even today courts make distinctions between "lost" and "mislaid" property, and the decisions are not in accord.

belonging to them but driven out as royal. "We know that many more were driven out, but we claim only for permits signed in his own hand," they said. Other "unrecorded sales" brought this indebtednesss to 32,508 pesos, and since the governor was only paying 13,096 pesos, the chest was 19,411 pesos short. Cattle which the missions had lost owing to Apache attacks (valued at the absolute minimum of 4 reales a head) plus their own legal costs in fighting the former governor's *bandos* increased the sum to 34,468 pesos. The figure even included a 740-peso fine assessed against Juan Andrés Travieso, in payment of which he had been obliged to part with his two pet buffalo. He had caught and raised the animals, and they were supposedly worth much more than the amount of the fine; Cabello had then sent them gratis to Spain. And thus the ranchers had been brought to utter ruin. While Indians, soldiers, and other marauders were stealing livestock, all the governor could do was use his men to kill their dogs in town. To be accused of being a *mataperros* ("killer of dogs") was, of course, about the worst reflection that could be cast on a man's personal valor. Attaching their names to this protracted indictment were Simón de Arocha, Francisco Travieso, Joaquín Leal, Santiago Seguín, Juan Joseph (José) Flores, Luis Mariano Menchaca, Joaquín Menchaca, Pedro Sambrano, Joaquín Flores, Juan José Bueno, and José Macario Sambrano.[19]

After the memorial was signed, an addition was tacked on—as if the author was reluctant to rest his case, perhaps fearing that more proof was needed—and signed again by all eleven ranchers. This addendum maintained that the first branding extension was published during an "impossible season" (July, 1783), when all the raisers either had to work crops or journey to the Saltillo fair to protect their credit. The subsequent two-month extension (November–December, 1784) was no help because their horses were "useless from the Saltillo trip" and because of the heavy rains, the cold, the crops to be harvested, and the *fiestas yuradas* (religious holidays).

To establish that Cabello had carried away "no telling how

---

[19] Ibid. Items 42–52 are devoted to establishing the second proposition of the "San Fernando Memorial," i.e., Cabello's motives for taking away the cattle belonging to the ranchers.

much" of their money, the signers made a separate itemization and attached it to the San Fernando Memorial. Apparently the attorneys obtained copies of Cabello's official records and the special reports he made at the conclusion of his administration, either with or without his successor's help. Otherwise, their calculations on *guías* issued, the contents of the strongbox, and so on, would have been extremely difficult to formulate. The final figure of 34,468 pesos had the following notation: "If this belongs to the King, whose interests we as good subjects do defend, let it be paid. If it belongs to his subjects—us—let it be tendered in hand, and we yield it to the King."[20]

The *vecinos* of Béxar were being very generous with money they wanted Domingo Cabello to pay. As with most other reports presented on behalf of vested interests, the San Fernando Memorial must be seen with the end it wished to accomplish in view. Its "facts" were designed to convince Governor Martínez Pacheco and others in high places of the rightness of the ranchers' cause. In this sense it is very much like the report of 1785 compiled by Father López. In all these appeals—even with their conflicting assertions and slanted statistics—a vivid picture of the struggle for dominance in eighteenth-century Texas ranching begins to emerge. It is to be expected that this picture will appear differently, viewed from different perspectives.

From the *asesor general*'s point of view, the situation still

[20] For these calculations, see BAT, 134:87.

looked the same. On September 11, Galindo Navarro responded to an *expediente*, designated number 74, "which was formed and pursued in this superior government with the backing of the missions and residents who are stock raisers in the province of Texas." Included were two *cuadernos* (memoranda) remitted by the Most Excellent Lord Viceroy with his official letter of July 3. These contained the appeals made by the *procurador* of the missions, Fray García, and the three petitions by the attorney for the resident stock raisers, Juan José Flores, in the summer of 1785, which had finally reached the viceregal level. According to Galindo Navarro, these appeals presented no new just grounds for changing the cattle laws. On the contrary, they tried to "attain their unfounded goals" by using surprise—since the viceroy was unaware of the situation or its precedents—and by obscuring and concealing the commandant general's resolutions. Because the petitions were initiated without stopping at either jurisdiction of two superior governments, the *asesor* considered them a low blow, aimed not only at a reversal of the unpopular law but at embarrassing his decisions—that is, him personally—before the viceroy. Added to all the true reasons why the stockmen's claims were unjust, said Galindo Navarro, their contentions of misery, necessity, revolt, and flight from the Indians and other exaggerations of like nature were "quite alien and far from the truth." The *asesor*, showing himself as prone to distortion as were the Tejanos, said that no evidence of such disruptions had reached him since the inception of Croix's decree in 1778, the basis for all subsequent resolutions. He suggested that in light of this the commandant general implement his decisions of February 22 and March 15, 1786, and order the governor of Texas to comply precisely with their provisions.[21]

On September 21, Commandant General Ugarte decreed, "Let that which seems appropriate to the *señor asesor* be done." His decree and letter to Governor Martínez Pacheco of the same date, however, show that the maze of branding extensions and the complexities of the past decade were beginning to take their toll. Ugarte was careful to point out that the extension

---

[21] Galindo Navarro to Ugarte, September 11, 1787, BAT, 136:154–55.

issued pursuant to Cabello's *bando* of October, 1784, had expired at the end of the following December. Of course, it was "normal and logical" that roundups should have been interrupted and suspended in the meantime, for anything else would have been an open and notorious infraction of existing superior resolutions. Therefore, he decreed, the suspension of roundups was effective from the first day of January, 1785. By so ordering, Ugarte was in effect pronouncing that no cattle roundups had taken place—"officially"—in the past two and a half years.

In his letter to Governor Martínez Pacheco the commandant general traced the circumstances which had led to the present state of affairs. It is interesting that he speaks of the mission petition as having been initiated by the padre attorney of "those" (San Antonio) missions, Fray Joseph Antonio de la Garza, indicating that he was as confused as everyone else—the *procurador*'s name was Fray José Antonio García, while the father *presidente* who had lodged the protest of 1784 against Cabello's two-month extension was Fray José Francisco Mariano de la Garza. Perhaps the two appeals became combined before reaching the viceroy. At any rate, the lord minister of the Royal Treasury had advised the viceroy to return both the mission and the resident petitions to the commandant general for his appraisal and decision, and it was this order from above which now required the *asesor* to repeat himself to the point of weariness. Ugarte transmitted Galindo Navarro's prior ruling as follows:

> Accordingly, in a decree of this date, and out of pure charity, I have granted a new, final, and peremptory term of four months to the missions and citizens, so that within that time they might mark and take possession of the number of head of said cattle that can be rounded up. They will have no right afterward to those which were not branded, as has been declared previously.[22]

Martínez Pacheco's sympathy for the ranchers' position becomes manifest at this point. Replying to the commandant general, he forwarded a list of the "restored" ranchers, fifty in all, who had made an agreement with the five Béxar missions and

---

[22] Ugarte, decree, September 21, 1787, ibid.; Ugarte to Martínez Pacheco, September 21, 1787, BAT, 146:114–15.

the one at La Bahía (listing lands and boundaries) in order to effect a roundup of their cattle up to the Guadalupe River, each one obligating himself to submit a report (see appendix B). The governor noted that they asked to be freed from such an obligation and that they had rendered to His Majesty "the rights they may have" to cattle above the Guadalupe. Thus was the leading concession of the San Fernando Memorial brought to the commandant general's attention. Martínez Pacheco offered his view that the situation was not their fault but should be blamed on Indian hostilities, an assessment diametrically opposed to the *asesor*'s stand. Furthermore, these people had endured untold hardships because of severe droughts and unusually cold winters, particularly in 1786, when there was much snow and ice, and because they frequently had to abandon their ranches for lack of adequate protection. These facts, stated Martínez Pacheco, accounted for the large numbers of unbranded cattle and stock, "many of which rightfully belonged to the ranchers and missions."[23]

All this was asked on behalf of the subjects' welfare, and, compared to Domingo Cabello's long-running hostility, must be considered strong prorancher advocacy. While waiting for a response, the governor addressed another matter. He wrote Ugarte about the costs involved in obtaining cattle around Béxar to feed Mescalero Apaches at the Valle de Santa Rosa, in Coahuila. The local residents paid vaqueros 1 peso a day, "without catching anything," he said. Nonetheless, he felt that he could find someone to deliver cattle at a price of 2 pesos each, handed over to an officer at the corral gate.[24]

Eager for a decision on his letter number 21, the governor again wrote the commandant general on December 1. This second plea on behalf of the ranchers, his number 35, did little more than restate the earlier objections to Ugarte's orders of September 21, and press for recognition of the cattle raisers'

---

[23] Martínez Pacheco to Ugarte, (no. 21) October 14, 1787, SA, 5:36–48.

[24] Martínez Pacheco to Ugarte, November 11, 1787, BAT, 148:49. For other Spanish attempts to induce hostile Indians to settle down to a "reservation" form of existence at this time, see John, *Storms*, pp. 728, 732–34; Max L. Moorhead, *The Presidio: Bastion of the Spanish Borderlands*, pp. 250–58.

rights to *orejano* stock found in their jurisdictions as far as the Guadalupe River. Reference was made to the new and absolute four-month grace period and how it was understood that afterward the citizens and missions would no longer have any right whatever to wild stock left unbranded. Reference was also made to the list of names of those "who are properly to be regarded as settlers, owners of ranchos, and as engaged in the business of raising cattle," all now firmly established on their properties thanks to peace with the Indians of the province. Martínez Pacheco reminded Ugarte that the citizens were willing to cede their claims to all cattle found above the Guadalupe River in return for being "absolved of the obligation of complying with the *orejanos*" found below it.

In other words, if the commandant general would permit the ranchers to take *orejanos* within the limits set forth in the roundup agreement of January, 1787, without paying any duties thereon, they would surrender all their claims to stock found elsewhere—including the regions beyond the Medina River, west, north, and south beyond Las Lomerías (the Hills). Within these limits the citizens and missions of Béxar were accustomed to pasture cows that had *chichiguas* (suckling calves). It was a sweeping concession, affirming the principle set forth in the *asesor*'s opinion that of their own free will the citizens should declare all wild cattle and horses to be crown property. In Martínez Pacheco's mind the ranchers were now willing to relinquish exactly what Galindo Navarro wanted, in return for one small guarantee: the unobstructed ownership of all *orejanos* taken in their recognized pastures.

As Castañeda has written, "The governor made bold to suspend the operation of the decree, pending the disposition of the request of the citizens and missionaries." At the same time Martínez Pacheco assured the commandant general that no roundup would be permitted until his final decision but ended by drawing attention to several more reasons why he had delayed putting Ugarte's order into effect. One of these was the serious difficulties which would arise from the need of guarding and protecting the royal herds, that is, all stock left *orejano* in the province after a roundup was held and the branding done.

He suggested that every unbranded cow would then require a sentinel to prevent its being taken by Indians from neighboring missions and private properties. "It will become necessary, therefore, to prosecute and punish such offenders, a problem that will not present much difficulty as far as Indians from the private estates are concerned but will lead into difficulties with the missions." Implied was a supposition that the padres would make trouble if the government tried to punish one of their Indians, even if *patrones* on the private ranches did not support their Indian vaqueros in similar fashion. No less a problem would be the citizens themselves, who would be "uncontrollable" if they saw one of their own number punished for something a mission Indian was allowed to do with impunity. As the old soldier saw it, even on private estates it would be no small matter to have a man hanged "for taking a cow," Indian or otherwise, but without punishment it would be impossible to restrain marauders. It goes without saying that Rafael Martínez Pacheco thought it foolish to lose the support of the citizenry over a trifle like a cow. He ended by asking Ugarte to bear these considerations in mind before coming to a decision so as to forestall further petitioning by the citizens and missions.[25]

The commandant general did not reply to this request, possibly believing that his ideas on the subject had already been made abundantly clear. For that matter, it is hard to say exactly when the First Big Roundup took place. In mid-December, Martínez Pacheco notified the Béxar cabildo that a sworn report was due "in view of the fact that you have made two sweeps in order to round up stray *orejano* cattle and horses on the indicated summer pastures and *linderos*." This had been their obligation since the month that the agreement was granted for this purpose, January of that year, 1787. He also reminded them that

[25] Martínez Pacheco to Ugarte, (no. 35) December 1, 1787, BAT, 149:10–13; SA, 5:43–48. This seems to be the document cited by Castañeda, *Catholic Heritage*, 5:30n.38, as "Ugarte y Loyola to Martínez Pacheco, December 1, 1787," from SA, 5:43–46, in which he claims that a *cédula* of September 21, 1787, was "summarized." This *"cédula,"* however, is only Commandant General Ugarte's letter of that date, forwarding the *asesor* Galindo Navarro's opinion of September 11. Thus even though Martínez Pacheco "made bold" to suspend the decree, he was not quite as bold as Castañeda supposes, since it was not royal in origin.

their reports should reflect the number of wild animals caught since the agreement made with Espíritu Santo, that is, in the preceding June, noting that several residents of Béxar had already complied.[26] Yet an entry in the records of the cabildo dated January 9, 1788, states that "by virtue of a decree sent to us by the governor, saying we should order the citizens to do their branding, we on the fourteenth of this month summoned the citizenry." Then they proceeded to brand nursing calves in town enclosures and, with the cabildo's consent, those at the ranches.[27]

Martínez Pacheco's own report to the commandant general was his number 48, dated March 16, 1788. In it he claimed that two roundups were made, one "from the twenty-first of January until the twenty-second of February, and the other [for] twenty days in July of the proximate past year of 1787." Castañeda has interpreted this to mean that both roundups took place in the winter and spring of 1787–88. The July roundup definitely took place in 1787, after the accord with Espíritu Santo, but it is uncertain whether the other was in January, 1787, or January, 1788. In his letter of December 17 the governor mentions two sweeps already made, but the cabildo records and the timing of the report indicate that the second occurred in January–February, 1788. In his general report Martínez Pacheco described the weather conditions during both efforts: "In the first, they did not continue their roundups of cattle on their pastures due to the frequent snows and heavy ice [storms] and because their tame horses, which they used for rounding them up, had died; and in the second [roundup], because of the heavy rains."[28]

In neither of the two roundups were the missions of Béxar able to participate owing to the near-total deterioration ("acausa

---

[26] Martínez Pacheco to Cabildo, December 17, 1787, BAT, 149:47.

[27] "Minutes, Resolutions, and Other Records of Cabildo . . . San Fernando de Béxar, January 1, 1783–May 10, 1807," entry of January 9, 1788, BAT, 115:10. This entry was signed by José Félix Menchaca, Juan Martín de Amondarain, Estanislao de Arocha, José Macario Sambrano, Juan de Arocha, Francisco de Arocha, Juan Flores, Gabino Delgado, Antonio Leal, and Pedro Flores.

[28] Martínez Pacheco to Ugarte, March 16, 1788, BAT, 153:55–57. This document is a copy sent to Nava on March 2, 1791, at a time when the administration of Martínez Pacheco was under intense scrutiny.

de la total decadencia") of their condition, both in men and in horses. Not one single *orejano* or mesteño were they able to catch, having neither the Indian neophytes nor enough tame horses for the job, despite all the work that had gone into the roundup negotiations. This speaks eloquently of the sad condition of the five Béxar missions as they neared secularization. The results of the First Big Roundup were as follows (taken from the original shown in facsimile, fig. 3):

Ranch or Mission	No. of Cattle	No. of Horses
Cattle raisers owning ranchos	6,231	183
Mission Espíritu Santo	1,418	—
Five missions of "this capital"	—	—
Total	7,649	183

Compared with previous attempts made at rounding up and branding cattle in Texas, the sweeps made in 1787 under the administration of Rafael Martínez Pacheco must be regarded as the largest rodeo ever. It clearly demonstrated the dominance of "private estates" over older mission *criadores* as the most industrious cattlemen of the province. Mission Espíritu Santo, however, was far from giving up the ghost, considering that even if the ranchers kept to their self-imposed 112-man limit they still must have enjoyed a five-to-one edge over the Bahía mission's Indian vaqueros.[29]

A better understanding of the roundup agreement of 1787, insofar as the Béxar missions are concerned, can be achieved by

---

[29] Martínez Pacheco's recap of the roundup appears in SA, 5:62–65, whose cover letter (no. 48) states that the five missions of Béxar got nothing, owing to their "total decadence," with respect to both men and horses. The original of this roundup tally is found in NA, and an even more fancifully executed copy sent to the commandant general is now in SA, cited above. There is ample evidence to support the notion that a number of mission Indian vaqueros went to work for private ranchers once the missions began to decline. Thus the padres were plagued by their own success as their former pupils entered the mainstream of colonial life, leaving the missions short of trained hands and hastening their demise.

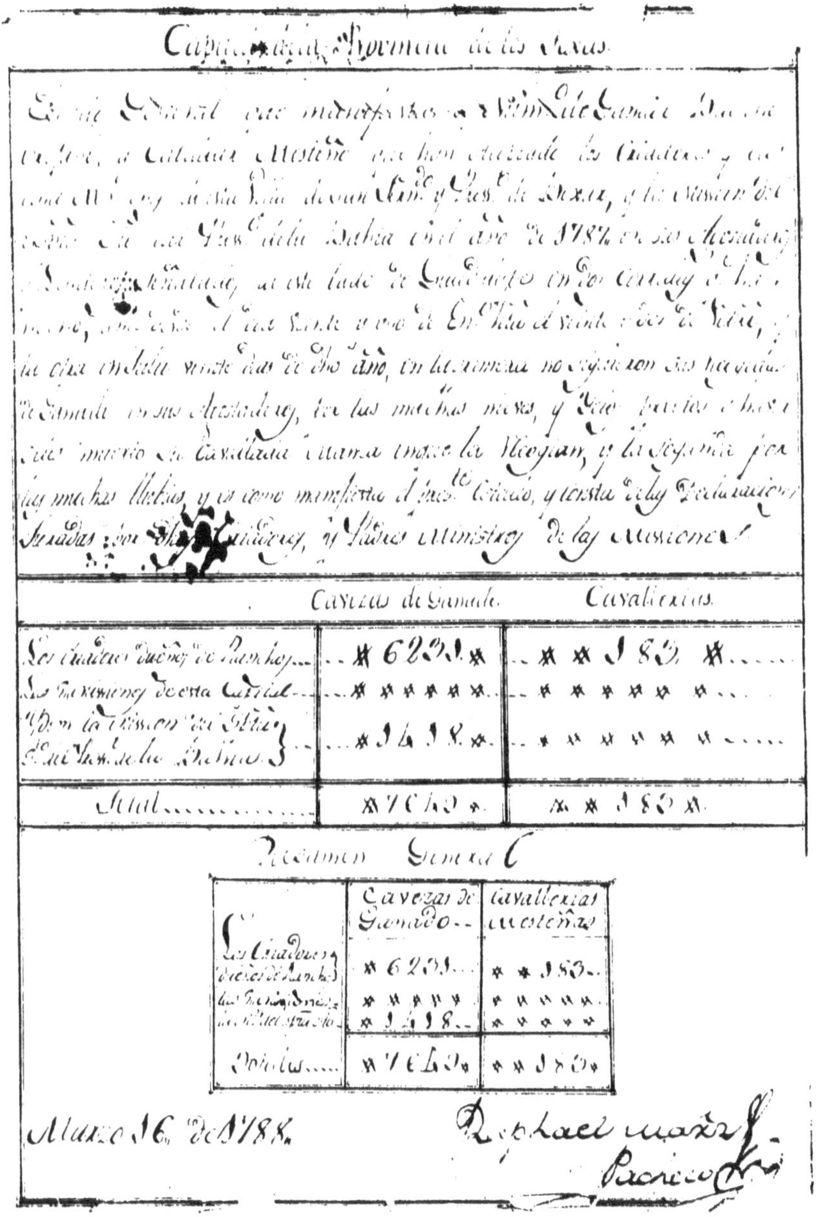

Fig. 3. Roundup report of Raphael Martínez Pacheco, March 16, 1788.

examining the documents found in Father Benedict Leutenegger's *Management of the Missions in Texas: Fr. José Rafael Oliva's Views concerning the Problem of Temporalities in 1788*. In a letter to Governor Martínez Pacheco written a month after the signing of the agreement, the new father *presidente* admitted that his missions were threatened with "total ruin." The temporal administration of the missions was a heavy burden that neither the priests in Texas nor those at the college wished to bear—a theme that Oliva would repeat the following year in his *problema*, a long discussion of the situation. He said that the missions of Texas in former times had had a goodly number of Indians and cattle which they had sold at a fair price because buyers had no other recourse than the missions. Today, however, everything was just the opposite; left were only a "few heads of cattle, and there is no one to buy them because there are many sellers."

Arguing the benefits of giving up the business end of running their missions, Oliva pointed out that in so doing the priests would be freed from matters pertaining to *orejanos*, lands, and cattle, "which is the one industry of this country and the source of scandal." Another comment on the padres' dire situation is found in Father Vasconcelos's journal, in which he noted that in October, 1787—while the rancheros were busily scouring the countryside for the thousands of *orejanos* in Texas—a drove of cattle left Zacatecas headed for the Texas missions. In the midst of plenty the missionaries had to be supplied with beef from afar in a perilous drive that took months to complete.[30]

Thus the ability of private ranchers to work the contested ground and exploit its wealth of wild cattle could no longer be

---

[30] Fr. Benedict Leutenegger, trans., *Management of the Missions in Texas: Fr. José Rafael Oliva's Views concerning the Problem of Temporalities in 1788*, pp. 31–32; Fr. Benedict Leutenegger, trans., *Journal of a Texas Missionary, 1767–1802: The Diario Histórico of Fr. Cosme Lozano Marvais, Pen Name of Fr. Mariano Antonio de Vasconcelos*, p. 24. A comparison of census figures between 1783 and 1786 indicates that, while the five Béxar missions actually gained in Indian population, the one at La Bahía suffered a dramatic loss. Nonetheless, it was still able to make a respectable showing in the Big Roundup of 1787, while the Béxar establishments could not even field a crew. Castañeda, *Catholic Heritage*, 5:32–33.

ignored, regardless of who held title to the land. As the missions continued to decline, Tejano ranchers tightened their grasp on what was formerly property of the padres, including even their neophytes, who were lured away to ride for men who could get the job done and pay them for their work. The process of decay was so far advanced that by the time the missions were secularized in the mid-1790s nothing remained of their once vast herds; they had been destroyed by hostile Indians, scattered in all directions, or branded by enterprising Españoles. Even so, Texas would not see another rodeo of this scale in the eighteenth century; it would be remembered as the Great Roundup of 1787.

The following year had a more settled aspect. Governor Martínez Pacheco reported that for the first twelve months of his administration a tax of 602 pesos was collected at Béxar on *orejano* cattle and mesteño horses. He elaborated on the condition of the Mustang Fund by sending a report to headquarters for taxes collected from December 3, 1786, to the end of 1787. Starting with a balance of 7,769 pesos, he collected another 1,036 pesos during the year (74 pesos from La Bahía, 360 pesos from Nacogdoches, and 602 pesos from Béxar), leaving the fund with a total of 8,805 pesos.[31]

Near the end of January, Alcalde José Félix Menchaca, the old captain's brother who was acting as agent for the citizens, filed a petition against the former Governor Cabello. Although only a fragment of this document remains intact in the Béxar Archives, it appears to be an outgrowth of accusations made in the San Fernando Memorial. It is also possible that Menchaca's efforts were offered as evidence in Cabello's *residencia*, the royal investigation which occurred at the end of an official's term of office. Designed primarily as a control and monitoring device to assure good administration, the *residencia* process

---

[31] "Tax on *Orejano* Cattle and Mesteño Horses Rounded up [at Béxar], 1787," BAT, 149:99; "Report on Taxes Collected on *Orejanos* and Mesteños [for the province of Texas], 1787," BAT, 153:24, also in SA, 5:56–57. For Gil Ybarbo's report of the Nacogdoches Mustang Fund, 1786–87, see R. B. Blake, Research Collection, Supplement ser., 2:219. When expenditures were made from the fund, the cashier issued a receipt "so that it may be reimbursed once the payroll is collected in San Luis Potosí."

could end the career of a blatantly corrupt officeholder. A ruling by a special judge, however, was subject to review by the Council of the Indies, as were any fines imposed. Menchaca charged Cabello with taking away the legitimate property of the residents—their stray cattle—selling them as unclaimed and belonging to the Royal Treasury, but misappropriating the proceeds, a rehash of the memorial's central theme. He blamed the estrayed condition of the ranchers' cattle on the "barbarous savages" who "encircled them from the four winds." It is possible that this petition was designed to gain restitution of the penalties and fines imposed on the ranchers during Cabello's administration, an end which would eventually be achieved.

Menchaca's power of attorney authorized him to follow through on all petitions, restraints, judicial letters, and so on, on behalf of the cattlemen. Evidence exists that he made some efforts along these lines. For example, there are two petitions filed in early February, both relating to the export of cattle during Cabello's term, both given to demonstrate that the former governor cheated the Royal Treasury by listing in his book of *guías* smaller herds than those that were actually taken out. Francisco Xavier Rodríguez swore before the attorney that he personally had seen 1,000 head at the corral of Marcos Hernández, assembled for a drive to Louisiana under the authority of Antonio "Blan" (le Blanc). José Antonio Saucedo, who accompanied the herd as far as Nacogdoches, testified that the herd contained 1,300 head, more or less, almost entirely *orejanos*. A number of other such complaints were directed against the former governor, and they eventually came to the attention of the viceroy, resulting in a complete review of the mesteño question in Texas and more trouble for Domingo Cabello.

Don Luis Antonio's brother was soon distracted from gathering evidence by a suit filed at the beginning of February. His old nemesis Juan José Pacheco again sued for payment of the bulls taken to Louisiana back in 1779. Thus Menchaca was drawn away from the ranchers' case against Cabello to defend himself personally from litigation launched during those hard times. This, of course, was José Félix's main defense, that is, that Juan José Pacheco's judgment against him was directly related to the oppressive rule of Domingo Cabello. He defended his flight from Cabello thus: "Fearful of the intensity with which he was persecuting me and all my household, as has been stated by the commandant general, I thought it best to leave and not appear in his court." Like his kinsmen before him, Menchaca cited an opinion of the *asesor*, dated July 2, 1782: ". . . this, at least, creates the strong suspicion that the Señor Governor has directed his actions against the Menchacas." The cattlemen's attorney was soon using his authority to appeal to Governor Martínez Pacheco for restitution of the 290 pesos that Cabello levied while he was imprisoned in 1783. This sum was perhaps deposited to cover the horses, mules, mares, cattle, and so on, taken from him in connection with the contraband charges that he and Juan de Ysurieta were facing at the time. Thus José Félix Menchaca's cause rapidly degenerated from a public to a private espousal. The governor, unwilling to become involved in Cabello's personal squabbles, ordered his petition on behalf of the ranchers returned.[32]

Another protest lodged at the same time was directed at ending the collection of the *diezmo* on slaughtered cattle. The *diezmero* Juan Barrera (according to the San Fernando cattle raisers) was still trying to collect tithes not only on cows killed to eat but also on those exported or "bought from the king." The raisers pointed out that they had to expend effort and risk personal safety in this work, not to mention paying their hands wages of a peso each per day. Sometimes they came back empty-handed even though they had gone as far as the Colorado River, 50 to 100 leagues away. If they had to pay a *machorraje* on cows eaten, claimed the raisers, next Barrera would want a *diezmo* for buffalo, bear, deer, turkey—"even on salt." The ranchers, it would seem, wanted to have the situation both ways: they wanted the wild herds recognized as belonging to them, yet they wanted the church to consider them products of nature. Since the tithe was applied only to agricultural and pas-

---

[32] Petition (fragment), January 29, 1788, BAT, 151:72. Documents relating to the suit of February, 1788, *Juan José Pacheco* v. *José Félix Menchaca*, contain additional information about the cattle drive of August, 1779, to Louisiana, one of the first if not the first conducted with official sanction. BAT, 152:5–48.

toral produce resulting from endeavors of the faithful, not to that emanating directly from the bounty of the Creator, they would have been home free.[33]

Some idea of the *diezmero*'s business relationship with Bishop Verger can be obtained from a contract, dated September 14, 1786, that Juan Barrera signed at Saltillo. In this agreement, effective for six years, were specified the conditions for securing the tithes in Texas. Barrera obligated himself to pay the bishop 400 pesos a year, in biennial installments of 800 pesos. Verger reserved the right to adjust this price should the value of tithes increase within the term of the contract. If an ecclesiastical cabildo was formed in the diocese during these six years, the agreement would be subject to its judgment. Tithes on *orejanos* were to be included "if all goes as planned." Barrera signed as the principal guarantor, but Vizente Flores and Santiago Seguín co-signed, all of them pledging their possessions as collateral for the tithes of the province. As suggested by the above reference to *orejanos*, Bishop Verger had not entirely given up on collecting tithes from the wild herds. Even the adverse ruling of the *asesor*, delivered just after this contract was negotiated, did not deter the bishop from pursuing the matter. See, for example, his request which the commandant general forwarded to the viceroy on August 26, 1791; it was rejected by the *fiscal* a month later. But from the Bexareños' petition of early 1788 it may be assumed that *diezmero* Barrera was exploring all possible avenues to make sure that his collections exceeded the sum soon to be due Bishop Verger.[34]

Several cattle cases developed at this time to relieve the monotony, especially at La Bahía. On February 18, Captain Luis Cazorla wrote the governor about problems associated with a recent roundup, mentioning in particular excesses supposedly

---

[33] BAT, 151:69.

[34] Tithe Contract, September 14, 1786, Protocolos, Archivo Municipal, Saltillo; "Demand of the Bishop of Linares [Nuevo León] for Payment of Tithes on Mesteños in Texas," 1791, AGN, Historia, Hackett Transcripts, 82:22, University of Texas Archives. Tithe records for the various districts of the diocese of Nuevo León, 1774–1800, are in the Eberstadt Collection, box 3N180, University of Texas Archives. The annual tithe for Texas remained at 400 pesos until 1792, when the amount began to climb, reaching a high of 1,749 pesos in 1795; the sum was insignificant compared with that in other districts.

committed by some residents of his presidio on lands of Rancho La Mora. These had to do with the slaughter of cattle. Cazorla said that a hunt was made at the request of the presidio chaplain for the purpose of catching some mesteño horses and killing several cattle for meat. When the boys came back, they admitted to having gone farther than they were supposed to, entering the ranch of "San Simón," which was the end of La Bahía's jurisdiction. Evidently they also went into Mission Valero's pastures, for one of the cows they killed bore a mission brand. This was not a problem in itself because the customary procedure was to pay rightful owners the legitimate worth of such stock slaughtered (the king, of course, was paid for any mesteños taken). While on his hunt one of the *muchachos* said that between San Simón (del Capote) and La Mora he met a foreman who claimed that all cattle in the area belonged to his master, Juan Martín de Amondarain. This, suggested the Bahía captain, was the source of the complaint. He told the governor that he had reproached the chaplain and all concerned, trusting that these annoyances would cease.[35]

They did not. Indeed, it was only a short time before Cazorla was involved in an export case of more serious dimensions. It seems that one Tomás Liendro had obtained permission from Governor Martínez Pacheco to drive 150 head out of the province. When Cazorla sent a man to inspect the herd, "many falsehoods" were discovered. Numerous head belonging to Mission Espíritu Santo were found in Liendro's herd, along with those of other owners. By the time they were all separated, there remained only 110 head, for which number the captain issued a *guía* and sent Tomás on his way. A group of citizens soon presented themselves, claiming that some of their cattle were missing and asking to go after Liendro. Permission was granted, but they returned downcast, unable to confirm their suspicions. Liendro had told them to go ahead and inspect the herd but added, with a cocked musket in his hand, that one of them or himself would die if they tried.

This news prompted Cazorla to send some men with an order to seize the herd and return it to the presidio. When he

[35] Cazorla to Martínez Pacheco, February 18, 1788, BAT, 152:77–79.

was caught, Liendro brandished his musket, threatened to kill himself, slashed his body with a knife, and then fled, leaving the herd behind. Sure enough, it contained 75 head more than the 110 of its permit, the excess cattle either belonging to Espíritu Santo and the citizens of Béxar or *orejano*. The captain wanted to use the *orejanos* for feeding his troops but was unsure how to establish their true ownership, a "critical point." In May he informed Martínez Pacheco that he had prepared charges against the fugitive Liendro because he had been caught redhanded and the affair had created a public scandal in the district. Failure to prosecute would doubtless open the door to greater disorders.[36]

While it is true that in Texas the death penalty could be imposed for stealing livestock, such extreme reprisals were rarely if ever taken. If the offender was an Indian or mixedblood, he would more likely be subjected to a severe public whipping and then banished from the province. At worst he would be sent to work in the mines for a specified period. If the culprit was a Spaniard, he would be fined heavily and perhaps required to render service in public works or in one of His Majesty's military companies. One of the remarkable features of the Spanish penal code on the frontier was that its bark was worse than its bite. For example, only one of the three murder trials recorded between 1778 and 1810 in the Béxar Archives resulted in the death penalty, the other two defendants being sentenced to serve time as soldiers. New Spain needed men on her exposed northern frontier too desperately to subject them to capital punishment, certainly not for cattle theft.[37]

Captain Cazorla reported in June that Lipans were killing much stock near the Nueces, from El Tepalcate to the head-

---

[36] Cazorla to Martínez Pacheco, April 19 and May 2, 1788, BAT, 154:11–14, 23–24. When a repentant Liendro surrendered to Cazorla in mid-September, the captain asked Governor Martínez Pacheco to show mercy so that the rustler could care for his family.

[37] The Texas legal code, based on the *Recopilación*, prescribed the death penalty for anyone who stole twelve sheep or goats, five horses, or hogs or beef cattle of comparable value (Gil Ybarbo's 1783 "Laws of Nacogdoches," art. 30, cited in Odie B. Faulk, *A Successful Failure*, p. 149, and found in its entirety in Nyal C. King, "Captain Gil Antonio Y'Barbo, Founder of Modern Nacogdoches, 1720–1809" [Master's thesis, Stephen F. Austin University, 1949], pp. 67–74).

waters of the Aránzazu. The sky was dark with circling scavengers, but the number of rotting carcasses exceeded even the buzzards' capacity to gorge themselves, said cattlemen who braved the stench of the area. Soon afterward Cazorla expressed some frustration with the way exports were being handled. Coming under fire because he had denied Martín de Amondarain permission to extract a herd of cattle, the captain defended himself to Martínez Pacheco, "since you are the one who must give it." Cazorla was miffed because he was expected to authorize such roundups yet was not informed by the governor of their terms. Because the herd in question, 1,100 head, was intended for Béxar Presidio, he issued a *guía*, noting that Fray Cárdenas had given no bond to assure payment for the herd. He asked for some sort of advance notice in the future on extractions of this kind, unaware that fate held his life in the balance and the scales were tipping.[38]

At Béxar the cattle cases—like the one in which José Félix Menchaca found himself embroiled—were mostly outgrowths of past events. For example, in May, Santiago de Zúñiga, a traveling muleteer and citizen of Guadalajara, sued Simón de Arocha for payment of a debt. Plying his trade, Zúñiga had brought some flour to Béxar and sold it to the *diezmero*, Juan Barrera, who gave him as payment a note against Arocha for 100 pesos. Don Simón, short of cash, told the *arriero* that he would pay him at the Saltillo fiestas, to which Zúñiga agreed. The muleteer was unable to attend the annual trade fair and showed up later at Arocha's ranch asking for his money. Upon learning that he wanted to buy some cattle, Arocha offered to pay his debt with cows and said that he would match any price quoted by the missions. Going to Espada, Zúñiga came away with a price of 3½ pesos each for "fat" ones but admitted in testimony that he had already made the deal with Arocha for 1 peso a head less. It was not his intention to take advantage of Arocha, avowed the mule driver, but when he later talked to Don Simón's wife about getting his cows, she told him that the only ones at the ranch

---

[38] Cazorla to Martínez Pacheco, June 22 and July 31, 1788, BAT, 155:62–64. Captain Luis Cazorla died early in October of a "painful colic." It is doubtful that he ever knew of Juan de Ugalde's letter to Martínez Pacheco of September 15, 1788, appointing him (Cazorla) interim governor of Coahuila.

were worth as much as 6 pesos, and she would not allow him to take any of them at the agreed price. Zúñiga maintained in his suit that they "only sought to put me off" and not pay anything. He asked the court for 93 pesos, 2 reales, considering all the expenses incurred and the four scroungy head that he eventually obtained.

Arocha's account, however, was considerably different. His petition said that Señora de Arocha had refused to give Zúñiga cows at the ranch because they were nursing stock and very docile. Zúñiga then agreed to go with him to his ranch on the Guadalupe, where he would receive and slaughter (for dried meat and tallow) enough cattle to repay the debt at the mission's price. Although Zúñiga was cautioned that the cattle would be very thin because of the drought, when they were penned, he could find only four head that suited him. Arocha charged that Zúñiga wanted value twice the amount of his 100 pesos, and when the dispute heated up, he claimed that his character had been libeled by the teamster's remarks. Nonetheless, he deposited 80 pesos in May, and Governor Martínez Pacheco certified the proceedings closed. Another such case was a lawsuit brought in violation of a cattle contract involving a drive to Saltillo. Like the Arocha affair, it was filled with contradictions of testimony, and this one dragged on for years before a decision was reached.[39]

A case that developed at Laredo during the summer gives an interesting contrast to the policy on corridas at Béxar. A petition was drawn up by citizens, *regidores*, and the *procurador*, stating that it was thirty-three years since the founding of their settlement and calling attention to a superior decree by the military governor forbidding them to "continue with the corridas that the residents of the villa have always been accustomed to make." Such roundups were necessary as a means of support and a help in collecting their strays. They asked that an exception be made since several members of "this poor community" supplied themselves with horses for the royal service by corridas.

At the request of the *procurador general*, a reply was made

---

[39] *Expediente*, May 14–July 2, 1788, BAT, 154:43–89; also BAT, 151:86–120.

by Melchor Vidal de García y Villena, colonel and military governor of Nuevo Santander at Villa San Carlos. He granted residents the right to continue making their corridas among wild stock after obtaining permission from the *junta mayor* of Laredo, with the express condition that such animals must be carried to the plaza, where those of known brands would be delivered to their owners: "The *mostrencos* must be set aside for the king, and the mesteños shall be for the use of those participating in the corridas. In their favor also shall be such stipends as the owners may give, according to custom, for the animals of known brands." As long as these conditions were observed, the corridas could continue. From this order it can be concluded that Laredo and the other Río del Norte towns in the jurisdiction of Nuevo Santander functioned under more traditional *mesta* regulations than those of the unruly province of Texas. It will also be noted that the military governor made no mention of fees due the king on mesteños taken, saying only that stray animals of unknown ownership must be turned over to proper officials for observation of the safeguards due *mostrenco* stock.[40]

In June, Governor Martínez Pacheco advised Don Macario Sambrano that a number of local cattlemen who owed money to their hired hands were presently engaged in driving a common herd to the Hacienda San Francisco de Patos. Pike's journals mention a "Hacienda of Pattos," possibly the destination of this cattle drive. Described as "a handsome place where the Marquis de San Miguel frequently spends his summers," it was the administrative center of a 15-million-acre estate, belonging to the Marqueses de Aguayo (it survives as the town of General Cepeda, Coahuila).[41] The drive in question was being made

[40] Grazing Papers, vol. 1, pt. 2, pp. 149–51; J. B. Wilkinson, *Laredo and the Rio Grande Frontier*, p. 76. The petition was signed by Josef Gonzáles, Josef de Jesús Sánches, Antonio Gonzáles, and Manuel Ygnacio Flores, all of Laredo.

[41] Donald Jackson, *Pike's Journals*, p. 429. For a detailed study of this *latifundio*, devoted primarily to sheep raising and the vineyards at Parras, see Ida Altman, "The Marqueses de Aguayo: A Family and Estate History: (Master's thesis, University of Texas, 1972). It was perhaps the same Hacienda de Patos, described as "vast land holdings which were located near Saltillo and also in the vicinity of Monclova," with which empresario James Hewetson became associated in 1833, when he married Josefa Guajardo, widow of Juan Rosillo (William H. Oberste, *Texas Irish Empresarios and Their Colonies*, p. 91).

to repay expenses occasioned by the general agent, Juan José Flores, in his defense of *orejano* cattle and horses appropriated by the Royal Treasury. The governor attached a list, along with an *auto* outlining the collection procedure he wished Sambrano to follow. Included among those tardy in paying their vaqueros were some of the most prominent ranchers in the province, and failure to comply with the governor's orders would cost each one a 6-peso fine.[42]

This indebtedness apparently had been incurred on another communal drive conducted the previous year for the same purpose: paying off the sum which the community owed Juan José Flores for his legal work on their behalf. Manuel Delgado, who took the herd to Saltillo, obligated himself as their agent to pay the trail hands 570 pesos, an amount for which Flores's brother Joaquín stood as guarantor. The cattle were delivered and payment received at 3 pesos, 4 reales, a head but the hands had not been paid, resulting in the attachment of Joaquín's property. Juan José protested the injustice of this affair and Martínez Pacheco agreed, ordering that the *ayuntamiento* divide the burden equally among the raisers of the province. This the council did in February, 1789, drawing up a list of fifty-two individuals and stating the amount that each was to contribute toward liquidating Flores's commitment. Although each raiser posted bond for the assessed amount, a few no doubt were slow to pay, justifying the governor's action with the mid-1788 drive to Patos. Carrying on a legal battle against the superior government, then as now, was clearly an expensive undertaking.[43]

An instance of interprovincial cooperation in attempting to collect taxes due on the export and sale of cattle came in November, when José Pereira de Castro wrote Martínez Pacheco about the "contraband trade" taking place between Béxar and

---

[42] The list of ranchers involved is cited in Myres, "Spanish Cattle Kingdom," p. 244. While a cover letter of the same date (Martínez Pacheco to Sambrano, June 7, 1788) is found in BAT, 155:6, the list is not attached.

[43] BAT, 158:60–70. Joaquín Flores made a habit of offering security for Texas herds; see the contracts dated September 20 and October 6, 1787, Protocolos, Archivo Municipal, Saltillo.

Saltillo. He sent the governor the names of three San Antonio citizens who had smuggled cattle into Saltillo, asking him to collect 178 pesos from them upon their return home. Felipe García brought in 447 head, valued at 1,564 pesos; Vizente Flores, 600 head, valued at 1,800 pesos; and Juan Romero, 310 head, valued at 1,087 pesos (the value ranging from 3 to 3½ pesos a head). Considering that the total number of animals was 1,357, the mere 178 pesos Castro wanted the governor to collect for defrauding the king seems insignificant, working out to little more than 1 real a head. The tax involved was the *alcabala*, a sales or excise tax levied on goods as they passed from one province to another. According to Ramos Arizpe, these numerous taxes were "exacted with so much cruelty and tyranny that they are irremissibly collected on the remnant of goods that a poor laborer buys in Saltillo in order to cover his naked wife and also on the rice, flour, and chickpeas that he buys for his domestic consumption." One can hardly blame the Texas trail drivers for trying to beat such an oppressive system, which appears to have been worse than the taxation that had driven English-speaking American colonists to revolt. The *alcabala* was not collected in Texas.[14]

That summer Martínez Pacheco sent the bishop of Nuevo León the cabildo's petition of January discussing the *machorraje* levied on the *diezmo* for fertile breeding (*de veintre fructifero*). He blamed the problem on a malicious report promoted by the local tithe collector and asked the bishop to hear the "just pleas of these subjects" and free them from the penalty and display of *machorrajes*. If there is any doubt that the governor sympathized with the ranchers' position, such doubts are dispelled by his statements on the question of *orejano* cattle abandoned because of the incessant wars in the province. He noted that such cattle had been claimed for the Royal Treasury "without a legal base which might support it." He thought, however, that once the issue was decided and its "hoped-for fulfillment"

---

[14] Pereira de Castro to Martínez Pacheco, November 13, 1788, BAM, roll 19, frames 400–402; for subsequent correspondence see BAT, 157:71; 158:5, 13, 52, and 159:14, 162. See also Weddle and Thonhoff, *Drama and Conflict*, p. 58; Nettie Lee Benson, trans. and ed., *Report of Ramos Arizpe*, p. 41.

achieved, the vindicated citizens as good Christians would pay to the holy precept of the *diezmo* what was now going into the king's coffers.[45]

Bishop Verger replied on October 14, obviously a bit ruffled that the governor wanted him to forgo even this modest source of income, refusing his request "lest I create echos from other places." His response sheds more light on the nature of this *amachorrado*, which was apparently a special tax on the extraction or slaughter of breeding cattle, applied because, once this type of stock was dispensed with, the church would be deprived of future revenue on its natural increase. Verger condemned the citizens of Texas who "go to the fields and, like beasts, destroy as many cattle as they please." He cited instances of wasteful meat hunts and said that his information came not from the *diezmero* (Barrera) but from citizens who, contrary to those who sought the absolute freedom to slaughter or export, had begged him to put a stop to such despotism.

Warming to the subject, Bishop Verger mentioned the totally disrespectful case of Pedro Flores, who had refused to pay the *amachorrado* "under the deliberate and malicious pretext that if the mission from which he bought the herd did not pay the *diezmo* neither should he pay the *machorraje*." The bishop reminded Martínez Pacheco that death came into the world because of sin; thus much loss of life and property could be expected in Texas, a land where this kind of remiss behavior—the cheating of both Holy Church and God—was rampant. He concluded by asking the governor to help Barrera do his job and to support the prohibition against slaughtering and extracting female stock, *mayor y menor*, "unless they have been rendered barren and *machorraje*."[46]

The San Fernando Memorial eventually reached the vice-

---

[45] Martínez Pacheco to Verger, August 6, 1788, BAT, 156:8.

[46] Verger to Martínez Pacheco, October 14, 1788, BAT, 156:32. John Wheat, who is translating the Béxar Archives, defines the *machorraje* as a fee for cutting out barren cows. Herbert Eugene Bolton, *Guide to Materials for the United States in the Principal Archives of Mexico*, p. 418, makes reference to an item in the Ecclesiastical Archives of Monterrey "concerning the prohibition of the exportation and killing of breeding animals, 1782," possibly of related interest.

roy, Manuel Antonio Flores, a short-term appointee to the position after the untimely death of Bernardo de Gálvez in November, 1786. Viceroy Flores forwarded it, along with a stack of other documents pertaining to the Texas cattle question, to the Junta Superior de Real Hacienda. On February 27, 1789, this distinguished body agreed that the best course of action would be to "place the aforesaid dispatch in the hands of the commandant of the before-mentioned Eastern Provinces," who was the tough Indian fighter Colonel Juan de Ugalde. After conducting a thorough investigation of the matter, including the validity of the citizens' memorial, Ugalde was to report back to Viceroy Flores so that he would be in a position to determine what measures in justice could be taken, granting them through proper channels whatever relief the law might provide. In the meantime, however, it was recommended that no departure was to be taken from the practices presently being followed and that "conditions should be left as they are."

While the matter was under study, the junta in Mexico City proposed a measure that doubtless was wildly celebrated by the stubborn cattlemen of Texas and their persevering legal agents: "And in order that the citizens whose petition we are considering may not feel wronged, we recommend they should be allowed an extension of one year's time to round up, mark, and brand such unmarked cattle of their own as they may have roaming free or straying on lands not privately claimed."[47]

This wonderful news soon reached Texas. In June, Governor Martínez Pacheco informed the *ayuntamiento* that their petition had finally borne fruit. He told them that the viceroy, in a letter written four months previously, had acknowledged the San Fernando Memorial "concerning their belief that they have a right to unmarked cattle." The viceroy was aware that this cattle had been declared property of the crown by Teodoro de Croix in 1778. Also acknowledged was receipt of the charges that Governor Cabello had misappropriated funds kept in the

---

[47] Resolution of the Junta Superior de Real Hacienda, February 27, 1789, found in Martin Henry's annotated translation under "Investigation of Claims," Grazing Papers, vol. 1; see also BAT, 159:52–81, and BAM, roll 19, frames 598–611. Ugalde had forwarded the memorial to Viceroy Flores on September 2, 1788.

Mustang Fund. Concerning the cattle-ownership question, the viceroy suggested that the citizens apply to the action of Ugalde the provisions of his decree-in-council, that is, the junta's decision of February 27. On the matter of wrongdoing by Cabello, he ordered the cabildo to take detailed testimony from the citizens for the *fiscal*'s information. The king's auditor would then be in a position to decide whether the former governor had cheated on his accounts.[48]

This decision caused a flurry of activity at Béxar, as the ranchers and their agents scrambled to document the improprieties of Cabello. Even though they had achieved an unprecedented new branding extension, the stockmen of the province immediately petitioned for more time and remained unwilling to drop their vendetta with the former governor. When Cabello, then in the king's service in Havana, was advised in mid-1790 of the accusations being made against him at San Antonio, he called them "absurd, unfounded, and unjust." He had difficulty obtaining a transcript of the charges necessary to form his defense. Martínez Pacheco, long after he left Texas, was still indignantly denying that he possessed papers which Cabello needed to exonerate himself. The viceroy, the *fiscal*, and the Junta Superior shuffled this case back and forth for years until it finally reached the office of the commandant general, where it apparently died in 1797.[49]

On the question of cattle ownership, a bundle of papers was also assembled at Béxar to establish the rights of the citizens to the unbranded mesteños of the province. Various petitions on the subject were extracted from the archives of the villa and recopied in mid-June, 1789, promptly after Governor Martínez Pacheco informed them of the viceroy's decision. Many were signed by an assortment of ranchers but others are

---

[48] Viceroy Flores to Martínez Pacheco, March 13, 1789, BAM, roll 19, frames 657–58; Martínez Pacheco to *ayuntamiento*, June 15, 1789, BAM, roll 19, frames 867–88.

[49] "Expediente promovido à representación del Ayuntamiento de la Villa de San Fernando, acusando al Coronel Don Domingo Cavello . . . de malversación con fondo de Mesteñas," 1793 (AGN, Historia, Bolton Transcripts, 93:281–88). For the citizens' response to the one-year roundup extension, see BAT, 160:92–94.

the sole handiwork of the cattlemen's attorney, Juan José Flores. Several documents, it appears from an inventory compiled by Leandro Martínez Pacheco (the governor's brother), had been gathered early in 1788 by José Félix Menchaca as an agent representing the citizens' claims.[50]

Of the four petitions authored by Juan José Flores, three are undated fragments. They all sought justice and recognition of the settlers' many sacrifices on behalf of His Majesty. It was a bitter experience for them to see their cattle taken away, especially when the "inaction of the authorities was the reason that their cattle were dispersed and were not branded in so many years." Mismanagement and neglect by the king's officials had caused the sad circumstances of the ranchers and had led to the ruin of the missions. Rosario, for example, was once prosperous—full of Indian families and cattle—but now was reduced to bare walls. Complaints had been directed to Viceroy Bucareli by the Béxar *ayuntamiento* as early as 1772, said the attorney, but no redress had been made. Mentioning his own efforts on behalf of the cattlemen, Flores asked the viceroy to permit him to return to Texas and gather a herd to help defray his expenses. A passport would be necessary for this endeavor lest Governor Cabello jail him, as he had threatened. It seems likely that these petitions were made in 1785–86, by which time Flores had despaired of securing remedy at the commandant's level and gone directly to the viceroy.

The fourth petition by Flores, dated June 27, 1786, is concise and to the point, perhaps reflecting the experience he had gained in composition during his exile from Texas (especially in the summer of 1785). Flores mentioned that the raisers had made contact with Croix several times concerning their cattle-ownership rights during the year that he visited Béxar. Nonetheless, Cabello dictated the offensive decree of July, 1783. It was very harmful to the *criadores*, Flores noted, because it "taxed us as if our property belonged to someone else," that is, the king.

---

[50] "San Fernando, Proceedings Concerning the Right of Citizens to Unbranded Mesteños . . . ," June 15–19, BAM, roll 19, frames 867–88, containing more than forty manuscript pages.

This *bando* was enforced, and the citizens' cattle were taken away, leaving every one of them without a shirt on his back. Thus the citizens had risked everything in the stock-raising efforts, yet today nothing was recognized as theirs.

These laws, he said, the people found very repugnant, hating both the decrees and their enforcers. His Majesty's officials, however, seemed intent on keeping their cattle, "just because they run loose, when it can be proved that the *vecinos* brought them here and they procreated and covered the land." This was allowed to happen, noted Flores, because nobody thought that there would be a tax, and therefore there was no reason for them to brand. If such a proposition as Croix's was accepted, then all livestock in the "entire Americas" would be recognized as belonging to the king. This was absurd, argued the attorney, because neither horses nor cattle were native to the New World, much less to Texas.

Flores maintained that stray cattle belonged to the citizens under an original title, that the seed stock had been purchased or had been given to them by His Majesty. He depicted Spanish civilization in glowing terms: "We are not one of those barbaric nations who do not give their citizens the necessary time to get the cattle together and mark it." The problem, he claimed, was that the inhabitants of Texas were busy defending their lives—this was the reason their cattle were wild. Flores enumerated all the problems of everyday life, noting that those who should be responsible for defense—and who were getting paid for it—did not do the job. Although some of the generals of the province were good, their chief concern was "not with the cattle but in taking care of themselves." The attorney tempered this charge of negligence by admitting that the distances involved were tremendous. Unfortunately, this isolation worked against the stockmen in many ways. Strangers and "bandits" had come in, had seen all the loose cattle, and had decided to stay. The governor was supposed to be responsible for controlling such matters, but under the circumstances Béxar's citizens had vested power in Flores to go to Chihuahua to make complaints. Flores closed by reiterating that the ranchers' claims were justified, and he made the amazing charge that Cabello had allowed 36,000 head of cattle belonging to his clients to be exported from the province, enclosing as proof a letter by the village priest, Pedro Fuentes. This petition was likely one of those mentioned by the viceroy as having been forwarded to the Junta Superior but was recopied into the proceedings for good measure.[51]

Commandant General Ugarte had other ideas on the subject, as did his veteran *asesor*. On September 25, Ugarte decreed that all wild cattle and horses should be considered the property of the crown just as before and that the 4-real duty per animal should be collected just as before. This order reflected the "no-departure" guideline set forth in the junta's resolution. It ignored the fact, however, that if the ranchers were allowed another year to round up and mark their stray stock before it became the king's property for the interval no duties would be added to the Mustang Fund.[52]

In any case, Colonel Ugalde was too busy waging war against the Apaches to do anything about the Béxar citizens' cattle petition. Acting upon instructions of the late viceroy Bernardo de Gálvez given to Commandant General Ugarte a few months before Gálvez's death, the intrepid colonel engaged in vigorous campaigns against both the Mescalero and the Lipan Apaches. He met with considerable success in Coahuila and Texas, abating the Indian raids to a large extent by bringing destruction to their camps. Ugalde was no doubt content to leave the paperwork associated with the viceroy's decision on wild cows in Texas to his nominal superior, Jacobo Ugarte.

Late in 1789 the redoubtable Ugalde was on another campaign, encamped near the old presidio on the San Sabá. Before attacking the Apaches, he sent to San Antonio for reinforcements and ammunition. As Castañeda describes it, "Spontaneous and instant was the response to the appeal for aid," with fifty-two citizens (mostly cattlemen) and eleven soldiers volunteering to join Ugalde's men. More wished to go, as Governor Martínez Pacheco later informed the viceroy, but lack of arms and ammunition prevented it. This combined force surprised

---

[51] Ibid., frames 881–87.
[52] Ugarte, decree, September 25, 1789, mentioned in Espadas to Muñoz, November 4, 1790, in Grazing Papers, vol. 1; see also BAM, roll 20, frame 870.

the enemy early in January and beat them badly, the citizens of Béxar giving good account of themselves. It is not known whether in the glow of victory a certain cattle petition was mentioned to Juan de Ugalde by his fifty-two stalwart volunteers from the rustic provincial capital of Texas; but the odds favor it. Uvalde Canyon received its name, in somewhat altered form, to commemorate the site of this significant battle.[53]

Governor Martínez Pacheco was also concerned with other problems than keeping tabs on wild cattle. Soon after he sent the volunteers to join Colonel Ugalde's men, six Lipans came to his residence intending to kill him. Angered by the governor's duplicity in professing peace while preparing for an all-out war of extermination, the warriors entered his bedroom unannounced early on the morning of December 29. Only Martínez Pacheco's quick wits kept him alive until a contingent of soldiers arrived to intervene. The Lipans drew knives from under their blankets, and a fight erupted during which the room was

---

[53] Castañeda, *Catholic Heritage*, 5:13–17; Herbert Eugene Bolton, *Texas in the Middle Eighteenth Century*, p. 127.

smeared with blood, including floors, walls, chairs, and the table. In his report to the viceroy, Martínez Pacheco said that not one of the six warriors escaped from the room to carry information to their tribesmen, thus ensuring Ugalde's surprise strike and victory.

But other accounts of the "scuffle" leaked out, accounts that appear to have led to Martínez Pacheco's dismissal as governor, with the "Arocha house" evidently playing a key role. The case against him had been building for a year, and in May, 1790, the new viceroy, the Conde de Revillagigedo (see chapter 10) acknowledged that he had received a petition concerning the governor prepared by agents of the Béxar *ayuntamiento*. A clue to its contents emerged in October, when the Conde del Campo de Alange wrote that the king was aware that Martínez Pacheco had been accused of murdering in cold blood within his own house six friendly Lipans and that other "exceedingly grave charges" had been made against him. Since the viceroy began issuing orders for the preservation of the wild herds in Texas soon thereafter, it seems likely that the petitioners also charged the governor with misconduct in this important realm.

In a letter written to the viceroy a year after departing Texas, Domingo Cabello had made similar charges, claiming that in the year of 1787 alone Martínez Pacheco allowed the citizens of Texas to export over 7,000 head of cattle to Coahuila and other places. His successor had permitted this sort of activity, said Cabello, "without attention to its serious consequences for the province, by which the species [of cattle] could be exterminated . . . in a very short time." Although the majority of Texas stockmen welcomed Martínez Pacheco's liberal policy with regard to mesteños, it is clear that others did not, and that the pressure on him had been steadily rising. He was to be recalled, said Alange, while his trial was being set, and another official would be sent to take his place.[54]

Two months earlier, in the spring of 1790, a very interesting petition had been submitted at Béxar by twelve citizens,

---

[54] Castañeda, *Catholic Heritage*, pp. 17–20; Edman, "Compilation," pp. 454–62; Cabello to Viceroy, November 25, 1787, AGN, Provincias Internas, Hackett Transcripts, 182:91.

many of them prominent ranchers, on the subject of certain election abuses recently perpetrated by the Arochas and other related families. While much of this petition centers on resentments about social and economic matters borne against this powerful clan by their less prosperous neighbors, quite a few details related to ranching emerge during the recitation. Its central aim, however, was to discredit the Arocha family, thereby vindicating the conduct of Martínez Pacheco. Marcos de Zepeda and Francisco de Arocha, who had gone to Mexico to complain about the governor, were denounced as ringleaders whose purpose was to have the governor removed because he served the inhabitants without any "self-interest." The petitioners made a point of declaring that the complaint being carried to the interior was the work of only "one individual," that is, the Arochas, and thus did not represent widespread dissatisfaction with the way Martínez Pacheco was running the province.[55]

As stated, the professed cause of the petitioners' grievance was a city-council election in which collusion took place to ensure the selection of certain individuals favoring the "Arocha house." The citizens charged that they had returned from Colonel Ugalde's campaign against the Apaches to find that this rigged affair had taken place, with the city council fraudulently assuring themselves of seats. When Martínez Pacheco opposed the Arochas by overturning the election, he incurred the wrath of Don Simón's clan. Perhaps more pleased than he would have cared to admit by the citizens' vote of confidence, the governor turned their petition over to his lieutenant governor, Juan Martín de Amondarain, for investigation of the charges made. Once the "evidence" was in, he sent the entire proceedings to

[55] Petition, ". . . grievances done to them by alcaldes, *regidores*, and *procurador* in 1789 . . . ," March 1–2, 1790, found in Blake, Research Collection, Supplement ser., 2:244–71. Signing were Juan Joseph de Santa, Miguel de Gortari, Santiago Seguín, Bartolomé Seguín, Francisco Flores, Vizente Flores, Joseph Francisco Péres, Francisco Xavier Rodríguez, Juan Antonio Romero, Sebastián Monjarás, Joseph Hernández, and Francisco Rodríguez. An addenda to this petition, giving information on the annual Saltillo fair and claiming that alcaldes and other city officials should have to "work like everyone else," was signed by Mariano Gortari (at request of Manuel Berbán); Vizente Flores (at request of Manuel Flores); Pablo Luciano Flores (at request of Gregorio Leal); Silvestre Joachín de Soto; Juan Antonio Romero; and Diego and Joseph Felipe [Félix] Menchaca.

the viceroy, saying in effect that this sort of thing happened frequently but most of the time was overlooked. He suggested depriving the guilty parties of offices for ten years to teach them some humility and respect for His Majesty's liberality in granting them self-government.

The success enjoyed by Don Simón de Arocha was obviously a source of agitation for many of his fellow citizens. After savagely attacking his conduct and that of his family, the petitioners moved on to an account of his stock-raising excesses. This was the real basis of their hostility, and central to it was the location of an Arocha-owned ranch on the other side of the Guadalupe River near its junction with the San Marcos. These lands were traditionally recognized as *realengas*, and it was maintained that if the Arochas were allowed to keep this ranch much detriment would result to the citizenry. While the wild cattle found there originated from that of all ranchers, only this powerful family would be able to enjoy its rewards, a situation that would cause endless dispute. The petitioners charged that the Arochas would not raise cattle on other, better lands because there were no "free" cattle to gather. At stake was the Mustang Fund, used among other things to ransom captives from the Indians, it being Simón de Arocha's object to deprive them of such benefits by taking stock without payment of the designated fees.

Another charge seems to imply that Don Simón was behind the idea of ceding to the king all stock beyond the Guadalupe—only to turn around and use his influence to locate a ranch on those lands. This had been accomplished by a ruling of the town corporation that the lands were vacant and that thus there was no impediment to the Arochas' obtaining them. But it was not possible, in the ranchers' view, for the members of the corporation to render an objective opinion about the location of such a ranch because the cabildo was "rigged with blood relatives who will ignore its damage to those not of the Arocha house." Besides Zepeda, who was related by marriage, there was Ignacio Calvillo, Simón's brother-in-law. *Regidor* Manuel Delgado was also married to a sister of Simón's. Then there was the first *regidor*, Francisco, Simón's son, and his brother Julián, who was high constable. To those who were not part of this clan the consolidation of power in the hands of Don Simón de Arocha must have assumed sinister proportions.

The petitioners asked Governor Martínez Pacheco to acknowledge this land grab, since the Arochas had not been able to turn him aside with their disputes and misrepresentations as they had other governors. They claimed that the missionaries also had many complaints against the Arochas, not the least of which was Simón's role in negotiating the roundup agreement of 1787. Pretending that they were being robbed, the Arochas were in fact doing the stealing, as the agreement supposedly made evident: ". . . and now finally it has been seen that the Arochas may have charge of our land and meat, of the cattle that they have stolen of others." Such an instance had occurred in 1789, when "all the Arochas" had asked for a license to make a gathering beyond the Guadalupe, where the king's cattle pastured. Since they controlled the town council, they had granted such permission to themselves, their brothers, and their nephews.

A tragedy had occurred on this outing, which Lieutenant Governor Amondarain reported obviously to show how cold-blooded the Arochas could be in their ruthless pursuit of every unmarked cow in the province. The Arocha party had crossed the Guadalupe into Espíritu Santo's pastures (the Arochas' new ranch fronted on the mission's upper lands) and proceeded to gather 200 head. In so doing, they had lost Simón's brother "when a cow ran a horn through his body." The injured man had asked for confession, but the vaqueros had been afraid to carry him to Fray Cárdenas lest, Amondarain said, their perfidious theft be discovered. Thus, to protect themselves, the Arochas had allowed their kinsman to die in a manner no good Catholic would countenance—at least so Amondarain charged. Not wishing to weary Martínez Pacheco, because if they spoke of the defects of the Arochas the list "would never be completed," the petitioners ended by lauding the governor's accomplishments and virtues. When the governor forwarded their endorsement to the viceroy, he also sent a defense of his record (number 11), indicating that the entire affair was conducted to counter the charges of his adversaries, the Arochas.⁵⁶

Apart from the eye-opening information that the enterprising Arocha clan was attempting to locate a ranch on lands that had traditionally been recognized as crown lands, higher above Béxar than Indian trouble had previously allowed ranching operations to be conducted, these proceedings of March, 1790, reveal that the success of the Arochas had provoked bitterness and opposition in many of their neighbors in El Rincón. Not content to be the bona fide owner of the 8-league San Rafael de Pataguilla, Don Simón had given others in his vicinity the distinct impression that he wanted to own everything in sight, including "our persons," as the ranchers expressed it. It is possible that he had somewhat exceeded common notions of propriety in his ambitions, yet the highly personal nature of the charges against him indicates that they were motivated to some extent by frustration and envy. In any case, it appears that these cattlemen had good reasons for not wanting the Arocha petition against Martínez Pacheco then being carried to the viceroy to prevail. If this state of affairs could be described as "peace" after forty years of disunity, then one must wonder what these frontiersmen considered war.

---

⁵⁶ The case (no. 10) was sent March 9, 1790, accompanied by Martínez Pacheco's defense (no. 11), ibid., pp. 278–98.

10

"RELEASED FROM THEIR OBLIGATION"

Slaughters and Secularization

During the same year, 1790, Juan Vicente de Güemes Pacheco de Padilla, the second Conde de Revillagigedo replaced Manuel Antonio Flores as viceroy of New Spain. He promptly ousted the energetic Juan de Ugalde from military command of the eastern sector of the Provincias Internas. Then Pedro de Nava took Jacobo de Ugarte's place as commandant general. To top off all this confusion, the governorship was suppressed in Texas. It was decided that a presidial captain could run the province, and on August 14, Martínez Pacheco turned over his office to Lieutenant Colonel Manuel Muñoz, another aging, ill veteran soldier sent to relieve him. Grown somewhat accustomed to the benign neglect of Martínez Pacheco concerning enforcement of Croix's cattle laws, the ranchers were doubtless apprehensive about the attitudes Muñoz would bring with him. Since these sweeping changes occurred under the weak and inept Carlos IV, son of the progressive Carlos III, who had died in December 1788, none of them bode well for Texas, which was more than ever exposed to bold incursions by the newly independent American colonies.[1]

Meanwhile, at La Bahía another attempt was being made to resurrect Mission Rosario. Both Captain Luis Cazorla and his second in command, Lieutenant José Santoja, had died during an epidemic in 1788, and the presidio was now in the hands of a "poor humble fellow who is not even a captain but only acting commander," as Father José Mariano Reyes described Manuel de Espadas. Reyes was serving as interim chaplain at Bahía Presidio when some of Rosario's former Indian neophytes appeared and asked that their mission be restored. According to Father Reyes, who wrote the viceroy on May 1, 1790, God used Espadas "as a tiny instrument to confound the haughty, and adorned him with those virtues which he giveth to men at times so that they may fulfill his purpose." In other words, Espadas told Father Reyes to go ahead with his plan to restore Mission Rosario, which the zealous friar soon did.

In his letter Reyes also sketched the history of the mission from the time it was abandoned, sometime between 1778 and 1781, when "even the minister departed." In 1783, according to Reyes, an inventory showed that Rosario owned more than 30,000 head of cattle, including many that were unbranded. It was then that the governor, Domingo Cabello, "declared the lands of these Indians to be the property of the king, and anybody who wanted to had the right to take out or kill the unbranded cattle"—a reference to Cabello's *bando* of July, 1783. Reyes charged that both soldiers and settlers slaughtered as many cattle as they pleased, even branded ones. At the same time the Lipan Apaches came and did immense damage, taking what they needed and killing the rest, and nothing was done to prevent such destruction. The governor and the Bahía captain

---

[1] Elizabeth A. H. John, *Storms Brewed in Other Men's Worlds: The Confrontation of Indians, Spanish, and French in the Southwest, 1550–1795*, pp. 735, 755; Odie B. Faulk, *The Last Years of Spanish Texas, 1778–1821*, pp. 19–20, 24–25. Carlos E. Castañeda, *Our Catholic Heritage in Texas*, 5:111–13, says that owing to the vigorous protests of Ugalde, the viceroy was convinced of the necessity of maintaining the office of governor in Texas. The king's approval of Muñoz on a temporary basis on October 18, 1790, set his salary at 3,000 pesos a year.

failed to come to Rosario's aid, Reyes said, "because they considered that this Mission was irretrievably ruined."[2]

Fray Reyes set about gathering neophytes for the resurrection of Rosario. By July he had forty-five Indians living at the ruins of the mission with more expected in October, when the crops could be harvested and enough cattle rounded up to provide a food supply for permanent residents. Unfortunately, Reyes was a somewhat controversial figure, and his efforts were not destined to be successful. Opposed by the father president, who declared that Reyes deluded the Indians with simple tricks (making them think that he could "catch the stars with his hands"), he was replaced early in 1791 with another priest, Father José Francisco Jaudenes. Reyes was recalled to face charges of disobedience at the Zacatecan college and did not return to Rosario, the infant given into his keeping "so that I could nourish it at my breast." Conditions were soon so bad at Rosario that Governor Muñoz asked the Bahía commander if it would be possible to round up wild cattle to help feed its Indians, suggesting that settlers might be offered a share of the animals taken for their work. Carlos Martínez, who owned Rancho de San José, managed to corral some of the mission's wild cattle, enabling Father Jaudenes to keep his flock together through the second winter.[3]

On October 18, 1790, former Governor Martínez Pacheco submitted a report of the Mustang Fund under his administration. The report showed an ending balance of 8,746 pesos. Of this total 5,905 pesos represented funds in the box, and 2,842 pesos was shown as having been spent to provision Colonel Ugalde's campaign against the Lipan Apaches. Attached to the report were five *cuadernos* (memoranda) explaining various

---

[2] Reyes, "Report on Mission Rosario," May 1, 1790, BAM, roll 20, frames 343–54; Charles [William] Ramsdell, [Jr.], "Spanish Goliad" (typescript, University of Texas Archives), p. 48.

[3] Castañeda, *Catholic Heritage*, 5:189. According to Father President Oliva, Reyes restored Mission Rosario at the "request" of Governor Martínez Pacheco. Oliva accused Reyes of contracting numerous debts totaling more than 3,000 pesos and asked the college to remove him from Espada, where he was stationed before going to Rosario. Fr. Benedict Leutenegger, trans., *Management of the Missions in Texas: Fr. José Rafael Oliva's Views Concerning the Problem of Temporalities in 1788*, p. 50.

entries, through which we learn that 573 pesos were spent "for rescue of captives from friendly northern tribes" during the period from December, 1786, to August, 1790 (*cuaderno* 5). Another entry of 511 pesos was noted as paid by the *vecinos* and soldiers at Béxar for *orejanos* killed and mesteños taken in 1787 (*cuaderno* 3). The sum of 360 pesos was collected at Nacogdoches in mid-November, 1787, indicating that the First Big Roundup was extended to loose cattle in that jurisdiction as well; La Bahía produced only 74 pesos for its efforts. In an accompanying report Martínez Pacheco stated that a total of 4,224 pesos was owed the fund by various individuals, including one entry of 3,870 pesos, which, of course, represented the 7,649 *orejano* cattle and 183 mesteño horses taken in the roundup of 1787. Despite the thoroughness of Martínez Pacheco's report, "shortages" in these accounts were noted as his trial progressed into February, 1791. By June he was on his way to Mexico. Thus it can be seen that, in facing his accusers, the former governor needed all the citizen support for his administration that he could get.[4]

At the same time that this report was submitted, Governor Muñoz wrote Lieutenant Commandant Espadas, informing him of Commandant General Ugarte's year-old decree that all wild cattle and horses should continue to be considered crown property. He told Espadas that the determination to carry out the provisions of this measure had been gravely weakened, "much to the injury of the Royal Treasury," and that he should proceed with all possible strictness in collecting the 4-real head tax. This tax was also to apply to animals found in the pastures of a cattle breeder or a mission. Further, Muñoz wanted similar measures taken with the capture and use of wild horses, even to the extent of putting "intelligent persons" to work on the task of reconnoitering droves rounded up for his post. Muñoz, it would seem, did not intend to give the ranchers any slack in the matter of *orejano* and mesteño stock.

---

[4] "Report of the *Ramo de Orejanas* (Mustang Fund) under Governor Rafael Martínez Pacheco's Administration, December, 1786–August, 1790, Submitted October 18, 1790," BAM, roll 20, frames 806–16.

Replying on November 4, Espadas told the governor that he would proceed according to the strictest possible interpretation of his orders. His only question was whether he himself was to decide on granting permission to local residents who wanted to hunt cattle in mission pastures or whether the missions alone were to enjoy this prerogative, subject to payment of the required 4 reales for each head taken. Learning of the presidio commander's uncertainty about allowing citizens to enter mission pastures and run down mesteños, Fray Cárdenas wrote Espadas the following day claiming all cattle that grazed on mission lands. This letter was promptly forwarded to the new governor, who jotted down his reply in the margin. He acknowledged the captain's report of income derived from the Ramo de Mesteñas from 1787 to 1789, along with the annoying claim submitted by the "teacher" at Mission Espíritu Santo. Muñoz now considered himself placed in a position where he must address the matter, like it or not.[5]

The problem at La Bahía was only beginning, as soon became evident. The viceroy hinted at what was to come in a letter to Muñoz dated October 26, 1790, in which he commended the governor for doing a good job in separating the soldiers' horses from *bestias* owned by the citizens. He suggested that by detailing six soldiers to help the *vecinos* maintain their own horse herd, many problems would be eliminated. But the real solution, noted Revillagigedo, would result from his order forbidding troops to run mesteños. Such a measure would contribute to harmony between the military and civilian populations. While this restriction on soldiers' roundups was very likely applauded by the people of Béxar, little did they suspect that it would soon be extended to them—first only in the neighborhood of La Bahía but later throughout the entire province. Also, in November the viceroy forwarded to Muñoz a copy of his predecessor's (Flores's) letter of March 13, 1789, concerning a one-year branding extension, the glad tidings of which had

[5] Ugarte's letter as cited in chap. 9, n.52. In Espadas's communication of November 4 both Muñoz's letter of October 16, 1790, and Ugarte's letter of September 25, 1789, are mentioned. See also Fray Cárdenas to Espadas, November 5, 1790, BAM, roll 20, frames 872–74.

already reached Texas at the end of Martínez Pacheco's administration. A comprehensive census was taken at La Bahía, showing most settlers as "su officio del campo" (making a living in the country), regardless of their caste (Spanish, Indian, mestizo, or mulatto). The equally detailed census of Béxar of 1790 reveals that the four largest households were maintained by *criadores* Juan Martín de Amondarain (fourteen male adults), Simón de Arocha (thirteen), Joaquín Leal (twelve), and Joaquín Menchaca (eleven).[6]

Thus the restoration of Mission Rosario and the attempts to collect the vestiges of its former herds created many problems—or at least brought those problems to the attention of policymakers—resulting in a clamp down on cattle slaughters and other abuses that endangered the breed. The limiting of corridas by soldiers, effected to smooth out differences between them and the citizens, was just the beginning. Governor Muñoz issued instructions to the Béxar *ayuntamiento* on January 10, 1791, directed toward resolving more conflicts—those between the ranchers and the churchmen responsible for administering the *diezmo*. Muñoz noted that much trouble had occurred during the recent branding, trouble which should have been prevented and could no longer be ignored. He told the city fathers that they must let the *herraderos* (branders) know in advance how much they would have to pay for their tithes. It would appear that *diezmos* were being required at a time which conflicted with or complicated the customary period for branding. Muñoz reasoned that, since the *criadores* had their own land and marked their cattle at a regular time, they should combine their operations with the titheman's, thereby rendering to Fray José Mariano Roxo the respect he was due. To avoid what had happened the previous December, the governor suggested that in the future the tithe collector should be present when the annual branding was regularly done.[7]

[6] Revillagigedo to Muñoz, October 26 and November 13, 1790, BAM, roll 20, frames 838, 877–78. See also the viceroy's letter of November 17 approving measures to prevent extinction of wild cattle and "Padrón Formado por el Tente de Cavalleria Don Manuel de Espadas, Comts. del Pres. de La Bahía de Sptu. Santo . . . ," 1790, BA, box 4C460.

[7] Muñoz to Justicia y Regimiento, January 10, 1791, BAM, roll 21, frame 101. Fray Roxo served at both Concepción and San José, 1790–92. "He was especially adept in

Reports of slaughters of cattle in the pastures of Mission Rosario begin to appear in March, 1791. Fray José Francisco Jaudenes complained to Muñoz on the eleventh that the mission was without food because of these outrages. He had experienced serious problems in catching cows and said that not enough were left to sustain the mission's needs; its existence he considered precarious. However, a party of twenty-three men had arrived "on a mission of mercy," loaded with meat, *sebo* (suet), and *manteca* (fat), and Father Jaudenes begged the governor to pay them. Muñoz evidently issued orders to Captain Espadas of Bahía Presidio on March 19, because the captain wrote back two weeks later saying that, as instructed, he had prohibited all citizens of the neighborhood either to hold corridas or to butcher cattle on Rosario's pastures.[8]

It was not long before the viceroy reinforced this edict. In April he notified the governor that a decision had been reached to forbid corridas entirely because of information that the *carneadores* took only the best parts, wasting most of what they killed. He ordered Muñoz to forbid destruction of breeding cows and to punish offenders. Discretion should also be used in subsistence slaughters, for which the *vecinos* must continue to pay the stipulated taxes. It should be noted that, at the same time, Viceroy Revillagigedo authorized a fact-finding junket in response to the king's instructions to investigate the possibility of extending the limits of Louisiana to the Sabine River, abandoning Nacodgoches in favor of Bucareli, placing a small fort on the coast, or opening a port for Texas. The fifth item of the viceroy's elaborate set of instructions, dated April 27, 1791, required his commissioner to determine "whether it would be useful to open up reciprocal trade . . . or more advantageous to shut it off entirely," a consideration which, as has been seen, refused to go away.

Interestingly, the sixth item on the viceroy's agenda called

teaching the Indians music and singing" but soon retired to the College of Zacatecas (Fr. Marion A. Habig, *The Alamo Chain of Missions: A History of San Antonio's Five Old Missions*, p. 252).

[8] Jaudenes to Muñoz, March 11, 1791; Muñoz to Espadas, March 19, 1791; Espadas to Muñoz, April 4, 1791, BAM, roll 21, frames 251–53, 303. Also on March 19, Muñoz told Fray Cárdenas that the duties on cattle could not be abolished until approved by the commandant general.

for a statement on the abundance or diminution of the number of cattle, horses, and ownerless stock, "which in Texas are commonly called *mesteños* or *alzados*," as well as a conservative estimate of the domesticated stock owned by both missions and inhabitants of the province. Although the inspection was suspended because of the expense involved, concern over the extent of the wild herds in Texas appears to have been on the rise in Mexico City and elsewhere. In August another letter from the viceroy on the same subject was addressed to Governor Muñoz, this one regarding complaints received from Fray José Mariano Reyes and Don Onofre Castillón, a chaplain at San Juan Bautista. They charged that citizens of Laredo were killing Rosario's cattle, and the viceroy ordered Muñoz to put a stop to such slaughters so that the herds could grow and the quality of life improve.[9]

Captain Manuel Espadas's successor at La Bahía, Juan Cortés, informed the governor on September 24 and 26 that he had not allowed corridas or the killing of mission stock and that he would keep the same policy in effect. Reflecting a bit of frustration, Cortés's second communication asked Muñoz to be more specific about who was committing these slaughters and to allow him enough time to do his duty. Despite all the fuss, Rosario's situation was little improved as the new year rolled around. Muñoz asked the Bahía captain to help the mission collect some cattle from *realengas*, reiterating the offer to pay citizens for their work with a share of the cows taken. Cortés answered on February 5, declaring that to keep the Rosario Indians happy he had tried on three different occasions to catch cattle for them on crown lands. He was ordering the *vecinos* to help and to be paid for their effort, and added that if the Indians did not get enough meat by these means he would take them out and hold a corrida himself. Rampant slaughtering in the mis-

---

[9] Revillagigedo to Muñoz, April 20, 1791, BAM, roll 21, frames 344–45; Charles Wilson Hackett et al., eds. and trans., *Pichardo's Treatise*, 3:452–62; Revillagigedo to Muñoz, August 6, 1791, BAM, roll 21, frames 624–25. For the correspondence relative to the Rosario killings by citizens of Laredo, see Onofre Castillón to Reyes, March 3 and August 9, 1791, ibid., frames 221–22; Jaudenes to Muñoz, March 11–19, 1791, ibid., frames 251–53.

sion pastures at La Bahía had taken its toll on the once-plentiful herds, and pressure was obviously being exerted to end such abuses, or at least to satisfy appearances. Meanwhile, Governor Muñoz continued to issue licenses for roundups of unbranded stock in other areas, and Father Vasconcelos's diary notes that in October a packtrain of supplies and a drove of cattle again left Zacatecas to sustain the Texas missions.[10]

The Béxar cabildo, acting on instructions dated October 3, 1791, formed a list of ranches which were populated and on which cattle was raised, along with the names of the ranch owners. Heading the "officially recognized" list, submitted on November 8, were Don Simón de Arocha with his Rancho San Rafael de Pataguiya and Don Luis Antonio Menchaca with his Rancho San Francisco de los Varais. The owners and ranches listed as unpopulated but with improvements were as follows:

> Don Tomás Travieso—San Vizente de las Mulas
> Don José Plácido Hernández—San Bartolo del Cerrito
> Doña Leonor Delgado—San José de los Alamos
> Don Salvador Rodríguez—Nuestra Señora de Candelaría
> Don Ygnacio Calvillo—Nuestra Señora de Guadalupe de las Mugeres
> Don Ygnacio Peña—San Eldifonzo del Chayopín
> Doña Manuela Móntes—Nuestra Señora de Guadalupe del Chayopín
> Don Macario Sambrano—Nuestra Señora de Candelaría de las Calaveras
> Don Diego Yrineo Corríquez—Santa Cruz de la Laja
> Doña Antonia de Armas—San Lorenzo de las Mulas
> Don Manuel Delgado—San Cristóbal de Espanta Perros
> Doña Josefa Quiñones—San Miguel de las Amoladeras

Thus in 1791 fourteen individuals were considered legitimate stock raisers—quite a drop from the fifty names submitted by Governor Martínez Pacheco just three years earlier. In *Drama and Conflict*, Thonhoff discusses the ranches included on this list, pointing out that by this time some of them were one gen-

[10] Cortés to Muñoz, September 24 and 26, 1791, ibid., frames 728, 730; Muñoz to Cortés, January 28, 1792; Cortés to Muñoz, February 5, 1792, BAM, roll 22, frames 55–57, 68–69.

eration removed from their founders and noting alterations in the original names.[11]

Such a list was considered necessary not only for the intendant's (and perhaps the viceroy's) information but because it was time for the annual branding. Muñoz had already issued a number of permits at Béxar for roundups, meat hunts, and the like. The procedure was to list the primary applicant along with the names of all the men who wanted to go on each outing. Generally the purpose of the outing was stated as "to catch and slaughter cattle on unclaimed lands," "for cattle to supply meat for their families," "for cattle and horses," and so on. Sometimes the location of the intended hunt was also mentioned: "on the Cíbolo," "to his ranch called San José," "to the other side of the Guadalupe," and so on. The summer of 1791 was a busy season for wild-cattle licenses, a trend which soon got out of hand and had to be drastically curtailed.[12]

On November 10, Governor Muñoz ordered the branding done and a list made as required by Croix's decree. Stating that certain raisers had made him aware of the provisions of this decree and that it was "an opportune time," he advised the cabildo to summon area cattlemen and tell them to go to their ranches on the fourteenth and commence branding. He also ordered the cabildo to notify the collector of tithes so that he could attend to the *diezmos*. The cabildo complied, and on the following day sixteen *criadores* met and acknowledged the governor's decree. They said that their livestock was far removed from normal pastures since fear of aggression from hostile Indians had prevented tending them. They asked for a license to round up beginning at the Guadalupe River "on all lands which are declared to be [un?]encumbered, separating them from the ranches which have been granted or licensed by the Lord Gov-

[11] Béxar cabildo, "Report on the Number of Villages, Haciendas, and Ranches in This Province" (as requested by the *señor intendente* on October 3, 1791), November 8, 1791, BAM, roll 21, frames 872–73. Frederick C. Chabot, *With the Makers of San Antonio*, p. 168, has this list but gives the name of Menchaca's ranch incorrectly. See also Robert H. Thonhoff, *The Texas Connection with the American Revolution*, pp. 13–17.

[12] See Chabot, *Makers of San Antonio*, pp. 168–69, for ten such permits, including a full listing of the participants.

ernors." The ranchers also asked Muñoz to request the missionaries to make available on behalf of each mission any people they could spare for the general roundup. However, they did not want the reverend fathers to be permitted to gather on royal lands but wished this right reserved for themselves. After the ranchers had caught as many head as possible, both branded and *orejano*, then the missions could come and remove their branded stock: "The *orejanos* acquired shall remain in the possession of the laborers, while the king shall be paid his royal duty."

The governor answered this bold proposal on the same day, saying that their reply ignored the second paragraph of his order, which specified that the ranchers were to provide individual tallies, which would be combined into a common report. This was necessary so that suitable measures might be taken in favor of legitimate and actual raisers. Muñoz was displaying all the signs of becoming another Domingo Cabello, except that now a certain amount of order in the cattle industry was being pressed by the raisers themselves, or at least by a few of them. Doubtless they were the ones who had called the governor's attention to Croix's original cattle law, although they were not named.[13]

Surprisingly, when the governor formally authorized the fall roundup on November 18, he granted at least some of the cattlemen's requests. But for the most part his instructions required the exercise of moderation in gathering and branding. Raisers were permitted to go as far as the Guadalupe River. They were to bring in the cattle and corral and count it by November 21—a Herculean feat. The raisers must recognize unbranded cattle as belonging to His Majesty, said Muñoz, and brand only what was theirs. They were forbidden to mark cattle belonging

---

[13] Muñoz to Cabildo, November 10, 1791; cabildo's reply, November 11, 1791; Muñoz to cabildo, November 11, 1791, all in "Minutes, Resolutions and Other Records of Cabildo . . . ," BAT, 115:22–26; see also BAM, roll 21, frames 875–78, for "Proceedings concerning General Roundup in Béxar." The ranchers' petition was signed by Tomás Travieso, Joseph Phélis Menchaca, Ygnacio Calvillo, Manuel de Arocha, Joaquín Flores, Vizente Flores, Joseph Macario Sambrano, Gavino Delgado, Julián de Arocha, Amador Delgado, Phelipe Flores, Miguel Gortaris, Diego Erineo Enríques, Francisco Rodrígues, Manuel Salinas, and Francisco Padrón.

to other provinces, although he did not say how such ownership was to be ascertained. Further, Muñoz wanted the ranchers to only mark enough for their "own needs," whatever that was supposed to mean, and ordered them to tell him specifically for what use cattle was taken beyond that limit. One suspects that the stockmen paid little attention to such vague guidelines, which were obviously designed to satisfy the viceroy and his junta.[14]

I have been unable to find roundup and branding reports for the administration of Manuel Muñoz, although he mentions that such tabulations were required. Nor are there detailed records of cattle exports to Louisiana or the southern markets for the period, as was formerly the practice. Evidence suggests that Texas in these years continued to send cattle to markets in provinces below the Río Grande, which traditionally concentrated on the raising of horses and *ganado menor* rather than bovine stock. That the Louisiana trade had been declared prejudicial to the needs of New Spain in 1786 would explain, of course, why no official reports exist for the years after Domingo Cabello's administration. That considerable trade did continue seems certain, regardless of the government's many attempts to forestall it. This subject will be more fully addressed in chapter 11. Suffice it here to say that, as the 1790s began, the very idea of trade between Texas and Louisiana—so filled with promise a decade earlier—was well-nigh discredited, even though both provinces were long since Spanish possessions. Trade's firmest advocates, José de Gálvez, his nephew Bernardo, Croix, Mézières, and Ripperdá, were either dead or gone from the scene.

It was at this time and in this connection that the activities of Captain Antonio Gil Ybarbo at Nacogdoches once again became suspect. Actually suspicion that Gil Ybarbo was engaged in smuggling had never completely left official circles from

---

[14] Muñoz, "Orders Regulating General Roundup," November 18, 1791, BAM, roll 21, frames 910–11. The governor's restriction on marking according to one's "own needs" was given in obedience to the viceroy's letter of April 20, 1791, in which hunts were ordered limited to what was needed "for maintenance." By such limitations it was hoped that breeding would be protected and the herds not depleted.

"Released from Their Obligation" 389

Oconor's day, as has been noted. Governor Martínez Pacheco was convinced of his guilt but feared to remove him lest the Indians over whom he exercised such great influence rebelled. Colonel Ugalde also gave bad reports on Gil Ybarbo, charging that he was an incapable administrator; that he engaged in illicit trade, being responsible for the constant sale of cattle and horses to Louisiana; that he was in contact with French and English traders; and that he was a "mulatto." Acting upon Ugalde's reports, as well as questions posed by the *fiscal*, the new viceroy instructed Muñoz to investigate secretly the doings at Nacogdoches. These and similar probes eventually led to the old pioneer's downfall.[15]

One such inquiry was precipitated by Gil Ybarbo's ongoing dispute over jurisdictions with the commander at Natchitoches, Don Louis Carlos de Blanc, a grandson of St. Denis. In 1789, to

[15] Gil Ybarbo's misfortunes are traced in Castañeda, *Catholic Heritage*, 5:113, 173–75; Chabot, *Makers of San Antonio*, p. 218; Nyal C. King, "Captain Antonio Gil Y'Barbo, Founder of Modern Nacogdoches, 1729–1809," pp. 92–101.

resolve the question, Blanc had suggested a solution that was ingeniously simple. It drew the line between his post and Nacogdoches at the Sabine, "the most equitable natural boundary for both." Among other things, this solution would supposedly eliminate all enmities between both settlements, promote intercourse and transit between them, push back the fierce Indians and bind more closely the friendly ones, and increase the benefits of stock raising by extending the pasturage available to his expanding post, substantially reducing the cost of animals. By redefining the situation, Blanc thus hoped to eliminate its objectionable features—in his favor, of course. He assured his superior, Estévan Rodríguez Miró, governor of Louisiana, that such a cooperative measure coincided with "the interests of His Majesty and of his loyal vassals in the two provinces, without the possibility of the least unfavorable result."[16]

On November 12, 1791, Blanc complained to Governor Muñoz that, although he was "little desirous" of extending his boundary line, Gil Ybarbo wanted to push his to midstream at the Natchitoches post. The Nacogdoches captain, as might be expected, had a different story. He said that the line had always been at the Natchitoches (Red) River until 1783, when Blanc began trading with the "Keechies" (Kichais) and trying to wrest control of all the ranches east of the Sabine from Gil Ybarbo's authority (nonetheless, when a list of these ranches was compiled in 1797, all the French owners indicated that they considered themselves to be in the Natchitoches jurisdiction). This squabble over jurisdictions in East Texas prompted plans for the fact-finding junket previously noted and resulted in a momentous decision by the king that on all such matters "no further steps [were to] be taken."[17]

That did little to solve the problem. Three weeks after the king had reached his determination to do nothing, Louis de

---

[16] Hackett et al., *Pichardo's Treatise*, 3:450–52.

[17] Ibid., pp. 452–62; R. B. Blake, Research Collection, Supplement ser., 2:239, 416, 422. It should be noted that J. Villasana Haggard, "Neutral Ground between Louisiana and Texas," *Louisiana Historical Quarterly* 28, no. 4 (October, 1945):1078, erroneously cites the king's decision as April 3, 1783 (perhaps a typographical error) but nonetheless correctly assesses its result.

Blanc reported to Governor Muñoz that Americans were entering Texas to kill wild cattle, capture horses, and trade with the Indians. He was as powerless as the captain at Nacogdoches to stop these incursions. When explaining the situation to his superior in New Orleans, Blanc said that his post, being very near the Texas frontier, was used as a "constant resort" by those with the object of trading cattle, horses, and mules for goods. Noting that this trade was prohibited, the commandant claimed that he could not prevent it and then described in glowing terms the livestock industry in the Natchitoches jurisdiction: "There are plenty of cattle, much more than needed for the consumption of the post, enough horses, many hogs, few sheep." Curiously, Blanc did not draw a connection between the prosperity of his people and the illicit trade which he admittedly could not control.

Only a few days later Viceroy Revillagigedo wrote the king's secretary concerning the opening of trade with Louisiana, which he considered impractical. Rather than try to encourage such trade, the viceroy wanted to discourage if not prohibit it altogether. He suspected that both the provincial officials and the citizens welcomed the idea because of the high profits to be made from smuggling, once restrictions were loosened somewhat. He therefore recommended severing all communications between the two provinces and abandoning Nacogdoches because, in his opinion, it served only as a refuge for intruders, smugglers, and other undesirables. Revillagigedo wanted no transients, traders, or settlers coming into East Texas from the neighboring province unless a strong garrison was there to maintain respect for Spain, check invasion, and stop illegal traffic, including that of livestock. Given such attitudes, it is small wonder that Antonio Gil Ybarbo's presence at Nacogdoches could no longer be tolerated.[18]

Concerning Gil Ybarbo's undoing, it should be observed that before the king decided on September 7, 1792, to reunite

---

[18] Blanc to Muñoz, April 26, 1793, in Sandra L. Myres, *The Ranch in Spanish Texas, 1691–1800*, p. 50, and in Castañeda, *Catholic Heritage*, 5:205; Revillagigedo to Gardoqui, April 30, 1793, cited in Castañeda, ibid., pp. 171–73, where this episode is outlined and related to Gil Ybarbo's removal.

the commandancy general of all five Interior Provinces (Sonora, Nueva Vizcaya, Nuevo México, Coahuila, and Texas) under Pedro de Nava, the eastern sector was administered by Ramón de Castro. Castro arrived in April, 1791, described as "Sir Commanding General of the Eastern Province and Governor Captain General of Porto Rico." It was he who engineered Gil Ybarbo's downfall, luring him to Béxar under the pretext of holding talks about locating a small garrison at Nacogdoches and placing him "under a state of arrest" in January, 1792. At the same time Castro ordered Captain Juan Cortés of La Bahía to conduct an investigation as soon as possible, saying that it should not be difficult to prove the charges against Gil Ybarbo. But before this transpired, the groundwork was carefully laid, and Governor Muñoz—who was still in the process of vilifying Martínez Pacheco—was called upon by the viceroy to help dispose of Gil Ybarbo. Indications are that Muñoz obliged.

While shortages were being discussed in the former governor's mesteño accounts, Muñoz was probing Gil Ybarbo's records for similar abuses. These were not hard to find. In March, 1791, Gil Ybarbo had submitted a breakdown of taxes he had collected from 1782 to 1789. By August, 1791, Muñoz had returned the report to him, calling it "confused" and lacking figures for various years. In the meantime Muñoz sent a special investigator to Nacogdoches, one Manuel Gaspar de Verazadi, and his report of June 15, 1791, which was not at all favorable to Gil Ybarbo, was forwarded to the viceroy by Castro the next day. It said that Gil Ybarbo's wealth was perhaps "imaginary." Although he possessed about seven hundred head of cattle and twelve herds of mares, including seven droves of asses, the captain supposedly owed more than 20,000 pesos to various creditors. Calling Gil Ybarbo a mixture of Spanish and Indian, Verazadi suggested that because of his influence it would be better to remove him. Other troubles began converging on the old Adaesaño. His former ally and business partner Nicolás de la Mathe filed three petitions with the viceroy, among other charges accusing Gil Ybarbo of maladministration of office at Nacogdoches. Then there was the captain's feud with Louis de Blanc. Finally the Piney Woods Giant was felled: Gil Ybarbo was

"Released from Their Obligation" 393

placed under house arrest, and Cristóbal de Córdova was named to take his place.[19]

By November, 1792, the case against him was formed. He was charged with exchanging muskets, balls, and other items with the Indians for horses stolen from Spanish owners elsewhere in the king's realm. Still detained under house arrest, he

---

[19] See Grace A. Edman, trans. and ed., "A Compilation of Royal Decrees Relating to Texas and Other Northern Provinces of New Spain, 1719–1799" (Master's thesis, University of Texas, 1930), p. 436; Nava to Muñoz, March 18, 1791, BA; Fr. Benedict Leutenegger, *Journal of a Texas Missionary, 1767–1802: The Diario Histórico of Fr. Cosme Lozano Narvais, Pen Name of Fr. Mariano Antonio de Vasconcelos*, p. 32; Blake, Research Collection, Supplement ser., vols. 2–4—almost all Gil Ybarbo–related—and his "Captain Antonio Gil Ybarbo of Nacogdoches" (typescript, Texas State Archives) for the documentation supporting this analysis. The captain's "confused" account entitled "Report of the Taxes Collected 1782–1789 for Mesteños, Horses and Cattle, Caught in the Nacogdoches Jurisdiction and Withdrawn toward Louisiana," given to Muñoz on March 22, 1791, is found in BA. It shows that in the period from 1782 through 1789, a total of 783 animals were captured (693 cows and 90 horses, charged at 4 reales and 2 reales respectively), and 901 head were recorded as sent to Louisiana (charged at 2 reales each). Exports in the year of 1787 produced over half of the revenue shown for the entire period, but almost no figures were given for five of the eight years involved. Gil Ybarbo's careless recordkeeping went heavily against him (Blake, Research Collection, Supplement ser., 2:337, 349, 3:27).

underwent trial at Béxar, which lasted until September, 1796, when Commandant General Nava declared it "governmentally finished." Although he was cleared—more or less—the old man was not allowed to remain in office or return to East Texas, so greatly feared was his power on the frontier. Shortly before his death Nava relented and allowed him to move to Louisiana "as he asks," but not to Nacogdoches. He retired to La Lunaca, his ranch on the Attoyac, where he died in late 1809 or early 1810. R. B. Blake was told by the family that he was buried where the Nacogdoches courthouse now stands, a fit ending for the man who had almost singlehandedly maintained the Spanish presence in that locale. But despite the government's attempt to cast Gil Ybarbo in the role of ringleader of illicit activities along the Louisiana border and its long-term effort to pull him from power, the smuggling continued with or without him. It was a way of life.[20]

While these events were transpiring, Muñoz was not without his own difficulties. On March 20, 1792, Commandant General Castro drew up a long list of petitions which the citizens of Béxar had presented against the governor—and each other. Castro said that the discords had plunged the province into misery and virtual civil war. Several of these *expedientes* were devoted to unhappiness with the way Muñoz was handling the livestock industry, although they covered a wide spectrum of grievances. One protested the manner in which the governor had chosen to supply meat to the presidio and villa, claiming grave damage to the rest of the stock raisers. Empowering him either to clear Muñoz or impose the appropriate fines, Castro ordered Manuel de Escandón, the second count of Sierra Gorda, to leave Nuevo Santander and conduct an investigation of these charges. The count spent the summer in Béxar, listening to a multitude of complaints. Some of these the viceroy sympathized with. He suggested that for their work on the Casa Real the citizens should be recompensed by being allowed to take wild cattle

[20] AGI, Audiencia de Guadalajara, 59:94 (Box 2Q143, University of Texas Archives), contains the investigation against Gil Ybarbo; see also R. B. Blake, "Béxar Archives Pertaining to East Texas" (Texas State Archives), which lists many relevant documents.

duty-free. Insofar as the provisioning of meat, Revillagigedo said that the poor folk in Texas deserved to be paid for their efforts because they were such "brave pioneers." The viceroy relieved Escandón of his chore and restored Muñoz to office in late August, declaring the governor free of "every charge."[21]

As the year 1792 drew to a close, the Junta Superior de Real Hacienda issued another resolution regarding "the alleged right" of the cattle raisers in Texas to unmarked, unbranded, and ownerless wild cattle. In following the principle discussed in its meeting of February 27, 1789, the junta recommended that the Texas cattlemen be "absolved from an obligation to make further payment into the Royal Treasury on the above-mentioned account as suggested by the Señor Fiscal in his letter of November 26, last." Also approved were other decisions reached in the *fiscal's* letter, including a similar disposition of the accounts of Captain Martínez Pacheco.

Viceroy Revillagigedo put the junta's resolution into effect in a decree of January 22, 1793, ordering that the commandant general (Nava) was to be given all necessary instructions for that purpose. The viceroy wanted Nava to inform the northern raisers that within one year's time they must subject all their cattle of unproved ownership to a roundup for the purpose of branding them and that they were excused from payment of arrears in their account with the Royal Treasury with the understanding that at the conclusion of the one-year period they would make payment of such taxes as Commandant General Croix had deemed fit. "If the present rate imposed for this equitable duty to His Majesty should seem to him excessive," Croix's successor was to suggest whatever reduction he thought appropriate.[22]

Although this decision represented remarkable victory for the cattlemen of Texas, it was another two and a half years before the measure was promulgated in the province. In the mean-

---

[21] "Causa formada al Governador de Texas [Muñoz] y otras á varias personas por incidencia," 1790–93, AGN, Historia, Hackett Transcripts, 82:82–99; R. B. Blake, Research Collection, Supplement ser., 2:29, 33–35.

[22] Resolution of the Junta Superior de Real Hacienda, December 14, 1792, Grazing Papers, vol. 1, under "Ordering Investigation . . ." (University of Texas Archives); Revillagigedo, decree, January 22, 1793, Grazing Papers, vol. 1.

time Muñoz proceeded in the footsteps of his predecessors. On July 20, 1793, for example, he reissued Cabello's *bando* of a decade before, with its twelve articles, "in order to obviate dispute, malversation, and misunderstandings." To tighten up on rampant lawlessness, however, the governor added a few more twists of the screw. Without express consent no one was permitted to round up cattle other than that bearing his own mark and brand. Rulings established by "authorities of higher jurisdiction" (the intendant at San Luis Potosí) required that the old marks were not to be used until they were thoroughly regulated. This was necessary "because persons who have no right to do so are rounding up illegally whatever cattle they require for maintenance and are marking animals at their discretion; and they wrongly assume, for similar reasons, that for the purpose of the law they are recognized as breeders of cattle."[23]

This ruling, as well as many future attempts at regulation in Texas, was aimed at restraining the activities of the increasing number of individuals who were systematically exploiting and destroying the wild herds. The Béxar Archives reveal that the numbers of applications to hunt and gather *orejanos* increased in 1791 and 1792, peaking in 1793, when Muñoz issued at least forty-eight roundup licenses, over twice as many as the preceding year or in 1791, when the trend started. The men desiring to take *orejanos* were not strangers to the area, as a survey of the licenses shows; but the numbers involved were formidable. Since many of them specified slaughter as their purpose, it can well be imagined that the stench on the pastures in the summer of 1793 was one reason for the swift-following protests by the established raisers and the governor's belated efforts to clear himself of any negligence or wrongdoing in the issuance of so many licenses to deplete the feral herds.[24]

Steps taken to curtail unwarranted slaughters of cows

[23] Muñoz, "Orders for the Publication of Cabello's Law of July 10, 1783, Concerning Licenses to Round up Cattle," July 20, 1793, ibid.; BAM, roll 23, frames 650–58.

[24] A survey of the Béxar Archives calendar by Wilson E. Dolman for his "Mission Cattle Rustling," *Texas Parks and Wildlife* 33, no. 3 (March, 1975), reveals the following totals of roundup permits in the 1790s: 1791, 17 permits; 1792, 21; 1793, 48; 1794, 4; 1795, 0; 1796, 11; 1797, 9; 1798, 4; 1799, 1. Those most frequently making application were the Delgado, Arocha, Menchaca, Flores, and Guerra families, in that order.

in their fecund years have already been mentioned, but these concerns were just gathering momentum. In August, in response to Governor Muñoz's request for a report on bovine *orejanos* in the area, the cabildo summoned citizens who regularly traversed the fields. Included in the evidence-gathering process were Joachín Menchaca, José Félix Menchaca, Pedro Sambrano, Manuel Delgado, Marcos Zepeda, Francisco Bueno, Clemente Delgado, Francisco Padilla, Toribio Durán, Cristóbal Guerra, and Mariano Guerra. They stated that the cattle had been "much diminished" even when Muñoz took office. *Orejanos* were extremely scarce, especially below the Guadalupe River. Very few *orejanos* could be found, compared with the numbers in former times. They must now be lassoed, a sure sign that they were becoming scarce. Perhaps the use of the lasso was mentioned to contrast present times with the "good old days," when *orejanos* were simply driven in herds to corrals and captured.[25]

The *ayuntamiento* then commented that roundups were not being conducted legally and efficiently. Repeated complaints from the missionaries and citizens proved it, as well as indicating the wanton destruction and fraud perpetrated against His Majesty. The ranchers asked that Muñoz establish a quota on roundup licenses, restricting them as much as possible, so as to amend the situation and thereby protect the royal revenue and the citizens' livelihood. While it is likely that the ranchers exaggerated the situation, it does appear that years of determined cattle chases had substantially reduced the once-plentiful wild herds. A map prepared in 1775 by Thomas Jefferys, geographer to the king of England, labels the interior of Texas as "Vast Plains . . . full of Wild Beeves." By the turn of the century, map legends speak mostly of wild horses, not cows. Other reports, given in the 1790s, bear this out, and it was possibly a factor in the increasing attention given to equine *mesteños*. During this final decade a great slaughter took place, antedating the one that

---

[25] "Minutes, Resolutions . . . of Cabildo . . . ," as citizens' response to Muñoz, August 23, 1793, BAT, 115:26–30. This statement was signed by thirteen men, headed by Juan Joseph de la Santa, Luis Mariano Menchaca, Manuel de Arocha, and Amador Delgado.

decimated the bison. Fortunately, the Spanish *carneadores* did not do as thorough a job as the Anglo Americans did in the nineteenth century.

Muñoz was alarmed by the cabildo's grim assessment of what had long been taken for granted in these parts as exploitation of an unlimited natural resource. He claimed that he had issued the permits because he thought that the *vecinos* were taking cattle only for subsistence purposes. He glossed over the more compelling reason, which had been to keep the citizens happy and prevent the constant strife that would have resulted if he refused to grant the licenses. The governor admitted that he had no idea where the cattle were or how many there were. He said that if he had made an error in being too generous with hunting permits he had done so from a desire to benefit the "common good" of the province. From now on, however, he vowed that he would be more attentive to such matters. He said that the cabildo members doubtless knew more than he about the true situation—where the wild herds were to be found, what their condition was, whether the corridas were wasteful, and so forth. He asked them to submit a report on how large the wild herds were so that they could be maintained and conserved.

The ranchers replied that they did not know the number of cattle left in the province and had no way of giving an estimate. They said that the only thing they could do was take possession of what was needed since the government was "washing its hands" of the matter. This comment on the dilatory policy of the viceroy and his cattle council could not have set Muñoz's mind at ease. On the following day he summarized the results of his inquiry into the relative abundance of cattle. According to the inhabitants, it was "much diminished," especially south of the Guadalupe; wild stock could still be found beyond the river but not as many as before. Very few were seen in the daytime, and to catch them a rope now had to be used. Thus, he was forced to conclude, cattle were as scarce in the *realengas* as in the lands which had been hunted out, such as those below the Guadalupe.

The corridas were done legally and without waste, Muñoz steadfastly maintained, though he obviously had no proof of this. He acknowledged that the missions and the raisers had

"*Released from Their Obligation*" 399

complained of destruction, waste, and fraud against His Majesty. He bristled, however, at their accusations of poor enforcement and illegal acts, commenting that he must answer the city-council members and tell them that the charges were false and that things had been done properly. Still, he said, he would propose a quota system limiting the number of roundup licenses in the future, "trying through this means to stop the disorder and vexation, to avoid whatever will menace the conservation of *orejanos* and the benefit of this neighborhood."[26]

While Muñoz did not press criminal charges against Texas cattlemen on the scale of those of Ripperdá or Cabello, several isolated cases were brought during his administration. Early in 1792, Francisco Hernández was charged with cattle theft. In proceedings that lasted throughout the summer of 1793, José Miguel Flores and others were charged with illegal slaughter of cattle, most likely to set an example for their errant peers. One item introduced by the presiding judge, Luis Mariano Menchaca, to establish that such *matanzas* (slaughters) were clearly prohibited was Viceroy Revillagigedo's decree of April 20, 1791. This ruling, as noted, had reference to the earlier Junta Superior's decision by which corridas had been forbidden and the commandant general had been ordered to approve and uphold the use of any enforcement means required, such as fines and penalties. Only necessary killing was to be allowed, for which the 4-real duty applied. One suspects that Muñoz offered this case to the viceroy as proof that he was not sitting on his thumbs when it came to stopping the slaughter.[27]

If this was his intent, it appears that Muñoz occasionally misjudged his vassals' willingness to be cowed by such tactics. The case of Pedro Flores, father of José Ignacio, one of those accused of disorders and stealing cattle, is a case in point. Don

---

[26] Thomas Jefferys, "The Western Coast of Louisiana and the Coast of New Leon," 1775, map no. 1420, Texas State Archives; ". . . Proposing a Quota System for Cattle Roundup Licenses," August 23–24, 1793, BAM, roll 23, frames 769–73. For confirmation of the extensive damage done to the wild herds in Texas through "disorderly slaughters" see Nettie Lee Benson, trans. and ed., *Report of Ramos Arizpe*, p. 21.

[27] ". . . Francisco Hernández, Charged with Cattle Theft," May 1, 1792, BAM, roll 22, frames 37–40; *expediente* no. 74: "Proceedings against José Miguel Flores and Others for Illegal Slaughter of Cattle in the Country . . . ," Luis Mariano Menchaca, pre-

Pedro, who was the son of Juan José Flores the elder and a brother of Juan José, the raisers' attorney, had a contract with Don José Félix Menchaca. Together they supplied beef to the friendly Indian delegations that visited Béxar from the north and to the troops of the presidio. For this they received 4 pesos a head, but they were still required to pay the Mustang Fund 4 reales for each animal so used. Menchaca landed this contract because of his "large cattle holdings"; Flores's function appears to have been more one of gathering cattle and presenting them in the Plaza de Armas, where sales took place. In so doing, Flores incurred the wrath of his neighbors, who claimed that their stock was often taken and who considered the governor's beef-supply system as detrimental to their interests. This was one of their grievances against Muñoz in the investigation just conducted.

Caught in this web of resentment was Pedro's son, Ignacio, who was prosecuted for killing seven head of branded cattle without the owners' authorization on one occasion and ten head on another. It was noted that a license was not needed to slaughter one's own cattle but was required when someone else's branded animals were killed—a point that Flores argued was irrelevant in his son's case because Ignacio was operating under his father's license as a beef purveyor. What was really the object of the prosecution, replied the ranchers of Béxar, was not these minor slaughter violations, but the "suspicious" manner in which Flores gathered and brought herds of cattle to the presidio, to his neighbors' detriment. When Muñoz ordered Flores's license cancelled, Pedro abandoned his hacienda, left the province, and carried his case to the viceroy.

At Chihuahua in August of 1793, Flores petitioned the commandant general saying that he had been run off his land, his cattle confiscated, his license as purveyor revoked, and his son slandered. Even though the former governor had assigned pastures for the use of different rancheros in a compromise agree-

---

siding judge, BAM, roll 23, frames 471–505. When the viceroy's ruling of April 20, 1791, was recopied for these proceedings (ibid., frames 504–505), its date was incorrectly noted as "20 de Octuvre."

ment with the padres—an arrangement which the stockmen continued to hold valid long after the First Big Roundup ended—Muñoz had refused to recognize their rights to these lands.

When confronted with these charges, Governor Muñoz indignantly denied them, claiming that they were motivated by Pedro's "duplicity" and "maliciousness" and that "his feigned desire to leave his land is only a trick in order to continue the haughtiness which his lawlessness inspires." Muñoz gathered evidence to justify his treatment of Flores, including a statement from the cabildo that no citizen had been denied use of pasturelands, as proved by the constant stream of beef to the plaza, and that licenses to gather cattle for sustenance had not been restricted. Flores's difficulties with the bishop over tithes were offered as further proof of his bad attitude. Muñoz declared that, in restricting Flores's activities, his only intention was to curb the excesses that had been permitted under the tenure of his predecessor, Martínez Pacheco.[28]

An offshoot of this affair was a suit brought in January, 1794, by Pedro Flores, who doubtless viewed the earlier proceedings in the standard fashion as persecution rather than prosecution. He notified the governor of his intention to go to his ranch, conduct a *"junta de mi ganado,"* mark his *orejanos*, and pay the appropriate tithes. Noting that his interests had been damaged by the laxness of his neighbors, he asked the governor that they be required to do the same. Muñoz submitted his petition to the cabildo, who in turn summoned the ranchers and notified them that they must gather their cattle, brand them, pay tithes to Barrera, and give grazing rights to Flores. Upon this resolution, Muñoz allowed Flores to go and get "what he needs"—a concession eventually expanded into a blanket permit for the recalcitrant rancher to catch and brand *orejanos* without a license. This arrangement assumed that Flores would pay the 4-real duty on each head taken and not slaughter in the pas-

---

[28] "Expediente no. 442. Año de 1793. Pedro Flores . . . se queja de la providencia que contra él tomó el Governador Dn. Manuel Muñoz por varias reces que mató en su rancho," SA, 5:263–303. Pedro was married three times, and José Ignacio, born 1769, was a son by his second wife, Sapopa Barrera (Chabot, *Makers of San Antonio*, p. 62).

tures. Muñoz therefore found it expedient to placate his subjects, in spite of lackluster prosecutions made to give the appearance that he was doing everything possible to enforce the ban on slaughters.[29]

Another case developed in the summer of 1793, not criminal but reflecting an official concern about the damaging effects of cattle exports and a determination that breeding stock must remain in Texas to restore the depleted herds. The *diezmero* Juan Barrera had accumulated a large herd of cattle, many of which were pastured at his coastal ranch in the jurisdiction of La Bahía. He wanted to conduct a drive to Coahuila and sell the cattle there, a plan that was bitterly resented by other ranchers. The *diezmero*'s problems with the drive had begun in late 1792, when he complained to the bishop that the governor of Texas had prohibited him from extracting cattle collected for the *diezmo* in "other times." His petition eventually worked its way through channels back to Muñoz, who defended his action by citing Viceroy Revillagigedo's order of 1791 that restricted the slaughter and exportation of breeding stock in Texas. Barrera's efforts to secure approval for his export at a higher level, contravening these instructions, could not have pleased Governor Muñoz, who ultimately would be held responsible for the depletion of the herds in the province.

Barrera was persistent, however, and unwilling to submit to the restrictions imposed on exports. By June, 1793, his activities had prompted six other cattlemen who suffered under the same yoke to complain that Barrera enjoyed a position harmful to their own, in that as *diezmero* he had been allowed to buy and collect more cattle than anyone else. This charge no doubt reflected the ranchers' resentment over Barrera's arrival year after year to collect tithes on the increase of the ranchers' herds (paid to him in cattle) and the suspicion that the collector had

---

[29] "Proceeding [no. 100] Concerning Pedro Flores's Petition to Have Ranch Owners Brand Their Cattle, Which Resulted from the Suit against His Son Ignacio for Disorders Committed on Other People's Stock and *Orejanos*. Year of 1793," January 8–10, 1794, BAM, roll 24, frames 424–27. Signing for the cabildo were Ramón de la Fuentes, Manuel Delgado, José Maria Sambrano, Plácido Hernández, Roberto Nuñez, and Francisco Galán.

managed to build his own considerable herd by virtue of his official position. The ranchers were right, of course, but Muñoz, perhaps still smarting from Barrera's insolence, noted only that Barrera's export permit should be considered carefully "lest the government be charged with favoritism."

When Barrera learned that his planned export was being protested by certain citizens on the grounds that it worked an injustice, he appealed to the governor. He did so through Captain Juan Cortés, who was apparently sympathetic to Barrera's position. Cortés admitted that the herd in question contained 697 cows, a few of which were *vacas de vientre* (cows with calf) but said that most of them were from corridas and brandings. The captain wrote that it had taken Barrera ten years to accumulate these cows and that it was only fair to allow him to export them. Muñoz replied that he preferred that area raisers buy the cattle so that they would remain in Texas, rather than allowing Coahuila to benefit from them, and instructed Cortés to find local buyers. One buyer who had expressed an interest was Joaquín Flores. The affair dragged on until July 7, when Captain Cortés was again moved to press the justice of Barrera's request, saying that either the buyers should come forth "with money in hand" or the *diezmero* should be allowed to take his herd south. The governor's disposition of this matter is unrecorded, but the subsequent prosperity of Don Juan Barrera and his son Manuel as cattlemen is well established.[30]

Apart from such distractions, the serious problem in enforcement for Muñoz and his successors remained cattle slaughters and unauthorized exports, with every raiser in the province claiming to be victimized. The residents of Béxar were convinced that those of La Bahía were making forays into their pastures, while priests on the coast charged citizens as far away as

---

[30] "Proceedings [no. 101] against Juan Barrera Concerning Exportation of Cattle," June 3–22, 1793, BAM, roll 23, frames 506–11; Cortés to Muñoz, July 7, 1793, ibid., frames 615–16; *expediente* no. 432, "Año de 1793," SA, 5:157–72. The petition of June 3 against Barrera was signed by ranchers Juan Joseph de la Santa, Manuel de Arocha, Luis Mariano Menchaca, Miguel Gortaris, Joseph Antonio Saucedo, and Ygnacio Pérez. For the list of 1792 of twelve Béxar raisers shown as owing a total of forty cows in tithes, see SA, 5:277. Joaquín Flores is called Barrera's "successor" in this document, a position he apparently held until the turn of the century.

Laredo with destroying their herds. At times they even protested cattle "requisitions" made by their fellow priests. Good examples of such proceedings appear in the correspondence between Father Cárdenas and Muñoz concerning damages caused by soldiers "coming from a neighboring mission" to round up Espíritu Santo's cows in October and November, 1793.[31]

These charges and others like them resulted in a lawsuit in December, presided over by the governor, in which the Béxar *ayuntamiento* held the soldiers and citizens of La Bahía liable for slaughter of their cattle. During the testimony it was revealed that Father Cárdenas had personally charged several citizens caught inside mission pastures with illegal killings and had made the culprits pay fines of 10 pesos a head. The priest had even jailed some of the offenders, including soldiers caught coming in at night loaded with meat. Although the *procurador general*, Joaquín Flores, had difficulty getting the names of the guilty, it was established that many raiding parties were active in the area, a revelation which caused the Béxar *vecinos* "great pain." Their investigation consumed twenty manuscript pages but accomplished little except to proclaim the grievances of the local folk and exhibit injuries inflicted upon them by certain worthless soldiers and citizens from La Bahía.[32]

Added to these enforcement woes were the extractions made by foreigners from Louisiana for the ongoing development of Opelousas and Attakapas as stock-raising centers. Most of this breeding stock had to be acquired in ways that circumvented official procedures, including payment of the king's 4 reales. Although Muñoz reissued Cabello's *bando* of July 10, 1783, which called for a 2-peso export duty in addition to the 4-real catching fee (making a total of 20 reales for each mature cow), there is little evidence that His Majesty's officers in Texas tried to get much more than the 4-real tax (2 reales for horses) on any herds at that time. Records kept at Nacogdoches by Captain Gil Ybarbo and his successor, Cristóbal de Córdova, indi-

---

[31] BAM, roll 23, frames 1004–1005. The damages were being caused, said Fray Cárdenas, by soldiers coming from the new mission of Refugio.

[32] "Proceedings [no. 78] against Soldiers and Citizens of La Bahía for Slaughter of Private Cattle," December 20–24, 1793, BAM, roll 24, frames 130–40.

cate that a flat 2 reales was levied on animals recorded as going across the border, usually specified as horses but presumably including some cattle. A few writers have suggested that Muñoz profited from this traffic but offer little evidence to support the charge, apart from his benign attitude toward Philip Nolan (see chapter 11). Collection efforts were no doubt hampered by the genuine uncertainty prevalent during the 1790s concerning Croix's decree and the extent to which Texas cattlemen were exempt from its provisions. Faced with orders from the viceregal level absolving the ranchers of all previous indebtedness and granting them a vaguely defined one-year breathing period, it is no wonder that Muñoz, who was in declining health, did not aggressively enforce the collection of royal duties.

In 1793 the long-sought goal of mission secularization was achieved at Béxar, more than fifty years behind schedule. Ironically, it resulted not from the greed-motivated proposals of local residents or the oft-enunciated desire of padres on the scene to be spared the temporal responsibilities of their spiritual ministry but from an overzealous priest whose primary reason for coming to Texas was to convert the Comanches and other *norteño* tribes. He was Fray Manuel Silva, and to help him in his great undertaking, he chose an old veteran of Texas missionary works, Father José Mariano de la Garza—the same Fray Garza who as father president had protested Governor Cabello's two-month branding extension late in 1784. Father Silva soon abandoned the bold idea of planting a mission among *los norteños* and decided instead to convert the coastal tribes, which had thus far eluded attempts to "reduce" them. To defray the costs to His Majesty of establishing such a new mission, Silva proposed secularization of Valero and reorganization of the other four Béxar missions into two missions. It was this proposal, coming from within the Zacatecan college itself, which set into motion the dismantling of the Béxar mission system. Father Silva obtained permission for his new coastal mission, Nuestra Señora del Refugio, but the San Antonio establishments paid the price.[33]

Valero was the first to go. Acting upon the suggestions of Manuel Escandón, who had gathered information on the situation during his brief stay at Béxar in 1792, the Junta Superior for once was decisive on the secularization proposals. After they were decreed by the viceroy, the plans were forwarded to Governor Muñoz, and on February 23, 1793, he issued a proclamation calling for the distribution of Valero's properties to its Indians. In April lands of the *labor de abajo* (lower farm) were subdivided among the twelve Indian families left at Valero, their governor, Esmeregildo Puente, acting as their representative. Each of the families received a yoke of oxen, farming implements, and a cow and a calf. The "surplus" stock, coming to 112 head of cattle and 10 saddle horses, was sent to Refugio. Witnessing the formal transfer of property at Valero were Manuel de Arocha, town alcalde, and Luis Mariano Menchaca, who signed as commander of Béxar Presidio.

Father Silva's proposal for the secularization of Valero included giving some of its remaining lands to the former inhabitants of Los Adaes who were still at Béxar. It will be recalled that this idea was not new: the destitute settlers had repeatedly asked to be granted such lands. Orders had even been transmitted by Hugo Oconor to Governor Ripperdá, and again by Commandant General Croix in 1779, calling for the distribution of Valero lands to the Adaesaños, but the orders were thwarted at the local level, though at whose instigation it is not clear. The governor, the Béxar cabildo, or someone else did not want these refugees to enjoy the improved lands of the ailing Mission Valero. Castañeda mentions that Ripperdá had entrusted Simón

---

[33] Castañeda, *Catholic Heritage*, 5:36–47.

de Arocha with the responsibility of carrying out the orders to secularize Valero and later suggests that collusion between Governor Cabello and Fray Salas kept the mission open. Of the sixty-three heads of families who had petitioned Croix for lands at Béxar in 1778, the count of Sierra Gorda reported that forty-five families were still there fifteen years later. Since the main reason for refusing to award them land—that not enough arable land was available for distribution without infringing upon the rights of others—no longer applied, the count suggested that the Adaesaños should be given land after the mission Indians had exercised first choice. This was apparently done, for Chabot lists thirty-nine individuals who received land grants in 1793, a figure confirmed by records in the General Land Office.[34]

While one mission was in its death throes at Béxar, another was being born on the coast. On February 4, 1793, Mission Refugio was founded at a place called Muelle Viejo (Old Wharf), near the mouth of the Guadalupe around present Tivoli, its pastures extending northward. Father Garza's first priority was a food supply for the 138 Karankawa Indians he managed to assemble there. He wrote to Governor Muñoz estimating that he would need 8 bushels of corn and 8 beeves a week. The priest wanted to buy 1,000 head of cattle, which could be obtained at 4 pesos each. These animals would be used to start a herd, thereby making the mission self-sufficient. In the meantime Muñoz sent Sergeant Mariano Rodríguez and thirteen soldiers to help Father Garza. They were soon engaged in hunting wild cattle to feed the neophytes (their orders specified that the pastures of Espíritu Santo were off limits) and in building a stockade and a *chamacuero* (log house). When Captain Cortés visited the mission site in April, he was so shocked by the Indians' destitute condition that he ordered Rodríguez to cross the Guadalupe to hunt wild cattle, even cattle belonging to the herds of Espíritu Santo. Governor Muñoz tried to help, sending Valero's excess cattle and authorizing the purchase of some slaughter bulls from Espíritu Santo at 10 reales a head.

---

[34] Ibid., 4:355, 5:39; Chabot, *Makers of San Antonio*, p. 216; Blake, Research Collection. Supplement ser., 2:37; *suerte* distribution of Mission Valero lands, GLO, "Béxar County Sketch Files," folder 54.

The site seemed doomed from the start, with sickness and other problems ever present. Rodríguez became seriously ill before the end of summer, and it was not long before the unhealthful climate forced Fray Garza's retirement and withdrawal to Zacatecas. Father Silva was obliged to return in August to take personal charge of the mission. On September 21, 1793, Father Silva petitioned Governor Muñoz for 4,000 pesos, pledging himself to erect the necessary buildings at Refugio and to purchase 1,000 cows with calves, 50 mares, 20 yoke of oxen, 25 horses, and the necessary mules. His request was granted in July of the following year, but in the meantime the new mission suffered severely. In October and November, Corporal Juan José Farías, who had taken Sergeant Rodríguez's place as head of the guard, turned to killing the semiwild Rosario stock. This brought protests from Fray Cárdenas, who was having trouble feeding his own Indians. Three citizens were employed at Refugio to teach the Indians how to tend stock; their wages were 5 reales a day and 6 reales for the overseer. They were unable to produce miracles. Although Refugio's situation improved somewhat in 1794 with a move to the healthier site of Rancho de los Mosquitos, all the Bahía missions remained in precarious condition throughout the decade and beyond, until final secularization in 1830.[35]

On New Year's Day, 1794, Muñoz submitted to the king a "Report on Texas." Several remarks in the report seem aimed at self-vindication, in case the dwindling herds in Texas should become a matter for affixing blame. Muñoz pointed out that he had "resettled" ten ranches in the vicinity of Béxar, including many of those listed as officially recognized in 1791.[36] The province, he said, was blessed with ample lands for the raising of cattle and horses, the only benefit that the present inhabitants

---

[35] Castañeda, *Catholic Heritage*, 5:79–89; Myres, *Ranch in Spanish Texas*, p. 14; BAM, roll 23, frames 350–52. On October 22, Corporal Farías gave Muñoz an inventory of Rosario's ranch, noting that its horses and mules were branded with the mission's mark (frames 905, 979), but not showing the design used.

[36] The ranchers José Plácido Hernández, Doña Leonor Delgado, Ygnacio Peña, Macario Sambrano, Diego Yrineo Corríquez, Doña Antonia de Armas, and Doña Josefa Quiñones do not appear on this list, being replaced by Joaquín Leal, Joaquín Menchaca, Juan Barrera, and Carlos Martínez.

had thus far enjoyed. This was true "notwithstanding the misapplication that they had in the extraction of these toward other provinces and destruction by killing, *until the day on which I received the government* [emphasis added]," an obvious attempt to pin responsibility on his predecessor, Rafael Martínez Pacheco. Muñoz and he had no doubt experienced problems in the changing of authority. The earlier excesses, his report continued, had placed the cattle and horses of Texas in the greatest impairment, but he suggested that Commandant General Nava's orders on the slaughter of breeding stock might help reestablish the herds. The last suggestion was another effort to shift the burden of responsibility.[37]

Perhaps irritated by Muñoz's maneuverings, Nava wrote the governor soon thereafter, reminding him that he had expressed concern on several occasions about what was happening to the wild herds in Texas and the scarcity "which has been reported." He proposed the proclamation of a *bando* forbidding the extraction or slaughter of breeding stock under penalty of *multas moderadas* (moderate fines). This protection was extended to all stock "fit for breeding" in the province, whether tame or wild. Coming on the heels of the viceroy's instructions of April 20 and August 6, 1791, this emphatic order could not be regarded lightly. Muñoz was finally spurred to take action on his promise to do something about the declining state of Texas' cattle. The old bureaucratic ploy "Obedezco pero no cumplo" ("I obey but do not comply") had been exhausted. In mid-February he wrote a set of regulations putting the edict into effect. This *bando*, number 67, established heretofore unheard-of restrictions on corridas and the way wild cattle could henceforth be exploited.[38]

First, Muñoz acknowledged that information received from citizens who caught *orejanos* for a living suggested that hunts had perhaps caused an extreme scarcity of wild stock. Recently not enough meat had been brought in to feed the *presidiales*

---

[37] Muñoz to the King, "Report on Texas," January 1, 1794, Blake, Research Collection, Supplement ser., 3:101. AGN, Historia, vol. 100, contains a report by Muñoz on the "excesses" of Governor Martínez Pacheco.

[38] Nava to Muñoz, January 18, 1794, BAM, roll 24, frames 451, 499–503.

stationed at Béxar or to maintain the friendly Indians who came visiting. In spite of the many licenses requested (or perhaps because of them), it was not possible to supply these needs, owing to the "notorious scarcity." Cattle were hiding in the hills and canyons, and it was impossible to run them; the few that were obtained had to be shot with guns, which was more trouble than the resulting meat was worth.

This proved, said the governor, that all the cows were gone, consumed. Such a sad condition had been brought on by the large drives made in former times to the other Interior Provinces, such as the drives ordered to supply the presidios of Nueva Vizcaya (he did not mention the herds sent to Louisiana). Documents in the Caja del Fondo de Mesteñas, he said, proved the continuous killing done in prejudice of state and church. Muñoz did not think the situation could be blamed on the people, but, he contradicted himself, it was still their fault. To remedy the evil, he said, the commandant general had agreed with him to forbid the slaughter of all breeding stock. It was now prohibited to kill any cow capable of reproducing, whether it was with milk (*clase de chichiguas*), mesteña, or *orejana*. The penalty for violation was set at a 5-peso fine and eight days in jail for a Spaniard; if the offender was of "broken color," the penalty was the same except that the time was to be spent on public works. For a second offense a Spaniard would suffer double the above penalty; an offender of another *casta* would keep working on public projects until he was ordered to stop by the commandant general. This, one suspects, meant that the poor mestizo or mulatto offenders would be working on the chain gang indefinitely. In this manner were corridas outlawed in Texas, and the torrent of forty-eight licenses issued in 1793 became a trickle of only four in 1794, two granted early in January, before the publication of the *bando*. On paper, at least, herd conservation was now the policy in force.[39]

On April 10, 1794, finishing the work begun in 1793, Commandant General Nava issued a decree ending the other Béxar

---

[39] Muñoz (no. 67), February 15 and 16, 1794, ". . . sobre el buen regimen que deven observar estos vecinos en las corridas del ganado orejano," ibid.

missions. It actually called for the secularization of all Texas missions that had been in existence more than ten years, the time previously considered necessary to "civilize" the Indians. Henceforth, declared Nava, mission Indians were to be considered *gente de razón* (beings endowed with reason) and were to enjoy all privileges, duties, and responsibilities of Spaniards. The role of the padres was now to be filled by *justicias* (justices). These officers were to supervise the converts and protect their material interests, responsibilities carrying the temptation of abuse for personal gain. Although Governor Muñoz protested that the Béxar missions were in no condition for a proper distribution of their goods, he nonetheless set about his task in July. As with Valero, nothing remained of the once considerable wealth in livestock except a few milk cows, yokes of plow oxen, and gentled saddle horses. Espada still owned over a thousand head of *ganado menor*, and of these 207 sheep (with their lambs) were not divided but left to be cared for as a flock. Joaquín Lerma agreed to tend them for 8 pesos cash, 2 bushels of corn, and 12 reales' worth of cigarettes a month, payable after shearing. It was understood that in the future any unbranded cattle caught or slaughtered by the Indians would cost them 4 reales each, the customary royal tax.[40]

Thus, as Castañeda has observed, the San Antonio missions as a formative institution of the Spanish frontier "passed away." When a list of San José's accounts was turned over to the governor in July of the following year, many well-known Béxar ranchers were found to owe money to the Zacatecan college, some of it undoubtedly for mission stock exported and sold. While most of the amounts were small, a few were substantial. Juan José Flores, for example, owed 2,533 pesos (by contract dated August 13, 1783), and in mid-1795, Fray Cárdenas suggested to Muñoz that he might turn over Flores's house to one of the mission's creditors, Ángel Navarro. Also noted was that the cattlemen's celebrated attorney was "now deceased." According to Chabot, Flores had been killed at his ranch by Apaches. He left a widow, Manuela de Aguilar. Another debtor of Mission San José was the French trader Nicolás de la Mathe, who owed 1,385 pesos, borrowed in cash, goods, cattle, and horses.[41]

The outlying ranches of the Béxar missions eventually became private property, coming into the hands of various prominent ranching dynasties. Many of these transactions were not made final until the nineteenth century. If the ranches were occupied during the eighteenth century by the families who eventually obtained them—say, through rental agreements with the various missions—I have not been able to find such contractual agreements. Valero's La Mora went to Erasmo Seguín, son of Santiago, son of Bartholomé. Concepción's El Paistle was claimed

---

[40] Nava, decree, April 10, 1794, Castañeda, *Catholic Heritage*, 5:46; Myres, *Ranch in Spanish Texas*, p. 14. The *inventarios* of 1794 are in SA, vol. 6; those for Espada and San José also appear in GLO, vol. 50.

[41] Castañeda, *Catholic Heritage*, 5:62–63. For one such instrument (Antonio le Blanc's promissory note given in payment of livestock bought at Espíritu Santo), see BAM, roll 26, frames 520–25, under date of April 18–29, 1796. See also Fr. Benedict Leutenegger and Fr. Marion A. Habig, comps. and trans., *San José Papers, 1791–1809*, pt. 2, pp. 193, 197; Chabot, *Makers of San Antonio*, p. 62; and the April, 1790, inventory of Flores's estate, where it was noted that he owned a saddle "Valenciana Borados con mochillas, corasa, anqueras, y rodiaduna," BA.

in 1834 by José María Balmaceda, a former soldier and a prominent politician. San José's El Atascoso Ranch went to José Antonio Navarro, whose merchant-father, Ángel, was owed 745 pesos by that mission at the time of secularization. Domingo Castelo thought that he had purchased the 11-league San Lucas Ranch west of Béxar as far back as 1766 (for a mere 130 pesos), but the missionaries sued and retained possession. Title was vested in the name of San José's Indians by the secularization of 1794, and part of this grant (named for the San Lucas Springs, on the Medina) later became the site of Castroville.

Espada's goat ranch became the property of Manuel Barrera, who in 1830 claimed that his father, the *diezmero* Juan, had possessed El Rancho de las Cabras Viejas for many years. Manuel secured 4 leagues, surveyed in two tracts; the first (survey 25) had its southern boundary at an old, wide ford on the San Antonio River called Caballo Crossing.[42] Not all of Mission Espada's Rancho de las Cabras went to the Barrera family. The daughter of Ignacio Calvillo obtained 3 leagues and a *labor* of land lying just above Barrera's grant, across the river from present Floresville. Included within its limits were the stone ruins of the ranch compound. Her father, according to Ramsdell, sought full title to the ranch in 1809, and his presence in the vicinity of Las Cabras went back thirty-five years, even before Juan Barrera's. As early as 1778 he was occupying land between Chayopines and Las Cabras "with permission of the reverend father," and

---

[42] Robert S. Weddle and Robert H. Thonhoff, *Drama and Conflict: The Texas Saga of 1776*, pp. 147–53, mention the disposition of these mission ranches. The original title documents are found in Spanish Archives, GLO, vol. 50, "Missions in Texas"; and, as noted, in the various county deed books for subsequent transfers. Seguín's title to Valero's La Mora, is in GLO, 31:66; Navarro's acquisition of San José's El Atascoso, GLO, 42:97; and Barrera's grants at Las Cabras, GLO, 31:314, and GLO, 49:9 (each of which has a plat map). Some transitional papers are more far-flung. Retired *alférez* Balmaceda's original petition of 1828 for four *sitios* on the "Arroyo llamado el Síbolo en el paraje que tiene nombre el Pastle" is found in SA, 23:60–62; also in GLO, 31:22. By the time this particular tract was surveyed, it had shrunk to one league on the west bank of the Cíbolo, one mile above the Sulphur Springs (Balmaceda was, among other things, land commissioner for the McMullen-McGloin Irish Colony at San Patricio). It is perhaps significant that no ranch properties were mentioned in the *inventarios* of 1793–94 (with the exception of San José's eleven-*sitio* tract, "San Lucas," and some small pasturage on the east bank of Leon Creek), but it is more difficult to say what it signifies.

by 1781 he was recognized as owning Rancho El Paso de las Mugeres, on the west bank of the river near "Women's Crossing," adjoining (and possibly overlapping) Espada's ranch.

Ignacio's wife, it will be recalled, was Antonia de Arocha, a sister of Don Simón, Juan, and the other Arocha brothers. Ignacio's and Antonia's daughter Ana María, born in 1765, married Gavino Delgado, son of Francisco. One of Gavino's brothers, Manuel, was married to Antonia de Arocha's sister, Angela, so the relationship between the three families was an involved one, typical of many in El Rincón. In 1811, María and her husband, Gavino, were living on Ignacio's ranch, La Santa Cruz y Paso de las Mugeres. Three years later her father was killed in an Indian attack; ten to twelve people, including women and children, escaped and reached Mission Espada. In 1833, María, in a petition for more pastureland behind her previous 2 leagues, stretched matters a bit by stating that both her father and her husband had died trying to defend the "present Government System." She was correct, however, in saying that her family had suffered much from Indian depredations.[43]

As the Béxar missions were being dismantled, it was becoming clear that those at La Bahía could not be dealt with easily. In 1793 the College of Zacatecas had reported to the viceroy that the economic life of Espíritu Santo was wholly dependent upon its cattle, since lack of irrigation made crops uncertain: "For this reason they get a supply of corn from the other missions and trade cattle for it."[44] But by the time Governor Muñoz journeyed to La Bahía in September, 1794, to review the missions there, the cattle herd of Espíritu Santo was a fifth its former size and steadily declining. Fray Juan José Aguilar, who had taken charge of the mission early in April, was desperately

---

[43] GLO, 31:75. Legend, supported by testimony found in "Sumaria Ynformación formada a los Paysanos que havitaban en el Rancho de los Calbillos . . . ," BAM, roll 53, says that Ignacio was murdered by his grandson, although several Lipans were among the raiding party. María's husband, who experienced troubles with both sides during the revolutionary decade, did not die in 1814 as the señora claimed. Doña María, living to be more than ninety years of age, from all accounts rivaled both Belle Starr and Sally Skull in her wild exploits, and "Doña Calvillo's Rancho" continued to be shown on landgrant maps as late as 1879 (W. C. Walsh, Map of Wilson County, no. 1830, Texas State Archives).

[44] Ramsdell, "Spanish Goliad," p. 22.

"Released from Their Obligation" 415

fighting a lost cause. After inspecting both Espíritu Santo and Rosario, Muñoz wrote the commandant general that he could not secularize either mission. The mission Indians were "as helpless as children," and to comply with Nava's decree would be to return them to "savagery." Muñoz commented that they owned an extensive herd of cattle which was roaming wild in the woods, "and to round it up is the hardest kind of task, whereas to leave it alone would be to destroy it and to allow it to perish in less time than you would think possible." Considering the state of the cattle—loose in many thickets and subject to inconveniences posed by the river bordering the pastures where they grazed—Muñoz said some of them could be saved only under the supervision of the minister who assisted the Indians. On May 10, 1797, Galindo Navarro, responding to Muñoz's decision, granted these missions a five-year extension in view of the circumstances.[45]

While the governor was at La Bahía, Fray Aguilar pleaded with him to spare Mission Espíritu Santo from having to pay the king's 4-real duty on *orejanos*. The logic was old, as old as the decision to tax wild cattle. He stated that the mission sorely needed an exemption from the tax on mesteños, just as it had been allowed to round them up freely in former times: "Your Lordship knows very well the condition it [the mission] is in, with no funds to subsist on, and every day it gets worse off, because of rustling and the laziness of the Indians." If there was no way to secure general exemption, Aguilar said, he would be patient and try to round up as many cattle as possible, "for in my opinion to round all of them up and brand them is out of the question." Most of the cattle were stubborn old bulls, scattered amidst tangled brush; to gather them would require a great deal of money to pay the hands. There was no money, and no one to provide it.

Even if he found the necessary means to have the cattle rounded up, Aguilar said, more time than a year would be needed. There was no use trying to have the Indians bring them in without help, "for they [the Indians] are very unreliable, and

---

[45] Muñoz to Nava, October 25, 1794, BA: Castañeda, *Catholic Heritage*, 5:65, 187, 191.

nothing worthwhile can be done with them." Since mission Indians had never been required to pay tribute, the padre wondered why they should not be free from other taxes. After all, the reason for their failure to brand the cattle was the attacks of hostile Indians and the fact that the cattle were widely scattered. Arguments such as these had failed to sway previous officials, but they worked with Muñoz, possibly because he realized that the position of the priests on the coast was almost hopeless. He granted the tax exemption request on August 8, 1795, an unprecedented concession.[46]

In January of that year Mission Refugio had formally reestablished itself at a better location. The final site chosen was near Rancho de Santa Gertrudis, also known as Cayo de Aránzazu, just north of present Aransas Pass, where the tithe collector Juan Barrera kept his cattle. On January 12, Fray Silva asked Muñoz for 1,452 pesos from the Mustang Fund to buy stock from Nuevo Santander for the mission. Enough cattle to feed the Indians for a year must be obtained at once, declared the priest, or the mission herd could not be saved, and the entire enterprise would be endangered. Nava vetoed the proposal, telling Muñoz that no cattle were to be brought in from outside the province. It is possible that Fray Silva meant to buy his cattle from ranches lying just across the Nueces, lands nonetheless in the jurisdiction of Nuevo Santander. Not only was Rancho de Santa Petronilla still there, but in 1785, Don José Evia charted the coastline and reported that the Nueces region was "poblado de Haciendas de Ganado" (filled with cattle ranches). Many of these isolated ranchers, originally from the lower Río Grande towns, could easily have supplied Fray Silva with cattle for Refugio, but it was evidently a traffic the commandant general did not wish to encourage.[47]

[46] Ramsdell, "Spanish Goliad," pp. 29–30; Castañeda, *Catholic Heritage*, 5: 187–88. Yet another drove of stock left Zacatecas for Texas in November, 1794. It appears that animals often accompanied the college's annual shipment, especially during those lean years.

[47] Silva to Muñoz, January 12, 1795; Nava to Muñoz, February 26, 1795, in Castañeda, *Catholic Heritage*, 5:94–95; Faulk, *Last Years*, p. 80; Dan Kilgore, *Nueces County, Texas, 1750–1800: A Bicentennial Memoir*, p. 7; Jack D. L. Holmes, ed., *José de Evia y sus Reconocimientos del Golfo de México, 1783–1796*, p. 183. Correspondence relative to cattle for Refugio Mission is found in BAM, roll 25, frames 313–14, 457–58.

Muñoz did his best with what was at hand. A total of 227 bulls were brought from La Bahía in April, and 133 more arrived the following month. Captain Juan Cortés delivered another 39 a few days later, brought in by Felipe Flores. Although it was agreed that one bull a day would be sufficient rations for the first year, this number was already exceeded by May. In that month, Captain Cortés wrote a report on the three Bahía missions, stating Espíritu Santo housed 124 Indians, Rosario 83, and Refugio 93. He said that Espíritu Santo had once owned many cattle but that large exportations and depredations on the herds committed by the hostile Indians "and even Spaniards" made it impossible now for the missions to supply his soldiers with meat. This mission had 200 head penned, but the loose ones were so wild that they could be gathered only with great difficulty. If depredations on the herds ceased, Espíritu Santo could recover, Cortés said, noting that the mission owned roughly 2,000 head (having once had 40,000). As for Rosario, things were terrible there owing to trouble caused by the notorious apostate José María. Its stock was reduced to a mere 34 head, and the minister routinely sent his Indians to the coast, where they could at least eat fish. Refugio he felt more optimistic about, saying that it had 2,000 head of stock, large and small. Refugio, being less exposed to hostilities than were the other missions, would be in a "very favorable condition" in four years' time, Cortés predicted.[48]

In the summer of 1795 the Junta Superior's cattle decisions were at last acted upon by Governor Muñoz. Commandant General Nava wrote in June that, "notwithstanding the representations contained in your letter number 67," he had decided to conform with the *asesor*'s opinion and come to an agreement with the Béxar governing body about the wild cattle of the province (the letter Nava referred to was Muñoz's quota proposal of August 24, 1793, based on the cabildo's opinion that *orejano* stock was much diminished over that of former times). Nava wanted the governor to convoke the city fathers and in-

---

[48] Cortés, "Report on La Bahía Missions," May 20, 1795, in Grazing Papers, vol. 1, pt. 2, pp. 159–60, also found in the Buquor Translations, box 2Q246, University of Texas Archives. An inventory for Mission Refugio of January 10, 1795 (ACZ, roll 3, frame 3860), indicates that Refugio had 2,500 head of livestock, large and small combined.

form them of the privileges of the one-year extension conceded for the rounding up and branding of unmarked cattle which had grown up wild or were for other reasons without ostensible private owners. Upon receipt of this news Muñoz was to work out details governing the roundup extension, making sure that the ranchers understood that at the end of the period all cattle found without marks or brands of known private owners would continue to be classifiable as *mostrencos* and property of the crown. As before, it would not be permissible to round up or slaughter such cattle without express written permission obtained from him against payment into the Royal Treasury of "the moderate tax of 4 reales a head for cattle and 2 reales for horses."

The best part was yet to come: pursuant to the junta's decision of December 14, 1792, all missions and citizens engaged in the raising of cattle were released from their obligation to pay arrears owed to the Mustang Fund during the governorship of Domingo Cabello and Rafael Martínez Pacheco. Muñoz was authorized to cancel such obligations immediately and return them to the interested parties, making the necessary entries to substantiate these "refunds."[49]

Thus, after seventeen long, tortuous years, the ranchers had come full circle. Although the slate was wiped clean, they were back where they had been at the beginning: after a specified period of grace the king owned all the wild stock in Texas, which, however, they could exploit by paying the same hated fees. If it was a victory—which it certainly was—it was the kind that left them wondering whether it was worth the price. But at least they had staved off the inevitable for almost two decades, during which time they had enjoyed the benefits of the wild herds of the province. Now they had another year, far better than their prospects had looked under Domingo Cabello. And who could say? Perhaps this latest reprieve could be stretched as in the past.

---

[49] Nava to Muñoz, June 18, 1795, Grazing Papers, vol. 1, under "Ordering Investigation . . ."; BAM, roll 25, frames 586–90, has this letter, ". . . enclosing decision of Junta Superior in settlement of dispute in Béxar concerning *mesteños*." These orders were no doubt the basis for Muñoz's tax "exemption" granted to Espíritu Santo in August.

On July 16, Governor Muñoz issued a notice to the members of the Béxar *ayuntamiento* concerning the agreement required by the commandant general. He told them that, to determine the manner and means of effecting a roundup during the year specified, a list of persons "legitimately engaged in the business of raising cattle" would be necessary. The *ayuntamiento* submitted the names of thirty-five men and ten widows (appendix C), consistent with a census taken that year which stated that sixty-nine heads of San Antonio families made their living working on the vicinity's *forty-five* ranches. Two days later the town council called these raisers together to acquaint them with details and procedures judged necessary for the roundup. It was requested that publication of the *bando* be deferred until July 26, and the following guidelines were established: (1) upon securing the necessary license, each owner would consult the others about his roundup plans, (2) a list of cattle taken would be presented to the governor, (3) cattle could be taken only on crown lands, not lands privately owned, (4) *orejanos* found on private lands belonged to the landowner, and (5) these *orejanos* must be branded to prevent future misunderstandings.[50]

Word of these proceedings was sent to the Spanish justices and to the Indian governors at the four missions, "in view of the fact that the missions are eager for cattle and can find on their pastures only a few head of cattle here and there." The custodians of the Indian populations still clustered about their missions, active or inactive, were told that they would be permitted to mark, brand, and breed wild stock, just as their Spanish counterparts could. (It should be noted that both San José and Espada continued to function as "central missions" after secularization, and the other two became *pueblos de visita*; Concepción was joined to and became a "sub-mission" of San José; while San Juan was administered from Espada. All four settlements elected officials, but missionaries resided at only San José and Espada.) Being unable to write, the Indian governors ac-

---

[50] Muñoz to *ayuntamiento*, July 16, 1795; Muñoz, "Report on *Ayuntamiento* Meeting," July 18, 1795, BAM, roll 25, frames 586–90; Chabot, *Makers of San Antonio*, p. 168; Odie B. Faulk, "Ranching in Spanish Texas," *Hispanic American Historical Review* 44 (May, 1965): 261–63.

knowledged these instructions by affixing a cross beside their names, which had been written by Spanish judges.[51]

More stipulations were hammered out at a council meeting on July 27. An area was set aside as a public reserve to supply the subsistence needs of the inhabitants and was to be off limits in the forthcoming roundup. Animals taken from offenders were to be brought alive to the main plaza, or, if they had "succumbed to the heat" and had been slaughtered for that reason, the hides were required for the purpose of showing that they were public property. Penalties of 5 pesos a head and fifteen days in prison were meted out to violators. The *ayuntamiento* expressed gratitude for this provision "in view of the great discord that has been prevailing in the export and slaughter of stock." It was further agreed that the proclamation should not be published until the first of the month, for unspecified reasons.[52]

It appears that the *bando* was published on August 1, 1795, but the *asesor* and the commandant general thought that confusion would result from several of the articles (3, 5, 9, 10, 11, and 14). Thus, to "eliminate doubts and questions," modifications were made, and new regulations for the roundup of *orejanos* during the one-year extension were issued by Muñoz on December 13. A copy was forwarded to the *ayuntamiento* and Nava in early February, 1796. This document, like the one it replaced, contains seventeen articles, and its introduction leaves no doubt what would happen to the wild stock of the province still remaining unmarked at the end of the year-long

---

[51] Castañeda, *Catholic Heritage*, 5:116; Habig, *Alamo Chain*, pp. 142, 220; Leutenegger, *Journal of a Texas Missionary*, p. 37.

[52] BAM, roll 25, frames 698–706. Odie B. Faulk, "Ranching in Spanish Texas," *Hispanic American Historical Review* 44 (May, 1965): 262, makes it appear that the viceroy himself issued this "new and sweeping code of regulations for the cattle industry," following closely the junta's recommendations. Myres, *Ranch in Spanish Texas*, p. 39, repeats this, citing Faulk and the same source: Muñoz, "Año de 1795. Copias de las providencias de la Junta Superior de Real Hazienda; Decretos . . . Acuerdos . . . y Bando publicado en uno y dos de Agosto del mismo Año sre Juntas Ganados por los Criadores," August 27, 1795, BA. Yet in his instructions to the *ayuntamiento* of July 16, Muñoz speaks of their "drawing up the agreement required by the Commandant General," and it seems clear that the *bando*'s seventeen articles were conceived locally by the ranchers in response to their own needs, rather than being handed down to them from distant Mexico City.

"Released from Their Obligation" 421

period granted for the roundups: it would belong to the king and would not be subject to roundup, use, or slaughter without a license, granted upon payment of the same old fees. The articles of Muñoz's proclamation (with subsequent revisions noted), are as follows:

1. The cattle breeders and missions have been absolved of the taxes on *orejano* cattle rounded up during Cabello and Martínez Pacheco's incumbency, and all amounts due are hereby canceled.

2. The roundup period commences as of August 1 [the date of the original order].

3. All cattle found in the districts of Las Lomas and Monte Galván shall be left free; penalties for entering this reserve without authorization and catching wild stock—fifteen days in jail and a fine of 5 pesos per animal [later reduced to fit the extent of the violation].

4. Failure to secure a permit and take part in the year-long roundup privilege will amount to a loss of rights in the matter.

5. All roundups must take place on crown lands and "wastelands" [*baldías*], not on lands owned in good faith by individuals, for willful entry into which violators will be responsible to the owner for damages [later qualified as "mistaken" entry].

6. Those who round up will not be allowed to slaughter stock taken, except for animals which are immediately consumed or which succumb to heat or other natural accidents.

7. Citizens not presently classified as cattle breeders may accompany the roundups and be paid with a few bulls and cows from those taken, in this manner establishing themselves as *criadores* for future maintenance.

8. On all roundups conducted a list and an account of cattle taken on crown lands must be submitted to the alcalde.

9. Wild cattle and horses found on the lands of missions or private breeders can legally be used by them, provided a report is given [this provision was later removed and a new article substituted—see below].

10. To stop the slaughter of cattle under pretext of subsistence, as evidenced constantly by the soap-boiling engaged in by individuals who have never been cattle breeders and have not at any time been owners of cattle, permits will now be issued only for the taking of one or two heads per inhabitant, and compliance must be publicly exhibited; penalties for violation—10 pesos a head for those taken in excess of the license and fifteen days on public works [later reduced to 5 pesos and eight days].

11. To limit the secret killing of cattle on the prairies for the purpose of soap manufacture, no grease can be purchased without prior notice to an alcalde, and the buyer must give a report of his source; penalties—20 pesos and fifteen days in jail for first offense; twice the fine for repeat offenders [later reduced to 10 pesos and eight days].

12. The person who reveals the identity of violators will be given the meat and grease secured, plus half the amount of the fine.

13. To feed the constantly arriving members of friendly Indian tribes, whom His Majesty has agreed to support during the time they may choose to remain within the precincts of this Quartel [presidio], meat purveyors will hunt from crown lands, not private estates; but so that no shortage occurs, exception will be made in the districts of La Lomería and Monte Galván.

14. Upon completion of the one-year extension period, animals remaining unbranded become *mostrenco* and belong to the Royal Treasury; they can no longer be legally slaughtered or taken alive without the explicit consent of this government; punishment for violators— if Spanish, 25 pesos a head besides confiscation of the cattle; if "a person not of the white race" (*quebrado*), 10 pesos a head plus one month on the chain gang doing public works; second offenders— twice the fine if a Spaniard; fifty lashes for persons of color [racially categorized penalties were later eliminated and those of article 3 above substituted].

15. To avoid these penalties, no cattle can be taken without a special license from the governor against payment into His Majesty's treasury of a very moderate tax [*el moderado impuesto*] amounting to 4 reales for cattle and 2 reales for horses; the amount of the tax is not subject to change.

16. Before this *bando* is promulgated, its contents will be made known to all members of the *ayuntamiento*, whose "resolutions and consensus" will be taken into account.

17. The official purveyor of meats for Indians will not be allowed to gather breeding cattle; in so doing he will be liable to the penalties of article 11 [above].[53]

The penalties set forth in several of the articles were evidently judged too harsh by the commandant general and his

---

[53] "Copy of Ordinances for Rounding up Cattle and Evidence of Publication," December 13, 1795–February 5, 1796, BAM, roll 26, frames 18–23. In Grazing Papers, vol. 1, is a translation made by Martin Henry under "Ordering Investigation of a Citizen of Béxar to Stock in Texas"; see also BAT, 159:52–81. Both, however, are from the initial ordinance (August, 1795, found in BAM, roll 25, frames 698–706), before the changes were initiated.

legal adviser. Most of them were restructured and reduced in the ordinance of December 13. The clause calling for stiffer penalties for mestizos and other *castas*, a typical feature of colonial regulations, was dispensed with, and the same punishments were applied to all—on paper, at least. The most notable revision took place in article 9, which originally gave owners of mission and private lands near-unrestricted use of the stock found there. Perhaps believing that this would lead to "doubts and questions," that is, endless wrangling, an entirely new article replaced it, stating that raisers had one year to hold a rodeo whereby they could collect and brand strays found inside their *own pastures*. After August 2, 1796, however, even these—if without mark or brand—would become the king's property. Beyond that date no more roundups would be permitted on private lands without the standard permit and royal fees, a drastic restatement of the original language.

This *bando* of 1795, issued by Governor Manuel Muñoz, and the proceedings surrounding it are perhaps the most elaborate attempt made in eighteenth-century Texas to regulate a roundup—with the possible exception of the agreement of 1787 made between missions and private raisers early in Martínez Pacheco's administration. Now, of course, the missions were not a serious contender. The benefits of their long stewardship would be reaped by the troublesome, "half-savage" Spaniards who had begun nipping at the vast mission herds three decades before. I have been unable to find any report of the wild stock taken during this final extension period. Also, it is not known whether Indian *vaqueros* of the former missions actually took part in the year-long rodeo. If they did, it was without the protection of the padres; they acted for themselves individually or as employees of other recognized—i.e., Spanish—raisers. Ready for it or not, these Indians—one generation removed from Stone-Age culture—were now officially *gente de razón*.

11
"AS MANY HORSES AS CIRCUMSTANCES PERMIT"

Neighboring Markets, Bold Smugglers

The year 1796 was hardly rung in before Governor Muñoz was petitioned by various citizens asking permission to take horses, mules, and breeding stock into Louisiana, requests that soon dominated the attention of Spanish officials from the viceroy to post commanders in the open frontier. For the next two decades it would be nothing but horses, horses, and more horses, driven eastward in defiance of His Majesty's laws to satisfy a growing demand. Although much time and energy were spent trying to control or shut off the traffic and many offenders were apprehended, tried, and found guilty, there is little evidence that the traffic was measurably slowed. Mustangs, so plentiful in Texas, were worth too much money in Louisiana for bold men not to consider the rewards worth the risks.[1]

Even though horses and mules supplanted cattle as Texas' chief export after the turn of the nineteenth century, cattle remained in demand. At the end of the eighteenth century they still brought 10 pesos a head at La Bahía, 12 pesos at Nacogdoches, and more in Louisiana. But cattle were no longer as scarce in Louisiana as they once had been, doubtless partly because of the many drives of previous decades. All accounts indicate that various districts, such as Natchitoches, Opelousas, and

---

[1] Both Sandra L. Myres, *The Ranch in Spanish Texas, 1691–1800*, pp. 49–50; and Odie B. Faulk, *The Last Years of Spanish Texas*, p. 91, mention the shifting emphasis to equine stock.

Attakapas, became transformed into stock-raising paradises during the waning 1700s, as did other areas on the east. In the Mississippi Valley, especially at Natchez, the industry was encouraged by the enactment of regulations similar to those in Texas. Various census reports taken in the 1780s and Spanish brand records of the mid-1790s for the district of "San Estéban Tombecbe" [Tombigbee] above Mobile Bay, indicate that cattle were considerably more plentiful along the southeastern Gulf Coast than they had been during the campaigns of Bernardo de Gálvez.[2] The dramatic increase of livestock in the former French possession at the same time that herds were rapidly diminishing in Texas is too pronounced not to invite closer examination.

Because of the many ways in which the two regions were linked and interrelated, it is proper at this point to present a brief scan of the development of the livestock industry in Louisiana and the lower Mississippi River valley, noting some similarities to the problems, practices, and regulations in neighboring Texas. As in Texas, the possibilities offered in Louisiana for livestock raising were obvious to many early observers. A report made in 1750 suggested the establishment of a post in the "beautiful and fertile prairies of the Atakapas," not only for growing tobacco "but also for the raising of cattle [to be made into] salted beef [for] Martinique." The post was founded in the following decade and augmented from 1764 until 1770, when the French gave up their posts in Alabama. Henry E. Chambers writes that the Acadian settlers "waxed fat and multiplied" in this favored region, the more enterprising of them becoming large landholders and cattle barons. This development was stimulated by a contract whereby each family was supplied with eight cows and a bull for six consecutive years starting in 1765. After the sponsoring captain, Antoine Bernard d'Hauterive, received back his seed stock, the increase was to be equally divided between him and the endowed cattlemen.[3]

---

[2] "Quaderno de Rexistro de las Marcas que usan los Havitantes que se establecen en este distrito [San Estéban Tombecbe] para marcar sus Animales. 1795," AGI, Sevilla, Papeles de Cuba, Legago 222-B, made available to the author by G. Douglas Inglis (see brand section C).

[3] Winston De Ville, *Opelousas: The History of a French and Spanish Military Post in America, 1716–1803*, p. 32; Henry E. Chambers, *A History of Louisiana: Wilderness-Colony-Province-Territory-State-People*, p. 270.

Evidently Attakapas (now Saint Martinville) prospered, as did other locales in southwestern Louisiana (brand section B shows a few of the marks registered in this region by eighteenth-century Cajun stockmen for their *vacheries* (ranches), a process that began as early as 1739). A report of a census of the province taken in 1763 reveals that it contained 206 horses, 4,510 sheep, and 6,784 cattle, the last spread evenly over the six districts reported. Another census of the province taken three years later shows 2,907 horses and mules, 7,736 sheep, and a rather unbelievable increase to 37,491 cattle (this figure was augmented by 15,000 indicated as the total for "old ranches in Atakapas"). More reliable seems the breakdown for the districts closest to Texas: Attakapas, 1,004; Opelousas, 1,350; and Natchitoches, 1,006. By 1769 it was reported to Governor Alejandro O'Reilly that the inhabitants of Opelousas owned over 2,000 head of cattle, double the number owned by their neighbors in Attakapas District. The next year two Irishmen—like O'Reilly, in the service of Spain—toured Louisiana for the governor. They took a circular route, starting in Attakapas, moving north to Opelousas and north-northwest to Natchitoches, and returning through "Rapido." In these four districts they found 5,752 head of cattle, noting that Opelousas and Attakapas enjoyed the most favorable conditions for stock raising. They were favorable indeed, for by the mid-1770s, according to census reports of the posts, these two areas boasted almost 10,000 head of cattle, along with a considerable number of horses and pigs. As has been discussed, Natchitoches, lying opposite the old Adaes Presidio and settlement, was conducting a livestock trade with Texas long before these southwestern population centers came into being. In time even the fur trade in Louisiana was surpassed by the "more stable and lucrative cattle trade, which was independent of the caprice of Indians."[4]

Some interesting information about stock raising in these

---

[4]Jacqueline K. Voorhies, trans. and comp., *Some Late Eighteenth-Century Louisianians: Census Records of the Colony, 1758–1796*, pp. 105, 163; John D. W. Guice, "Cattle Raisers of the Old Southwest: A Reinterpretation," *Western Historical Quarterly* 8 (1977):176; De Ville, *Opelousas*, p. 89. Louis Rafael Nardini, *My Historic Natchitoches, Louisiana, and Its Environment*, p. 81, notes that "Post des Opelousas" began in 1742, stock raisers buying land from the Indians soon after.

regions emerges from a set of regulations issued by O'Reilly just before he left office. Although his code mostly pertains to the granting of land, there are many references to the evils caused by estrays with which the province was "infested." Since the governor had received "divers complaints and petitions" from the inhabitants of Opelousas, Attakapas, and Natchitoches, he ruled that each property owner must enclose his land and limit the open grazing of cattle to the winter months (November 11 to March 15), after which time he would be held responsible for damages caused to his neighbors. Another article provided for the branding of cattle and the forfeiture of animals allowed to go unmarked after the age of eighteen months. The governor granted a period until July 1, 1771 (over a year), for residents to round up or dispose of strays; after that those still running wild could be killed by anyone who desired. These provisions were enacted, he said, because nothing was deemed "more injurious to the inhabitants than strayed cattle, without the destruction of which tame cattle cannot increase." O'Reilly further stipulated that possession of 100 head of tame cattle, some horses, sheep, and two slaves to look after them was a condition of eligibility for each tract 42 arpents square in the stock-raising districts. In relation to how much land was sought, this was "a proportion which shall always be observed." One arpent was a little less than an acre, and in 1799 a tract of 42 arpents square was simplified to a half league on each side (Morales, Regulation of July 17, 1799). At the time Alejandro O'Reilly firmly placed French Louisiana under Spanish control, landholding and stock raising were recognized as being closely intertwined in the western settlements.[5]

It was in the final quarter of the eighteenth century, however, that the Louisiana livestock industry developed markedly. The city of New Orleans relied heavily upon these outlying dis-

[5] O'Reilly, decree, February 18, 1770; Morales, regulation, July, 1779, both from *Regulations for the Granting of Land under the Spanish Government of Louisiana*. John D. W. Guice, "Cattle Raisers," pp. 184–85, thinks that the stipulation of two slaves to tend 100 cows means that blacks herded cattle from horseback, but in 1787 the Opelousas commandant Nicolás Forstall ordered that slaves were not to be provided with horses or allowed use of brands (De Ville, *Opelousas*, p. 99). This, of course, suggests that they were doing both.

tricts for its supply of beef. Until Spain took over, meat was mostly that obtained through bison hunts conducted around Natchez or salt beef imported from the French West Indies. In 1770–71 the New Orleans cabildo, in an attempt to resolve the constant problem of supplying beef, granted a monopoly on its meat market to bidders who in turn subcontracted to shed-site suppliers. Yet it was not until Opelousas and Attakapas became a stock-raising center that beef was readily available to the Crescent City. By 1782, at a time when the city's population was over 5,000, this trade had developed enough to merit the building of a new road to facilitate the large New Orleans–bound cattle drives, an accomplishment coming only two decades after the founding of the Attakapas post. The need for such a road was voiced by Hilario Bontet, the city's prime contractor from 1781 to 1784, who complained that these districts would only sell salted meats rather than drive in herds as the contract called for. In the fall of 1788, Estévan Rodríguez Miró, governor of Louisiana (1784–91), issued orders to Commandant Nicolás Forstall for the prompt payment of debts on this new cattle road.[6]

The scarcity of beef experienced by Bernardo de Gálvez when he launched his expeditions of 1780 and 1781 against English strongholds on the Gulf Coast has already been noted. Gálvez's reason for wanting large droves of cheap Texas cattle can be deduced from the fact that in 1781 beef sold for twenty-five dollars a barrel in Natchez. Gálvez found it necessary to employ well-paid vaqueros in Mobile to prevent the British and their Indian allies from stealing his stock. Profiteering individuals naturally took advantage of this situation, selling to both sides and driving the price as high as twelve dollars a head. Evidence exists that some stock raising was carried on around Mobile Bay and on the Tombigbee River plantations on the north before Gálvez landed his 2,000-man force there and began consuming the local herds. A map made in 1775 shows cow pens in this vicinity. Cattle raising was regarded thereabouts as

[6]John G. Clark, *New Orleans, 1718–1812: An Economic History*, pp. 57, 184–85, 259–61; De Ville, *Opelousas*, p. 81. Miró, in a decree of September 6, 1788, to the residents of Opelousas, also stated that no one could kill hogs or cattle except in the presence of two witnesses to identify the brands.

the best way to make a living well after the turn of the century. Mississippi tax lists for 1805 show over 36,000 head of stock, the greatest concentrations being near Natchez and along the Tombigbee and Chickasawhay rivers above Mobile.[7]

The cattle industry around Opelousas grew so rapidly that on July 17, 1783, Commandant Alejandro de Clouet (1774–86) was obliged to issue a special order in an attempt to control it (this was no doubt the "El Caballero de Clouet" who asked Ripperdá to permit a trade in livestock in 1774). The order provided that blacksmiths could not make branding irons without the commandant's consent (an examination of the Opelousas-Attakapas brand book shows that brands proliferated during these years). No one could own more than one brand, and all new brands had to be registered within one week of their use. Calves and colts were to be branded immediately, or they would be confiscated—if they were not stolen first. When a drive was organized to Avoyelles, Natchez, Manchac, Baton Rouge, or Pointe Coupée, the commandant must first inspect all brands. It will be noted that the movement contemplated was eastward, or to the north, indicating that these areas were not sufficient in cattle and that the breeding stock obtained in Texas was being used to establish and build herds throughout Louisiana and what was then called West Florida. While stock raising became important after Spain regained East Florida in 1783, most authorities consider the industry of little importance before that date. The early Florida herds were killed off or stolen by Carolinians in 1702–1704 and not replaced. There is little doubt, however, that the rise of stockmen in western Louisiana and points east was tied to the relative abundance and steady importation of Texas cattle and horses.[8]

That this trade flourished throughout the colonial period seems obvious from the many documents associated with it. Around Natchitoches it especially thrived, livestock being exchanged for slaves, tobacco, and other goods; but a lower road also ran to Opelousas. Jack D. L. Holmes writes that many horses

---

[7] Guice, "Cattle Raisers," pp. 177, 180–83.
[8] De Ville, *Opelousas*, pp. 90–92.

and cattle were imported into Louisiana and West Florida from Texas, suggesting that the flow was what prompted authorities to devise export duties, thus assuring themselves of "a constant source of revenue." Noting that cattle became scarce in Texas during the mid-1790s and that regulations were issued prohibiting the slaughter of breeding stock, Holmes concludes that the demand for meat and hides in Louisiana and West Florida continually encouraged smugglers to violate these laws. I must agree, for to argue that little Texas stock entered colonial Louisiana would be to ignore a half-century of Spanish documentation.[9]

Prices along the lower Mississippi Valley encouraged growth. In 1786 just south of Natchez, 107 head were bought for $1,800 at prices averaging $16 a head. The purchase included 66 cows two years old; 34 cows one and a half years old; and 5 bulls two years old—strictly breeding stock, not steers or old mossyhorns. In 1788 the adjutant of the Natchez fort paid $14 each for 300 head. These rich markets caused a boom in the Opelousas and Attakapas districts, a side effect of which was increasingly wild and difficult-to-manage herds. By 1787 cattle reverting to the wild were again a serious problem, for they would "mix with the tame," causing domestic stock to stray. When the commandant gave permission for settlers to shoot wild cows, rustlers and poachers abused the license; their number was not inconsiderable. One petitioner asked that all branded animals be penned and the rest declared fair game, but a solution was never found, and in those districts wild cattle continued to be a menace.[10]

In 1789 the beef market in New Orleans was made free, a relaxation possibly caused in part by the new cattle road from the west. The cabildo imposed a 3-real head tax on slaughtered animals to provide revenue for the city. It was also in that year that Manuel Gayoso de Lemos became governor of Natchez, and the district's nascent cattle industry began to flourish under his capable administration, which lasted until 1799. When François Louis Hector, Barón de Carondelet was appointed to the presi-

[9] Jack D. L. Holmes, "Livestock in Spanish Natchez," *Journal of Mississippi History* 23 (1961): 18–19.

[10] De Ville, *Opelousas*, pp. 90–92; Guice, "Cattle Raisers," p. 179.

dency of Quito, Equador, in 1797, Gayoso succeeded him as governor general of Louisiana and served in that capacity until his death two years later. Thus it was in the final decade of the century that Natchez profited from the Texas-based cattle corridor and became in itself a center for stock raising. By then Nueva Feliciana, just south of Natchez, had around 4,500 head of cattle (owned by 109 families); in 1788, Natchez had 7,000 head, and 36 of the 44 leading tobacco planters showed considerable herds. By 1792 one such planter, Anthony Hutchins, owned at least 1,000 head. Such figures begin to compare with those of the 1788 census of "Post du Oppeloussais," where 316 family units owned 17,350 head of cattle, a considerable increase from that outpost's total of 4,634 head in 1777 and 2,000 the decade before.[11]

High prices were only one of many reasons for the development of Natchez as an important center for cattle and horses. The region enjoyed excellent climate, good pastures in the river bottom, a prime location for trade, and—in addition to Gayoso's favorable guidance—a liberal policy of the Spanish government which allowed American immigrants to bring in livestock duty free. Many prosperous Anglos took advantage of this to introduce new strains of stock into the region and establish themselves as raisers. As governor of Natchez, Gayoso opposed Carondelet (who served from 1791 to 1797) when he forbade residents to go west of the Mississippi, observing on September 7, 1792, that it was essential for the welfare of both Natchez and Opelousas to continue the cattle trade between them. He allowed the residents to pasture stock west of the river, in the bottomlands near Vidalia, until widespread disturbances interfered. He argued for the right of Bayou Sara ranchers to graze on unoccupied lands in the district of Punta Cortada. He also encouraged drives between Natchez and Fort Nogales (later Vicksburg) and stimulated herd growth, especially in the districts of Bayou Pierre and Big Black. Under his term Natchez enjoyed a virtual monopoly in supplying beef to

---

[11] Clark, *New Orleans*, pp. 260–61; Jack D. L. Holmes, *Gayoso: The Life of a Spanish Governor in the Mississippi Valley, 1789–1799*, pp. 101–102; Guice, "Cattle Raisers," pp. 176, 183.

TABLE 9. Governor Gayoso's Count of Herds in Natchez, 1792 and 1794.

Year	Horses	Cattle	Sheep	Pigs
1784 (estimated) #	1,153	3,000	117	7,111
1792	3,506	15,181	1,131	13,953
1794	3,944	18,302	1,607	18,302

SOURCE: Jack D. L. Holmes, *Gayoso: The Life of a Spanish Governor in the Mississippi Valley, 1789–1799*, p. 103. Holmes notes that in 1794 there was a difference between the "actual totals" and the "Spanish totals."

Spanish posts along the Mississippi, although the Natchitoches vicinity has "generally been assumed" to have been the center of production. In addition to the Nogales market, beef was sold to Fort San Fernando de las Barrancas (Memphis), and some may have gone to New Orleans to compete with stock from Opelousas and Attakapas.[12]

The herds at Natchez grew remarkably fast. Gayoso provided figures for two years of his administration and an estimate for 1784 (based on a census), as shown in table 9. Such remarkable results are not achieved without problems. Theft, especially by Kentuckians, was common in Natchez. Gayoso tried to stop it, ordering on September 13, 1792, that recaptured stock was to be sold at auction with full notice given on public bulletin boards. Nonetheless, he admitted two days later to Governor General Carondelet that rustling was on the increase: "It is extremely difficult to halt the introduction of persons of low character, not only vagabonds, but those who live from nothing else than robbing cattle."

In 1793, partly to combat this problem, Governor Gayoso called together the principal stockmen of Natchez, most of them Anglos, to establish a set of rules governing the industry. This decree, dated February 28, contains fifteen articles primarily dealing with penning, branding (including provisions for

[12] Holmes, *Gayoso*, pp. 101–103; Holmes, "Livestock in Spanish Natchez," pp. 21–22.

a brand book), and giving proper advertisement of estrays (unclaimed animals reverted to the captor after a year). One article forbade anyone but a "settled inhabitant" to gather strays, and another regulated hunting in the woods, intended to curb incursions of "a great number of vagrants and others . . . that live almost altogether in the woods, under pretext of hunting, by whom the good and industrious inhabitants suffer in their stock." Also prohibited was the dumping of indigo wastes into stock water, and a five-dollar bounty each on "tygers" (pumas) or wolves killed within 5 miles of plantations was established.[13]

This proclamation was superseded the following year by a new one with a few modifications. It stated that the herds were increasing and scattered out, causing much intermixture and confusion of ownership. The previous regulation was of "dubious value," and the settlers and Gayoso met once again and tried to resolve their problems. This time penalties for violations were added, something the settlers' counterparts in Texas had experienced a decade previously. Each raiser was to build a pen, and anyone who claimed unbranded strays must first enclose them and give notice. Because many estrays (unmarked and over eighteen months old) were "running loose" throughout the district, owners were required to corral them and have two residents present at brandings. Brands had to be registered within two months, and unrecorded marks were illegal; a 1-peso fine was imposed for violation. Since driving stock back and forth to unmix it caused much injury, other owners' stock must be cut out before a drive and enclosed in some public place near the road. No stock killing was allowed in open pastures on penalty of a fine of 10 pesos a head.

Frauds and damages also resulted from killing cattle without brands. An animal eighteen months old could not be killed. Failure to comply would draw a stiff penalty of 20 pesos and a month in prison without bail. Notice of detained stock must be given within five days. If after a year and a day no owner appeared, the animal could be sold; semiannual advertisement of such animals was required, in April and September. A nonresi-

---

[13] Holmes, "Livestock in Spanish Natchez," pp. 24–30.

dent could not gather any lost animal unless he was employed to do so or had written permission detailing brands.

It was noted that a large number of swine without brands ran wild in various parts of the district. Thus hog hunting was forbidden without a landowner's license. If someone wanted to hunt, he must call owners and residents together and arrange a corral or traps set with lassos, bait, and so forth. Since vagrants caused much damage to various kinds of stock under the pretext of hunting, an alcalde's permission was necessary to hunt. No owner could allow his slaves to own swine, a regulation suggesting that abuses were also suffered from that quarter. Besides the usual provision against dumping indigo wastes in streams (and mention of a fund to encourage wild-beast extermination), rules for the gelding of horses were set forth so that the breed could be improved. In time Natchez became noted for its fine horses, indicating that such concerns paid handsome dividends. Beyond this elaborate livestock code adopted at Natchez in 1794, at New Orleans the following year, Carondelet issued an extensive set of regulations, some of which also pertained to estrays and fences.[14]

In 1799 the butchers of New Orleans protested a rise in the city tax rate, but an attempt by the Attakapas cattlemen to reinstitute a meat monopoly made shop owners swallow the increase without further protest. Street lights would be financed by the tax increase (not the cattlemen's association), and the market remained open. Figures given at the time of the Louisiana Purchase suggest the muscle of this association and indicate how justified were the butchers' fears of being required to buy from one organized supplier. In 1803, Consul Daniel Clark in New Orleans told Secretary of State James Madison that the Attakapas region had reported 7,315 horses and 58,871 cattle, totals which were "particularly defective" because of the cattlemen's fear of pending taxation. Clark's own estimate was 75,000 head of cattle and 13,000 horses. In Opelousas, according to an untitled return of 1805, there were well over 50,000 cattle, "exclusive of those roaming wild." One prairie alone grazed 10,000

[14] Ibid., pp. 31–37.

head, most of which were destined for the New Orleans market. The totals for Mississippi at this time, which have already been noted, were also considerable.[15]

In 1796, Victor Collot, writing of the advantage to be derived from this colony, commented:

... the multitude of cattle in certain parts of lower Louisiana might hold the first rank. The settlements which are more particularly productive are the Attacapas, the Apelousas, Baratarias, Chitamachas, and the Wachitas, all of which are on the right side of the Mississipi. The droves of cattle are so considerable in these countries, that few of the inhabitants are acquainted with the riches they possess.

While Collot said that the current price of a bullock was 4 piastres and horses brought 6 to 8 piastres, other sources say that at the turn of the century, upon reaching market, herders received about 18 piastres or less a head at Opelousas and that this price compared favorably with those at other posts.[16]

These, then, were a few of the attempts in the Mississippi Valley to encourage stock raising, which included swine raising to an extent unknown in Spanish Texas. That the Louisiana industry prospered cannot be questioned, and its many similarities to the precedents already at work in New Spain disprove notions that the two forms of ranching evolved independently. Thus it can be seen that the province east of Texas profited greatly from the trade in livestock, and as long as these inducements existed, the traffic continued, despite repeated efforts to curtail it. It can also be seen that when Anglo stockmen reached the lower Mississippi Valley from their Atlantic seaboard "cowpens" they found stock raising in an advanced stage, firmly based on Spanish procedures, techniques, and regulations—not to mention the livestock itself. Such stock was called "Spanish cattle" well into the nineteenth century.[17]

[15] Clark, *New Orleans*, p. 261; Guice, "Cattle Raisers," p. 176; De Ville, *Opelousas*, pp. 90–92.

[16] De Ville, *Opelousas*, pp. 90–92; Holmes, "Livestock in Spanish Natchez," pp. 16–17. At that time the dollar, the piastre, and the peso were roughly equivalent, the peso fuerte—"hard cash"—of Mexican mint being especially sought. As noted, the peso was equal to 8 reales, which the Anglos called "bits."

[17] Jordan takes everyone to task for falsely designating South Texas and its early occupants as the cradle of modern western ranching, preferring instead to bestow this honor upon transient herdsmen of South Carolina. What he seems doggedly determined

"As Many Horses as Circumstances Permit" 437

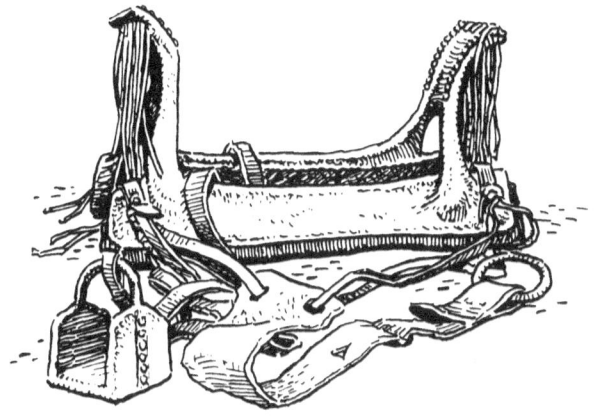

While Texas cattlemen like Ignacio Pérez were taking hunting parties as far away as the Río Colorado and in 1796 some licenses were issued, Indian hostilities may have caused less daring men to stay near home. Mule trains were attacked by Tonkawas, the Lipan Apaches continued to harass the region from Coahuila to Texas, and even the "peaceful" Comanches stole horses and cattle on their visits to Béxar, Laredo, and other settlements. On September 22 eight prominent ranchers protested that the continued thefts committed by Comanches and their allies were becoming unbearable. They claimed that neither cattle nor horses were safe in the vicinity of San Antonio, and they called for remedies, asking the governor to tell *norteño* chiefs that unless the depredations stopped, their plundering braves would be considered enemies by the settlers. Muñoz sympathized with the petitioners but recommended patience and moderation.[18]

to ignore (even though admitting it at times) is that those cattlemen were exposed to Hispanic ranching procedures—and their strains of livestock—all the way from the Atlantic shoreline to Texas (Terry C. Jordan, *Trails to Texas: Southern Roots of Western Cattle Ranching*, pp. 16–17, 151–57). For a survey of Spanish cattle and its distribution in the Americas—especially with regard to "Native American," i.e., northern European breeds introduced by the Anglos—see John E. Rouse, *The Criollo: Spanish Cattle in the Americas*, p. 79: "At the opening of the nineteenth century, the herds in Louisiana were pure Criollo."

[18] Signed by Salvador Rodríguez, Vicente Amador, Luis Menchaca, Joaquín Leal, José Antonio Saucedo, José Hernández, Félix Ruíz, and Manuel Derbón (Carlos E. Castañeda, *Our Catholic Heritage in Texas*, 5:118).

His health broken, Muñoz asked to be relieved early in the year. Nava thanked the governor and assured him that his request would be forwarded to the king, along with a full record of his service. Meanwhile, to assist him in governing the province, Nava selected Juan Bautista Elguezábal, who had earlier been sent to Texas to investigate conditions at Bahía Presidio. Thus was ushered in a bewildering succession of post commanders at La Bahía, Nacogdoches, and the capital itself. Antonio Cordero y Bustamante, the governor of Coahuila slated to relieve Muñoz, could not assume this duty, having become lieutenant governor of Nuevo Santander upon the death of the administrator of that province. La Bahía was in disarray; Manuel Espadas was under suspicion of having left unpaid debts. During Elguezábal's inspection Captain Cortés was retired to Béxar, and Bernardo Fernández took over until April, 1798, when he was replaced by José Miguel del Moral. In mid-1799, after del Moral was rotated to Nacogdoches, Francisco Xavier de Uranga took over at La Bahía.[19]

The administrative situation at Nacogdoches was just as unstable. José María Guadiana was in charge there from October, 1796, to May, 1799, when del Moral replaced him from La Bahía. It was suspected that Guadiana was lax in enforcing the contraband laws, a suspicion that few commanders of the post situated opposite Natchitoches managed to escape. He was also indulgent about foreigners, which greatly aggravated his superiors. Soon after Muñoz died in office in the summer of 1799 and Elguezábal became the acting governor, Commandant General Nava informed him that the commander at Nacogdoches was to be changed every four or five months. This action was deemed necessary to prevent officials from becoming "too intimate" with foreign intruders and *contrabandistas*. In spite of such precautions, every man who held the post was suspected of wrongdoing and closely watched. For example, when Juan Cortés, the former captain of La Bahía (who had also seen service in East Texas after Ybarbo's dismissal), wished to reside

[19] Ibid., 5:202–203; Faulk, *Last Years*, pp. 26–27, 45.

near the Louisiana frontier Nava forbade it, requiring him to retire to Coahuila. Each commander's term of office was closely monitored in regard to connections made, monies collected, and herds of stock passing through the jurisdiction.[20]

In the spring of 1797 Nava wrote Muñoz that Texas-based Comanches were raiding in Coahuila, especially in the vicinity of Mission San Bernardo, where they had run off 300 head of cattle. Pursuing them all the way to the old presidio site at San Sabá (a favorite base of operations of the Comanches), soldiers and mission Indians recovered some of the stock. Governor Cordero of Coahuila was not satisfied, however, and wanted steps taken to halt future depredations of this kind. To make sure that his intentions were understood, Cordero commissioned Captain José Menchaca—still in command at Presidio de Agua Verde—to take 121 men to the Comanches' camps and demand restoration of stock plundered from the Río Grande settlements.[21]

Nava, who had to approve Cordero's action for the sake of appearances, argued against the feasibility of such militant expeditions, pointing out that the Indians could very well interpret them as acts of war. Increased vigilance, he thought, was the key to preventing livestock thefts, not marching an armed force into Comanchería. In July both Nava and Governor Muñoz were much relieved to learn that Captain Menchaca had avoided a confrontation at San Sabá, retiring his men without serious incident.[22] Indians on the Louisiana frontier were also troublesome. In April, 1797, Governor Muñoz complained to Guadiana that Huasas, Tawakonis, and Tonkawas were carrying on an extensive trade with the Americans, exchanging stolen horses and

[20] Castañeda, *Catholic Heritage*, 5:208–209.
[21] Ibid., 5:119–21.
[22] Depredations continued, causing Nava to issue instructions on August 18, 1798, requiring soldiers to guard the horse herds of settlers on the frontier. This decision was prompted by a bitter lawsuit against Muñoz by the Béxar stockmen in view of their recent losses to Indians. They also accused the governor of sheltering a foreigner who was a lackey (*vasallo*) of the Louisiana militia captain, but Nava replied that Don Felipe Nolan had official business in Texas and that their accusations "had no proof" (SA, 9:1–24).

cattle for arms, powder, and lead. This trade was to become a growing concern in the near future.[23]

Some indication of the ranches east of the Sabine, in the vicinity of the old abandoned post of Los Adaes, can be obtained from a list prepared by Guadiana and given to Fray Bernardino Vallejo for purposes of urging these families to perform their Easter duties. The list, though unfortunately incomplete, is still of interest:

> Pablo Lafitte and Andrés Valentia [Valentine], on Arroyo Piedras
> José Gaviña [Lavigne], on Llano de los Cebollas [Cíbolos]
> Pedro Dolet [Dole] and Antonio Dubois, on Arroyo Cristal
> Francisco Prudhomme, in Adaes Pueblo [Village]
> Francisco Morbán, on Arroyo Durazno
> The widow [of Remigio?] Tutin, on Arroyo Tepalcate
> Manuel Prudhomme and Morfil [Murphy], on Arroyo Hondo [de los Adaes]
> Rouguier [Bouguier], on Adaes Lake
> Francisco Rouquier, on Laguna Purita [Prieto]
> José Piernas, on Rancho de Santa María de Adelaida
> "Sam the Englishman" [Santiago, James Wallace], on Arroyo de San Francisco [Juan]

This list should be studied with that given by Gil Ybarbo in 1792, which shows the names of twenty-nine foreigners who had "formed cattle ranches, cultivated the lands, built homes, and established themselves with their families and slaves . . . and otherwise engaged in trade with the Indians." These individuals—many of whom appear on Father Vallejo's list—had settled in his jurisdiction after Presidio Los Adaes was "demolished," said Gil Ybarbo, this dispersion of Frenchmen to Texas taking place with the Natchitoches commandant's permission. Included in his report of 1792 were Nicolás de la Mathe and "Don Felipe" [Nolan].[24]

---

[23] Muñoz to Guadiana, April 25, 1797, BA; Myres, *Ranch in Spanish Texas*, p. 50; Mattie Austin Hatcher, *The Opening of Texas to Foreign Settlement, 1801–1821*, p. 53; Castañeda, *Catholic Heritage*, 5:122.

[24] Castañeda, *Catholic Heritage*, 5:176; R. B. Blake, Research Collection, vol. 72. On August 18, 1792, the governor, the count of Sierra Gorda, asked Cristóbal de Cór-

From records in the General Land Office it appears that Captain Antonio Gil Ybarbo issued various land grants around Nacogdoches during his years there, most of them by "verbal permission" and vaguely defined. R. B. Blake suggests that the captain's problems intensified with the arrival of Cortés in April, 1792, and his review of the slipshod procedures that had been followed. High on the list were those in reference to grants of land made during his fifteen-year undisputed reign. Cortés promptly nailed a proclamation to the door of Gil Ybarbo's stone fort and set about establishing an orderly procedure for securing lands, which explains why the year 1792 is the starting point for many old East Texas titles.

According to Virginia Taylor, former Spanish archivist of the General Land Office, of the seventy land titles made during the Spanish era that still exist, fifty-two come from around Nacogdoches. Many of these ranches, Taylor notes, were abandoned between 1812 and 1821 and were not reclaimed. Other evidence suggests that a number of grants made during this formative era were lost during a chain of disturbances, particularly those associated with the Fredonian Rebellion of 1826 and the so-called Córdova Rebellion of 1838, in which many prominent descendants of original grantees were charged with treason and driven from their homes. Consequently, only twenty-five of these old Adaesaño grants are shown on modern-day maps, although a few fragmented records are preserved in various files in the General Land Office or are mentioned in litigation between subsequent owners.

Many of these grants are characterized by language calling for so-many leagues to each "wind," or cardinal point. The procedure for surveying was to begin at a central spot, such as a dwelling, and measure the specified distance by the throw of a rope from horseback. Other sources claim that the rope was coiled around a saddle horn and gradually fed out as the rider advanced toward the cardinal point. This explanation is more

dova to prepare a list of Frenchmen and other foreigners who had ranches east of the Sabine. I have been unable to find such a report unless it is the pitiful one given January 12, 1794, which listed an Englishman named "Simmes," who was married to a Bexareña, plus two creoles from Natchitoches (Blake, Research Collection, Supplement ser., 3:28, 106, 333).

likely considering that the rope, or *cordel*, used was customarily 50 varas in length. Since a league was 5,000 varas (1 vara being just under 1 yard), after 100 "tosses" the surveying party would stop and lay a boundary stone. Then the members of the team would return to their starting point and measure the same distance to another "wind," and so on. A grant of 1 league in each direction would therefore amount to 4 square leagues of land.

Although some writers have suggested that each boundary point reached served as a "corner," it can be seen that such a notion is incorrect, because if the four stones were connected by lines, only half as much land would result. The procedure was to extend the grant line outward in a perpendicular course to the path traversed, that is, at a right angle, where it would connect with the side boundaries at 90-degree angles, forming a square:

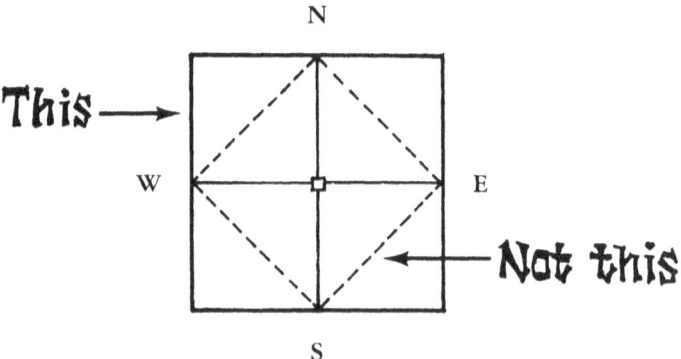

As most old titles show, there might be considerable variation between the grant and the actual survey, especially when the survey was conducted by such rudimentary methods. Nevertheless, as long as the surrounding country remained unsettled (and the neighbors friendly), the system evidently worked for the occupants of Spanish Texas.[25]

---

[25] Virginia H. Taylor, *The Spanish Archives of the General Land Office of Texas*, pp. 15–21, 72; Nyal C. King, "Captain Antonio Gil Y'Barbo, Founder of Modern Nacogdoches, 1729–1809," pp. 82, 89; interview with Herman Forbes, head of GLO Surveys

The grants along the Río Grande, many of which were issued in the 1790s and early 1800s, fared better, in both their preservation and their eventual recognition. A number of works are available on the ranches founded around Escandón's river villas as they gradually expanded northward in search of broader pastures. While that area, properly considered Nuevo Santander, is beyond the scope of this work, a few of the most prominent ranching dynasties of the region should be mentioned.[26]

As at Béxar, stock raising thrived along the Río Bravo, and by the time José Tienda de Cuervo made his report in 1757, Camargo already had seventeen ranches in its vicinity and Revilla twenty-nine. When lands were assigned to the *primitivos* (first) settlers in 1767, many ranchers had established operations on the north bank. Captain Tomás Sánchez, of Laredo, for example, had a ranch on the Nueces, 20 leagues away. La Fora said that it was on the Arroyo San Casimiro, where many horses were raised. Don Tomás also owned El Pato (the Duck), fifteen *sitios* located 4 leagues northeast of the Laredo ford. At one time the Sánchez family as a group held 100,000 acres on both sides of the river.

The location of Hacienda de Dolores, Don José Vásquez Borrego's ranch on the north bank of the Río Grande, has already been mentioned, as has Santa Petronilla, the ranch started near the lower Nueces by Blás María de la Garza Falcón, founder of Camargo. When Captain Blás María died in 1767, the year of the land assignments, his son Joseph Antonio de la Garza Falcón became captain in his place. He received *porción* 80, and his brother Juan was awarded *porción* 81 (see map on page 445, keyed to appendix M). Besides the Nueces River ranch, which

---

Department, November 29, 1983; Blake, Research Collection, 28:381–85, 50:54–58, 53:251–352. Carolyn Reeves Ericson, *Nacogdoches, Gateway to Texas: A Biographical Directory, 1773–1849*, notes involvement in the Nacogdoches–San Augustine "treason trials" and other disturbances which dispossessed or dislocated the older settlers. For insight into how nineteenth-century litigation contributes to an understanding of early ranches, their owners, boundaries, etc., see R. B. Blake, "Records . . . Relating to the Edmund Norris Four League Grant," Texas State Archives, a collection of documents surrounding the defense of Rancho Naconiche's title by Norris's heirs which extended well into the 1870s.

[26] Both Robert S. Weddle and Robert H. Thonhoff, *Drama and Conflict: The Texas Saga of 1776*; and Myres, *Ranch in Spanish Texas*, include good bibliographies for information on the Río Grande settlements and their ranches.

was guarded by a garrison of troops, Blás María also established ranch headquarters on the left bank of the Río Grande, high on a hill at a place called Carnestolendas. It became the present Rio Grande City (situated in *porción* 80). Nine miles to the west his father-in-law, Don Nicolás de los Santos Coy, ran a ranch called Guadado (now Garceño). On Guadado and another place south of the river called Rancherías, Don Nicolás had 100 vaqueros working for him. Escandón allowed this wealthy hacendado 100 *sitios de ganado mayor*—twice the size of the Borrego spread. The colonizer reserved for himself and his heirs 642 leagues (2,850,000 acres) with 100 miles of river frontage starting at the coast and going up the right bank of the Río Grande.[27]

As Florence Johnson Scott has pointed out, the land grants made to ranchers based on the Río del Norte were of three types: (1) *porciones* given in 1767: 2 leagues for pasture (8,856 acres) plus 12 *caballerías* fronting on the river for farming (1,500 acres; later arrivals received less than the *primitivos*), (2) larger tracts to the elite for grazing only (1767–1810), and (3) assignment of vacant lands (1770–1810). While the effect of the Visita General of 1767 was to scatter the settlers, most remained along the river. The typical rancher either built a *casa fuerte* of stone or stayed in town, placing the ranch in the hands of a trusted *majordomo*—often a nephew, son-in-law, or other relative. From Laredo downriver to Camargo most of the ranchers were of *gente de razón* and enjoyed relatively equal status. This was not the case at Reynosa, where most of the land was owned by six clans, a circumstance creating a vast gap between the rich and the poor, even though Reynosa was an offshoot of Camargo founding families. Around Reynosa the Canos, Hinojosas, Garzas, Garza Falcones, Cavazoses, and Ballís were as close to being eighteenth-century cattle barons as anyone could be in the territory that is now Texas. Like their later Anglo counterparts and their contemporaries at Béxar, these powerful families intermarried, producing even more vast empires in the *brasada* country between the Río Nueces and the Río Grande.[28]

[27] See "Acts of the General Visit," GLO (5 vols.), for *porciones* granted along the Río Grande.

[28] Florence Johnson Scott, *Historical Heritage of the Lower Río Grande*, pp. 99–102; see also pp. 60–98 for a full listing of river *porciones*.

"As Many Horses as Circumstances Permit" 445

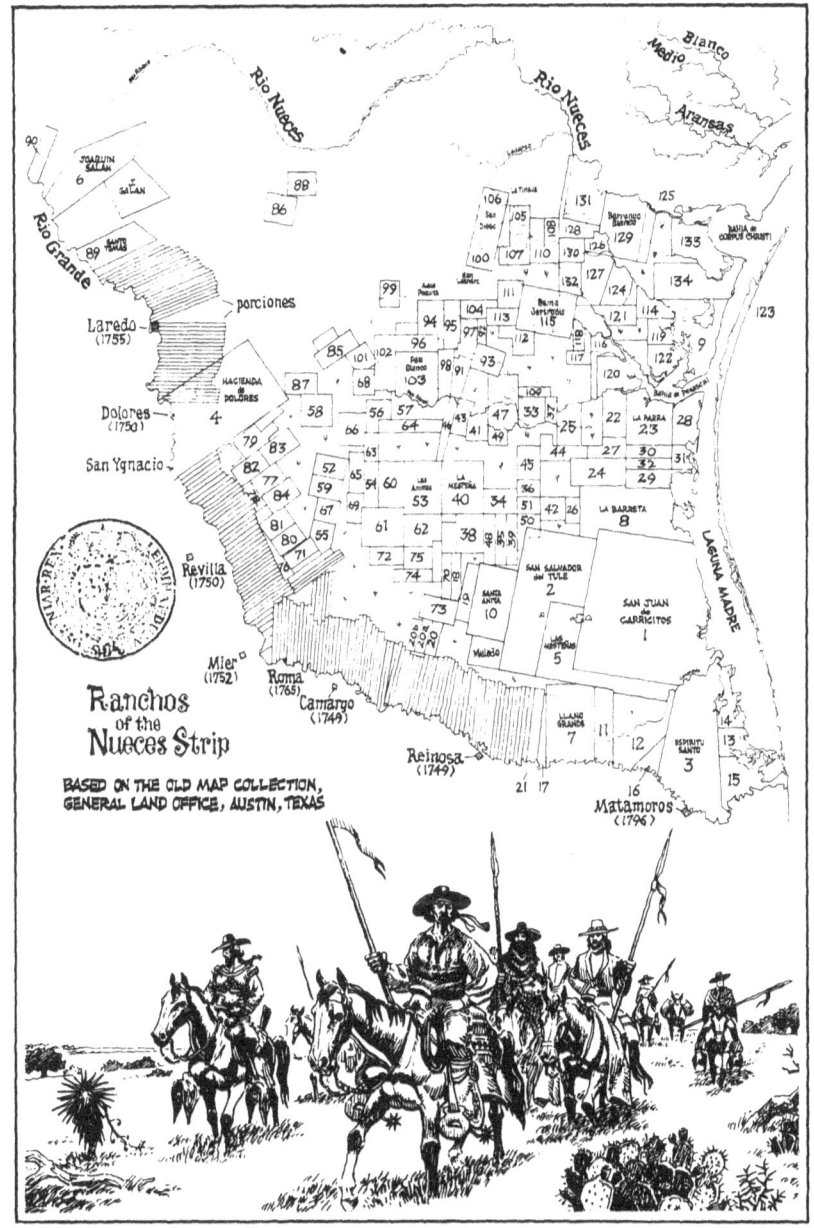

Perhaps none of these dynasties was greater than the one started by Juan José (or Juan Joseph) de Hinojosa, the captain and chief justice of Reynosa. A simplified diagram of his family (there having been nine children) may prove useful:

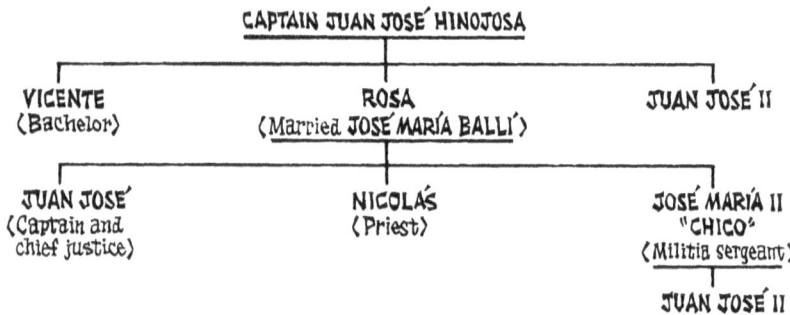

Juan José Hinojosa's daughter, Rosa, married José María Ballí, the son of Nicolás Ballí, a primitive settler. In 1774, Rosa's father and her husband made joint application for Llano Grande, 25½ leagues lying just below the Reynosa *porciones*, with more than 11 miles of frontage on the north bank of the river. Both men had died by the time the grant was approved in 1790, and Doña Rosa acquired her husband's 12 leagues, La Feria, putting it in her own name. She also received one-eighth of her father's Llano Grande. Meanwhile, she and her brother Vicente had received 12 leagues each from their father in 1788. Since Vicente was unmarried, he bequeathed his part to Rosa. She and her son Nicolás had a ranch there, near present Donna, from 1788. Rosa also helped Vicente obtain the 35-league grant Las Mesteñas, near present Harlingen, taking 12 leagues for herself and calling it Ojo de Agua. She and her children inherited this as well.

In 1794 she made application for San Salvador del Tule (72 leagues) in the name of her son, Captain Juan José Ballí. It lay just north of Reynosa's *porciones* and contained the valuable salt deposits known as El Sal del Rey (the King's Salt). Included was a 9-league tract called El Melado, which Rosa intended to give her brother, Juan José Hinojosa II. The application struck snags, but the property was acquired anyway at public auction in 1798. Another son, José María ("Chico") Ballí, a militia sergeant, applied for Santa Anita, a 95,202-acre tract which adjoined San Salvador del Tule on the west. He withdrew in favor of a family friend, and Doña Rosa bought Las Casteñas from Eugenio and Bartolomé Fernández out of their Concepción de Carricitos grant. She died in 1803, leaving her heirs an incredibly large estate.[29]

Perhaps the best-known member of this remarkable family was Doña Rosa's son Nicolás, the padre for whom Padre Island is named. In 1790 he inherited all his father's and half his mother's land; his brothers, Juan José and Chico, shared the other half. Before Padre Island was known as such, it was called Las Islas de Malaguitas, and the southern part, called San Carlos de las Malaguitas, was owned by Nicolás's brother Juan José. When Nicolás came home about 1794, he helped his mother, Rosa, run the various ranches. They applied for the part of the island called Brazos de San Iago, took forty-seven persons to the island, and established Rancho Santa Cruz, about 15 miles above the Brazos Santiago Pass. In 1800, Nicolás made a new claim to the island with his nephew Juan José Ballí II, Chico's son. When Captain Juan José died childless in 1804, brother Nicolás took over his interests and continued to guide the fortunes of the Ballí family. During this period he was the administrator of tithes for the five "northern" villas, presumably those along the river. The priest's name is also linked with the little ranching settlement planted near the mouth of the Río Grande in 1792 by a group of settlers from Reynosa. It was known as Congregación del Refugio (later becoming Matamoros), and Padre Ballí served there, his mother having built its first chapel.[30]

Another large grant on the north bank of the lower Río Grande was El Potrero del Espíritu Santo, a 59-*sitio* tract bestowed upon José Salvador de la Garza. Garza married María Gertrudis, the daughter of Captain Blás María de la Garza

---

[29] Minnie Gilbert, "Texas' First Cattle Queen," in Valley Byliners, *Roots by the River: A Story of Texas Tropical Borderland*, 2:15–25; Scott, *Historical Heritage*, pp. 103–106, 159–60.

[30] Agnes G. Grimm, *Llanos Mestenas: Mustang Plains*, pp. 18–19, 44–45; Scott, *Historical Heritage*, p. 109; Clotilde P. García, *Padre José Nicolás Ballí and Padre Island* (application for a historical marker), kindly sent to the author by Lionel Garza, of Kingsville.

Falcón. Although this grant, stretching all the way north to the Arroyo Colorado, was contested by José Narciso Cavazos, Garza was sustained. As a consolation Cavazos was awarded the largest single tract of all: 106½ leagues, or 601,657 acres. Called San Juan de Carricitos, the tract lay along the coast above the disputed grant, in present Kenedy and Willacy counties. These large holdings were generally sold at 50 centavos per *sitio* or league (4,428 acres), and the Cavazos grant—over half a million acres—later exchanged hands for a mere 53 pesos. Many other large grants were adjudicated near the turn of the century, but the assignment of practically all river lands was accomplished by 1781. After that there was no place to go except north—to the Nueces—as many ranchers did.[31]

The acquisition of huge tracts of land, however, was almost

[31] Scott, *Historical Heritage*, pp. 107–109, 148–49, 163–65. For a brief survey of all the lower Río Grande ranches see Weddle and Thonhoff, *Drama and Conflict*, pp. 161–65; Tom Lea, *The King Ranch*, 1:376–81.

a thing of the past. The Superior Council on Royal Lands decreed in May, 1802, that grants to wealthy applicants could be no more than 3 or 4 square leagues, whereas the poor could receive one or two *sitios*. Three years later another royal *cédula*, aimed at populating the vast expanses of the frontier, was issued. It ushered in a new policy regarding grants of *realengas*, rejecting the old concept of the absentee hacendado who presided over vast cattle empires in favor of numerous rancheros operating on a smaller scale. It was evidently felt that the frontier could best be developed by encouraging cattlemen of scant resources to start their own operations rather than remaining landless wage earners bound to a *patrón*. Thus the king stipulated that in the future all royal lands obtained for stock raising must be occupied and improved at once.[32]

It was not long, of course, before ways were found to circumvent these limitations. Many grants, such as Barranco Blanco (awarded in 1806) and Casa Blanca (awarded a year earlier, in 1805), both lying on the Nueces, were applied for in contiguous tracts. In the former Vicente López de Herrera asked for land totaling 20 leagues for himself and his three sons. Then his son-in-law Gregorio Farías applied for and received a grant called El Diezmero, which further increased the family's holdings. In the award of Casa Blanca, Juan José de la Garza Montemayor and his three sons received 16 leagues, and then Montemayor's father-in-law, Benito López de Xaen (or Jaen), acquired San Antonio de Agua Dulce next to their ranch. Usually such nepotistic combinations were winked at, owing to the overriding advantages obtained by the settling of thinly populated areas, especially those along the Nueces, where many earlier attempts at colonization had failed.[33]

---

[32] Reference to these shifting royal land policies is found in Lea, *King Ranch*, 1:381; Castañeda, *Catholic Heritage*, 5:319–21.

[33] For information on the Nueces Strip ranches and their owners see Nueces County Historical Society, comp. and ed., *The History of Nueces County*, pp. 29–32; Dan Kilgore, *Nueces County, Texas, 1750–1800: A Bicentennial Memoir*, pp. 5–8; Lea, *King Ranch*, 1:376–81; Paul Schuster Taylor, *An American-Mexican Frontier: Nueces County, Texas*, pp. 179–88; Virginia H. Taylor, *Index to Spanish and Mexican Land Grants in Texas*; Grimm, *Llanos Mestenas*. Appendix M and its map, page 445, list the largest.

While these ranches in upper Nuevo Santander were developing and expanding, Juan Elguezábal, assistant to the ailing Governor Muñoz, devised a proposal aimed at benefiting both the Bahía missions and the neighboring province. On February 4, 1798, he suggested that Rosario and Refugio be allowed to trade their excess cattle for the wild horses so plentiful in Nuevo Santander. In such a manner enough money could be raised to build irrigation canals at Espíritu Santo and Rosario, the only way Elguezábal saw of alleviating the impoverished condition of these missions. As a possible center for the exchange he mentioned Laredo, to which the missions could drive their cattle each year on a prearranged date. Elguezábal considered the Bahía missions important in controlling the coastal tribes and believed that they merited consideration, noting that their funds were inadequate for the task expected of them. Despite the constant complaints of incursions made on the Bahía mission herds, Refugio was still able to respond in late 1798 to the king's call for loyal citizens to help in the war effort against England. The mission donated 100 cows. Captain del Moral sold 89 head at auction for 10 pesos each, and the other 11 brought 6 pesos a head, netting for the war fund three times the entire amount collected from the soldiers and citizens of La Bahía.[34]

Early in 1799 attention was once against focused on the Louisiana border and its flourishing contraband trade in cattle and horses. On February 19, the viceroy, Marqués de Branciforte, informed Commandant General Nava that there was entirely too much illegal traffic, which was no news to anyone on the frontier. Nonetheless, in May, Elguezábal issued a decree prohibiting all trade with Louisiana and calling for the confiscation and sale at public auction of property seized from such trade. This order was perhaps founded on the king's decision of 1793 that on the question of trade between the two provinces no changes be made in existing policy. Other equally stringent regulations were applied against the admission of foreigners. José María Guadiana dutifully replied that he was doing all he could to exclude foreigners

[34] Castañeda, *Catholic Heritage*, 5:104–109. For the list of those who bought the auctioned cattle, see del Moral to Muñoz, February 4, 1799, BAM, roll 28, frames 714–15.

from the Nacogdoches area and that he was keeping an eye on the operations of Reymundo (Samuel) Davenport and Guillermo (William) Barr. While both Samuel Davenport and his associate William Barr had recently been permitted by the government to trade with the Indians, the activities of these two men were viewed with suspicion from the beginning. Future developments, at least in regard to Davenport, would prove such doubts entirely justified.[35]

The House of Barr and Davenport was organized in 1798 by these two men (natives of Ireland and Pennsylvania, respectively) and two other traders, Luther Smith and Edward Murphy. Murphy brought to the partnership a tract of land 4 leagues square (16 leagues) called La Nana, just east of the Sabine. It lay squarely astride the trade route to Natchitoches. In 1798 Barr was also granted 5 leagues of land called San Patricio, situated on the Angelina River straddling the Camino Real headed toward Béxar. In addition to these extensive tracts Murphy located a trading post about 1801 at the old mission for the Aís Indians (now San Augustine). Dwarfing all these, Davenport bought the Las Hormigas grant of 6 leagues square (207,360 acres, or 24 square miles) in 1805; this grant lay above La Nana. Thus the partnership was easily the largest landowner in the Nacogdoches region and admirably suited to stock raising or the pasturing of animals.

Trade, however—more specifically the Indian trade—the endeavor for which these men joined forces, was a privilege formally conferred on Barr by the Spaniards in 1800. In order to maintain friendly relations with the many tribes, the government had adopted a lavish policy of bestowing presents on them, entrusting the distribution of these gifts to various traders. It was the Spanish equivalent of the "factory" system adopted by the United States, pushing westward into Indian territory. In Texas this system provided the Indians with manufactured goods, in exchange for which the commissioned agents received, among other things, horses. They were entitled to ex-

---

[35] Marqués de Branciforte to Nava, February 19, 1799, Holmes, "Livestock in Spanish Natchez," p. 19; Elguezábal, decree, May 20, 1799, in Castañeda, *Catholic Heritage*, 5:206; Charles Wilson Hackett et al., eds. and trans., *Pichardo's Treatise*, 3:462.

port these animals to Louisiana and sell them in consideration of their expenses (upon paying the king 2 reales a head), all as part of a scheme to keep the Indians happy and attached to the interests of Spain. After Captain Gil Ybarbo's removal, this supply function was increasingly important in the area he had dominated by personal sway for so many years.

Barr and Davenport handled business affairs in Texas, while their two partners operated in Louisiana. For example, from 1803 to 1807 Natchitoches-based Luther Smith made annual trips between Nacogdoches and West Florida, "usually driving large herds of horses and mules from Texas to be sold in the district of New Feliciana." One such trip netted the firm 2,720 pesos. Since horses obtained from the Indians were valued at about 10 pesos a head, considerable profit resulted when they were sold on the other end. At one time Barr obtained 800 steers in Béxar and drove the herd to Nacogdoches, where he disposed of it to the garrison. The partners' ranches were ideally situated for such operations, and their trading house prospered. Because of their origin and many contacts with *extranjeros* (foreigners), their success was always the object of deep concern in official places.[36]

Even so, the threat which Spain sensed on her borderlands at the close of the century was personified in another foreigner, a young Irishman of extreme vigor named Philip Nolan. Much has been made of Nolan's contacts in high places, his mapmaking skills, and his ulterior motives; but whatever else this brazen adventurer was, he was a mesteñero of no small ability. The conjecture about Nolan's reasons for journeying to Texas is endless, but one fact is clear: while he was in the province, he engaged in the lucrative business of catching and breaking horses intended for Louisiana markets. Nor did he enter Texas

---

[36] For an account of lands and trading privileges enjoyed by this firm, see J. Villasana Haggard, "The House of Barr and Davenport," *Southwestern Historical Quarterly* 49 (July, 1945): 72–77; J. Villasana Haggard, "Neutral Ground between Louisiana and Texas," *Louisiana Historical Quarterly* 28, no. 4 (October, 1945): 1089–1101; Nardini, *Historic Natchitoches*, pp. 112, 114. An abstract of title for La Nana is in University of Texas Archives, box 2R125. See also U.S. Cong., *House Exec. Doc.* no. 49, 24th Cong., 1st sess., 1824 [ser. 287], "Land Claims between the Rio Hondo and the Sabine," pp. 69–73.

without authorization, regardless of how officials may have later repudiated their involvement. On his first trip, in 1791, he traveled with a letter and passport issued by Governor Miró of Louisiana. After his trade goods were confiscated at Nacogdoches, Nolan went to live among the Indians for two years, returning to Louisiana with 50 mustangs. When he reappeared, the new governor of Louisiana, Barón de Carondelet, considered him "as a person risen from the dead."[37]

Nor was this an isolated example. Since the Louisiana cavalry was in the habit of importing Texas horses for mounts, Nolan could not have had much trouble convincing Carondelet that he was just the man to supply such needs. It is known that Governor Muñoz wrote Carondelet on April 30, 1794, concerning proposals to send range horses from Texas to Louisiana.[38] By June, Nolan was back in Nacogdoches with five citizens of Louisiana and a slave. He was also armed with a letter from the baron and a passport, and the Nacogdoches commander allowed him to enter Texas and catch horses as the governor of Louisiana had requested. Carondelet wrote Muñoz soon after: "I have given permission to Don Philip Nolan, a young Irishman of talent and experience who has resided four years in Nacogdoches, for him to pass to San Antonio in order to procure as many horses as circumstances permit, and to return here with them."[39]

On this expedition, which could not exactly be termed covert, Nolan managed to capture 250 horses, which, after they were sufficiently tamed, were driven to Natchez. He sold the best there, taking the rest to Kentucky. As Holmes has observed, evidence exists that Nolan and Governor Gayoso at Natchez were at one time partners in cattle and horse speculations but later had a falling out and became mortal enemies. Perhaps Gayoso's perilous situation with certain Americans thought to be loyal Spanish citizens in Natchez also contributed to his dis-

---

[37] An account of Nolan's activities in Texas is found in Castañeda, *Catholic Heritage*, 5:232–46; see also Gerald Ashford, *Spanish Texas, Yesterday and Today*, pp. 174–88. The most detailed study is Maurine T. Wilson, "Philip Nolan and His Activities in Texas" (Master's thesis, University of Texas, 1932).

[38] Lawrence Kinnaird, ed., *Spain in the Mississippi Valley, 1765–1794*, American Historical Association Annual Report for 1945 (1946), 3:274–75.

[39] Carondelet to Muñoz, September 9, 1794, Faulk, *Last Years*, p. 117.

like of Nolan, causing him to warn Carondelet against the intrepid "dealer in horses."[40]

In any case, Nolan reappeared in San Antonio in the summer of 1797 and presented his credentials to Muñoz, claiming to have a special commission to go to Nuevo Santander to secure horses for the Louisiana regiment. While the request may have aroused his suspicion, on October 31, Nava issued Nolan a license to obtain the horses, instructing Muñoz to assist him as he deemed proper. In fact, it was the commandant general who suggested that Nolan would have to travel to Nuevo Santander to collect the horses he wanted, inviting him also to visit Chihuahua. A check with Carondelet—who, it seems, had been swayed by Gayoso's advice—resulted in Nolan's downfall. Admitting that he had permitted Nolan to enter Texas, the baron wrote that a commission from him to buy horses in Nuevo Santander was as false as the letter of recommendation said to have been lost. The joke of all this, of course, is that the enterprising mesteñero had no intention of "buying" horses when the plains were full of them. Nolan, who had already established contacts in the river villas, merely wanted to see for himself how extensive the herds were on the Llanos Mesteños.

Ironically, while he doubtless smuggled many horses out of Texas, Nolan did pay some of His Majesty's duties—at least until his operations were ordered terminated. A "Statement of Those Who Took Horses to Louisiana" filed in 1795 by Cristóbal de Córdova, acting commander of Nacogdoches, for the Mustang Fund account for 1792–94, includes Nolan entries (104 horses at 26 pesos). Later correspondence demonstrates the sly way Nolan manipulated the system. In January, 1800, José Miguel del Moral wrote that Nolan had paid him 132 pesos due on the export of horses. It so happened that this was the exact amount that the soldiers at Nacogdoches and La Bahía owed Nolan's business partner, Antonio Leal, for trade goods he had advanced the troops (items that Nolan had most likely brought with him from Louisiana). Governor Elguezábal wrote Cordero the next month, mentioning that Nolan had covered his indebtedness

---

[40] Holmes, "Livestock in Spanish Natchez," p. 20.

with a draft; Nava replied that Leal's voucher was to be reimbursed from the Mustang Fund, reminding his officers to pay residents punctually for stock, dried meat, corn, and other supplies purchased to sustain the friendly Indians. Thus Nolan's mustang duties were "laundered" through the fund and came back to his agent, Leal, whom Muñoz had appointed trader to *los norteños* in 1794 with sweeping authority. One suspects that Nolan sweetened the pot with other goods, such as the late-model carbines and fowling pieces he made a habit of presenting to ranking officials and influential priests and the bolts of cloth and other duty-free merchandise that Leal's wife, Gertrudis, sold with ease from their ranch house.[41]

Certain it is that Carondelet's news caused Commandant General Nava to make an immediate about-face. On March 20, 1798, he wrote Muñoz revoking Nolan's permit to import 2,000 pesos' worth of goods for the purpose of defraying some of his expenses, which had been granted the preceding January. Following Carondelet's example, Nava cited the royal decree of 1780 as his basis for allowing stock to pass from the Interior Provinces to Louisiana, although he must have known that he was on shaky ground. Meanwhile, Nolan was off somewhere catching horses, and the new viceroy, Miguel José de Azanza, was beginning to make inquiries about the elusive Irishman—inquiries which resulted in orders for Nava to keep Nolan out of Nuevo Santander altogether. It was not until April, 1799, that the commandant general learned much to his surprise that Nolan was still in Texas, assembling horses at a corral near the Trinity River. Nava wrote Muñoz, ordering him to evict Nolan immediately and warn him not to return. Surely, added Nava, sufficient time had elapsed for the gathering of horses "which I permitted in order that he fulfill his contract with the governor of Louisiana for remounts." Muñoz, with only one month to live, defended Nolan, explaining that his delays were caused by difficulties in roundups and the trip to Nuevo Santander. Nolan made his way back east that fall with more than 1,200 horses.

---

[41] Blake, Research Collection, Supplement ser., 3:104, 258, 346, 347, 362, 364, 369, 375, 4:54; Grazing Papers, Texas State Archives.

Considering that, according to André Michaux, wild horses brought $50 a head in New Orleans, it is not difficult to justify Nolan's sojourns in Texas on the profit motive alone, $60,000 being a considerable sum of money in 1799.[42]

But Philip Nolan's web was almost spun. Gayoso de Lemos, now governor general of Louisiana and Nolan's implacable foe, wrote Nava on June 10, 1799, denouncing General Wilkinson's suspected protégé as a sacrilegious hypocrite who obtained passports by fraud. Gayoso wanted Nolan captured and imprisoned "where he would never be seen again." The mustanger was not unaware of Gayoso's hostility. After returning to Louisiana in November with his latest catch of horses, he wrote Jesse Cook, his agent in Nacogdoches, informing him that Gayoso had ordered the governor of Texas to arrest and hold him (Nolan) under close confinement. Nolan urged Cook to brand their remaining horses with Gertrudis's iron and await further instructions. In August, 1800, Commandant General Nava, his wavering trust in the Irishman finally shaken beyond further procrastination, issued orders for his arrest should he return to the province.

The bold mesteñero dared to make one last expedition—this one definitely unauthorized. He met his death as dawn was breaking on the morning of March 21, 1801, in Tawakoni country, where he and his twenty-odd men had erected corrals and several log structures as a defense against the Indians. After a battle involving Spanish troops sent from Nacogdoches to arrest the mustanger, William Barr, "moved by his well-known love for the king," took Nolan's ears to Governor Elguezábal, who forwarded the grisly trophies to Nava. According to declarations made by Nolan's companions, their purpose in entering Texas had been simply to catch mustangs and return with horses left behind on the last expedition. For their work in building corrals and catching wild horses, they were to receive a share of the

---

[42] Faulk, *Last Years*, p. 118; Castañeda, *Catholic Heritage*, 5:235–37; Ashford, *Spanish Texas*, p. 181; Holmes, "Livestock in Spanish Natchez," p. 19; Guice, "Cattle Raisers," p. 182. Among the other things Nolan accomplished on this extended trip was to father a child, born August 20, 1798, by Gertrudis Quiñones ("Baptismals of San Fernando," vol. 3, entry no. 268). These unpublished records have been compiled and translated by John Ogden Leal.

haul, but if the job took longer than their three months' enlistment period, they were to receive an additional peso a day. However, a man who had deserted Nolan's party in the early going, Mordecai Richards, gave a more sinister account of the expedition's purpose, and it was his version that the Spaniards chose to believe. Elguezábal, in addition to sending Nolan's ears to the commandant general, sent him a list of the adventurer's confiscated horses and mules, carefully noting their brands. Nolan's men were sent to prison in Chihuahua and paid dearly for their ostensible desire to get-rich-quick by entering Texas and taking His Majesty's mesteños without permission and without payment of the stipulated 2-real fees.[43]

Not only foreigners suffered in the Nolan affair. Seven of Nolan's twenty-seven men were Spaniards: Luciano García, Vicente Lara, Refugio de la Garza, Juan Joseph Martínez, Lorenzo Hinojosa, Joseph Berbán, and Joseph de Jesús de los Santos, a brother of Nolan's mistress, Gertrudis. They were perhaps chosen for their expertise as mesteñeros and *jinetes* (broncobusters), as well as their knowledge of the country. Over the years Nolan had developed business relationships with certain rancheros, such as the one with Juan Antonio Leal and his wife, Gertrudis de los Santos. Natives of Béxar, the couple owned Rancho Señor San Antonio, conveniently near the Sabine River, and this property was used for collecting and pasturing horses until Nolan could drive them across the border. This mutually beneficial arrangement, it appears, was conducted under per-

---

[43] Castañeda, *Catholic Heritage*, 5:238; Elguezábal, "List of Horses, Mules and Brands Belonging to Prisoners," November 3, 1801 (Nolan Documents, vol. 796, box 2Q241, University of Texas Archives). One of these brands is shown as "fierro de la Misión de San Juan [Bautista?] entero."

mits which Muñoz issued every three months, with the knowledge of the commandant general. In addition, Nolan "owned" ranches on the Medina and the Trinity, where he employed hands to tend horses destined for Louisiana. According to testimony he registered several *fierros*, one for pastured animals and another used as a road brand. It was a well-organized network, regardless of the king's feelings on restricted trade or the cry of innocence which was raised in the aftermath.

After Nolan's death, Leal and his wife were arrested as accomplices to the mustanger's crimes and prosecuted in what the *Handbook of Texas* calls one of the "most famous trials in Texas history." They were hauled to Béxar, where they underwent intensive examination. More testimony was taken at Nacogdoches and sent to the capital. Leal was obliged to sell property to raise money for his defense, receiving 400 pesos in cash from Pedro Buigas on March 30, 1801. The lost ranch extended "two leagues to each wind." Included in the sale price were all the horses pastured there bearing the husband's and wife's brands, which were shown in the deed of transfer. Commandant General Nava decided in November that they and two other men, Santiago (Jesse) Cook and Pedro Longueville, alias "Big Foot," were guilty of considerable contraband trade and should be removed to the interior.[44] The affair was no doubt intended to be an object lesson to other Spaniards who might be tempted to befriend foreigners and pursue the forbidden

---

[44] "Año de 1801 (no. 168): Criminal: Contra el Americano Santiago Cook, Antonio Leal, su muger Gertrudis de los Santos y el Frances Pedro Goremias Longueville indicados de Correspondiencias secretas con Don Felipe Nolan," January 23, 1801, BAM, roll 29. It was noted that Cook was planning to go to Monclova and the Leales to San Fernando (Coahuila); Longueville was permitted to stay in Béxar and opened a bakery, later marrying a local girl and becoming a rancher. Some writers have suggested that Leal's wife was the mother of a child by Nolan. While Gertrudis herself admitted that she maintained the "illicit intercourse of a frail woman" with him, such a sensational fact would doubtless have emerged in the detailed testimony taken by authorities to establish the exact nature of her relationship with the slain mustanger (Nolan Documents, vol. 793, box 2Q241, University of Texas Archives). For information on the ranch used as Nolan's staging area see R. B. Blake's entry on Leal in *Handbook of Texas*, 2:42; see also GLO, 37:355–64. Edmund Quirk (a partner of Edward Murphy) bought the 4-league tract on Ayish Bayou from Buigas, paying 600 pesos, at which time it was called Ranch of Tihuatina.

trade. Nowdays we call such elaborate displays "media events," and such it was to the inhabitants of colonial Texas.

Apart from viewing Nolan's mustanging activities as an infraction of the laws of the province governing mesteños and *orejanos*, the incidents surrounding his last entry and defeat on the Arroyo Blanco (now Nolan River) created a great paranoia in Nueva España and set the entire frontier in an uproar. Suspicion of outsiders who might be entertaining revolutionary designs similar to Nolan's resulted in a clampdown on all contact with Louisiana. When Juan Bautista Fortiere (or Forten) arrived in Nacogdoches a month after the Nolan crisis with sixteen horses, which he claimed he had caught near La Bahía, they were confiscated since the unfortunate fellow was unable to produce a passport. The horses were sold at auction, and Fortiere was put to work on the new church being built at Nacogdoches. Don Miguel de Músquiz, the military and political commander—the one who had led the assault against Nolan's "fort"—reported to Governor Elguezábal his compliance with orders that horses brought into the jurisdiction without proper license were to be attached and sold. The proceeds, he noted, were put on deposit until the commandant general should decide their disposition. Road guards (*cortaderos de caminos*) soon began scouting little-used routes into Louisiana for livestock smugglers.[45]

Nor were the restrictions on trade limited to hapless *vecinos* who wandered into the hornet's nest stirred up by Nolan. In May a letter was addressed to Elguezábal by Vicente Fernández Tejeiro, commander of a Spanish post on the Ouachita River.[46] Tejeiro, declaring that the military governor had so ordered him, asked permission to extract 300 horses, 300 mules, 300 mares, 16 jennies, and 8 jacks over the next several years. These animals were intended for Barón Felipe Enrique Neri de Bastrop's new settlements in Louisiana. Tejeiro urged the governor

---

[45] Myres, *Ranch in Spanish Texas*, p. 49; Castañeda, *Catholic Heritage*, 5:226; Músquiz to Elguezábal, May 9, 1801, Grazing Papers, vol. 2; Músquiz to Elguezábal, April 20, 1801, BAM, roll 30, frames 24–25.

[46] On his final trip to Texas, Nolan had written this officer a note saying that since his party did not possess a passport he would spare him "embarrassment" by not passing through his post, located near present Bastrop, Louisiana.

to use his "powerful influence" with the commandant general to gain approval of his request. Confident that Elguezábal would do so, the Ouachita commander sent at this time "the free mulatto, Lador Harmand, one of the most prosperous residents of this post, in order to bring back 100 horses. He will pay the required duties."[47]

Nava, however, rejected this seemingly legitimate request, doubtless because of the excitement over Nolan. It was no longer enough to have an accredited official of Spanish Louisiana backing a proposed stock transaction; Nolan had abused such methods beyond repair. Juan Lastrope found that contracts made before the trouble were no longer binding. He wrote Elguezábal in October, 1801, explaining that he had contracted with Manuel Barrera, son of the former *diezmero*, for the delivery of about 190 head of cattle and a drove of horses. In view of the current ban on export of both cattle and horses, Lastrope begged for an exception to be made in his case, but Nava refused.[48] The frenzy did not soon burn out. The restrictions on trade with Louisiana were still further tightened, but the horse-smuggling business was not easy to stop; on the contrary, it was just gathering momentum.

As the nineteenth century began, Spain's policy on trade across the thinly guarded frontier would, as always, remain out of touch with reality and be its own worst enemy. Concern was expressed, a few requests for information were made, and distant officials like Manuel Muñoz in Texas asked questions, formed lists, and tried their best to window-dress. But if the barriers remained, so did the time-tested ways of circumventing them. Except that now, along with the criminal frame of mind necessary to conduct such trade successfully, would come "heretical" political doctrines brought in by the Americans pushing ever westward into Spain's cloistered dominions. As Arthur Preston Whitaker has ably demonstrated, it was the demand for

---

[47] Myres, *Ranch in Spanish Texas*, p. 49, where it is noted that Fernández Tejeiro wrote inquiries on the purchase of stock as early as January, 1796; for his letter to Elguezábal of May 23, 1801, see Grazing Papers, vol. 1, pt. 2, p. 162.

[48] Castañeda, *Catholic Heritage*, 5:226.

trade, more than political or diplomatic considerations, which shaped the Spanish-American frontier during these years and defined the nature of its conflicts. "Trampling down with pitiless determination every obstacle to prosperity," the approaching American frontiersmen had a rainbow in sight. At its end was the fabled pot of gold, represented in real terms by broad, fertile lands and numberless herds of Spanish livestock. Nolan had showed the way, and for the next decade many others would attempt to succeed where he had failed.[49]

---

[49] Arthur Preston Whitaker, *The Spanish-American Frontier, 1783–1795: The Westward Movement and the Spanish Retreat in the Mississippi Valley*, p. 32; and Arthur Preston Whitaker, *The Mississippi Question, 1795–1803: A Study in Trade, Politics, and Diplomacy*, p. vii.

12
"BY RISKING THEIR HIDES A LITTLE"

At Revolution's Threshold

REGARDLESS of the strong influence that Philip Nolan's horse-stealing exploits may have had on Spanish borderlands policy, life in the province of Texas continued much as before. After all, this bold Irish-American only did what generations of Adaesaños had been doing long before him. The work of catching and breaking wild horses did not originate with young Philip Nolan. His was a quantitative contribution, not a qualitative one, despite the fact that historians have traditionally placed his accomplishments in a symbolic, if not heroic, context. And the notion that the Spaniards of Texas excelled in working horses was not new when Zebulon Pike expressed it soon after Nolan's downfall. This skill was common knowledge everywhere along the frontier.

The Reverend Edward Everett Hale, whose fictional treatment "The Man without a Country" (first published in *Atlantic Monthly* in 1863) unwittingly made Philip Nolan's name a household word for generations of Americans, later tried to atone for his blunder by researching the "real" Nolan. In a letter written in 1901 to the Mississippi Historical Society (accompanied by a translation of the trial documents of the Leales, Cook, and Longueville), Hale gave his verdict on the historic Nolan's significance. He believed that his "murder" in 1801 was the "beginning of that hatred of the Spanish and Spain which characterizes the whole of the Southwest up to the present moment." Such views may have had currency in 1901, but tracing Spanish-Anglo difficulties considerably past Philip Nolan should have presented no problem even to Hale, writing a century after the fact. Nolan's fate sent a message loud and clear to every other American adventurer: he entered Texas at peril to his life. Perhaps because the mustanger lost his in the wilderness on a cold, blustery day in 1801 accounts for Nolan's true significance to a culture obsessed by such symbolic "last stands." In this sense he was the first, and his party's fate was a legitimate precursor of the Alamo, Goliad, Santa Fe, Mier, and other such defeats for Anglo-Texans at the hands of an "alien" people. Spain's frontier guardians made their point, with Nolan's men, but they little reckoned with the obstinate nature of their opponents.[1]

While the dramatic climax on the Brazos River was building, events at Béxar were considerably more ordinary. In January, 1800, Elguezábal, who had just completed his first six months as governor, sent a report on the mesteño taxes collected at Nacogdoches under the commandancy of José María Guadiana. Assuming that the 132 pesos reported were collected on horses exported at 2 reales each, the sum represents only 532 animals, not many for the three years Guadiana had held his post. Although it is not certain whether this report was confined to Nolan's fees or represented all exports, surely it must have been the former. By comparison, however, Cristóbal de Córdova reported that at Nacogdoches, in the years 1792–94, he collected a total of 112 pesos, on 153 cows and 142 mustangs and that Nolan's exports during the period accounted for 60 percent of the total. Such poor showings perhaps contributed to

---

[1] E. E. Hale, "The Real Philip Nolan," Mississippi Historical Society *Publications* 4 (1901):228.

Nava's decision to rotate the Nacogdoches command several times a year.[2]

On May 8 the king issued a royal *cédula* on improving the livestock cared for by *dueños de ganado* (owners of cattle) of his kingdom. It called for separating bulls from cows and choosing the best bulls so as to improve the quality of the herds. Those that were not selected for breeding were to be fattened in different pastures and used as oxen or sent to market. Unfortunately, it was difficult to put the king's suggestions into effect on the broad grasslands of the Interior Provinces, especially where hostile Indians kept the ranchers' surveillance and control of the herds at a minimum. Nor were the incentives present to encourage development of better breeds, though many rancheros doubtless made attempts to do so simply out of pride in their stock. There is little evidence that His Majesty's decree had much impact in Texas, but it stands as an early example of progressive ranching techniques. Hard reality did not permit their implementation.[3]

Acting on a more realistic level, Governor Elguezábal wrote the governor of Nuevo Santander in October, 1800, regarding the proper season to catch wild horses, orders dictated by long-term experience. Hunts must be suspended from the end of February to the end of August, he said, because the colts died or were killed either during the roundup or inside the corrals. Pike's description of such corridas and the "insupportable" stench emanating from corrals packed with putrid carcasses leaves little reason to doubt the wisdom of Elguezábal's advice, especially when colts were vulnerable. The Spanish stockmen had special words to describe these scenes of mayhem and death. The word *hediondo* ("stinking") was applied to a pen clogged with animals that had died of *despecho*, the indignation, wrath, or nervous intensity resulting from being captured.

---

[2] Elguezábal to Cordero, January 22, 1800, Grazing Papers, Texas State Archives. For Córdova's reports, dated October 19, 1795, see R. B. Blake, Research Collection, Supplement ser., 3:253, 256, 258 (University of Texas Archives).

[3] *Cédula*, May 8, 1800, in Carlos E. Castañeda, *Our Catholic Heritage in Texas*, 5:204–205, and in Sandra L. Myres, *The Ranch in Spanish Texas, 1691–1800*, p. 30; Nava to Governor of Texas, August 26, 1800, BAM, roll 29, frames 642–43.

Other animals, like the colts, doubtless perished during the *susto*, the scare, that led to penning. Some animals simply died of *sentimiento*, a broken heart, unable to adjust to the loss of freedom. The governor of Nuevo Santander was instructed that when the customary time arrived to perform roundups he might send his soldiers for the task or ten other men responsible to royal justice.[4]

Captain José Miguel del Moral, who had taken Guadiana's job at the Nacogdoches post, wrote Elguezábal on June 26 that Choctaws had raided the ranch of José Ignacio Ybarbo near the settlement. Actually this ranch, Amoladeras, lay along the arroyo of the same name, a branch of the Attoyac about eighteen miles east of Nacogdoches. When Guadiana granted title in 1798, José claimed that he had "inherited" the place from his grandfather, Captain Gil Ybarbo, but he was really the captain's nephew, the son of Mariano. After killing two friendly Aís Indians and cutting off their heads, the marauders tied up a Spaniard and ran off the ranch's cattle. While the so-called Five Civilized Tribes were known to own valuable herds of cattle in the Creek country around the turn of the century—and also to engage in horse breeding—del Moral believed that the Choctaws' admission, then being proposed by the commander of the Rapides post, would bring no benefits whatsoever. He considered them under the influence of the English and hostile to the Texas tribes and feared their connections in Louisiana, including those that might be used in Rapides Parish for trade of illegally acquired stock.[5]

---

[4] Elguezábal to Governor of Nuevo Santander, October 17, 1800, Grazing Papers, vol. 1, pt. 2, p. 161, in response to Governor José Blanco's letter of July 22. In addition to Pagès's and Pike's vivid accounts of roundups, see Jean Louis Berlandier, *Journey to Mexico during the Years 1826 to 1834*, 2:545–46, for an even more detailed description of mustanging, including the roles played by *aventadores* (drivers), *puestos* (outriders), and *encerradores* (corralers); see also J. Frank Dobie, *The Mustangs*, pp. 215–34; Myres, *Ranch in Spanish Texas*, p. 27.

[5] Del Moral to Muñoz, June 26, 1800, in Castañeda, *Catholic Heritage*, 5:224; Nyal C. King, "Captain Antonio Gil Y'Barbo, Founder of Modern Nacogdoches, 1729–1809" (Master's thesis, Stephen F. Austin University, 1949), pp. 7–8. According to Berlandier (*Journey to Mexico*, 2:544), the Lipans and other Indian tribes caught and broke wild horses, which they sold to travelers and rancheros. They also branded their own animals with a mark "which the authorities have given them for their use," a practice Berlandier said was much abused; see the undated fragment of marks issued, doubt-

Early in 1801—at the time Nolan was busy catching mustangs near the Brazos—proceedings were being conducted in Béxar on the way beef was supplied to visiting Indian delegations. Juan José Curbelo submitted a report on the cost of such gifts, noting that in the month of January just ended fifty-five cows, valued at 10 pesos a head, had been distributed. Three steers had been supplied at the same rate. In April the price was down slightly to 9 pesos a head, bulls going for 7 or 6 pesos a head, depending upon the animal's condition. Juan José (born in 1771) was the son of Joseph Antonio Curbelo, who had conducted the royal buffalo to Spain. He, like many of his fellow citizens, was an Indian agent acting, as Frederick C. Chabot notes, in very "precarious" times.

Testimony continued into the summer. On May 23, Antonio Rodríguez Vaca (or Baca, as it was often spelled) appeared to explain why he, Governor Muñoz's meat contractor, had collected 1 peso per arroba (25 pounds) for several arrobas of fresh meat delivered. Rodríguez Vaca's contract obligated him to supply bulls at 4 pesos a head, either on the hoof or slaughtered and delivered from the country. Dried meat apparently being more valuable, the purveyor's defense was that he had substituted fresh meat only when supplies of *carne seca* were scarce. Yet, having charged the same price, 1 peso per arroba for fresh meat, was apparently enough to cause him problems, indicating that there was money to be made from Indian beef contracts in Spanish times, just as there was at a later date. These expenditures came out of the Mustang Fund, and it behooved government officials to keep their records in order, as trivial as the matter might seem.[6]

At the beginning of 1802, Governor Elguezábal issued a

---

less for their horses, to the Tancague, Comanche, Lipan, and Tahuacan tribes in BA, box 4D314, University of Texas Archives.

[6] Curbelo's report of January 31, 1801, is in Grazing Papers, vol. 2, as is the testimony of Indian beef contractor Rodríguez Vaca, as well as Curbelo's monthly reports for the entire year of 1807; see also Frederick C. Chabot, *With the Makers of San Antonio*, p. 156. A similar document for the year 1795, "Relación de los Gastos Erogados en la Manutn, de Sietecientos Ochenta y Dos Yndios de las Naciones Comancha, Tancahue, Tahuacanes, Ays, Vidais, Guichitas y Ahuaes . . . ," listing expenditures made from the Mustang Fund to maintain visiting Indians, is at this writing in the possession of the Jenkins Company, Austin.

proclamation addressing certain "long-time abuses" and their serious consequences to the public welfare. Several of the articles pertained to cattlemen. Owners of ranches must ask permission before going out to inspect their herds or making "raids" to gather stock. A report was required on all meats, fats, and animals taken. Owners of ranches were forbidden to add to their personnel without the knowledge and permission of judges. No hunting expeditions for unbranded stock could be conducted between March 1 and September 1 but were permitted the rest of the year. Owners of milk cows, calves, sows ("vulgarly called *sanchas*"), or hogs in the villa had to keep them enclosed. Otherwise, if someone's property was damaged, they would be deprived of their animals and subjected to fines.[7]

A few days later the governor turned his attention to a request for *mesta* information initiated by the Intendencia of San Luis Potosí. Although the intendancy system was devised in 1786, it was not until 1790 that Texas and Coahuila were put under the jurisdiction of San Luis Potosí, from which place the fiscal affairs of these provinces were then administered. When the five Interior Provinces were reorganized under Nava two years later, this Superintendencia Subdelegada de Real Hacienda was joined to his realm. As a practical matter, it took the new system another decade to penetrate distant outposts of New Spain and to affect ranching in Texas very much. The *intendente* (superintendent), Onesimo Durán, was apparently attempting to correct this situation in 1801. He required Elguezábal to submit a sworn statement of all *mostrencos* within the boundaries of Texas, indicating their number, classes, colors, and brands. Further, he wanted the report to indicate when they first appeared, in whose possession they were found, and whether or not due notice had been given "in order to see if the owners appear, as the law requires." All of this energy, it would seem, was directed to the end of auctioning off those *mostrencos* which had been held over a year and properly advertised without being claimed. Durán ordered such animals valued by two experts of integrity and sold to the highest bidder. This apparently was an estab-

---

[7]Elguezábal, proclamation, January 10, 1802 (supplemented on January 15 and 20), in Grazing Papers, vol. 1, pt. 2, pp. 164–65.

lished source of revenue in areas where strict *mesta* ordinances controlled stock raising.

Elguezábal answered with as much politeness as could be expected that within the province under his jurisdiction there were perhaps "some *mostrencos*" which were unbranded. He pointed out that in other years these *bestias* had been recorded, the proceeds of which were used for the ransom of captives from Indian tribes. After noting that the general superintendent was circulating a royal decree requiring all funds to be transmitted to the royal coffers, Elguezábal stated that such monies had been faithfully sent to Saltillo until the end of 1800. It is not known whether he ever bothered to compile the "certified report" Durán asked for, or whether he seriously considered such a ridiculous request. No one in Texas would have acknowledged that a single head of unbranded stock on their "haziendas, ranchos, y demas parages" was *mostrenco*, even if the governor had asked. After all the years of haggling over ownership of the wild herds, that much was certain.[8]

Smuggling was on everyone's mind in 1802. On April 3, Elguezábal ordered José María Guadiana, back in favor at Nacogdoches (as he would be, off and on in the coming years) to improve his watchful measures. The governor had been informed that exportations of horses to Louisiana were "excessive," and he wanted a corporal made directly responsible for controlling the situation. Ten days later Nava wrote Captain Francisco Xavier de Uranga at La Bahía, telling him that the export of horses and mules to Louisiana must be stopped. Exceptions were to be made only in legitimate cases, where the exporter had permits and passports. Nava repeated his protests of excessive exports in a letter written from Valle de San Bartolomé on October 27, having received word that 381 horses and mules had left the province without authorization. Nemesio

---

[8]Grace A. Edman, trans. and ed., "A Compilation of Royal Decrees Relating to Texas and Other Northern Provinces of New Spain, 1719–1799" (Master's thesis, University of Texas, 1930), p. 449, for the king's intendancy order of July 6, 1790; Viceroy to Muñoz, November 1, 1790, BA, noting same; Fr. Benedict Leutenegger, trans., *Journal of a Texas Missionary, 1767–1802: The Diario Histórico of Fr. Cosme Lozano Narvais, Pen Name of Fr. Mariano Antonio de Vasconcelos*, p. 32; Durán to Governor of Texas, November 28, 1801, and Elguezábal's reply, January 20, 1802, BAM, roll 30, frames 428–29, 538; also in Grazing Papers, vol. 1, pt. 2, pp. 163, 165.

Salcedo y Salcedo, whom the king had appointed commandant general in place of the retiring Nava, added his voice to the chorus. On December 21 he wrote Elguezábal forbidding either the export of stock to New Orleans or the admission of foreigners without passports. Salcedo had sent similar orders from Chihuahua back in April but repeated them for emphasis. An annual report filed at Nacogdoches was mentioned in the new commandant general's letter of December 21. For the year just ended, 1,187 horses and mules had passed through that jurisdiction bound for New Orleans, said to be probably one-tenth of the actual number taken from the province. Apparently the situation did not improve, because Juan Manuel de Salcedo, the governor of Louisiana, issued orders in May, 1803, again prohibiting the importation of cattle and horses from Texas.[9]

Indians struck a party of meat hunters at a place called Las Peñitas early in 1803, killing nine of them. From a report on the province made by Elguezábal in June, it seems that without the semiannual buffalo slaughters conducted in May and October most of the families would probably have starved. "It has been found that no profit will result from raising sheep," he said, adding that there were no more than a thousand head in the entire region. There was a "notable scarcity" of cattle as well. The other matter occupying the attention of Texans was "the catching of wild horses (a species in which the province greatly abounds)." At Nacogdoches, claimed Elguezábal, there were only a few horse ranches, most of the others being cattle spreads. This locality was considered far enough east to be safe from the plains Indians.[10]

Commandant General Salcedo wrote the governor on

---

[9] Elguezábal to Guadiana, April 3, 1802; Nava to Uranga, April 13, 1802, Grazing Papers, vol. 2; N. Salcedo to Governor of Texas, April 12, 1802, BAM, roll 31, frame 180; Nava to Governor of Texas, October 27, 1802; N. Salcedo to Governor of Texas, December 21, 1802, BAM, roll 30, frames 871–72, 1022–23. Odie B. Faulk, in both "Ranching in Spanish Texas," *Hispanic American Historical Review* 44 (May, 1965): 265; and *The Last Years of Spanish Texas, 1778–1821*, p. 91, mentions the report of 1802 of the Nacogdoches "lieutenant governor."

[10] "Minutes, Resolutions and Other Records of Cabildo," entry of February 14, 1803, BAT, 115:1; Elguezábal, "Report on Conditions in Province," June 20, 1803, in Mattie Austin Hatcher, *The Opening of Texas to Foreign Settlement, 1801–1821*, p. 67, app. 5, and referred to in Faulk, "Ranching in Spanish Texas," p. 263; also in Grazing Papers, vol. 1, pt. 2, pp. 151–55 (under date June 30); and in Blake, Research Collec-

March 14 asking for a report on the number of stock exported to Louisiana during Captain Uranga's tenure at La Bahía. The letter demonstrates the increasing concern that herds were being headed out from points near the coast, probably to avoid guards posted on the main road. The governor's reply was rather equivocal. He stated that Uranga was no longer available but that he had been told that the captain had done what he was "supposed to do." The governor said that he accepted Francisco Amangual's report of what had transpired during his absence and noted that passports had been issued. Subsequent investigation evidently proved otherwise, for Captain Uranga was convicted of disobeying orders and allowing horses to be transported to Louisiana. Juan Cortés, who had served at La Bahía previously, did not fare much better. Not only was he convicted of a shortage in his accounts but also the charge of smuggling was brought against him—ironically, by Captain Gil Ybarbo, whom he had been sent to investigate for similar offenses. The arrest of Cortés, and that of his son-in-law José de Jesús Alderete, had been approved by the commandant general as early as August, 1797, along with the usual confiscation of property. Cortés's exclusion from retirement privileges of settling near the frontier has already been mentioned.[11]

On August 11, 1803, the Béxar cabildo made reference to the fact that alcaldes of former mission settlements had been ordered to report all "roving outsiders" staying there and also to inform such transients of the possible unpaid fees they might be subject to on mesteños taken from August 1, 1799. Mention of this date, the approximate beginning of Elguezábal's term of office, could have been intended as intimidation, or possibly as a hint to move on. The judges of the Indian communities were forbidden to grant permits to squatters for roundups of mesteños without the governor's permission.[12]

---

tion, Supplement ser., 4:211–14, though the latter overstates the figure for sheep in the province, reading 1,000 as 10,000.

[11] N. Salcedo to Governor of Texas, March 14, 1803, and reply, BAM, roll 31, frames 136, 146–47. Uranga took del Moral's place at La Bahía in May, 1799. See Faulk, *Last Years*, p. 45; Blake, Research Collection, Supplement ser., 3:37; Nava to Governor of Texas, August 8, 1797, BAM, roll 27, frame 618.

[12] "Minutes, Resolutions . . . of the Cabildo," August 11, 1803, BAT, vol. 115.

It was not long before Guillermo (William) Barr, on behalf of his firm, formally protested the orders forbidding exports of stock to Louisiana. The House of Barr and Davenport's dealings with the Indians—along with their various ranching establishments and livestock interests—have already been mentioned. A report submitted at the end of November, 1803, by yet another new commander at Nacogdoches, Captain José Joaquín Ugarte (a report that was likely the basis for Elguezábal's subsequent report), sheds some additional light on Barr's activities. The agent presented for inspection animals that he wished to export, at which time an examination was conducted of those without brands. Excepted from this scrutiny were mustangs and colts from the herds of Indians, "all those [horses] purchased with the goods for their [the Indians'] use being furnished him without passport." Without passport, perhaps, but not without payment to the king of the standard 2-real head tax. For the goods they distributed they were allowed to receive horses, peltries, and so on, from the Indians in lieu of cash payment from the government, but the Mustang Fund was another matter entirely, and payment of the duties was a condition Barr well understood. His protest was not against the tax but against the prohibition on export of stock—in his case, at any rate.

The authority for Barr and Davenport's stock exporting arrangement was cited as the approval granted to Lieutenant del Moral on May 29, 1800. Ugarte established the agent's yearly acquisition of Indian horses as follows: "from the Bidais, 80 head; Tawakonis, 100; Nacogdochitos [Nacogdoches], 60; Aíses and Tejas, 100; Keechies [Kichais], 60; and Tonkawas, 100." At the time Barr had 250 Indian horses besides another 80 horses and mules used to conduct the trade, which Ugarte deemed very necessary to the maintenance of good relations with the various tribes. Reference to a possible increase of duties to 1 peso per head "in place of the 2 reales which is stipulated" indicates that Barr's trading privileges were also being reviewed in terms of their profitability to the Royal Treasury.

In his report to the commandant general on the following January 18, Elguezábal noted that in 1800 the government had placed Barr in charge of supplies for *los norteños*, a concession amounting to exclusive trading rights. The provision allowing him to drive stock to Louisiana had been canceled, however, when Salcedo's predecessor, Nava, curtailed trade. Elguezábal estimated that Barr handled 300 horses a year under such terms. Salcedo replied on February 14 that Barr was not included in his orders to prevent exportation. Consequently, he would be allowed to trade, a concession which the Nacogdoches commander acknowledged on April 3, 1804. Barr apparently abused this privilege, because two years later Salcedo ordered his exportations controlled.[13]

In December, 1803, the United States took possession of the Louisiana Purchase and camped troops outside New Orleans. On the twentieth the French colors were lowered, and "a few cheers" greeted the new flag, though more than four hundred Spanish soldiers were still in control of the city. It was an uneasy transition for all concerned, especially since no one really knew where "Louisiana" ended and "Texas" began. The tide of petitions from Spain's former vassals reached flood proportions even before the transfer took place. His Majesty, touched by these supplications, decreed on September 24, 1803, that loyal subjects in Louisiana might emigrate to other Spanish possessions and take their property with them duty-free.[14]

Added to this impending arrival of refugees was a call for more new settlements between Nacogdoches and Béxar, which eventually resulted in the founding of villas on the Trinity and San Marcos rivers and schemes for other settlements. At Nacogdoches, Captain José Joaquín de Ugarte[15] expressed the idea

---

[13] Barr, protest of orders forbidding export of stock, August 17, 1803, BAM, roll 31, frame 494; Ugarte to Elguezábal, November 26, 1803, Blake, Research Collection, Supplement ser., 4:241; Elguezábal to Commandant General, January 18, 1804; N. Salcedo to Elguezábal, February 14, 1804; Ugarte (at Nacogdoches) acknowledges permission for Barr to trade, April 3, 1804, all in Grazing Papers, vol. 1, pt. 2, pp. 166–69; N. Salcedo to Cordero, December 9, 1806, BAM, roll 35, frames 271–79.

[14] For a study of the transfer of Louisiana to the United States, and its implications for Texas, see Hatcher, *Opening of Texas*; Castañeda, *Catholic Heritage*, 5:293–94; Faulk, *Last Years*, p. 91.

[15] Although Commandant General Salcedo's letter to the governor of Texas dated November 10, 1803, speaks of the Nacogdoches captain as Juan, he evidently meant José Joaquín. Most writers (Castañeda, Hatcher, etc.) continue to credit a "Juan" Ugarte with the idea of new settlements.

that new centers of population would make it easier for his outpost—if there were a confrontation with the Americans—to obtain supplies. Replying on January 1, 1804, Elguezábal admitted that the intervening region was vast and contained many fertile spots suitable for settlements. But, he said, there were equally good or better locations close to the capital, as well as large bodies of irrigable lands. "Although they are very well cleared, the greater part of them are left uncultivated each year, as well as without stock for grazing." The lack of cultivation, he thought, was due to the disinclination of the settlers for agriculture and their scant numbers. The latter circumstance was attributed to the constant attacks upon them and their ranches by hostile Indians in past years, with the result that Béxar was one of the few populated areas in the province. Ugarte's proposal would not work, declared Elguezábal, unless settlers could be brought in and then offered protection from the Indians. Elguezábal was not opposed to new settlements or to immigration; he was simply a realist. Commandant General Salcedo had already instituted a set of procedures for admission to the region, and colonization had the blessing of the bishop of Nuevo León, not to mention the king himself. Thus, while the locations of prospective new settlements were being debated, asylum was given to those who wished to resettle in the Interior Provinces—preferably away from Nacogdoches and the temptations of contraband trade.[16]

Of these refugees perhaps none is more fascinating than José (Joseph) de la Baume. Born in France in 1731, he came to America and fought in the Revolution with Lafayette, after which he became "stranded" in Louisiana upon the outbreak of the French Revolution in 1789. He entered Spanish military service, becoming a lieutenant in the Ouachita militia and making the acquaintance of the Barón de Bastrop, which turned into a life-

---

[16] Hatcher, *Opening of Texas*; Castañeda, *Catholic Heritage*, pp. 287–88; Elguezábal to N. Salcedo, January 18, 1804, Grazing Papers, vol. 1, pt. 2, p. 166. Also useful to an understanding of this period is Odie B. Faulk, "The Penetration of Foreigners and Foreign Ideas into Spanish East Texas," in Archie P. McDonald, ed., *Eastern Texas History*, pp. 11–28; and J. Villasana Haggard, "Neutral Ground between Louisiana and Texas," *Louisiana Historical Quarterly* 28, no. 4 (October, 1945): 1001–1128.

long friendship. After the Louisiana Purchase he moved his family to Nacogdoches and petitioned Commandant General Salcedo to settle his family in Béxar or La Bahía, "wishing to continue following the Spanish flag." As this request was being decided, La Baume remained in East Texas, where he married a thirty-year-old mulatta named Feliciana (his third wife), and acquired a small rancho apparently in the Moral-Loco Creek vicinity, east of Nacogdoches below the Camino Real. Narciso la Baume was listed on the census of 1809 as a forty-year-old native of Ouachita who had the "ranch of La Baume sold him by Ortolant." He was no doubt the "mulatto" shown attending the La Baume Ranch in 1810 who registered a cattle brand at Nacogdoches as José Narciso Labomba. Perhaps Narciso was a son by José's first marriage, to Ana María Kentree, back in Ouachita.

Arriving in Béxar in 1806, La Baume built a stone house in the cottonwood grove near Mission Valero and applied for a 6-league grant of land for stock-raising in the vicinity of El Capote, the hills lying just below the Guadalupe River. He stated at that time that he had six sons, all employed in farming and raising stock. When title was received to 1 league of land in East Texas by José in 1834 (the year of his death at age 103), the tract was located in Angelina County, near Lufkin, not at the old ranch. The José de la Baume who joined other old-time Nacogdoches citizens in signing Córdova's manifesto of August 10, 1838, declaring that they were "tired of suffering the injuries and usurpations of their rights" was most likely a relative of the old French roustabout—either José Narciso or son Joseph, the latter born in Texas to La Baume's second wife, Louise Cuturie.[17]

Another interesting immigrant was Vicente Micheli. He was a native of Brecia, Italy (born about 1755), married to a woman from Natchitoches. Evidently Micheli was involved in the Indian trade, as were many other foreigners in the borderlands. In

[17] Chabot, *Makers of San Antonio*, p. 260; *Texas and the American Revolution*, pp. 51–53; Willie Mae Weinert, *An Authentic History of Guadalupe County*, p. 1. For La Baume's petition for admission of August, 1803, see Hatcher, *Opening of Texas*, p. 62 and app. 4.

1799 he persuaded Barr and Davenport to pay him 1,125 peltries for a claim held against the Nadaco and Nacogdochito Indians representing merchandise delivered—a claim the trading firm had trouble collecting. Early census reports of foreigners in Nacogdoches list him as a "suspicious character." Many new arrivals fell into this category, and Micheli freely went about his business. In 1796 he purchased 2,134 pesos' worth of Captain Gil Ybarbo's livestock, which was being auctioned to satisfy debts to Natchitoches creditors. The stock, sequestered at the captain's Attoyac ranch, consisted of mules, valued at 25 pesos; horses, 12 pesos; burros, 70 pesos; and wild cows, 8 pesos. Micheli also bought four slaves for another 1,100 pesos. In 1801 he was in Béxar petitioning Nava to grant him exclusive rights to establish the province's first cotton gin.[18]

Before moving to Béxar, Micheli, who appears to have been something of a speculator and "wheeler-dealer," acquired several ranches in East Texas. His principal holdings were a tract on the Angelina, south of Nacogdoches (a title for 2 leagues granted in 1810), and another 8 leagues straddling the Sabine at the Salinas Crossing (granted in 1797, the title mentioned in General Land Office records but the location in question).[19] He had help running these ranches, such as José Lucobiche, also a native of Italy, who arrived in Nacogdoches in 1796 and engaged himself as a merchant and "attendant" to Micheli. Lucobiche received title to Rancho Durazno, 6 leagues south of Nacogdoches; the General Land Office title shows 4 leagues granted in present Angelina County, across the river. The application papers of 1802 state that the "place named Durazno" was next to the lands belonging to Estévan Goget—where Micheli's grant was—although the Arroyo de Durazno (Peach Creek) empties into the Angelina some distance below this point.

In 1802, Micheli purchased the lands of Joaquín Córdova

---

[18] Blake, Research Collection, Supplement ser., 3:218; Micheli to Nava, April 17, 1801, and Nava's reply, April 20, ibid., 4:100; J. Villasana Haggard, "The House of Barr and Davenport," *Southwestern Historical Quarterly* 49 (July, 1945):76.

[19] In 1840, 4 leagues of this 8-league tract and one of 4 leagues on the Attoyac were sold for $5,000 by Micheli to Henry Wax Karnes (for whom Karnes County is named). Blake Research Collection, 53:239, 393; GLO, 37:301.

from his widow, Juana María Sierra, "at the place called the Aylitos on the River Attoyac," but a son, José Córdova, later contested the sale. In 1792, when Captain Cortés awarded the grant to Doña Juana María, it was described as being at the crossing of the Aylitos, 8 leagues above the rancho of Antonio Gil Ybarbo, 1 league to each cardinal point. When she sold it to Micheli, one of the conditions was that her sons could pasture their animals there, which suggests that the Italian land baron arranged for them to tend his stock also.[20] Besides these tracts Micheli had a ranch on the Trinity River near Villa de Salcedo, when this settlement was established in 1806; he appears on a list of brands for Trinidad along with his minor son Francisco. In 1810, however, he and his family are shown owning Rancho de San Francisco in the Béxar jurisdiction, where it seems they settled. The former Menchaca spread was listed in the *síndico* of Manuel Salinas, along with San Bartolo, La Mora, and the Guerras' ranch.[21]

The story of how Micheli came by this property, one of the earliest recognized ranches in Texas, is an interesting one. Captain Luis Antonio Menchaca died on September 29, 1793, at age eighty. The death of his wife, Doña Ignacia Nuñez Morillo, followed in 1800. Her will, dated September 12, makes no mention of a ranch, only several slaves, presumably body servants. Their son Luis Mariano died on June 22, 1803, aged fifty, survived by his wife, María Concepción de Estrada. Mariano's will lists Rancho de San Francisco as part of his real property. The year after he died, his brother José sold to Vicente Micheli "la mitad del Agostadero del paraje que llaman San Franco" (his half of the pastures named San Francisco), for 440 pesos. Possibly this sale was negotiated as early as 1794. In any event, on July 17, 1806, Micheli petitioned Governor Cordero saying that Captain José Menchaca had not kept his part of the agreement and allowed him to occupy the purchased land. It was ruled that Micheli had the right of formal possession and that he was to be permitted to build his house somewhere south of "palo

---

[20] GLO, 37:258, 376; GLO, 41:65.
[21] *Síndico* of Manuel Salinas, January 2, 1811, BA.

quemado" (Burnt Wood, apparently a ranch or ranching community), as long as he did not infringe on the rights of Los Hernándezes.[22]

Because the prominent land speculator José Cassiano later acquired part of the lower Menchaca grant from Vicente Micheli, documents relating to the transaction are found in the Cassiano-Pérez Collection in Daughters of the Republic of Texas Library. The documents include a power of attorney given to P. L. Buquor in 1844 by Petra Villarreal, shown as Micheli's wife (the Nacogdoches census of 1809 lists an earlier wife, Susana "Moro," as a widow from Natchitoches, age thirty-nine, with two children, José and María Josefa). Another document is a statement dated February 2, 1835, which confirms that Micheli had sold to Cassiano two *sitios* of Menchaca land on the lower part of the San Antonio River next to the Hernández grant. Cassiano consolidated four large tracts of land in El Rincón through various negotiations and in 1844 tried to develop it into a town called Capote. His partner, Alexander Henry Bourgeois de'Orvanne, was unable to attract people to the area, and the scheme fell through. A decade later fellow land merchant John Twohig sold three hundred acres of Hernández land to Polish emigrants, and the town of Panna Maria (Virgin Mary) was founded. This colony rapidly expanded into a flourishing Polish community, its roots deep in unguessed-at ranching tradition.[23]

Unlike many who took advantage of the king's generosity in this stockman's paradise, Vicente Micheli seems to have remained a staunch supporter of the Spanish crown after moving to Texas. As suggested, his land dealings were complicated, and it was perhaps some unhappiness over the Republic's treatment of them that caused Micheli to become involved in the Córdova Rebellion; he died in 1847. But this Italian and the Frenchman

---

[22] John Ogden Leal, "Burials of San Fernando," 2:82; will of Luis Mariano Menchaca (University of Texas Archives, box 2Q236); Bexar County Deed Book F1, pp. 44–48, BCSA.

[23] Cassiano-Pérez Collection, folders 63, 113, 114, 118, 208, Daughters of the Republic of Texas Library at the Alamo; Hedwig Krell Didear, *A History of Karnes County and Old Helena*, pp. 22–32; *Herndon v. Cassiano* (1851), *Reports of Cases Argued and Decided in the Supreme Court of the State of Texas*, 7:161–69; hereafter cited throughout as *Texas Supreme Court Reports*.

La Baume were perhaps exceptional men. Many other newly arrived colonists simply lingered around Nacogdoches and caused Spanish authorities to worry over both their loyalty and their contraband activities, especially the unruly American element.[24]

On February 4, 1804, Captain Ugarte mentioned the ranch of Don Antonio Gil "Ibarrero" at "Atoyaque" and the cattle left there ten years before, which had multiplied in great numbers. Now the captain's son-in-law Juan Ignacio Guerrero wanted title to the ranch, said Ugarte, and other heirs were also pestering him. In addition to children and grandchildren by his first wife, María Padilla, the old pioneer had remarried after his "exile" to Bexar. There was so much dispute over his estate that Ugarte doubted that any of the heirs would ever enjoy the benefits of the feral cattle grazing on Gil Ybarbo's ranch. Consequently, he suggested that these animals be declared wild or stray so that the local inhabitants, and the Royal Treasury as well, could derive some benefit from them.[25]

This was far from the first time that the former captain's descendants (said to number more than seventy) had requested disposition of stray stock at the Attoyac rancho. Beginning in 1798, Gil Ybarbo himself had asked Nava's permission to gather up and dispose of scattered stock in his summer pastures, 20 to 30 leagues from Nacogdoches. Amazingly, permission was granted on September 18, with the strict proviso that he could go to Nacogdoches for such purposes but could not remain there. Muñoz, who was carrying on a running feud with Gil Ybarbo at the time, nonetheless gave him approval in mid-1799 to "receive the properties belonging to him" in the area. Lieutenant Guadiana reported on July 13 that Gil Ybarbo had appeared in Nacogdoches with an altered passport (to give himself more time there) and had gone to a ranch "where he had left his baggage." In November, del Moral informed Elguezábal

---

[24] Ericson, *Nacogdoches, Gateway to Texas: A Biographical Dictionary, 1773–1849*, pp. 100, 196.

[25] Ugarte to Elguezábal, February 4, 1804, BA. On February 2, 1804, the governor submitted a report on the Mustang Fund as of the end of 1803, showing a balance of 2,051 pesos (Grazing Papers, vol. 2).

that the old pioneer had left the jurisdiction, his mules loaded with fats and some household items such as jars and carpenter tools, "without being included the least thing of contraband." Apparently he voluntarily returned to Béxar, where he was living in 1800 when his will was probated in response to the demands of his first wife's children. Among the possessions listed was Rancho "Atoyaque," on which stood a house of wood with a thatched roof and iron nails; also mentioned was stock, including those found in summer pastures, that is, running wild. In January, 1802, Nava granted Gil Ybarbo permission to move to Louisiana, but Governor Elguezábal kept him at Béxar because of some debts incurred by a son-in-law, for which the former captain as surety was responsible. In the spring of 1803, Lieutenant Guadiana wrote Governor Elguezábal that the family still had not gathered the cattle as planned but that, when they did, notice was to be given by agent Juan Ignacio Guerrero, "as well as the rest of the heirs making the chase and butchering cattle in the summer pastures of the Attoyac Ranch, bearing among them notice of the herds of cattle that each one may avail themselves for proving it when they come to carry out a division of said properties." In other words, they were to keep track of their cattle hunts. From Ugarte's recommendation of February 14, 1804, it is obvious that they did not and that he was disgusted with the whole situation.[26]

Commandant General Salcedo issued a proclamation on February 16, 1804 (supplemented on October 22, 1807) setting forth various provisions he wanted applied to stock raising. For every 1,000 head of cattle a *caporal* (range boss) and four men—two mounted and two on foot—must be provided as tenders. Three men were specified for each 1,000 sheep or goats in a flock. Ranch owners who suffered enemy raids without immediately notifying a judge and arranging pursuit would be fined 25 pesos. The idea, of course, was to let hostiles know

[26] Muñoz to Nava, June 12, 1799; Guadiana to Muñoz, July 13, 1799; del Moral to Elguezábal, November 14, 1799; Nava to Elguezábal, January 19, 1802; Elguezábal to Nava, February 17, 1802; Guadiana to Elguezábal, March 9, 1803, all in Blake, Research Collection, Supplement ser., 4:24, 33, 40, 159, 166, 193; Gil Ybarbo to Nava, August 22, 1798; Nava to Muñoz, September 18, 1798, ibid., 3:403, 410.

that they could not commit depredations with impunity. Finally, all persons found in settlements or ranches without passports or permits were to be evicted and returned by the *jueces de partido* (district judges) to their place of origin.[27]

Salcedo issued several other directives in 1804. One, issued on May 28, authorized Elguezábal to allow 120 horses to pass through Texas to New Orleans, where they were needed for cavalry mounts. They had been requested by Pedro (Pierre Clément de) Laussat, prefect of Louisiana under France, and were to be charged off at 2,150 pesos, 4 reales, "total cost of said mounts" (averaging about 20 pesos). Exceptions of this sort were made from time to time. Elguezábal, for example, allowed Celestino St. Maxent, a captain in the regiment stationed in New Orleans, to move a large number of horses to Louisiana. This officer had taken his mother to Puebla and had received the viceroy's permission to travel overland on the return trip. The horses, he claimed, had been used to transport baggage from Puebla to the Rancho del Palo Blanco, near Mier, and St. Maxent wanted to continue with them by way of La Bahía. In view of the circumstances—it was November, 1801, at the height of the Nolan backlash—Commandant General Nava had agreed. In 1781, Gilberto Antonio St. Maxent had been given a contract by the Spanish king to supply the West Florida Indians with French goods, as he had been doing since O'Reilly's day. He was Governor Bernardo de Gálvez's father-in-law, the marriage of Felicité de St. Maxent d'Estrehan and Gálvez having occurred in 1777. Antonio, a son of Gilberto's, was in charge of the new Spanish post at Gálveztown in 1781, and the father, called a "rich merchant," was commander of militias in New Orleans in 1789. If Celestino was also his son, this would largely explain why permission was granted in this unusual export of horses to Louisiana, for the memory of Don Bernardo de Gálvez was held dear in New Spain.[28]

On July 31, 1804, Salcedo forwarded the *asesor*'s opinion

---

[27] N. Salcedo, proclamation, February 16, 1804, Grazing Papers, vol. 2.

[28] N. Salcedo to Elguezábal, May 28, 1804, ibid.; Castañeda, *Catholic Heritage*, 5:228; Edman, "Compilation," p. 442.

in reference to stock taken from smugglers: it was to be sold at public auction and the proceeds placed in the Mustang Fund. This was in accordance with existing policy; still, it helped to have solid legal opinion behind operational procedures. Involved was the seizure of thirty-eight horses and mules (a number which later grew to seventy-three) belonging to the free mulatto Dionisio Denis. Joseph Navor Menchaca and Santiago Flores were driving them to Louisiana when they were caught. The commandant general ordered the prisoners released, after "first threatening them with a greater punishment in case of repetition." Many similar smuggling cases were prosecuted until the end of the decade, but Pedro Galindo Navarro would not assist in their resolution. He died in 1805, somewhat out of favor with the commandant general because he had recommended leniency in the trial of Nolan's men.[29]

On November 15, Don Nemesio ordered Elguezábal to permit no outlaw animals in the caballadas of horses and mules. He was advised not to add such animals in the future or allow them to be purchased as remounts; experience had shown that they were too troublesome and unfit for duty. On December 20 he also forwarded to the governor orders—based on a royal decree of June 22—that all tallow, meat, salted meat, and rice were now duty-free. These orders were acknowledged on February 1, 1805, by Dionisio Valle, newly appointed commander of the Nacogdoches post. His letter also noted that, by official letter of January 6, "I have been informed that I am to prevent the driving of horses and mules from this province to Louisiana without making any exceptions for privileged persons." Only animals that were brought in could be taken out again, and Indian agent Barr's traffic was limited to pack mules used in his trading.[30]

Several reports were given in the summer of 1804, possibly

---

[29] N. Salcedo to Governor of Texas, July 31, 1804, Grazing Papers, vol. 2. One such case occurred in May, when Manuel de León, "trader for the Comanches," left the main road with his caballada of thirty-five horses and mules. Since this was considered a "suspicious act," he was placed in prison, and his animals were confiscated, a list being made of their brands (ibid., vol. 1, pt. 2, p. 170).

[30] N. Salcedo to Elguezábal, November 15, 1804; Valle to Elguezábal, February 1, 1805, ibid., pp. 174–75; Blake, Research Collection, Supplement ser., 5:9.

aimed at providing information on the question of new settlements. Nacogdoches, which had 68 foreigners in its environs at the beginning of the year, contained a total of 791 persons according to a report made by Captain Ugarte on August 1. He noted that exports of horses from the Indians were 400 head annually. The citizens lived by hunting, including wild horses and cattle; and although 3,000 cattle (worth 12 pesos each), 1,000 horses (worth 15 pesos each unbroken), 100 mules, 20 burros, 600 hogs, 100 sheep, and 15 goats were reported, Ugarte said that there was no stock raising in the jurisdiction. Similarly, on June 30 a report was sent to the governor from La Bahía. It showed some statistics under section 7, "Stock Raising," as follows: cattle—5,600 at 10 pesos each (if grown); sheep—1,370 at 2 pesos each; hogs—17 at 6 pesos each; goats—168 at 1½ pesos each; horses—1,500 (no price shown); mules—250 (no price shown); and burros—7 (no price shown).[31]

The long, exposed border below Nacogdoches along the Sabine River was mentioned by Captain Ugarte in a letter to Elguezábal dated November 4, 1804. To keep herds of horses from being driven up the coastline into Louisiana, he suggested sending a twelve- to fifteen-man detachment to Orcoquisac or

[31] Report to governor from La Bahía Presidio, June 30, 1804; Ugarte to Elguezábal, August 1, 1804, Grazing Papers, vol. 1, pt. 2, p. 171. This report is also found in Blake, Research Collection, Supplement ser., 4:362. Ugarte noted under "Exports" that 20,000 hides were sold in Louisiana yearly at 3 reales each; presumably these were pelts and skins rather than cowhides. Faulk, *Last Years*, p. 122n.40, mentions the census of 1804.

the old ranch called Atascosito so that they could "continuously reconnoiter" that section. Ugarte wanted the patrol to range north, up the Trinity River, to the place known as Santa Gertrudis. The clampdown on horse traffic into Natchitoches had obviously encouraged smugglers to seek new routes considerably off the Camino Real. Opelousas and Attakapas lay beyond the lower Sabine, which flowed one hundred miles below Nacogdoches before reaching the coast, if one was bold enough to try the direct route across the lowlands (it was called the Opelousas Road, for obvious reasons). The higher, more established corridor could still be used simply by moving stock off the main road and crossing them at places not frequented by *cortadas de caminos* (road guards).

Actually, Elguezábal had suggested to Commandant General Salcedo the previous August 15 that Orcoquisac was an ideal place to stop the illegal horse herds bound for the region of Attakapas. He pursued this measure in January, 1805, ordering Sergeant Juan Antonio de Urrutia to take a squad "from the new detachment of Orcoquisac," join other men stationed at Arocha's ranch, and proceed to Atascosito by the shortest route. While he was to maintain good relations with local Indian tribes, the primary object was to reconnoiter as far as La Bahía and the crossings immediately above and below the Trinity River, "as well as places where horses might travel, so as for the time being to prevent them from being driven to Louisiana." He was especially to try to catch persons like the mulatto Denis and Pedro Procela, notorious for their past doings.[32]

At year's end Father Bernardino Vallejo, residing at the partially secularized San José, gave a dismal report on the Texas missions. Rosario and Espíritu Santo had only a few cattle, lately placed there by the priesthood. He was careful to point out that the livestock did not belong to the missions but was strictly for the needs of the missionaries and the Indians. None of these establishments (those at Béxar at any rate) had funds, since their properties were distributed among the converts, "who

---

[32] Ugarte to Elguezábal, November 4, 1804, Grazing Papers, vol. 1, pt. 2, p. 173; Blake, Research Collection, Supplement ser., 4:378, 5:4.

have kept but little." Fray Huerta's census of 1803 at Mission Rosario shows 600 head of cattle, no doubt considered insufficient by past standards.[33]

Juan Bautista de Elguezábal's term effectively ended in July, 1805, when because of illness he was forced to turn the day-to-day affairs of the province over to another. A few months later he died in office, as did his predecessor, Manuel Muñoz. Still, on May 22 the ailing old veteran of His Majesty's service wrote a letter welcoming the newly designated commandant general, Pedro Grimarest, to his post. Elguezábal trusted that he would land safely on the coast of Nuevo Santander, commenting that according to reports, it was better stocked with herds of cattle and horses than were the other three provinces. Texas had no large horse herds "because of the severe drought which has prevailed for many months." Grimarest was prevented from assuming his appointment by Spain's latest war with England. At one point he wrote Elguezábal that he intended to slip through the English blockade and land near the Río Grande. Nemesio Salcedo continued to act as commandant general until 1813, although the province of Nuevo Santander was under viceregal control, not administered by his commandancy.[34]

The man appointed to assume Elguezábal's responsibilities was Antonio Cordero y Bustamante, governor of neighboring Coahuila. As noted, he had been chosen earlier to relieve Muñoz but had been unable to break away from pressing duties at Monclova. No sooner had Cordero made a survey of Texas than he reported his priorities to the commandant general. In his mind, in importance second only to strengthening the military defenses at the three posts (San Antonio, La Bahía, and Nacogdoches), was the founding of new civil settlements. The empty spaces must be filled with colonists and ranchers if the province

[33]Vallejo, "Report on Missions," December 31, 1804, Grazing Papers, p. 175; also in Fr. Benedict Leutenegger and Fr. Marion A. Habig, comps. and trans., *The San José Papers, August, 1791–June, 1809*, pt. 2, pp. 228–36; Fr. Marion A. Habig, *The Alamo Chain of Missions: A History of San Antonio's Five Old Missions*, pp. 105, 220; Fray Huerta, Rosario Census, May 10, 1803, ACZ, roll 3, frame 3988.

[34]Faulk, *Last Years*, pp. 21, 28; Castañeda, *Catholic Heritage*, 5:290–93. For a comparison of ranching in the four eastern provinces at this time, see Nettie Lee Benson, trans. and ed., *Report of Ramos Arizpe*, pp. 21–22.

was to be permanently occupied. Thus did the proponents of immigration to Texas win a strong advocate in the first decade of the new century.[35]

Cordero's opinion could not be brushed aside lightly. He had long experience on the frontier, having served under all the commandants general from Croix to Nava. Pike, who was considerably impressed by Cordero's abilities, left a crisp picture of the governor, calling him "by far the most *popular man* in the *internal provinces*." Cordero, born in Spain, was said to be a man of great learning who spoke Latin and French. He was universally beloved and respected, being generous, gallant, brave, and sincerely attached to his king and country. Physically, said Pike, the new governor of Texas was about 5 feet 10 inches tall, was fifty years of age (in 1807), and had a fair complexion and blue eyes. He wore his hair "turned back," and in every area of his deportment was legibly written "The Soldier." "He was," said Pike, "one of those select officers who had been chosen by the court of Madrid to be sent to America about 35 years since, to discipline and organize the Spanish provincials and had been employed in all the various kingdoms and provinces of New Spain."

Cordero was thus a member of the elite *gachupín* class of Spanish administrator so familiar to the native-born creoles of New Spain. Although friction had been building between these two classes for generations—especially at Béxar and other frontier settlements with strong mestizo infusions—Pike thought that both Cordero and his counterpart in Nuevo León, Simón de Herrera, were adored by the masses. The American visitor, focusing on the military aspect of what he saw, apparently missed the love-hate dichotomy that would soon plunge Mexico into tortured revolution. This is not to say that Pike was oblivious to class distinctions in New Spain. He commented, in fact, on how the government had multiplied the difficulties of Europeans intermarrying with the creoles or "Metifs" (mestizos) to such a degree that it was difficult for such marriages to take place. Such

---

[35] Castañeda, *Catholic Heritage*, 5:309–69, notes Cordero's advocacy of "unrestricted immigration."

niceties vanished where daughters of officers with the rank of captain or upward were concerned. "Rank purifies the blood of the descendants," Pike wryly observed.

Nor did Pike miss the nuances of polite society, although to the Protestant outlook of his culture these activities seemed to border on "gratification of the sensual passions" or "voluptuous dissipation" or to be reminiscent of "Turkish" society. "The general subjects of conversation among the men are women, money and horses, which appear to be the only objects, in their estimation, worthy of consideration." More to the point, he noticed the staggering number of beggars living in a land so rich in gold and silver, concluding that it could only be accounted for by the tyranny of the government and the luxuries of the privileged class. That Cordero himself maintained a greatly embellished residence in "Montelovez" (Monclova), before being required to relocate in San Antonio after the United States took possession of Louisiana, did not seem to classify him as a tyrant. On the contrary, Pike found both Cordero and Herrera, who was in charge of Spanish troops near the Neutral Ground, united in their hatred of "tyranny of every kind." Such were the contradictions of a people on the brink of civil war.[36]

Despot or not, Cordero wasted no time addressing the laxities he saw around Béxar. In September, 1805, he conveyed to the cabildo a decree of seven articles regulating different aspects of town life, including idleness and restrictions on travel. He wanted the citizens to maintain arms and horses for possible military duty, to build walls around their houses, and to plant trees. He forbade them to go on roundups or journeys when there was "work to be done" and required settlers, transients, and residents to obtain passports before traveling. After these permits were issued, plans could not be changed, for instance, in the matter of hunting and rounding up wild stock. The governor wanted to keep tabs on his subjects, especially those considered of lower extraction and few responsibilities, and article 7 was designed to end the thefts of livestock common among those classes. Thus he prohibited those of "low birth and few

---

[36] Donald Jackson, ed., *Pike's Journals*, 1:439–41; ibid., 2:83–84.

obligations" to travel to ranches unless they first presented themselves to a justice and received a permit. Such people must report upon leaving and returning; exceptions were to be made only in urgencies, and even then the ranch owner had to submit an account of the circumstances. Cordero assured his subjects that upon compliance with these measures would depend the safety of the hacendados' property and that of all raisers with stock on the range. This *bando* was promulgated at Béxar on November 10, 1805, following closely on the heels of a decree of September 21 aimed at controlling the contraband trade in cattle and horses.[37]

Another matter that Cordero took under consideration was management of the public food supply, a previously haphazard affair left to individual *carneadores*. On October 25, Cordero wrote the commandant general that he had called for the establishment of a public slaughterhouse and meat market in Béxar. Following Salcedo's wishes, he asked for bids from contractors, but none came forward. This, thought Cordero, could be remedied by an exclusive license issued by the cabildo for two weeks or a month. It was a privilege that could be divided among the capital's residents and raisers, other slaughtering forbidden during each license period except for the sustenance of families. As one license to kill and deliver beef was nearing termination, another could be issued so that the citizens would suffer no lapses of supply. A commissioner would be appointed to see that all beef offered for sale was good, only cows and steers being used. Each fifteen-day licensee must include two beeves obtained from a "reputable widow" or other needy person in the community.

On October 29, 1805, these provisions were published by *bando* establishing Texas's first public butcher shop. It called for fifteen-day licenses, as approved by the commandant general, and decreed that meat could be sold only at a house to be built for this purpose. Rates were set at 1 real per 4 pounds of meat and bone. A report filed the following January gives additional insight into the operations of the *carnicería* (slaughter-

---

[37] See BAT, 115:51, for the *bando* of September 21, 1805; Grazing Papers, vol. 1, pt. 2, p. 177, gives the date of its publication as November 10; see also BAT, 33:622.

house). A royal tax of 3 reales was levied on each head butchered, from which amount the wages of a meat cutter were paid. For a twenty-day period of the preceding November this "servant" drew 4 pesos, 5 reales, which worked out to a mere 1.7 reales a day. Detailed records continued to be kept on this operation.[38]

The settlement of Trinidad de Salcedo, one of Cordero's main projects, was accomplished in January, 1806. Where the Camino Real crossed the Trinity River, 5 families from Béxar joined 23 other immigrants from Louisiana in founding what Spanish authorities hoped would become a flourishing villa. These Bexareño families were headed by Pedro Cruz, José Borrego, José Manuel Casanova, Francisco Travieso, José Luis Durán, and José Aldrete (who soon died)—a total of 16 persons. The first three of these registered stock brands at Trinidad. By 1809 the settlement had 101 inhabitants, bolstered by the relocation of 11 families that had gathered at the outpost of Atascosito, near the mouth of the river, under William Barr's sponsorship. Cordero, writing the commandant general on January 28, spoke out on the benefits to be derived from immigration since the province, in its present condition, could not defend itself and had to import subsistence even to feed local troops.[39]

On the same day he told Don Nemesio that his precedessor's (Nava's) orders of August 18, 1798, requiring soldiers to guard settlers' horses were working a hardship. The Indian threat which had necessitated such orders, he said, was no longer present, not to mention that the horses—mostly wild—were continually stampeding, wreaking havoc, and causing the loss of many mounts belonging to the soldiers. This information had come from Captain José Joaquín de Ugarte, commander at Béxar, who had expressed favorable views on the need for new settle-

---

[38] BAT, 115:64, also in Grazing Papers, vol. 1, pt. 2, pp. 179–82, as is Cordero to commandant general, October 25, 1805, and the report of January 3, 1806, on the Béxar *carnicería*. Chabot, *Makers of San Antonio*, p. 239, gives an account of Cordero's meat market.

[39] For the settlement of Trinidad de Salcedo see Cordero to commandant general, January 28, 1806, Grazing Papers, vol. 1, pt. 2, p. 183; Castañeda, *Catholic Heritage*, 5:310–18; Faulk, *Last Years*, p. 126.

ments while stationed at Nacogdoches; no doubt he regaled the new governor with those views at the capital. Cordero wanted the settlers to have their own *situado* and guard it themselves, freeing his troops for more pressing duty. The commandant general responded favorably to this request a year later, as shown by Captain Ugarte's letter of March 23, 1807, in which he reported that the military's and the settlers' stock had been separated as ordered. Interestingly, as late as February 17, 1827, the Béxar alcalde, José Flores, was protesting the refusal of the military to let citizens put their stock with soldiers' animals, "which lessens chance of theft by Indians."[40]

The duty that Governor Cordero had in mind for his troopers was most likely related to protecting the new colony on the Trinity, apprehending smugglers and contrabandists, and recapturing stock taken by the Indians. A report submitted on April 19, 1806, by Sergeant Vizente Tarín of horses and mules which he took from the Comanches illustrates such activity. This list, complete with brands, is one of many such records kept throughout the remainder of the Spanish and Mexican periods, now in the Béxar Archives. While some of these animals were claimed by their owners upon publication of the brands, it would seem that most of them were distributed to soldiers in need of mounts. A list of branded animals taken in 1821 by troops in a mustang roundup describes the procedure as follows: "The horses were distributed among the said troop, with the understanding that they are to return them to their legitimate owners as soon as these obtain their release." Otherwise, they were to be entered into the treasury by an appraisal of the horses' or mules' value, an evaluation "which will be made as the governor of this province may determine."[41]

The recaptured animals that displayed known brands were "in justice delivered." Four of those taken by Tarín were recognized as belonging to Corporal Coy, of the Río Grande Company, and delivered to him. Most other lists also indicate the company

---

[40] Grazing Papers, vol. 1, pt. 2, p. 187; ibid., vol. 2. Captain José Joaquín Ugarte later served as lieutenant governor of the province during Manuel de Salcedo's inspection tour of 1810.

[41] "Report of the Branded Horses That Were Captured in the Corrida of Mesteños Performed by Troops under Captain Juan de Castañeda," August 22, 1821, ibid., vol. 2.

of soldiers to whom retaken horses of uncertain ownership were awarded. When strays bearing unknown brands were turned in by settlers, they were duly recorded and held for six months, after which time they were auctioned, supposedly to the benefit of those who had brought them in. At least this was the policy recommended by Commandant General Rengel's decree of December 9, 1784, in which he dispensed with Croix's fanciful schedule of recapture fees. It appears that as a practical matter such animals—like those confiscated from smugglers—"benefited" either the Royal Treasury or the soldiers who took them, as long as legitimate owners did not appear. The appraised value of these animals was then charged against the pay of the soldiers receiving them.[42]

Perhaps to expedite transfers of this nature, brand lists were formed. Two such Texas lists of brands have survived, both undated but from around this time. The first list, entitled "Northern List for the Recognition of Brands," contains fifty-five names, many of them from Béxar. The list cannot predate 1788 because that was the year in which Juan de Arocha died, and his widow, Doña Manuela Móntes, is shown. Most of the names—such as Manuel Barrera, Doña María Josefa de la Garza, Santiago Seguín, and Félis (de) Arocha—suggest that the list was drawn up between 1800 and 1810. The other list is for Nacogdoches and Trinidad and shows earmarks as well. Since it contains the brand of "Guillermo Barr y Davinport," a partnership which was dissolved upon Barr's death in 1810, and sets the jurisdiction of Trinidad apart from Nacogdoches, the period 1806 to 1810 seems appropriate. Many of these brands, like those in the Béxar list, were doubtless in use before this compilation. As might be expected, the East Texas list contains a number of hispanicized Anglo names—Guillermo Quark (Quirk), Santiago Dil, Reymundo Noris, Henrico Cheriden, Miguel Quin,—while that of San Antonio contains none (see brand sections D and E).[43]

A document written by José Luis de la Bega on March 7, 1807, gives additional information about the ranches around

[42] "List of Horses and Mules Which Sgt. Vizente Tarín Took from the Comanches," April 19, 1806, ibid., vol. 1, pt. 2, p. 184.

[43] "Northern List for the Recognition of Brands" (n.d.), BA; Nacogdoches and Trinidad, "Fierros y Señales" (n.d.), BA.

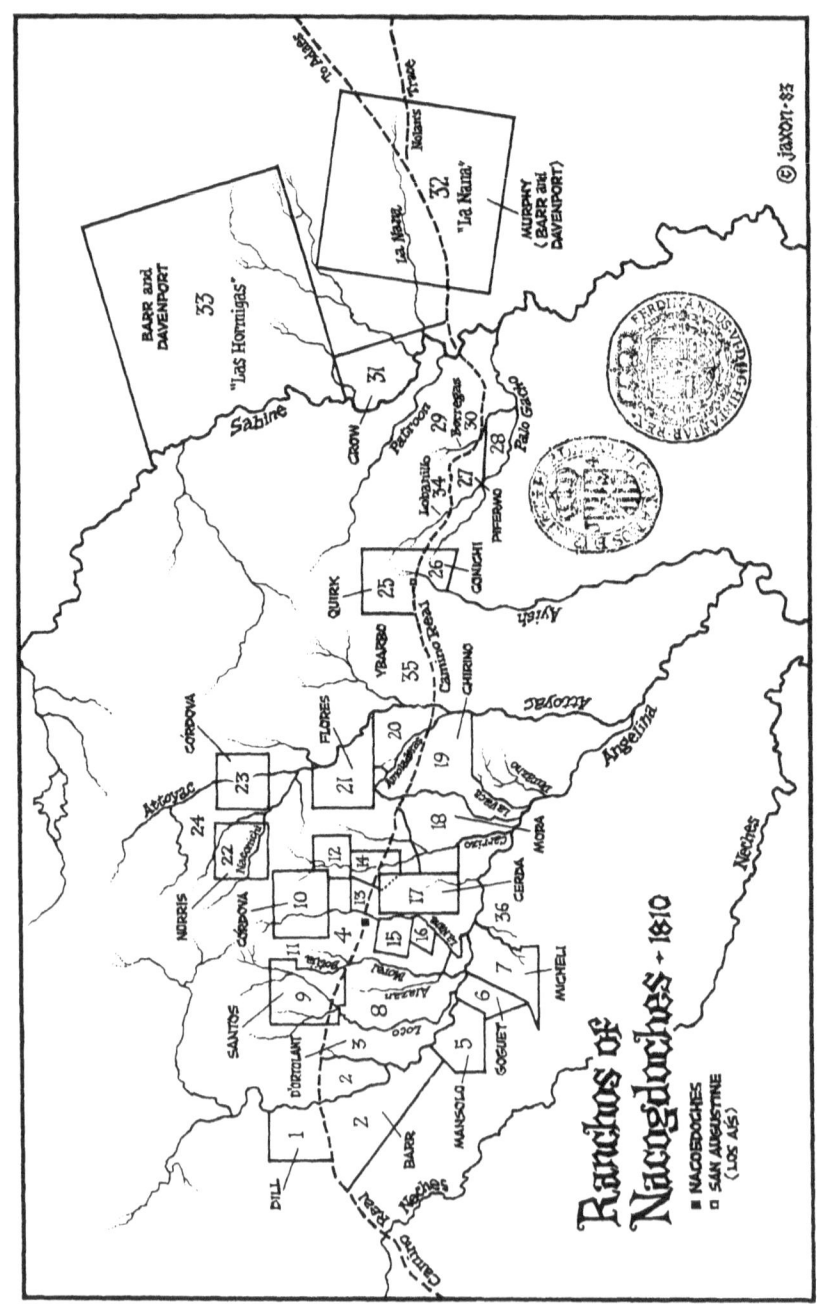

Nacogdoches ("los Ranchos de este Pueblo"). Bega notes the name of each establishment and the intervening landmarks, beginning with "Rancho de Manuel Mora." From there he lists the ranches and place names as follows: José Morilla, Cerda, "su yerno" Estévan Morín, La Biña, Goguete, Los Monsolos, Don Guillermo Barr, Don Bernardo Dortelan, El Salto, José Antonio Cruz, Juan de Acosta, de Labome, Juan José Sánches, La Botija, Manuel Raso, Francisco de los Santos, Guerrero, Mariano Cruz, Pedro Padilla, José Córdova, José de los Santos Coy, Martín Cruz, and "Nacanichi," a bayou named for those Caddoan Indians. Then Bega passed El Guajolote and Tortuga to the ranches of Martín Ibarvo, Villalpando, Don José Flores, José Ignacio Ibarvo, Baltasar de la Garza, El Atascoso, Don José María Mora, Gerónimo Hernández, Pedro Bartolomé Orrachal, José Antonio Chirino, and de Amoladeras to the Atollaque River. Beyond that point the listings are brief: Conichi, Rechar, Cuerque, El Patrón, Sonca, Berván, Yonson, La Leone, Chichi, Cidra, and La Biña again, ending with Juan Boden "de Borregas."[44]

A careful study of this route, along with the brand lists and other records compiled at Nacogdoches in the years 1809 and 1810, sheds considerable light on outlying ranches at the turn of the century. For example, the March, 1806, patrols of carbineer Juan Galbán and José María Guadiana in pursuit of horse smuggler Enrique (Henry) Quirk, brother of the trading-post operator Edmund Quirk, provide many details about routes, ranches, and the contraband trade of the time—through the medium of a diary kept by Guadiana. Most important are the records kept at the General Land Office supporting these grants, whether or not they were eventually recognized. Thus from a variety of sources we can arrive at a fairly clear picture of the East Texas ranches when Anglo stockmen were just beginning to establish themselves among the older Hispanic settlers.[45]

[44] José Luis de la Bega, "Direcsión que se deve tomar para ir a los Ranchos de este Pueblo . . . ," March 7, 1807, Blake, Research Collection, 28:378.
[45] Diary of José María Guadiana, March 11, 1808; patrol of Juan Galbán, March 2, 1808, Grazing Papers, vol. 1. See also the case "against foreigners Enrique Kuerke, José Megui, Juan Macfarson and José Brenton for contraband trade in livestock," January 19, 1809, ibid.

While some of the ranches visited by José Luis de la Bega, who bought the Old Stone Fort from Gil Ybarbo in 1805 and then sold it to Barr the following year, are easy to place, others are not, suggesting that they were less important establishments (the numbers in the following text refer to the numbered grants shown on the map "Ranchos of Nacogdoches, 1810"). Of the Mora family it is known that José María Mora owned Rancho San Francisco, granted by Lieutenant Guadiana in 1810. It was slightly over 4 leagues, situated on "Atascosito" Creek (no. 18). "Cerda" probably referred to Nepomuceno de la Cerda, born about 1752 at Los Adaes. He owned Rancho San Antonio, extending half a league in each direction, granted by Captain Cortés. It lay west of Mora's ranch, and while the customary method of marking distance would have yielded only 2 square leagues, the records of the General Land Office show that the fortunate Don Nepomuceno was awarded 3½ leagues in 1792 (no. 17). Doubtless his son-in-law Estévan Morín lived nearby.[46]

The next ranches mentioned by Bega clearly indicate that he was well to the southwest of Nacogdoches, traveling up the Angelina River. Goguete was Estévan Goguet (also spelled Gouget, Goget, etc.), and his ranch, called Goguet or Angeline, lay below the river (no. 6). A trader-farmer from the Arkansas Post, he married Juana de Lara, the "half-caste" daughter of grantee Pedro de Lara Pasos (or Posos), who had received the land from Captain Juan Cortés. It was shown on the census of 1809 as having a 1-league frontage, 4 leagues in depth, and it appears to have been part of the basis for sales made to Barr and Davenport and Micheli. According to Haggard, the House of Barr and Davenport acquired part of the old Lara grant from Goguet in payment for a note of 800 pesos. Early maps also show the Micheli tract as part of the original Pedro de Lara grant.

[46] For supporting documentation on this scan of East Texas land grants see primarily the Nacogdoches census of 1809, in Carmela Leal, comp. and trans., "Translations of Statistical and Census Reports of Texas, 1782–1836 . . . ," (microfilm), roll 2; personal research of Linda Flores Bowen, an Adaesaño descendant, kindly shared with the author; Blake, Research Collection, vols. 18, 19; GLO records, by name of grantee (which is cited for each ranch discussed), i.e., José María Mora, GLO, 37:471; Nepomuceno de la Cerda, GLO, 37:201.

Before continuing west, Bega listed "Los Monsolos," apparently the ranch of Tomás Mansolo (no. 5). Lieutenant Guadiana promised this "half-caste" native of Adaes his place in 1799, and it was granted in 1810 for 1½ square leagues. "Mansolo Road" connected Nacogdoches to the Angelina River ranches below the Camino Real, indicating that his residence was both early and well known. According to R. B. Blake, the King's Highway to La Bahía left Nacogdoches in a southerly direction, fording the Angelina at the "Don Joaquín" (later known as the Procela Crossing), where Highway 35 now crosses. The mouth of Bidias Creek, in Angelina County, is near the "Paso Tomás Monsola" of olden times (the confusion in name spellings is also typical of those days).[47]

Adjoining Goguet upriver was the property of William Barr, the ranch San Patricio of 5 leagues (no. 2) mentioned in the census of 1809 as "had in sale" authorized by Lieutenant Guadiana. Granted to Barr in 1798, it was adjacent to the concession of Bernardo D'Ortolant, "which is next to the old Presidio and east and west above the King's Highway," measuring 2½ leagues square. Title was confirmed in 1804 and again in 1810 to the firm of Barr and Davenport. It is shown on grant maps under Juan (John) Durst, Davenport's adopted son, title given in 1832, consisting of 8 leagues, 23 *labores*. In 1829, Durst and another heir swapped their possessions in Louisiana and Texas, Durst remaining in Mexican Texas. This ranch was likely the one Pike described as a settlement 2 miles east of the Angelina, a little over "four hours" from Nacogdoches. Davenport also left Durst another 10,000 acres in his will, part of the Posos grant that the firm obtained from the old man's son-in-law in 1810.

Above the river east of Barr was Bernardo D'Ortolant's Rancho San Bernardo (no. 3), granted by Guadiana in the neighborhood of Loco Creek and apparently an important establishment. Previously the ranch was the site of Presidio de los Dolores, which would put it 8 leagues west of Nacogdoches along the King's Highway, just below present Douglass. Don Bernardo had served in the campaigns of Gálvez and was active

[47] Estévan Goguet, GLO, 37:385; King, "Captain Antonio Gil Y'Barbo," pp. 31–33.

in the militia at Natchitoches and later at Nacogdoches, where he was shown as captain in 1804. The title to D'Ortolant's ranch was no doubt jeopardized by his role in the revolutionary decade; he was one of the three "foreigners" refused pardon in Arredondo's decree of 1813. General Land Office title records show a tract of 4 leagues given in 1797, but its location is uncertain. Other accounts have it on the left bank of the Angelina, opposite Tomás Mansolo, bounded on the north by lands of Francisco de los Santos and on the west by Barr.

Although it was not visited by Bega, there was another important ranch in this vicinity, the one belonging to James Dill (no. 1). One of the Anglos who arrived early, about 1793, Dill was a licensed trader among the Nacono, Nasoni, and Anadarko tribes until he fled to Natchitoches in 1813 as a result of the revolution. He returned to Nacogdoches in 1821, when Erasmo Seguín escorted Stephen F. Austin through the country, and was installed as alcalde. Several years later Dill was ousted from office by a junta of disgruntled residents; he died around 1825. Title to his 4-league grant was vested in his widow, Helena Kimble, in 1828. Their daughter Delilah Dill married Joseph Durst, brother of John (mentioned above), both of whom were active in the Texas Revolution and affairs of the Republic.[48]

It seems there was a waterfall ("El Salto") between D'Ortolant's ranch and José Antonio Cruz's El Moral, although the location of the latter is hard to place. Perhaps it was near the tract acquired by Mariano Santa Cruz from Matías Peña in an extrajudicial sale, although some evidence suggests that "Nabato" was near Naconiche. Similarly with the Juan de Acosta Ranch, but because "de Labome" (José de la Baume) was mentioned next and appears to have acquired land from Bernardo D'Ortolant, it is likely that these men lived between Loco and Moral creeks, below the road to Béxar. Mention of La Botija, a branch of the Moral, and the ranches of Juan José Sánches and Francisco de los Santos strengthens this assumption.

[48] William Barr (John Durst), GLO, 30:259; Bernardo D'Ortolant, GLO, 37:273; James Dill, GLO, 38:593, 68:124; *Texas and the American Revolution*, pp. 49–50; Hatcher, *Opening of Texas*, app. 25.

Santos' Rancho Loco (no. 9) was on the arroyo of that name. Title to 3½ leagues was confirmed in 1827 under the name of Francisco's sons, "Manuel Santos Coy and brothers." On the east was the Sánches place, La Botija (no. 11), described as "three leagues in width and two in length" lying along the Arroyo Botija. It was sold to José de la Bega, but Mariano Sánches remained there and worked the place "as his own." Mariano's brother Manuel had part of it by sale, and their brother-in-law Ramón Chavana lived on a nearby ranch, El Moral, which had been sold by the clan's patriarch Juan José Sánches to José "Piefrnas" [Pifermo?], a transaction authorized by Lieutenant Guadiana. Despite these sales this old Adaesaño family remained active stock raisers, since they were the ones staying and doing the work.[49]

From these ranches Bega moved in an eastward sweep above Nacogdoches, mentioning the Padillas' Rancho Santo Domingo (no. 4), one of the oldest in the area. As previously noted, it was said to have been one of the first places reoccupied in 1779, and perhaps Captain Gil Ybarbo stayed there at his father-in-law's while the settlement was being shaped up. Don Pedro Silverio Padilla died in Louisiana about 1814 or 1815, a poor man possessing only "5 or 6 cows," another of the many refugees from royal authority following the failure of the Gutiérrez-Magee filibuster. The next large spread belonged to the Córdova family, 3½ leagues on La Nana Creek; title was granted in 1810, but it was another old one. Given to Joaquín Córdova by verbal permission, it was run by sons José, José María, and Manuel (no. 10), who also managed their mother's ranch on the Attoyac, although Bega did not mention the widow Juana María Sierra's 4-league grant (no. 23). Since present landgrant maps show José de los Santos (Coy) claiming 1 league of this tract and his name was noted, perhaps this explains why hers was omitted. The other stops on Bega's route of 1807, Manuel Raso, Guerrero, and Mariano and Martín Cruz, are difficult to place.

Not so "Nacanichi." Belonging to Reymundo (Edmund)

---

[49] Juan José Sánches, GLO, 18:15, 19; Francisco de los Santos, GLO, 37:491.

Norris, Rancho Naconiche (no. 22) was originally granted to Saragoza Santa Cruz, who sold it to Matías Peña, who sold it to McWilliams, "all in informal sale." Norris acquired the place in 1806, although the exact transaction was never pinned down. His claim was acknowledged in 1810 and again in 1824, but the title caused his heirs considerable litigation. The grant was described as situated 12 to 14 miles northeast of Nacogdoches and west of the Attoyac, with Norris's house squarely in the center. Again, it was one of those league-to-each-direction grants, amounting to 4 square leagues of land. Peña lived four or five miles away, possibly at the place called Guajolote (Turkey), and testimony reveals that his land came to him through his wife, María Villador Arriola, a daughter of Marcelino. Norris died in 1828, but sons Samuel and Nathaniel were involved in various scrapes, including the Haden Edwards trouble and the Córdova Rebellion. Above the Norris place was another ranch, Santa Rita (no. 24), which Bega omitted. It was on the Attoyac at some ill-defined spot ("en el paso real de la tortuga") and was owned by José Caro. It was not the present site of Caro, however, which is in the José Antonio Caro 1-league grant north of Nacogdoches. Santa Rita, 1 square league, was granted by Francisco Viana in 1808, although title to 2 leagues was recognized. Caro, an Indian born about 1771, was listed on census reports as "servant" or "farmer."[50]

Going down the right bank of the Attoyac, Bega then turned toward town. He passed José Flores's Rancho Tortuga (Turtle Ranch) of 4 leagues, which later documents cite as "lying on the River Atoyaque and the Bayou Tortuga" (no. 21), granted in 1792 and confirmed in 1810. He was the son of Gil Flores, an old-time Adaesaño and compatriot of Antonio Gil Ybarbo. José's first wife was Ana Guerrero, a granddaughter of Gil Ybarbo, and their daughter Cleta married neighboring rancher José Ignacio Ybarbo, who was the captain's nephew. Flores was listed "as attorney of this place" on the Nacogdoches

[50] Pedro Padilla, GLO, 37:163; José [Joaquín] Córdova, GLO, 37:483; Juana María Sierra, GLO, 41:65; Reymundo Norris, GLO, 37:47; José Caro, GLO, 37:452; R. B. Blake, "Records . . . Relating to the Edmund Norris Four League Grant" (typescript, Texas State Archives); Blake, Research Collection, vol. 32.

census of 1804. Next door was his son-in-law's Rancho Amoladeras (no. 20), the site of the Choctaw attack mentioned earlier. José Ignacio's father, Mariano, was deceased, and this grant of approximately 4 leagues was made in his name by Lieutenant Guadiana in 1798. Also living there were his mother, four brothers, and a Sánches brother-in-law.

Closer to the villa was the ranch of José Ignacio's uncle, Martín "Ibarvo" (Ybarbo). It was called El Carrizo (no. 12) and consisted of 2 square leagues "had by sale" from Captain Cortés. A native of Adaes, the captain's brother was married to María Josefa Arriola, another half-caste, and title was granted under her name in 1810. Across the Arroyo Carrizo lay Antonio Arriola's square league (no. 13) "inherited from his parents, who had it by sale authorized by Captain Don Juan Cortés." This and María Josefa's tract were doubtless the old Arriola Rancho described in former times as being on the outskirts of Nacogdoches. Also in this area was the ranch of Francisco Villalpando, a native of New Mexico and an Indian trader rejected by the Tonkawas in 1800 because of his "ungovernable and captious nature." José Flores also owned another tract, El Carrizo (no. 14), 1 league, used "to plant corn and beans." It was granted by Captain Valle and confirmed in 1829 to his son Vital. According to testimony given by Vital in 1871, José Flores, already noted as an attorney, and José Luis de la Bega were the two men commissioned in 1810 by Governor Manuel Salcedo to "grant titles to lands in this Nacogdoches Municipality."

Almost back to his starting point, Bega came to San José, the ranch of Baltasar de la Garza. It was east of Cerda and was described as bounded on the north by the lands of Captain Gil Ybarbo and occupied earlier by Dimas Moya (as shown in the census of 1809). Also in this vicinity (between the Carrizo and its branch the Atascosa, south of the Camino Real) was a ranch owned by Pedro Procela, made to him by Gil Ybarbo in 1780 or 1782, and west of Cerda was a small ranch owned by Pedro José Esparza (no. 16). Gerónimo Hernández and Pedro Bartolomé Orrachal were apparently in the same area. Back to the east, between the Carrizo and La Vaca creeks, was the Mora Ranch already noted; and east of it, bordering the Attoyac, was the big spread of José Antonio Chirino (no. 19). A native of Los Adaes (born about 1755), he married María Antonia de Mora in 1792 and, after her, María Antonia de los Santos in 1804. In 1792 title was granted in his name to 5 leagues, and in 1833 he received 9 leagues, both tracts in Nacogdoches County. Documentation of these two large grants, including several excellent plat maps by Thomas McFarland, is in the General Land Office.[51]

Across this stream, of course, was the Rancho Attoyac of the exiled Captain Gil Ybarbo (no. 35). It was being operated by his grandson Francisco Guerrero, but, curiously, Bega does not mention it. Yet Gil Ybarbo soon returned to his house built with nails that stood near La Lunaca, where he died soon afterward. The commandant general wrote Governor Cordero the year after Bega's survey that the seventy-nine-year-old Adaesaño could live "in any post except Nacogdoches or one on the Louisiana border," a safeguard which presumably did not include his ranch.[52]

Once beyond the Attoyac, foreigners abounded. Because the process of acquiring land from the crown was a long and involved one, it is not to be expected that many Anglo or French colonists would be shown as ranch owners at this early date. On the contrary, it is surprising that so many newcomers were recognized as ranchers, having obtained land through sale or trade with the original grantees—or, in a few cases, as grantees themselves. Landed or otherwise, they were rapidly moving in, as Pike noted. Some of them professed "great attachment" to the government in the presence of crown officers; once out of their hearing, however, they voiced contempt for all things Spanish. This attitude was part of what worried those officials who advocated a liberal admission policy.

One of the more notorious Anglo-Celtic enclaves was "Tiquitania," owned by Edmund Quirk (no. 25), whose name

---

[51] José Flores, GLO, 37:174; José Ignacio Ybarbo, GLO, 37:347; Antonio Arriola, GLO, 37:121; Baltasar de la Garza, GLO, 37:402; Pedro Procella, GLO, 38:501; José Antonio Chirino, GLO, 33:313, 327; and GLO, 37:154.

[52] N. Salcedo to Cordero, September 14, 1808, in King, "Captain Antonio Gil Y'Barbo," pp. 103–105. See also ibid., pp. 115–17, for the petition of 1810 of his daughter María Antonia Ybarbo de Guerrero for her deceased father's ranch at Attoyac, including the place called "La Lunanca."

was spelled by the Spaniards as Quark, Cuerque, Kuerk, and Kuerque. His ranch, as seen, was that granted to Antonio Leal and wife by Gil Ybarbo when he was captain of militia. Ironically, title was not received until February, 1800, just a year before Nolan died and the Leales were obliged to part with the property. It consisted of 4 leagues on both sides of "Aies Bayou," north of the highway. Upon obtaining it in 1801, Quirk established a trading post there with the backing of Edward Murphy. It was something of a settlement. Living at Tiquitania were Quirk's wife, Anna Alsop; his son William (married to Edmund Norris's daughter Anna); his son-in-law Anthony Parrott; Denis Quinelty; Rafael Sims (Symes); and various "squatters" from time to time, such as the Rechar (Richards) family that had been involved with Nolan. Some eventually obtained land from the Spanish government, among them Santiago Conilte, or "Conichi" (James Quinelty); "Cidra" (James Cedar); Richard Symes; and Miguel Cro (Michael Crow). Crow owned the property called San Miguel de los Patrie (no. 31), granted to Miguel Viciente by Governor Oconor in 1769 and bought by Crow thirty years later. It straddled the Camino Real at Paso Chalán, a ferry on the Sabine. Crow's home was situated on an island overlooking the ford. He maintained a way station and was able to avoid expulsion during the Neutral Ground disturbances, although in 1812 he was briefly arrested by Americans, his house sacked, his stock killed, and his wife's earrings stolen.

Quite a few Frenchmen were settled near the Sabine River. In addition to Cedar at Rancho Borregas (no. 30), there was James Lepine at Rancho Patroon (or Patrón), a square league occupied by virtue of a sale (granted by Músquiz) but not later recognized (no. 29). Lepine, a native of New Orleans, had lived in Nacogdoches since 1797 and called himself a carpenter. Bega's list also mentions a Juan Boden living on Arroyo Borregas and a man named Berván in the vicinity. Below the road was Cristóbal Chonca (also spelled Sonca, Yonca, Yucante, and Yocante) at Rancho Palo Gacho (no. 28). This grant, possessed with the verbal permission of Captain Gil Ybarbo since 1782, was not later recognized. Many other French families settling on Sabine tracts suffered the same fate. Chonca was a French-

Canadian, born around 1739 and married to Mariana (identified as an Apache). Above the road was Pedro Tessier (or Tesie). Also a Canadian, he was shown occupying a ranch on Lobanillo Creek (no. 34) in 1809 "without judicial document." Yet another Canadian, José Tessier (relationship unknown) was shown at the ranch called Salinas, or Salinillas, purchased from Santiago León, who had settled and cultivated it with the permission of Captain José Joaquín Ugarte. Another José Tessier, a veteran of Gálvez's campaigns from Islas Negras, Louisiana, had a ranch on the Angelina River near Nacogdoches.

Juan Ignacio Pifermo owned Rancho Lobanillo (no. 27), 2 leagues square (4 leagues, granted in 1794) obtained from Miguel Larrua upon authorization of Captain Ugarte. It must have adjoined Borregas Creek because Santiago Sidre (James Cedar) was shown living there in 1809–10 "on land of Pifermo." This appears to have been the vicinity of Captain Gil Ybarbo's once-prosperous establishment which authorities considered a blemish or "wart" on their attempts to control smuggling across the frontier. Pifermo also owned "Chichi," a rancho of 1 square league on the Arroyo de la Agua, granted by Lieutenant Cristóbal de Córdova.[53]

It is interesting to note that José de la Bega's list did not take into account the many ranches beyond the Sabine River, including Barr and Davenport's extensive holdings. But, as later lists and the testimony taken by U.S. commissioners in 1824 to establish Neutral Ground land claims show, there were many French, Spanish, and Anglo stock raisers in the Bayou Pierre region, down to Juan de Mora Lagoon (Spanish Lake) and old Adaes. Also, Bega modestly did not reflect his own landholdings, having acquired several choice tracts in addition to occupying various administrative posts at Nacogdoches. Besides the Sánches ranch described in item 11, he owned a tract (no. 15) 6 leagues by 1½ leagues (a sale authorized by Cortés) and 1 square league bought from "citizen Guerrero" which in

---

[53] Edmund Quirk, GLO, 37:355; Santiago Conichi [Quinelty], GLO, 38:673, 63:138; Richard Symes, GLO, 22:669, 68:18; Cristóbal Chonca, GLO, 37:57; Juan Ignacio Pifermo, GLO, 37:240; Louis Rafael Nardini, *My Historic Natchitoches, Louisiana, and Its Enrivonment*, pp. 108–14, 134.

1809 was being worked by Andrés Acosta. Another small holding was being tenanted by Damián de Arocha and family. One thing does emerge from a scan of the list of ranches of the Nacogdoches jurisdiction formed by this middle-aged native of Castile: stock raising was indeed practiced in East Texas, and the Anglo herdsmen who were spilling into the area did not find it devoid of an actively practiced ranchero tradition, regardless of their professed hostility toward Spanish culture.

Soon after Bega made his tour (if he did not in fact compose the list sitting behind a desk), Zebulon Pike and his party passed through Texas. Reaching Natchitoches on July 1, Pike confessed that he felt a surge of patriotism as they once again beheld the American flag waving aloft. His graphic descriptions of manners, morals, and customs have already been alluded to, along with his description of Spanish saddles, mustang roundups, and the Spaniards' superior horsemanship. Certainly this bright young American lieutenant did not hold the Mexican horse culture in contempt, nor did he share the backward views expressed by an American named Johnson (doubtless Bega's "Yonson") who had moved his family west of the Sabine, that is, across the "line." And if there was a shortage of wild horses in Texas, from drought or any other reason, Pike did not notice it, commenting that the inhabitants traded them to New Orleans by way of Natchitoches. This trade, "being contraband, is liable to great damage and risks," he added, almost as an afterthought. While he began seeing wild horses the first day after passing the Río Grande and continued to encounter them all the way to the Trinity, Pike is curiously silent on the subject of cattle, wild or otherwise. Either his route did not take him near wild bovine herds, or the herds *were* depleted; or perhaps the officer's mind was on horses and mules to the exclusion of cattle. Since Pike's *Expeditions* (published in 1810) was read by many adventurous Americans as an encyclopedia of the wealth that awaited them beyond the Sabine River, one is led to the conclusion that Texas was indeed no longer as rich in cattle as it had been in former times. On the other hand, Louisiana's relative richness in cattle could have caused him to emphasize the commodity this province needed: horses, of which Texas had an abundance.[54]

Most stock-smuggling cases during the decade so indicate. Typical is one in September, 1807, in which José Antonio de León, a native of Camargo, was found guilty of stealing four horses from a herd belonging to Don Vicente Micheli and selling them in Opelousas. For this offense de León was sentenced to six months in chains, doing public works in the barracks of the company of San Carlos de Parras; he was advised not to return to Nacogdoches. José María Rioxas, a resident of La Bahía, was convicted of the theft of horses and mules in that vicinity during the month of November. His sentence: one year in jail. But since he had a family to support, he was allowed to work during the day and return to confinement at night. Another case "por Extración de Cavalleda para la Provincia de la Louisiana" was pressed against five persons at La Bahía in 1809–10. Castañeda mentions a suspected exportation scheme involving William Barr, his packtrain privileges, and an "enterprising character" named Francisco de la Rosa. Evidently there were many such enterprising characters on the frontier during those years.[55]

Apart from the clamors of immigrants attempting to gain admission and those of residents trying to get horses and mules out, conditions in the province were rather dull. After much

---

[54] Jackson, *Pike's Journals*, 1:446, 2:77. Pike did not include cattle in his "Animals" section for the province of Texas, mentioning only horses and "wild hogs." On his trip to Texas, in 1805, Bishop Marín de Porras also commented on the wealth of wild horses, saying they went in herds of 4,000 to 6,000 (Sandra Lynn Myres, "The Development of the Ranch as a Frontier Institution in the Spanish Province of Texas, 1691–1800" [Ph.D. diss., Texas Christian University, 1967], pp. 79–80).

[55] Faulk, "Ranching in Spanish Texas," p. 265 (also in his *A Successful Failure*, p. 144); Faulk, *Last Years*, pp. 91, 111; Castañeda, *Catholic Heritage*, 5:32.

deliberation on the idea of rebuilding Mission Rosario (including an opinion from the *fiscal*), orders were given on December 15, 1806, to consolidate Refugio and Rosario. During the following year this problem was further discussed. In February, Commandant General Salcedo wrote Cordero on the decision to move the Indians and their priest to Refugio while repairs were being made at Rosario. Estimates on new buildings and other improvements came to 500 pesos, but by August, 1808, the 200 head of cattle that were supposed to underwrite this expense had been used for other purposes. It would seem that the scheme hardly justified all the paperwork generated, for a detailed report given in June, 1809, by Governor Cordero showed that Rosario's Indian population was "greatly diminished" by runaways; he reported that Refugio's Karankawa Indians spent most of the time at the seashore. Fray José María Huerta de Jesús called it a "true fact" and well known that Rosario's Indians had been living in the woods for a long time because there was not sufficient stock to support them. A report on the Mustang Fund at La Bahía tallied 100 pesos for the year ended 1807. In one entry, dated October 10, future empresario Martín de León paid 32 pesos' royal duty on 128 mustangs rounded up, working out to the usual 2 reales a head.[56]

In July a group of citizens from San Fernando (Coahuila) were charged with violation of the ban on chasing mustangs, which limited such corridas to the period September through March. Cordero instructed the first-ranking alcalde to send them home after confiscating their *bestias* (mesteños) and *herradas* (marked animals). The former were to be sold at auction, the proceeds going into the chest, while the latter would be disposed of in the proper manner, that is, held as *mostrencos* and advertised for the required period. During the following month Mariano Varela, captain at Béxar Presidio, reported to Cordero that the balance in the Mustang Fund was 7,660 pesos.

---

[56] Much correspondence on the consolidation of Rosario and Refugio is found in BAM, rolls 34, 35. See also Huerta to governor, April 17, 1806, Grazing Papers, vol. 1, pt. 2, p. 183. For mention of Martín de León's early mesteñero activities see H. B. J. Hammett, *The Empresario: Don Martín de León*, pp. 6–7; C. L. Douglas, *Cattle Kings of Texas*, pp. 9–23.

His company had repaid 7,609 pesos for the "small loans made to it by your order," spent to take care of the great amount of business that came up in 1806. These expenses, which it appears had drained the fund almost dry, were perhaps associated with the interception of the Freeman-Custis Expedition, the negotiation of the Neutral Ground, and the founding of Trinidad de Salcedo.[57]

Governor Cordero in the meantime was pushing ahead with plans for another settlement, this one where the King's Highway crossed the San Marcos River. It will be recalled that various plans had been advanced over the years to locate settlers in this fertile region so conducive to stockraising but that Indian hostilities had ruled them out. In contrast to Trinidad, Cordero wanted to populate San Marcos de Neve with colonists drawn from the interior of Mexico. There is evidence that he had personal interests in so doing, spending a considerable sum of money to establish the settlement and introducing livestock of all kinds, owned by him but tended by vaqueros working under Felipe Roque de la Portilla.

The governor negotiated with Portilla for the enterprise, which included bringing sixteen families of herdsmen from Nuestra Señora del Refugio (Matamoros), the little village on the lower Río Grande. On August 29, 1808, Portilla wrote Cordero from Rancho Santa Rita informing him that he was leaving and would be at the Nueces River by mid-September. He expected an escort of twenty men to be awaiting him at the Santa Margarita Crossing (a mile below the site later chosen for the Irish colony San Patricio), on Don Martín de León's ranch. Also, he expected to be met with the 200 pesos for forty horses wanted by Captain Varela. Portilla explained that great danger to the caballada was expected from *mesteñadas*, wild horse herds encountered along the way. He stated that he was bringing 24 herds of horses and mule colts with 17 trained burros in front, a total of over 1,200 animals. Fifteen mules would carry the expedition's supplies, and thirty men would be employed to tend the stock, which would be herded in two divisions. Unfortunately, dry weather had already cost them 400 head. Cordero

---

[57] Cordero, decree, July 22, 1808; Valera to governor, August 25, 1808, BA.

replied that he would send soldiers from La Bahía to conduct the settlers to their destination. Other families were drawn from the river towns, as well as from Béxar and Nacogdoches, but the settlement proved short-lived and was abandoned before 1814. By that time Cordero was back in Coahuila, where he remained in an official capacity until 1817.[58]

In the summer of 1808 a new governor for the province of Texas arrived from Spain. He was Manuel María de Salcedo, a nephew of Don Nemesio, the commandant general, and a son of Juan Manuel de Salcedo, the last governor of Spanish Louisiana. Manuel had assisted his ailing father for a time in New Orleans just before the province was ceded to France. Thus he was not a complete stranger to some of the problems facing his new administration, especially those touching trade. His uncle, Don Nemesio, nonetheless ordered Cordero to remain in Texas for a while and help Manuel get acquainted with his difficult task. This he did, even after formally turning over the governorship to the thirty-two-year-old Salcedo on November 27, 1808. Meanwhile, Cordero received a promotion as deputy to the commandant general in Coahuila and Texas. With Cordero, Herrera, Governor Salcedo, and another distinguished "governor," Brigadier General Bernardo Bonavía (who soon arrived from Durango with a commission to strengthen colonial defenses), San Antonio de Béxar was overpopulated with top brass. Cordero, eager to return to Monclova, now had not only young Salcedo to brief but the new military coordinator as well.[59]

In April, 1809, the commandant general advised Bonavía that soldiers were henceforth to function with only two horses and one mule per man, a considerable reduction from the six horses that frontier cavalry duty had previously been considered to require. All animals above this number were to be placed in the custody of the Trinidad post commander to prevent fraud and loss. This idea was not new, Croix having vig-

---

[58] Castañeda, *Catholic Heritage*, 5:332–36; William R. Oberste, *Texas Irish Empresarios and Their Colonies*, pp. 87–90; Jean Louis Berlandier, *Journey to Mexico during the Years 1826 to 1834*, trans. Sheila M. Ohlendorf et al., ed. C. H. Muller et al., 2:547.

[59] Faulk, *Last Years*, p. 31; Félix D. Almaráz, Jr., *Tragic Cavalier: Governor Manuel Salcedo of Texas, 1808–1813*, pp. 23–33; Castañeda, *Catholic Heritage*, 5:349–50.

orously advanced it during his term as commandant general. Besides reducing the expense involved for the average soldier, it was part of his plan to make light troops less encumbered by horse-tending duties. Subordinates like Ugalde opposed the scheme with equal vigor until Croix yielded, which perhaps accounted for his disdainful remark that too many frontier officers (and soldiers) felt that being a good vaquero was sufficient measure of a man's Indian-fighting abilities.

After reaching Texas, Bonavía solicited written opinions from his three cohorts on how best to defend and develop the province. Salcedo's reply, given on May 7, 1809, indicates that the young governor already possessed a considerable knowledge of conditions on the frontier. Speaking of the contraband trade, he stated that, although the greatest efforts were being made to stop it, "the evil not only still exists but will grow worse daily unless the government entirely changes its plan and system for preventing it." Then he set forth reasons why the illegal trade flourished, rhetorically asking what the citizens, living 500 leagues from Veracruz, could reasonably be expected to do under existing circumstances. The supplies for their subsistence necessarily advanced in price by passing through the various commercial "gullets" up to Saltillo, arriving at Béxar priced at outrageous figures. Yet, "by risking their freedom and hides a little, they know that they have a chance to secure items for their families at the nearby post of Natchitoches at a ridiculously low sum." And what were the citizens of Texas and Nuevo Santander to do with the great herds of horses and mules they raised and the mustangs they caught but try to dispose of them at the best price offered (even though they risked the commission of a crime in so doing) especially considering the unsettled condition of the province's immense spaces and the inhabitants' intimate knowledge of the country, which afforded them so many roads unknown to the authorities? Young Salcedo knew the inevitable result, and he told Bonavía as much:

> We deceive ourselves if we think that, pending the opening of a port ordered for this and the other Interior Provinces by His Majesty—thus permitting the settlers to secure what they need by legal and lawful means, and export their stock and other products—they will not, at all risks, get them otherwise. The government will be forced to see its

most industrious and useful citizens and its most devoted parents turned into criminals.[60]

These were remarkable words of insight, coming from one fresh from Cádiz, justifying John Sibley's impression of him (en route to Texas) as having "sense enough to govern such people as he will find there." Like the parade of administrators before him, Salcedo felt that Texas enjoyed many riches and bright prospects, not the least of which were the "great numbers of horses and mules that, at little cost, are increasing in great numbers, and even without care are producing thousands of head of wild stock." Again, there is no mention of the herds of cattle that had once run wild in the province.

The great reformer Miguel Ramos Arizpe, writing just two years later, echoed many of these views to the Spanish Cortes, saying that the unfortunate inhabitants of the northern frontier seemed "destined to be the slaves of four greedy merchants of Querétaro, San Luis [Potosí], etc." Advocating free trade, a port on the Texas coast, and the opening of a *consulado* at Saltillo, he went on to confirm that mounted hunters had indiscriminately destroyed wild cattle in Texas until the herds dwindled to an alarming scarcity. Texas had formerly been covered with millions of wild cattle and horses, he wrote, but because the government had permitted their disorderly slaughter and their exportation for the "miserable sum" of "*un medio duro por cabeza*" (half a peso per head), Texas now had hardly enough cattle for its small population. Further, he charged that the Spanish inhabitants were "mere spectators" to the natural bounty of the province, its profits being reaped by native Indians and Anglo-Americans through an extensive trade network. But regardless of their basis in truth, Ramos Arizpe's ideas were ahead of the times—so much so that they augured modern concerns over the squandering of other natural resources once thought to be without end.[61]

---

[60] N. Salcedo to Brigadier General "Boncura" [Bonavía], April 22, 1809, BA; Max L. Moorhead, *The Presidio: Bastion of the Spanish Borderlands*, pp. 191–95; M. Salcedo, "Views on Development of the Province," May 7, 1809, Grazing Papers, vol. 1, pt. 2, pp. 188–90, and vol. 2.

[61] Benson, *Report of Ramos Arizpe*, pp. 21, 23; Vito Alessio Robles, *Coahuila y Texas en la época colonial*, pp. 607–608.

Although Bonavía advanced Manuel Salcedo's ideas on trade to the commandant general, including the logic—nay, necessity—of smuggling for the basically pastoral people of Texas, Don Nemesio found them much too liberal for his liking. He opposed the idea of a port and wanted the frontier closed to all future immigration. As far as he was concerned, the people being admitted from Louisiana were libertines, smugglers, fugitives from justice, atheists, or restless rovers who had been nothing but trouble. These ungrateful opportunists, predicted the commandant general, regardless of race or nationality, were "crows who some day will peck out our eyes."[62] Likewise, he tersely rejected his nephew's plan to locate incoming immigrants on the vacant lands of the secularized Béxar missions, reminding him that the main purpose behind encouraging colonization was to develop new lands, not to have newcomers reap the benefits of a prior occupation. Another junta called in June, 1809, nonetheless explored the possible use of these extensive lands, including turning the former missions into municipalities or haciendas and subdividing the surrounding lands into "tract homes" and small farms.

In forming these recommendations, Governor Salcedo found it necessary to conduct a census and a survey of the mission lands under consideration. Their boundaries were noted as follows: Concepción: from the mission 1 league south to El Paso del Nogal, 1 league east to Salado Creek, 1 league north to the Bahía Road, 8 leagues to the Cíbolo, then back to the mission, for a total of 15 square leagues. San José: bounded by Arroyo de la Piedra on the south, by the ranch of the curate Valdés[63] on the north, by the San Antonio River on the east, and by the Medina on the west. In addition to these lands, the mission still claimed eleven *sitios* in San Lucas, on the Medina, bought from the king in 1766.[64]

---

[62] This remarkable prediction is found in N. Salcedo to Bonavía, August 21, 1809, Castañeda, *Catholic Heritage*, 5:390.

[63] The *bachiller* who was granted land in 1798 along San José's Acequia Madre, a tract still to be seen on Bexar County land maps as "Padre Gavino Valdez."

[64] The documentation to the dispute between the friars at San José and Domingo Castelo over San Lucas is found in GLO, 50:50–129; included is the *inventario* of 1794 for Mission San José. The Castelo family seems to have pursued its claims to this land, even after it was awarded to San José in November, 1766.

San Juan Capistrano's boundaries extended 5 leagues east to El Águila, on the Bahía Road; down the road 10 leagues to "Pataguillos" Lake; and from the headwaters of the Cíbolo 7 leagues to San Bartolomé. Doubtless many of the ranchers in El Rincón—particularly the Arochas and the Traviesos—would have argued with such a demarcation. Espada's lands were vague (said the governor), but according to old-timers its limits were, for the north: from the back of the mission to a small dam on the river; for the west: from there to the lake (La Laguna); for the east: from the lake to ranch of Luis Pérez; for the south: from the lake down the Río Grande Road to Atascosa Creek. Also, Espada's lands (Las Cabras) were bounded by the riverbanks from Los Chayupines to La Parrita; on the east by the Delgado lands; on the south by El Atascoso; and on the west by the Peña Ranch.[65]

Governor Salcedo felt that these valuable lands were being held without yielding a return, since the few Indians (120) still at the missions were incapable of doing anything with them. Worse, the missions had become havens for idlers and gamblers, perhaps the kinds of people earlier described as of "low birth and few obligations." The lands of Valero also lay fallow, not developed as agreed to by the assignees. As Castañeda notes, these distributed lands were far less productive under their new owners or "renters" (a total of 186 Spaniards), than they had been when tended by mission Indians under the guidance of their padres. How the optimistic junta members were able to shake off this decade of nonperformance and forge ahead with their community planning is unknown. Perhaps they envisioned a better sort of citizen for their model subdivisions than the foregoing century had been able to provide.

On November 9, Gavino Delgado, justice of ranches, was instructed to divide the ranchos of Béxar into eight groups. Over each he was to nominate a *síndico*, an official to assist in the orderly conduct of area stock raising. The *síndicos*' main duty was to make sure that men killed only cattle belonging to

---

[65] Castañeda, *Catholic Heritage*, 5:367–68, 407–408. For the exact language on these boundaries, see AGI, Audiencia de Guadalajara, Dunn Transcripts, 61:223–25 (Box 2Q143, University of Texas Archives); and Leutenegger and Habig, *San José Papers*, pt. 2, pp. 270–77.

them and to punish those who violated this rule. Delgado complied, submitting a "Notizia de los ranchos" four days later (appendix D). An attempt was also made that November to resume the annual roundup and branding. At this time Alcalde Manuel Barrera, on the order of Governor Salcedo, notified the citizens that all "criadores [de] ganados y Dueños [de] los Ranchos" were required to have their cattle rounded up by November 15. Other owners' stock would be singled out and an examination made to discover the brands; a 10-peso fine was set as penalty for failure to participate in the rodeo. Further, written notice was to be given requiring the citizens to pasture animals caught on the outskirts of town to prevent crop damage, for the corn harvest was to begin on December 1. This order was followed by another on November 24 ordering all the ranchers to assemble at the corral of José Antonio Saucedo, possibly for the operation of *mesta* regulations concerning *mostrencos* taken on the roundup. From the tenor of Barrera's roundup order it appears that Governor Salcedo was trying to put the Texas cattle business on more formal footing.[66]

The multitude of proclamations which followed in rapid succession so indicates. For example, on November 19 Barrera was told that shelter was no longer to be given at ranches without the knowledge of the authorities. On December 23 the governor ordered the cattlemen notified that henceforth the supplying of beef to visiting Indians would be consigned at auction on a two-year basis. On January 10, 1810, he issued a long ordinance of twenty-eight articles, eight of which pertain to livestock. Under the ordinance town officials were to familiarize themselves with the brands of raisers in their districts so that lost animals could be returned to their lawful owners. When a resident slaughtered cattle at his ranch, he was required to send one of his hands to the *síndico* with a "piece of flesh" to show that it was from his own brand and mark. When a sale was made, it had to be conducted in the presence of a *síndico*: "Thus we hope to end cattle thefts and fraudulent sales that constantly occur." The fine for violation was set at the price of the cow killed, or twice that in case of theft (half to the informer, half to the Royal Treasury).

Owners were acknowledged to have a right to what was taken on their land. Thus anyone who took cattle from private lands was obliged to pay the owner for damage plus a fine of 6 pesos to the Royal Treasury. *Síndicos* were to make frequent visits to ranches in their jurisdictions, reporting any violations they found. They were charged with keeping a "register of all citizens living on ranches," that is, taking a census, including totals of their stock. Since the employable ranch workers of the province were "generally of vicious character," the ordinance read, strict discipline was considered necessary to keep them in line. If an employee owed his boss money, he could not quit, a situation amounting to indentured servitude. "Public justice" would take care of negligence, insults, and so forth (in case the vaquero tried to avenge himself on a *patrón* for detaining him and requiring his labor). A master, however, was allowed to pro-

---

[66] Barrera, decree on branding, November 5, 1809, BAM, roll 43, frames 318–20; Delgado, "Notice of Ranches . . . ," November 13, 1809, ibid., frame 339.

tect his interests by granting an advance on wages, "if necessary to avoid losing all." If a vaquero could show abuses, everything within reason would be done on disputes concerning loans and advances.

The *síndico* would see that cattle had proper guards, that is, that a *caporal* in charge of four mounted men and two on foot were assigned to each 2,000 head; only three men were to be assigned to *ganado menor* (goats and sheep) or to keeping hogs out of fields. Violators were subject to a 10-peso fine (half to the informer, half to the Royal Treasury) or a month at public labor. Finally, all roundups and markings of cattle were to be done between November 1 and November 30, every year without fail. Circuit Judges Vicente Travieso and Gavino Delgado were assigned to take charge of the roundup, calling for assistance from the *síndicos*, so that everything would proceed with order. Among the *síndicos* in 1810 were Ignacio de Arocha, Francisco Móntes de Oca, Joaquín Leal, Vicente Gortari, and Manuel Salinas, each with his own jurisdiction.

On January 12, Governor Salcedo added another pronouncement, this on the subject of fences. Telling landowners to keep their lands fenced, he noted, was not enough, owing to the evil practice of stealing fence posts for firewood. Therefore, he commanded the residents to build good, strong fences fastened with leather thongs and, once the fences were built, to watch for thieves. Neighbors should report forays on the fences so that offenders could be brought to justice. Theft of fence posts cost the culprit eight days in jail plus repair of the damage.[67]

On February 12 a list was made of ranches along the San Antonio River and the Cíbolo and Salado creeks which made donations to the latest war effort (against the French). Writing from Rancho del Salado, José Ignacio de Arocha itemized each contributing resident and vaquero at the various establishments, thereby providing useful information to latter-day gene-

---

[67] M. Salcedo, proclamations, December 23, 1809, and January 10 and 12, 1810, Grazing Papers, vol. 2. For Vicente Travieso's appointment on August 21, 1810, as *juez de campo* and the various duties entailed, see Mattie Alice Austin, "The Municipal Government of San Fernando de Béxar, 1730–1800," Texas State Historical Association *Quarterly* 8, no. 4 (April, 1905): 350–52.

alogists. The ranchos listed were as follows: Vicente Travieso (4 donors), Juan de Veramendi (9), José Andrés Hernández (2), Erasmo Seguín (3), Ignacio Calvillo (8), Francisco Farías (3), Ignacio Villaseñor (3), Manuela Móntes de Oca (3), Tomás de Arocha (4), Manuel Barrera (6), Manuel Nuñez (3), Francisco de Arocha (1), Ignacio de Arocha (4), José Piernas (4), Francisco Móntes (4), José Antonio Carvajal (1), Andrés Courbiere (4), José Flores (3), "retired sgt." Mariano Rodrígues (2), and Francisco Flores (1).[68]

Salcedo was short of funds for many of the projects he had in mind for the development of the province. It appears that he toyed with the idea of using livestock from the Trinity River outpost and its environs to provide such income. This plan fell through, however, when the officer in charge of the post, Pedro López Prietto, wrote that the cattle and horses in the area were in such bad condition that they could not be driven to the capital. Expenditures were often covered from the Mustang Fund, as in February, when Salcedo authorized the Nacogdoches commander, José María Guadiana, to make a withdrawal from the *caja* (box) kept at the post. Also, when Governor Salcedo went to East Texas in the summer of 1810 to clear squatters from the Neutral Ground, he was instructed by Bonavía to deduct all expenses, as well as costs of future expulsions, from the Mustang Fund.[69]

In August more ordinances were proclaimed on the matter of slaughtering cattle. Apparently private kills were cutting into the monopoly of the public slaughterhouse, and Salcedo made it virtually illegal for anyone to slaughter except "certified paupers" to whom beef had been given as charity. Those who would kill cattle at their homes must first give notice to the *síndico* (district commissioner). Failure to do so would result in the confiscation of the meat or an equivalent fine. The number killed and their brands were to be noted and steps taken to see that a sale did not compete with the villa's slaughter cattle. Sales were permitted only for the increase of area herds. If

---

[68] BAM, roll 44, frame 207.
[69] Almaráz, *Tragic Cavalier*, pp. 42–48.

a citizen was not a raiser, he had no right to slaughter even for his own consumption. This ordinance sounds suspiciously as though it was effected at the instigation of the licensed public beef contractors in an effort to bolster their business, which would also increase public revenues in the process, a point bound to win the governor's favor.[70]

Several comprehensive lists of Texas ranches are available for this period, the best to date. They were made in an effort to assess the resources of the province and also to enumerate the foreigners within its borders. The hostility of Commandant General Nemesio Salcedo to these interlopers has been observed. Alarmed that their numbers were growing, he ordered his nephew to make a thorough inspection of the situation. Governor Salcedo stalled but finally set out in March, 1810. After making a half-hearted survey of Villa de Salcedo on the Trinity, defending to Don Nemesio all of its supposedly twenty-seven *extranjeros*, he moved on to Nacogdoches. Guadiana, to expedite the governor's task, prepared several different lists for his examination.

One, dated April 14, 1810, gives the names of twenty-nine foreigners living in Bayou Pierre, east of the Sabine above old Adaes, but considered to be in the jurisdiction of Nacogdoches. As might be expected, some of the names on the fragment of 1797 are also on this list, and, far from being "foreigners," many of them—such as Marcelo Soto, a grandson of St. Denis—were long-time residents. Included was a count of the number of children in each family; their slaves were likewise enumerated, thirty-five in all (see appendix E).[71] Another list formed from May 8 to May 12 (also bearing twenty-nine names) was of the foreigners living in the Nacogdoches vicinity, most of them re-

---

[70] M. Salcedo, ordinance, August 5, 1810, BA. Castañeda, *Catholic Heritage*, 5:414, refers to a "public abattoir" ordinance of July 25, 1810, as well as others enacted that year.

[71] Guadiana, "Relación de los Extrangeros . . . ," April 14, 1810, Blake, Research Collection, 74:102–103. Castañeda, *Catholic Heritage*, 5:430, presents information from a census of 1809 of Bayou Pierre (above old Adaes), including many on this list. Compare also with Nardini's list of Bayou Pierre of the same date, but with considerable spelling variations (*Historic Natchitoches*, p. 123), and the listing shown in Haggard, "Neutral Ground," app. C, p. 1110.

siding on their ranches. It contains many of the names shown on José de la Bega's travel route. The distance of each ranch from Nacogdoches is given, as well as family information (appendix F).[72]

Of even more interest to the subject of ranching is the list dated April 14 of ranches, their owners, and their locations in relation to Nacogdoches. It shows thirty-seven individuals—some of them evidently occupying the same establishment or the immediate vicinity—and mostly foreigners, although it is not labeled as such. It contains many of the names in the list just mentioned (appendix G).[73] Finally, there is a compilation of East Texas ranchers, prepared by Captain Guadiana, this one grouped under five *síndicos*: José Flores, Bernardo Dortolan, José María Mora, José Antonio Chirino, and Juan Ignacio Pifermo. It indicates the general direction of each jurisdiction from Nacogdoches, as well as mentioning distances between ranchos (appendix H). Apparently Governor Salcedo's *síndico* orders for Béxar raisers were extended to the eastern region. Most of these ranchers appear on the Nacogdoches-Trinidad brand list, indicating that the two lists (of ranchers and of brands) may have been made at the same time. If so, it fits into a larger attempt to gain fiscal control over frontier ranching. Lists of stockmen and their brands were also being made in Nuevo León by orders of Intendant Manuel de Acevedo, dated July 23, 1810. Part of this *expediente* can be seen in the State Archives at Monterrey.[74]

All of the prying and questioning necessary to put these lists together, combined with the detailed census inquiries made in 1809, frightened away many of the East Texas settlers. Gover-

---

[72] Guadiana, "Relación de los Extrangeros . . . ," May 8–12, 1810, Blake, Research Collection, 74:116–17. See Castañeda, *Catholic Heritage*, 5:425–28, for an interesting discussion of how these foreigners were viewed by their Spanish hosts.

[73] Guadiana, "Noticia de los ranchos . . . ," April 14, 1810, Blake, Research Collection, 74:104–105; also found in Haggard, "Neutral Ground," app. D, pp. 1111–12.

[74] Guadiana, "Lista de los Vecinos . . . ," June 14, 1810, Blake, Research Collection, 74:189–91. For the badly torn original, see BAM, roll 45, frame 697; see also BAM, roll 46, frame 250. See also Allende, "Lista de los fierros de herrar, y nombre de los sugetos . . . ," September 15, 1810, State Archives of Nuevo León, box marked "Fierros de Herrar, 1810–1826."

nor Salcedo tried without success to reassure them. When the frontier seemed to be threatened with depopulation, he issued a proclamation at Nacogdoches on July 29, 1810, promising a pardon to all who had left out of fear of prosecution for possession of contraband or for other reasons. This upset his uncle Nemesio somewhat, for he was already convinced that his subordinates in Texas were ignoring orders and doing things their own way. In this connection it is interesting to note that when Marcelo Soto, a resident of Bayou Pierre (and a rival trader), charged Barr and Davenport with using their Las Ormigas Ranch in the Neutral Ground for smuggling livestock to Louisiana, Governor Salcedo defended them, claiming that they had a right to pasture stock there in order to maintain legal title to the ranch. One of Salcedo's responsibilities while he was at Nacogdoches was the matter of land titles, many of which he carried back to Béxar for review, causing more concern among the inhabitants. These titles, deeds, applications, and so forth, became lost in the aftermath of revolution and Governor Salcedo's brutal murder, no doubt accounting for the fragmented condition of some early land records in East Texas.[75]

This comprehensive survey of the ranchers along the ill-defined Louisiana border supplemented a detailed census made at Béxar earlier in the year. As at Nacogdoches, the itemization was taken by jurisdiction of *síndicos*, as provided by Governor Salcedo's proclamation of January 10, 1810. The report of Ignacio de Arocha, dated January 1, 1811, lists eleven establishments; Francisco Móntes's report, dated December 15, 1810, shows only three; Joaquín Leal's, dated December 18, 1810, has five; Vicente Gortari's dated December 31, 1810, has five; and Manuel Salinas's, dated January 2, 1811, has eleven (Delgado's list of 1809 shows seven ranches on the Medina and León under *síndico* Ignacio Pérez). Castañeda gives a detailed listing of fourteen of these ranchos, noting that they contained 172 persons, with livestock reported as follows: 3,928 head of cattle,

---

[75] M. Salcedo to Bonavía, September 12, 1809, in Haggard, "House of Barr and Davenport," p. 79; Castañeda, *Catholic Heritage*, 5:431–33. Davenport later testified that the Nacogdoches commander, Bernardo Montero, evacuating the town in 1812, had carried the archives to San Antonio, where many were destroyed.

673 horses, 42 mules, 12 burros, 168 oxen, 3,720 sheep and goats, 85 hogs, and 21 carts (it is to be assumed that the actual stock far exceeded the number reported, as was customary with most official accountings). Strangely, Castañeda does not show the neighboring ranchos of Arocha's and Gortari's syndicate, or Los Guerras under Salinas. One explanation for this oversight is that Castañeda used the records found in the Nacogdoches Archives (Transcripts, vol. 15) while the Arocha and Gortari tallies became part of the Béxar collection. All of these *síndico* lists of 1810 have been assembled and are presented in appendix I along with brief annotation.[76]

In addition to the count of these ranches in the vicinity of Béxar, beginning in 1809 a count was taken of several above the Nueces River, in the jurisdiction of La Bahía. In December, 1809, these establishments were listed as El Carrizo, belonging to Don Manuel Básques; San Pedro, the ranch of José Miguel Delgado, on which Antonio Montreal and others were living; and the ranch of Martín de León. Typical of the reports on these outlying ranches is the one made on November 10, 1811: El Carrizo: Manuel Vásquez (age fifty-nine, of Serralbo, "four years here from Monterrey"), wife, Ana María García (fifty-two), and four children; San Miguel de Buena Virtud: José Miguel Delgado (thirty-eight, Crucillas, "twelve years here from Colonia"), wife, María de Jesús de la Garza (thirty-five), and six children; and brothers Francisco and Manuel Delgado, their families, and their in-laws, a total of twenty-six persons.[77]

I have been unable to discover Spanish-era ranch lists for the Bahía (Goliad) region itself. A rare exception is the "Lista de

---

[76] Frederick C. Chabot, ed., *Texas in 1811: The Las Casas and Sambrano Revolutions*, pp. 120–22; Castañeda, *Catholic Heritage*, 5:416–21; Leal, "Translations of Statistical and Census Reports . . . ," roll 2; BAM, roll 47, frames 696–98, 803–10.

[77] "Census of Ranches under Jurisdiction of La Bahía," December 11, 1809, BAM, roll 43, frames 542–46; "Reports . . . of Families Living on Their Ranches," November 10, 1810, BAM, roll 47, frames 202–207; list, dated November 10, 1811, NA, in Chabot, *Texas in 1811*. The list of December, 1809, has de León's children as Fernando, María Candelaría, José [Silvestre], María Guadalupe, and José Félix. For the report of November 22, 1810, of families living on Don Martín's Rancho de Santa Margarita, see BAM, roll 46, frame 986. Oberste, *Texas Irish Empresarios*, p. 68, has the census of 1811 list of de León's family. For more on this distinguished clan, see Victor Rose, *Victor Rose's History of Victoria*, ed. J. W. Petty, Jr., pp. 10–13, 151–55; Hammett, *The Empresario*, pp. 4–5.

los Individuos á quinen se les concidio tierras desde el año de 1824 a 1834," which contains the following twelve names: Padre José Antonio Váldez (4 *sitios*), Gerónimo Muizas (?) (4 *sitios*), Ermengildo de la Cruz (1 *sitio*), Juan Bautista Serck (1 *sitio*), Antonio Sedek (1 *sitio*, 7 *labores*), Nicolás Seguín (1 *sitio*, 6 *labores*), Nicolás Carabajal (1 *sitio*, 4 *labores*), Gertrudis Barrera—possibly descended from the *diezmero* (4 *sitios*, 4 *labores*), Tomás Buentello (1 *sitio*), María de Jesús Ybarvo (5 *sitios*, 8 *labores*), Juan Cameron (4 *sitios*, 11 *labores*), and El Cura Váldez (4 *sitios*). Of these, the first four were granted in 1824–25 (around the time of contemplated secularization), and the others—as suggested by the appearance of Anglo names—around 1833. John B. Sidick and his son Anthony, two of those named above, were neighboring ranchers of Don Carlos de la Garza, and they were saved by him from execution with Fannin's men, as were Nicholas and John Fagan. Most likely, one of Padre Váldez's tracts was Rancho de Apaches, where the San Antonio and Guadalupe rivers meet. Just below Váldez's ranch was the old Rancho de los Mosquitos, once used by Mission Refugio.

The fact that the missions retained their land so long (until 1830) at La Bahía perhaps accounts for the fragmentary state of records pertaining to ranching in the area. But quite a few residents of the presidio had long engaged in chasing mesteños and raising cattle, an endeavor which on occasion put them in conflict with their upriver brethren and the missionaries close by. Further, a tally dated January 4, 1811, of livestock kept by settlers in the jurisdiction of Bahía Presidio proves that private ranching took place there at the same time that detailed *síndico* lists were being formed elsewhere in the province. It shows the following totals: 383 horses, 758 mares, 219 mules, 1,114 yoke of oxen, 2,658 cattle, 3,430 sheep and goats. Lands were awarded to many of the region's ranching clans under the Republic (suggesting prior occupancy), but in most cases only the very prominent were able to retain them. In the chaotic situation that characterized these years, prominence was often not enough to save one's property. In several notable instances it worked just the opposite: the more prominent one was (and the greater one's holdings), the greater were the abuses suffered.[78]

A wealth of information emerges from these reports, hinting at the complexity and broad scope of ranching in Texas. The network of humanity at these ranches discredits the notion that they were isolated from contact with the outside world. We find broken-down vaqueros hailing from Punta de Lampazos, Aguascalientes, Mayapíl, and as far away as Old Castile. There were caretakers from Chihuahua and Nuevo León, young families from Río Grande villas, sheepherders from Monterrey, free blacks from Guinea, youthful Lipan horsebreakers from Béxar, and even one woman, Manuela Pérez, listed as a ninety-year-old Indian "slave." As always, several of the ranches were run by women.[79] Some establishments were admittedly not very prosperous, inhabited by "motley groups," while other were noted as flourishing (Las Mulas) or as forming a small rural community (San Bartolo). By this time they were something like "mini-haciendas," attracting a number of hired hands in addition to their extended family members. But the primitive aspect of the land and its tenacious native inhabitants kept the operations from expanding into estancias anywhere on the scale of those to the south.

Other factors worked against this as well. Besides Indian hostilities, which kept the population down and retarded development, in Texas there were few disproportionately wealthy families to absorb smaller estates or foster an encomienda-type system as there were in Mexico. Also, no strong, centralized organization—such as a stockmen's *mesta*—ever wielded au-

---

[78] "Lista de los Individuos . . . ," cited as from GLO, book 56 (Cassiano-Pérez Collection, folder 40); BAM, roll 43, frame 749. William H. Oberste, *History of Refugio Mission*. pp. 320–26, deals with the final secularization at La Bahía. Perhaps the best census of ranches in this area is the "Padrón General de toda la Jurisdicción de la Bahía del Espíritu Santo," January 4, 1810, BA, which incorporates the fragments cited above into a fuller report.

[79] For an excellent treatment of women in colonial Mexico, see Colin M. MacLachlan and Jaime E. Rodríguez O., *The Forging of the Cosmic Race: A Reinterpretation of Colonial Mexico*, pp. 228–48. The authors' observations on the "special position" in society occupied by widows are especially applicable to Texas.

thority or controlled or directed the province's livestock industry. As in later times, custom among the stockmen regulated their conduct, occasionally assisted by decisions of the cabildo, whose members were generally raisers of a self-reliant stripe. Owing to the ease with which small operators could exploit mesteño stock and set themselves up as *criadores* (after a fashion), there was little reason for even a poor man to bind himself to the Texas version of a *patrón*. This was especially true if the aspiring cattleman was *español*, less true if he was an Indian or a *casta*. But it is also a fact that many mestizos and mulattoes were shown as ranchers throughout the colonial period, particularly at La Bahía and Nacogdoches. In short, rugged individualism triumphed on the frontier, even though it was a shabby existence by full-blown hacendado standards.

Most of all, the lack of easily accessible, dependable, crown-sanctioned markets doomed the aspirations of "big-time" stock raisers from the start. Deprived of their logical market, a trade with the occupants of Louisiana, early-nineteenth-century ranchers, like those in the beginning, had only the small beef demands of a few military garrisons to satisfy. Despite repeated appeals for a port on the Bay of San Bernardo, an option which could have stimulated the production of hides, tallow, dried meat, and other items, nothing was accomplished toward this end.[80] Nor was Texas ever permitted its own annual fair, an idea suggested in conjunction with the opening of a port since it would have encouraged the sale of imported goods as well as those produced locally. *Ganaderos* continued to be dependent upon the yearly marketplace at Saltillo and its "ruinous" domination of their lives and financial affairs. Thus the province found itself in virtual economic thralldom, its condition succinctly posed by Ramos Arizpe in a simple question: "Of what advantage can it be to the hungry to have flour if it costs him more than the whole is worth to make it into bread?" Spain did not provide answers to this basic dilemma, and the ranches of distant Texas were unable to realize their rich potential.

---

[80] The king authorized the opening of this port on September 18, 1805, but Nava frustrated the project (Haggard, "Neutral Ground," p. 1078).

"By Risking Their Hides a Little" 523

    These census reports of 1809–11 provide a sharply focused picture of the Texas ranching establishments standing on the precipice of revolution. All of them would suffer from the internal disorders of the coming decade; some would be entirely destroyed. By the time Stephen F. Austin's colonists made their appearance, not one of these ranchero clans stood unshaken by Father Hidalgo's *grito* or the many troubles that followed in its wake. With society in turmoil and survival itself in the balance, peaceful pursuits like stock raising would not be much on anyone's mind during the next ten years.

13

"HOPELESSLY LOST IN THEIR MISERY"

Disruptions of a Decade

ECHOES of Father Miguel Hidalgo y Costilla's revolutionary call of September 16, 1810, to end Spain's rule of Mexico were not long reaching Texas. Signs of discontent had been observed in the province as early as the summer of 1808, as indicated by Governor Cordero's concern with the comings and goings of various individuals. Suspicious meetings were being held in Béxar. Tomás de Arocha was labeled a troublemaker in these "discords" and was denounced for circulating a petition aimed at returning the cabildo to its original structure, although more sinister purposes were inferred. The 1808 situation had grown out of Cordero's heavy-handed reduction of the local governing body to five members in mid-1807, which had outraged the proud descendants of the Isleños. Vicente Travieso was also implicated in these political maneuverings. He escaped from confinement, but in October he was back in Béxar with a safe conduct from the Audiencia de Guadalajara. Upon his arrival more meetings were held, and the king's provincial officials fumed.[1]

[1] Texas was subject to the Audiencia de Guadalajara in judicial affairs at this time. See Nettie Lee Benson, trans. and ed., *Report of Ramos Arizpe*, p. 32, for the complex

The revolt came to Béxar with the overthrow of Royalist rule in January, 1811, and it was not long before many prominent families were drawn into the conflict. As the revolution turned into counterrevolution, only to flare again before being brutally extinguished in 1813, one after another of the old ranching dynasties would be touched and seared by the struggle for freedom. Family was turned against family, kin against kin, and the fabric of ranchero society was torn asunder, never fully to recover. The revolutionary turmoils were often used for personal gain, such as the confiscation of a neighbor's coveted house, lands, and cattle, and for other outrages even more difficult to forgive. What little emerged from the convulsions of insurrection was then swept away by the depredations of hostile Indians attracted like carrion birds to the ravaged Spanish settlements. It is the devastation to ranching as an institution and to the ranchers themselves that concerns us here, not the complex political upheavals of the period per se.

Most writers agree that revolutionary sentiment was widespread in San Antonio de Béxar by the time Juan Bautista de las Casas, a former officer of the Nuevo Santander militia, decided to make his move. Las Casas was supported at the outset by members of Canary Island families such as Francisco Travieso, the ranking alcalde, and Gavino Delgado, the son-in-law of Don Ignacio Calvillo, both of whom were ranchers. These men, by their resolute support, made possible a *coup d'état* and lent prestige to the usurpation of Spanish authority. They must have had general sympathy, for such a feat requires more than an isolated handful of conspirators.[2]

---

system that controlled every aspect of life in colonial Texas—religious, judicial, fiscal, political, etc.—all in different and very distant places: "From this chaos come a thousand confusions and a necessary complication of affairs that makes the prompt administration of justice impossible and necessarily results in a thousand vexations for those respectable and worthy Spaniards." The "discords" in the villa are found in BA, June–October, 1808.

[2] For the story of Hidalgo's movement in Texas, see Frederick C. Chabot, ed., *Texas in 1811: The Las Casas and Sambrano Revolutions*; J. Villasana Haggard, "The Counter-Revolution of Bexar, 1811," *Southwestern Historical Quarterly* 43, no. 2 (October, 1939): 222–35; Julia Kathryn Garrett, *Green Flag over Texas: A Story of the Last Years of Spain in Texas*; Félix D. Almaráz, Jr., *Tragic Cavalier: Governor Manuel Salcedo of Texas, 1808–1813*; Carlos E. Castañeda, *Our Catholic Heritage in Texas*,

It appears that once Las Casas took control of the villa he became intoxicated with his new power. He launched a campaign against all vestiges of Royalist influence, sequestered the property of certain residents, jailed others, and in a generally undiplomatic manner alienated himself from many prominent citizens, including some of those who had helped bring him to power. While proof is lacking, some accounts suggest that Las Casas set about confiscating the livestock of many suspected "loyalists" and *gachupines* (European-born Spaniards), compiling a brand list of those whose animals were forfeit. I have been unable to find such a list, but it is established that one of Las Casas's first official acts was to "confiscate the property of all Europeans," presumably including their cattle. As the names of the families who rallied behind the counterrevolution indicate, many prominent ranchers were among those either affected or antagonized by his measures.[3]

Las Casas, recently arrived in San Antonio, may have been ignorant of the zeal with which Bexareños traditionally defended their stock. Men like Travieso and Delgado, however, being from old families, should have known better. Not only did the arbitrary seizures (and there were many) cause problems, but when Las Casas failed to reward his fellow insurgents according to their expectations, he drove such supporters away. Resentment toward the new ruling clique was not long in forming.

When the shift came, it centered around Juan Manuel Sambrano, son of the ranching dynasty founded by Don José Macario Sambrano. Born in 1772, Juan Manuel was a tempestuous character, described as a man of "questionable virtue" who had been briefly exiled from the province in 1807 because of his frequent indulgence in worldly pleasures. Yet he was a subdeacon of the San Fernando Church, and his position as a

---

6:1–120; Harris Gaylord Warren, *The Sword Was Their Passport: A History of American Filibustering in the Mexican Revolution*, pp. 1–72. One of the best studies from the standpoint of the various families involved is Elizabeth May Morey, "Attitude of the Citizens of San Fernando Toward Independence Movements in New Spain, 1811–1813" (Master's thesis, University of Texas, 1930).

[3] Hortense W. Ward, in *Cattlebrands and Cowhides*, pp. 178, 183, mistakenly associates a confiscation list of brands with Las Casas, but the list is for the insurgents that opposed Arredondo two years later, dated February 28, 1814 (see note 26 below and brand section F); Haggard, "Counter-Revolution," p. 224.

minor clergyman helped him gain permission from the Audiencia de Guadalajara to return to Texas. When Salcedo opposed Sambrano's reinstatement first by threatening to resign and then by arresting the subdeacon and placing him in jail, the governor found himself excommunicated by the bishop of Nuevo León. This episode no doubt left a bad taste in Salcedo's mouth and did little to improve his opinion of the flamboyant cleric.

From the Sambrano ranch, La Laguna de las Ánimas, 20 leagues away, Juan Manuel followed developments in the capital. Two of his brothers, José Dario and José María—the former an ordained priest—kept him fully informed. José María, also designated by some a priest, was nonetheless twice married and received a grant of four *sitios* of grazing land at the "place of the lagoon" in 1809. Toward the end of February, Juan Manuel quietly entered Béxar and met with others determined to oust Las Casas. They were soon joined by Gavino Delgado and Captain Antonio Sáenz, who still had revolutionary sympathies but were disenchanted with Las Casas. Sambrano, by pretending that his actions were directed against the depotism of Las Casas, was able to exploit their disaffection. They struck on the night of March 2 and took the reins of government without a fight.[4]

Other powerful families, however, were not as easily reconciled to the hasty restoration of Ferdinand VII. They included the Menchacas, the Arochas, the Traviesos, the Leales, and most of the Delgados. It soon became necessary to arrest the curate José Clemente de Arocha because of his opposition to the junta, a task performed by Captains Francisco Ruíz and Juan de Veramendi. Others fled the reinstatement of Royalist authority and appeared with the Gutiérrez-Magee Expedition of the following year, the next phase of the *grito de Dolores* in Texas. After carting Las Casas off to trial and execution in Chihuahua, the junta busied itself in restoring order and authorizing the trade of

[4] Frederick C. Chabot, *With the Makers of San Antonio*, p. 196; Castañeda, *Catholic Heritage*, 6:34; and R. B. Blake, Research Collection, 6:30 (University of Texas Archives), contain profiles of the subdeacon. Members of the new ruling junta were Juan Manuel Sambrano, president; José Antonio Saucedo, secretary; Captain Antonio Sáenz; Ignacio Pérez; Miguel Eca y Músquiz; Luciano García; Erasmo Seguín; Luis Galán; Manuel Barrera; Juan Josef Sambrano (another brother); Gavino Delgado; and Vicente Gortari.

Texas horses for rations and other supplies needed from Louisiana. One proposal called for the establishment of a school with money from the Mustang Fund. In June regulations were issued pertaining to slaughters and penalties for ranchers who killed stray cattle on their land. Governor Salcedo had instituted similar orders the previous November in an attempt to curb mesteño hunts outside ranch boundaries. Then, in July, 1811, the junta proclaimed an end to its rule and returned the government to Simón de Herrera until Governor Salcedo could resume command of the province. The head of Las Casas was boxed up and sent back to Texas for public exhibition on a pole in the Plaza de Armas, a grim reminder to those who still harbored seditious ideas.[5]

J. Villasana Haggard, in his study of the counterrevolution, lists the ten newly elected members of the town council (an election held at the order of the ruling junta). That most of those "elected" were leaders of the disaffected clans possibly represents an an attempt to consolidate authority at Béxar. They were displaced by a more conservative cabildo in May, 1812, however, when Salcedo reduced their number to eight and sold each office to the highest bidder. That summer an "honor roll" of the junta members and all other citizens who had supported the Spanish government in Texas was sent to Commandant General Salcedo. Included were the names of Delgado and Sáenz; it was said that they knew how to mend their ways. Special praise was lavished on all these men for their vital service to the crown, but especially singled out for honors was Juan Manuel Sambrano. Manuel Salcedo reassumed the governorship in December, 1811, his pride no doubt severely galled by the knowledge that his office had been restored to him largely by the efforts of the subdeacon, his bitter personal enemy. In the face of his "grievous task" at Béxar the governor was further mortified by the deterioration of his working relationship with the commandant general, Don Nemesio. Convinced that within the ashes of the old revolution yet smoldered embers that would

---

[5]Almaráz, *Tragic Cavalier*, p. 123; Juan Manuel Sambrano, "Slaughter Regulations," June 2 and 27, 1811, BAM, roll 48, frames 665, 825; M. Salcedo, "Orders for Roundup and Branding," December 20, 1810, BAM, roll 49, frame 773.

flame forth anew, Manuel could only swallow his pride, follow his uncle's instructions, and resign himself to the inevitable.[6]

The new revolution was not long in coming. As expected, it loomed from neighboring Louisiana, where many who had taken up Padre Hidalgo's fallen banner found shelter and refuge. There they allied themselves with restless American adventurers, some with former military training and others with long-standing interests on the frontier. The figurehead for this movement was José Bernardo Gutiérrez de Lara, a rancher, blacksmith, and skilled propagandist from Revilla, who fled to the United States in the summer of 1811. Guiding him to exile was the retired captain, Don José Menchaca, the old captain's son, who was on the run from anticipated prosecution by Commandant General Salcedo.

They established themselves at Natchitoches with the help of sympathetic Americans. After a sojourn in Washington, D.C., Gutiérrez began spreading subversive literature throughout Texas calling upon the "sons of Montezuma" to rise up and "shake off the barbarous and ignominious yoke" that had oppressed them for three hundred years. The original plan—for Menchaca to enter Texas and pave the way for armed revolution—was disrupted by the captain's decision to switch sides again. Even so, Gutiérrez had no difficulty finding ready recruits in the Neutral Ground for his plan to revolutionize Texas. Samuel Davenport, a loyal Spanish subject until the summer of 1812, was one who actively supported the goals of Gutiérrez and was made quartermaster general of the "Republican Army of the North." His role, however, was much greater than that of supplying goods to the army. The formation and early success of the enterprise was due in no small part to the steady influence Davenport had exercised on the border for almost twenty years.[7]

[6] Haggard, "Counter-Revolution," p. 230; Morey, "Attitudes of the Citizens," pp. 80–83.

[7] Garrett erroneously identified Miguel as the Menchaca who helped Gutiérrez escape to the United States, beginning the confusion between these two individuals (*Green Flag*, p. 84). Gutiérrez's diary (copy of the original in the Texas State Archives; translated by Elizabeth West in *American Historical Review* 34 [October, 1928]: 57–71) and his "Memorial to the Mexican Congress" (C. A. Gulick et al., eds., *The Papers of Mirabeau Buonoparte Lamar*, 1:7–11) refer to Menchaca only as "Captain"

While the second phase of the revolution was taking shape east of the Sabine, efforts were being made to reorganize stock raising in the province. On June 1, Sambrano submitted a tentative proposal of *síndico* candidates, a list apparently amended at a later date. The candidates and their territories were as follows: José Barcenas, San Bartolo and Las Mulas; José María Sambrano, from La Mora to Manuel Barrera's ranch; Gavino Delgado (scratched out and Francisco Móntes's name entered), from Arocha's ranch to Los Chayopines; Joaquín Leal (scratched out), from Candelaría to Francisco Treviño's ranch; name omitted, from *los cimados* (the upper regions) of the Arroyo Salado and Salitrillo; and Ignacio Pérez, from the upper extents of the Arroyo de León and the Medina. Four days later Governor Salcedo asked Ignacio Pérez, Manuel Salinas, and Joaquín Leal to return their former commissions as *síndico*, which they soon did. By August a complete list of *síndicos de ranchos* was formulated, offering us the last glimpse of post-junta cattlemen just before Texas came loose at the seams (see appendix J).[8]

Although provincial officials at Béxar were aware that trouble was brewing at Natchitoches, Sambrano learned of the impending invasion the hard way. At Nacogdoches in August, 1812, he attempted to obtain a safe passage across the Neutral Ground for a packtrain of sixty mules laden with wool and specie from Béxar. The subdeacon's 100 mule drivers were armed, but he dared not risk the passage to Natchitoches because of the large number of bandits infesting the area. Finally, however, despairing of receiving either a safe conduct or an escort from local United States authorities, Sambrano started across the Neutral Ground on his own. It was a rash decision.

Near the Sabine he met a vanguard of the Republican Army and was rapidly put to flight. Retreating from Nacogdoches, he and about ten loyalist soldiers were all that remained after the local militia abandoned them and returned to welcome the revolutionary forces. Sambrano left his cargo behind and rode hard to Béxar to warn the governor that East Texas was in the hands of insurgents and their American coconspirators. Estimates of

---

and "Colonel," but West correctly notes that he was José. Likewise BA, July–October, 1811, confirm that the fugitive was "el Capitán retirado" José Menchaca, not Miguel.

[8] BAM, roll 51, frames 381, 423, 425, 431–32; BAM, roll 52, frame 335.

his losses vary, but some sources place them at 100 bales of fine wool (said to amount to 40 tons) and 300 to 400 mules and horses, the whole valued by William Shaler at $100,000. As an example of the intensity of emotion being displayed after Nacogdoches fell to the rebels, perhaps the letter that Vizente Flores wrote to Governor Salcedo on September 1 is representative. Flores said that if Salcedo molested Travieso and the other citizens in his power he would be publicly burned alive.[9]

Virtually unopposed, the Gutiérrez-Magee Expedition took Trinidad and La Bahía and marched on to San Antonio. First, however, the blacksmith from Revilla smoothed the way for conquest by assuring the citizens that his cause was dedicated to securing liberty for them and protecting their rights. Among the promises that Gutiérrez made to those who supported him were land and "the right of taming and disposing of the wild horses and mules which roam unclaimed over an immense tract of country." The right to these mesteños would henceforth be "common to all of you"; in effect the traffic in animals to Louisiana would no longer be restricted. After the expenses of the expedition were paid, the surplus property confiscated from all Royalists was to be divided among his soldiers. Years of discontent, not to mention news of the sweeping victory as far as the Trinity River, made Béxar highly susceptible to this propaganda. Thus by the time rebel troops reached the outskirts of the capital in March, 1813, they had been joined by a large number of citizens, guaranteeing the capitulation of the province.[10]

Facilitating this easy conquest were recent Indian troubles, of which the citizens were growing decidedly weary. The settlement on the San Marcos River had been abandoned the preceding summer owing to Comanche hostilities, with the loss of all

---

[9] Garrett, *Green Flag*, pp. 138, 150–52; Castañeda, *Catholic Heritage*, 6:82–84; Warren, *Sword*, pp. 34–35; Lamar Papers, Texas State Archives, fragment, box 2917A; Ted Schwarz, "Forgotten Battlefield of the Texas Revolution" (typescript), pp. 27–31. Castañeda notes that trade with Natchitoches figured importantly in the survival of the ruling junta of 1811, regardless of its "official" posture and reverses suffered later by prosperous individuals like the subdeacon (*Catholic Heritage*, p. 50).

[10] Hatcher, *Opening of Texas*, p. 229; Garrett, *Green Flag*, p. 160; J. Villasana Haggard, "Neutral Ground between Louisiana and Texas," *Louisiana Historical Quarterly* 28, no. 4 (October, 1945): 1069.

livestock pastured in the vicinity. When Dr. John Robinson visited Béxar in the spring of 1813, he was told that the Indians had killed fifty-five persons and stolen 5,000 sheep and 10,000 head of horses and mules. After the insurgents triumphed in a skirmish on the Rosillo, a creek just east of the Salado, Colonel Samuel Kemper was nonetheless able to capture 3,000 horses by raiding the presidial corral. These successes attracted even more recruits to the Republican encampment at Mission Concepción, causing great divisions in the ranks of the inhabitants and sowing the seeds for bitter retributions in the future.[11]

When Governor Salcedo and other Royalist officers surrendered, Gutiérrez formed a junta of his own to try them, apparently packing it with Menchacas to guarantee a guilty verdict. The Menchacas were avowed sympathizers of Mexican independence and vehement opponents of the Royalists. As anticipated, the revolutionary junta found the prisoners guilty of betraying the Hidalgo movement and sentenced them to death. Some of the charges involved the seduction of Captain José Menchaca, who the rebels claimed was lured back to the Royalist fold with promises of a pardon, only to be treacherously tried, found guilty, and sent to Chihuahua in chains. The documentation supports such a view. But ironically, José—after entertaining notions of supporting the revolutionary cause in its early, successful stages—had been instrumental in Hidalgo's capture at the Wells of Baján. After joining Elizondo at Monclova to help restore the "lost government," Menchaca set out to clear his name at Béxar, traveling with Commandant General Salcedo's recognition of his loyalty to the king. He presented the junta with justification of his earlier actions and apparently intended to visit Don Nemesio, but something made him change his mind.

By mid-July reports of his "escape" toward La Bahía were coming from the line presidios. Gutiérrez noted his arrival at Revilla shortly thereafter, saying that José was fleeing "on account of the persecution of the Commanding General Salcedo, who was seeking to take his life." Upon reaching Louisiana with Gutiérrez, he evidently decided to abandon the rebel cause.

[11] Garrett, *Green Flag*, pp. 176–77.

Herrera notified headquarters of José's arrest and transfer to Béxar on November 13, 1811, and on December 24 the commandant general reprimanded his nephew for granting Menchaca a pardon. In a letter dated January 15, 1812, José thanked Governor Salcedo for securing this pardon, news of which was communicated to the commandant general four days later. The governor said that Menchaca would travel to Chihuahua "as soon as his legs and age let him," but Elizabeth May Morey cites documents to prove that Manuel Salcedo wanted to make an example of the retired captain, feeling that he was lost to religion and honor, as well as being a drunk. Likewise, Almaráz mentions José's trial on charges of sedition (the trial lasting from February 20 to March 8, 1812) and his removal to Chihuahua "under protective custody." Antonio Menchaca's "Memoirs" and biographical notes in the Lamar Papers say that he died there about 1820, "still in chains." Even though Don José's actions had helped bring about the downfall of Hidalgo's revolution and he was led to believe that they merited him a royal pardon, his fate was bound to be resented by those at home.[12]

Menchaca's defection to Royalist troops on the Sabine River in mid-October, 1811, severely damaged Gutiérrez's credibility in Washington, forcing him to rely almost entirely on American aid in accomplishing the liberation of the province. Still, Gutiérrez believed Menchaca to be an honorable man, dedicated to the cause of freedom, and his suffering at the hands of Salcedo and Herrera perhaps justified such sentiments. Certainly the clan at Béxar felt that José had been betrayed, and they blamed the governor for his harsh treatment. It is small wonder, then,

---

[12] José's early correspondence with Pedro de Aranda, insurgent governor of Coahuila, and other Hidalgo subalterns is found in BAM, roll 48, under dates January 20, 21, 23, 26, and 27, February 9, 17, 20, 23, and 26, and March 1 and 7, 1811; his decision to support the king can be traced: BAM, roll 48, March 15, 17, 24, and 29, April 8 and 19, May 7 and 21 (when he submitted his military record to Nemesio Salcedo, frame 847); his flight to Louisiana with Gutiérrez: roll 49, items dated July 12, September 19 and 26, and October 3 and 6; his surrender, arrest, and trial: roll 49, November 13, December 24, and roll 50, January 15, 20, and 21, February 20, and March 2, 1812, at which time Menchaca was noted as having reached Monclova, en route to prison in Chihuahua. See also Morey, "Attitudes of the Citizens," pp. 84–85; Almaráz, *Tragic Cavalier*, p. 134; Antonio Menchaca, "Memoirs" (University of Texas Archives); and Menchaca's biographical notes in Gulick et al., *Papers of Lamar*, 4(2):71–72.

that Gutiérrez considered his kinsmen as good as a death squad in the mock trial he arranged for Salcedo and other officers of the crown. Out of the confusion cloaking this notable family eventually emerges the fact that the Menchacas were staunch advocates of social change and deadly foes of the *gachupines*.[13]

Other foes were just as deadly, as demonstrated by the fate of Salcedo, Herrera, and twelve of their fellow officers. They were marched a few miles down the Bahía Road by Antonio Delgado, a corporal of the militia; Pedro Prado, a soldier in the Alamo Company; and between sixty and one hundred men. At a lonely spot known as La Tablita the Royalists' throats were cut, and their mutilated bodies were left to be devoured by wild animals. Delgado returned to Béxar, "battle trophies" bloodily hanging from his saddlehorn, and proclaimed the foul deed. Delgado told the assembled throng that Governor Salcedo had killed his father and brother and dragged their heads through the streets because they favored liberty and received revolutionary messages from Natchitoches. Many accepted his retribution as just. Although the murder shocked some of Gutiérrez's American allies, it did not seem to perturb overmuch the native Texans who had cast their fates on the side of independence. They may have reasoned that one did not kill a snake without cutting off its head, and the *gachupín* elite at Béxar was but the fanged appendage of a vast, wriggling colonial empire dedicated to their oppression.[14]

This butchery did, however, cause crown officials to take the situation in Béxar very seriously. They dispatched an army under Joaquín de Arredondo, newly appointed commandant general of the Eastern Interior Provinces, to crush the rebellion and restore the province to Spanish rule. This he accomplished

---

[13] Gutiérrez, "Memorial to the Mexican Congress," in Gulick et al., *Papers of Lamar*, 1:7–11.

[14] Garrett, *Green Flag*, pp. 180–81; Almaráz, *Tragic Cavalier*, p. 171. For a lively but unsubstantiated account of these and other events climaxing in the Battle of the Medina, see John Warren Hunter's three-part series—supposedly based on the "autobiography" of a participant, one Carlos Beltran—in *Frontier Times* 3, nos. 1-3 (October–December, 1925). José Antonio Navarro discounted Delgado's professed motives in his more reliable narrative *Apuntos Históricos Interesantes de San Antonio de Béxar: Escritos por el C. Dn. José Antonio Navarro en Noviembre de 1853...*, p. 15.

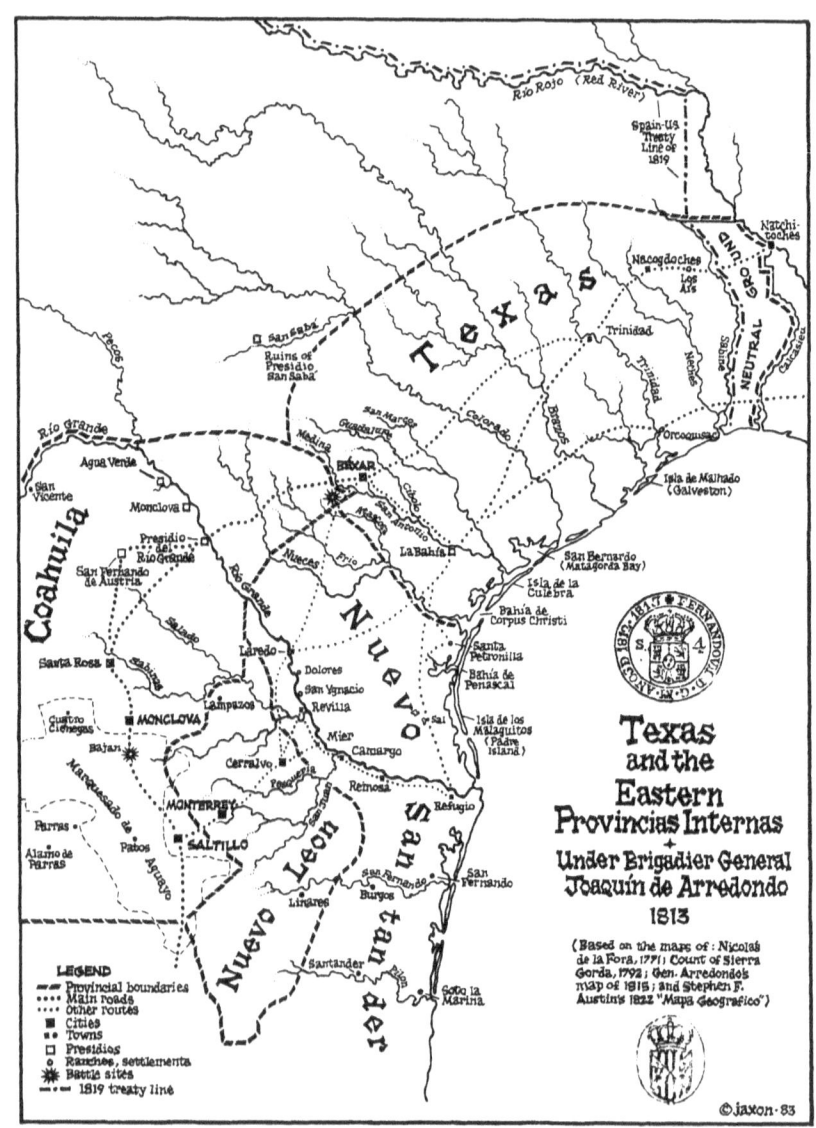

in August, 1813, routing the insurgents in an *encinal* (oak grove) below the Medina River and scattering them to the four winds. He did not stop until Texas was purged of republicanism and many of its prominent citizens killed, stripped of their possessions, or driven into exile. The Arochas, Delgados, Traviesos, and Leales were among those families who took the Camino Real to Louisiana. Some were caught at the Trinity River. Antonio Delgado was shot instantly for his part in the killing of the governor's party. Two of Joaquín Leal's sons were "judicially murdered" on the Trinity, and the old man died before he reached Béxar. Other rebels were bound and hauled before Arredondo, ultimately meeting the same fate. The suffering intensified at Béxar as the hot summer of 1813 wore on. Learning of a popular ribald ditty about the "one-eyed general" (and a Bexareña's earlier boast that she would eat his roasted *huevos*), Arredondo taunted the rebellious Tejanos as he brought them to their knees.

Peace, it is said, though not prosperity, returned to Texas with the victory at El Encinal de Medina,

but from San Antonio to the Sabine the country had been laid waste. More than a thousand terrorized residents and Indians had fled to the Neutral Ground and into Louisiana. The scars of merciless war were visible on every side. Vacant homes, neglected crops, untended herds, desolation, and destruction bespoke the price of victory. The stillness of death proclaiming the restoration of order was broken only by the low moaning of women inside the Quinta, heightened by the shrill blasts of the north winds signalling the advent of winter.[15]

Those who could, escaped. Francisco Ruíz, for example, fled into the wilderness, where he lived with Indians, returning only when independence was assured. José Antonio Navarro and other young men who had fought at the decisive encounter sought refuge in Louisiana, where many of them were reduced to laborers in the districts of Opelousas, Attakapas, and Bayou Pierre.

[15] Schwarz, "Forgotten Battlefield," pp. 165–76; Castañeda, *Catholic Heritage*, 6:120; see also Garrett's description in *Green Flag*, p. 228. When the division of the Interior Provinces took place in 1813, Bonavía was given command of the western part, Arredondo the eastern.

Litigation on old land grants is replete with references to how the province was emptied as a result of Arredondo's purge. In the testimony gathered in defense of Edmund Norris's title to Rancho Naconiche years later, old settler Vital Flores (born about 1790) said that almost everyone left Nacogdoches and fled to Louisiana for safety. A "general stampede" ensued when Ignacio Elizondo's troops ranged as far as Spanish Bluff, on the Trinity, it being "unsafe . . . to remain in this section of Texas," as far removed as it was. Norris, like many others, did not return until years later. In 1873 his son John—at peril of endangering the estate's land title because of technical "occupancy" provisions—gave a deposition saying that Nacogdoches was entirely evacuated and that "no one remained here that I know of. All left in order to save their lives." His father took the family and settled near Logansport Ferry, Louisiana, where he built a house, worked a small farm, and stayed until 1820, "when the Mexican authorities invited all the citizens to come home." Such testimony exemplifies the plight of all early East Texas grantees, not just the Anglo claimants, as demonstrated by the death of Pedro Padilla beyond the Sabine in humble circumstances.[16]

Those who remained at Béxar did so under the most trying circumstances. José Menchaca's "melancholy fate"—the expression Antonio Menchaca later used to describe it—has been mentioned. According to Menchaca's memoirs, one of the first casualties of the Gutiérrez-Salcedo difficulties at Béxar was "old Antonio Baccha [Baca]," who perished of sunstroke on the road to La Bahía. Correct in substance, Menchaca (who was a boy at the time of the revolt) was somewhat inaccurate in the details; San Fernando Burial Records show that Antonio Baca died on June 26, 1813. This puts his death after the heady rebel victory at the Alazán but before Arredondo's army arrived to crush the rebellion. Baca, whose gift of 5,000 pesos to the insurgent cause had gained him the appointment as "Governor of La Bahía," was doubtless attempting to escape the anticipated conflict when death overtook him. Chabot calls Baca one of the richest mer-

[16] R. B. Blake, "Records . . . Relating to the Edmund Norris Four League Grant" (typescript, Texas State Archives); R. B. Blake, Research Collection, 28:361 (University of Texas Archives).

chants of his time, which indicates that colonial-era beef-supply contracts paid off handsomely.

Among those imprisoned in the political turmoil was the old French revolutionary José de la Baume, who was supposedly fined "7,000 doubloons" after spending seven months in jail. Like those of many other citizens suspected of liberal principles, all of his papers and property were confiscated by the Royalists. It is said that of all the immigrants admitted to Texas during the preceding years only Daniel Boone and Vicente Micheli remained in the province after Arredondo had exacted his vengeance.[17]

The disruptions the period brought to ranching were incalculable. Even the victors were soon petitioning Arredondo for relief. On September 17, Juan Manuel Sambrano, José Antonio Saucedo, Ignacio Pérez, and ten other stockmen from the vicinity of San Antonio stated that they had suffered such severe losses as to force them to abandon their ranches. Sambrano claimed to have lost more than 10,000 head of sheep (not cattle, as some have written) to the rebels and Indians. But the subdeacon was not long in taking measures to recover his losses. Soon he had so much livestock in his possession, cattle as well as sheep and goats, that it was necessary to conduct an investigation to ascertain whose they were. Since the brands in question belonged to men either dead or departed, no one could

---

[17]Chabot, *Makers of San Antonio*, p. 75; Menchaca, "Memoirs" (University of Texas Archives, box 2F32 for the original, box 2R115 for the transcript); John Ogden Leal, comp. and trans., "Burials of San Fernando," vol. 3; John Ogden Leal, comp. and trans., "Marriages of San Fernando," vol. 2; Hatcher, *Opening of Texas*, p. 236; Florence (Nina) W. Bruns, "El Capote Ranch," in *Bicentennial Minutes of Seguin-Guadalupe County, 1976*, pp. 22–23, contains information on La Baume's ranch near the Capote Hills. La Baume was still seeking a pardon in 1816 (letters dated October 24 and December 19 which Ignacio Pérez wrote to Arredondo in reference to his situation, both in BA). Although La Baume hired Stephen F. Austin as a lawyer, he had not succeeded in recovering his title to El Capote at the time of his death in 1834. His prior claims were recognized, however, as in 1828, when José Antonio Navarro tried to claim 4 *sitios* of land around "el ojo de agua del Capote" (told that the tract was not available, Navarro then chose Mission San José's former rancho, El Atascoso). Documentation relating to La Baume's historic Guadalupe County ranch and its later acquisition by the Erskine family is found in the Claude Elliott Collection, Texas State Archives, folder 12; see also *Michael Erskine et al. v. Joseph de la Baum et al.* (1848), *Texas Supreme Court Reports*, 3:406–23.

refute Sambrano's claim that he had bought them. Ignacio Pérez was another who went out to gather cattle from the ranches of Travieso, Veramendi, and other insurgents in the Cíbolo basin. He found that "Indians" had already swept the country clean.[18]

The lands of all those who had participated or lent aid to the rebels were, also soon confiscated, the militaristic cleric seizing several choice tracts declared vacant. Among them were lands belonging to Manuel Delgado and Joaquín Leal (brothers-in-law of the deceased Simón de Arocha), who "because of their traitorous crimes fled toward the United States," as well as some belonging to José Antonio de la Garza. The acting governor Lieutenant Colonel Cristóbal Domínguez noted that the property was worth more than the purchase price but recommended that it be given to Sambrano in consideration of his many services against the insurgents.

While confiscation and sale documents drawn up by Domínguez on November 19, 1813, state that Joaquín Leal was "slain," a defense of his land title made by heirs in 1838 has him dying of "grief and hardship" soon after his sons were killed on the Trinity. San Fernando burial records indicate that he was alive until 1819. In any case, his wife, Anna María de Arocha, later appealed the confiscation and won restitution, although some doubt remained as to which lands were restored. Garza also appealed the sale of his lands to the subdeacon, but lost. Not one to give up easily, Garza (called "the skinny one") gathered testimony of his loyalty, including a statement given by Francisco Antonio Rivas. It hints at some of the motives behind this Royalist-insurgent witch hunt: "I have known for some time that Sambrano nourished hatred for de la Garza because he never would consent to sell the said land to him." According to Chabot, Garza won, and his lands were returned, Sambrano keeping Leal's and Delgado's *suertes* but asking for the return of

---

[18] Castañeda, *Catholic Heritage*, 6:121. Also signing statements were Manuel Barrera, Alvino Pacheco, Thoribio Durán, Vicente Gortari, and Manuel Nuñez—some of whom were in jail and were noted as "Republicano" (BAM, roll 53, frames 204–209). Chabot says that Sambrano owned 77,000 sheep in 1812, a figure difficult to reconcile with Governor Elguezábal's estimate of 1803 that there were only 1,000 head in the entire province.

a third of his payment to the Royal Treasury. Many other valuable properties no doubt exchanged hands in the same roguish fashion.[19]

In October Acting Governor Domínguez appointed a committee to appraise the confiscated rebel property—and perhaps to keep it from slipping through the king's fingers. The committee consisted of Manuel Barrera, José Antonio de la Garza (whose land Sambrano coveted), and Vicente Gortari. They were considered to be experts in assessing values of cattle, sheep, goats, and so on. Others were appointed to fix a value on real estate, both committees eventually arriving at a total figure of 62,642 pesos. All deductions from this estimate were carefully noted, including cattle "eaten by the army" or subsequently returned to exonerated owners. A few stockmen, such as José Félix de Arocha, managed to elude this dragnet. Arocha was allowed to keep his father's ranch, along with some corn and goats, even though his father was a rebel in hiding. This concession was apparently granted to him for helping Elizondo in August, 1813. All in all, the actions taken against rebel property seem to have considerably profited those who managed to convince Arredondo and his minions of their loyalty to the king.[20]

In later years many land grantees experienced problems because of damage to their titles and papers during the revolutionary decade. Ignacio de Arocha, son of the "traitor" Tomás who fled with Leal and Delgado, stated in his petition of 1834 to the Mexican government that the documents to his grandfather's (Simón's) land grant were lost for reasons "well known since those who persecuted us as insurgents had very evil intentions and tried by all possible means to harm us." He claimed

---

[19] Chabot, *Texas in 1811*, section on documents concerning Juan Manuel Sambrano; GLO, "Bexar County Sketch Files," folder 55; SA, 16:227–36; John Ogden Leal, "Burials of San Fernando," vol. 2, item no. 942.

[20] Rebel Property Folders, BCSA. Some of those whose houses, lands, etc., were confiscated include Francisco de Arocha, Vicente Travieso, Manuel Delgado, Juan [Martín de] Beramendi, Antonio Baca, José Manuel Delgado, José Delgado, Clemente Delgado, Francisco Rodríguez, Juan Manuel Enríquez, Manuel Pérez, Erasmo Seguín, Tomás de Arocha, Francisco Borrego, José Antonio Curbelo, Gertrudis Móntes, and Luciano Menchaca. Morey, "Attitudes of the Citizens," pp. 113–16.

that the original Arocha title was deliberately despoiled by Arredondo and enemies of the republican system. The Leal descendants claimed the same thing. Ángel Navarro, alcalde in 1832, said that the Béxar Archives passed through many hands during this time and that after Arredondo took possession of them most were lost, and the rest were carried away to Laredo. According to Navarro, this was done to "add misery" to the lives of those suspected or known to be rebels against the crown. Damage came from both sides, however. Governor Antonio Martínez noted the wretched state of the public records on several occasions, saying that it was impossible to find anything before the "entrance of the revolutionary forces."[21]

These disruptions were not limited to the proud old ranching families of San Antonio de Béxar and Nacogdoches. They were common along the entire northern frontier. Perhaps no better example can be found than the fate of Hacienda de Dolores, on the Río Grande. The sons of old Captain José Vásquez Borrego, the rancho's founder, were evidently ardent in Hidalgo's cause; even if they were not, they nonetheless paid the price. One son, Juan José, a priest, was executed in Chihuahua for his support of the movement. Soon afterward a party of Royalists raided the ranch at midnight, taking Macario and Fernando Vásquez Borrego prisoners and forcing them to deliver up keys to the strongbox. Claiming that they were looking for papers from the "Liberal Party," the Royalists then ransacked the place and scattered or destroyed the title documents. They finally left, taking Don Macario to Chihuahua to answer charges. When he returned three months later, he found everything in hopeless disarray, and it became necessary to sell part of the family's Hacienda de Encinas at public auction to pay off a mortgage.

José Marjil de Vidaurri, a grandson of the founder, related the rest of the sad story before a Laredo alcalde in 1828, trying to establish title to the original grant. He said that Don Macario ran away and later died intestate in Monterrey; his son Francisco

---

[21] Virginia H. Taylor, trans. and ed., *The Letters of Antonio Martínez: Last Spanish Governor of Texas, 1817–1822*, p. 244; Virginia H. Taylor, *Spanish Archives of the General Land Office of Texas*, pp. 24–25; Simón and Juan de Arocha grant title, GLO, 31:47.

became insane. Don Anastacio Borrego, "the heir," had died in the Battle of Alazán—a prelude to the decisive Battle of the Medina—and his minor children had been carried away by an aunt. Thus José Marjil held the fort at Dolores until Indian hostilities forced him away in 1814. Such were the hardships of the Borrego-Vidaurri clan, ushered in by Mexico's struggle for freedom. It should be noted that Charles H. Harris, in his study of the northern Mexican latifundio system, claims that this family was also instrumental in the capture of Hidalgo in March, 1811, and the restoration of royal authority. It appears that, like the Menchacas, other men of wealth and property suffered in the turmoils, regardless of their conduct.[22]

It was not long before impending starvation and other critical problems necessitated a more conciliatory policy toward the insurgents at Béxar. On October 10, 1813, Arredondo issued a proclamation of amnesty—a conditional pardon—for those who had fled the province with the broken Republican Army. It was supposedly granted in response to many pleas received from refugees in Louisiana and the Neutral Ground. Excepted from this amnesty were Francisco (de) Arocha, Francisco Ruíz, Juan (de) Veramendi, Vicente Travieso, Pedro Prado, and others whose "accursed" deeds had placed them beyond forgiveness. Among those refused pardon was Samuel Davenport, who carried a price on his head of 250 pesos. He was declared to be a scoundrel, "ungrateful at the kind treatment given him by his government, and who abused the good faith with which he was made a subject of the Spanish monarch." All lands, cattle, and other property that Davenport had accumulated in Texas were, of course, forfeit. He retired to Natchitoches and experimented with sugarcane until his death a decade later.[23]

Providing food continued to be a major problem, with the economy wrecked and the province in tatters. Raids by Lipans

---

[22] Virgil N. Lott and Mercurio Martínez, *Kingdom of Zapata*, pp. 132, 136–38; Jerry Thompson, *Sabers on the Rio Grande*, p. 16; Charles H. Harris, "A Mexican Latifundio: The Economic Empire of the Sánchez Navarro Family, 1765–1821" (Ph.D. diss., University of Texas, 1968), pp. 271–78.

[23] Hatcher, *Opening of Texas*, app. 25; Castañeda, *Catholic Heritage*, 6:123; Haggard, "House of Barr and Davenport," pp. 86–87.

and Comanches, along with rumors of more rebel invasions, prompted an order by Ignacio Pérez in January, 1814, telling the settlers to abandon the ranches and retire to Béxar for safety. Not long afterward Arredondo ordered the confiscation of herds being driven from Texas and the summary trial and execution of "traitorous owners and persons engaged in such trade." This harsh measure was intended to alleviate the plight of the hungry people at the capital, for area ranchers were supposedly worsening the meat shortage by shipping their cattle to "adjacent provinces," that is, Louisiana.

In an opinion dated January 16, 1823, regarding the disposition of stray animals around Béxar, Erasmo Seguín described stock raising during this chaotic period. He said that from 1794 to 1806 raisers began establishing their herds in different places near the villa as well as 20 leagues away. At this time there were no *orejanos* to be found, a fact considered indisputable because ranch hands were dependent on the semi-annual hunts of buffalo to sustain themselves. Beginning in 1807, however, there were so many "raising places" (*criaderos*) that a survey ordered by the government in 1813 found 36,000 head of bovine stock at Béxar. "In that same year Brigadier Arredondo took over this plaza and ordered some of this cattle seized from the ranches. The rest was abandoned in the country because of the war with the barbaric Indians." These ongoing disturbances, noted Seguín, were responsible for the scattered condition of their cattle and the presence of so many strays and *orejanos* a decade later.[24]

One raiser, Doña María Josefa de la Garza, tried in a small way to alleviate the suffering of Arredondo's troops. She donated ten head of cattle to feed the soldiers, patriotically avowing that, if necessary, she would donate the rest of her herd and all her property in defense of her beloved king and master, Fernando VII. Other accounts of the situation of women in the

---

[24] Arredondo to Governor of Texas, January 31, 1814, and Arredondo to Armiñán, February 2, 1814, in Castañeda, *Catholic Heritage*, 6:122; Morey, "Attitudes of the Citizens," p. 117. Seguín's letter and those of M. Arciniega, Barón de Bastrop, Eugenio Flores, and others on the same subject are found in a miscellaneous records folder, described as "Decision on Roundup and Cattle Breeding, 1823," BCSA.

aftermath of defeat are not so positive. One, a petition to the cabildo by Doña Luisa de Luna, suggests utter ruin. Because her husband, Vicente Travieso, was one of those "carried away by caprices and want of judgment to help the iniquitous party of the insurrection," the Royalists had confiscated everything that belonged to him. She and her four small children were reduced to misery and want. Doña Luisa prayed that the cabildo would be moved by pity and have the charity "to give to me one of the rooms of the house known as mine," along with a milk goat so that her unhappy and unfortunate babes might be nourished. In this case restitution was made, but as Félix D. Almaráz Jr., concludes, "generally this was the exception and not the rule." When Señora de Travieso made her will (dated September 29, 1828), among the possessions she listed was "that part of range which I have at the ranch of that place called Las Mulas," along with a house in Saltillo originally owned by her father-in-law, Don Tomás. Regardless of this family's difficulties in preserving their land under the Republic, it appears that at the time of her death title to the Traviesos' Las Mulas was still recognized. In that she was indeed fortunate.[25]

On February 28, 1814, a detailed list was compiled of cattle confiscated from the insurgents "who have left this capital [Béxar]." The number of head involved was 4,577, amounting to 27,462 pesos when evaluated at 6 pesos per animal. Of this total Commissioners Francisco del Pardo y Arce, José Antonio Saucedo, and Luis Galán noted that 400 animals taken from Mariano Rodríguez and 40 from Remigio Leal had been returned to their wives, plus another 646 head consumed by the army, leaving 20,814 pesos for the Royal Treasury. The list not only provides a picture of republicanism at San Antonio but also shows these rebels' cattle brands (brand section F). Perhaps the number of cattle confiscated from each can be taken as a measure of their relative importance as ranchers, if not as revolutionaries. At any rate, there can be little doubt that the Battle of

---

[25] Ford, *Texas Cattle Brands*, p. 2; Almaráz, *Tragic Cavalier*, p. 180; Cassiano-Pérez Collection, Daughters of the Republic of Texas Library at the Alamo, folder 45. For Tomás Travieso's attempt in 1808 to secure title in the name of his son Vicente, see ibid., folder 24.

the Medina dealt a crushing blow to area stock raising and caused severe dislocation of its most prominent breeders, a situation that would not rectify itself while Texas remained in vassalage to Spain.[26]

The deplorable condition of the province was described to Arrendondo by the governor in a letter of May 22, 1814. The citizens, he said, were "hopelessly lost in their misery." No crops were grown above subsistence level, and his garrison was forced to live entirely on meat with no possibility of supplying itself with even a tortilla. From a report made early the following year, the missions were not in much better shape. Father Vallejo observed that the natives to whom property had been given were practically destitute. Of all the formerly flourishing establishments only Mission Refugio was still self-supporting. He said that at the close of 1814 many of its 3,000 head of cattle were left unbranded because of a lack of horses for a roundup.

Hostile Indians raided the mission ranch at will, and the insurgents had also taken a heavy toll on its herds, reducing them down from "10,000 or 12,000 to its present number." Mission Espíritu Santo was in ruins and completely abandoned. Its Indians had fled during the recent disturbances, which had also resulted in the closing of the church at Nacogdoches. Worse than this, almost all of the records for all the missions (kept at San José) were destroyed during the Gutiérrez-Magee invasion and occupation. Padre Vallejo declared that the missions, without proper protection, were constantly exposed to attacks and raids by every hostile tribe from the north.[27]

Such attacks thwarted attempts to reestablish stock raising until the end of the decade, resulting in an almost total pullback from the exposed ranches. Beginning in 1811 and 1812 these

---

[26] This brand list was found at the CA Chancery Office in Austin among the documents now filed in SA, vol. 12, 1807–13, on the 1813 confiscation and sale of the insurgents' property at Béxar (noted in Herbert Eugene Bolton, *Guide to Materials for the United States in the Principal Archives of Mexico*, p. 431, *exp.* 663). Two slightly varying versions of this list, both dated March 21, 1814, are in the Samuel A. Maverick Papers, box 3G8, University of Texas Archives. For a list of those insurgents and their families still in jail at that time, see BAM, roll 53, frames 547–50.

[27] Governor of Texas to Arrendondo, May 22, 1814, in Hatcher, *Opening of Texas*, p. 247, and Grazing Papers, vol. 1; Vallejo, "Noticia de los Misiones," February 11, 1815, Castañeda, *Catholic Heritage*, 6:125–26.

extensive raids swept away the cattlemen not only from around Béxar and along the Nueces but from most of the lands bordering the Río Grande as well. The whole region, where many ranches were beginning to be settled, was depopulated. The former ranchers took refuge in towns along the Río Grande, leaving their stock behind to fend for itself in the *brasada* thickets and *mesquitales* of the lower coastal plains, but not even in town were the terrified settlers safe from Comanche incursions. These raids received much of their impetus from the revolutionary troubles. A report on the Indians of Texas by Juan Antonio Padilla later declared that up until this time the Comanches had not been as well armed, or warlike, nor had they penetrated into places where they were later frequently seen. His views were shared by the Béxar *ayuntamiento*, which stated that the "barbarous" Indians had at all times been masters of the possessions and lives of the unfortunate inhabitants of Texas, "but never with such tenacity and frequency as since the year 1813." These Indians, after making away with cattle, horses, and other property in Texas—killing and capturing a considerable number of its citizens—proceeded to do the same in Coahuila, Nuevo Santander, and parts of Nuevo León.

Padilla's report leaves little doubt that these relentless raids were spurred by the disorders of the revolution and that the hostiles took advantage of the troops' preoccupation with domestic duties. He even charged that foreigners and various rebel Spaniards, survivors of the crashing defeat at El Encinal de Medina, introduced guns among the Indians and encouraged them in laying waste to haciendas and ranchos as remote as Villa Colonia. "They were not lacking Spaniards, still worse, who led them and incited them to kill and burn whatever came their way." Besides all the other plunder, this munitions trade was conducted in exchange for stolen animals, "making a well worn road through the unsettled region towards Natchitoches." The Lipan Apaches joined in, looting exposed ranches of horses and mules, which they sold along with mesteños taken in roundups, as was their custom.[28]

---

[28] Juan Antonio Padilla, "Report on the Barbarous Indians . . . ," December 27, 1819, and Béxar *ayuntamiento* "Instructions for Its Provincial Deputy," November 15, 1820, both in Mattie Austin Hatcher, trans., "Texas in 1820," *Southwestern Historical*

The botanist Jean Louis Berlandier, who visited Texas soon afterward, left a similar description. Where once the countryside had been dotted with ranches and covered with "immense herds" belonging to the inhabitants or missions, very few of these survived. Besides Erasmo Seguín's fortified establishment, already noted, were mentioned only "Los Arrochitos" and another ranch on the opposite bank—most likely the Floreses' Chayopines. San Bartolo stood abandoned, and only the remains of herders' cabins could be seen at various places along the Cíbolo, as on other streams throughout the province. Speaking of former years, Berlandier said that when the friars who managed the missions of Espíritu Santo, Refugio, and Rosario established themselves in these lands they began raising livestock and that toward the end of the previous century ("when these religious establishments began to wane") the number of animals pastured around their domains was so large that the cattle were counted by the thousands.

Since the abandonment of the missions, the war of independence, and the constant hostilities of various Indian tribes who continually invaded these regions, that part of their wealth had never been "exactly known," wrote the young botanist. The herds which once covered the wilderness had disappeared "from the surface of the earth." But if cattle had vanished from Texas, wild horses were "not lacking" in Berlandier's day. They were found in every locality where there was water. Some traveled in herds conservatively estimated at 1,000 to 1,200 head, numbers so large that they "scarcely opened a passage for us." It was noted that many of them appeared to have been formerly domestic stock, perhaps wearing faint *fierros* on their shaggy flanks.[29]

There was little the ordinary stockman could do to withstand all these forces of destruction except pray for deliverance

---

Quarterly 23, no. 1 (July, 1919):47–68; Béxar *ayuntamiento*, "Report on Condition of Texas," May 1, 1821, and Béxar *ayuntamiento*, "Instructions to Its Constitutional Representative," January 30, 1822, both in Blake, Research Collection, 10:228–36, 249–56.

[29] Jean Louis Berlandier, *Journey to Mexico during the Years 1826 to 1834*, trans. Sheila M. Ohlendorf et al., ed. C. H. Muller et al., 1:390, 2:372–73, 544–45, 553–56.

and bide his time. It seems clear that horror and devastation were visited upon the industry during these years, "great numbers of animals both horses and mules" being lost in Texas and on the frontiers of neighboring provinces. Report after report stressed that, if the revolution had partly ruined these lands, the Indians almost completed their destruction. Only when they retired could herdsmen return to gather the scattered remnants of their flocks and herds. The hostile tribes, however, gave them little peace. Most applications for grants of lands and petitions for confirmation of these grants under the Mexican Republic speak of the many Indian troubles suffered during these times, troubles which almost invariably resulted in abandonment of the ranchos. Weakened by the revolutionary turmoils, few families were able to resist the savage onslaughts directed against their possessions, properties, and lives by both Lipans and Comanches.[30]

The raids on Hacienda de Dolores have been mentioned. José Marjil de Vidaurri described his brave attempt to remain on the ranch, saying that Indians first attacked the place in the year 1813. Because his family was living there, José built a stone tower "in order to perpetuate the occupation." When the hostiles menaced Alías Clareño, Colonel Felipe de la Garza furnished him with a guard of three soldiers and saddle mules to remove his family and household goods. But the Indians hit again, carrying away stock and killing a servant; afterward they returned and killed his oldest son, who had been left in charge. Vidaurri had thus built his *torreón* to no avail. Another ranching family left in such haste that they took nothing from the house "or any of the extensive herds on the range." Los Ojuelos was abandoned by Eugenio Gutiérrez, and although his son Isidro returned several years later, he too was forced away by the Indians. San Antonio Viejo was another establishment which succumbed to such attacks.

Around the Nueces, Comanches killed fourteen people at the Tithesman's Ranch in 1814, and their continual raids de-

---

[30] Virginia H. Taylor, comp., *Index to Spanish and Mexican Land Grants in Texas*, touches on the problems faced by grantees in the Nueces Strip, including Indian raids; see especially pp. 11–12.

stroyed the "fort" of Casa Blanca. Martín de León, Enríque Villarreal, and other stockmen were forced to leave. Villarreal, however, held out at Rincón del Oso until 1817, visiting the ranch only at branding time. The attack on Calvillo's ranch, near Las Cabras, in the spring of 1814 has already been noted; Carlos Martínez was another old cattleman who met his end, killed in 1815 by Indians at his Rancho del Señor San José. Above Laredo the Villa of Palafox was destroyed in 1818, when raids were especially severe. Two years later the ranch Las Comitas was attacked by Comanches and burned to the ground. In a Laredo census, given on April 30, 1819, Alcalde Ildefonso Ramón noted that of the forty-four ranches in the vicinity thirty-seven had been abandoned "on account of the desolating war with the barbarous Indians of the North." The other seven ranches were operated only at great risk, and those who suffered most acutely were the owners in outlying areas.[31]

These troubles extended well past the Spanish era, but it appears that they lessened somewhat as Mexico entered its pe-

---

[31] Lott and Martínez, *Kingdom of Zapata*, pp. 22, 137–38; Eugene George, *Historic Architecture of Texas: The Falcón Reservoir*, p. 28; Grimm, *Llanos Mestenas*, pp. 24, 66; NCHS, *History of Nueces County*, pp. 31–32; Thompson, *Sabers on the Rio Grande*, pp. 42–43; Robert S. Weddle and Robert H. Thonhoff, *Drama and Conflict: The Texas Saga of 1776*, p. 159.

riod of independence. Perhaps this was due to a national surge of optimism over the change and increased tenacity by frontier stockmen. Evidence also suggests that the ranches along the lower Río Grande were less seriously affected by the raids that consumed Texas and Coahuila, despite Padilla's assertion that the plundering reached as deep as Villa Colonia (Nuevo Santander). Such evidence is contained in a long report prepared by Felipe Roque de la Portilla in December, 1814, at the order of Arredondo, for the jurisdiction of Villa del Refugio (Matamoros). He, of course, was the same man who had attempted to establish a stock-raising colony for Governor Cordero on the San Marcos River before Indian trouble caused the project to be abandoned. Portilla moved back to his Rancho de Santa Rita, in the brush country. His report of 1814 indicates that it was a large operation, jointly occupied by a number of prominent cattlemen of the lower valley and guarded by a troop of soldiers. It seems that he remained there until his move to the Irish settlement on the Nueces, for which empresario contract he was an adviser following his daughter's marriage to colonizer James Power. Portilla's list contains the names of twenty-eight ranches and an enumeration of the people at each ranch (appendix K). He said that his jurisdiction contained 7,623 head of cattle, 25,310 horses, 27,082 sheep and goats (*ganado cabrío*), and 275 hogs. Such figures reflect relative prosperity at a time when royal troops in Béxar had difficulty finding a single tortilla to eat.[32]

Following Arredondo's brutal suppression of republicanism at Béxar, Texas experienced a succession of short-term military governors, most of whom were unable to deal with the many problems plaguing the province. At times the turnover of interim administrators was so rapid that communications were simply addressed "Governor of Texas." One such was the letter of mid-February, 1817, which Intendant Manuel de Acevedo directed to Béxar from San Luis Potosí. It called attention to the viceroy's letter of January 21 of the same year concerning regu-

[32] Felipe Roque de la Portilla, "Lista varios Ranchos . . . y sus dueños," December 22, 1814, MA, 16:47, box 2Q269, University of Texas Archives; John Brendan Flannery, *The Irish Texans*, p. 32.

lations on the wholesale slaughter of stock rampant in the Interior Provinces. Acevedo claimed that a good part of the small stock had recently been slaughtered, being considered superfluous; these animals, however, were of importance in preserving the growth of the flocks. The higher branches of government, said the *intendente*, were not in a position to correct these abuses but could not ignore them.

Acevedo continued to quote from the viceroy's letter, which noted that regulations concerning these matters had been established before 1787. Therefore, he said, the Audiencia had directed him to say that in no respect should changes be made in practices "known to have been previously established." His decree further stipulated that individuals interested in obtaining a cattle brand or slaughtering unneeded or unfit animals, "provided the increase of the species is not hindered by such killing," should apply to higher authorities, that is, his *intendencia*. When permission was sought to slaughter cattle, the viceroy required applications to be accompanied by documents attesting that the stock in question was actually unfit or unneeded. In such cases, a judge, a local priest, or two citizens of capable intelligence must testify that the slaughters were not harmful to future propagation. These measures, Acevedo said, were being circulated to district officials in his *intendencia* for their guidance.[33]

Acknowledging these orders on March 27 was Manuel Pardo. Of all interim appointees perhaps he held the record for serving the shortest time as governor of Texas, from March 20 to May 27, 1817.[34] Two days before this colonel of cavalry turned his office over to his successor, he issued a decree to the

---

[33] Acevedo to Governor of Texas, February 17, 1817, Grazing Papers, vol. 2. For information on the frontier trade in horses, ammunition, etc., at this time, see Governor of Texas to the commandant general, August 29, 1816, BA, enclosing testimony of Edmund Quirk and companions; see also *expediente*, August 13–October 29, 1816, BA, dealing with the protest of an embargo on stock by Irinco Castellón, Leandro San Miguel, Juan José Ybarbo, etc. (along with some belonging to Quirk).

[34] Castañeda (*Catholic Heritage*, 6:127) says that Mariano Varela served only one week as governor and that his term was the shortest, but Odie B. Faulk (*The Last Years of Spanish Texas, 1778–1821*, p. 36, citing *Handbook of Texas*, 2:334), names Pardo as enjoying this dubious distinction.

citizens on controlling their stock. All owners of hogs and calves were required to keep them confined. If the animals wandered loose in the streets, a fine of 4 reales per head would be levied against the owner. Stock found in planted fields was to be seized and owners held responsible for damages. Owners who permitted their animals to drink from the main ditch crossing the city would be fined 1 peso. The next article forbade washing clothes in the canal, tossing garbage into it, or otherwise fouling it, since this ditch provided drinking water for the inhabitants.[35]

Pardo was succeeded by Colonel Antonio María Martínez, who served until April 11, 1822. He was, therefore, a transitional figure, the last Spanish governor and the first Mexican chief executive of Texas. At first Martínez refused the governorship, but when Viceroy Juan Ruíz de Apodaca promised aid and assistance to the province, he accepted the job. Martínez, like many others before him, was bitterly disappointed. His administration was little more than a holding action; he was frustrated by his inability to protect the eastern frontier against foreign aggression, block the heavy contraband trade, or defend the citizens from repeated Indian attacks. Much of his concern was directed against internal disorder and the activities of the Spaniards who continued to wage guerrilla war against the king.

Scarcely had Martínez taken office when his communications began to reflect his consternation over the movements of the "infamous Spaniard" Vicente Travieso, who was said to be advancing on Bahía Presidio with a force of men in conjunction with Anglos who had landed at Matagorda Bay. Martínez received word that Travieso intended to pass through the vicinity of La Bahía with 100 rebels to join his "fellow traitor" Gutiérrez.

Other letters contain similar hints of ongoing civil disturbances in the province. Claudio Hernández, a *vecino* of Béxar, was noted as having been in jail for nearly two years on charges of disloyalty. Hernández, after being kept in chains for twenty months, appealed to Martínez for release. In October, 1817, de-

---

[35] Pardo to Acevedo, March 27, 1817, BAM, roll 58, frame 215; Pardo to the Public, May 25, 1817, Grazing Papers, vol. 2.

spairing of mercy, he escaped from prison, taking with him a local boy, a servant, and some stock stolen from various citizens. Pursuit was ineffectual, and the governor commented on the breakout, made with the help of two of Hernández's guards, saying that his escape to the United States, and others, had led him to draw unpleasant conclusions about local security. Although he suspected some citizens of corresponding with traitors in those lands, his active confidential investigators had not discovered much. The zeal and "constant suspicion" that Martínez promised to maintain availed him little in this particular instance. Two years later Hernández was still at large.[36]

Nor was this an isolated case. In August, 1817, Pedro Procela, alias "El Chino," appeared before the governor asking to take protective advantage of the "recent pardon" (perhaps the king's decree of amnesty of September 29, 1815). He had returned from the United States and also from the interior after soliciting amnesty on the charge of insurrection. Governor Martínez detained Procela until a decision was reached by his superiors, but the supplicant soon fled back into the interior taking with him *vecinos* Rafael Martínez, José Antonio Carvajal, José Antonio Farías, and several others, not to mention nineteen head of stolen stock. "El Chino" faded from view, but it is safe to guess that he eventually turned up among his children and kinsmen in East Texas. In connection with these dispersed people, it is interesting to note that in November, 1818, Juan Manuel Sambrano asked Martínez to instruct Captain Juan de Castañeda (who was being sent to eject the French from Champ d'Asile, on the Trinity River, and to eject foreigners from East Texas) to treat the old residents of Nacogdoches with consideration since they did not take part in rebellions against the king and might help control the restless Indians.[37]

---

[36] Martínez to Arredondo, July 6, August 2, November 3, 1817, and October 13, 1819, in Taylor, *Letters of Martínez*, pp. 17, 33, 73, 272; SA, 14:1–51. For a detailed account of various insurgent movements during this time, see Fane Downs, "Governor Antonio Martínez and the Defense of Texas from Foreign Invasion," *Texas Military History* 7, no. 1 (Spring, 1968):27–43.

[37] Martínez to Arredondo, August 27 and September 30, 1817, in Taylor, *Letters of Martínez*, pp. 44, 65; Sambrano to Martínez, November 1, 1818, BA.

Throughout the decade others charged with rebellion managed to clear themselves. On October 4, 1815, Juan Martín de Veramendi was exonerated by Arredondo, and his property was restored. He was one of the few who had specifically been denied amnesty in October, 1813, yet he won fairly rapid restitution. Erasmo Seguín was not cleared of treason until March, 1819, when the governor was notified that the señor auditor de guerra had reached this decision. The charge against Seguín: receiving a letter from Natchitoches written by the infamous José Álvarez Toledo and the rebel Tomás de Arocha. On account of "his miserable condition and that of his family," however, he was allowed to plead his case at Saltillo in 1815.

After Seguín's pardon an order was issued for the return of his confiscated property by the *intendente*, the official responsible for disposition of all impounded rebel possessions. At the time Don Erasmo's house was being used as a public school. In regaining his property—and his status as a militia captain—Seguín was more fortunate than others, such as the Arochas. The former home of this rebel family, situated behind the guardhouse, was offered at auction, as were many other confiscated estates. Martínez suggested that the *intendencia* at San Luis Potosí reduce its price so that the Arocha structure, valued at 600 pesos, could be purchased as a granary for the Béxar Company.[38]

All these assaults on their honor and property left deep scars on the proud descendants of Canary Island hidalgos. Speaking of citizens in exile, the Béxar *ayuntamiento* later said that "those who are still living wish only to come back to the bosom of their families, notwithstanding the regret of being deprived of their property, which has been confiscated, and of living in a wretched country doomed to the dangers of incessant Indian aggressions." Unable to make a fair estimate of the property loss caused by the revolutionary struggle, the council could only observe that since its reconquest the province had

---

[38] "Sumaria información formada contra Dn. José Erasmo Seguín . . . acusado de infidente," SA, 13:1–114; Martínez to Arredondo, April 19, June 28, November 25, 1819, Taylor, *Letters of Martínez*, pp. 221, 240, 282; Chabot, *Makers of San Antonio*, p. 119.

advanced at an amazing rate toward ruin and destruction. Soon after Mexican independence, however, the city fathers stated in no uncertain terms their feelings on the property sequestered when residents fled Arredondo's wrath. They wanted it restored to its former owners, as done in cases where the property had not already been sold. Going one step further, they suggested that the same should be done for estates that had passed into the hands of another, if the "original and legitimate owners" claimed their rights. The difficulties that would arise from such restitution were provided for. It was considered to be a question of equity, now that the horrors of the past decade were over. By this time the damage had long since been done, even when something tangible could be salvaged from the shambles.[39]

On several occasions Governor Martínez expressed his repugnance at pardoning traitors. When he was informed that Lieutenant Colonel Ignacio Pérez had provisionally pardoned thirty-four citizens found living in wretched circumstances at Nacogdoches and in the Neutral Ground at Bayou Pierre, Los Adaes, Vallecillo, and Tres Llanos, he told the commandant general how he felt in no uncertain terms. In his opinion "these are the most detrimental inhabitants this province could have," not only because they took part in and supported the revolutions which were fomented, but also because they traded with the Indian nations, equipping them with arms, munitions, and other effects "with which they then make war on us."

Still, when Martínez sent Erasmo Seguín, Juan Martín de Veramendi, and several other pardoned rebels to meet colonizer Moses Austin and escort him to Béxar, these delegates had another mission to fulfill. It was described by the deceased empresario's son Stephen F. Austin, writing from Natchitoches in July, 1821: "Don Joseph Erasmo Seguín, a Spanish gentleman from San Antonio was dispatched by governor Martínez for the express purpose of informing my father of the confirmation of his grant by the governor general, and to invite back all the

[39] Béxar *ayuntamiento*, "Report on Condition of Texas," May 1, 1821, NA; Béxar *ayuntamiento*, "Instructions to Its Constitutional Representative," January 30, 1822, NA. The subject of restoring confiscated property was also addressed in a set of instructions the *ayuntamiento* drew up for its provincial deputy on November 15, 1820, BA.

fugitive Spaniards who fled in the revolution of 1812, most of whom, I am informed, will return to their country again." As noted, quite a few former residents returned to their homes west of the Sabine at this time.[40]

Most of Governor Martínez's time was spent on more routine matters, such as keeping his soldiers fed and mounted. It is difficult to say which of the two consumed the greater part of his energy, for both were constant preoccupations. From the moment the governor entered Texas, food was a priority. On May 31, 1817, he told the viceroy that the garrison at Béxar had not one serviceable horse and that the ragged, half-starved troops could scarcely walk. He informed the commandant general that the troops had been living entirely on field roots for several days. On June 28 he reported that the men of the garrison were near revolt and could no longer endure the hunger and want oppressing their families. He had convoked a council of ways and means but admitted that nothing was offered but "promises of a few cattle." A party was sent to gather and ration them to avoid starvation.

In his attempt to assess the region's food supply he ordered a list drawn up of those possessing livestock. The list, signed by Francisco Flores and José Manuel Granados, was submitted on June 26 (appendix L). Typical of results Martínez gained from local stockmen, the itemization was delivered "sin expresar el numero" (without noting the number). So it would go for the remainder of his term, poverty and hunger constantly menacing the province. Three years later Martínez was still complaining that the "great need" of his troops forced them to eat every roasting ear as soon as it appeared in the cornfields. He was as powerless as ever to restrain them or to satisfy the incessant protests of local *vecinos* about their livestock and crop losses.[41]

No less a problem was keeping his men in the saddle. Ignacio

---

[40] Martínez to Arredondo, November 13, 1819, in Taylor, *Letters of Martínez*, p. 280; Austin to ———, July 1, 1821, in Eugene C. Barker, ed., "The Austin Papers," pt. 1, p. 399; for the general pardon to Anglo-Americans who had borne arms in favor of the insurgents, see Martínez to Seguín, August 29, 1820, BA; see also Seguín to Martínez, June 23, 1821, Blake, Research Collection, 10:241.

[41] Martínez to Arredondo, June 28, 1817, July 21, 1820, in Taylor, *Letters of Martínez*, pp. 15, 351.

Pérez informed the governor in November, 1817, that the horses of the Bahía Company were useless and that he had sent twenty men to the Nueces to catch mustangs so that his squad could be mounted. Pérez ordered that the mesteños caught were to be branded and returned to the presidio. Despairing of receiving mounts from the commandant general—even the troops of Nuevo Santander were "on foot"—Martínez wrote on November 12 concerning the difficulties to be expected in using wild horses. He told Arredondo that his predecessor (Pardo) had made every effort to round up mustangs and use them as mounts for provincial troops and that he had followed this policy. However, the governor was "extremely doubtful" that mustangs would ever serve this purpose, despite the commandant general's instructions for him to redouble his efforts to capture them. He assured Arredondo that he would nonetheless avail himself "of every opportunity to mount these troops, even on mustangs which is my only recourse."

A year later Martínez was still resorting to mustang round-ups to provide animals for a contemplated expedition. Although no gentle animals could be found, thirty-one colts were captured and brought in "without the rough treatment which is sometimes necessary." Breaking mustangs was always a problem, and on more than one occasion the governor complained that his soldiers could not use them because of their half-wild condition. In 1818 he noted that the small herd of horses left at Béxar was in a deplorable state because of continual thievery. On September 4 of the next year he purchased thirteen horses from a visiting party of soldiers at 10 pesos each. He noticed that the animals were branded with a P, the brand of remounts belonging to that officer's party. Suspecting that something was amiss, Martínez questioned the officer and relayed his explanation—a likely story—to the commandant general: the officer had marked them as royal property so that in case they were lost "he would have more right to claim them should they be found."[42]

As previously noted, horses recaptured from the Indians or

---

[42] Pérez to Martínez, November 1, 1817, Grazing Papers, vol. 2; Martínez to Arredondo, November 12 and 30, 1817, October 30, 1818, September 4, 18, and 19, 1819, in Taylor, *Letters of Martínez*, pp. 77–78, 82, 191, 259.

gathered as strays were often awarded to soldiers needing mounts. Instructions for the disposal of branded stock taken from Indians had been forwarded to Texas in the spring of 1817, but the problem was a long-standing one. The practice of sequestration was put to good use by Martínez. For example, on February 8, 1820, Lieutenant Colonel Pérez presented to Martínez a list of 147 mules and 350 horses captured by various soldiers on the frontier (brand section G). This list showed the animals' brands and supposedly the individuals to whom they belonged. On February 14, Martínez sent the documents to Arredondo with a cover letter explaining that they were for the commandant general's information and decision about their disposition. This is one of the longer samples of early-nineteenth-century Spanish brands I have found. Like most other military lists, it does not attempt to identify the proper owners, but it is possible that such compilations were posted at various presidios to give notice to area stock owners.

The governor was careful to explain that some of the above animals were missing, stolen by deserters. By April 26, Martínez had received a reply informing him that the recaptured animals were to be delivered to their legitimate owners, if claimed, and that he was to proceed in this case with "due circumspection." Martínez told Arredondo that the animals had already been distributed to his troops for use in the performance of routine duties which had to be left undone when the men were without mounts. The distribution was made, he noted, on condition that if any individual proved his full and rightful ownership to an animal payment for it would be credited to the soldier's company according to a valuation made at that time. Thus, for all practical purposes, such horses belonged to the troopers using them until other ownership was proved. Such a policy, said Martínez, was consistent with superior orders effected "in former times."[43]

[43] Martínez to Arredondo, February 14 and April 26, 1820, Taylor, *Letters of Martínez*, pp. 300, 319; Ignacio Pérez, "List of Recaptured Animals . . . Showing Brands with a Description," February 8, 1820, BA, box 4D101, University of Texas Archives. See also the brand lists: Francisco García to Martínez, June 8, 1822, BA; José Salinas, "Brands on Animals Taken from the Comanches and Given to Soldiers," June 22, [?], BA; Fernando Rodríguez, "Brands on Horses and Mules Taken from the Indians and Others Belonging to the Crown Which Were Given to Soldiers" (n.d.), BA.

All this horse catching was evidently confined to the military, a restriction that did not sit well with the restless, impoverished citizens. Since the revolution Texas had literally been under martial law and its livestock industry suspended. Any benefits from the exploitation of mesteños and *orejanos* during this period were derived by soldiers through the slaughter of cattle in the pastures for sustenance; the off-the-record personal appropriation of *mostrencos* for the soldiers' caballadas; the capture of mustangs, horses of unknown brands, and others for their own use; and the collection of the customary fees from private citizens—none of which monies accrued to the public good.

Finally in 1820 the Béxar *ayuntamiento* addressed these issues in a set of instructions to its provincial deputy, Don Ambrosio Aldasoro. It asked that citizens be permitted to round up wild horses, saying that roundups had been prohibited by Arredondo "because it is alleged that they wish to make this their sole occupation." The prohibition had evidently been instituted to combat rampant smuggling, a practice which the councilmen claimed citizens engaged in not to accumulate riches but to alleviate ever-present sufferings and supply themselves with bare necessities. No doubt the subjugator of Texas was touched by this tale of woe. He was perhaps less amused at the *ayuntamiento*'s call for all branded horses captured from the Indians or in other military operations to benefit a new city mesteño fund, not the royal service and its hard-pressed soldiery.[44]

The name Ignacio Pérez is important in any consideration of ranching during this time. He was generally regarded as the foremost cattleman in the province at the end of the Spanish era, as suggested by the appearance of his name at the top of the raisers' compilation of 1817. Governor Martínez called him the only individual in Béxar who possessed any material resources, adding that from what he had observed "it seems that he [Pérez] wishes to keep all the citizens submerged in poverty while he assumes an attitude of superiority over all of them." This, said the governor, was especially true of Pérez's wife, and he obviously resented the prosperous couple's "arrogance" and their lack of support for his measures on behalf of the public welfare. The governor's correspondence with the commandant general nevertheless shows that time and again he was forced to rely on Pérez's capable services in managing the province and that the lieutenant colonel was in fact his right-hand man.

Pérez, born in 1761, was the descendant of a Canary Island family—if not through Joseph Antonio Pérez Casanova and Paula Granados, as Chabot says, then through his father Domíngo's being the son of Isleño Antonio de los Santos's daughter María and her husband, Josef Pérez, whose family came to Texas from Coahuila. In 1781 Ignacio married Clemencia Hernández, the granddaughter of old Don Andrés Hernández, the founder of Rancho de San Bartolo. Ignacio had seen service in the Interior Provinces as a captain of cavalry and had also served as an alcalde before the Hidalgo revolt, during which he appears to have remained firmly loyalist. He was one of the principal counterinsurgents in the coup against Las Casas and sat on

---

[44] Béxar *ayuntamiento*, "Instructions for Its Provincial Deputy," November 15, 1820, BA.

Sambrano's ruling junta. From his post as commandant of the militia of the province, he was temporarily elevated to the governorship in 1816, serving nine months before turning the office over to Manuel Pardo for his brief tenure. Unlike some of his fellow citizens, who switched from royalism to republicanism and back again, Pérez was a steady defender of the crown. He prospered from his constancy. One of his daughters married Governor Antonio Cordero in 1806, and a son, José Ignacio, on his death in 1852 left "one of the most formidable estates in the community," including twenty-eight different properties. Among them was the building known as the Governor's Palace, which had been bought from the Menchacas in 1804.[45]

On April 25, 1818, an incident came to light which resulted in what was possibly the first major attempt by the citizens to resume their normal ranching activities since the upheavals of the revolution. José Antonio de la Garza complained to the governor about the difficulty he had experienced in branding his stock according to custom. It seems that the greater part of his herd had wandered into the pastures of Pérez, who would not allow them to be removed. Martínez searched the archives for some document "that might reveal the proper procedure to follow, possibly some order that you [the commandant general] may have issued for the guidance of my predecessors," but found nothing. Consequently, he referred the case to the ciudad's councilmen for their opinion.[46] In view of Don Ignacio's position, the governor was very reluctant to commit himself without having the "necessary knowledge or experience" to guide a decision.[47]

In reply, the cabildo seized the opportunity to solicit per-

---

[45] Frederick C. Chabot, *San Antonio and Its Beginnings*, p. 30; Chabot, *Makers of San Antonio*, p. 179; Will of Antonio de los Santos, 1756, Bexar County Protocol Book 1, item no. 6, BCSA, brought to my attention by Mrs. Gloria V. Cadena. After Cordero died, Ignacio's daughter married José Cassiano in 1828; hence the importance of the Cassiano-Pérez Collection, in the Daughters of the Republic of Texas Library at the Alamo.

[46] San Antonio de Béxar was elevated from villa (town) to ciudad (city) status as a result of citizens' efforts to topple Las Casas in 1811 and restore royal authority. Its coat of arms proclaimed the motto "Loyalty Conquers Perfidy."

[47] Martínez to Arredondo, April 25, 1818, in Taylor, *Letters of Martínez*, pp. 119–20; Castañeda, *Catholic Heritage*, 6:44.

mission for a roundup, as did the garrison's officers and various citizens. Corridas were long overdue because of past proclamations forbidding the molestation of breeding stock plus the unsettled conditions brought on by civil disorders and Indian depredations. In a petition dated May 14 the cabildo reported to Martínez that citizens were only exercising lawful rights over their property by urging a roundup, stressing that cattle found in summer pastures should be recognized as belonging to the raisers. Their ranches had been abandoned for five years (since 1813) owing to the Indian raids. The frequent incursions had kept them from gathering the stock they had raised, especially cattle, "which is wandering along the plains, and it is sure that the longer they take to gather it the farther it goes."

They pointed out the benefit to be derived from a general roundup by citizens, as well as by troops of the presidio, saying that its greatest significance would be to relieve the unfortunate situation of the whole population, deprived of meat and other products, such as lard, candles, and soap. Another request was mentioned by the cattlemen: they asked for a detachment of soldiers to be stationed midway between Béxar and La Bahía, a move which would provide them with the opportunity to take cattle found in outlying summer pastures and establish themselves again as stock raisers. They emphasized the service such a guard could render in blocking the way the Indians "so frequently enter the town." Furthermore, with a detachment at that location it would be easier to give opportune notice of the presence of an enemy, whoever it might be.[48]

This last request was for something like the former outpost on the Cíbolo, impossible to provide because Governor Martínez had not received the promised support from the viceroy. The enemy, "whoever it might be," was an obvious reference to the threat still posed by armed adventurers and unreconciled revolutionaries. Faced with the task of expelling foreigners from Galveston Island and Atascosito with soldiers not only on foot but "barefooted as well," the governor must have been slightly irritated by the citizens' request for a military post to guard their cattle roundup and future grazing opera-

[48] Béxar cabildo to Martínez, May 14, 1818, Grazing Papers, vol. 2.

tions. He evidently told them that such roundups were forbidden, expecting to hear no more on the matter. If so, he seriously misjudged the obstinacy of his subjects.[49]

Undaunted, the cabildo and the garrison of the city, led by Joseph María Sambrano, addressed another petition to Martínez on July 23. They informed him that they intended to call a meeting on the twenty-sixth to discuss the easiest and best way to collect from summer pastures all stock possible, both branded and unbranded. Their stated purpose was to help alleviate the emergencies that Béxar continued to suffer because of the aforementioned scarcities. Their petition again pressed the advantages to the general welfare that would result from such a roundup and chided the governor for his decree of May 6: "... it is not just to deny this community the last resource [a roundup] that remains for its subsistence as it is impossible to apply to another means on account of lack of resources." They proposed to share the unbranded stock in proportion to the number of branded stock they owned, assuring the governor that their conduct would be such as to trouble him no longer. In closing, they asked for a reply and hoped that Martínez would help the stock raisers by furnishing troops. The signers were Joseph María Sambrano, José Antonio de la Garza, Albino Pacheco, and Manuel Salinas.[50]

The first signer was, as noted, a brother of Juan Manuel Sambrano, and since the intended meeting was being called in response to a written message received from "the colonel," it is evident that the subdeacon was a key figure in the determination to hold a corrida. Just the preceding March, Governor Martínez had received orders from the commandant general that Lieutenant Colonel Juan Manuel Sambrano was to be admitted to the *compañía volante* ("flying company") of Parras, which was stationed at old Mission Valero, with the rank of captain.[51] Although it would not be long before the soldiering

---

[49] Martínez to Arredondo, May 8, 1818, in Taylor, *Letters of Martínez*, pp. 123–24.

[50] The cabildo and garrison of the town to Martínez, July 23, 1818, Grazing Papers, vol. 1, pt. 2, pp. 193–97.

[51] The company hailed from Alamo de Parras, in Coahuila, hence "Alamo." The resulting settlement (after 1801) was known as Pueblo de San José y Santiago del Alamo.

clergyman incited "disgraceful scandals" and caused serious problems for the governor, at the time of the roundup sessions it does not appear that his activities had yet prejudiced Martínez against the idea.

On July 26 the cabildo met in extraordinary session and decided to call various owners together for the purpose of agreeing on the best roundup procedure. This convocation took place two days later, and after discussion a detailed plan was adopted by unanimous vote. It was submitted to the assembled eighteen cattlemen, each of whom signed the proposal, thereby "renouncing in particular the rights and privileges belonging to him, submitting in all particulars to the enforcement of the articles ... by the illustrious *ayuntamiento*." Members of this governing body were shown to be José María Sambrano, presiding first alcalde; the Barón de Bastrop, second alcalde; José Yturri, Agustín Ruíz, José Antonio de la Garza, and Alvino Pacheco, *regidores*; and Manuel Salinas, *procurador* (clerk). Don Ignacio Pérez was not among those petitioning for the roundup; he was on the San Marcos River with one hundred men, chasing Indians.[52]

The agreement contains eight articles, some of which reflect a new mood of communalism and cooperation. Cattle taken and assembled on the first drive were to be divided by lot according to owners' brands. Such work would be performed by those who followed on foot, a procedure specified for all other roundups as well. Owners were permitted to mark and brand all unbranded stock which belonged to them after distribution was made according to the above proportion. In any disputes over strays, "this legislative body shall decide what is proper"; its decision was final. Persons who did not attend the roundups would be charged 4 reales a head for cows and calves and 2 reales a head for bulls allotted to them, this charge to

[52] Martínez to Arredondo, June 2 and 7, 1818, in Taylor, *Letters of Martínez*, pp. 137–41. Signers of the document, besides the cabildo members who also signed, were José Flores, Francisco Xavier Bustillos, José María Granados, Ygnacio Villaseñor, Juan Manuel Sambrano, Francisco García, Francisco Móntes, Juan Martín de Veramendi, Francisco Flores, Juan Francisco de Móntes, Francisco Flores, Fernando Rodríguez, Remigo Pérez, Luis Galán, Vicente Mich[e]li, Juan Courbiere, Francisco Farías, and José María de Arocha.

benefit those who incurred costs by riding out to hunt, the chief herdsman, and the cabildo.

Those owners who desired to leave their cattle in the pasture were permitted to do so; cattle left that belonged to another were to be delivered to that owner. The council was entrusted with electing a person to attend the roundups and preside over the separation and distribution; the results would be reported back to that body. If some cattle were left over which owners did not wish to kill or otherwise use, they could guard them in common, each one contributing in proportion to the number owned. Such a communal effort would reduce the number of herdsmen needed to guard the stock against Indians. Failure of owners of pastures and stock to attend the roundups would result in the loss of any *orejanos* they might be entitled to; for branded cattle assigned to them, they must pay the costs specified in article 3. Last, it was agreed that cattle could be pursued on all pastures and public lands, provided the ranchers on the west would hunt there until they had assembled their cattle. On the south, ranchers could gather all along the Laredo Road to the Nueces; on the north, "as far as they can go."

The agreement assigned roundup areas to the ranchers of the San Antonio River and its tributary the Cíbolo, much as the land had been divided for hunting purposes in the past. These jurisdictions were as follows: (1) ranches on the Salado, on the banks of the river, and at Calaveras, (2) ranches on the river prairies, or the lower Calaveras, to the junction of the Cleto, (3) ranches of the "other part of the river," and (4) ranches of the Chayopin. The first two categories covered lands east of Béxar toward the old hunting areas bounded by the San Antonio and Guadalupe rivers to the Cleto, and most likely beyond. The latter two centered on the lands between the San Antonio and Nueces rivers lying mostly east of the Laredo Road. If in fact cattle sweeps were made all the way to the "mouth of the Nueces," as outlined, they would have intruded into the pastures of Mission Refugio. Most likely the intention was to strike south from the junction of the Ecleto and the San Antonio, touching the Nueces in the vicinity of present George West, and working back up to Borrego Creek. This would put the "ranches of the Chayopin" west of them, in present Atascosa County. The latter were probably the cattlemen in the vicinity of the Floreses' Rancho de Chayopines, that is, those along the right bank of the river above modern-day Floresville. Picosa Creek (one of the limits mentioned) runs in this area, joining the river opposite Floresville, just above Las Cabras Ranch.[53]

It is unknown whether Governor Martínez permitted this roundup, but considering all the plans laid by the ranchers, their resolute nature, and the governor's tendency toward ineffectualism, the chances are that the corrida was held. It is interesting to note that the plans do not mention any taxes accruing to His Majesty for the "privilege" of catching mesteños or *orejanos*. The fees involved were now being levied against absentee owners, to the benefit of those who organized and participated in the roundups—and this for gathering cattle already owned and branded. In any case, no mention was made of this troublesome situation to Commandant General Arredondo. Martínez continued to harangue him about failures to deliver needed foodstuffs and his own inability to "promote the agricultural industry" in Texas, which the governor considered his primary duty. For some curious reason Martínez seemed uninterested in the more obvious benefits to be derived from promoting stock raising, preferring instead to nag the admittedly few farmers of Béxar to cultivate crops, though he was unable to provide them with seed.

That the roundup negotiations of 1818 marked an important turning point for stock raising, as far as the ranchers were concerned, is confirmed by a letter from Erasmo Seguín to the governor five years later. On the subject of *orejanos* and the social disruptions producing them, he said that since the troubles of 1813 their cattle had not grazed locally but were widely scattered owing to the ongoing disturbances. He said, "Now if—as I have shown—at that time there were no *orejanos* and those under care were abandoned for said reasons, can it be believed that the cattle at present has any other origin than that produced by these events?" Logic dictated that strays be-

---

[53] Cabildo session, July 28, 1818, Grazing Papers, vol. 1, pt. 2, pp. 193–97.

longed to the raisers, and if the *orejanos* were their property, such rights should be respected by all as "sacred." Let it not be argued, said Seguín, that the laws relating to marks and brands should govern (as in a dispute of ownership in which each raiser could claim his property), because here no brands existed and the evidence was compelling.

Don Erasmo continued: "Thus was it recognized by *ayuntamiento* in 1818, and all the raisers in a solemn act agreed to impose upon themselves rules for strays (*ganado alzado*) and they should adhere to it." Seguín added that this was his opinion, even though he was a raiser himself, implying that it might have been more profitable for him to exploit unmarked animals on his own rather than abide by the accord of 1818. His observations were largely sustained by eleven other accounts written in January, 1823, in what appears to have been a local junta on the question. But also implied by the "solemn act" taken in the year 1818 is that it was taken to a purpose and that the rules adopted were applied to a roundup which did indeed occur.[54]

Even if plans were made for the roundup without Don Ignacio Pérez's assistance, the governor still considered him the most substantial *criador* of Béxar. Writing in July, 1818, about an expedition being planned to rout foreigners from their nests in Atascosito, Martínez told Arredondo that it was necessary to secure some cattle to be driven in front of the division. He estimated that 300 head were required because after the column left Béxar there would be no other source of supply, not even buffalo. Efforts to obtain such stock locally had failed "because these *vecinos* have none." Only Pérez, he noted, kept his cattle in good condition, and was able to do so because it was pastured near the city. This pasturage was doubtless on the 4 leagues of land lying along the southwest side of the Medina granted to the lieutenant colonel on March 27, 1808. Its lower boundary was at La Barranca (called Bluff Bank in later survey notes), near the Laredo Ford (Garza's Crossing), extending upriver to Dolores

---

[54] Louis Lenz Collection, box 3J326, University of Texas Archives, contains a rather awkward translation of these documents; originals in the Office of the City Clerk, City Council Minutes Record Book, San Antonio (see also note 24, above for their location in BCSA).

Crossing. The latter crossing, one of three fords on the Medina, later known as Pérez Crossing, sat astride the lower Camino Real to Presidio San Juan Bautista. Pérez owned another league of land—opposite the river inside its fork with the León—with a thoroughfare linking these adjacent grants to the beef market in Béxar.[55]

But if he was admirably situated and suited to exploit this market, it must be wondered what the prosperous Don Ignacio did with all his prime beef. For example, in early March, 1820, Martínez had yet another fiasco to report to his *comandante*. Pending the arrival of "aid which you are pleased to send me," the governor arranged for Pérez to gather some cattle in his pastures to furnish food for the troops. The cattle were so poor that the troops did not wish to accept them, however. They were turned loose, and Ignacio promised that others would be gathered. This was done, "and we find they are even worse than the first." Most of them were old and "very poor" or recently castrated steers. When they too were rejected, Martínez had the commandants of the companies present themselves and suggested that they advise the troops to take the cattle, considering that stringy beef was better than none at all. They refused, not because the price (which would be deducted from the soldiers' pay) was exorbitant but because Pérez's price for an old cow in bad condition was 10 pesos, the price normally asked for a fat cow or young bull in its prime.

Recognizing the justness of their claim, Governor Martínez tried to influence Pérez to be fair, but the lieutenant colonel would come down only 1 peso a head. As a last resort he persuaded the men to accept this price, but the officers immediately protested. Thereupon Martínez appealed to the commandant general to set a fair price for the cattle. Perhaps a bit annoyed that his top executive in Texas could not arrive at the value of a skinny cow without his assistance, the indomitable Arredondo told him to consult "experts." According to the condition of cattle when they were delivered and other circum-

---

[55] Martínez to Arredondo, July 10, 1818, in Taylor, *Letters of Martínez*, p. 158; GLO, 43:119, 121; GLO, 49:100; Cassiano-Pérez Collection (oversize documents); Schwarz, "Forgotten Battlefield," p. 118.

stances, the accounts could be adjusted once their proper value was ascertained. Martínez tried to defend himself for soliciting assistance in such a routine matter; still it is obvious not only that Pérez was gouging the soldiers but also that the governor was unable to deal with the situation. In lame fashion he announced the conclusion of his beef-buying experience, saying that he had made no further effort to supply the troops with meat and that Pérez, "seeing that they are reluctant to accept it and that no statement has been offered, has refrained from furnishing any more."[56]

In defense of Pérez it must be admitted that he was doing nothing that generations of soldier-ranchers before him had not done. It was so customary as to be expected that men in his exalted position would use their leverage to advantage. Martínez even hinted at the prerogatives enjoyed by individuals who had just rendered a service to the sovereign, berating Don Ignacio only because he "did not take into consideration the present afflictions of this government." Pérez no doubt felt justified in demanding as much as he could get, perhaps aware of his superior bargaining position and mindful of his many sacrifices on behalf of the king. Nonetheless, some months later, when he was sick in bed and not expected to live, citizens were reported killing cattle in his pastures. The governor suggested that these *vecinos* were perhaps motivated by the "pitiful condition" of Pérez but did not elaborate on the condition of the cattle being slaughtered—whether they were scrubs or sleek ones held back from the presidio.[57]

Before he died later in the decade, Colonel Pérez compiled a formidable military record. It was he who captured the noted filibuster General James Long, at La Bahía in October, 1821. Before that, in 1819, he led a 550-man expedition that cleared East Texas of American intruders, systematically burning all the squatters' cabins and destroying their property to discourage reoccupation. On the way to Nacogdoches he razed thirty farms and ranches, noting that his men ate well thanks to the many

---

[56] Martínez to Arredondo, March 6 and April 26, 1820, in Taylor, *Letters of Martínez*, pp. 309, 318.
[57] July 2, 1820, ibid., p. 345.

pigs and chickens the squatters had left behind. A few cows and horses were reported seized; perhaps others went unreported, because the efficient commander returned to Béxar laden with spoils.

Among the members of General Long's "Supreme Council" who had situated themselves at Nacogdoches and issued a declaration of independence on June 23, 1819, were old-timers Samuel Davenport, James Gaines (the son-in-law of Edmund Norris), Bernardo Gutiérrez, Edmund Quirk, Pedro Procela, and one José Menchaca, doubtless another member of that obstreperous clan. Perhaps he was the José Tomás who appears on the Nacogdoches-Trinidad brand list, or the soldier José, who, based at Nacogdoches, figured in the Gutiérrez-Magee affair after the old captain's son of the same name was carted off to Chihuahua. There were Menchacas in East Texas, as well as at Béxar. One of them, Antonio, was later involved in the Córdova trouble, which has led some historians to confuse him with Captain Antonio Menchaca, the veteran of San Jacinto who left his "Memoirs." When Colonel Pérez rode into Nacogdoches on October 28, 1819, he found the place deserted; Long and his council had fled into the Neutral Ground, where they would reorganize for a second attempt two years later. On that occasion Pérez would have more luck catching his prey. But for now the intruders had been expelled, even though they would return again and again.[58]

Typical of these—if trailblazers can be considered "typical" in any sense of the word—was Nicholas Trammell. He represented the spirit of the Anglos pushing westward out of the Kentucky heartland, down the Ohio River, and into the vast, unexplored Louisiana Purchase. His great-grandfather Gerrard Trammell had been appointed surveyor of Fairfax County, Virginia, in 1754. Gerrard's son Philip had helped establish government in southern Illinois and to secure trails of migration west of the Mississippi. His son Nicholas, Sr., was a founder of

---

[58] Castañeda, *Catholic Heritage*, 6:164–68; Warren, *Sword*, pp. 235–39; Blake, Research Collection, vol. 28; *Handbook of Texas*, 3:586–87. Although Pérez died October 7, 1823 (Leal, "Burials of San Fernando," vol. 3, no. 1202, p. 51), his will is dated March 7, 1826 (Cassiano-Pérez Collection, folder 389), and another copy, in the GLO, is dated 1825.

Nashborough (later Nashville), Tennessee, and was killed there in 1784 defending the settlement against Cherokees. Uncles, brothers, and cousins of young Nicholas ranged the entire frontier from Kaskaskia to Shawneetown; from Eaton's Station to the "Georgia settlement," near Logan County, Kentucky; and on down into Arkansas. They were hunters, trappers, scouts, tavern keepers, and salt manufacturers—men with names like Carnes, Chisholm, Lafferty, Armstrong, Trimble, Kelly, McFarland, Bean, and Creig—a restless breed always one jump ahead of the migratory wave behind them.[59]

There is little doubt that Nicholas Trammell the younger blazed his trace to Nacogdoches, connecting the Great Southwest Trail to the old Spanish Camino Real as a means of exploiting trade possibilities in Texas, like those opened up by the wholesale devastation of ranching which occurred during the revolutionary decade. Likewise, the route he chose for this "nefarious traffic" was most likely an old Indian trail used for procuring Texas mustangs. Some evidence indicates that Trammell's Trace received its impetus from two factors: the terrible earthquake of 1811, which drove settlers toward the Red River, and the lawlessness of the Neutral Ground, which made trade between Nacogdoches and Natchitoches unsafe after 1806. The deterioration of this region as a haven for bandits and criminals has been noted by most authorities. Haggard in particular discusses how this "bridge" for trade coming out of Texas was severely affected by the infestation of outlaws. Some, of course, were clothed in garments of legitimacy, and their acts—culminating in the extensive losses suffered by Sambrano and other Spaniards in August, 1812—shut off the flourishing commerce between Nacogdoches and Natchitoches.[60]

---

[59] James W. Dawson and Mary Dawson, "Texas Trammel's [sic] Trace" (typescript, University of Texas Archives), pp. 17–22; Rex W. Strickland, "Miller County, Arkansas Territory: The Frontier That Men Forgot," *Chronicles of Oklahoma* 18 (1940): 17–18; Rex W. Strickland, "Anglo American Activities in Northeast Texas, 1803–1845" (Ph.D. diss., University of Texas, 1937), pp. 93, 282.

[60] Davenport to Governor of Texas, February 6, 1820, BA: Castañeda, *Catholic Heritage*, 6:48–60, 82–84; Haggard, "Neutral Ground," pp. 1074, 1099–1101.

"Hopelessly Lost in Their Misery" 573

As was to be expected, alternative trade routes were soon being sought. Besides the old, lower route known as the Opelousas Road, from present Orange to Lake Charles, Trammell's Trace linked what was left of Nacogdoches with the bustling American trade and population center at Saint Louis. A number of documents and early maps (such as Father Puelles's effort of 1807 for Pichardo's monumental study of the Louisiana border question) note the presence of Americans along the upper Red River. These initial thrusts hastened the settlement of Miller County, Arkansas. Although Colonel Pérez knew of the existence of Puente Pacana (Pecan Point) and of Jonesborough nearby, he was unable to destroy them on his expedition of 1819, as he suggested should be done.

When young Stephen F. Austin was serving as a judge of Hempstead County, before the area was reorganized into Miller County, he and his brother-in-law James Bryan were selling lots in the new townsite of Fulton. This site was squarely on Trammell's Trace, which the future empresario termed in his promotional literature the "most direct road from Missouri and the eastern states." Dr. John Robinson's detailed map of 1819 does not show this road linking the upper regions to Nacogdoches. However, Austin's first contribution to the cartography of Texas, his "Mapa geografico" of 1822, does. The trace crosses the Red River near a point labeled "U.S. Factory," a trading post operated by John Fowler at the confluence of Sulphur Fork and the Red River. Austin's more elaborate map of 1829 shows this road extending down from "villeta de Washington" (the Hempstead county seat) and crossing into Texas at Long Prairie. Terán's map of 1826 shows Trammell's Trace terminating at "Bean," near Nacogdoches.[61]

Besides guns, powder, and shot, one item men like Trammell had to trade was salt, an essential commodity which he, his relatives, and his friends extracted in quantity from various frontier salt licks. Salt sold for $30 a bushel in many Tennessee settlements, and the federal government imposed a heavy tax on all salt shipped through the port of New Orleans, perhaps suggesting the reason for reports that western scouts were smuggling packtrains of salt into Texas. One report also suggests that Trammell used this trail to run horses out of Texas, back to his neighbors on the White River. In another report the Cherokees in Arkansas charged that he stole horses from them and drove them down the trail to Nacogdoches! That is not likely, for if there was one commodity war-torn Texas did not need, it was more horseflesh.

But if the trace was not used to convey Texas livestock northward in the beginning, with the new Red River settlements it was soon so used. When United States troops from Fort Smith also arrived the year of the Pérez expedition, telling settlers they must vacate the district, Trammell cut a trail to

---

[61] Dawson and Dawson, "Texas Trammel's Trace," pp. 7, 28, cited from *Arkansas Gazette*, December 11, 1819; Robert S. Martin, "Maps of an Empresario: Austin's Contribution to the Cartography of Texas," *Southwestern Historical Quarterly* 85, no. 4 (April, 1982): 372–90; John H. Robinson, "A Map of Mexico, Louisiana, and the Missouri Territory . . . 1819," Special Collections, University of Texas at Arlington.

connect them with his trace. It crossed the Sulphur River at Stephenson's Ferry, forming a junction at Old Unionville. By this route many people of the "well-nigh broken up" Red River settlements made their way illegally to Nacogdoches and San Augustine. Countless others soon followed, traveling down the main branch into Texas. Like Trammell, they plagued Spanish authorities throughout the 1820s and formed the vanguard of a more critical revolution during the next decade. As Bernardo de Gálvez noted as early as 1784, the lack of established routes was no deterrent to the hardy American frontiersmen because, "far from desiring the facility of roads, they prefer the woods," being better adapted to the Anglos' method of entering Spain's coveted dominions.[62]

That many Americans did not leave the Red River district is indicated by a letter William Rabb wrote in the summer of 1821 to the governor of Texas from "Jonesborough, south side of the Red River." He claimed that settlers on the north bank were carrying on a direct trade with the Comanches, supplying them with weapons and receiving in exchange a great number of horses, many of which bore Spanish brands. Perhaps it was this "selfish and illegal traffic" being conducted up Trammell's Trace in a manner Rabb thought "very injurious to your government" which prompted Governor Martínez in September, 1820, to prohibit the trade of horses and mules to friendly Indians, a prohibition he also wanted applied to foreigners. The commander at La Bahía was specifically ordered to prevent the removal of animals to "a foreign country" according to existing regulations. Needless to say, the stockade-corrals which Nicholas Trammell and others erected along the trace bearing his name remained familiar landmarks for years to come. The Red River settlements might be just as lawless and dangerous as

[62]Dawson and Dawson, "Texas Trammel's Trace," pp. 22–25, 28–29, 34–36; Gálvez to the King [should be Bernardo de Gálvez to José de Gálvez], February 6, 1783 [should be 1784], in Haggard, "Neutral Ground," p. 1076. Empresario Haden Edwards sold land to Trammell and gave him the right to operate a ferry on the Trinity River in 1826, ejecting the former occupant, Ignacio Sartuche. When Alcalde Samuel Norris sent militiamen to evict Trammell and other "bad men" accused of cattle theft, they fled to Pecan Point, sparking the Fredonian Rebellion (NA, Transcripts, 29:94–95, 114, 144; 30:251–52). This was only one of Trammell's many scrapes during the decade.

the trade route through Bayou Pierre, as Castañeda suggests, but it appears that many Anglos were willing to brave the risks, even if Spaniards no longer were. By the same token, many Indians besides the Comanches regularly plundered the Spanish settlements and had need of middlemen for their stolen merchandise. As Ramos Arizpe mentioned, Tejanos became "spectators" of a lucrative trade carried on by the eastern tribes and aggressive Americans like Trammell.[63]

When Colonel Pérez left on his East Texas expedition in September, 1819, taking with him almost every able-bodied soldier between Béxar and Monclova, Governor Martínez found it necessary to shore up the capital's defenses. He organized a company of "faithful royalists" composed of forty-seven men. Having written earlier that the local militia was more detrimental than helpful, he nonetheless named as his officers Manuel Barrera, José Flores, and Manuel Yturri Castillo, deemed the best and most capable men available. Martínez then complained about those citizens who, by claiming exempt-officer status, overburdened others in the community. Since the result of this privilege was "completely injurious to the rest," the governor asked for an examination of the records of Juan de Veramendi, José Ángel Navarro, Francisco Flores, José Manuel Sambrano, Domingo Bustillos, and Erasmo Seguín to see whether they could be modified and service required of these men.[64]

Since disputes over pasture infringements are generally an indication of renewed vigor and incipient prosperity, it is worth noting that several such squabbles took place in the years 1820 and 1821. They involved citizens of Béxar, Bahía, and even the Río Grande towns. In April, 1820, Erasmo Seguín protested that La Mora was being entered by *carneadores* from La Bahía who were doing damage to his cattle. Ignacio Flores defended his fellow citizens, saying that they were innocent of killing Seguín's stock on the former ranch of Mission Valero. He ad-

---

[63] Strickland, "Anglo Activities," pp. 106–107; Martínez to La Bahía Commander, September 16, 1820, Grazing Papers, vol. 2; Nettie Lee Benson, *Report of Ramos Arizpe*, p. 21.

[64] Martínez to Arredondo, September 13, 1819, in Taylor, *Letters of Martínez*, p. 263.

mitted, however, that a few servants had left the households of Lieutenant Jesús Alderete and Juan José Hernández to gather a little meat. Permission had been given for this outing because these men (supposedly) had a right to abandoned cattle in surrounding pastures. Flores maintained that the hunting party had proceeded along Arroyo de Cuchillo, far from the pastures of Erasmo Seguín. Even if they had gone as far as the Escondida, they were within their rights, he claimed, because those pastures belonged to Sergeant Antonio Vásquez, who had given permission for the foray. Flores ended by saying that apparently the killing at Mora Pass and nearby was done by fifty men from the capital, not by the good citizens of La Bahía.

Governor Martínez showed remarkable firmness in the matter of Seguín's complaint, issuing orders the same day to the presidio commander at La Bahía. Since Seguín had established that his pastures extended to the Cañon de la Escondida, the governor wanted Sergeant Vásquez kept out. Vásquez "pretends there is his father's cattle in those pastures," but that was not sufficient proof. Martínez forbade the granting of slaughter permits except to reliable men. Furthermore, no killing was to be done in the pastures; all stock must first be driven to the presidio. Not even an owner was allowed to slaughter stock unless it had been previously inspected. The governor emphasized that a "worthy man" should be put in charge of all such tasks, not a complimentary reflection on Vásquez's character.[65]

A similar complaint was made in December, 1820, this one by José María Sambrano, Juan Manuel's brother. By this time the subdeacon had vexed Martínez to the point that he had ordered Sambrano's military salary suspended and declared his presence in the city no longer desired. Sambrano, it seems, was in the habit of picking a fight with former rebel Manuel Delgado every time they met. It was only one of Sambrano's many traits which the governor found intolerable. Perhaps to distract attention from his brother's affairs, José María charged the inhabitants of La Bahía with catching cattle grazing along creeks flowing into the Nueces, such as the Chiquihuitillo, Tordillo, Pitahayas,

[65] Martínez to La Bahía Commander, April 22, 1820, and Ignacio Flores to governor, April 30, 1820, Grazing Papers, vol. 2.

San Cristóbal, Santo Domingo, Puente de Piedra, and Cunillo. Sambrano admitted that these raiders paid the 4 reales—an indication that His Majesty's Mustang Fund was still being administered—but believed that most of the cattle being taken belonged to him, not the king. Martínez ordered the alcalde of Espíritu Santo to restrict issuance of licenses for roundups other than those in the pastures of ranchers seeking permits and to issue permits only to men of unquestioned character. Upon receipt of this directive, Second Alcalde Vásquez protested the innocence of his neighbors. On the contrary, he said, it was the citizens of Béxar who came to Bahía and took cattle.[66]

Martínez took an oath of loyalty to the new Republic while holding office under the old government, and on July 18, 1821, he required his subjects to do the same. Independence brought a few changes to the frontier even before the official ceremonies. Constitutional cabildos and provincial deputations were restored before Agustín de Iturbide published his Plan of Iguala in February, 1821. Martínez, for example, wrote to José Encarnación Vásquez in December, 1820, congratulating him on having been appointed second alcalde of La Bahía's new *ayuntamiento* the preceding September. Concerning such officiating duties, of interest is the letter of February, 1821, which Vásquez wrote to First Alcalde de los Santos about the Mustang Fund at La Bahía. He said that he had not collected the 4-real duty "since no citizen of this town has ever presented any stock [for taxation]." Further, the new alcalde had no plans to do so, "considering it is just that the owners or stockraisers be exempt from said royal taxes, according to the new plan of government."[67]

It seems that after Mexican independence a discretionary fund (*fundo de arbitrios*) was established to replace the old Mustang Fund, the beneficiary of this tax revenue now being the municipality rather than the king. In the early years one still

---

[66] Martínez to José Encarnación Vásquez, alcalde of Espíritu Santo, December 5, 1820; Alcalde Vásquez to Martínez, December 10, 1820, ibid.

[67] Martínez to Alcalde Vásquez, December 5, 1820, BAM, roll 65, frames 969–70; Vásquez to Santos, February 21, 1821, Grazing Papers, vol. 2; Colin M. MacLachlan and Jaime E. Rodríguez O., *The Forging of the Cosmic Race: A Reinterpretation of Colonial Mexico*, pp. 329–30.

finds documents referring to the National Treasury as the destination for funds once due the Real Hacienda. Evidence suggests that the Béxar *ayuntamiento* worked diligently to assure that this revenue would remain in Texas and benefit local projects. It instructed its provincial deputy to work toward this end, even going so far as to demand an accounting and restitution of fees collected during the revolutionary period 1814–20. Apparently these orders were somewhat successful because, as Erasmo Seguín expressed it in January, 1823, the issue was whether *orejanos* found outside recognized pastures or all *orejanos*, wherever found, should benefit the new fund.

Instructions drafted by the Béxar governing body to their constitutional representative (who happened to be Erasmo Seguín) declared that the customary fees should henceforth be considered a branch of revenue of "this capital," as should the proceeds of horses and cattle of unknown brands gathered in the chase—including animals taken in war from the Indians or other enemies. In this manner, it was hoped, sufficient funds could be raised to benefit public works, start a school, and renovate the jail, the government house, and so on. It was observed that before the revolution mesteños produced 15,000 to 18,000 pesos in revenue, but instead of being set aside for public use, the fund had been exhausted by the military. Now, even the account books and other documents formerly kept in the chest of *mesteñas y público* were gone; the box was empty.[68]

Perhaps to remedy this situation, the Béxar *ayuntamiento* drew up a "Plan de Arbitrios," or a municipal revenue proposal, on October 20, 1823. It regulated the renting of town *propios* (lands) and set forth fees for such things as entertainments, cargos leaving the district, and so forth. Horses exported to the United States were taxed at one real per head while mules were levied at two reales. Article 7 implemented the discussions on *orejanos* held at San Antonio the preceding January. If taken above the Guadalupe, in a broad area defined as within the council's jurisdiction, wild horses were taxed at two reales and

---

[68] Seguín, "Decision on Roundup and Cattle Breeding," January 16, 1823, BCSA; Béxar *ayuntamiento*, "Instructions to Its Constitutional Representative," January 30, 1822, NA.

cattle at four reales "como está acostumbrado" (as is the custom). Provision was also made for the capture, recording, and disposition of *mostrencos* of unknown brands in order to rid raisers of this problem.[69]

These proposals for municipal revenue were repeated virtually unchanged in an 1825 plan under the new state government, recognized by Coahuila y Texas State Decree No. 98 in the year 1829. Section 9, "On the Creation of Municipal Funds," closely resembles Béxar's earlier plans. Other towns adopted similar ordinances, such as the one for Goliad embodied in Decree No. 99. Nonetheless, questions on regulating—and taxing—the livestock industry continued to plague state and local authorities during the period of Mexican rule. Tejano spokesmen never ceased to press their claims to these tax revenues, despite the contrary views held by state politicians.[70]

On the subject of stock losses the Reynosa cabildo members became involved soon after their northern neighbors did. In March, 1821, they complained about the incursions that citizens of both Béxar and La Bahía had been making into their district for years, carrying off horses and mules. The interim commandant general, José María Echeagaray, to whom the charge was sent, forwarded it to Governor Martínez and ordered the raids stopped. That they nonetheless continued is established by a letter which Martínez wrote on July 31 of the following year, this time to Juan José Hernández, alcalde of La Bahía. The governor of Nuevo Santander had complained to the commandant general that stock from around Mier was being stolen by thieves from La Bahía. Groups of these people were frequently encountered herding cattle and catching mustangs: "When asked for a permit, they answered that their permit is in the mouths of their rifles." Nuevo Santander's administrator asked help in preventing such "disagreeable" events, stating that the Reynosa cabildo could not stop them and that, if something

---

[69] Béxar *ayuntamiento* to Provincial Deputation, "Plan de Arbitrios," October 20, 1823, BA.

[70] Béxar Municipal Regulations, March 20, 1825, BA; Coahuila y Tejas, *Ordnanzas municipales . . . de Béjar*, 1829; *Exp.* no. 777, "Accounts of the Collection and Disbursement of Export Duties on Horses and Mules, and of the Consumption Tax on Foreign Goods in Texas," 1824–25, SA, 16:1–30.

was not done, the region would soon be desolate of stock. These thefts, he added, were being perpetrated against the villas of the river under the excuse that the stock was stray (*alzado*).[71]

It was not long before countercharges were leveled by the citizens of Béxar and those of the coastal settlement. Late in May, José Guadalupe de los Santos, first alcalde of La Bahía, answered the governor's letter of the seventeenth concerning the large-scale driving of cattle from Béxar pastures to the Río del Norte. Although the results of the alcalde's investigation were inconclusive, he thought that those guilty of committing the excesses must be breeders of the northern villas (the Río del Norte settlements) or fugitives who lived there. Neither the people of Béxar nor those of Bahía were engaged in this traffic, he assured Martínez. They were incapable of conducting drives down the many trails to the interior owing to their poverty and the high price of stock in Villa Colonia, meaning perhaps that this would more likely motivate thefts by those living closer to such markets.[72]

On a related topic José Ángel Navarro answered a complaint lodged by the senior member of the Presidio del Río Grande cabildo in October of the year. Navarro denied that Béxar mustang hunters were going in three or four groups to the jurisdiction of Coahuila, as the official claimed. Mesteñeros took the presidio route, but not past the corrals of Rosales on Chacon Creek, 8 to 10 leagues from Béxar. These corrals, declared Navarro, had been used by the citizens of Béxar "since time immemorial," and he refused to forbid their use since no harm was done to other inhabitants.[73]

Such disputes on tax revenues and livestock continued to rage into the era of Anglo presence in Texas. In 1823, José Miguel Aldrete was still defending the citizens of La Bahía against cattle-rustling charges made by the governor of Nuevo Santander. More promises were made that La Bahía would cooperate with Béxar authorities in stopping unauthorized roundups

---

[71] Complaint of Félix de León, *regidor* of the Reynosa cabildo, March 31, 1821; Martínez to Hernández, July 31, 1822, Grazing Papers, vol. 2.

[72] Santos to Martínez, May 26, 1821, ibid.

[73] Navarro to governor, regarding complaints of *regidor de cano* of the Villa Presidio de Río Grande, October 29, 1821, ibid.

of mesteños and illegal brandings. The coastal missions, which were facing secularization and the final distribution of their lands, continued to be raided for wild stock, just as they had been during more prosperous years. As late as 1827 reports were still being written on mesteños and unbranded cattle, with remittances submitted as in former times. The changes were of degree, not of substance, as the Spanish-Mexican stock raisers began to witness the arrival of their Anglo counterparts.[74]

When Don Erasmo Seguín conducted Stephen F. Austin and his party of prospective colonists to meet Governor Martínez, the members of the Béxar cabildo were busily at work on the old problem of how to reduce losses of cattle in their pastures. On July 2, 1821, they sent the governor a proposal, aimed particularly at the depredations being committed by soldiers of the presidio. It was brief and to the point: (1) only owners had a right to hunt and kill in their pastures, and (2) no other person was entitled to solicit a license for roundups on said lands. The cabildo members admitted that much of the stock in question was semiwild, owing to the Indian wars from 1813. But because the cattle clearly belonged to the raisers, they asked for restrictions on licenses granted to soldiers. These men were neither "raisers nor ranch owners, but go to the country and hunt with the pretext of a mouthful of meat." The petition was signed by José Ángel Navarro, José Manuel Granados, Gaspar Flores, Francisco Montes, and José Manuel de la Garza.

Governor Martínez was sympathetic and agreed on the need for such an ordinance. He reminded the petitioners, however, that the government was in dire straits and lacked the money to feed its soldiers. Under such circumstances he considered it only fair to permit them to chase mesteños for subsistence. The governor avowed that he did not like the practice but had to allow it, promising to advise the raisers of licenses issued and do everything possible to minimize their losses. Per-

---

[74] Aldrete, "Defense against Accusations Made by Governor of Nuevo Santander," January 9, 1823, BAM, roll 73, frames 1001–1004. See BAM, roll 75, frames 14–15, 276–80, for more promises to control unauthorized roundups of mesteños; and BAM, roll 107, frames 431–32, for Carvajal to de la Garza, September 22, 1827, regarding remittance of La Bahía report on mesteños and unbranded cattle.

haps the form of reimbursement (if any) would come in IOUs, for some stock raisers had already advanced cattle to the garrison on that basis.[75]

Austin, who arrived in Béxar the following month, was no doubt impressed by the methods he saw being used in Spanish Texas to cope with the problems presented by open-range stock handling. Still, he needed coaxing. After he drew up what he considered to be a full code of civil and criminal regulations under which to govern his colonists, two more articles were suggested by José Antonio Saucedo, the political chief at Béxar. One provided for the registration of brands, and the other for the disposition of strays; both suggestions were incorporated in Austin's Civil Code of 1823, as articles 31 and 32. As Wortham says, "It was the first important lesson in connection with cattle-raising that the Americans learned from the Mexicans."[76]

[75] Béxar cabildo, resolution, July 2, 1821, and Martínez to Cabildo, July 3, 1821, Grazing Papers, vol. 2. In connection with this decision see "List of Animals of Known Brands Taken in Corrida," by Juan de Castañeda, captain of La Bahía, August 22, 1821, BA; Béxar *ayuntamiento* to Commandant General, "Proceedings on Creation of a Municipal Fund from Tax on Wild Stock, Animals with Unknown Brands, and on the Dispute with Juan de Castañeda concerning Tax on Animals Rounded Up," August 23, 1821, BAM, roll 68, frames 198–200; "List of Animals Captured by Erasmo Seguín," August 14, 1821, BA; and his views on *orejanos* already discussed.

[76] Louis J. Wortham, *A History of Texas from Wilderness to Commonwealth*, 5:135; J. Frank Dobie, *The Longhorns*, p. 29. An excellent treatment of livestock regulations during the Mexican period is found in Andrew Anthony Tijerina, "Tejanos and Texas: The Native Mexicans of Texas, 1820–1850" (Ph.D. diss., University of Texas at Austin, 1977), pp. 74–76, 140–74.

14

A LOOK BEYOND 1821

The Legacy's Impact

A Look beyond 1821

IT must not be imagined that Spanish influence on ranching ended with the beginning of formal Anglo colonization in Texas. On the contrary, its impact continued to be felt long after the institution passed to Anglo ownership. Austin's colonists, enjoying the protection of legitimate authority—unlike the earlier wave of Anglo intruders, or "squatters"—were at last in a position to examine the benefits to be derived from the Spanish-Mexican ranching experience. If they wanted to, that is, for it appears that most of the families introduced by Austin to the rich Brazos-Colorado river bottoms came to pursue agriculture, not stock raising. While it is true that many of these early arrivals brought considerable stock-handling expertise with them, there seems little basis for supposing that they did not learn from and profit by contact with the established system they found in Texas.[1]

---

[1] Walter Prescott Webb, *The Great Plains*, pp. 206–208; J. Frank Dobie, *The Longhorns*, pp. 29–30; Terry C. Jordan, *Trails to Texas: Southern Roots of Western Cattle Ranching*, p. 16.

That this system was fundamentally a going concern is demonstrated by a century of documentation in the Béxar Archives and—perhaps more important—by the many Spanish elements preempted by Anglo cattlemen and incorporated into their own way of doing things. Thus it cannot be maintained with accuracy that Spanish ranching institutions lacked the vigor to shape or influence their new neighbors simply because other aspects of Spanish life succumbed to Anglo domination. The passing of the *ganaderos* and *criadores* from the historical stage in Texas was not because their ranching institutions, practices, and techniques lacked functional integrity. Rather, their capitulation was directly related to the overall balance of power in Texas and the shifts that occurred as Anglos moved into positions of control—military, political, and economic. One must look behind the scenes, explore aspects of the cultural conflict that are not generally advertised, to discover the real reasons for the so-called rapid decline of Hispanic ranching following the Texas Revolution. The picture that emerges is often not a pretty one, which perhaps accounts for the silence of most authorities on the subject.

As has been noted, there had been mingling of cultures in the Spanish borderlands for several generations before Austin successfully established an Anglo colony in Texas. People of many nationalities and races—French, Spanish, Irish, Scottish, black, Italian, English, German, and Indian (from a wide variety of tribes)—constantly defied the official policies of whatever government was presuming to control their conduct and rubbed shoulders with each other from Pensacola to Quebec to Nacogdoches. In short, they became "Americans," a new breed of social creature. Not for nothing has American been called a melting pot, and nowhere was this experience more pronounced than on expanding frontiers, which were beyond many of the restrictions common to settled societies. Sometimes these frontiersmen switched flags with remarkable ease, and many other behavioral traits were modified as the need or impulse presented itself.

Arthur Preston Whitaker writes that the Anglo westward migration was not because of discontent with the "older societies," that is, to escape what was behind, but simply to improve their own situation within that system. Perhaps so, but the spontaneous and highly individualized pattern of westward movement blurred the distinction. Those who pushed into the wilderness to escape intolerable circumstances soon found themselves needing more "elbow room" as the older society closed in. Thus the bolder and more restive spirits on the frontier were obliged again to move on, a process that historians have chosen to recognize as "trailblazing" rather than the retreat that it sometimes more closely approximated.

Daniel Boone, for example, helped lead the American migration west, but neither he nor his kinsmen were enamored of what they left behind them, as demonstrated by the fact that his nephew and namesake settled in Spanish territory out of anger at the way the United States had treated his pioneering uncle. In 1806 the younger Daniel, who had been residing in Opelousas for twelve years, petitioned for admittance to Texas with his family and goods because Louisiana had "passed into the possession of the Anglo-Americans and it does not suit me to live under their laws." Boone himself chose to end his days on the lower Missouri River, where he had been welcomed by the Spanish government in 1799. Even there he was hounded by creditors from Kentucky. Other trailblazers, it may be discovered, had antisocial motives similar to the Boones', that is, escaping their culture's version of "civilization," not inflicting it on unspoiled places.[2]

The evidence shows that Texas livestock served to establish a flourishing industry in French Louisiana which spread eastward as early as the final quarter of the eighteenth century. With the cattle went vaquero know-how and the time-tested Spanish system, which had already undergone a process of "creolization" in the hinterlands before it encountered the westward march of the Anglo vanguard. It was a system that was readily adapted by the new people who continued to meet it all along the extended line of contact on the Spanish-American frontier. This transfer of knowledge was a gradual process, and the

---

[2] Arthur Preston Whitaker, *Spanish-American Frontier, 1783–1795: The Westward Movement and the Spanish Retreat in the Mississippi Valley*, p. 32; Paul O'Neil, *The Frontiersmen*, pp. 63–70; Daniel Boone, Entrance Petition of 1806, in Mattie Austin Hatcher, *The Opening of Texas to Foreign Settlement, 1801–1821*, p. 322.

blending of cultures was subtle. There was not necessarily a conflict between the two, or, for that matter, a drastic difference between them, as some writers have suggested. Nor were the Spanish methods completely strange to Anglo emigrants approaching the Sabine and Red rivers.

When Austin's "Old Three Hundred" entered Texas, many of them had already been exposed to facets of Hispanic ranching filtered through at least a generation of crosscultural modification in Louisiana and the Mississippi Valley. In most cases Austin's colonists themselves were a result of the melting pot experience, not merely touched by it in passing. If not—if they came to Texas directly from foreign countries or northeastern population centers, rather than being a product of the gradual, leap-frog migratory pattern that characterized westward expansion—then the first "white" people they encountered upon reaching Texas were so initiated. These earlier arrivals who penetrated Texas before the empresario system dominated colonization policy, were well versed in the Hispanic ranching tradition by Austin's time; some of them had married into old French and Spanish families, and they had lived in the polyglot of races and cultures generally unmolested by the token government at Béxar. As one might expect, this cultural assimilation is reflected even in such things as the early cattle brands seen in the Nacogdoches-Trinidad list. At least this was the case with the first migratory waves, before the rapid polarization of attitudes after the Texas Revolution.

Moreover, merely because some Anglo stockmen continued to prefer their own highly simplified type of brands, most of which were based on their initials or a combination of numbers, does not mean that they had no contact with the Mexican variety. Terry C. Jordan, in his study of the trails that led to Texas, seems to believe that the designs the Anglos chose when they arrived were a measure, or an indicator, of their segregation from all things Spanish insofar as stock raising was concerned. Such a conclusion does not necessarily follow, nor do the brands in Texas lend themselves to such simplistic classification.[3]

---

[3] Jordan, *Trails to Texas*, pp. 92–94. For the diversity of midcentury stock brands see W. H. Jackson and S. A. Long, *Texas Stock Directory, or Book of Marks and Brands*.

A better argument could be made that this meant only that Anglos were less subtle than their Mexican counterparts, whose brands sometimes incorporated the owners' initials into artistically pleasing devices reminiscent of Oriental characters but firmly based on a long-standing Old World tradition of trademarks, merchant seals, guildmarks, watermarks, and other heraldic symbols of proprietorship. As Walter Prescott Webb put it, for ingenuity of design "no one can beat a Mexican." Whether he meant it as a compliment or a criticism is beside the point, for the observation was correct, in his day and long before. The Spanish-Mexican stockmen took great pride in the marks they conjured up for their cattle, and few were content with anything as mundane as block letters. Authorities like J. Evetts Haley and Hobart Huson have observed that in time this became the case with many Anglo ranchers as well. Still, it must be acknowledged that early Anglo stockmen found the Tejano *fierros* "peculiar," a view that did much to determine their conduct toward cattle found wearing these elaborate marks. This culturally myopic attitude was to have ominous implications for the owners of such "peculiar" *fierros* during the stormy years to follow.[4]

That the Spanish-Mexican brands would reflect "Moorish crescents" or "Indian-inspired" figures is to be expected considering the long evolutionary path these *ganaderos* had traveled to reach Texas with their livestock. At a loss to explain such complexities, later Anglo-Celtic ranchers (obviously long out of touch with the intricately decorative motifs their own forefathers had once used on everything from fieldstones to their faces) came to call them *quién sabe*? ("who knows?") brands. Some however, especially members of the older generation, did display a certain amount of ingenuity in using their initials, often combining them with circles, diamonds, crosses, hearts, curlicues, and squiggles, the resulting brands strongly suggesting Old World origins. Those registered at Opelousas and points east indicate that this style was not unique to Texas, being rather common in the borderlands among various ethnic groups.

[4]Webb, *Great Plains*, p. 259; J. Evetts Haley, *The Heraldry of the Range*, p. 5; Hobart Huson, *Refugio: A Comprehensive History of Refugio County from Aboriginal Times to 1953*, 2:219.

One such mark was the one adopted by Stephen F. Austin, a form of hispanicized *F*. The brands of Miguel Quin, the Quark (Quirk) family, David Valtemore, San Miguel Noris, James Carruthers, James White, Frederico Stocman (Esctozman), Adolphus Sterne, Humphrey Jackson, and a host of other early cattlemen show distinctly European features, many of them, like Austin's, influenced by the Spanish style. This holds true, incidentally, even to the time of Richard King and his famous "Running W," which Mexicans easily recognized as a fast-moving snake (*la viborita*). One suspects that, beyond strictly utilitarian considerations, the design selected was more a matter of personal taste and artistic inclination than anything else.[5]

None of this should detract from the realization that Texas was a cattle kingdom long before footloose heirs of early South Carolina's marginal stockmen viewed Spanish mission ruins along the San Antonio River and marveled at the richness of the surrounding prairies. From their first contact with these "mighty plains" the newcomers recognized them as perfect for raising stock, requiring only a little attention to prevent animals from straying away or becoming wild. The grazing lands they judged superior to anything they had ever seen before, and they spread the word abroad that "not a single country in the whole world is better suited for every kind of cattle-breeding than is Texas." Others proclaimed that in all other places man was obliged to work for his cattle but that in Texas the cattle worked for him.

Scores of books and pamphlets were written over the years in several languages to spur immigration to Texas, and all of them extolled the virtues of this new land as a stockman's paradise. Typical are the remarks written in 1838 by Frédéric Leclerc: "Already it is not rare to find colonists having 1500 to 2000 head of cattle which they have not taken the slightest trouble to raise. All animals are in liberty; the owner marks them with his brand and then leaves them alone; in summer they graze in the prairies; in winter they know how to hunt out for themselves the fresh and succulent grass of the bottoms." If

---

[5]Hortense W. Ward, *Cattlebrands and Cowhides*, pp. 29–43; Nacogdoches-Trinidad, "Fierros y Señales," n.d., (see brand section E); "Brand Book for Opelousas and Attakapas Districts, 1739–1888" (transcript, Louisiana Room, University of Southwestern Louisiana Library; see brand section B); Jordan, *Trails to Texas*, p. 93.

one did not know better, one might think that this gentleman was describing a Mexican rancho operated by indolent *ganaderos*, not a grand stock-raising venture run by vigorous Anglo-Celts. Yet this was the pattern of ranching in Texas until the end of the open range.[6]

Most of these enthralled observers barely guessed at the long odyssey of toil, frustration, and suffering behind the open-range stock-handling regulations that had permitted the wild herds to flourish on the beckoning expanses of grazing land. They discounted the long years of experience amassed by the civilization that had built the quaintly picturesque "spoiled temples" they saw at Béxar and La Bahía, crediting neither the former splendor of the edifices nor the bounty of the feral herds to the "negligent, idle" Mexicans or the "half-civilized" Indians clustered around the old missions in "wretched circumstances."

[6] Frédéric Leclerc, *Texas and Its Revolution*, trans. James L. Shepherd III, p. 137. Almost all early travel accounts or immigration guidebooks contain sections on the rich potential for stock raising. See, e.g., Col. Edward Stiff, *The Texas Emigrant...*, pp. 11, 30, 39–40, 134; Viktor Bracht, *Texas in 1848*, trans. Charles Frank Schmidt, pp. 51–55; David Woodman, Jr., *Guide to Texas Emigrants*, pp. 168–70; Ferdinand Roemer, *Texas ...*, trans. Oswald Mueller, p. 9; J[acob] de Cordova, *Texas: Her Resources and Her Public Men*, pp. 23, 54; Francis Moore, Jr., *Map and Description of Texas...*, p. 9; *A Visit to Texas...*, p. 23; Carl, Prince of Solms-Braunfels, *Texas: 1844–1845*, pp. 27–28, 49, 119; the Rev. C[hester] Newell, *History of the Revolution in Texas...*, pp. 170, 176–77; George W. Bonnell, *Topographical Description of Texas*, pp. 69, 71.

This blindness was likely one reason Mexican officials at Béxar were anxious to impress upon Austin an awareness of their open-range regulations. Moreover, a century of hard experience had taught them the need to minimize the disputes that invariably accompanied exploitation of the feral herds; their intuition must have told them to expect no less conflict from these brash new colonists from a traditionally hostile and overbearing culture.[7]

Despite all the official Spanish protestations that wild cattle were "much diminished" over former times and that the herds had been slaughtered to the point of extinction, the Béxar ranchers' concern over *orejanos* demonstrates that such was not entirely the case. Indeed, the *ayuntamiento*'s instructions of January, 1822, to its constitutional representative said that the province was "overrun by large droves of wild horses and cattle." A report submitted by the same body the previous summer had suggested that the only monetary relief in sight was a possibility of authorized trade with the United States, "where goods are cheap, and the price of horses, the number of which is very great in this province, is high." Padilla's report of December, 1819, noted that the cattle, horses, and mules of the province elicited the admiration of all who saw them, and other accounts likewise attest that Texas was far from stripped of wild stock. Assessment rolls of the lower river towns, for example, show that in 1835, just before the Texas Revolution, more than *3 million* head were grazing between the Nueces and the Río Grande alone (a figure given United States commissioners in 1859 by J. L. Haynes, later customs collector at Brownsville). Juan Almonte's "Statistical Report on Texas" says that in 1806 in the region above the Nueces there were more than 100,000 head of cattle and about 40,000 to 50,000 tame horses. Dobie writes that not all—"probably not a majority"—of such stock ran wild.[8]

---

[7] Beale's journal, quoted in William Kennedy, *Texas: The Rise, Progress, and Prospects of the Republic of Texas*, pp. 120–36.

[8] Béxar *ayuntamiento*, "Instructions to Its Constitutional Representative," January 30, 1822, NA; Béxar *ayuntamiento*, "Report on Condition of Texas," May 1, 1821, NA; Padilla, "Report on the Barbarous Indians . . . ," December 27, 1819; U.S. Congress, "Texas Frontier Troubles," *House Rept.* no. 343, 44th Cong., 1st sess., 1876, pp. ii–iii; Juan N. Almonte, "Statistical Report on Texas" (1835), trans. Carlos E. Castañeda, *South-*

Wortham, perhaps relying a bit too heavily on sources like Almonte and Berlandier, did not think that there were many wild cattle in Texas when Anglo colonists arrived, the herds supposedly having been killed off by Indians or filibusters between 1810 and 1820. This notion gained credence with other writers until it achieved mythic proportions, sweeping from the vast plains not only the herds but their herdsmen as well. No better example can be found than the treatment in *Prose and Poetry of the Live Stock Industry*, where fallacy and fact become intertwined in a self-serving paean of Anglo superiority. The Bible would have supplied the American pioneers in Texas with "about as much practical knowledge of stock raising as they ever acquired from their Mexican neighbors," it said. The range industry would have developed as it did even "if there had never been a herd of Mexican cattle nor a flock of Mexican sheep on Texas soil." Common sense, energy, the opportunities of the country itself—these were the things that made Americans stockmen without peers in Texas. "At home he [the Mexican ranchero] is all filth," and in his hands the Texas stock business "would have slumbered indefinitely in primitive simplicity." Also, it claimed that the numbers of the Mexican herds had been subject to a "great many exaggerations." In such a manner did a proud legacy fall and the Hispanic contribution become reduced to bare bone.[9]

These notions, after suffering somewhat from the broad knowledge and intellectual integrity of a generation of Texan authorities like Bolton, Castañeda, Webb, and Dobie, are coming to life once again; now, however, repudiations of Spanish influence walk the land in scholarly guise rather than in the trappings of prose and poetry. For example, in *Trails to Texas: Southern Roots of Western Cattle Ranching*, author Terry C. Jordan, a cultural geographer, clearly wants to acknowledge Anglo colonists' place in the development of ranching (a place that should be obvious anyway). As he does this, he diminishes,

western Historical Quarterly 28, no. 3 (January, 1925):181, 189–91, 202–203, 215; Dobie, *The Longhorns*, p. 21.

[9] Louis J. Wortham, *A History of Texas from Wilderness to Commonwealth*, 5:135; James W. Freeman, ed., *Prose and Poetry of the Live Stock Industry of the United States* . . . , pp. 387–91.

if not entirely disavows, the Hispanic contribution, in spite of his disclaimer that this is not his intent. He even writes about the "rapid decline" of the Mexican rancheros of South Texas without mentioning the real reasons for this decline, as if it had been caused by some kind of debilitating virus to which only Nordic peoples were immune.

Perhaps it is sufficient to observe that his list of practices that supposedly distinguished the Anglo herding tradition from the Hispanic shows at least two-thirds common to both. Except for such details as the use of dogs and whips, scattering salt on the range or setting fire to it, the two traditions were closely akin. The grand scale of ranching in Texas made them more so, not less, and the Spanish system prevailed, for it was already adapted to the land and its unpredictable vicissitudes. Jordan concedes the Spanish *ganaderos* and *criadores* a certain amount of "horsemanship and related paraphernalia," plus a few surviving linguistic terms, but he labors prodigiously to find someone else to wear the laurels, even transporting us back to the herding cultures of darkest Africa. In my view such things as the frequency with which modern-day residents of northeast Texas have heard words like *corral* rather than *cow pen* are questionable proofs of the origins of western range stock-handling. Better proofs can be found in places like the Béxar Archives.[10]

In addition to the South Carolina–origin "school," which tends to downplay vigorously the Spanish-*Mexican* influence on ranching, other useful Hispanic contributions are now being questioned. The western stock saddle with its characteristic horn, we are being told, did not originate with Spanish *ganaderos* but magically appeared when Anglo traders began to ply the Santa Fe Trail in the 1820s. Should this trend continue, we can expect to hear that Mexicans rode bareback—if at all—and that Longhorns were simply figments of our imagination; that in reality the thundering herds that once covered Texas were white-faced Herefords, Durham shorthorns, or Jersey milk cows. After this, of course, we will discover that Captain Richard King

[10] Jordan, *Trails to Texas*, pp. 15–17, 25, 98–100, 150–57. For a more balanced expression of this school of thought, see D. W. Meinig, *Imperial Texas: An Interpretive Essay in Cultural Geography*.

learned all his ranching techniques as a waif in the Brooklyn slums before arriving at Rancho de Santa Gertrudis to put them into practice.

Nonsense aside, Frank Goodwyn, who grew up on the King Ranch, says that from the beginning King hired Mexican hands because they were good on a horse (which he was not) and knew the land, their ancestors having settled there long before. That the Kineños taught the former Yankee riverboat captain much about how to ranch in the brush country around present Kingsville goes without saying. For generations these people have remained with the King-Kleberg dynasty, making themselves an integral part of the operation. Their value has heretofore been recognized by knowledgeable Texans, certainly by the family itself. Yet Jordan and others would have us believe that the contribution of these mayordomos and vaqueros was inessential to the evolution of western ranching.[11]

Men like Erasmo Seguín hinted that Texas on the eve of the Anglo era was not lacking in cattle or horses, and early Anglo accounts confirm the impression he gives. Actually, most newcomers of the 1830s and 1840s were amazed by the abundance of wild livestock throughout the province and described it in glowing terms. Austin's maps of 1829 bear the notations "Immence herds of wild horses" and "Ganado vacuno mesteño en

---

[11] Beatie, *Saddles*, pp. 50, 54, 57; Frank Goodwyn, *Life on the King Ranch*, p. 30; *King Ranch: 100 Years of Ranching, 1853–1953* (Reprint from *Corpus Christi Caller-Times*, July 12, 1953), pp. 64–67, 75, 98.

el gran numero" (great numbers of feral cattle). It was soon observed that the natural increase of these animals was enormous, providing instant financial independence for those who shifted their energies from farming to stock raising. For settlers who were not large slaveholders, the attractions offered by such a switch were very appealing. Even the Irish colonists of the lower coast, coming directly from predominantly farming areas, soon turned to ranching, "a form of animal husbandry with which they had not been theretofore familiar." The success enjoyed by a few of these families is astonishing, considering their modest beginnings. Short of miraculous intervention it can perhaps best be explained by their close proximity to the fountainhead of Texas stock raising and the many advantages associated with such contact. Local historian Victor Rose did not mince words, acknowledging that many well-to-do spreads were established through frequent applications to the "doby [dogie] foundation," that is, by zealous appropriation of the region's abundant *orejanos*.[12]

The incoming Anglo-Celtic stock tenders were well aware of the source of their newfound wealth, though most of them feigned ignorance or indifference. A few men who reached cattle-baron status preferred humorous explanations for the inexplicable number of mavericks and "swamp angels" (coastal mavericks) found wearing their brands. Shanghai Pierce, for example, was fond of attributing his success to the remarkable reproductive powers of a pair of old oxen that he brought to South Texas after the Civil War. But the first generation of Anglo Texans, especially those arriving before 1836, were remarkably candid about where their cattle came from. Wild stock found in the valley of the San Marcos River, for example, John Linn acknowledged as being the offspring of "Don Felipe Partilleas's herd," left there after Comanches forced the settlers to leave. This was a fairly accurate description; the cattle were the leavings of Governor Cordero's attempt to plant a stock-raising center on the Río San Marcos just after the turn of the century.

---

[12] John Brendan Flannery, *The Irish Texans*, pp. 53–54; Hobart Huson, *Refugio: A Comprehensive History of Refugio County from Aboriginal Times to 1953*, 2:217–40; Victor Rose, *The Texas Vendetta; or the Sutton-Taylor Feud*, pp. 5–9; maps nos. 917 and 1411, Texas State Archives.

Other aspiring Anglo cattlemen and prototype "cow boys" were not as curious about where the mustangs and cattle originated or to whom they might have once belonged. After the revolution fine distinctions, such as whether animals were unbranded or branded with those abstract motifs favored by Mexicans, also lost their meaning. That they were there for the taking was sufficient. This, it should be remembered, was no different from the traditional attitude of energetic Spanish-Mexican ranchers about semiwild mission cattle that the long-suffering padres and their Indian converts had been powerless to protect.[13]

Regardless of who enjoyed preeminence when it came to exploiting mesteños and *orejanos*, it should not be supposed that the Hispanic contribution lagged or halted after Anglo stockmen entered the scene in strength. Mexican officials continued promulgating stock ordinances up until the revolution. An example was the decree issued by the government of Coahuila y Texas on August 31, 1827, on special brands that all city councils should adopt to mark wild stock sold at auction. In August, 1831, Ramón Músquiz sent a copy of the brand chosen at Béxar to the Nacogdoches *ayuntamiento* for its future reference. Slaughter regulations were passed, and strict controls were exercised over professional livestock traders (*mercaderos*) who conducted business in Texas. State law required them to register sales and purchases with alcaldes, indicating the number of head and their brands. Roundups were regulated, as in former times, by a bill which Miguel Arciniega introduced into the legislature in 1827. "Corredurías de mesteñas" were limited to the traditional period from October to February, a provision covered by State Decree No. 8. Included were state taxes for unbranded livestock caught on vacant lands, charged at the same rates earlier adopted by the Béxar municipality.[14]

As suggested, mesteño taxes proved as controversial under Mexican rule as under Spanish. One of the concessions granted

---

[13] To establish that wild cattle were found throughout Texas when Anglo colonists arrived, Dobie listed his sources (*The Longhorns*, pp. 352–54); see also Wayne Gard, *The Chisholm Trail*, pp. 7–19.

[14] Músquiz to Nacogdoches *ayuntamiento*, August 10, 1831, NA; Andrew Anthony Tijerina, "Tejanos and Texas: The Native Mexicans of Texas, 1820–1850," (Ph.D. diss., University of Texas, 1977), pp. 149–53.

in 1824 to empresario Martín de León was the right of his colonists to take wild horses free of duty for a period of ten years. At first the Béxar *ayuntamiento* instructed its constitutional representative to seek this right, that is, free exportation of horses to the United States for a ten-year period, for all the citizens of Texas. However, local officials soon realized the benefit such an impost would have at home and reserved it for themselves, along with Croix's old catching fees. No doubt the new Bexareño political figures felt imposed upon when Decree No. 8 usurped some of these taxation prerogatives. Finally, in 1831 the legislature of Coahuila y Texas declared livestock exempt from taxes for six years (Decree No. 176), but only in the Béxar and Monclova departments. Perhaps seeing that they could not keep these revenues in Texas led Tejano statesmen to work to have them abolished altogether—a decision no doubt applauded by the stockmen of the state.[15]

Lists of stray animals and their brands continued to be kept at the Río Grande villas, San Antonio, Nacogdoches, and other population centers (although places like Liberty reported surprisingly few strays). One of these lists, maintained at Béxar by various officials for the years 1827 to 1834, reflects an ongoing concern about returning strays to their proper owners (see brand section H). A typical entry, made in April, 1830, notes that a *novillo* was given to Doña Luisa Laza (Lazo), who claimed the young bull until her husband, "Señor Dimit" (Philip Dimitt, later of Goliad fame), could attend to the paperwork. The last entry was made by political chief Juan Nepomuceno Seguín in June, 1834, for a black mare found by citizen Juan María Salinas on the road to Nacogdoches. Later that year Seguín called what Dudley G. Wooten has described as the "first strictly revolutionary meeting in Texas," signaling this prominent ranching family's strong stand for independence.[16]

[15] A. B. J. Hammett, *The Empresario: Don Martín de León (The Richest Man in Texas)*, pp. 19, 22, 26–27; H. P. N. Gammel, ed., *Laws of Texas*, 1:178, 291. Another enactment (Decree no. 241, Gammel, 1:334) continued to tax the activities of livestock traders but not raisers; strays were further defined in Decree no. 321, dated May 19, 1835 (Gammel, 1:418).

[16] "Libro en que se anotan las Bestias Mostrencal de fierros no conosidos con arreglo al Decreto n. 8 del Congreso Constitucional del Estado," 1827–34, NA; Liberty alcalde, "Report of Strays," Grazing Papers, Texas State Archives; "Lista de los individuos

It was a call soon answered by many of Seguín's neighboring clans—an astonishing fact from a socio-ethnic perspective and especially considering the damage these rancheros had suffered for their revolutionary sympathies over the preceding two decades. Arredondo's savage campaign must have left a scar on Juan, who was barely seven years old at the time. His father's generation, of course, knew only too well the devastation such conflicts engendered. Still, family after family aligned itself on the side of freedom: Flores, Navarro, Ruíz, Menchaca, Rodríguez, Carvajal, Sambrano, de León, Benavides, Aldrete, to name a few, all of them important cattle raisers.

This sentiment was not restricted to Béxar; Nacogdoches, Goliad, and Victoria were also represented in the revolutionary ranks. Many patriotic sons of old Tejano ranching dynasties rendered valuable service against Mexico in 1835–36, some even shedding their blood at the Shrine of Texas Liberty. Unfortunately, in many instances their rights were brushed aside in the turmoils of revolution, republic, and statehood simply because they were "Mexican"—that is, of the same extraction as the defeated nation. The proof of this is not lacking for those meddlesome enough to wish to examine such cruel twists of fate. For the most part, past generations have deemed it proper to leave this skeleton hanging in the closet rather than giving it an honorable burial—or its deserved place in our history books.[17]

It is no great secret that the so-called "cow boy" stock depredations began legitimately on August 8, 1836, when President David G. Burnet authorized a company of Independent Rangers, numbering one hundred men or more, to be employed in col-

que tienen vestias de fierros no conocidos . . . ," June 1, 1826, and "Asientos de bestias de fierros no conocidos," 1827, MA, 6:66–68, 11:55–57; "Libro de Arriento de bestias . . . ," October 9, 1837, and "Libro de vienes mostrencos," 1844–45, LA, rolls 11, 13, 14; Dudley G. Wooten, *A Comprehensive History of Texas, 1685 to 1897*, 1:162.

[17] Reuben M. Potter, *The Texas Revolution: Distinguished Mexicans Who Took Part in the Revolution of Texas, with Glances at Its Early Events*; Victor Rose, *Victor Rose's History of Victoria County*, ed. J. W. Petty, Jr., 104–106, 154–55; Citizens of Bexar to Stephen H. Darden (state comptroller), January 12, 1875, Texas State Archives. For the authoritative treatment of the period 1836–42 see Joseph Milton Nance, *After San Jacinto: The Texas-Mexican Frontier, 1836–1841*; and Joseph Milton Nance, *Attack and Counterattack: The Texas-Mexican Frontier, 1842*. Tejano views toward and participation in the conflict are detailed in Fane Downs, "The History of Mexicans in Texas, 1820–1845" (Ph.D. diss., Texas Tech University, 1970).

lecting and driving the large herds of cattle found between the Nueces and the Río Grande, "which have no ostensible owner." Such raids continued long after they were needed to provision the army and soon became dominated by a lawless set of men who fancied themselves a "Band of Brothers" and defied any legally sanctioned body to contest their rule over the frontier. An act by the First Congress of the Republic four months later, providing for the registration of cattle brands, had little impact on such rapaciousness, except perhaps to provide a means for legalizing the spoils of war so acquired.

Moreover, evidence exists that prevailing Anglo attitudes favored the cattle forays as retaliation for losses suffered during General Santa Anna's booty-gathering march through Texas. Widespread expropriation of livestock escalated, affecting friend and foe alike. In 1839 it became necessary for Congress to pass a law to prohibit the driving of cattle from the country lying below the Guadalupe River. Before order was eventually restored to the ravaged land and this business was brought to a halt, untold numbers of cattle bearing "peculiar" Mexican brands were driven northward and sold, with few questions asked or answers given. That many of the animals carried away by the victorious Texians were unbranded, falling into the class of mesteño, *alzado*, or *mostrenco*, did nothing to diminish the losses suffered by old rancheros, who for generations had defended their rights to such stock.

"Texans did not create their cattle industry, they simply took over. It was one, and perhaps the greatest and most profitable, of the spoils of the Texas Revolution and the Mexican War." So wrote the compilers of the Grazing Industry Papers—after assembling and studying a mass of evidence on the origins of Texas ranching—in their unpublished work of 1935, "The Range in Colonial Times." One of their sources was a Refugio County item in the *Texas Almanac* of 1861, which stated that armed companies from East Texas, operating under the "Cow Boy system," were the prime movers in frontier stock raids:

From their secure position when they had driven the cattle to their homes, and the proximity to a market in Louisiana, the eastern men became more anxious to obtain the wild stock than even those of the west, and on the wild herds becoming exhausted, they did not scruple to push their expeditions to the very doors of the Mexicans on the Rio Grande, and drive off their gentle cattle.

To these and similar events must be attributed the "rapid decline" of Hispanics as cattlemen of substance in the coming years, not to the inert or moribund nature of their livestock methods. It was not a virus that struck Tejano stock-raising aspirations but hot lead and cold steel, finished off by the stroke of a quill pen.[18]

In some ways the transition that took place was nothing new; only the roles changed, not the play itself. Ranching in Texas had always been a violent and risky business, subject to savage molestations by Indians or periodic maulings by awesome natural forces. It was also brutal in the sense that some men acquired large tracts of land and many cattle and then bound other, less fortunate men to their service. The Hinojosas, the Ballís, the Sánchez Navarros and many other powerful Spanish ranching dynasties did not become wealthy hacendados without being accused of greediness and ruthlessness along the

---

[18] Grazing Papers, vol. 1, pt. 2, pp. 1–2. Burnet's order and a sampling of eyewitness reports dealing with early "cow boy" activities are found in ibid., pp. 275–300. A typical one is the account extracted from John H. Linn, *Reminiscences of Fifty Years in Texas*, pp. 322–24. For laws of the Republic of Texas pertaining to strays, brands, and other aspects of the livestock industry, see Gammel, *Laws of Texas*, 1:1249, 1251, 1272–75, 2:53, all firmly based on Spanish-Mexican precedents.

way, just as were their later Anglo counterparts. The bitter dispute in which the Menchacas managed to gain control of their ranch at the expense of the Hernández family has been discussed, as has the fight for ownership of the 59-league Potrero del Espíritu Santo between the de la Garzas and José Narciso Cavazos. Frederick Law Olmsted, rambling around Texas in 1854, saw these forces at work—but by then the issue of who should own the land and profit from its blessings had different overtones. Speaking of the old ranchos in El Rincón, he predicted: "These small landholders are almost certain to disappear before the first American settlers who approach. A quarrel is immediate and the weaker is pushed off the log. But throughout the South the same occurs—the small whites are everywhere crowded upon and elbowed out before the large planters."

The big fish eat the little fish; sad but true. But if this universal truth was operative in Texas after the Mexican War, it was also true that being considered part of the "conquered race" made it no easier for these proud old Tejano ranching clans to yield their land to new masters—even harder if they had fought for the winning side and imagined themselves part of the new order. Olmsted noted that dispossessed Mexicans had already proved of value in furnishing a temporary though ill-regulated supply of cheap labor, being familiar with the details of local agriculture and "especially adapted to its most profitable branch of stock raising." Whether he realized it or not, this observant Free-Soiler was defining the occupational roles that many of these people would fill in Texas for the next century. Other accounts also acknowledge the usefulness of Mexican vaqueros in handling stock, though it soon became fashionable to denigrate them for a lack of fidelity to their Anglo benefactors, general untrustworthiness, impudence, cruelty to animals, and so forth. Their skills as herdsmen, however, were rarely denied.[19]

The subject of Anglo-Spanish rivalry for the control of Texas and its great wealth has long excited attention and controversy. Too often, though, "scholarship" has settled for arrang-

---

[19] Frederick Law Olmsted, *A Journey through Texas: Or, A Saddle-Trip on the Southwestern Border . . .* , pp. 272, 427.

ing "facts" in such a manner as to simply confirm the authors' predispositions, formed under the influence of class and kin. Moreover, often overlooked is the fact that the confrontation in Texas was between two peoples basically of European stock—of a closely related "gene pool," so to speak, even if they differed greatly in language, culture, and inclination. How the Indian part of the Hispanic population was dealt with by both groups is another matter entirely.

No one has begun to tell the story of these Christianized aborigines, many of whom were forced into virtual serfdom by opportunistic *patrones* after the mission doors were closed. Victimized by a system they did not fully understand, unable to go back to "unspoiled" primitivism yet denied full participation in the Spanish *gente de razón* social order, the Indians often turned to stock tending to survive. Not being recognized landowners in the sense of *dueños de ganado* or *criadores*, they had to hire themselves out for below-subsistence wages, which meant that they were soon bound to employers by perpetual indebtedness. This, incidentally, is the skeleton that contemporary Hispanic scholars must eventually haul out of their own cultural closet and dust off. For when it is argued that Anglos stole the land from them, sooner or later comes the realization that their European ancestors did likewise to the aborigines—a bitter truth that has convulsed Mexico off and on for centuries. The fight of these domesticated Indians for human dignity is easily comparable to the struggle Spanish dons waged against Anglo barons for control of the cattle kingdom in Texas, yet it remains virtually unrecognized in the prose and poetry of the Old West.

The reasons for this lopsided historical treatment of America's expanding frontiers are, paradoxically, as complex as they are simple. Aside from religious issues and the Anglos' horrified fascination with ramifications of the Black Legend, there was the long-standing urge to plunder New World Spanish dominions so ably practiced by Sir Francis Drake and associates in the late sixteenth century. This sack-and-pillage mentality endured among "Carolina's children" and was very much in evidence as the conflict in Texas passed beyond political philosophies and took on increasingly racial and cultural connotations. Greatly bolstering the Anglos' Moral Right to Rule—in their own eyes at least—was the fact that the greater part of the population of Texas was mestizo, showing strong evidence of Indian and perhaps Negro blood. Therefore, the Indian-hating, slave-holding Anglos lumped the entire Mexican population—with all its fine caste distinctions, *español, indio, negro, mestizo, mulato, coyote, lobo, zambo,* and so on—into one "despicable" race. While this sort of categorization perhaps made the expropriation of Mexican property a bit easier on Protestant consciences, it ignored the reality behind the prevailing social order in Texas, which was that "Indians" owned no property to speak of. It also completely submerged the plight of this Spanish-speaking Indian-mestizo class beneath the greater (or at least more discernible) losses of their masters, the light-complexioned rancheros who possessed all the accouterments of civilization.

Ironically, the dons, whose own society and system of justice had routinely exploited the noncomprehending Indians, now found themselves manipulated by hordes of condescending politicians, sharp land speculators, and merciless attorneys—whiter than they. As Weber notes, the upper-class, fair-skinned *ricos* were generally safe in their persons if not in their property. It did not matter a whit either way to the victors, especially those sharing Mirabeau B. Lamar's imperialistic views. They had a self-appointed job to do, and in bulldog fashion they set about obtaining the riches they had come for—horses, cattle, land titles, political power, and whatever else the *ricos* had that was worth taking. The darkskinned *pobres* they considered hardly worth a passing glance.[20]

Nowhere are the devious workings of the Texian imperialistic mind better illustrated than in the ill-considered Santa Fe Expedition of 1841. Meaning to capture for the Republic of Texas the lucrative trade going up and down the Santa Fe Trail, Presi-

---

[20] David J. Weber, ed., *Foreigners in Their Native Land: Historical Roots of the Mexican Americans,* pp. 68–70, 135–38, 154–56; Rodolfo Acuña, *Occupied America: The Chicano's Struggle toward Liberation,* pp. 7–19, 34–36. For the popular nineteenth-century view of Texas Hispanics, see Alex E. Sweet and J. Armoy Knox, *On a Mexican Mustang through Texas: From the Gulf to the Rio Grande.*

dent Lamar was obliged to devise a way to take it without appearing unduly vandalistic. Central to his plan of pacifying New Mexico without a struggle were its many mestizos and Pueblo Indians, to whom he extended full constitutional rights in a proclamation dated April 14, 1840. Instructions to his messengers (traders William G. Dryden, John Rowland, and William Workman) pontificated thus: "Should it be objected that Indians, under our Constitution, cannot enjoy the rights of citizenship in the fullest sense of the term, you are authorized to reply, that the term 'Indian'... does not embrace civilized Indians, but applies to the barbarians only." Secretary of State Abner S. Lipscomb went on to say that many Texas citizens at Béxar were Indian but civilized, enjoying equal privileges with the whites. Perhaps to prove it, José Antonio Navarro was sent along the following year when the expedition finally got under way.

By that time, however, the Executive Department had entertained second thoughts about extending the blessings of its liberal constitution to the numerous Pueblos of New Mexico, civilized or not. Commissioner Navarro was instructed that if the foregoing agents had not already made an explanation of what it meant to be an Indian in Texas "it is thought advisable that it should not now be done"—unless, of course, it was absolutely necessary to the mission's success to deceive them. One must wonder about the thoughts Don José carried with him as his wagonful of trade goods rattled across the Llano Estacado, heading for benighted Santa Fe. Francisco Ruíz was not there to steady his shaking hand this time, for the only other Tejano signer of the Texian independence manifesto had passed away some months before the armed-to-the-teeth "Pioneers" and their little "commercial venture" rolled westward.[21]

When Olmsted reached Texas, this imperialistic frame of mind was in full flower, well on the way to achieving its goals. His *Journey through Texas* mentions many instances of racism at work: dispossession at Goliad, disturbances associated with the Cart War, prejudice based upon the degree of Indian or Negro blood, alarm over Mexican complicity with slaves, meet-

---

[21] Harriet Smithers, ed., *Journals of the Sixth Congress, Republic of Texas*, 3:287–97; Noah Smithwick, *The Evolution of a State*, pp. 271–86.

ings to expel the Tejano population of various counties, and so on. But the stark picture of a priest living hand to mouth in the ruins of Goliad's presidio chapel sums the situation up nicely: "The Mexicans, he [the priest] said, certainly once owned all the land about here. Now it was all held by Americans, and no Mexican had received any pay for it. He did not know, but his people said it really belonged to them." Such a feeling has proved tenacious, whether or not grounded in fact.

The priest's flock told him that they were not well treated by the Americans: the Americans thought the Mexicans a bad people; the Mexicans thought the same of them. The Anglos, they said, cheated them in "every business," such as not allowing them to get wood for their fences in the customary places. But they were too poor and too ignorant to do anything toward insisting upon their rights. "The Americans, he heard, talk very hard about the Mexicans, as if they had no business in the neighborhood; but he was sure the treaty declared they should have the rights of citizens, and continue to hold their property." When Olmsted said he hoped the priest would be able to help them secure just treatment, the cleric answered that his duty was not to mingle in their "temporal concerns," but that he hoped to do them some moral benefit.[22]

Since these unfortunate people were universally acknowledged as the best hands that could be procured for the management of cattle, horses, and other livestock, this would be their avenue of survival under Anglo rule as under Spanish. Many former hidalgos were reduced to similar circumstances, but "people of color" invariably fared worse. Much has lately been made of the contribution of black cowboys, and rightly so, for they and Mexican vaqueros figured prominently in the story of Texas ranching, trail driving, and so on. But in keeping with the modern need to expurgate our ancestors' lamentable characteristics, rarely mentioned is the fate of those few blacks who tried to establish themselves as stock raisers in the Republic of Texas. If John Warren Hunter's "Life of Creed Taylor" can be believed, this grizzled old Texian said that in olden times things happened

---

[22] Olmsted, *Journey through Texas*, p. 265. For a detailed treatment of racism see Arnoldo de León, *They Called Them Greasers: Anglo Attitudes toward Mexicans in Texas, 1821–1900.*

during the formation of cattle empires which some of his contemporaries later wanted "turned to the wall," unseen by future generations. Such an unpleasant picture must have been etched on many minds in the mid-1850s in the coastal-bend counties of Orange and Jefferson, near the mouth of the Sabine River.

This area, around Madison, had the largest enclave of free blacks in the state. Most of them were of mixed ancestry— quadroon or octoroon, three or four generations removed from undiluted Negro blood—and "considerably less black than the hearts of their persecutors" as W. T. Block says. They had come to Texas early, and many of them fought during the revolution— men with names like Ashworth, Bunch, Perkins, and Thomas. After independence from Mexico they prospered and became wealthy cattlemen. In 1850, Aaron Ashworth, for example, was reported to be the richest resident of Jefferson County, worth more than $30,000. He had accumulated large tracts of choice lands, grazed upon by many sleek cattle. That was his "cardinal sin." Racial tempers flared, and envious neighbors drove him and more than thirty such mulatto families across the Sabine into Calcasieu Parish. A few returned later but by then Ashworth's herd of 3,000 cattle had "disappeared." Abner and William Ashworth, each of whom also owned large numbers of livestock, lost everything, and the sixty-two-year-old William was reduced to the status of a day laborer. An isolated illustration? Not really, just one executed on too big a canvas to be successfully turned to the wall.[23]

What was the result of such dispossessions? Rage, in most instances, some of it muted, some manifested. The Juan N. Cortina uprising at Brownsville in 1859 provides an example of the rancheros' intense frustration at their losses. Seguín's memoirs

---

[23] John Warren Hunter, "Life of Creed Taylor, Mason County, 1901" (manuscript, Texas State Archives), pp. 159–61; W. T. Block, *A History of Jefferson County, Texas, from Wilderness to Reconstruction*, pp. 93–95; and W. T. Block, "Meanest Town on the Coast," *Old West* 16, no. 2 (Winter, 1979):10–11, 28–30. For many brands of this mulatto enclave see F. W. Dibble's compilation in the Grazing Papers volume titled "Cattle Brands" (box 2R232); Aaron Ashworth's mark dates from 1837. Evidence abounds to support the thesis that nineteenth-century cattle drives, though Anglo bossed, had considerable Mexican and black participation. Nora E. Ramírez, "The Vaquero and Ranching in the Southwestern United States, 1600–1970" (Ph.D. diss., Indiana University, 1978), pp. 102–77, contains a good summary.

of the previous year about those who were preying upon landed Tejanos are almost as scathing. Because he did not resort to violence (except earlier, in the uniform of a Mexican soldier), his views amounted to little; all the concern focused instead on the hell-raising Cortina. Both said that they found themselves strangers in their homeland, and Cortina recklessly proclaimed that the Anglos "shall not possess our lands until they have fattened it with their own gore." Seguín's rebuke to the land grabbers was milder; he simply called attention to the many suits that encumbered the Béxar County docket and the evidence elicited in such cases, whereby one "will readily discover the base means adopted to deprive rightful owners of their property." A case he had in mind was perhaps the decision in *Paul v. Pérez*, reviewed by the Supreme Court of Texas in 1851, in which, in an attempt to divest him of the redoubtable colonel's pasturelands along the Medina, Ignacio Pérez's son José was charged with being an enemy alien. A multitude of others could be cited. These issues continue to smolder in South Texas, as evidenced by the activities of various land-claimant groups and litigation relating to oil and natural-gas revenues on several old Spanish grants which changed hands during turbulent times, usually for a pittance. Ironic in light of Cortina's *grito*, generations of Anglo lawyers, not grantee descendants, have waxed fat on such issues.[24]

Although most accounts agree that the early "cow boys" were acting extralegally, it is not generally recognized (or at least admitted) that their violent tactics made life untenable for Mexican stockmen in the Nueces Strip, thereby paving the way for eventual Anglo ownership of the land. Paul S. Taylor has boldly stated the conditions these grantees faced: "They were not simply individual holders of property selling of their own free will; they were selling *because they were Mexicans* who, in a time of chaos, could no longer occupy their land, and who saw

---

[24] Insight into Anglo land acquisition can be had from John Bost Pitts III, "Speculation in Headright Land Grants in San Antonio from 1837 to 1852" (Master's thesis, Trinity University [San Antonio]); for the Cortina "difficulties on the southwestern frontier" see U.S., Cong., *House Exec. Doc.* no. 52, 36th Cong., 1st sess., 1859–60 (ser. 1050); Juan N. Seguín, *Personal Memoirs* . . . ; *Paul v. Pérez* (1851), *Texas Supreme Court Reports*, 7:169–74; Robert J. Salazar et al., *Asociación de Reclamantes v. the United Mexican States: Texas Land Grant Heirs Seek Justice*.

the imminent American military and political domination." Thus they sold under stress, and generally under conditions advantageous to the buyers, a fact still remembered with some bitterness by empty-handed heirs of the original title holders. As Taylor notes, this takeover was mostly accomplished in then-sprawling Nueces County before the Civil War. It occurred earlier in the Goliad area, where forty of the forty-nine Tejano ranches had passed into Anglo hands by 1845.

Andrew A. Tijerina says that many of the dispossessed stockmen "received no recompense at all," and were simply driven from their lands. D. W. Meinig, in *Imperial Texas*, gives a similar analysis: "By 1860 the Anglo had gotten control, by fair means or foul, of nearly every ranch worth having north of the Nueces, but they still needed a few vaqueros to work them." Speaking of the confrontation between the two socioeconomic systems, plantation and hacienda, he adds that it was an unbalanced encounter of forces in which the military triumph of the one drove out the leadership of the other, "so that both institutions were now ruled by the Anglo, the one worked by the Negro slave, the other still worked by the Mestizo vaquero."[25]

Strangely, one finds admissions of this sort in the oddest places. *Prose and Poetry of the Live Stock Industry*, after a long-winded essay on how inessential the ranchero contribution was, concedes that headright holders descended on the Río Grande Valley and "in repeated instances located them on property which for a century had been in the quiet possession of the descendants of the old Spanish colonists." The latter, "hopeless of the results of litigation, and sometimes in fear of their lives," fled and sought refuge below the river. In such a manner were large districts "pounced upon" and afterward devoted to stock raising by newcomers. In Texas it has been customary not to speak of these things in polite circles, but the truth persists. One suspects that the way Texans choose to regard such truths in the coming years will have much to do with the unity, if not survival, of our unique society. Viewed in the cold light of objective inquiry, such transgressions are harder for modern inves-

---

[25] Paul Schuster Taylor, *An American-Mexican Frontier: Nueces County, Texas*, pp. 25, 71, 179–90; Tijerina, "Tejanos and Texas," pp. 317–24; Meinig, *Imperial Texas*, pp. 54–55.

tigators to suppress or ignore than they were in the past. Like it or not, it will become more difficult to keep that dusty, antiquated picture facing the wall. In my view, it behooves historians to square the time-worn myths of our heritage with the realities, lest coming generations, in discarding a brazen forgery, abandon or lose interest in the subject entirely.[26]

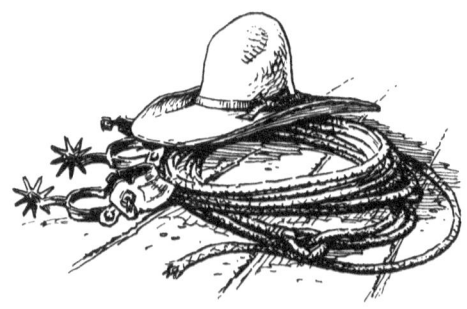

Just as it must not be imagined that the Hispanic contribution to ranching ended in Texas with the arrival of Anglo stockmen, neither should it be pretended that Mexicans gave up after the conquest. When they could no longer ride for themselves, they rode for others, passing on their knowledge and customs to subsequent generations of "buckaroos" (the word itself, a corruption of "vaqueros"). As always, their services were highly sought, and still are in the brush country, where cattle continue to be raised in large numbers. There, in this now-maligned "diamond-shaped area" elucidated by Webb, Dobie, and others, the herds of former *criadores* took refuge and multiplied without number. There the first Anglo cattle empires began to take shape, by hook or by crook, and there the Spanish influence on Anglo ranching techniques was most profound. Down through the years Texans rode into this area for cattle and emerged wearing chaps, *sombreros*, *bandanas*, *ponchos*, silver-inlaid spurs, and most of the other trappings that we now associate with the well-dressed western cowpoke. Perhaps the main thrust of population moved east to west, as Jordan painstakingly demonstrates,

---

[26] Freeman, *Prose and Poetry*, pp. 391–92. For one such proposal see Hobart Huson, *A New Approach To the Teaching of Texas History In Our Schools and Colleges*.

but the indisputable truth is that cattle moved south to north, for the simple reason that the large herds were in South Texas, not elsewhere. Quite a bit more came out of these drives than livestock, as was the case a century before with colonial Louisiana and its hardy Tejano culture carriers.

In this region Anglo saddlemakers began to produce new, improved types of stock saddles based on the standard *silla vaquera*. It was an innovation soon to make Texas famous wherever men tended cattle from horseback. Prince Carl said that in Texas "everyone rides a Spanish or Mexican saddle" but advised his German immigrants to buy Hungarian models before they came because they were cheaper and not quite as rough as the Tejano rigs. Nonetheless, when Germans at New Braunfels, Yorktown, and elsewhere soon set about tanning leather and making saddles, the native variety served as their model. Many old Anglo saddleries throughout the West employed Mexican helpers, who were noted for their craftsmanship in fashioning saddletrees and working leather. These saddle coverings might in time be attached to the tree and called "Mother Hubbards," but any Texan worth his salt knew that they came from *mochilas*, and he also knew that the protuberance in front was a horn. If he did not know what it was for (since eastern saddles were "muleys"), he soon learned by watching Mexican vaqueros. The flow of functional knowledge in a rough-and-tumble frontier setting is rarely impaired by prejudice, even if other dimensions of the human experience become stigmatized by its touch.[27]

In these and many other ways diverse ethnic forces met, fused, and shaped for the future a frontier ranching experience recognized as unique to Texas. From there this integrated system of practices reached out to touch the similarly Spanish-derived systems in New Mexico, Arizona, and California, and the resulting synthesis spread throughout the northern High

---

[27] Webb, *Great Plains*, pp. 207–15, 224–49; Dobie, *The Mustangs*, pp. 99–108; J. Frank Dobie, *A Vaquero of the Brush Country*, pp. 44–71, 255–70; Sandra L. Myres, *The Ranch in Spanish Texas, 1691–1800*, pp. 23–25, 53; Prince Carl, *Texas: 1844–1845*, p. 133; Lee M. Rice and Glenn R. Vernam, *They Saddled the West*, pp. 9–19; Richard E. Ahlborn, ed., *Man Made Mobile: Early Saddles of Western North America*, pp. 2, 18, 39, 41, 59.

Plains. Because the main thrust of Manifest Destiny was ever westward and California was at the "end of the trail," Texas continued to exercise a great influence on the progressive development of ranching. In his study of the range-cattle industry, Edward Everett Dale wrote, "Any history of the cattle industry in the West must begin with Texas since that state was the original home of ranching on a large scale in the United States." Glenn R. Vernam, in *Man on Horseback*, tells us that it diffused from there: "The Texas cowboy set the pattern for most range life east of the Continental Divide." How did we come by this knowledge? Paul I. Wellman, in *The Trampling Herd*, says that the "cow-knowledge" of the old vaqueros of Spanish days had been "so well taught to the more modern white cowboys of Texas" that such things as long trail drives were undertaken without concern, "as a matter of routine." At the core of this newly acquired competence were the essential working tools— saddle, rope, and branding iron—all bequeathed to nineteenth-century buckaroos by vaqueros of the eighteenth.[28]

Such was admitted by most men who knew the Old West and the way things were. No less an authority than Frederic Remington gave Owen Wister, the author of *The Virginian*, benefit of his keen observations when the latter was seeking information on the evolution of the cowboy. Nice young men who ambled around wire fences were not to be mistaken for the "wild rider of the Plains," said Remington. Yankees coming west had merely improved on Spanish and mestizo ranching techniques. "You want to credit the Mexican with the inventing [of] the whole business," wrote the Artist of the American West— about as forthright an assessment as can be found. This is not to say, of course, that the experience in California, along with many other places, did not make important contributions. The question of *origins*, however, is quite another matter. Texas was where the vast herds of cattle came from, as well as where ranching became an institutionalized, enduring way of life. Its dominance in this respect should not be diminished by modern-

---

[28] Edward Everett Dale, *The Range Cattle Industry: Ranching on the Great Plains from 1865 to 1925*, p. 3; Glenn R. Vernam, *Man on Horseback*, pp. 296–99, 317; Paul I. Wellman, *The Trampling Herd: The Story of the Cattle Range in America*, pp. 29, 31–34, 107–10.

A Look beyond 1821

day revisionism in favor of an ephemeral Carolinian "hearth," nor should its Spanish roots be disinterred from Texas soil.[29]

The truth is that many Hispanic Texans continued to ranch for themselves after 1850, although Jordan maintains they had "very nearly disappeared" by that time and implies that those who were left were not men of substance but small-time operators whose culture was in decline and who were therefore incapable of exercising an influence on their more "vital" Anglo rivals. Such an interpretation does not agree with the facts. One has only to examine the exquisitely detailed "Mapa del Río Grande" showing Mexican ranchos strung all the way from Paso del Águila (Eagle Pass) to Bagdad at the river's mouth to realize that ranching had not completely passed out of their hands. And

---

[29] Stan Steiner, *Dark and Dashing Horsemen*, pp. 164–66; *Grazing Papers*, vol. 1, pt. 2, pp. 300–16, contain a review of the vaquero influence on cowboys, an influence solidly documented in Ramírez, "The Vaquero," and Tijerina, "Tejanos and Texas."

one has only to read the voluminous document that accompanied it, *Reports of the Committee of Investigation Sent in 1873 by the Mexican Government to the Frontier of Texas*, to learn that brush-country Tejanos were still giving cattle barons like Captain King and Mifflin Kenedy a run for their money. Further, the investigating commissioners give us startling insight into exactly how such baronial estates were built, another picture that some may wish would remain turned to the wall. Beyond presenting evidence to support the charge that there was "no justice for the Mexicans in Texas," this compendium almost does for ranching in the Nueces Strip what Pichardo's treatise of 1812 did for the boundary question on the Louisiana border. In short, taken with the congressional inquiry that followed, the Mexican report offers an unparalleled view of nineteenth-century stock raising in South Texas.[30]

Even in the Cradle—the old *agostaderos* (pastures) along the San Antonio River valley—a number of Hispanics were still actively ranching in 1865, as the *Texas Stock Directory* shows. It should be remembered, however, that the stock raisers represented there (1) had to pay two dollars for each mark shown (cattle agents handled many brands) and (2) had to know about the book and consider it of importance to their interests. Those conditions excluded many Mexicans, but the directory nonetheless provides a wide selection of brands used in the Hill Country and south of the Guadalupe River by various ethnic groups in post–Civil War Texas. As usual, it is almost impossible to group these *fierros* along ethnic or cultural lines, and very many marks used by Irish, German, Czech, Polish, and Anglo stockmen appear to be of Spanish origin or to reflect such influence.

Only three counties, Bexar, Wilson, and Atascosa, show

---

[30] Jordan, *Trails to Texas*, pp. 150–51; Comisión Pesquisidora de la Frontera del Norte, *Reports of the Committee of Investigation Sent in 1873 by the Mexican Government to the Frontier of Texas* (1875). The Mexico City edition (1874) contains M. T. Martínez's map, dated Monterrey, December, 1873 (kindly made available to me by Dorothy Sloan); a reprint of the translation is in *The Mexican Experience in Texas*, intro. Carlos E. Cortés. Arnoldo de León, *The Tejano Community, 1836–1900*, pp. 50–62, 77–82, offers further proof of the rancheros' post–1850 viability, as does the extensive testimony taken by the Committee on Military Affairs relating to "Texas Border Troubles" (U.S. Cong., *House Misc. Doc.* no. 64, 45th Cong., 2d sess., 1878 [ser. 1820]).

many Spanish-surnamed ranchers. Of these, Bexar County had 72 such individuals (18 percent of the county total); Atascosa County, 24 (14 percent of the county total); and Wilson County, stronghold of the old Rincón rancheros, 90 (70 percent of that newly formed county's total). Most districts list no Mexicans at all: Karnes, Gonzales, Goliad, Guadalupe, DeWitt, Live Oak, Refugio, San Patricio, and Nueces. Eleven Mexican raisers, however, were shown as clustered at San Diego. These areas were where mavericking was at its worst (as Dobie shows) and the "alien" Mexican *ganaderos* hardest hit. No doubt the families at San Diego were forted up to protect themselves from such enterprising activities.[31]

A more valid impression of postwar Tejano activity in stock raising can be gained from the brand books of these counties, housed in the respective county courthouses. They reveal a far greater percentage of Hispanic brands, especially below the San Antonio River before the 1880s, when the open range was fenced. Fences cut out not only the Tejano "free-grass men" but also their landless Anglo counterparts. The practice resulted in virtual open war from Karnes County to the coast, a lesson any student of the disturbances associated with large-scale use of barbed wire has already learned. By that time most rancheros had sold their properties above the river and retreated from the Anglo onslaught. Typical of these was Juan Seguín's brother-in-law Manuel Flores. His brand, one of the earliest registered in Guadalupe County (1847), thus appears in the Bexar County Brand Book in 1853, where he is listed as living on the Atascosa River, "about thirty miles from the city." This followed the sale of the renowned Flores Rancho and his subsequent move south to Atascosa County.[32]

Along the Guadalupe near present Seguin, there once existed a flourishing Tejano community of ranchers, including such notables as José Antonio Navarro and José Cárdenas. Flores's

---

[31] Jackson and Long, *Texas Stock Directory*, pp. 83–97, 117–40, 182–233; Dobie, *Vaquero of the Brush Country*, pp. 44–71, 107–28.
[32] Rose, *The Texas Vendetta*, pp. 53–57; Huson, *Refugio*, 2:217–40; Guadalupe County Brand Book 1 (first brand was issued August, 1846; Flores's on January 26, 1847); Bexar County Brand Book A, BCSA (begun in 1848; Flores's brand entered in 1853).

place was one of the more prosperous, and people ranging from Mary Maverick to Ferdinand Roemer left accounts of it. The latter viewed it on the eve of statehood, calling the ranch "a valuable piece of property." But conditions being what they were, Flores sold it, and a dispute over its title reached the Texas Supreme Court in 1853. In the same year Navarro sold to a native of Alabama his San Gerónimo Rancho, which he considered "the most perfect in Texas for farming and stockraising." In the 1870s, Seguín finally sold the family's last surviving piece of property in Wilson County, the "Juan Seguin League," and retired below the border, where some of his children had already relocated.[33]

Among the many prominent Tejano cattlemen victimized during the earliest turmoils was a man who had held his nephew's hand steady at the signing of the Texas Declaration of Independence, Colonel Francisco Ruíz. Ruíz, a veteran of former rebellions, had a son-in-law named Blás Herrera (said to be a mestizo), who had also taken the warning of Santa Anna's approach to William Travis and Juan Seguín at the Alamo. Writing his "beloved son" from the seat of government on December 27, 1836—back in the days when that seat was still shaky—Don Francisco gave Blás some advice. Even though it might mean a separation from his family, he said, Herrera was to leave Béxar if Mexican troops came and he felt endangered. Blás could be of no service to the family if he was killed or taken prisoner:

> If for any reason you should remain, then by no means should you take up arms against the Texans. Give the same advice to your friends for only God could possibly return the territory of Texas to the Mexican Government. Texas has the arms and money for her defense and shall remain forever free.[34]

---

[33] Velma Huber, "Spanish Land Grants," *Bicentennial Minutes of Seguin–Guadalupe County, 1976*, pp. 44–49; Wanda Timmermann, "Wings over Navarro Territory," ibid., pp. 63–70; Roemer, *Texas*, p. 145; *Charle v. Saffold* (1854), *Texas Supreme Court Reports*, 13:47–114; Guadalupe County Deed Book D (County Clerk's Office, Guadalupe County Courthouse, Seguin), p. 849; "Juan Seguin League," Wilson County Deed Book B, pp. 291–94, and Plat Records D, p. 70.

[34] Richard G. Santos, ed. and trans., *Biographical Sketches, Letter from Columbia, Texas, December 27, 1836*. For cattle brands belonging to this clan, see Bexar County Brand Book A: Blás, Francisco and Manuel Herrera; Francisco Antonio, José, and Antonio Ruíz; Miguel (Blás's son-in-law), José de Jesús, and Antonio de la Garza, among others.

A Look beyond 1821

After offering these firm convictions, the senator told Blás to remind his son Francisco Ruíz to hurry with the cattle he had requested. There was a buyer waiting, and a sale to be made. The flag might have changed again—to old freedom fighters like Ruíz a welcome change—but one thing had not changed: Texas was still a kingdom held together with rawhide, and that meant that men like Ruíz sat high in the saddle, as always. They continued to do so, even when they began riding for other men, herding other men's cattle.

Blás Herrera was only one of many Hispanic Texans who kept the ranching traditions of his ancestors alive—who kept the well of knowledge flowing—until his death in 1879. He was laid to rest in the cemetery of the Ruíz-Herrera family ranch, on the shady banks of the Medina River. His sons and sons-in-law carried on the legacy, however, as did many other nineteenth-century Tejano descendants. Their "peculiar" *marcas y fierros* have come down to us and can still be seen emblazoned in old brand books throughout the southern part of the state. Such brands continued to be registered alongside Anglo designs well into the end of the era. The story of western ranching cannot easily be extricated from these deeply planted Spanish roots. They are a source, an essence, that will remain in Texas "until the cows come home"—be they wild-eyed mesteños or some tamer variety.

APPENDICES

APPENDIX A

Cattle, Branded and *Orejano*, Exported from Texas under Governor Domingo Cabello, 1779–86

Exporter	1779	1780	1781	1782	1783	1784	1785	1786	Total
Simón de Arocha		306	{423, 419}	186	330		760	802	3,226
Luis Mariano Menchaca			300, with Sambrano	243	{130, 427} with A. Delgado	{144, 612}	360		2,216
Felipe Flores				770			104	412	1,286
Vizente Flores			200		75		551	433	1,259
Juan José Flores		440	120		{108, 229}				897
Juan Barrera				84	274			373	731
Julián de Arocha	441							266	707
Santiago Seguín						300		281	581
Manuel de Arocha				215		119		208, with Calvillo	542
José Antonio Curbelo			414 (308, with M. Delgado)						414
Marcos Hernández		1,234							1,234*
Antonio (le) Blanc				1,200					1,200*
José Andrés Hernández	19						160		179
Francisco de Arocha	281								281
Sebastián Monjarás	170			(330, with F. Flores)					170

Name									Total
Joaquín Flores y Zendeja	138								138
Manuel Gonzáles	30				80				110
Mission Espada		208							208
Manuel Delgado			308 with Curbelo						308
Juan Monjarás			188						188
Ignacio Calvillo				50	{55 / 35}			35 (with M. de Arocha)	175
Francisco Flores					330, with S. Monjarás			330	330
Francisco Péres					118			70	188
José de Cárdenas						143			143
Francisco X. Rodríguez						139		165	304
Juan José Pacheco						369			369
Amador Delgado							(427, with Menchaca)	140	140
Carlos Martínez							50		50
Félix Gutiérrez							16		16
Macario Sambrano							150	103	253
Various			(300, with Menchaca)				50	224	274
Total	1,079	1,980	2,084	3,194	2,151	2,132	2,123	3,374	18,117[†]

SOURCE: BA.

NOTE: Some rancheros made more than one drive in a given year; this is noted by dual figures for that year, joined by a brace. Some made occasional joint drives with other rancheros; this is noted by giving the joint figure both places and the name of the partner. For one partner the information is given in parentheses, and these parenthetical numbers are not figured into the totals. Thus, joint drives contribute only once to the column and row totals.

*To Louisiana.

[†] Cabello's total was 18,449, an addition error of 332.

APPENDIX B

List of "Restored" Ranchers Sent to Commandant General Ugarte by Governor Martínez Pacheco, October 14, 1787, with Letter No. 21 (From Saltillo Archives)

Simón de Arocha
Tomás Travieso
Juan de Arocha
Francisco Flores
Macario Sambrano
José Péres Casanova
Francisco de Arocha
Miguel Gortari
Francisco Travieso
Vizente Flores
Joaquín de la Garza
Luciano Martínez
Plácido Hernández
Francisco Cano
Manuel Delgado
Joaquín Leal
Joaquín Flores
Doña Leonor Delgado
Santiago Seguín
Manuel Casanova
Estanislao de Arocha
Manuel Delgado
Mariano Delgado
Francisco Móntes de Oca
Amador Delgado

Francisco Xavier Padrón
Doña Juana de Ollos
Luis Menchaca
Félix Menchaca
Joaquín Menchaca
Clemente Delgado
Josef Andrés Hernández
Francisco Hernández
Francisco Xavier Rodríguez
Julián de Arocha
Francisco Pérez
Sebastián Monjarás
Carlos Martínez
Pedro Flores
Philipe Flores
Manuel Salinas
Juan José Bueno
Diego Hernández
Ignacio Calvillo
Fernando de Arocha
Ignacio de la Peña
Gavino Delgado
Juan Martín Amondarain
José Antonio Curbelo
José Hernández

APPENDIX C

List of Those "Legitimately Engaged in the Business of Raising Cattle," July 18, 1795 (From Béxar Archives)

José Félix Menchaca
José Luis Menchaca
Joaquín Menchaca
Simón de Arocha
Francisco de Arocha
Julián de Arocha
Ygnacio Calvillo
Salvador Rodríguez
Joaquín Leal
Tomás Travieso
Joaquín Flores, "for his father"
Miguel Gortari
Clemente Delgado
Marcos Zepeda
Plácido Hernández "and brothers"
Pedro Flores
Felipe Flores
Manuel Salinas
Ygnacio Pérez
Francisco Travieso
Francisco Rodríguez
Gavino Delgado
Manuel Delgado
Ygnacio Casanova
Cristóbal Guerra
Diego Enríquez
Vizente Flores
Amador Delgado
Santiago Seguín
Juan Martín Amondarain
Ygnacio Peña
Francisco Móntes
José Francisco Farías
Carlos Martínez
Antonio Leal
Widows of *criadores*:
  Doña Leonor Delgado
  Doña Juana Ocontrillo "and sons"
  Doña Josefa Quiñones
  Doña Manuela Aguilar
  Doña Manuela Móntes
  Doña Vicenta Travieso
  Doña Micaela Menchaca
  Doña Antonia Granados
  Doña Josefa Granados
  Doña Josefa Cortenas

APPENDIX D

"Notizia de los ranchos..." (Notice of Ranches...), Written at "Santa Cruz y Paso de las Mujeres" by Gavino Delgado, November 13, 1809 (From Beẍar Archives)

Síndico Manuel Salinas
   José Francisco Flores
   Josef Andrés Hernández
   Francisco Hernández
   Juan Martín de Veramendi
   Vicente Travieso
   Francisco Guerra

Ranches of the Salado

Síndico Vicente Gortari
   Mariano Rodríguez
   José Flores
   Andrés Corbiere
   Pedro Longeville
   Francisco Chaves

Ranches of the Medina and León

Síndico Ignacio Pérez
   Father Bernardino Vallejo
   Luis Galán
   Ángel Navarro
   José Antonio de la Garza
   Antonio de la Garza
   Joaquín Pérez [?]

Síndico Francisco Móntes
   (Rancho Puente de Piedra)
   Francisco Perei [?] g [?]
   [illegible]
   Francisco Pérez
   Joachín Estrada

Síndico Joachín Leal
   José Antonio Carvajal
   José Flores
   Ignacio Rodríguez

Síndico Francisco Farías
   Manuel de Arocha
   Ignacio Villaseñor
   Ignacio Calvillo

Síndico Juan José [?] de Arocha
   Tomás de Arocha
   Francisco de Arocha
   Joachín [?] Menchaca
   Manuel Nuñez
   Manuel Barrera

Síndico Esmerehildo Seguín [1]
   Vicente Micheli
   Juan Manuel Sambrano

---

[1] Ermeregildo was a half-brother of Erasmo Seguín's father, Santiago, and it is probable that he was living at Erasmo's La Mora when this list was formed (Frederick C. Chabot, *Makers of San Antonio*, p. 128).

APPENDIX E

"Relación de los Extrangeros . . . de la Jurisdicción de Nacogdoches situados en Bayupier" (Account of the Foreigners . . . of the Jurisdiction of Nacogdoches Living in Bayou Pierre), by José María Guadiana, April 14, 1810 (From Béxar Archives)

Marcelo Soto[1]
Pedro Dolé[1,2]
Miguel Ramben
Luis Beltran
María Ramben
Francisco Prudome[2]
Andrés Balentin
Pedro Lafita
Pablo Lafita[2]
Bautista Prudome
Juan Palvado
Miguel Vicente
Carlos Grullal
Bautista Colet
Antonio Dubua[2]

María de Soto[1]
Santiago Guales [Wallace]
Jacobo Guales [Wallace]
Tomás Guales [Wallace]
Benjami Guales [Wallace]
Remigio Cristin
Pedro Rublo [Rubio?]
Vicente Rolan
Lucas Morly
José Morván
Pedro Morván
Bele Buguer
Pedro Boluco
Miguel Cro[w]

[1] Owning 7 to 8 slaves.
[2] Noted in list of 1797.

APPENDIX F

"Relación de los Extrangeros . . . en esta
Jurisdicción de Nacogdoches"
(Account of the Foreigners . . . in This
Jurisdiction of Nacogdoches),
by José María Guadiana, May 8–12, 1810
(From Béxar Archives)

Bernardo Dortolan
Antonio Paret
Cristóbal Jonca
Denis Quinelty
Estévan Goguet
Guillermo Barr
Pedro Samuel Davenport
Guillermo Pallar
Nicolás Pont
Pedro Tesier
Timoteo Barnet
Guillermo Querque
Reimundo Querque
Juan Biens
José Lucovichi

José Tesier
Luis Forten
Rafael Simes
Reymundo Noris
Santiago Dil
Santiago Sidre
Santiago Lepin
David Haltman
Guillermo Bebé
Guillermo Suel, "fugitive"
Cristian Esser
Francisco Bruno
Pedro San German
Juan Sarnac

APPENDIX G

"Noticia de los ranchos . . . , Jurisdicción
de Nacogdoches,
el nombre del praxe, el de el dueño,
y la distancia . . ."
(Notice of the Ranches . . . , Jurisdiction
of Nacogdoches,
the Name of the Place, That of the Owner,
and the Distance . . .),
by José María Guadiana, April 14, 1810
(From Béxar Archives)

Ranch	Owner	Location (Leagues from Nacogdoches)
San Bernardo	Bernardo Dortolan	4 W
San Patricio	Guillermo Barr y Davenport	6 W
Santa María Adeleide		25 NE
La Nana		30 E
Palo Gacho	Crisostomo Sonca	18 E
Aices	Antonio Paret	14 E
Aices	Denis Quinelty	
Angeline	Estévan Goget	4 S
Aices	Guillermo Querque	15 E
Durazno	José Lucobichi	6 S
Salinillas	José Tesie	6 S
Aices	Rafael Sims	15 E
Naconiche	Reymundo Norris	6 NE
Borregas ("in land of Pifermo")	Santiago Sidre	20 E
Patrón	Santiago Lepin	16 E
Aices	Ana Alsop ("wife of Reimundo Querque")	15 E

Paso del Chalán ("Legitimate residence of Cro[w]")	Miguel Cro	26 E
"At the mid-Sabine pass to Baypier"	Miguel Cro	25 E
	Marcelo Soto	37 E
Bayupier	Antanacio Poesó	37 E
	Andrés Valentin	33 E
	Pedro Dolé	33 E
	Antonio Duboa	33 E
	Bautista Prudom	33 E
Tierras Blancas ("White Lands")	Santiago Cristin	42 E
	María Ramben	40 E
Ballupier	Carlos Crullal	38 E
	Bautista Colet	38 E
	Pedro Lafite	37 E
	Luis Beltran	37 E
	Juan Palvado	39 E
Ballupier, el de los Ingleces ("English section")	Santiago Wales ("and his brothers")	40 N (of Bayou Pierre)
	Pedro Rublo	38 E (of Bayou Pierre)
	Pablo Lafite	37 E
	Silbestre Poisó	37 E
Bacilio	Francisco Prudome	39 E
Morbán	José Morbán	43 E
Laguna de Juan de Mora	Bugen	40 E
La Iglecia	Pedro Balille	45 E

APPENDIX H

"Lista de los Vecinos que pueden ser nombrano síndicos de Ranchos . . ." (List of Citizens Who Can Be Designated Commissioners of Ranches) by José María Guadiana, June 14, 1810 (From Béxar Archives)

Síndico José Flores ("at Atascoso"), 7 leagues east:
   José Caro, Matías Peña (at Guajolote), Martín Ybarbo, Remundo Norris (at Naconichi), José Santos, Villalpando, Martín Cruz, José Córdova, Pedro Padilla, Andrés Acosta, Antonio Arriole, Mariano Cruz, Mariano Garza

Síndico Bernardo Dortolan, 5 leagues west:
   Guillermo Barr (2 leagues distant), Francisco Santos, Tomás Mansola, José Labine, Visente Micheli, Manuel Procela, José de la Bega (owner of Botija), Manuel Raso, Mariano Sánches, Labaume,[1] Francisco de los Santos, Juan de Acosta, Ramón Chavana

Síndico José María Mora, 4 leagues east:
   José Flores (El Carriso), José Ignacio Ybarbo, Estévan Morín, Baltasar de la Garza, Nepomuceno de la Cerda, Estévan Mora

Síndico José Antonio Chirino, 7 leagues east:
   Amoladeras, Atoyaque, Antonio Paret, Los Querques, El de Rechar y el de Conichi seis leguas y todos le quedan al Oreiente (Those at Rechar[2] and Conichi,[3] 6 leagues, and all those left to the east).

Síndico Juan Ignacio Pifermo, 23 leagues east:
   El Palo Gacho, [Santiago] Lepin, [Santiago] Sidre,[4] Pedro Laviña

---

[1] José de la Baume's ranch was being looked after by a mulatto named Narciso.
[2] Rechar was perhaps the dwelling of Mordecai and Estévan Richards.
[3] Conichi was perhaps the James Quinelty who lived with his two brothers near Los Aís.
[4] Sidre was James Cedar.

APPENDIX I

Síndico Reports of the Béxar Jurisdiction, Taken in the Year 1810 (From Béxar Archives and Nacogdoches Archives)

Jurisdiction of *Síndico* Ignacio de Arocha:
1. San Rafael de Pataguia: Ignacio de Arocha (son of Simón); wife, María Josefa Salinas (age 34, Béxar); children José Félix (14), María Gertrudis (12), José Antonio (10), 2 servants and families.
2. Nuestra Señora de Guadalupe y Paso del Chayopin: Doña Manuela Móntes (55, widow of Juan de Arocha); children Manuel (33), José María (30); 3 servants and families.
3. Los Dolores y Chayopin: Ignacio Villaseñor (45, Saltillo); wife, María Gertrudis Flores (36, Béxar); daughter María Josefa (13); 3 servants.
4. San Ildefonso de los Chayopines: Francisco Farías (45, Béxar); wife, Encarnación Rosales (43, Béxar); children José Antonio (20), Domingo (11, "adopted"); niece Antonia Rodríguez (4); 2 servants. (In 1791 this ranch was owned by Ignacio Peña.)
5. La Santa Cruz y Paso de las Mugeres: Ignacio Calvillo (77, Aguascalientes); and wife, Antonia de Arocha (65, Béxar, sister of Simón de Arocha); grandchildren Ignacio Casanova (22); Francisco Casanova (10); 3 servants. Also *agregados* (tenants) Gavino Delgado (55) and wife, María Calvillo (45, Ignacio's daughter); José Saucedo (46); wife, Juana Calvillo (35); 3 children; 4 servants.
6. San Juan Nepomuceno y Pataguias: José Clemente de Arocha, curate (45); 11 servants (see no. 1 above).
7. Pataguia: Tomás de Arocha; 2 servants and families (see no. 1 above).
8. La Soledad, in Pataguia: Francisco de Arocha; 2 servants. (Nos. 6–8 were divisions of Simón and Juan de Arocha's 8-league grant, along with no. 2. Juan died in 1788; Simón, in 1796.)
9. San Antonio del Sabinito: Manuel Nuñez, who lived in Béxar; 3 servants.
10. Santa Gertrudis, in Las Cabras Viejas: Manuel Barrera (son of the *diezmero* Juan), who lived in Béxar; ranch kept by 3 servants and families.

11. La Laguna de las Ánimas (Lagoon of the Souls): Juan Manuel Sambrano (38, "subdeacon," son of José Macario); 32 servants and 2 slaves.

   Jurisdiction of *Síndico* Francisco Móntes (de Oca):
12. San Juan Bautista en Puente de Piedra: Francisco Móntes (54); wife, María Josefa Sambrano (daughter of José Macario); children Juan, Antonio, and María Antonia; and 2 manservants.
13. Nuestra Señora del Refugio: Doña Josefa de la Garza, the widow of Francisco Pérez (Casanova); her children Dolores, Anacleto, and Juan Díaz; 5 helpers plus a tenant, José Leal (a soldier) and his wife. (This ranch was at Paso de José Miguel.)
14. Del Sabinitos: Félix Estrada (35); wife, Josefa Rodríguez (19); son José Manuel; mother-in-law Luisa Guerrero (widow of Salvador Rodríguez); her son José María; 4 servants.

   Jurisdiction of *Síndico* Joaquín Leal:
15. Santa Rita de las Yslitas: Joaquín Leal; wife, Ana María de Arocha (sister of Simón); grown children Clemente (21); Simón (20); Antonio (19); Juana (18); Consolación (17). (Employing 5 helpers, this ranch was opposite the little settlement of Las Islitas, just above the present Wilson-Bexar county line on the San Antonio River. It appears on grant maps under the name José [Leonardo] de la Garza, who married Joaquín's daughter Consolación.)
16. San Cayetano y Paso de los Huitas (Vintas [?] in the manuscript): José Antonio Carvajal (40); wife, María Gertrudis Sánchez (33); children Teodora, José Luis, and José María. (José María was later noted as a Federalist leader, founder of the "Republic of the Sierra Madre," etc.)
17. San Nicolás, Paraje de Maldonado (near the Maldonado Crossing on the San Antonio River): José Flores; wife, María Antonia Rodríguez (daughter of Salvador Rodríguez and Gertrudis de la Peña); children Manuel, Josefa, José María, Salvador, Gertrudis, and José Ignacio; 2 servants. (This family was active in the Texas Revolution. As noted, Gertrudis Flores married Juan N. Seguín, and her brother José María married Juan's sister Leonidas.)
18. La Candelaría: Ygnacio Rodríguez (son of Salvador); wife, Antonia Bueno; 3 helpers.[1]

---

[1] Candelaría was perhaps situated in the sandy stretch of land described by Jean Louis Berlandier (*Journey to Mexico* . . . , 2:554) as "most remarkable." It was a dense stand of oaks one league above the then large stream Las Calaveras, part of the topographical zone still known to residents as the "sandhills"; much of it is covered with blackjack

19. San Juan Nepomuceno, Paraje de los Arroyos: Miguel Flores; wife, María Antonia de Abrego; children María Gertrudis, María Antonia, María de Jesus, Miguel, and José Francisco. (This ranch, situated at Los Arroyos, had 5 helpers, including 50-year-old Concepción Abrego from Coahuila.)

Jurisdiction of *Síndico* Manuel Salinas:

20. San Bartolomé: Manuel Salinas (42); wife, María Ignacia Flores (37, daughter of Juan José Flores and Leonor Delgado); children Margarita, Gertrudis, Pablo, Antonia, and José María; 5 servants and families.
21. San José, en el Arroyo del Cíbolo: Juan Martín de Veramendi (32); wife, Josefa (Navarro), (18); 6 servants, some with families.
22. San Bartolo: Fernando de Veramendi (he and Juan Martín, in no. 21 above, were sons of Fernando de Veramendi and María Josefa Granados); wife, Antonia Flores (21). Besides their 2 helpers were 3 other family units which *síndico* Salinas listed individually, nos. 23–25 below.)
23. San Bartolo: José Andrés Hernández (65, "widower," a son of Andrés); children José Vicente (25), José Felipe (20), Juana (16); 1 servant.
24. San Bartolo: Francisco Hernández (50, a nephew [?] of Andrés); wife, Rafaela de León (Frederick C. Chabot, *Makers of San Antonio*, p. 37, shows her as Rafaela de Ávila), (50); and children José, Juan Nepomuceno, and Candida; 1 helper.
25. San Bartolo: Bárbara Sánchez (widow of José Hernández); son José; 1 helper.
26. Las Mulas: Vicente Travieso (44, son of Tomás, grandson of the *alguacil* Vicente Álvarez Travieso); wife, María Luisa de Léon [Luna] (24); children Juan, Jacoba, and Melchor. (This ranch, "one of the more prosperous," had 7 servants.)
27. San Juan Nepomuceno de la Mora:[2] José Erasmo Seguín (28, son of Santiago, son of Bartolomé); wife, Josefa Becerra (19, from La Bahía, the daughter of Miguel Becerra and Bárbara Sánchez-Navarro); children Juan Nepomuceno, María, and Leonidas; 5 servants and families.

---

and post oak. The impenetrability of this region was noted as early as the Aguayo Expedition, when Father Peña, calling it "Monte Grande," spoke of the difficulties of travel (Peter P. Forrestal, trans. *Peña's Diary of the Aguayo Expedition*, p. 18).

[2] This was Mission Valero's old La Mora Rancho, although the name San Juan de Nepomuceno was also applied to Don Erasmo's later acquisition of part of the Arocha grant, just above present Floresville, where he built his home, Casa Blanca.

28. San Francisco: Vicente Micheli (51, native of Brecia, Italy); wife, María Susana Maro (36, Natchitoches); children José Bicente (18) and María Nieves (18); 2 helpers. (This was formerly the Menchaca ranch.)
29. San Bartolo: Francisco Flores (28, son of Pedro, grandson of Juan José); wife, Josefa Móntes (27, daughter of Francisco Móntes and his second wife, Josefa Sambrano); children Pedro, Manuel, and María Clara.
30. Los Guerras: Francisco Guerra (40, son of Miguel); wife, Teresa del Valle (40, Béxar).

Jurisdiction of *Síndico* Vicente Gortari

31. Rancho Salado, at La Laja Pass: Doña Estacia Sambrano (53, widow); children ("that she has raised") Juan Manuel Móntes (12), María Antonia Seguro (33), Ignacio de León (35); his wife, Manuela de la Garza (30); a *caporal* (foreman) Manuel Muñoz; 3 servants.
32. Rancho del Paso de la Casita: Doña [María Feliciana] Durán (45, widow of Andrés Courbiere), children Dona (?) Josefa, María Herlinda, Juan, and Manuel; her unmarried sister, Ana María Durán (38); *majordomo* Bisente Durán; 6 servants.
33. Rancho del Paso de los [torn]: Pedro Teremias Longovíe (Longueville), one of the men tried in the Leal-Nolan case, a native of Bordeaux, France; wife, Doña Josefa [del Carmen Leal] (22), native of Béxar; child María (2). Tenants Francisca Ximénes (56), "widow" (of Francisco Leal), children Miguel, Juan Andrés, and Bisente Leal; 9 servants.
34. Rancho de la Loma Prieta: Francisco Chaves (soldier, native of New Mexico, 50); wife, Juana Francisca Padrón (40, Béxar); children María Gertrudis, María del Refugio, Manuel, Bisente, Francisco, and Leonardo.
35. Rancho del Paso de las Cucharas: Francisco Treviño (52); wife, Josefa de la Garza (32, both of Béxar); daughter María del Refugio; 2 servants.

APPENDIX J

"Síndicos de Ranchos," (Commissioners of Ranches), August (?), 1812 (From Béxar Archives)

Francisco Móntes, *Síndico*: Francisco Móntes, Doña Josefa de la Garza, Manuel Granados, Félix Estrada, Joaquín Leal, José Antonio Carabajal, José Flores de Abrego, José Ignacio Rodríguez, José Miguel Flores

Ignacio de Arocha, *Síndico*: Francisco Farías, Manuel de Arocha, Ignacio Villaseñor, Ignacio Calvillo, Ignacio de Arocha, Tomás de Arocha, Francisco de Arocha, Manuel Nuñez, Mariano [?] Rodríguez

José María Sambrano, *Síndico*: Manuel Barrera, Juan Manuel Sambrano, Vicente Micheli, Erasmo Seguín

José Barcenas, *Síndico*: Manuel Salinas, Francisco Flores, José Andrés Hernández, Francisco Hernández, Juan Martín de Veramendi, Vicente Travieso, Francisco Guerra [?]

José Ignacio Pérez,[1] *Síndico* (Medina y de León): José Ignacio Pérez, Ignacio Pérez, Bernardino Vallejo, Joaquín Pérez, Clemente Delgado, José [scratched out] Antonio de la Garza, Remigio Leal, José Ángel Navarro, José Antonio de la Garza

Ranchos de Salado: Doña Anastacia Sambrano, Doña Feliciana Durán, Pedro Longueville[2]

---

[1] Son of Lieutenant Colonel Ignacio Pérez
[2] He was killed by Indians at his ranch in 1824.

APPENDIX K

"Lista varios Ranchos y Haciendas g. sitan en este Jurisdicción [Villa del Refugio] y sus dueños"
(List of the Various Ranches and Haciendas That Are Situated in This Jurisdiction [Villa of Refugio] and Their Owners),
by Felipe Roque de la Portilla,
December 22, 1814[1]
(From Matamoros Archives)

Rancho del Chiguibuite: Alejandro Longoria, Francisco Longoria, Cayetano de la Garza
Canasta: Miguel Longoria, Juan Longoria y Garza, Diego de Ynojosa, José Antonio Salinas
San Juan: Rosa María Treviño, Juan Chapa, Antonio Chapa, Gregorio Chapa
Caja Pinta: Nepomuceno Cisneros, Rafael García, Margarita de la Garza
Porla Buelta: Sergeant Irineo Gómez, José María Treviño, Nepomuceno Cisneros (soldier)
Loma de las Manadas: Xavier Salinas, Francisco Gonzáles
Soledad: Rafael Ramírez, Margarita Ramírez, Nicolasa Longoria, Miguel Salinas
Naguahuytas: José Antonio García
Algodones: Ramón García
Trabuco: Ionacio Longira, Ángel Olivaras
Sacramento: Francisco Ramírez, Margarita de la Garza, Juan Bautista García, Tiburcio Pérez
Mesteñas: Juan José Cárdenas ("curate of Reynosa")
Miguete: José María Flores
Tirerita: Juan de la Garza (soldier), Francisco García
Rucias: Blás María de la Garza Falcón, Juan Treviño, Patricio Ernández, Domingo Ernández (soldier), Solas Guerra, Lino Cobos, Teodoro Montalvo, José Antonio Chazarretas

[1] These ranchers were shown as owning 275 pack mules, 56 saddle mules, and 450 tame horses.

Soledad de Arriva: Chrisostomo Longoria, Leonardo Basan [?], José María de la Garza
Tahuachal: José María Guerra, Ignacio de la Garza, Juan José de Abrego, Alejandro de la Garza
Potrero: Luys Antonio García ("of Camargo"), Matías García y Garza, Antonio López, Francisco Venavide, Francisco García, Lino Cavazos
Barrancas: Ramón Longoria, Joaquín García, Manuel Longoria (soldier), Pedro García, Vivano Vela, Urbano Longoria, Damasio de la Garza, Adapto García
Sauces de los Solises: Marcelin Longoria, Matías Longoria (sergeant), Juan Longoria (corporal), Santiago Solís, Marcelino Solís, Alvino García, Matías García, Francisco Pérez, Manuel Solís (soldier)
Palma de Avajo: José de Ynojosa, Fernando Cavazos
Orcon de Áfuera: Balentin García (corporal), Basilio García, José María Cantu, Bartolo Casas, José Antonio García
Palma de Arriva: Santiago Galván
Bastón y Feria ("to the north on the other side of the Río Grande are the following ranches"): Nicolás Bally, Antonio Trinidad
Florida y Santa Rosa: Felipe Abarca, Félix Treviño, Antonio Sánchez
Carricitos del Río y de Áfuera: Pedro Villarreal, Enrique Villarreal (*alférez*), José María Villarreal, Rafael Uresty, Julián Munguia, Guadalupe Cavazos
Santa Rita: Salvador de la Garza (in Reynosa), Francisco Farías (in Mier), Pedro Ignacio García (Camargo), Félix Villarreal (soldier), Santos Flores, Manuel Cavazos, Martín de León, Petra Ramírez, Felipe Roque de la Portilla, Rafael Rubio, Francisco Salinas, Guillermo Rubio (foreman of Pérez), Maximo Delgado
Tanque: Ignacio Treviño (on ranch), Leonardo Treviño (in Camargo), Francisco Treviño, Lorenzo Villarreal, the widow of Cesario Leal

APPENDIX L

"Noticia de los vecinos en este ciudad [Béxar] que tienan ganado mayor y menor, caballos y mulas . . . sin expresar el numero"[1] (Notice of the Citizens of this City [Béxar] Who Have Cattle, Sheep, Horses, and Mules . . . without Showing Their Number), by Francisco Flores and José Manuel Granados, June 26, 1817 (From Béxar Archives)

Ignacio Pérez
Doña Josefa de la Garza
José Antonio de la Garza
Francisco Móntes and Manuel Rodríguez
José Flores
Doña Antonia de Arocha
Sergeant Remigio Pérez
Ignacio Villaseñor
Francisco Flores
Manuel Granados
Doña Antonia Bueno
Alférez Francisco Colbamas [?]
Padre [Juan Manuel] Sambrano
Manuel Nuñez
Manuel Diomicio
Doña María Calvillo
Ignacio de León
Francisco Rolen
José de Sosa
Agustín Brori [?]
José Manuel Garza
Manuel Salinas
Mariano López
Juan José Mañ[?]
Juan Delgado
Juan de Veramendi
Manuel Barrera
Ignacio Cortinas
Joaquín Pérez
Juan José de Arocha—"very few"
Manuel Quiñones
Damián Rodríguez
José Dolores de los Santos
Miguel Bustillos
Santiago Dortolan

[1] This list omitted those owning only "one, two, three, four, and up to eight head."

APPENDIX M

Partial List of Nueces Strip Ranches, Showing Acres in the Survey and Amount of Land Confirmed by the Texas Legislature, 1850–52 [1]

1. Cavazos, José Narciso: San Juan de Carricitos—601,657 (confirmed, 106½ leagues to "Cabazos")
2. Ballí, Juan José: San Salvador del Tule—315,391
3. Garza, José Salvador de la: Espíritu Santo—284,418 (confirmed, 59½ leagues)
4. Borrego, José Vásquez: Hacienda de Dolores—276,350
5. Ynojosa, Vicente: Las Mesteñas—146,670 (confirmed, 35 leagues, Las Mesteñas Pititas and La Abra)
6. Galán, Joaquín: Balconcitos—139,482; Palafox—66,975
7. Ynojosa de Ballí, Juan José: Llano Grande—127,625 (confirmed, 25½ leagues)
8. Ballí, José Francisco: La Barreta—124,297
9. Rey, José Pérez; José María Pérez Rey; Manuel García: Rincón de los Laureles—100,848
10. Gómez, Manuel: Santa Anita—95,202 (confirmed, 14 leagues) [2]
11. Ynojosa de Ballí, Rosa María: La Feria—53,104 (confirmed, 12 leagues)
12. Fernández, Bartolomé and Eugenio: Concepción de Carricitas—57,569 (confirmed, 11½ leagues)
13. García, Rafael: Santa Isabel—32,355 (confirmed, 7 leagues)
14. Garza y Soza, Manuel de la: Buena Vista—30,217 (confirmed, 6+ leagues to "Garza Lasa")
15. Treviño, José Ignacio de: San Martín—27,289 (confirmed, 5½ leagues to "Travenio")
16. Villarreal, Pedro: San Pedro de Carricitos—12,730 (confirmed, 3 leagues) [3]

[1] Extracted from Virginia H. Taylor, *Index to Spanish and Mexican Land Grants*, and keyed to the map on page 445.

[2] This "top ten" should also include Antonio Rivas, 125,834 acres (25 leagues) in Maverick County.

[3] Grants 11 through 16 are in present Cameron County. Many of these grants extend into adjoining counties; for simplicity they have been listed where the larger portion is situated. Space limitations prohibit showing most grants of less than 10,000 acres.

17. Cabazos, Lino: La Blanca—24,060 (confirmed, 2 leagues)
18. Farías, Alejandro: San José—17,713 (confirmed, 4½ leagues)
19. Farías, Julián: San Roman—22,602 (confirmed, 4 *sitios*)
20. Flores, Segundo: Los Guajes—13,322 (confirmed, 2½ leagues, Los Guages)
20a. Salinas, Nicolasa: Los Magueyes—12,260 (confirmed, 2½ leagues)
20b. Flores, Ygnacio: El Panal—9,854 (confirmed, 2 leagues)
21. Treviño, Juan José: El Gato—23,067 (confirmed, 5 leagues)[4]
22. Ballí, Juan Antonio: El Paistle—25,790 (confirmed, 5 leagues, El Pastle)
23. Garza, Alvino and Domingo de la: La Parra—66,426 (confirmed, 10 leagues for Alvino; 5 for Domingo)
24. Garza, Juan Nepomuceno de la: Los Finados—51,484
25. Garza, Pedro de la: Santa Rosa—28,784 (confirmed, 6½ leagues)
26. Garza, Teodoro: El Alazán—18,532 (confirmed, 3 leagues)
27. Gomez, Irineo: Las Barrosas—24,660 (confirmed, 5 leagues—Borasco)
28. Ramírez, Rafael: Rincón de Penascal—39,390 (confirmed, 8 leagues)
29. Salinas, Leonardo: La Barreta—22,140 (confirmed, 5 leagues, La Bereta)
30. Salinas, Xavier: San Pedro de las Motas—22,140 (confirmed, 5 leagues)
31. Villarreal, Ygnacio: Rincón de Mirasoles—23,837
32. Ynojosa, Miguel: El Palmito (also called San Pedro de las Moras)—22,140 (confirmed, 5 leagues)[5]
33. Chapa, Francisco Guerra: Los Olmos and Loma Blanca—22,142
34. Chapa, José Manuel and Luciano: La Encantada—39,855
35. Díaz, Juan Garza: Vargas—17,712
36. Elizondo, Antonio: El Lucero—13,358
37. García, Antonio: El Tule—10,839
38. García, José Antonio Morales, and Apolinario Morales García: San Antonio—27,812
39. García, Pedro: El Perdido—17,712
40. García, Rafael, Ysidro García, and Rafael García Salinas: La Mesteña—22,140 each (confirmed, 15 leagues)

[4] Grants 17 through 21 are in present Hidalgo County. Not shown: Juan José Ynojosa: Los Torritos—12,799.

[5] Grants 22 through 32 are in present Kenedy County.

41. Guerra, Juan José: Charco Redondo, or Tule—22,538 (confirmed, 5 *sitios*)
42. Guerra, Ramón Cabazos: Santa Quintería—22,140 (confirmed, 5 leagues)
43. Guerra, Ysidro: Palo Blanco—17,713 (confirmed, 4 *sitios*)
44. León, José Antonio Leal de: San Antonio del Encinal—27,878
45. Martínez, Estévan: La Noria de Tío Ayala—18,756
46. Peña, Ygnacio: Los Magueyas de Palo Blanco—16,004 (confirmed, 4 *sitios*)
47. Peña, Ygnacio de la: Los Olmos de Loma Blanca—44,284 (see no. 33 above)
48. Sánchez, Guadalupe: La Rucia—22,140 (confirmed, 5 leagues)
49. Vargas, Leonardo: Guadalupe del Encinal—13,285
50. Zarate, Gil: La Blanca—22,140
51. Zarate de Bayareña, Pilar: La Alameda—13,132 (confirmed, 3 *sitios*)[6]
52. García, Antonio: El Rendado—22,140 (confirmed, 5 leagues)
53. García, Nicolás and Bruno: Las Ánimas—66,426 (confirmed, 15 leagues, under García y García)
54. Garza, Dionisio: Santo Domingo de Abajo—17,889
55. Gonzáles, Victoriano: Las Cuevitas—17,412 (confirmed, 4+ leagues)
56. Montalba, Francisco: Las Viboritas, Santa Rita, and Loma del Sordo—17,713
57. Peña, Antonio: Palo Blanco—18,939 (confirmed, 4+ leagues; also 1+ league for Francisco)
58. Peña, Felipe de la: Las Ánimas, or Alberca de Abajo—22,140 (confirmed, 5 leagues)
59. Peña, Rafael de la: Las Moritas—22,140 (confirmed, 5 leagues)
60. Ramírez, José Miguel: Agua Nueva de Arriba—35,427 (confirmed, 8 leagues)
61. Ramírez, Juan Manuel: Agua Nueva de Abajo—44,284 (confirmed, 10 leagues)
62. Rivas, Ygnacio, and Maximo Villarreal: San Rafael—13,873 (confirmed, 2 leagues; also 3 *sitios*)
63. Sais, Rafael Garza: Palitos Blancos—13,472
64. Salinas, José Luis: San Antonio de Baluarte—22,140 (confirmed, 5 leagues)
65. Silva, Antonio: La Noria de Santo Domingo—22,140

[6] Grants 33 through 51 are in present Brooks County.

Appendix M 641

66. Vela, Luis: Agostadero del Sordo—22,229 (confirmed, 5 *sitios*)
67. Vela, Xavier: San Antonio Viejo—17,713 (confirmed, 4 leagues)
68. Ynojosa, Simón de: Las Noriacitas—22,142
69. Ysaguirre, Antonio: Santa Domingo de Arriba—18,018 (confirmed, 4 leagues)[7]
70. Farías, Francisco: Santa Cruz—17,713 (confirmed, 4 leagues)
71. Flores, Juan: Agostadero del Javali—17,712 (confirmed, 4 leagues, El Javeli)
72. Garza, Andrés de la: Las Comitas—13,285 (confirmed, 3 leagues)
73. Morales, José Antonio: El Venadito—22,648 (confirmed, 5 leagues)
74. Sais, Juan José: Los Retaches—13,285
75. Sais, Vicente: La Sal Colorada—17,889 (confirmed, 4 *sitios*, but to Gregorio Sais)[8]
76. Benavides, Jesús: El Pedernal—9,809
77. Bustamante, Pedro: Las Comitas—22,142
78. Canales, José María: El Socorro—8,856
79. Davila, Eduardo: San Antonio de Miraflores—22,453 (confirmed, 5 leagues)
80. García, Anastacio: Charco Redondo—22,140 (confirmed, 5 leagues)
81. García, Onofre: El Grullo—17,713 (confirmed, 4 *sitios*)
82. Pereda, Andrés B.: Charco de la India—17,713
83. Pereda, José M.: Cerrito Blanco—17,713
84. Zapata, Antonio: Villa—22,142[9]
85. Arispe, Mariano: Santa María de Los Angeles—22,140
86. Domingo y Gonzáles, José: Las Pintas—18,795
87. Fuentes, Valentin de las: Alberca de Arriba—22,142
88. Fuentes, Valentin de las: San Casimiro—17,713
89. Gonzáles, Antonio: Santo Tomás—53,136 (confirmed, 6 leagues)
90. Guerra, Antonio: Palafox—13,953 (confirmed, 3 *porciones*)[10]
91. Cordente, Francisco: Agostadero de la Santa Cruz de Concepción—22,140 (confirmed, 5 leagues)
92. Elizondo, Dionisio: El Señor de la Carrera—10,078
93. Falcón, Juan Joseph Manuel de la Garza: San Francisco—20,721 (confirmed, 4 leagues)
94. Flores, Santos: Agua Poquita—26,745

[7] Grants 52 through 69 are in present Jim Hogg County.
[8] Grants 70 through 75 are in present Starr County.
[9] Grants 76 through 84 are in present Zapata County.
[10] Grants 85 through 90 are in present Webb County.

95. García, Andrés: San Andrés—23,042
96. García, Santos: El Charco de Palo Blanco—22,142 (confirmed, 5 leagues)
97. Gonzáles, José Antonio: La Huerta—23,781
98. Ramírez, Rafael: San Pedro del Charco Redondo—22,142
99. Ramírez, Rafael: Santa Rosalia—22,584 (with no. 98, confirmed, 10¹/₁₀ leagues)
100. Salinas, José Rafael García: San Leandro—17,712
101. Vela, Trinidad: El Mesquite, or Santa María de los Angeles de Abajo—22,142
102. Ynojosa, Diego: San Rafael de los Encinos—42,072 (confirmed, 5 leagues)
103. Ynojosa, José Marcelo: Palo Blanco—61,992 (confirmed, 14 leagues)
104. Ynojosa, Vicente: Las Anacuas—16,026 (confirmed, 3+ leagues)[11]
105. Barrera, Manuel: La Tinaja de Lara—25,684
106. Flores, Julián and Ventura: San Diego—39,680
107. García, José María: La Vaca—22,142 (not confirmed, but 5 leagues confirmed to José María García y García: La Noria de San Domingo)
108. Garza, Apolinario: Las Presenas—11,626 (confirmed, 2 leagues)
109. Garza, Ramón de la: El Paisano, or Los Olmos—11,070 (confirmed, 2½ leagues)
110. López, Marcelino: Las Presenas—16,149 (confirmed, 4 leagues)
111. Moreno, Santos: La Trinidad—17,157 (confirmed, 4 *sitios*)
112. Ramírez, Antonio: Los Jaconcillos—25,860 (confirmed, 5 leagues, Javoncillos)
113. Ynojosa, Vital: La Anima Sola—20,009 (confirmed, "—½" leagues)[12]
114. Falcón, Blás María: El Chiltipin and San Francisco—26,605
137. García, Bernardo: El Infernillo—18,502 (confirmed, 5½ leagues)
115. Garza, José Lorenzo, José Domingo Garza, and José Julián de la Garza (for heirs of José Pérez Rey): Santa Gertrudis—78,228
116. Garza, Leonardo Longoria de la: El Rincón del Grullo—28,640 (confirmed, 6 leagues)
117. Gutiérrez, Antonio: El Pasadizo—13,243
118. Gutiérrez, Miguel: Santa Gertrudis—11,683 (confirmed, 2+ leagues)

[11] Grants 91 through 104 are in present Duval County.
[12] Grants 105 through 113 are in present Jim Wells County.

Appendix M 643

136. Mindiola, Juan: Rincón de Santa Gertrudis—15,499
119. Treviño, Andrés: Las Comitas—20,509 (confirmed, 5 leagues)
120. Treviño, Gabriel (patented to Manuel Elisondo): Rincón de la Boveda—28,784
121. Ynojosa, José Antonio: Los Sauces—28,007
122. Ynojosa, Vicente: El Rincón del Alazán—29,374 (confirmed, 6 leagues)[13]
123. Ballí, Nicolás and Juan José: La Isla del Padre—50,925 (confirmed, 11½ leagues, Padre Island)
124. Cabazos, José Antonio: Santa Petronilla—28,437 (confirmed, 8+ leagues)
125. Farías, Gregorio: El Diezmero—17,704
126. Fuentes, Andrés: Puentecitas—17,713 (confirmed, 4 leagues, to "Andrés Fernándes de la Fuentes")
127. García, Matías: Palo Alto—30,998 (confirmed, 7 leagues)
128. García, Rafael: Agua Dulce—26,131 (confirmed, 5+ leagues)
129. Herrera, Joaquín López de (18,640), José Vicente López de Herrera, (18,525), Mariano López de Herrera, (20,602), and Vicente López de Herrera, (18,039): Barranco Blanco—75,806
130. Longoria, Antonio: Los Sauces—17,712 (confirmed, 4 *sitios*)
131. Montemayor, Juan José de la Garza, and his three sons, José Manuel, Perfecto, and Agustín: Casa Blanca—70,848 (confirmed, 16 leagues)
132. Rivas, Luciano: Paso Ancho de Abajo—11,070
133. Villarreal, Enrique: Rincón del Oso—42,840 (confirmed, 10 leagues)
134. Ynojosa, Ramón de: Rincón de Corpus Christi—81,407 (confirmed, 10 leagues?)[14]

---

[13] Grants 114 through 122, 136, 137 are in present Kleberg County.
[14] Grants 123 through 134 are in present Nueces County.

APPENDIX N

Brands

Brand Section A*

Some of the First Brands Found Recorded in the Béxar Archives

 Nicolás Saez (October 4, 1742)

 Francisco Joseph de Estrada (January 16, 1748)

 Juan Joseph Flores (July 1, 1762)

 Andrés Hernández, for his son Joseph Miguel (January 28, 1765)

Lieutenant General Simón de Arocha's Export License Book Entry Dated May 19, 1778

 Don Tomás Trabiesso (his father and brothers)

 Sebastián Monjarás

 Francisco Xabier Rodríguez

 Vizente Flores (his father's)

 Mission Espada

 Don Luis Menchaca

*Names throughout the brand sections are as spelled in the original records, except that abbreviations are spelled out.

Appendix N

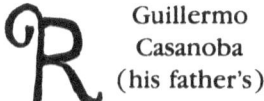 Guillermo Casanoba (his father's)

 Martín de la Garza

Brand Section B

Brand Book for Opelousas-Attakapas Districts, 1739–1888 (Louisiana): A Selection of Marks Used in Saint Martin Parish and Saint Landry Parish

Louis Grevemberg (1739)

Jacob Prudhomme (1816)

Jangais Guilbeau (1793)

Barthelemy Grevemberg (1739)

Nicolás Provost (1762)

Humphrey Jackson (1808)

François Gansanling (1789)

Ferdinand Prades (1780)

John Joachin (1793)

Étienne Lacaze (178?)

Solomon (1785)

Nathaniel West (1824)

Zini Leblanc (1776)

François Stelly (1826)

John Jenkins (1816)

Simón Leblanc (1770)

Thomas Steane (1826)

Jean Bautiste Longley (1823)

Litette (1760)

Simón Broussard (1762)

Michel Trahan (1790)

Appendix N

Mark	Name	Mark	Name	Mark	Name
	Julián Oliver (1809)		Bouté, pére (1768)		Louis James (1823)
	Sarah Patello (1825)		Jean Broussard (1767)		Elisha Wallace (1818)
	Jordan Perkins (1827)		John Jackson (1820)		Jean Pére Bérard (1767)
	Celeste Arguve (1815)		François Grovenberg (1775)		James Carruthers (1808)
	Lise Ardain (1821)		Pierre Grangl (1805)		Sarah Smith (1809)
	Baptiste Leblauve (1770)		Claude Broussard (1769)		Sally Parrott (1809)
	Basile Landry (1778)		Joseph Joachin (1823)		Saul Martin (1809)
	Comme Leblanc (1771)		James White (1809)		James Theall (1808)
	Joseph Priney (1780)		Pierre Trahan (1790)		Andre Guilbaut (1808)
	Antoine Bonin (1764)		Joseph Duhon (1790)		Edward White (1809)

Appendix N 647

Mark	Name
	Alexandre (1760)
	Lazard Lafayette Arseneaux (1823)
	Baptiste Guillory (178?)
	Balthazar Arseneaux (1825)
	Etienne Guiguan (178?)
	Guilbeau (1793)
	Creed Ouest (1748)
	François Provost (1783)
	Joseph Silvain (1827)
	Baptiste Barra (1783)
	John Abscher (1782)
	Michel Boson (1770)
	Adolphe Frederic Smith (1809)
	François Guidry (1808)
	Robert Bundik (1808)
	Auguste Villeneuve (1808)
	Simonet Leblanc (1808)
	John Dunman (1808)
	Jean Baptiste Mouse (1808)
	Valery Martin (1808)
	Marie Adelaide Mouton (1790)
	Charles Guidry (1766)
	John Abscher (1782)
	Marguerite Richard (1809)
	Louis Chiaffon [?] (1809)
	James Argraw (1799)
	Joseph Dunman (1798)
	Jesse White (1806)
	George Tellier (1761)
	Claude Broussard (1769)

648   *Appendix N*

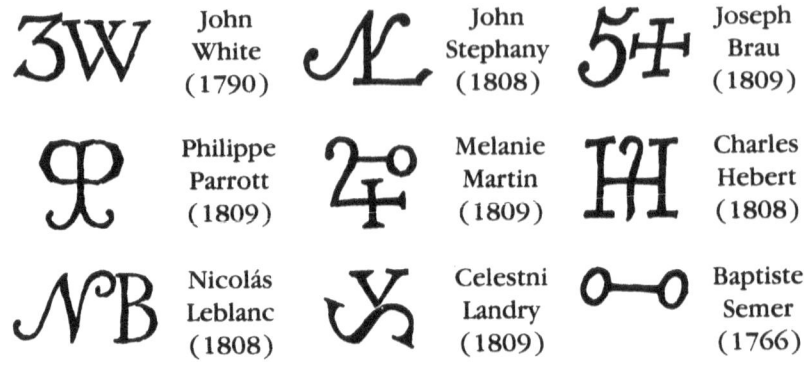

Brand	Name
3W	John White (1790)
ℳ	John Stephany (1808)
5H	Joseph Brau (1809)
℘	Philippe Parrott (1809)
♃	Melanie Martin (1809)
H	Charles Hebert (1808)
𝒩B	Nicolás Leblanc (1808)
𝒴	Celestni Landry (1809)
o–o	Baptiste Semer (1766)

Brand Section C

Register of the Marks Used by the Inhabitants of This District (San Estéban Tombecbe) to Mark Their Animals, 1795 (From Archivo General de Indias)

Brand	Name	Brand	Name	Brand	Name
AH	Adam [H]enchen	ⓎG	Ana Young	F◇	Alejandro Foúlan
⊡L	[?]	BC	¹Agustín Charran [?]	2	Jorge Brua
BH	Ira Banto [?]	DJ	Daniel Yancen [?]	MS	Hesekiah Wat
CR	Cornelia Rens [?]	⌘	Carlos Brua [?]	PC	Pelipe Sartan
4E	Elijah Thompson	F15	Francisco Sartan	69	Gurllirmo Paubel [?]
FB	Francisco Bouquin	ⓎJ	Ysavel Le Tutona	Nh	Enrique Nail

¹ Also Bacilio Sartan and Eduardo Chartan.

Appendix N 649

Brand	Name	Brand	Name	Brand	Name
JC	Juan Sartan	JB	Juan Buan	CT	Julian de Castro [?]
DL	Jaime Daniel	JM	Juan Mignar[s]	JB	Juan Bouquin
♀	Toven Yimi	W	Roberto Welch	Ⓜ	Juan Machan [?]
mw	James M. Grau [McGraw?]	CI	Luis Sartan	IJ	Juan Yonein [Yohnston]
3B	Natalis Blaquel [Nathan Blackwell]	R	Tobaes Rims [Tobias Roams]	B	Thomas Baset [?]
SJ	Solomon Yanzan [?]	OS	Dens Suliben	RB	Ricardo Brashed [?]
TW	Tomas Wit	SW	Salomon Wit	CI	Zenon Sartan

Brand Section D

Northern List for the Recognition of Brands (Undated) (From Béxar Archives)

Brand	Name	Brand	Name	Brand	Name
	Manuel Barrera (raiser)		José Salinas (raiser)		Satiernino Gusman
	José Antonio Salinas (raiser)		Luis Chirino		Juaquín Ramón
	José Antonio Salinas		Romano Rodríguez		José María Robalin [?]

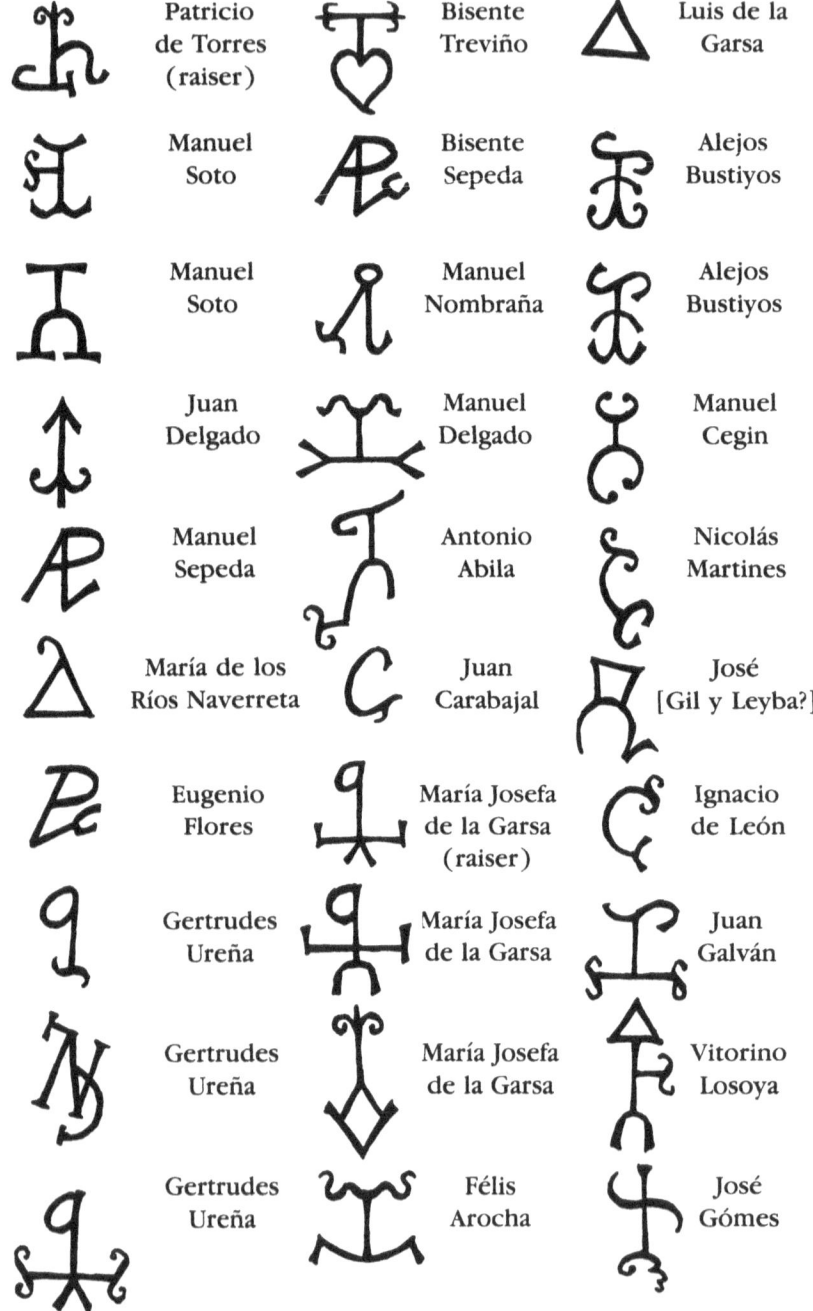

Appendix N

Gertrudes Ureña	José María Ramíres	Luisa Ramos [Ramón?]
Gertrudes Ureña	Francisco Móntes (raiser)	Francisco Ruís [?]
Gertrudes Ureña	Francisco Móntes	Don José Antonio [de la Garza?]
Don Ventura [?] de la Garza	Captain [Ygnacio?] Péres	José Manuel de la Garza
Pedro Quiñones	María Josefa Sola [Soto?]	José Manuel de la Garza
Pedro Quiñones	José María Sambrano	José Manuel de la Garza
Gavino Delgado	Santiago Seguín	[Marcelo?] Váldes
Tomás Péres	Agustín Ruíz	Josefa Ruíz
Captain Luciano García	Manuel Nuñez	Doña Saragosa Rodrígues
José Fragoso	Francisco Días	Manuela Móntes

652   *Appendix N*

Brand Section E

Brands and Marks, Nacogdoches-Trinidad (Undated)
(From Béxar Archives)

NACOGDOCHES:

Brand	Name	Brand	Name	Brand	Name
	Mariano Sánches		José Tomás Menchaca		María Morín, widow of Juan de Mora
	Dionisio Quinelty		Christian Hesser		Pedro al Cantara de Alamio
	Domingo Gonzáles		Manuel Sánches		José María Mora
	Matías Peña		Mariano Santa Cruz		Julián Rosales
	Patricio Torres		José de los Santos Coy		José Dionisio Lópes
	Francisco de los Santos		Francisco Billapando		Antonio Cierra
	Tomás Mansolo		Juan José Ernándes		Guillermo Bebe
	José Locubiche		Antonio Rodrígues		Francisco Guerrero
	Pedro Crisofogo		Juan José Ybarvo		José Tesie

Appendix N

Brand	Name	Brand	Name	Brand	Name
	Juan Baptista Prosela		Pedro Gonzáles		Santiago Lepine
	María Josefa Arriola		José Córdova		Luis Forten
	José Flores		José Narciso Labomba		Antonio Parrett
	Antonio Arriola		Juan de Díos Acosta		José Ybarbo
	Nepomuseno de la Zerda		José Candido San Miguel		Richard Simis
	Melchora del Río		Anastasio Ybarbo		Gregorio Mora
	Guillermo Quark		Pedro Tesier		Jose Luis de la Bega
	Reymondo Quark		Mariano Garsa		José Sánches
	Ana María Quark		Francisco de los Santos		Antonio Córdova
	Juan José Sánches		Francisco García		José Mariano Sánches

Appendix N

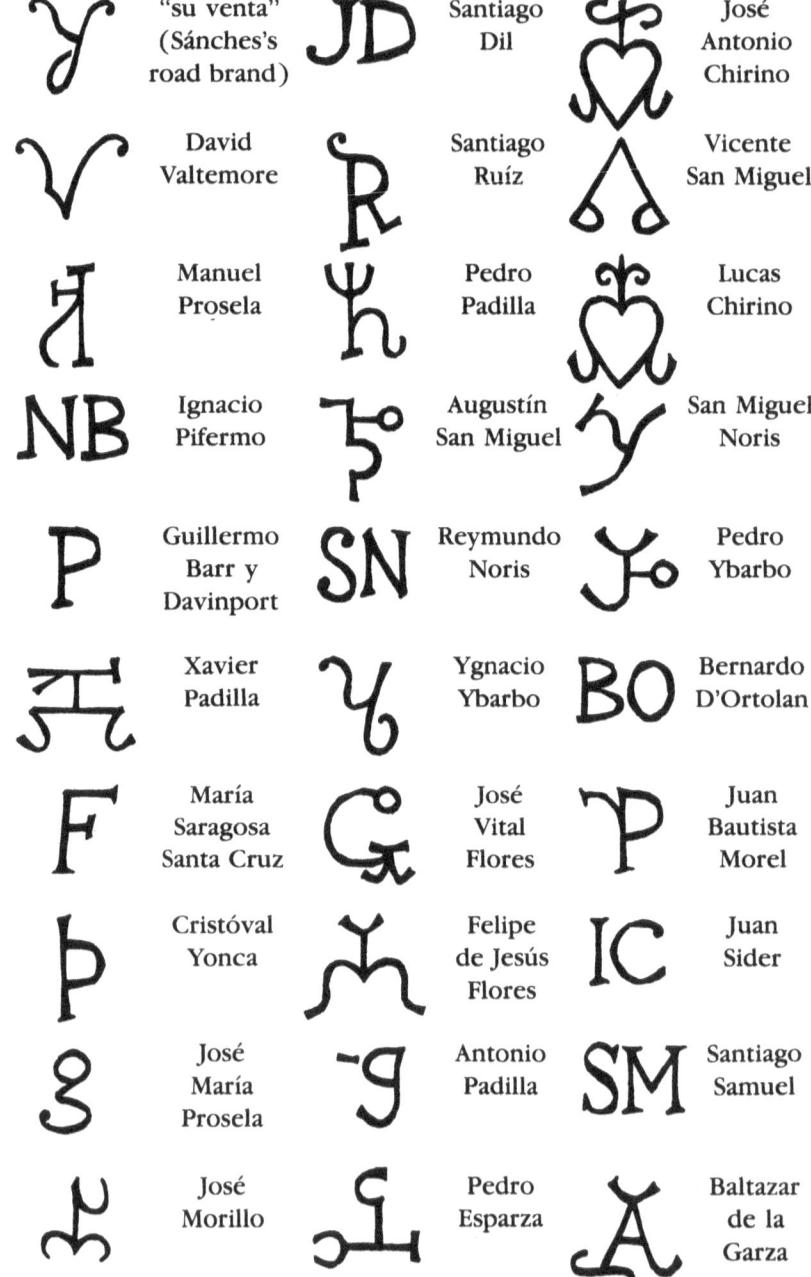

Appendix N

TRINIDAD:

Mark	Name	Mark	Name	Mark	Name
⏉	Ponciano Ybarbo	IB	Juan Lorenzo Bodin	22	Elias Nelson
J	Jaime Miglahan	M	Juan Magee	HS	Henrico Cheriden
⌐	Luis Grande	&	Magee's wife, Celestina Borges		
ℛ	Carlos Trahan		José María Cortinas		
R	Pedro Santa Cruz		Miguel Quin		
M	Vicente Micheli	⅄	José Borrego		
ƐM	Micheli's minor son, Francisco		Juan Si		
₽	Pedro Lartigue		Manuel Casanova		
G'S	Frederico Stocman [Esctozman]	⊥	Juan Lum [Lunn]		
I⟑	Santiago Fier		José Giroud		

Appendix N

Brand Section F

List of Cattle Confiscated from the Insurgents Who Have Left This Capital, Their Number and Brands, February 28, 1814 (From Saltillo Archives)

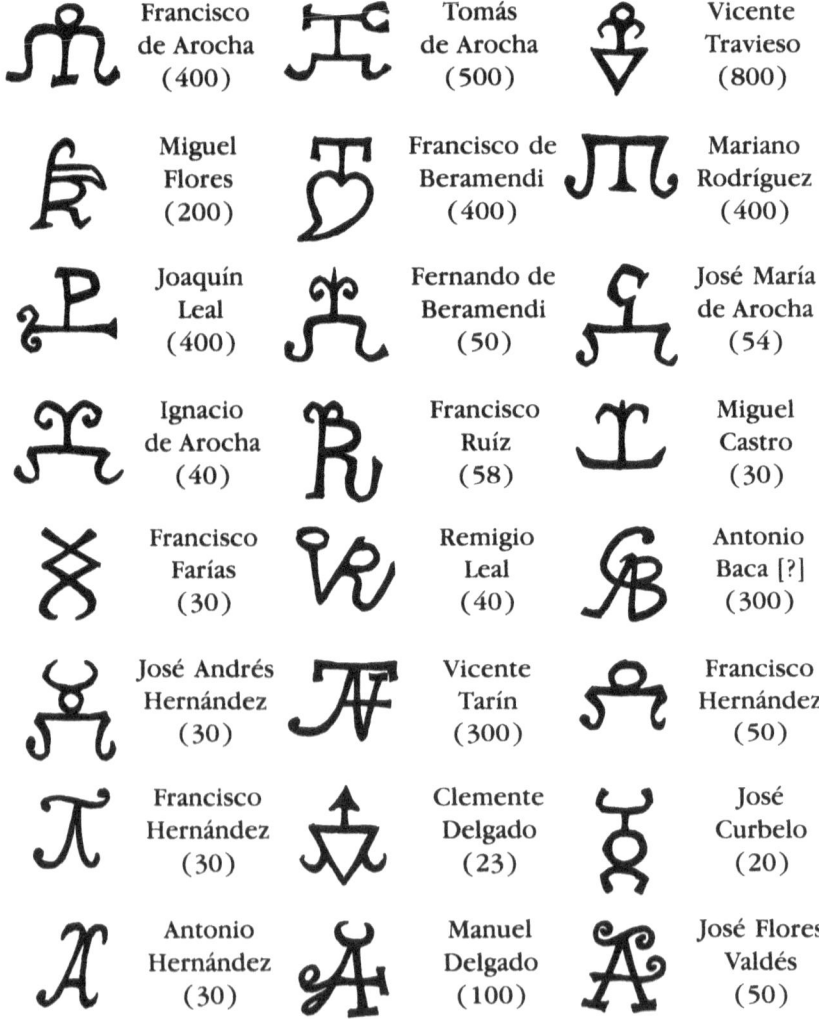

Francisco de Arocha (400)

Tomás de Arocha (500)

Vicente Travieso (800)

Miguel Flores (200)

Francisco de Beramendi (400)

Mariano Rodríguez (400)

Joaquín Leal (400)

Fernando de Beramendi (50)

José María de Arocha (54)

Ignacio de Arocha (40)

Francisco Ruíz (58)

Miguel Castro (30)

Francisco Farías (30)

Remigio Leal (40)

Antonio Baca [?] (300)

José Andrés Hernández (30)

Vicente Tarín (300)

Francisco Hernández (50)

Francisco Hernández (30)

Clemente Delgado (23)

José Curbelo (20)

Antonio Hernández (30)

Manuel Delgado (100)

José Flores Valdés (50)

Appendix N   657

Brand Section G

*List of Recaptured Animals Formed for the Commandant General,
Showing Brands with a Description, February 8, 1820
(From Béxar Archives)*

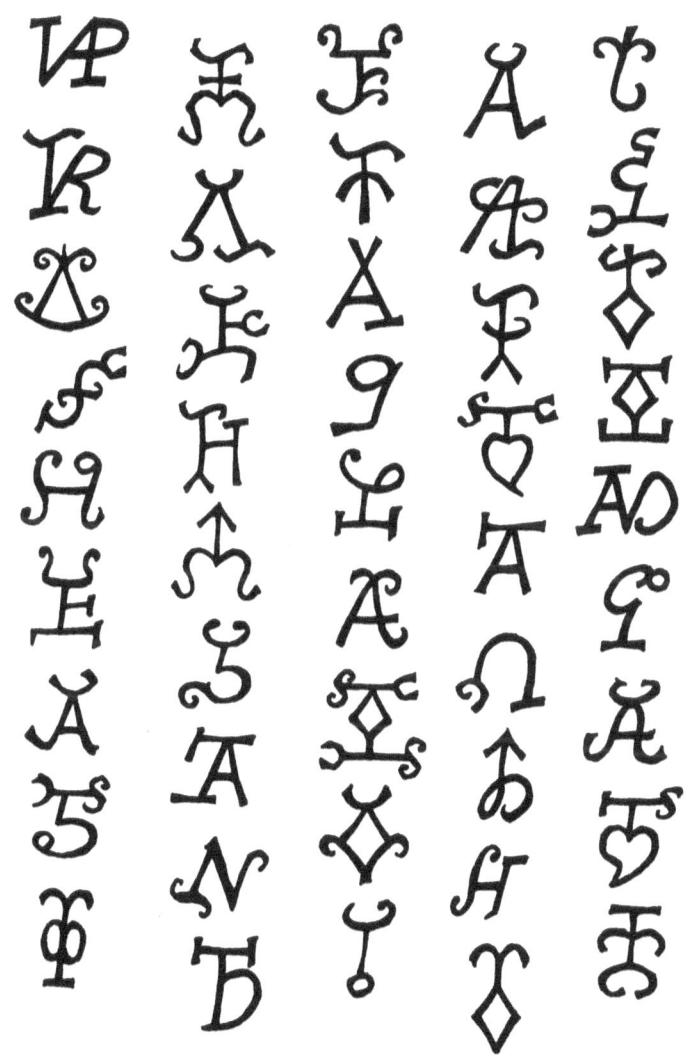

658 Appendix N

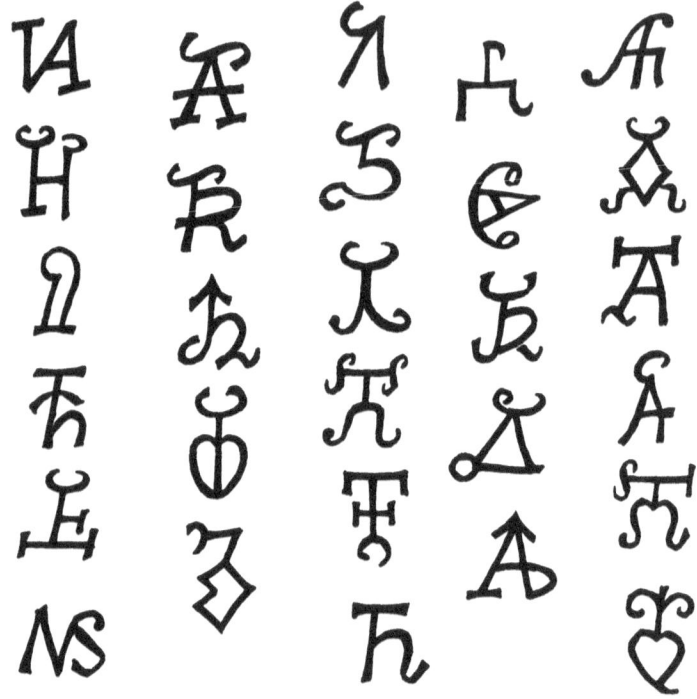

Brand Section H

List in Which Are Noted Brands of Stray Animals (bestias mostrencal)
Kept at Béxar for the Free State of Coahuila y Texas, 1827–34 (From Nacogdoches Archives)

Appendix N

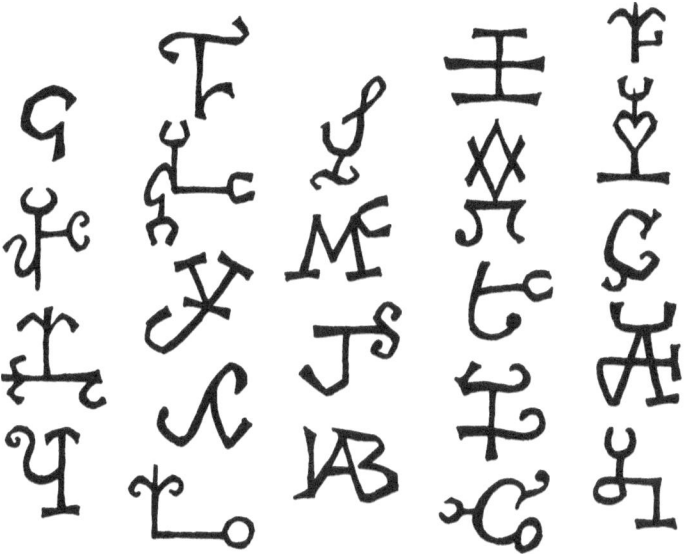

BIBLIOGRAPHY

Primary Sources

Spanish Archives

Archivo del Convento de Guadalupe (Zacatecas). Microfilm (11 roles) concerning activities of the Franciscan missionaries in Texas, College of Zacatecas, with calendar. Abbr. ACZ. Old Spanish Missions Research Library. Our Lady of the Lake University, San Antonio. Abbr. OSMRL.

Archivo General de Indias (Seville, Spain). Documents (transcripts) relating to Texas, found in: Audiencia de México, 73 vols., and Audiencia de Guadalajara, 53 vols. University of Texas Archives, Austin. Abbr. AGI.

Archivo General y Público de la Nación. Documents (transcripts) relating to Texas. In Audiencia de Guadalajara (1582–1821), 54 vols., and Provincias Internas (1617–1821), 88 vols. University of Texas Archives, Austin. Abbr. AGN.

Archivo San Francisco el Grande. 1673–1800. Franciscan documents copied by Carlos E. Castañeda from Biblioteca Nacional. 36 vols. University of Texas Archives, Austin. Abbr. ASFG.

Béxar Archives. 1717–1836. Manuscript Collection, with calendar. 172-roll microfilm series. Also in Béxar Archives Translations, series 1 (160 vols. to date, covering 1730–89), and series 2 (38 vols., covering 1804–1808). University of Texas Archives, Austin. Abbr. BA, BAM, BAT.

Bexar County Spanish Archives. Multivolume holdings retained at San Antonio when the Béxar Archives were transferred to the University of Texas in 1899. Contains Deed Books, Plat Books, Land Grant Books, Brand Books, Water Book, Protocol Books, and Miscellaneous Documents. Bexar County Courthouse, County Clerk's Office, San Antonio. Abbr. BCSA.

Catholic Archives of Texas. Extensive collection of colonial documents gathered from many sources. Chancery Office, Austin. Abbr. CA.

General Land Office of Texas, Spanish Archives. Multivolume holdings concerning Spanish-Mexican period land grants. Austin. Abbr. GLO.

Laredo Archives (City Records, 1749–1836). Manuscript Collection. Also available in 16 rolls of microfilm, no calendar. Saint Mary's University, San Antonio. Abbr. LA.

Matamoros Archives (City Records, 1811–59). Photostats, with calendar. 68 vols. University of Texas Archives, Austin. Abbr. MA.

Nacogdoches Archives. 1731–1836. Manuscript Collection. Also available in transcripts (89 vols.) and on microfilm (27 rolls, with guidebook). Texas State Archives, Austin. Abbr. NA.

Saltillo Archives (Civil Records of the State of Coahuila). Photostats (gathered by Carlos E. Castañeda), with calendar. 50 vols. University of Texas Archives. Abbr. SA.

Manuscript Collections

Austin [Stephen F.]. Papers. Manuscript Collection. 1676–1889. University of Texas Archives, Austin.

Bexar County. Brand Book A. County Clerk's Office, BCSA.

Blake, R. B. "Records . . . Relating to the Edmund Norris Four League Grant." Typescript. Texas State Archives, Austin.

———. Research Collection. 75 vols. with "supplement" series of 18 vols. University of Texas Archives, Austin. An impressive compilation of transcripts and translations of documents (mostly from NA and BA). Other sets are housed in the Texas State Archives, the Houston Public Library, and the Special Collections of Stephen F. Austin University.

Brand Book for Opelousas and Attakapas Districts. 1739–1888. Transcript. Louisiana Room, University of Southwestern Louisiana Library, Lafayette, La., formerly in possession of Saint Martin's Parish, La. Original in Saint Martinville County Courthouse, La.

Buquor, P. S. Papers. 1730–1829. University of Texas Archives, Austin.

Cassiano-Pérez. Collection. Daughters of the Republic of Texas Library at the Alamo, San Antonio.

City Council Minutes. Record Book. Office of the City Clerk, San Antonio.

Comptroller's Military Service Records (Texas). Texas State Archives, Austin.

Eberstadt, [Edward]. Collection. University of Texas Archives, Austin.

Elliott, Claude. Collection. Texas State Archives, Austin.

Garay, Richard C., comp. Garay Transcripts. From AGN. Provincias Internas.

García, Genaro. Collection. 1325–1921. Benson Latin American Center, University of Texas, Austin.

Grazing Papers ("History of Grazing in Texas"). Of interest to the student of Spanish ranching is "The Range in Colonial Times," 2 vols. in 3 pts., a collection of bound typescripts, translations, and extracts from various sources. Historical Records Survey by WPA, 1935. University of Texas Archives, Austin. Also, see loose assortment of these items in Box 2-23/1028, Texas State Archives, Austin.

Guadalupe County. Brand Book No. 1. County Clerk's Office, Guadalupe County Courthouse, Seguin, Texas.

Hunter, John Warren. "Life of Creed Taylor, Mason County, 1901." Manuscript (with alterations by James DeShields). Texas State Archives, Austin.

Lamar, Mirabeau Buonaparte. Papers. Texas State Archives, Austin.

Leal, Carmela, comp. and trans. "Translations of Statistical and Census Reports of Texas, 1782–1836, and Sources Documenting the Blacks in Texas, 1603–1803." 3 rolls of microfilm. Institute of Texan Cultures, San Antonio.
Leal, John Ogden, comp. and trans. "Baptismals of San Fernando" (1731–1858). 8 vols. From San Fernando Church Records, BCSA.
———, comp. and trans. "Burials of San Fernando" (1744–1860). 3 vols. From San Fernando Church Records, BCSA.
———, comp. and trans. "Marriages of San Fernando" (1742–1856). 3 vols. From San Fernando Church Records, BCSA.
Lenz, Louis. Collection. 1688–1962. University of Texas Archives, Austin.
Maverick, Samuel A. Papers. 1825–88. University of Texas Archives, Austin.
Menchaca, Antonio. "Memoirs." Manuscript and typescript. University of Texas Archives, Austin.
Nolan, Philip. Papers. 1797–1808. University of Texas Archives, Austin.
Travieso, Vicente Álvarez. Papers. 1771–83. Translation. University of Texas Archives, Austin.
Wilson County Deed Books C and B, Plat Book 1, and Brand Book A. County Clerk's Office, Wilson County Courthouse, Floresville, Texas.

Published Works (Books and Journals)

Almonte, Juan N. "Statistical Report on Texas" (1835). Translated by Carlos E. Castañeda. *Southwestern Historical Quarterly* 28, no. 3 (January, 1925).
Arizpe, Miguel Ramos. See Benson, Nettie Lee.
Barker, Eugene C., ed. "The Austin Papers." Pt. 1. In *Annual Report of the American Historical Association for the Year 1919*, vol. 1. pt. 2. In *Annual Report . . . for the Year 1922*, vol. 2. Washington, D.C.: Government Printing Office, 1924–28.
Benson, Nettie Lee, trans. and ed. *Report That Dr. Miguel Ramos de Arizpe . . . Presents to the August Congress on the Natural, Political, and Civil Condition of the Provinces of Coahuila, Nuevo León, Nuevo Santander, and Texas*. University of Texas Institute of Latin-American Studies, vol. 11. Austin: University of Texas Press, 1950.
Berlandier, Jean Louis. *Journey to Mexico during the Years 1826 to 1834*. Translated by Sheila M. Ohlendorf et al.; edited by C. H. Muller et al. 2 vols. Austin: Texas State Historical Association, 1980.
Bolton, Herbert Eugene, ed. *Athanase de Mézières and the Louisiana-Texas Frontier, 1768–1780*. 2 vols. Cleveland: Arthur H. Clark Co., 1914.
Bonnell, George W. *Topographical Description of Texas*. Austin, Tex.: Clark, Wing, and Brown, 1840. Reprint. Waco, Tex.: Texian Press, 1964.
Bracht, Victor. *Texas in 1848*. Translated by Charles Frank Schmidt. San Antonio: Naylor Co., 1931.
Céliz, Fray Francisco. *Diary of the Alarcón Expedition into Texas, 1718–1719*. Translated by Fritz L. Hoffman. Los Angeles: Quivira Society, 1935.

Cervantes, Rafael, ed. *Diario del padre fray Gaspar José de Solís en su visita a las misiones de Texas 1768*. Guadalajara: Editorial Font, 1981.

Comisión Pesquisidora de la Frontera del Norte [de México]. *Reports of the Committee of Investigation Sent in 1873 by the Mexican Government to the Frontier of Texas*. New York: Baker & Godwin, 1875.

Dabbs, J. Autry, trans. *López's Report of the Texas Missions in 1785*. Preliminary Studies of the Texas Catholic Historical Society 3, no. 6 (1940). Austin.

de Cordova, J[acob]. *Texas: Her Resources and Her Public Men*. Philadelphia: J. B. Lippencott & Co., 1858. Reprint. Waco, Tex.: Texian Press, 1969.

Foik, Paul J., and Peter P. Forrestal, eds. and trans. *The Solís Diary of 1767*. Preliminary Studies of the Texas Catholic Historical Society 1, no. 6 (1931). Austin.

Fora, Nicolás de la. See Kinnaird, Lawrence.

Forrestal, Peter P., trans. *Peña's Diary of the Aguayo Expedition*. Preliminary Studies of the Texas Catholic Historical Society 2, no. 6 (January, 1935). Austin.

Gulick, C. A., et al., eds. *The Papers of Mirabeau Buonaparte Lamar*. 6 vols. Austin: A. C. Baldwin & Sons, 1921–27.

Hackett, Charles Wilson, et al., eds. and trans. *Pichardo's Treatise on the Limits of Louisiana and Texas*. 4 vols. Austin: University of Texas Press, 1931–46.

Hatcher, Mattie Austin, trans. "Texas in 1820." *Southwestern Historical Quarterly* 23, no. 1 (July, 1919).

Holmes, Jack D. L., ed. *José de Evia y sus Reconocimientos del Golfo de México, 1783–1796*. Madrid: Ediciones José Porrúa Turanzas, 1968.

Jackson, Donald, ed. *The Journals of Zebulon Montgomery Pike*. 2 vols. Norman: University of Oklahoma Press, 1966.

Jackson, W. H., and S. A. Long. *Texas Stock Directory, or Book of Marks and Brands*. San Antonio: Herald Office, 1865.

Kennedy, William. *Texas: The Rise, Progress, and Prospects of the Republic of Texas*. 2 vols. London, 1841. Reprint. Fort Worth, Tex.: Molyneaux Craftsmen, 1925.

Kinnaird, Lawrence, ed. *The Frontiers of New Spain: Nicolás de la Fora's Description, 1766–1768*. Berkeley, Calif.: Quivira Society, 1958.

———, ed. *Spain in the Mississippi Valley, 1765–1794*. Vols. 2–4. American Historical Association Annual Report for 1945. Washington, D.C., 1946.

Leclerc, Frédéric. *Texas and Its Revolution*. Translated by James L. Shepherd III. Houston: Anson Jones Press, 1950.

Leutenegger, Fr. Benedict, ed. and trans. *Inventory of the Mission San Antonio de Valero, 1772*. Office of State Archaeologist, Report no. 1. Austin: Texas Historical Commission, 1977.

———, trans. *Guidelines for a Texas Mission: Instructions for the Missionary of Mission Concepción in San Antonio (ca. 1760)*. Documentary 1. San Antonio: Old Spanish Missions Historical Research Library, 1976.

Bibliography 665

———, trans. *Journal of a Texas Missionary, 1767–1802: The Diario Histórico of Fr. Cosme Lozano Narvais, Pen Name of Fr. Mariano Antonio de Vasconcelos.* Documentary 3. San Antonio: Old Spanish Missions Historical Research Library, 1977.

———, trans. *Management of the Missions in Texas: Fr. José Rafael Oliva's Views concerning the Problem of Temporalities in 1788.* Documentary 2. San Antonio: Old Spanish Missions Historical Research Library, 1977.

———, trans. "Memorial of Father Benito Fernández Concerning the Canary Islanders, 1741." *Southwestern Historical Quarterly* 82, no. 3 (January, 1979).

———, trans. *The Zacatecan Missionaries in Texas, 1716–1834: Excerpts from the Libros de los Decretos of the Missionary College of Zacatecas, 1707–1828.* "Biographical Dictionary" by Fr. Marion A. Habig. Office of the State Archaeologist, Report no. 23. Austin: Texas Historical Survey Committee, 1973.

———, and Fr. Marion A. Habig, comps. and trans. *The San José Papers, 1719–1791.* Pt. 1. San Antonio: Old Spanish Missions Historical Research Library, 1978.

——— and ———, comps. and trans. *The San José Papers, August, 1791– June, 1809.* Pt. 2. San Antonio: Old Spanish Missions Historical Research Library, 1983.

Linn, John J. *Reminiscences of Fifty Years in Texas.* 1883. Reprint. Austin: Steck Co., 1935.

Martínez, Antonio. See Taylor, Virginia H.

Menchaca, Antonio. *Memoirs.* San Antonio: Yanaguana Society [1937].

Moore, Francis, Jr. *Map and Description of Texas*.... Philadelphia: H. Tanner, Jr., 1840. Reprint. Waco, Tex.: Texian Press, 1965.

Morfi, Fray Juan Agustín de. *Diario y Derrotero (1777–1781) por Fray Juan Agustín de Morfi.* Edited by Eugenio del Hoyo and Malcolm D. McLean. Monterrey, Mex.: Instituto Tecnológico, 1967.

———. *Excerpts from the Memorias for the History of the Province of Texas.* Translated and edited by Frederick C. Chabot. San Antonio: Privately published, printed by Naylor Co., 1932.

———. *The History of Texas, 1673–1779.* Translated and edited by Carlos E. Castañeda. 2 vols. Albuquerque, N. Mex.: Quivira Society, 1935.

———. *Viaje de Indios y Diario del Nuevo México.* Edited by Vito Alessio Robles. Mexico City: Bibliófilos Mexicanos, 1935.

Navarro, José Antonio. *Apuntes Históricos Interesantes de San Antonio de Béxar: Escritos por el C. Dn. José Antonio Navarro en Noviembre de 1853*.... San Antonio: Published by friends, 1869.

Newell, Rev. C[hester]. *History of the Revolution in Texas*.... 1838. Reprint. New York: Arno Press, 1973.

Olmsted, Frederick Law. *A Journey through Texas: Or, A Saddle-Trip on the Southwestern Border*.... New York: Dix, Edwards & Co., 1857. Reprint. Austin: University of Texas Press, 1978.

Padilla, Juan Antonio. "Report on the Barbarous Indians of the Province of Texas." Translated by Mattie Austin Hatcher. *Southwestern Historical Quarterly* 23, no. 1 (July, 1919).

Pagès, Pierre Marie François de. *Travels round the World in the Years 1767, 1768, 1769, 1770, 1771.* 2 vols. Printed for J. Murray. London, 1791.

Peña, Manuel de la. See Forrestal, Peter P.

Pichardo, José Antonio. See Hackett, Charles Wilson, et al.

Pike, Zebulon Montgomery, See Jackson, Donald.

Potter, Reuben M. *The Texas Revolution: Distinguished Mexicans Who Took Part in the Revolution of Texas, with Glances at Its Early Events.* [New York, 1878?].

Ramos Arizpe, Miguel. See Benson, Nettie Lee.

Regulations for the Granting of Land under the Spanish Government of Louisiana. Printed by Order of the House of Representatives. No. 114. Washington, D.C., April 19, 1820.

Reports of Cases Argued and Decided in the Supreme Court of the State of Texas. Vol. 3 (1848), Austin: State Gazette Office, 1851. Vol. 7 (1851–52), Houston: E. H. Cushing, 1883. Vol. 13 (1854–55), Houston: E. H. Cushing, 1876.

Roemer, Ferdinand. *Texas: With Particular Reference to German Immigration and the Physical Appearance of the Country.* Translated by Oswald Mueller. San Antonio: Standard Printing Co., 1935. Reprint. Waco, Tex.: Texian Press, 1967.

Seguín, Juan N. *Personal Memoirs of John N. Seguin: From the Year 1834 to the Retreat of General Woll from the City of San Antonio, 1842.* San Antonio: Printed at the Ledger Book and Job Office, 1858.

Smithers, Harriet, ed. *Journals of the Sixth Congress, Republic of Texas.* Austin: Texas State Library, 1945.

Smithwick, Noah. *The Evolution of a State.* Austin: Gammel Book Co., 1900. Reprint. Austin: Steck-Vaughn Co., 1968.

Solís, Gaspar José De. See Foik, Paul J., and Peter P. Forrestal; Cervantes, Rafael.

Solms-Braunfels, Carl, Prince of. *Texas: 1844–1845.* Houston: Anson Jones Press, 1936.

Stiff, Col. Edward. *The Texas Emigrant....* Cincinnati: G. Conclin, 1840. Reprint. Waco, Tex.: Texian Press, 1968.

Sweet, Alexander E., and John Armoy Knox. *On a Mexican Mustang through Texas: From the Gulf to the Rio Grande.* Hartford, Conn.: S. S. Scranton & Co., 1883.

Taylor, Virginia H., trans. and ed. *The Letters of Antonio Martínez: Last Spanish Governor of Texas, 1817–1822.* Austin: Texas State Library, 1957.

United States. Congress. *House Exec. Doc.* no. 49, 24th Cong., 1st sess., 1824 (ser. 287).

———. *House Exec. Doc.* no. 52, 36th Cong., 1st sess., 1859–60 (ser. 1050).

———. *House Misc. Doc.* no. 64, 45th Cong., 2d sess., 1878 (ser. 1820).

———. *House Rept.* no. 343, 44th Cong., 1st sess., 1876 (ser. 1709).

A Visit to Texas: Being the Journal of a Traveller through Those Parts Most Interesting to American Settlers. New York: Van Nostrand and Dwight, 1836. Reprint. Austin: Steck Co., 1952.
Voorhies, Jacqueline K., trans. and comp. *Some Late Eighteenth-Century Louisianians: Census Records of the Colony, 1758–1796.* History Series. Lafayette: University of Southwestern Louisiana, 1973.
West, Elizabeth, ed. and trans. "Diary of José Bernardo Gutiérrez de Lara. *American Historical Review* 34 (October, 1938–January, 1939).
Wilber, Marguerite Eyer, ed. *Vancouver in California, 1792–1794.* Los Angeles: Glen Dawson, 1954.
Woodman, David, Jr. *Guide to Texas Emigrants.* Boston: M. Hawes, 1835. Reprint. Waco, Tex.: Texian Press, 1974.

Secondary Sources

Manuscripts and Typescripts

Altman, Ida. "The Marqueses de Aguayo: A Family and Estate History." Master's thesis, University of Texas, 1972.
Blake, R. B. "Captain Antonio Gil Ybarbo of Nacogdoches." Typescript. Texas State Archives, Austin.
Dawson, James W., and Mary Dawson. "Texas Trammel's [*sic*] Trace." Typescript. University of Texas Archives, Austin.
de Burgos, Francis. "The Administration of Teodoro de Croix, Commander General of the Provincias Internas de Mexico, 1776–83." Master's thesis, University of Texas, 1927.
Downs, Fane. "The History of Mexicans in Texas, 1820–1845." Ph.D. diss., Texas Tech University, 1970.
Edman, Grace A., trans. and ed. "A Compilation of Royal Decrees Relating to Texas and Other Northern Provinces of New Spain, 1719–1799." Master's thesis, University of Texas, 1930.
Faulk, Odie B. "Texas during the Administration of Governor Domingo Cabello y Robles, 1778–1786." Master's thesis, Texas Technological College, 1960.
Harris, Charles H. "A Mexican Latifundio: The Economic Empire of the Sánchez Navarro Family, 1765–1821." Ph.D. diss., University of Texas, 1968.
King, Nyal C. "Captain Antonio Gil Y'Barbo, Founder of Modern Nacogdoches, 1729–1809." Master's thesis, Stephen F. Austin University, 1949.
Morey, Elizabeth May. "Attitude of the Citizens of San Fernando toward Independence Movements in New Spain, 1811–1813." Master's thesis, University of Texas, 1930.
Myres, Sandra Lynn. "The Development of the Ranch as a Frontier Institution in the Spanish Province of Texas, 1691–1800." Ph.D. diss., Texas Christian University, 1967.

Pitts, John Bost, III. "Speculation in Headright Land Grants in San Antonio from 1837 to 1852." Master's thesis, Trinity University (San Antonio), 1966.
Ramirez, Nora E. "The Vaquero and Ranching in the Southwestern United States, 1600–1970." Ph.D. diss., Indiana University, 1978.
Ramsdell, Charles William, Jr. "Spanish Goliad." Typescript. University of Texas Archives, Austin.
Scherer, R. B., Jr. "James Taylor White." Anahuac Historical Marker Research Paper, n.d., possession of author.
Schwarz, Ted. "Forgotten Battlefield of the Texas Revolution." Typescript in the possession of the author.
Strickland, Rex W. "Anglo American Activities in Northeast Texas, 1803–1845." Ph.D. diss., University of Texas, 1937.
Tijerina, Andrew Anthony. "Tejanos and Texas: The Native Mexicans of Texas, 1820–1850." Ph.D. diss., University of Texas, 1977.
Wilson, Maurine T. "Philip Nolan and His Activities in Texas." Master's thesis, University of Texas, 1932.

Published Works (Books and Articles)

Acuña, Rodolfo. *Occupied America: The Chicano's Struggle toward Liberation.* San Francisco: Canfield Press, 1972.
Ahlborn, Richard E., ed. *Man Made Mobile: Early Saddles of Western North America.* Washington, D.C.: Smithsonian Institution Press, 1980.
Alessio Robles, Vito. *Coahuila y Texas en la época colonial.* Mexico City: Editorial Cultura, 1938.
Almaráz, Félix D., Jr. *Tragic Cavalier: Governor Manuel Salcedo of Texas, 1808–1813.* Austin: University of Texas Press, 1971.
Ashford, Gerald. *Spanish Texas, Yesterday and Today.* Austin: Jenkins Co., 1971.
Austin, Mattie Alice. "The Municipal Government of San Fernando de Béxar, 1730–1800." Texas State Historical Association *Quarterly* 8, no. 4 (April, 1905).
Bancroft, Hubert Howe. *History of the North Mexican States and Texas.* 2 vols. San Francisco: History Co., 1884–89.
Beatie, Russel H. *Saddles.* Norman: University of Oklahoma Press, 1981.
Block, W. T. *A History of Jefferson County, Texas, from Wilderness to Reconstruction.* Nederland, Tex.: Nederland Publishing Co., 1976.
———. "Meanest Town on the Coast." *Old West* 16, no. 2 (Winter, 1979).
Bolton, Herbert Eugene. *Guide to Materials for the United States in the Principal Archives of Mexico.* Publication no. 163. Washington, D.C.: Carnegie Institution, 1913.
———. "The Spanish Abandonment and Reoccupation of East Texas, 1773–1779." Texas State Historical Association *Quarterly* 9, no. 2 (October, 1905).
———. *Texas in the Middle Eighteenth Century: Studies in Spanish Colonial*

History and Administration. Berkeley: University of California Press, 1915.
Brinckerhoff, Sidney B., and Odie B. Faulk. *Lancers for the King: A Study of the Frontier Military System of Northern New Spain, with a Translation of the Royal Regulations of 1772.* Phoenix: Arizona Historical Foundation, 1965.
Bruns, Florence [Nina] W. "El Capote Ranch." In *Bicentennial Minutes of Seguin-Guadalupe County, 1976.* Seguin, Tex.: Research Committee of the Seguin Bicentennial Commission, 1976.
Buck, Samuel M. *Yanaguana's Successors: The Story of the Canary Islanders' Immigration into Texas in the Eighteenth Century.* San Antonio: Naylor Co., 1949.
Castañeda, Carlos E. *Our Catholic Heritage in Texas.* 7 vols. Austin: Von Boeckmann–Jones Co., 1936–58.
Caughey, John Walton. *Bernardo de Gálvez in Louisiana, 1776–1783.* Berkeley: University of California Press, 1934.
Chabot, Frederick C. *San Antonio and Its Beginnings.* San Antonio: Artes Gráficas, 1936.
———. *With the Makers of San Antonio.* San Antonio: Artes Gráficas, 1937. Reprint. San Antonio, Tex.: Graphic Arts, 1970.
———. ed. *Texas in 1811: The Las Casas and Sambrano Revolutions.* San Antonio: Yanaguana Society 6, 1941.
Chambers, Henry E. *A History of Louisiana: Wilderness-Colony-Province-Territory-State-People.* Chicago: American Historical Society, 1925.
Chevalier, François. *Land and Society in Colonial Mexico—The Great Hacienda.* Berkeley: University of California Press, 1963.
Clark, John G. *New Orleans, 1718–1812: An Economic History.* Baton Rouge: Louisiana State University Press, 1970.
Cortés, Carlos E., intro. *The Mexican Experience in Texas.* New York: Arno Press, 1976. [Contains translation of Comisión Pesquisidora report of 1875.]
Cox, I. J. "The Early Settlers of San Fernando." Texas State Historical Association *Quarterly* 5 (July, 1901–April, 1902).
Dale, Edward Everett. *The Range Cattle Industry: Ranching on the Great Plains from 1865 to 1925.* Norman: University of Oklahoma Press, 1930. New ed., 1960.
Dary, David. *Cowboy Culture: A Saga of Five Centuries.* New York: Alfred A. Knopf, 1981.
de León, Arnoldo. *The Tejano Community, 1836–1900.* Albuquerque: University of New Mexico Press, 1982.
———. *They Called Them Greasers: Anglo attitudes toward Mexicans in Texas, 1821–1900.* Austin: University of Texas Press, 1983.
Denhardt, Robert M. *The Horse of the Americas.* Norman: University of Oklahoma Press, 1947. New ed., 1975.

Deuvall, Aurelia Flores, and Peggy A. Rodríguez, comps. *Our Family Heritage.* San Antonio: Graphic Arts, 1975.
De Ville, Winston. *Opelousas: The History of a French and Spanish Military Post in America, 1716–1803.* Cottonport, La.: Polyanthos, 1973.
Didear, Hedwig Krell. *A History of Karnes County and Old Helena.* Austin: San Felipe Press (Jenkins Publishing Co.), 1969.
Dobie, J. Frank. *The Longhorns.* Boston: Little, Brown and Co., 1941.
———. *The Mustangs.* Boston: Little, Brown and Co., 1952.
———. *A Vaquero of the Brush Country.* Dallas: Southwest Press, 1929.
Dolman, Wilson E. "Mission Cattle Rustling." *Texas Parks and Wildlife* 33, no. 3 (March, 1975).
Douglas, C. L. *Cattle Kings of Texas.* Dallas: Cecil Baugh, 1939.
Downs, Fane. "Governor Antonio Martínez and the Defense of Texas from Foreign Invasion." *Texas Military History* 7; no. 1 (Spring, 1968).
Dunn, William Edward. "Apache Relations in Texas, 1718–1750." Texas State Historical Association *Quarterly* 14, no. 3 (January, 1911).
Dusenberry, William H. *The Mexican Mesta: The Administration of Ranching in Colonial Mexico.* Urbana: University of Illinois Press, 1963.
Ericson, Carolyn Reeves. *Nacogdoches, Gateway to Texas: A Biographical Dictionary, 1773–1849.* Fort Worth: Arrow/Curtis Publishing Co., 1974.
Esparza Sánchez, Cuauhtémoc. *Historia de la Ganadería en Zacatecas, 1531– 1911.* Zacatecas: Departamento de Investigaciones Históricas de la Universidad Autónoma de Zacatecas, 1978.
Faulk, Odie B. *The Last Years of Spanish Texas, 1778–1821.* The Hague: Mouton and Co., 1964.
———. *The Leather Jacket Soldier: Spanish Military Equipment and Institutions of the Late 18th Century.* Pasadena, Calif.: Socio-Technical Publications, 1971.
———. "The Penetration of Foreigners and Foreign Ideas into Spanish East Texas." In Archie P. McDonald, ed. *Eastern Texas History.* Austin: Jenkins Publishing Co., 1978.
———. "Ranching in Spanish Texas." *Hispanic American Historical Review* 44 (May, 1965).
———. *A Successful Failure.* Austin: Steck-Vaughn Co., 1965.
Flannery, John Brendan. *The Irish Texans.* San Antonio: Institute of Texan Cultures, 1980.
Ford, Gus L., ed. *Texas Cattle Brands: A Catalog of the Texas Centennial Exposition Exhibit.* Dallas: Clyde C. Cockrell, 1936.
Freeman, James W., ed. *Prose and Poetry of the Live Stock Industry in the United States....* Denver, Colo., and Kansas City, Mo.: National Livestock Historical Association, 1905.
García, Clotilde P. *Padre José Nicolás Ballí and Padre Island.* Corpus Christi, Tex.: Grunwald Publishing Co., 1979.
Gard, Wayne. *The Chisholm Trail.* Norman: University of Oklahoma Press, 1954.

Garrett, Julia Kathryn. *Green Flag over Texas: A Story of the Last Years of Spain in Texas.* New York and Dallas: Cordova Press, 1939. Reprint. Austin: Pemberton Press (Jenkins Publishing Co.), 1969.
George, Eugene. *Historic Architecture of Texas: The Falcón Reservoir.* Austin: Texas Historical Commission, 1975.
Gilbert, Minnie. "Texas' First Cattle Queen." In Valley ByLiners. *Roots by the River: A Story of Texas Tropical Borderland.* Mission, Tex.: Border Kingdom Press, 1978. Anthology.
Goodwyn, Frank. *Life on the King Ranch.* New York: Thomas Y. Crowell Co., 1951.
Grimm, Agnes C. *Llanos Mestenas: Mustang Plains.* Waco, Tex.: Texian Press, 1968.
Guice, John D. W. "Cattle Raisers of the Old Southwest: A Reinterpretation." *Western Historical Quarterly* 8 (1977).
Habig, Fr. Marion A. *The Alamo Chain of Missions: A History of San Antonio's Five Old Missions.* Chicago: Franciscan Herald Press, 1968.
———. *The Alamo Mission: San Antonio de Valero, 1718–1793.* Chicago: Franciscan Herald Press, 1977.
Haggard, J. Villasana. "The Counter-Revolution of Bexar, 1811." *Southwestern Historical Quarterly* 43, no. 2 (October, 1939).
———. "The House of Barr and Davenport." *Southwestern Historical Quarterly* 49 (July, 1945).
———. "Neutral Ground between Louisiana and Texas." *Louisiana Historical Quarterly* 28, no. 4 (October, 1945).
Hale, E. E. "The Real Philip Nolan." Mississippi Historical Society *Publications* 4 (1901).
Haley, J. Evetts. *The Heraldry of the Range.* Canyon, Tex.: Panhandle-Plains Historical Society, 1949.
Hammett, H. B. J. *The Empresario: Don Martín de León.* Waco, Tex.: Texian Press, 1973.
———. *The Empresario: Don Martín de León (The Richest Man in Texas).* Kerrville, Tex.: Braswell Printing Co., 1971.
Hatcher, Mattie Austin. *The Opening of Texas to Foreign Settlement, 1801–1821.* Austin: University of Texas Press, 1927. Reprint. Philadelphia: Porcupine Press, 1976.
Holmes, Jack D. L. *Gayoso: The Life of a Spanish Governor in the Mississippi Valley, 1789–1799.* Baton Rouge: Louisiana State University Press, 1965. Reprint. Gloucester, Mass.: Peter Smith, 1968.
———. "Livestock in Spanish Natchez." *Journal of Mississippi History* 23 (1961).
Huber, Velma. "Spanish Land Grants." In *Bicentennial Minutes of Seguin-Guadalupe County, 1976.* Seguin, Tex.: Research Committee of the Seguin Bicentennial Commission, 1976.
Hudson, William R., Jr., et al. *Walker Ranch: An Archaeological Reconnaissance and Excavations in Northern Bexar County, Texas.* Office of the

State Archaeologist, report no. 26. Austin: Texas Historical Commission, 1974.
Huson, Hobart. *A New Approach to the Teaching of Texas History in Our Schools and Colleges*. Refugio, Tex.: Snooks Publications, Refugio Timely Remarks, [1971?].
———. *Refugio: A Comprehensive History of Refugio County from Aboriginal Times to 1953*. 2 vols. Woodsboro, Tex.: Rooke Foundation, 1953.
Ivey, James, and Anne Fox. *Archaeological Survey and Testing at Rancho de las Cabras, Wilson County, Texas*. Center for Archaeological Research, Archaeological Survey Report no. 104, University of Texas at San Antonio, 1981.
Jaeggli, J. T., Jr. *The Court House Story*. [Wilson County Historical Committee, 1971].
John, Elizabeth A. H. *Storms Brewed in Other Men's Worlds: The Confrontation of Indians, Spanish, and French in the Southwest, 1540–1795*. College Station: Texas A&M University Press, 1975.
Jordan, Terry C. *Trails to Texas: Southern Roots of Western Cattle Ranching*. Lincoln: University of Nebraska Press, 1981.
Kilgore, Dan. *Nueces County, Texas, 1750–1800: A Bicentennial Memoir* [Corpus Christi: Friends of the Corpus Christi Museum, 1976].
———. "Texas Cattle Origins." *Cattleman* 69, no. 8 (January, 1983).
King Ranch: 100 Years of Ranching, 1853–1953. Reprint from *Corpus Christi Caller-Times*, July 12, 1953.
Klein, Julius. *The Mesta: A Study in Spanish Economic History, 1273–1836*. Cambridge, Mass.: Harvard University Press, 1970.
Lea, Tom. *The King Ranch*. 2 vols. Boston: Little, Brown and Co., 1957.
Lott, Virgil N., and Mercurio Martínez. *Kingdom of Zapata*. San Antonio: Naylor Co., 1953.
MacLachlan, Colin M., and Jaime E. Rodríguez O. *The Forging of the Cosmic Race: A Reinterpretation of Colonial Mexico*. Berkeley: University of California Press, 1980.
McLean, Malcolm D. "Our Spanish Heritage in Texas." *Sobretiro de Humanitas* 17 (1976, Universidad de Nuevo León).
Martin, Robert S. "Maps of an Empresario: Austin's Contribution to the Cartography of Texas." *Southwestern Historical Quarterly* 85, no. 4 (April, 1982).
Mathes, W. Michael, ed. and comp. *Cattle Brands of Baja California Sur, 1809–1885*. Los Angeles: Dawson's Book Shop, 1978.
Meinig, D. W. *Imperial Texas: An Interpretive Essay in Cultural Geography*. Austin: University of Texas Press, 1969.
Moorhead, Max L. *The Presidio: Bastion of the Spanish Borderlands*. Norman: University of Oklahoma Press, 1975.
Mora, Jo. *Californios: The Saga of the Hard-Riding Vaqueros, America's First Cowboys*. Garden City: Doubleday & Co., 1949.

———. *Trail Dust and Saddle Leather.* New York: Charles Scribner's Sons, 1946.
Myres, Sandra L. *The Ranch in Spanish Texas, 1691–1800.* El Paso: Texas Western Press, 1969.
———. "The Spanish Cattle Kingdom in the Province of Texas." *Texana* 4 (1966).
Nance, Joseph Milton. *After San Jacinto: The Texas-Mexican Frontier, 1836–1841.* Austin: University of Texas Press, 1963.
———. *Attack and Counterattack: The Texas-Mexican Frontier, 1842.* Austin: University of Texas Press, 1964.
Nardini, Louis Rafael. *My Historic Natchitoches, Louisiana, and Its Environment.* Natchitoches, La.: Nardini Publishing Co., 1963.
Nueces County Historical Society, comp. *The History of Nueces County.* Austin: Jenkins Publishing Co., 1972.
Oberste, William H. *History of Refugio Mission.* Refugio, Tex.: Timely Remarks, 1942.
———. *Texas Irish Empresarios and Their Colonies.* Austin: Von Boeckmann–Jones, 1953.
O'Connor, Kathryn Stoner. *The Presidio La Bahía del Espíritu Santo de Zúñiga, 1721–1846.* Austin: Von Boeckmann–Jones, 1966.
O'Neil, Paul. *The Frontiersmen.* Alexandria, Va.: Time-Life Books, 1977.
Rice, Lee M., and Glenn R. Vernam. *They Saddled the West.* Cambridge, Mass.: Cornell Maritime Press, 1975.
Rincón Gallardo y Romero de Terreros, Carlos. *El Libro del Charro Mexicano.* Mexico City: Librería Porrúa, 1939. Reprint. 1977.
Rose, Victor. *The Texas Vendetta; or the Sutton-Taylor Feud.* New York: J. J. Little & Co., 1880. Reprint. Houston: Frontier Press of Texas, 1956.
———. *Victor Rose's History of Victoria County.* Edited by J. W. Petty, Jr. Laredo, Tex.: Daily Times Print, 1883. Reprint. Victoria, Tex.: Book Mart, 1961.
Rouse, John E. *The Criollo: Spanish Cattle in the Americas.* Norman: University of Oklahoma Press, 1977.
Salazar, Robert J., et al. *Asociación de Reclamantes v. the United Mexican States: Texas Land Grant Heirs Seek Justice.* [Denver, 1981?].
Santos, Richard C., ed. and trans. *Biographical Sketches, Letter from Columbia, Texas, December 27, 1836.* San Antonio: James W. Knight, Bexar County Clerk, 1966.
Scott, Florence Johnson. *Historical Heritage of the Lower Río Grande . . . , 1747–1848.* San Antonio: Naylor Co., 1937. Reprint. Waco, Tex.: Texian Press, 1966.
Serrera Contreras, Ramón María. *Guadalajara Ganadera: Estudio Regional Novohispano, 1760–1805.* Sevilla: Escuela de Estudios Hispano-Americanos, 1977.
Sibley, Marilyn McAdams. *Travelers in Texas, 1761–1860.* Austin: University of Texas Press, 1967.

Steiner, Stan. *Dark and Dashing Horsemen*. San Francisco: Harper and Row, 1981.
Strickland, Rex W. "Miller County, Arkansas Territory: The Frontier That Men Forgot." *Chronicles of Oklahoma* 18 (1940).
Taylor, Paul Schuster. *An American-Mexican Frontier: Nueces County, Texas*. Chapel Hill: University of North Carolina Press, 1934.
Taylor, Virginia H. *The Spanish Archives of the General Land Office of Texas*. Austin: Lone Star Press, 1955.
―――, comp. *Index to Spanish and Mexican Land Grants in Texas*. Austin: Lone Star Press, 1974.
Texas and the American Revolution. San Antonio: Institute of Texan Cultures, University of Texas at San Antonio, 1975.
Thompson, Jerry. *Sabers on the Rio Grande*. Austin: Presidial Press, 1974.
Thonhoff, Robert H. "The First Ranch in Texas." West Texas Historical Association *Yearbook* 40 (October, 1964).
―――. *The Texas Connection with the American Revolution*. Burnet, Tex.: Eakin Press, 1981.
Time-Life Books, Editors of. *The Spanish West*. New York: Time-Life Books, 1976.
Timmerman, Wanda. "Wings over Navarro Territory." In *Bicentennial Minutes of Seguin–Guadalupe County, 1976*. Seguin, Tex.: Research Committee of the Seguin Bicentennial Commission, 1976.
Tjarks, Alicia V. "Comparative Demographic Analysis of Texas, 1777–1793." *Southwestern Historical Quarterly* 77 (January, 1974).
Vernam, Glenn R. *Man on Horseback*. New York: Harper and Row, 1964. Reprint. Lincoln: University of Nebraska Press, Bison Books, 1972.
Ward, Hortense W. *Cattlebrands and Cowhides*. Dallas: Story Book Press, 1953.
Warren, Harris Gaylord. *The Sword Was Their Passport: A History of American Filibustering in the Mexican Revolution*. Baton Rouge: Louisiana State University Press, 1943.
Webb, Walter Prescott. *The Great Plains*. New York: Grosset & Dunlap, 1931.
―――, and H. Bailey Carroll, eds. *The Handbook of Texas*. 2 vols. Austin: Texas State Historical Association, 1952.
Weber, David J., ed. *Foreigners in Their Native Land: Historical Roots of the Mexican Americans*. Albuquerque: University of New Mexico Press, 1973.
Weddle, Robert S., and Robert H. Thonhoff. *Drama and Conflict: The Texas Saga of 1776*. Austin: Madrona Press, 1976.
Weinert, Willie Mae. *An Authentic History of Guadalupe County*. 1951. Reprint. Seguin, Tex.: Seguin Conservation Society and the Seguin Enterprise, 1976.
Wellman, Paul I. *The Trampling Herd: The Story of the Cattle Range in America*. 1951. Reprint. New York: Cooper Square Publishers, 1974.
Whitaker, Arthur Preston. *The Mississippi Question, 1795–1803: A Study in*

Trade, Politics and Diplomacy. New York: American Historical Association, 1934. Reprint. Gloucester, Mass.: Peter Smith, 1962.

———. *The Spanish-American Frontier, 1783–1795: The Westward Movement and the Spanish Retreat in the Mississippi Valley.* Boston, 1927. Reprint. Lincoln: University of Nebraska Press, Bison Books, 1969.

White, Gifford. *James Taylor White of Virginia and Some of His Descendants into Texas.* Austin: Privately published, 1982.

Wilkinson, J. B. *Laredo and the Rio Grande Frontier.* Austin: Jenkins Publishing Co., 1975.

Williams, J. W. *Old Texas Trails.* Edited and compiled by Kenneth F. Neighbors. Burnet, Tex.: Eakin Press, 1979.

Wooten, Dudley G. *A Comprehensive History of Texas, 1685 to 1897.* 2 vols. Dallas: W. G. Scarff, 1898.

Wortham, Louis J. *A History of Texas from Wilderness to Commonwealth.* 5 vols. Fort Worth: Gammel, 1924.

INDEX

Acadians, stock raising by, 425–36
Acevedo, Manuel de, 517, 551–52
Acosta, Andrés, 503
Acosta, Juan de, 493, 496
Adaes, Misión San Miguel de Linares de los (Tex.), 97, 117n, 335
Adaes, Presidio de Nuestra Señora del Pilar de los (Tex.), 11, 12, 52, 73, 74, 97, 98, 107, 112–23, 152, 182–85, 190, 195, 406–407, 427, 440, 463, 494–95, 497–503, 516, 556
Agreda, José Guadalupe de, 207n
Agreda, María de Jesús de, 55
Agua Verde, Presidio de (Coahuila), 198, 216n, 263, 266, 303, 308, 439
Aguayo, Marqués de (governor of Texas), 11, 12, 13n, 15, 55
Aguayo, Marquesado de, 160, 361
Águila, Arroyo del, 40, 93, 238, 511
Aguilar, Fr. Juan José, 414–16
Aguilar, Joseph Marcos de, 224n
Aguilar, Manuela de, 256, 412
Aguirre, Matías, 14
Ahlborn, Richard E., 82
Aís, Misión de Nuestra Señora de los Dolores de los (Tex.), 96, 97, 114, 115, 118, 182–83, 451, 501. *See also* San Augustine
Alamo, Battle of the, 63n, 464, 599, 616
Alamo, Hacienda del, 24
Alamo de Parras, Villa de (Coahuila), 564
Alamos, Arroyo de los, 286
Alange, Conde del Campo de, 371
Alarcón, Martín de, 11, 13, 55, 61, 63, 95
Alazán, Battle of, 538, 543

alcabala, 121, 363
alcaldes, 98, 132; duties of, 17, 22, 140, 156–57, 179, 188, 197, 217, 225–27, 246, 272, 406, 421–22, 435, 471, 490, 505, 512, 550, 578, 580–81, 597–98; selection of, 496. *See also ayuntamiento*; cabildo
Aldasoro, Ambrosio, 560
Alderete, José de Jesús, 471, 577
Alderete, Vicente de, 27–29
Aldrete, José, 489
Aldrete, José Miguel, 581
Alegre, Fr. José Ignacio María, 88
Almaráz, Félix D., Jr., 534, 545
Almazán, Juan Antonio Pérez de. *See* Pérez de Almazán, Juan Antonio
Almonte, Juan, 592–93
Alonzo, Arroyo de, 95, 165, 168–69, 219, 330
Alsop, Anna, 501
Álvarez Toledo, José. *See* Toledo, José Álvarez
Álvarez Travieso. *See* entries under Travieso
Amador, Vicente, 437n
Amangual, Francisco, 305–308, 471
Amoladeras, Rancho de las (on Cíbolo), 93, 385. *See also* Guerra, Miguel; Quiñones, Josefa
Amoladeras, Rancho de las (near Nacogdoches), 466, 493, 498–99. *See also* Gil Ybarbo, José Ignacio
Amondarain, Juan Martín de, 349n, 357, 359, 372–75, 382
Angelina County, 475–76, 495

Angelina River, 451, 476, 494–96, 502
Ánimas, Arroyo de las, 237, 268
Apaches, Lipan: and Comanches, 16, 155; depredations of, 15, 18, 20, 31, 34, 35, 56, 61, 87, 88, 107, 133–34, 146, 157, 186, 194, 208n, 221, 244, 246–48, 293–94, 342, 358–59, 378, 412, 437, 543, 547–51; peace treaty with, 21, 48, 57, 66; policy toward, 173, 182, 369–71, 379, 466n. *See also* Indians
Apaches, Mescalero, 346, 369
Apaches, Rancho de (los), 520
Aranda, Pedro de, 534n
Aránzazu, Cayo de, 359, 416
Arbitrios, Plan de, 578–80
Arciniega, Miguel, 544n, 597
Areche, José Antonio de, 122
Arenoso, Arroyo del, 104, 137–38
Arenoso, Juntas del, 137
Arizpe, Sonora, 211, 259, 297
Armas, Antonia de, 414
Arocha, Anna María de, 62n, 72, 540
Arocha, Damián de, 503
Arocha, Estanislao de, 330n, 349n
Arocha, Félix de, 491
Arocha, Fernando de, 289
Arocha, Francisco de (father), 69, 71, 117n
Arocha, Francisco de, 198, 240, 241n, 349, 372–73, 515, 541n, 543
Arocha, José de, 138
Arocha, José Félix de, 541
Arocha, José Ignacio de (son of Simón), 514–15, 518–19
Arocha, José Ignacio de (grandson of Simón), 62n, 541
Arocha, Juan de, 72, 105n, 237–39, 289, 309, 330n, 349n, 414, 491
Arocha, Julián de, 198, 245n, 309, 312, 373–74, 387n
Arocha, Manuel de, 271n, 309, 312, 330n, 387n, 397n, 403n, 406
Arocha, Rev. José Clemente de, 207n, 287n, 528
Arocha, Simón de: land grant of, 71, 237–39; as provincial official, 71, 90n, 91, 102, 116, 149n, 164, 289, 323, 327–30, 371–75, 406–407; as rancher, 71–72, 129n, 139, 143–44, 146, 179, 198, 207n, 219, 226–28, 230, 245n, 263, 271, 286, 287n, 301, 330, 342, 359–60, 373–75, 382, 385, 414, 540. *See also* San Rafael de Pataguiya, Rancho de
Arocha, Tomás de, 515, 525, 541, 555
Arredondo, José Joaquín, 496, 527n, 535–42, 546, 551, 558–61, 567, 599; livestock regulations of, 544, 568–70
Arriola, Antonio, 499
Arriola, Marcelino, 498–99
Arriola, María Josefa, 499
Ashworth, Aaron, 607
Ashworth, William, 607
Atascosa County, 325, 567, 614–15
Atascosa River, 94, 511, 615
Atascoso, Rancho del, 47, 66, 91, 94, 511; and José Antonio Navarro, 413, 539n; and Mission San José, 40. *See also* San José y San Miguel de Aguayo, Misión de
Atascosito, Rancho del (Orcoquisac), 97, 484, 489, 563, 568
Attakapas Post (La.), 120, 122, 404, 426–33, 435–36, 484, 537. *See also* Saint Martinville
Attoyac, Rancho de, 182–83, 394, 476, 479–80, 500. *See also* Gil Ybarbo, Antonio
Attoyac River, 96, 183, 466, 476n, 477, 493, 498–500
Austin, Moses, 556
Austin, Stephen F., 95n, 496, 523, 539n, 556–57, 573–74, 582–85, 588, 590, 595
Avila, Blás de, 138
Avoyelles Post (La.), 430
ayuntamiento, 20, 235, 362, 382, 397, 565, 568, 597; Bahía, 578, 581; Béxar, 224, 367, 371–75, 404, 419–22, 547, 555–56, 560–61, 579–80, 592. *See also* cabildo
Azanza, Miguel José de, 455
Azlor y Virto de Vera, José Ramón de. *See* Aguayo, Marqués de

Bagdad (Tamaulipas), 613
Babia, La. *See* San Antonio Bucareli de la Babia, Presidio de (Coahuila)
Bahía, La. *See* Espíritu Santo de Zúñiga,

Index

Misión de Nuestra Señora del; La Bahía del Espíritu Santo, Presidio de Nuestra Señora de Loreto de; La Bahía Road
Baján, Wells of, 533
Ballí, José María, 446–47
Ballí, José María "Chico," 446–47
Ballí, Juan José, 446–47
Ballí, Juan José (nephew), 447
Ballí, Padre Nicolás, 447
Balmaceda, José María, 413
Baño, Rancho del, 97
barbed wire, 615
Barcenas, José, 531
Barker, Samuel, 69
Barr, William, 451–52, 456, 472–73, 476, 482, 489, 491, 493–96, 502, 504, 518
Barrancas, Corral de las, 331
Barranco Blanco, Rancho del, 449
Barrera, Gertrudis, 520
Barrera, Juan, 177n, 261–62, 305, 312, 355–56, 359, 364, 402–403, 408n, 413, 416
Barrera, Manuel, 403, 413, 460, 491, 512–13, 515, 528, 531, 540n, 541, 576
Barrio Junco y Espriella, Pedro del, 67
Barrios y Jáuregui, Jacinto de, 35, 47, 101, 118–20
Bastrop, Barón Felipe Enrique Neri de, 459, 474, 544n, 565
Baton Rouge, La., 430
Bayou Pierre (La.), 502, 516–18, 537, 556, 576
Bega, José Luis de la, 491–503, 517
Berbán, Joseph, 457, 493, 501
Berbán, Manuel, 372n
Berlandier, Jean Louis, 62, 96n, 466n, 548, 593
Bermúdez y de Soto, Antonio Manuel, 194. *See also* St. Denis, Louis Juchereau de; Soto, Marcelo de
Bethencourt, María Robaina de, 65, 66n, 93, 164n, 177, 332
Béxar. *See* San Antonio de Béxar, Presidio de; San Fernando de Béxar, Villa de
Bexar County, 71n, 88n, 325, 608, 614–15
Bidais, 467n, 472

Bidias Creek, 495
bison: as gift to king, 246–47, 342, 467; as natural resource, 17, 96, 129, 336, 339, 355, 397–98, 429, 470, 544, 568
Blake, Robert B., 394, 441, 495
Blanc, Antonio le, 236–37, 239, 312, 354, 412n
Blanc, Louis Césaire de, 118, 119, 236
Blanc, Louis Charles de, 236, 315, 389–92
Blanc, Louis Pierre Villenfre de, 236
Blanco, Arroyo (Nolan River), 459
Blanco, José, 465–66n
Block, W. T., 607
Boden, Juan, 493, 501
Bolton, Herbert E., 120, 593
Bonavía, Bernardo, 507–11, 515, 537n
Bontet, Hilario, 429
Boone, Daniel, 587
Boone, Daniel (nephew), 539, 587
Borregas, Arroyo de las, 493, 501–502, 566
Borregas, Paso de las, 88
Borrego, Francisco (Vásquez?), 541n
Borrego, José (Vásquez?), 489
Botija, Rancho de la, 493, 496–97
Bourgeois de Orvanne, Alexander Henry, 478
Branciforte, Marqués de, 450
branding: abuses of, 135–36, 146, 265–66, 268–69, 275, 305–309; described, 43, 142–43, 144–46, 152, 185–87, 223, 281, 306, 368, 472; regulations for, 121–22, 156, 160, 162, 179, 199–201, 218–19, 229–31, 244–46, 252–53, 257–59, 273–74, 276–77, 302, 311, 322–31, 382, 386–88, 396, 401, 428, 430, 433–35, 511–14, 531, 552, 562–68, 597. *See also* ear marks; marks; roundups; tallies
Brazos River, 75, 96, 191, 456, 459, 467, 585
Brazos Santiago Pass, 447
Brownsville, Tex., 592, 607–608
Bryan, James, 573–74
Bucareli, Pueblo de la Nuestra Señora del Pilar de (Tex.), 192, 251, 383; abandonment of, 181, 183; colony at, 129, 177, 184; and contraband, 116, 121,

123; founding of, 115; abandonment of, 181, 183. *See also* Gil Ybarbo, Antonio
Bucareli y Ursúa, Antonio María de, 110, 122, 123, 125, 135, 242, 367
Bucheli, Lic. José M., 288
Bueno, Francisco, 397
Bueno, Juan José, 323, 342
Buentello, Tomás, 520
Buigas, Pedro, 458
Buquor, P. L., 478
Burnet, David G., 599
Bustamante, Antonio, 335
Bustillos, Domingo, 576
Bustillos, Francisco Xavier, 565n
butcher shop: at Béxar, 488–89, 515–16; at New Orleans, 429, 431, 435

Cabello y Robles, Domingo, 135, 159, 171, 185, 321–25, 332, 371, 387, 399, 405, 407, 418, 421; disputes of, with cattlemen, 174–76, 189–90, 205–207, 215, 231–35, 238, 249–50, 254–57, 261–70, 274–76, 280–89, 302–309, 317–19, 334–46, 353–55, 365–69, 378; Indian policy of, 173–74, 181–82, 212–14, 223, 239, 246–47, 257, 279, 315–16; regulations of, 179–80, 187–88, 197–201, 204, 207–209, 218–19, 221, 226–30, 237, 240, 244–45, 252–54, 257–58, 270–74, 277, 309–12, 396, 404
cabildo, 20, 73, 186, 254, 348–49, 406, 487, 522, 578, 580–82; composition of, at Béxar, 69, 71, 150, 167, 233, 310, 372–75, 525, 529; decisions of, at Béxar, 184–85, 322–32, 385–88, 401, 417–23, 471, 545, 562–67, 582; New Orleans, 429, 431, 435; protests of, at Béxar, 66, 70, 101–103, 107–10, 152, 363–64, 366–69, 394, 397–99. *See also* ayuntamiento
Cabras, Rancho de las, 45, 48, 49, 62, 90, 105, 113, 148, 216, 219, 231, 325, 511, 567; and Barrera family, 413; and Calvillo family, 413–14; Indian depredations at, 104, 224, 550; and Mission Espada, 41. *See also* Espada, Misión de San Francisco de; missions

Cacaste, Arroyo del, 138
Caddos, 21, 493
Cadena, Antonio, 216
Cádiz, Spain, 121, 122, 247, 509
Calaveras, Arroyo de las, 72, 91, 93, 96n, 218, 385, 566
Calcasieu Parish (La.), 607
California, 44, 82, 238n, 242–43, 301, 611–12
Calvillo, Ana María del Carmen, 413–14
Calvillo, Ignacio, 164n, 526, 550; land claims of, 413–14, 515; as rancher, 72, 163, 385; and wild cattle, 207n, 230, 309, 373, 387n
Camargo, Villa de (Nuevo Santander), 23, 24, 98, 133, 443–44, 504
Cameron, John, 520
Cañada de la Concordia, 330
Cañada del Quatralbo, 227, 249
Cañada Verde, 137, 138
Canary Islanders. *See* Isleños
Candelaría, Encinal de la, 96n, 385, 531
Capitán, Rancho del, 89, 90. *See also* Ramírez de la Piscina, Manuel
Capitaneño, Rancho del, 62
Capote, El: hills of, 58–60, 89, 170, 184, 219, 233, 475, 539n; proposed settlement named, 478
Cárdenas, José de, 615
Cárdenas, Fr. José Luis Mariano do, 374; at Espíritu Santo, 247–48, 267, 281, 296, 408, 412; and illegal roundups, 404; and land claims, 326, 328; at San Juan Capistrano, 90; and wild cattle, 267–70, 323, 359, 381
Cárdenas, Rev. Juan Ygnacio de, 90
Carlos IV, 83, 377
Carlos III, 102, 241, 246–47, 291, 299, 377
Carnestolendas, Rancho de las, 444
Caro, José, 498
Caro, Tex., 498
Carondelet, François Louis Hector, Barón de, 431–35, 453–55
Carrizo, Arroyo del, 95n, 137, 140, 170
Carrizo, Rancho del, 499. *See also* Gil Ybarbo, Martín
Carrizo, Rancho del, 519. *See also* Vásquez, Manuel

Index 681

Carruthers, James, 590
Carvajal, Bernabé: as alcalde, 87; and burning of ranch, 65, 94; lands of, 41, 58–60, 65, 93, 141, 144, 169, 326, 328, 332
Carvajal, Cristóbal, 54
Carvajal, José Antonio, 515, 554
Carvajal, Manuel, 63
Carvajal, Mateo, 54
Carvajal, Nicolás, 520
Carvajal y de la Cueva, Luis, 77
Casa Blanca, Rancho de la (of Erasmo Seguín), 62n
Casa Blanca, Rancho de la (of Garza Montemayor), 449, 550
Casafuerte, Juan de Acuña, Marqués de, 15
Casanova, Francisco, 133
Casanova, Guillermo, 127n, 165
Casanova, José Manuel, 226n, 489
Casa Real (government building), 107, 289, 315, 394. *See also* San Antonio de Béxar, Presidio de
Cassiano, José, 238n, 478, 562n
Castañeda, Juan de, 490n, 554, 583n
Castelo, Domingo, 413, 510n
Casteñas, Rancho de las, 447
Castillón, Onofre, 384
Castro, José Pereira de, 362–63
Castro, Marcos de, 128n, 136–37, 140, 144, 164n, 179n, 207n, 226n, 233, 245n, 323
Castro, Ramón de, 392–94
Castroville, Tex., 413
Cavazos, José Narciso, 448, 602
Cazorla, Luis, 162, 266–70, 304, 326, 333, 356–59, 378
Cedar, James, 493, 501–502
Céliz, Fr. Francisco, 11, 55
Cerda, Nepomuceno de la, 493–94. *See also* San Antonio, Rancho de; Zerda
Cervantes, Rafael, 95
Chabot, Frederick C., 53, 63, 73n, 407, 412, 467, 538, 540
Chacón, Arroyo de, 581
Chalán, Paso del (on Sabine), 501
Chambers, Henry E., 426
Champ d'Asile, 554
Chapman Ranch, 98
Chavana, Ramón, 497

Chayopines, Arroyo de los, 40, 92
Chayopines, Rancho de los, 148, 219, 230, 249, 310, 385, 413, 511, 531, 548, 566–67; Francisco Flores and, 91n; location of, 91–93. *See also* Peña, Ignacio de la
Chevalier, François, 77, 78n
Chichi, Rancho, 493, 502
Chiflónes, Paso de los (on Guadalupe), 223
Chihuahua City, 175, 454, 528, 542, 571; Croix in, 259; Flores in, 284, 299n, 368, 400; headquarters at, 160, 259; Menchaca in, 533, 534; Nolan's men in, 533, 534
Chiquihuitillo, Arroyo de, 577
Chirino, José Antonio, 493, 499–500, 517
Choctaws, 466, 499
Chonca, Cristóbal, 493, 501–502
Cíbolo, Arroyo del, 16, 38–40, 59–73, 88, 93, 94, 105, 107–12, 128, 137–38, 141, 144–46, 148, 153, 165, 168–70, 179–80, 184, 208, 218–19, 235, 238, 240, 286, 305, 413n, 510–11, 514, 548, 566
Cíbolo, Fuerte de Santa Cruz del (Tex.), 133, 137, 145, 148, 152, 184, 200, 236n, 563; abandoned, 235; Adaesaños at, 115; built, 109–10; Indians and, 209, 214, 223; Lt. Menchaca at, 189, 195n; soldiers at, 149n, 181, 203, 212; supplying of, 231–33
Ciprián, Fr. Ignacio Antonio, 35
Cisneros, José, 82
Ciudad Acuña, Coahuila, 263n
Civil War (American), 3, 75, 238n, 596, 609, 614
Clareño, Alías, 549
Clark, Daniel, 435
Cleto, Arroyo del (Ecleto Creek), 137, 139, 145, 332; Indians along, 153, 187; and La Bahía, 95; and land claims, 41, 58, 59, 60, 141, 144, 166, 234; roundups near, 165, 168, 206, 218, 227, 271, 330, 566
Clouet, Alejandro, Cabellero de, 122, 430
Coahuila, Province of, 10, 12, 23, 25, 98, 106, 160, 251, 261, 335–36n, 392,

468, 485, 507; Indian depredations in, 369, 437–39, 547, 551; livestock trade with, 130–33, 138–39, 149, 205–207, 212, 215–17, 221, 226–27, 252, 255, 263–68, 304–305, 312, 314, 371, 402–403, 581. *See also* Monclova, Villa de Santiago de la; Saltillo; San Juan Bautista del Río Grande, Presidio de
Collot, Victor, 436
Colorado, Arroyo, 448
Colorado River, 96, 191, 196, 209, 309, 355, 437, 585
Comanches: and Apaches, 16, 35; depredations of, 21, 87, 107, 125, 145, 174, 182, 186, 200, 209–14, 219, 223–25, 229, 235, 257, 294, 323, 437, 439, 532, 544, 547–51, 596; peace with, 155, 173, 214, 279, 296, 298, 311, 315, 405, 467n, 482n, 490, 575–76. *See also* Nations of the North
Comisión Pesquisidora, report of, 613–14
Comitas, Rancho de las, 550
Concepción, Misión de Nuestra Señora de la Purísima (Tex.): founding of, 33; land grant of, 38–40, 70, 101–102, 144–45, 153, 239, 510; ranching at, 36, 41–44, 46, 94, 104–106, 113, 127, 143, 145, 177, 180, 219, 231, 290, 323–26, 331, 349–53, 382n; secularization of, 411–13n, 419, 533. *See also* missions; Paistle, Rancho del
Concepción de Carricitos, Rancho de la, 447
consulado, 314, 509
Cook, Jesse, 456, 458, 464
Cordero y Bustamante, Antonio, 438–39, 454, 477, 485–90, 500, 505–507, 525, 551, 562, 596
Córdova, Cristóbal de, 209, 393, 404, 440n, 453, 464, 502
Córdova, Joaquín de, 183, 196, 476–77, 497
Córdova, José de, 477, 493, 497
Córdova, Juan Joseph de, 98
Córdova, Miguel de, 117n
Córdova Rebellion, 441, 475, 478, 498, 571
Cornide y Saavedra, Diego Antonio, 101–103

Corpus Christi, Tex., 98
Corralitos, Rancho de los, 87, 93, 94; and Bernabé Carvajal, 58, 59; and Mission Espíritu Santo, 60, 141, 169
Corralitos, Rancho de los (of Vásquez Borregos), 24
Corríquez (Enríquez?), Diego Irineo, 385, 387n, 408n
Cortés, Juan, 392, 402, 407, 417, 438, 441, 471, 477, 494, 499, 503
Cortina, Juan Nepomuceno, 607–608
Cortina, Xavier, 133
Costales, Paso de, 105
Cotulla, Tex., 133
Courbiere, Andrés, 246, 515
Courbiere, Juan, 565n
Croix, Carlos Francisco, Marqués de, 107, 111n, 129
Croix, Teodoro de: cattle law of, 6, 155–60, 164–66, 170, 174–76, 179–80, 197, 204, 219, 228, 241–44, 252–56, 266–70, 291–95, 336–40, 365, 377, 386–88, 395, 598; as commandant general, 68, 72, 129, 140, 147–55, 161, 163, 183–84, 190–94, 207–208, 211–14, 224, 235, 239, 250–52, 266, 276–77, 313–14, 367–68, 406–407, 491, 507–508; as viceroy of Peru, 252, 259, 284
Crow, Miguel, 501
Cruz, Ermengildo de la, 520
Cruz, José Antonio de la, 493, 496
Cruz, Pedro, 489
Cuatitlán, Mex., 14
Cuchillo, Arroyo del, 95, 137, 140, 227, 232, 234, 577
Cuero, Tex., 94n, 95n
Cuervo, Arroyo del, 96
Curillo, Arroyo del, 89, 578
Curbelo, José Antonio, 164n, 318, 541n; as alcalde, 188; as cattle exporter, 227, 236–37, 312; as lieutenant governor, 202, 206, 207; in Spain, 246–47, 248, 467
Curbelo, Juan, 69
Curbelo, Juan José, 467
Curbelo, Mariana, 207n, 248–49
Cuturie, Louise, 475
Czestochowa, Tex., 61

Index 683

Dale, Edward Everett, 612
Davenport, Samuel, 451–52, 472, 476, 491, 494–95, 502, 518, 530, 543, 571
Delgado, Amador, 138, 143, 264, 387n, 397n
Delgado, Antonio, 535, 537
Delgado, Clemente, 226n, 245n, 397, 541n
Delgado, Francisco, 66, 70n, 414
Delgado, Francisco (of Nuevo Santander), 519
Delgado, Gavino, 349n, 387n, 414, 511–14, 518, 526–30, 531
Delgado, Jacinto, 129n, 139, 164n, 165
Delgado, José Miguel, 519
Delgado, Joseph Martín, 127n
Delgado, Leonor, 140, 186, 238, 385, 408n
Delgado, Manuel, 72, 90n, 414, 577; as alcalde, 246; on cabildo, 402n; ranch of, 385; as rebel, 540–41; as *regidor*, 373; and wild cattle, 129n, 143, 207n, 312, 330n, 362, 397
Delgado, Mariano, 323, 330n
Denis, Dionisio (St.?), 482, 484
Derbón, Manuel, 437n
De Witt County, 325, 330, 615
Días, José, 310
Días del Castillo, Pedro, 330n
Diezmero, Rancho del, 449, 549
Dill, Delilah, 496
Dill, James, 491, 496
Dimitt, Philip, 598
Dimmit County, 133
Dobie, J. Frank, 3, 10, 197n, 592–93, 597n, 610, 615
Dole, Pedro, 440
Dolores, Grito de, 523–30
Dolores, Hacienda de, 542, 549; founding of, 23, 24, 443
Dolores Crossing (on Medina), 568–69
Dolores y Viana, Fr. Mariano Francisco de los, 29, 35, 36, 45, 66, 71, 99–101, 103, 105, 295
Dolores Viejo, Rancho de los, 62
Domínguez, Cristóbal, 540–41
Donna, Tex., 446
D'Ortolant, Bernardo, 475, 493, 495–96, 517
Douglass, Tex., 495

Drake, Sir Francis, 603
drought, 145, 301, 503; and Texas ranching, 30, 127, 152, 275, 346, 506
Dryden, William G., 605
Dubal, Francisco, 14, 15
Durán, José Luis, 489
Durán, Onesimo (*intendente*), 468–69
Durán, Toribio, 226n, 397, 540n
Durasno, Arroyo del, 268
Durazno, Rancho del, 476
Durst, John, 495–96
Durst, Joseph, 496

Eagle Pass, Tex., 613
ear marks (*señales*), 9, 47, 163, 233, 267, 306, 491. *See also* branding; *fierros*
Eca y Músquiz, Blás María de, 266–70, 302, 304, 317
Eca y Músquiz, José Antonio de, 268
Echavarri, Francisco Antonio de, 60n
Echeagaray, José María, 580
Edwards, Haden, 498, 575n. *See also* Fredonian Rebellion
Elguezábal, Juan Bautista, 438, 450, 459–60, 464–74, 479–85
Elizondo, Ignacio, 533, 538, 541
Encinas, Hacienda de las, 542
Enríquez, Juan Manuel, 541n
Erskine, Michael, 539n
Escamilla, Juan de, 132
Escandón, José de (first Conde de Sierra Gorda), 23–27, 30, 31, 98, 443–44
Escandón, Manuel de (second Conde de Sierra Gorda), 394–95, 406–407
Escobar, Fr. Joseph, 162, 179, 197, 205, 243–44
Escondida, Arroyo de la, 38, 89, 90, 91, 93, 126, 208n, 577
Espada, Misión de San Francisco de la (Tex.): founding of, 33; land grant of, 41, 101, 239, 332, 511; ranching at, 21, 36, 44–46, 48–49, 104–106, 113, 165, 219, 227–28, 231, 257, 323–25, 349–53, 359, 379n; secularization of, 411, 413–14, 419. *See also* Cabras, Rancho de las; missions
Espadas, Manuel de, 378–84, 438
Espanta Perros, Arroyo de, 38, 91, 105, 385
Esparza, Pedro José, 499

Espíritu Santo de Zúñiga, Misión de Nuestra Señora del (Tex.): disputed pasture of, 60n, 126–28, 136–37, 141, 144, 153, 162–63, 177–80, 199–201, 240, 323–33, 381; Indian damage to, 66, 200, 209–11, 247–48, 293, 296, 546; land grant of, 41, 58–60, 164n, 326–28; ranching at, 24, 34, 36, 37, 47, 93, 95, 192, 197–98, 203–206, 208, 219, 225–26, 236–37, 243–44, 248, 264, 266–70, 281, 291–94, 300, 302, 350–53, 414–17, 425, 450, 484, 546, 548, 591; rustling at, 136–37, 144–46, 165–70, 174, 249, 357–58, 374, 404, 407, 582. *See also* La Bahía del Espíritu Santo, Presidio de Nuestra Señora de Loreto de; missions; Rosario, Misión de Nuestra Señora del
Estrada, Francisco Joseph de, 67
Estrada, María Concepción de, 263, 289, 477
Evia, José, 416

Fagan, John (son), 520
Fagan, Nicholas (father), 520
Falcón Mariano, Fr. Josef Agustín, 283
Fannin, James Walker, 520
Farías, Francisco, 515, 565n
Farías, Gregorio, 449
Farías, José Antonio, 554
Farías, Juan José, 408
Ferdinand VII, 528, 544
Feria, Rancho de la, 446
Fernández, Bartolomé, 447
Fernández, Bernardo, 438
Fernández, Eugenio, 203–205, 447
Fernández de Jáuregui y Urrutia, Joseph Antonio, 18–20
Fernández de Santa Ana, Fr. Benito, 21
Fernández Tejeiro, Vicente, 459–60
fierros, 45, 46, 67, 306, 457, 548, 589–90, 614, 617. *See also* branding
Flores, Cleta, 498
Flores, Eugenio, 544n
Flores, Gerónimo, 105n, 210n
Flores, Gil, 183, 498
Flores, Francisco Antonio, 167
Flores, Ignacio, 576–77
Flores, José, 493, 498–99, 517
Flores, José Miguel, 399

Flores, Manuel Antonio, 365, 379, 381
Flores, Manuel Ignacio, 361n
Flores, María Josefa de, 133–34, 179n
Flores, Martín, 70n
Flores, Pablo Luciano, 372n
Flores, Santiago, 482
Flores, Teresa, 207n
Flores, Thadeo, 29n
Flores, Vital, 499, 538
Flores de Abrego, Francisco, 68, 178
Flores de Abrego, Gertrudis, 68
Flores de Abrego, Josefa, 69
Flores de Abrego, José María, 68
Flores de Abrego, Joseph Antonio, 68, 490, 515, 565n, 576
Flores de Abrego, Joseph Joaquín, 220, 224n, 403; arrest of, 138, 167; on Cabello, 342; land of, 164n; and mission cattle, 138, 177–79, 300; as *procurador general*, 404; and roundups, 245n, 323, 330n, 387n
Flores de Abrego, Manuel, 615–16
Flores de Abrego y Valdés, Felipe, 208, 268, 312, 330n, 387n, 417
Flores de Abrego y Valdés, Francisco (brother of Juan José, the elder), 56n, 178n, 227; arrest of, 141, 167; as cattleman, 68, 129n; in disputes, 248, 372n; and Indians, 224n; land of, 91n, 164n; and roundups, 140, 225–26, 330n; versus missions, 137, 141, 167, 169–70, 178n
Flores de Abrego y Valdés, Francisco (grandson of Juan José), 91, 515, 557, 565n, 576
Flores de Abrego y Valdés, Gaspar, 257, 582
Flores de Abrego y Valdés, Joaquín, 178n, 186, 362
Flores de Abrego y Valdés, José Francisco, 179n, 186
Flores de Abrego y Valdés, José Ignacio, 399
Flores de Abrego y Valdés, Juan José (father): death of, 185–88; as *diezmero*, 67; as rancher, 60, 65, 68, 87, 91, 105, 128n, 137–47, 150, 154, 161, 164n, 165–69, 174, 177n, 178n, 205, 208, 241, 318, 330, 332, 400
Flores de Abrego y Valdés, Juan José (son): death of, 412; as rancher, 186,

205–207, 220, 226–27, 244, 245n, 256, 262–63, 268, 312; as stockmen's advocate, 262, 284–86, 296, 298, 299n, 317, 318, 323, 328–30, 332, 334–44, 349n, 362, 367–69, 400. *See also* San Fernando Memorial of 1787
Flores de Abrego y Valdés, Pedro, 186, 349n, 364, 399–401
Flores de Abrego y Valdés, Vizente, 91n, 271, 318; arrest of, 167; in disputes, 232, 248–49, 372n, 532; as exporter, 312; and roundups, 164, 227–28, 245, 330n, 387n; and taxes, 318, 356, 363
Flores Galán, Francisco, 196, 205, 330n
Flores Rancho, 615–16
Floresville, Tex., 40, 41, 64n, 413, 567; name of, 68, 69
Flores y Valdés, Manuel, 224n
Flores y Valdés, Nicolás, 15, 68
Forstall, Nicolás, 428n, 429
Fortiere, Juan Bautista, 459
Foucher, José, 209
Fowler, John, 574
Franquis de Lugo, Carlos, 17–20, 61, 63
Fredonian Rebellion, 441, 498, 575n
Freeman-Custis Expedition, 506
Fuente, Manuel de la, 90n
Fuentes, Ramón de la, 402n
Fuentes, Rev. Pedro, 261, 310, 369
Fulcher Creek, 330

Gaines, James, 571
Galán, Francisco, 402n
Galán, Luis, 528n, 545, 565n
Galindo Navarro, Pedro (*asesor*), 104n, 123, 152–53, 161–63, 272, 481–82; opinions of, 175–76, 180, 195, 241–44, 250–52, 253–56, 259–60, 266, 275, 285–86, 295, 297–300, 302, 310, 344–45, 369, 415, 417, 420. *See also* livestock taxes
Galván, Juan, 493
Galván, Manuel, 268
Gálvez, Bernardo de, 190, 192–94, 197–98, 202, 211, 220–21, 237, 280, 289, 291, 301, 365, 369, 388, 426, 429, 481, 495, 502, 575
Gálvez, José de, 110n, 123, 190, 194, 251–52, 313–14, 388
Gálvez, Matías de, 280

Gálveztown Post (La.), 481
Gámes, José Miguel, 305, 307
García, Ana María, 519
García, Felipe, 363
García, Francisco, 193, 197–98, 565
García, Fr. José Antonio, 280–84, 290, 297, 299, 344–45
García, Fr. Joseph María, 326
García, Luciano, 457
García, Matías, 54
García Larios, Francisco, 67
Garcitas Creek, 34
Gard, Wayne, 75n
Garza, Antonio de la, 237
Garza, Baltasar de la, 493, 499
Garza, Carlos de la, 520
Garza, Felipe de la, 549
Garza, Francisco de la, 138
Garza, Fr. José Francisco Mariano de la, 266, 272, 274–75, 290, 300, 345, 405, 407–408
Garza, Joaquín de la, 90, 164n, 220, 226n, 245n, 330n
Garza, José Antonio de la, 132, 540–41, 562–65
Garza, José Manuel de la, 582
Garza, José Salvador de la, 447–48
Garza, Leonardo de la, 164n
Garza, María de Jesus de la, 519
Garza, María Josefa de la, 491, 544
Garza, Martín de la, 90n, 165, 226n
Garza, Miguel de la, 105n, 127
Garza, Nicolás de la, 23
Garza, Refugio de la, 457
Garza Falcón, Blás María de la (father), 98
Garza Falcón, Blás María de la (son), 98, 443–44, 447
Garza Falcón, Joseph Antonio de la, 443
Garza Falcón, Juan de la, 443
Garza Falcón, María Gertrudis de la, 447
Garza Falcón, Miguel de la, 98
Garza Montemayor, José de la, 449
Garza's Crossing, 568
Garzía, Fr. Joseph Juaquín, 59, 163
Gayoso de Lemos, Manuel, 431–35, 453–54, 456
Geneva, Tex., 97
George West, Tex., 566
Gillett, Tex., 110
Gil Ybarbo, Antonio: as Nacogdoches

captain, 182–83, 195–96, 209n, 237, 276, 288, 300n, 353n, 358n, 388–94, 404, 438, 440–41, 452, 466, 494, 497–99, 501; as rancher, 96–97, 114–17, 129, 182–83, 190, 335, 471, 476–77, 479–80, 500. *See also* Nacogdoches, Pueblo de; smuggling
Gil Ybarbo, José Ignacio, 466, 493, 498–99
Gil Ybarbo, María Antonia, 182, 500n
Gil Ybarbo, María de Jesús, 520
Gil Ybarbo, Mariano, 466, 499
Gil Ybarbo, Martín, 493, 499
Gil Ybarbo, Matheo Antonio, 96, 97
Goguet, Estévan, 476, 493–95
Goliad County, 615
Goliad, Tex., 12, 71, 239, 325, 464, 580, 598–99, 605–606, 609. *See also* La Bahía del Espíritu Santo, Presidio de Nuestra Señora de Loreto de
Gonzáles, Antonio, 361n
Gonzáles, Josef, 361n
Gonzáles, Manuel, 215–18
Gonzáles, Fr. Manuel, 323
Gonzáles, Pedro, 330n
Gonzales, Tex., 325, 330
Gonzales County, 325, 330, 615
Gonzáles de Cosio, Tomás, 27, 29n
González, José, 98, 117
Goodwyn, Frank, 595
Gortari, Mariano, 372n
Gortari, Miguel de, 128n, 164n, 178n, 207n, 224n, 226n, 245n, 372n, 387n, 403n
Gortari, Miguel Ignacio, 268
Gortari, Vicente, 514, 518–19, 528n, 540n, 541
Governor's Palace, 63, 150, 562. *See also* Plaza de Armas; San Antonio de Béxar, Presidio de
Granados, Corral de los, 137, 140
Granados, José Manuel, 557, 582
Granados, José María, 565n
Granados, Juan Francisco, 164n, 207n
Granados, Manuel, 207
Granados, Pedro, 226n, 245n
Graytown, Tex., 88n
Grevembert, Agustín de, 122
Grimarest, Pedro, 485
Guadado, Rancho de (Garceño), 444

Guadalajara, Audiencia of, 104n, 285, 525, 528
Guadalajara, Bishopric of, 67, 177n
Guadalupe, Virgin of: religious festivals of, 139, 140, 154, 295
Guadalupe County, 219, 325, 615–16
Guadalupe River: as boundary of royal lands, 52, 59–60, 89, 94–96, 115, 127–28, 143–44, 162, 166, 169, 206, 219, 237, 240, 255, 271, 309, 325, 330, 335, 338–39, 346–47, 386–87, 397–98, 566, 579; Indian attacks near, 209–10, 223, 233; ranching on, 34, 41, 47, 58, 184, 360, 373–75, 407–408, 415, 475, 520, 600, 614–16
Guadiana, José María, 440, 515, 516, 517; and contraband, 438, 450–51, 469, 493; and Gil Ybarbo, 479–80; land deals authorized by, 466, 494, 495, 497, 499; and mesteño taxes, 464
Guajolote, Rancho del, 493, 498
Güemes Pacheco de Padilla, Juan Vicente de. *See* Revillagigedo, second Conde de
Guerra, Cristóbal, 397
Guerra, Francisco, 136–37, 144, 249–50
Guerra, Mariano, 136, 167, 245n, 397
Guerra, Miguel, 60, 65, 68, 93, 105, 136–37, 140, 144, 250. *See also* Amoladeras, Rancho de las
Guerra, Vicente, 23
Guerras, Rancho de los, 218–20, 230, 323, 328, 519
Guerrero, Ana, 498
Guerrero, Félix, 196
Guerrero, Francisco, 500
Guerrero, Juan Ignacio, 182, 479–80
Gutiérrez, Eugenio, 549
Gutiérrez Barona, Fr. Félix, 27
Gutiérrez de Lara, José Bernardo de, 497, 528, 530, 532–35, 553, 571

Habig, Fr. Marion A., 48, 90, 106, 113n
hacendados: observations about, 23, 25, 77, 148, 361, 443–49, 488, 522, 542–43, 601–604. *See also* haciendas; *latifundios*; ranchos
haciendas, 24, 102, 148, 263, 361, 400, 443–44, 469, 521, 542–43, 547–51.

Index

See also hacendados; *latifundios*; individual haciendas
Haggard, J. Villasana, 494, 529, 572
Hale, Edward Everett, 463–64
Haley, J. Evetts, 589
Harlingen, Tex., 446
Harmand, Lador, 460
Hasinai, 21
Hauterive, Antoine Bernard de, 426
Havana, Cuba, 44, 122, 194, 315, 366
Haynes, J. L., 592
Hays, John C., 71n
Hempstead County, Ark., 573–74
Hernández, Andrés, 71, 90, 164n, 178; brand of, 67, 87; death of, 185, 186–87, 188; heirs of, 186–87, 206, 332, 561; oldest Texas ranch owned by, 60, 146; ranch of, 60–62, 63–64, 65, 70, 93, 105, 187, 238. *See also* San Bartolo, Rancho de
Hernández, Claudio, 553–54
Hernández, Clemencia, 561
Hernández, Domingo, 178n
Hernández, Francisco (early soldier), 54, 61, 63, 64n
Hernández, Francisco, 186, 237, 399
Hernández, Gerónimo, 493, 499
Hernández, Jacobo, 70, 71n, 249
Hernández, Josef Andrés, 165–69, 179n, 187, 241, 245n, 515
Hernández, Josef Joaquín, 187
Hernández, Josef María, 217
Hernández, José Miguel, 87, 186
Hernández, José Plácido, 178n, 186, 330n, 385, 402n, 408n
Hernández, Juan José, 577, 580
Hernández, Marcos, 208–209, 214, 311, 354
Hernández, Rosa Hermenegilda, 68, 178
Herrera, Blás, 616–17
Herrera, Simón de (governor of Nuevo León), 486–87, 529, 534–35
Herrera, Vizente de, 280–84, 290, 296, 299
Hewetson, James, 361n
hidalgos: attitude of, 107, 109; observations about, 149–50, 156–59, 189, 265, 272, 296, 556–57; privileges of, 14, 15, 65; after Texas Revolution,
596–97, 599–604, 606, 608–10, 614–17. *See also* Isleños
Hidalgo y Costilla, Miguel, 523, 525, 530, 533–34, 542–43, 561
Hinojosa, Juan José de, 446
Hinojosa, Lorenzo, 457
Hinojosa, Rosa de, 446–47
Hinojosa, Vicente de, 446
Hochheim, Tex., 95
Holmes, Jack D. L., 430–31, 453
Hondo, Arroyo, 126, 208n
Hormigas, Rancho de las, 195n, 451, 518. *See also* Barr, William; Davenport, Samuel
Huerta de Jesús, Fr. José María, 485, 505
Huizar, Pedro, 236n
Hunter, John Warren, 606
Huson, Hobart, 589, 610n
Hutchins, Anthony, 432

Iguala, Plan de, 578
Indians: battles with, 209, 229n, 369–71; brands of, 466–67n; depredations of, 15, 16, 35, 66, 94, 104, 107, 110, 113, 125, 129, 133–34, 153, 174, 181, 186–87, 194–96, 200–202, 209–12, 215, 219, 223–24, 229, 231, 235, 239, 244, 247–48, 257, 263–65, 314, 335, 358–59, 368, 378, 414, 417, 437, 439, 465–67, 470, 489–90, 532, 539–40, 543–51, 556, 563; as mission vaqueros, 34, 41–49, 128, 145–46, 158, 169–70, 184–85, 263, 281–82, 291–95, 326–32, 348–52, 367, 379, 406–408, 411–13, 415–17, 419, 423, 505, 511; peace with, 21–23, 35, 57, 279, 296, 298, 311, 315–17, 346; policy toward, 77, 155, 157, 173, 182, 191, 212–14, 225, 246–47, 260, 390, 405, 410, 411, 422, 451–52, 455, 467, 472, 484, 496, 565, 574; trade with Americans, 391, 427, 439–40, 509. *See also* individual tribes
Isleños (Canary Islanders): arrival of, 13–22; attitudes of, 54, 65, 69, 99, 141–42, 525–28; observations about, 20, 57, 71, 72n, 149–50, 157, 167n, 189, 237, 265, 272, 288–89, 296, 335–36, 371–75, 395, 537, 555–56, 561

Islitas, Las (settlement at), 88
Iturbide, Agustín de, 578

Jacames, 257
Jackson, Humphrey, 590
Jalisco, Colegio de Santiago de, 106. *See* missions; San Juan Bautista, Misión de
James, John, 238n
Jaranames (Xaranames), 144–45, 168, 200
Jaudenes, Fr. José Francisco, 379, 383
Jefferson County, 607
Jefferys, Thomas, map of, 397
Jesuits, expulsion of, 105
John, Elizabeth, 160, 210n, 279n, 301, 317n, 322n
Johnson, William, 493, 503
Jonesborough, 573, 575
Jordan, Terry C., 436n, 588, 593–95, 610, 613
Jourdanton, Tex., 325
juez de campo (field judge): role of, 156, 200–201, 219, 229, 244–45, 481, 514–15. *See also síndicos*
Junta Superior de Real Hacienda, 365–69, 395, 406, 417–18, 420n

Karankawas, 405, 407, 450, 505
Karnes County, 59, 64, 71, 208n, 325, 476n, 615
Kemper, Samuel, 533
Kenedy, Mifflin, 614
Kenedy, Tex., 208n
Kenedy County, 448
Kentree, Ana María, 475
Kerlérec, Louis de, 119
Kichais, 390, 472
Kilgore, Dan, 55
Kimble, Helena, 496
King, Nyal C., 183
King, Richard, 590, 594–95, 614
King Ranch, 594–95
Kingsville, Tex., 595

La Bahía del Espíritu Santo, Presidio de Nuestra Señora de Loreto de (Tex.): *ayuntamiento* at, 578; cattle disputes at, 161–62, 198–201, 208–209, 263, 266–70, 356–59, 378–84, 402–404, 407–408, 414–17, 459, 504, 576–78, 580–82, 595–96, 600; founding of, 34; military command at, 45, 58, 89, 108, 110, 126, 129, 137, 202–203, 235, 266–67n, 272, 302, 321, 326, 333, 353, 378, 384, 392, 438, 450, 483, 519–20, 538, 558; revolutionary activity at, 532–33, 553, 570, 599; smuggling from, 117, 204–205, 469–71, 484, 575. *See also* Espíritu Santo de Zúñiga, Misión de Nuestra Señora del; Rosario, Misión de Nuestra Señora del; soldiers
La Bahía Road, 45, 71, 91, 109, 145, 210, 218, 510–11, 535, 538
La Baume, José de, 474–75, 479, 493, 496, 539
La Baume, José Narciso de, 475
labor: devices for controlling, 21, 37, 38, 120, 149, 155–58, 185, 348, 487–88, 603; division of, 128, 137, 143–46, 148, 177, 187, 199–201, 215–16, 264, 373–75, 387, 400–401, 444, 447, 449, 456–57, 475, 480, 521–22, 565–66, 595, 601–602; indebtedness of workers, 361–62, 513–14, 561, 601–603; Indian menace to, 34, 88, 133–34, 148, 209–15, 224, 263–65, 470, 546–51; at missions, 11, 34, 42–44, 47, 49, 348, 379, 407–408, 411–12, 415–17, 511; on public works, 15, 22, 107, 109, 358, 421–23, 504; recruitment of, 153, 167, 196, 315, 355, 379, 421, 477, 497, 506–507; shortage of, 19, 20, 43. *See also* missions; slavery; vaqueros
Ladrón de Guevara, Baltazar, 122–23, 193
Lafitte, Pablo, 440
La Fora, Nicolás de, 88, 89, 92–98, 443
Laguna, Corral de la, 227
Laguna de las Ánimas, Rancho de la, 528. *See also* individual Sambrano entries
Laja, Paso de la, 59, 60, 94, 168, 385. *See also* Rocky Ford Crossing
Lake Charles, La., 572
Lamar, Mirabeau B., 604–605
La Mathe, Nicolás de, 129, 181, 194–96, 247, 257, 260, 271–72, 315, 392, 412, 440

Index 689

land grants: acquisition of, 24, 38–41, 54, 56, 126, 182–85, 237–39, 361, 407, 412–14, 428, 441–48, 451, 457–58, 475–78, 491–503, 518, 520, 528, 568–69; Anglo acquisition of, 451, 458n, 495–98, 500–501, 520, 603–604, 606–10; disputes over, 63, 64, 69–71, 101–105, 128, 141–46, 151–53, 162–64, 168–70, 178, 206, 208, 233–34, 249, 273–74, 285, 326–28, 373–75, 448, 479–80, 538, 540–43, 555–56, 576–78, 601–602; limitations on, 449; recognition of, 59–61, 185–87, 443, 510–11; survey of, 331–32, 441–42, 498

land measurements: arpent, 428; *caballería*, 63n, 444; *labor*, 520; *legua* (league), 24n, 64, 441–42; *porción*, 443; *sitio*, 24n, 60, 101, 447–48; *suerte*, 189, 407n, 540; *vara*, 22, 442

Lanzarote (Canary Islands), 167
Lara, Vicente, 457
Lara Posos, Juana de, 494
Lara Posos, Pedro de, 494–95
Laredo, Villa de (Nuevo Santander), 23–25, 89, 117, 133, 360–61, 384, 404, 437, 443–44, 450, 542, 550
Laredo Road, 41, 566, 568
Larrua, Miguel, 502
La Salle, Robert Cavelier Sieur de, 34, 55
La Salle County, 133
Las Casas, Juan Bautista de, 526–29, 561
Lasgarda Hernández, Juana, 96
Lastrop, Juan, 460
latifundios, 13, 261, 361, 543. See also hacendados; haciendas
Laussat, Pierre Clément de, 481
Lava, Fr. Ignacio María, 295n
Lavaca River, 96
La Vernia, Tex., 38, 40
Lavigne, José, 440
Lazo, Luisa, 598
Leal, Antonio, 127, 349n, 454–59, 501
Leal, Bernardo, 238
Leal, Gregorio, 372n
Leal, Joaquín, 72, 164n, 238, 537; and illegal cattle, 138; lands of, confiscated, 540; protests by, 129n, 179n, 224n, 342, 437n; as raiser, 382, 408n, 515,
518, 531; in roundups, 245n, 323, 330n, 514
Leal, Remigio, 545
Leal Goraz, Juan, 14–18
Leclerc, Frédéric, 590–91
León, Alonzo de, 11, 54, 55, 96, 149
León, Arroyo de, 102, 105, 413, 518, 531, 569
León, José Antonio de, 504
León, Manuel de, 482n
León, Martín de, 505–506, 519, 550, 598
Lepine, James, 501
Lerma, Joaquín, 411
Leutenegger, Fr. Benedict, 352
Liberty, Tex. (Old Atascosito), 598
Liendro, Tomás, 357–58
Linares, Bishopric of. See Nuevo León, Bishopric of
Linn, John J., 596
Lipscomb, Abner S., 605
Live Oak County, 615
livestock prices: in Coahuila, 139, 216, 332, 362; in Louisiana, 196, 425, 429, 431–32, 436, 456; in Texas, 18, 22, 42, 74, 138, 186, 188, 192, 206, 215, 220, 231, 253, 346, 359–60, 400, 407, 425, 450, 452, 467, 476, 481, 483, 545, 558, 569
livestock taxes: collection of, 174, 219, 237, 249–50, 256–57, 262, 264, 317–18, 332–33, 353, 362–63, 379–80, 392–93n, 464; in Louisiana, 431, 433–35; petitions against, 244, 257, 274–75, 280–86, 290–95, 296–300, 333–43, 353–56, 363–64, 415–16; regulations for, 155–60, 162, 165, 179, 188, 193, 197, 207–209, 211n, 212–14, 221, 226–29, 232n, 239–41, 253–57, 260, 267, 270n, 276, 302, 309–10, 365, 369, 380–81, 404–405, 418–23, 451–52, 489, 578–80, 598. See also Mustang Fund
livestock trade: with frontier presidios, 17, 42, 74, 127, 130–34, 138–39, 145, 149, 164, 177–80, 198, 205–207, 215–18, 226–29, 240–41, 263–71, 301, 303–10, 333, 357–58, 361–63, 371, 402–403, 410, 468–69; with Louisiana, prohibited, 118–23, 313–

15, 388, 391, 425–26, 450, 459–61, 469–71, 483–84, 503–504, 544, 575–76; with Louisiana, regulation of, 190–98, 204, 207–12, 236–37, 255–56, 260, 451–59, 472–73, 481; with Louisiana, views about, 11, 117, 129, 192, 220–21, 250–52, 314, 318, 404, 430–31, 436, 466, 482, 508–10, 522–23, 532, 592; within Texas, 76, 126, 231–35, 359–60, 394, 400–401, 416–17, 450, 467, 488, 512–13, 515–16, 569–70, 597. *See also* missions; ranching; smuggling; trail driving

Llano Grande, Rancho de, 446
Lobanillo, Rancho del, 96, 97, 114, 116, 129, 182, 502
Loco, Rancho, 497
Logansport Ferry, 538
Lombrana, Tomás de, 29n
Lomerías, Las, 347, 421–22
Long, James, 570–71
Longueville, Pedro, 458, 464
López, Fr. José Francisco, 290–95, 312–13, 323, 331, 337, 343
López de Herrera, Vicente, 449
López de Jaen, Benito, 449
López Prieto, Pedro, 515
López de Santa Anna, Antonio, 600, 616
Lorenzo de Armas, Antonia, 177, 385, 408n
Lorenzo de Armas, Ignacio, 65, 66
Lorenzo de Armas, Martín, 60, 65, 93, 94, 105, 140, 164, 167, 169, 177, 328, 332
Louisiana Purchase, 435, 473, 475, 487, 571
Lucobiche, José, 476
Lufkin, Tex., 475
Luna, Felipe de, 215
Luna, Luisa de, 545
Lunaca, Rancho de la, 183, 394, 500

McFarland, Thomas, 500
Macfarson, Juan, 493n
McQueeney, Tex., 325
Madison, James, 435
Madison, Tex., 607
Magee, Augustus William: expedition of, 497, 528, 532
Malaguitas, Las Islitas de (Padre Island), 447

Manchac, Fort (La.), 430
Manifest Destiny, 5, 612
Mansolo, Tomás, 493, 495–96
Marcelino, Arroyo de (Marcelinas Creek), 93, 238
Marín de Porras, Feliciano, 504n
marks: of Anglo stockmen, 588–90, 601n, 614–15; lists of, 165, 212, 426–27, 466n, 489–91, 517, 545, 559, 598–99n, 607n, 614–17; registration of, 67, 87, 117, 242, 583. *See also* branding
Marmolejo, Fr. Ildefonso Joseph, 36n, 47
Martínez, Antonio María, 542, 553–70, 575–83
Martínez, Arroyo de, 38
Martínez, Carlos, 89n, 94, 125–26, 136, 150, 163, 164n, 169, 179n, 239, 268, 379, 408n, 550. *See also* Señor San José, Rancho del
Martínez, Juan Joseph, 457
Martínez, Rafael, 554
Martínez Pacheco, Leandro, 367
Martínez Pacheco, Rafael, 310–11, 332–33, 337, 353, 355, 379–80, 382, 389, 392, 401, 409, 418, 421, 423; dismissal of, 371–77; early career of, 112, 125, 315–17, 321; Indian relations under, 370–71; livestock regulations of, 322–31, 359; as rancher advocate, 322, 345–53, 361–64, 366–67
Martos y Navarrete, Ángel de, 28, 29, 45, 59, 66, 67n, 70, 71n, 98, 101, 120, 144, 163, 316, 321
Masse, Monsieur de, 120
Matagorda Bay, 553
Maverick, Mary, 616
Medina, Battle of, 537, 545–47
Medina, Fr. Lorenzo, 326, 327–28n
Medina River, 41, 102, 105, 229n, 257, 347, 413, 458, 510–11, 518, 531, 568–69, 608, 617
Megui (Magee?), José, 493n
Meinig, D. W., 609
Melado, Rancho del, 446
Menchaca, Antonio (of Nacogdoches), 571
Menchaca, Antonio (veteran of Texas Revolution), 534, 538, 571
Menchaca, Diego, 372n
Menchaca, Joaquín, 164n, 207n, 215,

234, 271, 323, 328, 342, 382, 397, 408n
Menchaca, José: at Béxar Presidio, 57, 110, 150, 189, 195n, 196, 202, 209, 214–15, 308, 477; at line presidios, 263n, 303–306, 439; in Royalist counterrevolution, 530, 533–35, 538, 571
Menchaca, José Antonio (Francisco), 56, 63
Menchaca, José Félix, 110, 128n, 143, 164, 179, 189, 194–96, 202n, 204–205, 207, 215, 250, 287–88, 305–309, 317, 349n, 353–55, 359, 367, 372n, 387n, 397, 400
Menchaca, Joseph Navor, 482
Menchaca, José Tomás, 571
Menchaca, Luciano, 541n
Menchaca, Luis Antonio: death of, 477; land grant of, 63, 93, 105, 238–39; as presidio captain, 56, 64, 67, 71, 104, 107, 150, 321–22; as rancher, 57, 65, 90, 110, 163–65, 187, 189–90, 207n, 215, 227, 231, 236n, 245n, 257, 260, 264–65, 270, 273, 288, 304–309, 317, 385. *See also* San Francisco, Rancho de
Menchaca, Luis Mariano, 263–66, 271, 287–89, 302–308, 312, 317, 323, 330n, 342, 397n, 399, 403n, 406, 437n, 477
Menchaca, Miguel Jorge, 189, 196, 215, 257, 263
Mesquite, Arroyo de, 206
mesta: in northern provinces, 201n, 241–43, 361, 468–69, 512, 522; origin of, 135
Mesteñas, Corral de las, 219
Mesteñas, Rancho de las, 446
mestizos, 189, 382, 494–99, 522–23; defined, 13; punishment of, 22, 358, 410, 422–23; under Spanish rule, 148, 392, 486; after Texas Revolution, 593, 599, 602–606, 609, 611, 614–15
Mexican War, 52, 76, 600, 602
Mexico City, 63, 69, 70, 103, 116, 198n, 283–84, 286, 297, 316, 365, 372, 380, 384, 420n
Mézières, Athanase de, 134, 182, 190–93, 201, 236, 251, 388
Michaux, André, 456

Micheli, Francisco, 477
Micheli, Vicente, 475–79, 494, 504, 539, 565n
Mier, Villa de (Nuevo Santander), 23, 464, 481, 580–81
Mier y Terán, Manuel, 574
Miller County, Ark., 573
Minchaca, Joseph, 29n
mining: absence of, in Louisiana, 250–52; and minting of coins, 436n
Miró, Estévan Rodríguez. *See* Rodríguez Miró, Estévan
mission inventories: 1772, 106, 112–13; 1794, 406, 411–12n, 510n
missions: foundations of, 25, 33, 34, 378–79, 406–408, 416; land disputes of, 60n, 69, 70, 101–105, 141–46, 150, 153, 162–64, 166–71, 176–80, 208, 234; land grants of, 38–41, 59, 60, 203–204, 510–11, 520; livestock trade of, 42, 119, 176–80, 192, 197–206, 208–10, 236–37, 266–70, 293; neophytes at, 35, 37–38, 41–44, 49, 66, 77, 101, 105, 113, 144–46, 152, 158, 169–70, 184–85, 200, 248, 257, 263, 268, 281–83, 291–95, 378–79, 408, 419, 423, 505, 511, 591; revolutionary damage to, 546, 548; and rustling, 17, 18, 21, 126–28, 135–46, 248, 383–84, 404; secularization of, 27, 28, 100, 184–85, 295, 405–406, 410–14; stock raising at, 12, 21, 27–31, 34–37, 54, 88, 93, 95–102, 247–48, 281–82, 296, 322–32, 349–53, 378, 381, 407–408, 416–17, 450, 484; and taxation, 257, 260, 272–75, 280–84, 290–95, 299, 344–46, 414–16; and colleges, 105, 106, 112, 113, 295. *See also* individual mission
Mission Valley, Tex., 47
Mississippi River, 123, 129, 252, 426, 428–29, 431–36, 571
Mobile Bay, 426, 429
Mojoneras, Arroyo de las, 104, 105
Monclova, Presidio de (Coahuila), 139, 266
Monclova, Villa de Santiago de la (Coahuila), 24, 54, 139, 216n, 266, 277, 361n, 458n, 485, 487, 507, 533, 598

Monjarás, Sebastián, 138, 143, 163, 164, 177–80, 198, 206, 215–18, 241, 252, 272, 300, 372n
Montalvo, Thadeo, 29n
Montalvo, Xavier, 29n
Monte Galván, Rancho de, 38, 94, 113, 331, 421–22
Montero, Bernardo, 518n
Monterrey, Nuevo León, 23, 54, 335n, 517, 542
Móntes, Josef María, 167
Móntes de Oca, Francisco, 224n, 245n, 259, 330n, 514–15, 518, 531, 565n, 582
Móntes de Oca, Gertrudis, 541n
Móntes de Oca, Juan Joseph, 105, 207
Móntes de Oca, Marcos, 224n
Móntes de Oca, María Manuela, 72, 385, 491, 515
Móntes de Oca, Teodora, 68
Montreal, Antonio, 519
Moorhead, Max, 189, 203n
Mora, Gregorio de la, 196n
Mora, Jacinto de la, 196n. See also Hormigas, Rancho de las
Mora, José María de la, 494, 517
Mora, Juan de la, 195
Mora, Laguna de Juan de la (Spanish Lake), 502
Mora, María Antonia de la, 500
Mora, Rancho de la, 45, 105, 148, 215, 325, 357, 531; conflict over, 208; Erasmo Seguín and, 412–13n, 576–77; livestock at, 113, 143, 145, 165, 218–20, 230–31, 245; Mission Valero and, 38, 40. See also missions; Valero, Misión de San Antonio de
Moraín, Juan Antonio, 117
Moral, José Miguel del, 438, 450, 454, 466, 472, 479–80
Moral, Arroyo de la, 475, 496
Moral, Rancho del, 496–97
Morbán, Francisco, 440
Morey, Elizabeth May, 534–35
Morfi, Fr. Juan Agustín de, 21, 55, 91, 96, 146–50, 157–59, 332
Morilla, José, 493
Morín, Estévan, 493–94
Moro (Mora?), Susana, 478

Mosquitos, Rancho de los, 408, 520
Mound Creek, 110. See also Tetillas, Las
Moya, Dimas, 499
Muelle Viejo (Old Wharf), 407
Mugeres, Rancho de las, 230, 385, 414
Muizas, Gerónimo, 520
Mulas, Rancho de las, 93, 133, 140, 148, 163, 169, 186, 201, 225, 238, 271, 286, 323, 332, 385, 521, 531; conflict over, 70, 71, 234, 248–49, 545; Indian attacks at, 209; livestock at, 131, 137, 218–20, 230–33, 244–45; Vicente Álvarez Travieso and, 56, 65. See also Rincón, El; Travieso, Vicente Álvarez
mulattoes, 132, 189; punishment of, 22, 358, 410, 422–23, 482; under Spanish rule, 130, 148, 289, 389; as stockmen, 186, 382, 460, 475, 522–23; after Texas Revolution, 604, 606–607
muleteers: dangers to, 133–34, 437, 531–32; traffic of, 130–32, 213, 359–60
Muñoz, Manuel, 179n
Muñoz, Manuel (governor of Texas), 236n, 331, 377, 425, 438, 450, 485; death of, 438, 455, 471, 485; Indian relations under, 437, 439; livestock regulations of, 254n, 380–83, 385–88, 395–96, 398–99, 402–405, 408–10, 417–23; and mission secularization, 406–407, 410–12, 414–16; and Philip Nolan, 405, 453–60; quarrels of, with citizens, 394–95, 399–402, 479
Murillo, Ramón de, 78, 84
Murphy, Edward, 440, 451–52, 458n, 501
Músquiz, Miguel de, 459, 501, 528n. See also Eca y Músquiz
Músquiz, Ramón, 597
Mustang Fund: controversies over, 229–30, 243–44, 255–56, 261–62, 266, 283–84, 291–95, 311, 341–43, 365–66, 410, 415–16, 438–39; modification of, 188, 369, 395, 404–405, 418, 422, 472, 561, 578–80; origin of, 155–57, 160; reports on, 174, 208, 219, 225, 246, 258–59, 275–76, 296, 300, 332–33, 353, 379–80, 392–93n, 454, 464, 505–506; uses for, 287, 298, 373, 380, 416, 455, 467, 469, 482, 515, 529, 579. See also livestock taxes

Nacogdoches, Misión de Nuestra Señora del Pilar de (Tex.), 118
Nacogdoches, Pueblo de (Tex.), 75, 117, 195–96, 209, 235, 288, 333, 353–54, 380, 383, 425, 464, 597–98; founding of, 112, 182–83, 441; ranching near, 52, 97, 98, 466, 475–77, 479–80, 483, 491–504, 516–17; revolutionary disturbances at, 530–32, 538, 546, 554, 556, 570–71; smuggling activities at, 388–94, 404, 438, 450–60, 469–76, 483–84, 503–504, 518, 572–75. *See also* Adaes, Presidio de Nuestra Señora del Pilar de los; Bucareli, Pueblo de la Nuestra Señora del Pilar de; Gil Ybarbo, Antonio
Naconiche, Rancho de, 443n, 493, 496–98, 538
Nana, Arroyo de la, 183, 497
Nana, Rancho de la (La.), 451
Nardini, Louis R., 97, 98, 117
Nashville, Tenn., 571–72
Natchez, Miss., 426, 430–36, 453
Natchitoches Post (La.), 78, 97, 98, 112, 114, 117–23, 190–92, 194, 236, 315, 389–94, 425, 427–28, 430, 433, 440, 451–52, 475–76, 484, 496, 503, 508, 530–31, 535, 543, 547, 556, 573
Nations of the North, 21, 87, 88, 107, 113, 125, 134, 155, 173–74, 182, 194, 221, 224, 225, 247, 254, 260, 263, 279, 316, 380, 400, 405, 437, 439, 455, 467n, 472, 546, 550. *See also* Comanches; Indians
Nava, Pedro de, 349n, 377, 392, 409–11, 415–23, 438–39, 450, 454–60, 468–70, 473, 479–81, 486, 489, 522n
Navarro, Ángel, 412–13
Navarro, José Ángel, 542, 576, 581–82
Navarro, José Antonio, 210n, 413, 537, 539n, 605, 615–16
Navarro, Juan, 207n
Navidad River, 96
Neutral Ground, 97n, 196n, 487, 501–503, 506, 515, 518, 530–35, 543, 556, 571–76
Neve, Felipe de, 242, 258–60, 262, 265–66, 276
New Braunfels, Tex., 128, 184, 611

New Mexico, Province of, 301, 392, 499, 605–606, 611
New Orleans, La., 119–22, 192, 197, 251, 314, 391, 428–29, 431–36, 456, 470, 473, 481, 501, 503, 507, 574
Nogal, Paso del, 510
Nogales, Arroyo de los, 170, 178, 208, 209, 237, 330
Nogales, Fort (Vicksburg), 432–33
Nolan, Philip, 287, 439n, 440, 452–64, 467, 481, 482, 501
Noreña, Fr. Pedro, 323
Norris, Anna, 501
Norris, Edmund, 443n, 491, 497–98, 501, 538, 571
Norris, Nathaniel, 498
Norris, Samuel, 498, 575n
Noris (Norris?), San Miguel, 590
Nueces County, 609, 615
Nueces River, 24, 98, 208n, 358, 416, 443–49, 506, 519, 547, 549–51, 558, 566–67, 577, 592, 600, 608–11, 614–15. *See also* Nuevo Santander, Province of
Nueva Estremadura, Province of, 13, 54. *See also* Coahuila
Nueva Feliciana, District of, 432, 452
Nueva Vizcaya, Province of, 13, 160, 286, 289, 301, 392, 410
Nuevo León, Bishopric of, 261, 291, 335, 356n, 474, 528
Nuevo León, Province of, 10, 11, 13, 54, 77, 130, 149, 220, 251, 287, 314, 335n, 486, 517, 547. *See also* Monterrey
Nuevo Santander, Province of, 52, 211n, 251, 261, 287, 335n, 394, 438, 526, 568; Indian raids in, 547–51; livestock trade with, 122, 130, 212, 220, 361, 416, 454–55, 465–66, 508, 580–81; river towns in, 23, 24. *See also* Camargo; Laredo; Mier; Refugio, Congregación de Nuestra Señora del; Revilla; Reynosa; Río Grande
Nuñez, Manuel, 515, 540n
Nuñez, Roberto, 402n
Nuñez Morillo, Ignacia, 289

Ocón y Trillo, Pedro, 169–70n
Oconor, Hugo de, 83, 107, 113, 115–17,

121, 123, 125, 190, 389, 406, 501
Ojo de Agua, Rancho, 446
Ojo de Agua [Martínez] Creek, 58, 59, 89n, 94
Ojuelos, Rancho de los, 549
Oliva, Fr. José Rafael, 290, 323, 326–28, 352–53, 379n
Olivares, Fr. Antonio de San Buenaventura y, 10, 25
Ollos, Juana de, 64n, 87, 129n, 164n, 179n, 186, 187n, 207n, 220, 230
Olmos, Arroyo de los, 95, 141, 168–70, 178, 227, 249
Olmsted, Frederick Law, 602, 605–606
Opelousas Post (La.), 122, 192, 194, 196, 198, 204, 208, 220, 236, 404, 425–33, 435–36, 484, 504, 537, 587, 589
Opelousas Road, 236, 430–31, 484, 572–73
Orange, Tex., 572, 607
Orcoquisac, Presidio de Nuestra Señora de la Luz de (Tex.), 97, 108, 112, 114, 120, 316, 321, 483–84
O'Reilly, Alejandro, 191, 427–28, 481
Orobio y Bazterra, Prudencio de, 61
Orosco, Julián de, 196, 205
Orrachal, Pedro Bartolomé, 493, 499
Ortiz, Fr. Francisco Xavier, 34–36, 45, 46
Ortolant, Bernardo de. *See* D'Ortolant, Bernardo
Oso, Arroyo del, 208
Ouachita Post (La.), 436, 459–60, 474–75
Oyos, Juana de. *See* Ollos, Juana de

Pacheco, Albino, 540n, 564–65
Pacheco, Juan José, 195–96, 207, 271, 287–88, 305, 307, 354–55
Padilla, Francisco, 397
Padilla, Juan Antonio, 547, 551, 592
Padilla, Pedro Silverio, 183, 493, 497, 538
Padre Cárdenas, Rancho del, 90. *See also* Cárdenas, Rev. Juan Ignacio de
Padre Island, 447
Padrón, Francisco, 387n
Padrón, Joseph, 22, 70n, 105n, 167, 177–80, 252, 300
Pagès, Pierre Marie François de, 73–78, 80, 88, 96, 98, 130, 466n

Paistle, Rancho del, 94, 113, 218–19, 231; conflict over, 70, 169, 177; Indian depredations at, 145, 223; and José María Balmaceda, 412–13n; and Mission Concepción, 40, 46. *See also* Concepción, Misión de Nuestra Señora de la Purísima; missions
Pajaritos, Arroyo de los, 64n, 93, 96n, 238
Palafox (settlement at), 550
Palo Blanco, Rancho del, 481
Palo Gacho, Arroyo del, 96, 501
Palo Gacho, Rancho del, 501
Palo Quemado, Rancho del, 477–78
Panna Maria, Tex., 478
Pánuco River, 77
Pardo, Manuel, 552–53, 558, 562
Pardo y Arce, Francisco del, 545
Parras, Hacienda de Santa María de las (Coahuila), 211n, 361n
Parrita, Arroyo de la, 105, 511
Parrita, Rancho de la, 89. *See also* San Simón del Capote, Rancho de
Parrott, Anthony, 501
Pataguilla, Laguna de, 40, 64, 72, 90, 148, 238, 511
Pato, Rancho del, 443
Patos, Hacienda de San Francisco de los (Coahuila), 361
Patrón (or Patroon), Rancho del, 493, 501
Paul v. *Pérez*, 608
Pawnee, Tex., 325
Pecan Point, 573, 575n
Peña, Fr. Juan Antonio de la, 11, 12
Peña, Ignacio de la, 91, 104, 133, 164n, 224n, 230, 385, 408n
Peña, Martín de la, 105
Peña, Matías, 496–98
Peña, Rev. José Antonio Ildefonso de la, 92
Peñitas, Las, 470
Pénjamo, 75
Péres, Joseph Francisco, 372n
Péres, Miguel, 133
Pérez, Balthazar, 105n
Pérez, Domingo, 561
Pérez, Francisco, 196
Pérez, Ignacio, 403n, 437, 518, 528n, 531, 539, 544, 556–65, 568–71, 576, 608

Pérez, José, 22
Pérez, Josef, 105n, 165, 179n, 207n, 561
Pérez, José Ignacio, 562, 608
Pérez, Luis, 105n, 511
Pérez, Manuela, 521
Pérez, Remigio, 565n
Pérez Casanova, Joseph Antonio, 561
Pérez de Almazán, Juan Antonio, 14, 15
Peyotes, Misión de Dulce Nombre de Jesús de (Coahuila), 132
Pichardo, Fr. José Antonio, 55, 573, 614
Picosa, Arroyo de la, 567
Piedra, Arroyo de la, 510
Pierce, Abel Head "Shanghai," 596
Piernas, José, 497, 515
Pifermo, Juan Ignacio, 502, 517
Pike, Zebulon M., 78, 81–85, 130, 361, 463, 465, 486–87, 495, 500, 503–504
Pimería Alta, 105
Pinilla, Fr. José, 28, 29, 45
Pinilla, Fr. Miguel, 28
Pitahayas, Arroyo de las, 577
Plaza de Armas (Military Plaza), 150, 175, 225, 400, 529. See also San Antonio de Béxar, Presidio de
Pleasant Hill, La., 97
Pleasanton, Tex., 41, 325
Pointe Coupée (La.), 129, 430
Portilla, Felipe Roque de la, 506–507, 551, 596
Posada, Ramón de, 236n
Poteet, Tex., 41
Potrero del Espíritu Santo, Rancho del, 447–48, 602
Power, James, 551
Prado, Pedro, 535, 543
presidios. See soldiers; individual presidios
Procela, Pedro, 484, 499, 554, 571
Procela Crossing (on Angelina), 495
Prudhomme, Francisco, 440
Prudhomme, Manuel, 440
Provincias Internas, Comandancia General de los, 73, 78, 82, 83, 120, 147, 212–13, 224, 241, 251, 297, 314, 365, 410, 455, 465, 474, 486, 508, 526n, 551–52; command of, 252, 258–59, 276, 301, 377, 485, 507, 535, 580; formation of, 129, 160, 190; jurisdiction of, 301, 391–92, 468, 537n

Puelles, Fr. José María de Jesús: map by, 573
Puente, Esmeregildo, 406
Puente de Piedra, Arroyo del, 578

Quemado, Tex., 139
Querétaro, Colegio de la Santa Cruz de, 27, 28, 33, 34, 45, 46n, 88, 105, 106, 112, 113, 295. See also missions
Quinelty, Dennis, 501
Quinelty, James, 493, 501
Quinn, Miguel, 491, 590
Quiñones y Flores de Abrego, Gertrudis, 456n
Quiñones y Flores de Abrego, Joseph, 68
Quiñones y Flores de Abrego, María Josefa, 68, 93, 144, 385, 408n
Quirk, Edmund, 458n, 493, 500–501, 552n, 571
Quirk, Henry, 493
Quirk, William, 491, 501

Rabb, William, 575
Ramírez de Arellano, Fr. Pedro, 66, 127n, 162–63, 177, 180, 185–87, 193, 197–200, 209, 290
Ramírez de la Piscina, Manuel, 45, 58, 63, 89, 90, 91, 126, 208n, 321
Ramón, Andrés, 66, 70n
Ramón, Diego, 55, 56
Ramón, Domingo, 11, 55
Ramón, Ildefonso, 550
Ramós, Rev. José Félix de, 209
Ramós Arizpe, José Miguel, 37n, 130–31, 297, 363, 509, 523, 576
Ramsdell, Charles William, Jr., 36, 47, 58, 128, 159n, 163n, 225, 280, 413
ranching: and agriculture, 16, 18–20, 66, 93, 99, 102, 185, 251, 355, 414, 432–35, 450, 474, 512, 557, 567, 585, 595–96; in early Texas, 15–22, 34, 36, 44, 48, 53–73, 88–99, 104, 146, 182–83, 335–36; in French Louisiana, 97, 98, 117–23, 391, 404, 425–36; importance of, 6, 54, 108, 291, 428–29; and northern provinces, 13, 23–31, 49, 52, 73, 77, 98–100, 122, 242, 314, 361–63, 368–69, 410, 465–66, 468–69, 506–507, 521–23; observations about, 11, 52, 106, 125–28, 134, 149, 157,

171, 173, 176, 188, 203–204, 220–21, 224, 240, 250–51, 254–55, 271, 280, 286, 313–14, 318, 332, 343, 350, 352–53, 368, 375, 388, 396–98, 408, 418, 423, 436, 465, 470, 485, 503–504, 520–23, 526, 539, 546–51; Spanish influence on, 3, 5, 75, 80, 81, 436, 463, 493, 503, 582–617. *See also* livestock trade; missions
ranchos: censuses of, 65, 89–98, 104, 105, 148, 163, 345–46, 382, 385, 408, 419, 440–50, 491–503, 511–12, 514–20, 531, 557; description of, 45–49, 61, 62, 112, 126, 146, 182–87, 224, 237–39, 248–49, 263–65, 303–309, 412–14, 443, 457–58, 475–78, 487–88, 607, 614–16; Indian depredations at, 87, 88, 94, 153, 194, 209–11, 263, 281, 293–94, 437, 466, 474, 543, 546–51; livestock figures at, 23, 34–37, 46–48, 67, 75, 97, 98, 106, 113, 189, 218–20, 230, 245, 248, 258–59, 281n, 292–93, 378, 392, 406, 411, 417, 483, 518–20, 544–46, 551; social organization at, 51–53, 57, 71–73, 98, 108–109, 169, 323–24, 330, 371–75, 407, 414, 428, 444, 511, 521, 549, 590–91. *See also* haciendas; missions; individual ranches
Randolph Air Force Base, 94, 331
Rapides Post (La.), 427, 466
Real de Joaquín, 105, 238
Real de Manuel, 238
Real Hacienda (Royal Treasury), 27, 155–57, 160, 193, 201, 242, 259, 269, 281, 291–94, 334, 339, 341–43, 345, 354, 362–64, 380, 395, 418, 422, 468, 472, 479, 491, 513, 540, 545, 579. *See also* Junta Superior de Real Hacienda
Recopilación, 243n, 358n
Red River, 78, 98, 107, 390, 572–75, 588
reducciónes, 31n, 55, 61
Refugio, Congregación de Nuestra Señora del (Matamoros), 447, 506–507, 551
Refugio, Misión de Nuestra Señora del (Tex.), 404n, 406–408, 416–17, 450, 546, 548, 566
Refugio County, 600, 615
Remington, Frederic, 612
Reñe, Lorenzo, 196

Rengel, José Antonio, 276–77, 279, 284, 287, 296, 299–301, 491
Revilla, Villa de (Nuevo Santander), 23, 443, 530, 533
Revillagigedo, first Conde de (Güemes y Horcasitas), 27, 119
Revillagigedo, second Conde de (Güemes Pacheco y Padilla), 291n, 371, 377, 381, 383–84, 389, 391–95, 409, 420n
Reyes, Fr. José Mariano, 378–79, 384
Reynosa, Villa de (Nuevo Santander), 23, 444–47, 580–81
Richards, Mordecai, 457, 493, 501
Rico, Bentura, 127n, 133
Rincón, El: Indian attacks in, 88, 187, 194, 214–15, 263, 548; land grants in, 61–73, 105, 116, 237–39, 248–49, 375, 412–14, 477–78, 511, 602; stock raising in, 40, 72–73, 87, 91–94, 107–10, 133, 135, 148, 170, 184–88, 206, 208, 216–19, 227–33, 244–45, 258–59, 264–66, 303–309, 332, 385, 401, 513–15, 518–19, 531, 540, 566, 614–15. *See also* Cíbolo, Arroyo del; San Antonio River
Rincón del Oso, Rancho, 550
Rincón Gallardo y Romero de Terreros, Carlos, 10
Río Grande, 15, 23–31, 52, 55, 62, 78, 98, 99, 127, 212, 215, 266–68, 416, 443–50, 503, 542, 547–51, 580–81, 592, 600, 609–10, 613–14
Río Grande del Norte, Presidio del (Coahuila), 13, 25, 133, 138, 180, 198, 205, 581. *See also* San Juan Bautista del Río Grande, Presidio de
Riojas, Carlos, 167
Riojas, José María, 504
Ripperdá, Juan María, Barón de, 122, 123, 149, 164, 182, 184, 190, 204–206, 214, 228, 241, 249, 250, 254, 264, 304, 317, 332, 339, 388, 399, 406, 430; versus cattlemen, 103, 107–10, 113–17, 125–28, 133, 150–53, 155, 157, 159–62; rustling trials of, 134–47, 154, 165–71, 174–76, 186–88
Rivas, Francisco Antonio, 540
Rivera, Pedro de, 15
Robeline, La., 97
Robinson, John Hamilton, 533, 574

Rocky Ford Crossing (on Cibolo Creek), 59, 60. *See also* Laja, Paso de la
Rodrígues, Agustín, 152n, 183
Rodríguez, Fernando, 565n
Rodríguez, Francisco Xavier, 71n, 110, 127, 129n, 133, 136n, 137–46, 154, 160, 164n, 165, 179n, 207n, 245n, 249, 271n, 272, 309, 354, 372n, 387n, 541n
Rodríguez, Mariano, 407–408, 515, 545
Rodríguez, Salvador, 217, 385, 437n
Rodríguez Baca, Antonio, 467, 538–39, 541n
Rodríguez Granado, Juan, 65
Rodríguez Miró, Estévan, 315, 390, 453, 429
Roemer, Ferdinand, 616
Romero, Juan, 363, 372n
roping, 76, 77, 81, 82, 397
Rosa, Francisco de la, 504
Rosales, Corrals of, 581
Rosali, Juan, 186n
Rosario, Mision de Nuestra Señora del (Tex.), 34, 41, 47, 60n, 89, 126, 162, 198–99, 203, 226, 293, 326–27n, 367, 378–79, 382–85, 417, 450, 484–85, 548. *See also* La Bahía del Espíritu Santo, Presidio de Neustra Señora de Loreto de; missions
Rosé, Francisco, 194, 220
Rose, Victor, 596
Rosillo, Arroyo del, 331, 533
roundups, 4, 29, 34, 58, 117, 127, 128, 153, 164–66, 168–70, 225–26, 237, 240, 248, 357–58, 394, 401, 437, 479–80, 546, 558; described, 75, 77, 78, 136–46, 199–201, 227–34, 237, 263–70, 309–10, 348–53, 374, 415–16, 465; regulations for, 22, 23, 26, 155–57, 161–62, 179, 188, 205–208, 218–19, 243, 252–54, 257–58, 272–75, 285–86, 298–99, 322–31, 360–61, 365, 380–81, 383–85, 387–88, 395–99, 409–10, 417–23, 428, 433–35, 465–66, 468, 487–88, 505, 511–14, 531, 562–68, 576–83, 597, 601n. *See also* branding
Rouquier, Francisco, 440
Rowland, John, 605
Roxo (Rojo), Fr. José Mariano, 382

Royal Regulations of 1772, 75, 82, 110–12, 182, 203, 216, 263n
Rubí, Marqués de, 74–76, 82, 88, 89, 94, 95, 110, 112, 120, 129, 182, 216, 251
Ruíz, Agustín, 196, 205, 565
Ruíz, Félix, 437n
Ruíz, Francisco, 528, 537, 543, 605, 616–17
Ruíz, Marcos, 316, 321
Ruíz de Apodaca, Juan, 553
Runge, Tex., 59, 95, 208n
rustling: at missions, 17–19, 133, 152–54, 248, 326, 374, 378, 383, 404, 415, 417; from private owners, 357–58, 368, 400, 403–404, 539–40, 554, 576–78, 580–82; regulations to control, 22, 23, 155–62, 243, 254, 273, 433–35, 513–14; after Texas Revolution, 595–97, 599–601, 604, 607–608; trials for, 135–46, 165–71, 176, 264–66, 399–400

Sabinas, Real Santiago de las (Nuevo León), 67
Sabine River, 97, 117, 383, 390, 440, 451, 457, 476, 483–84, 501–504, 516, 531, 534, 537, 588, 607
saddles, 14, 42, 43, 75, 132, 186, 192, 232, 412n, 441, 503, 535; description of, 74, 78–80, 84, 85; evolution of, 81–83, 594, 611
Sáenz, Antonio, 528–29
Saez (Sáenz?), Nicolás, 67
St. Denis, Louis Juchereau de, 10, 11, 117, 118, 191, 194, 236, 389, 516. *See also* Natchitoches Post
St. Denis, María de, 194
Saint Martinville, La., 427. *See also* Attakapas Post
St. Maxent, Celestino, 481
St. Maxent, Gilberto Antonio, 481
St. Maxent d' Estrehan, Felicite, 481
Salado, Arroyo del, 38, 88, 91, 105, 331, 510, 531, 533, 566
Salado, Rancho del, 514
Salas de Santa Gertrudis, Fr. José María, 40, 208n, 217, 257, 259–60, 270, 273, 281n, 407
Salazar, Fr. Francisco Xavier de, 37n
Salcedo, Juan Manuel de, 470, 507

698　　　　　Index

Salcedo, Manuel María de, 490n, 499, 507–18, 528–37
Salcedo, Nemesio, 474, 484–85, 505, 507; on foreigners, 510, 516, 518; livestock regulations of, 469–70, 473, 480–82, 488–90; in Royalist counterrevolution, 529–35
Sal del Rey, El, 446
Salinas, Juan María, 598
Salinas, Manuel, 387n, 514, 518–19, 531, 564–65
Salinas, Pedro Xavier, 226n
Salitrillo, Arroyo del, 531
Saltillo (Coahuila), 14, 68, 69, 121, 129–33, 139, 167, 178, 198n, 216, 256, 287, 303–305, 332, 342, 356, 359, 361n, 362–63, 469, 508, 523, 545, 555
Sambrano, José Macario, 129n, 163, 164n, 186, 207n, 220, 227, 229–30, 240, 244–46, 257–59, 323, 330n, 334, 342, 349n, 361–62, 385, 387n, 408n, 527
Sambrano, José María, 402n, 528, 531, 564–65, 577–78
Sambrano, Juan Josef, 528n
Sambrano, Juan Manuel (subdeacon), 527–29, 531–32, 539–41, 554, 562, 564–65, 572, 576–77
Sambrano, Pedro, 323, 342, 397
Sambrano, Rev. José Dario, 528
San Agustín de Ahumada, Presidio de (Tex.), 316
San Antonio, Rancho de, 494. *See also* Cerda, Nepomuceno de la
San Antonio Bucareli de la Babia, Presidio de (Coahuila), 266, 317
San Antonio de Agua Dulce, Rancho de, 449
San Antonio de Béxar, Presidio de (Tex.), 130, 197, 458; founding of, 13, 68; Indian affairs at, 56, 66, 117, 125, 155, 173, 181–82, 213–14, 223–24, 279, 296, 369–71, 437, 467–68; livestock disputes around, 14–22, 29, 31, 54, 108–109, 135–46, 152–61, 165–70, 174–80, 217, 231–34, 254, 264–66, 283, 301–308, 317, 322–31, 359–60, 366, 382, 387, 394, 409–10, 417–23, 487–88, 562–67, 576–78, 582; military command at, 55–56, 64, 146, 149–50, 171, 189, 202, 215, 235n, 247, 315–16, 377, 438, 464, 482, 485, 505, 507, 526–28, 533–37, 541, 551–53, 578; missions near, 33–40, 42–44, 349–53, 405–407, 410–14, 510–11, 591. *See also* San Fernando de Béxar, Villa de; soldiers
San Antonio del Cíbolo, Rancho de, 65, 94, 177
San Antonio River: Indian attacks near, 210, 215, 223; land grants along, 38–40, 89–93, 102–105, 238–39, 413–14, 478, 510–11, 576–78; ranching along, 6, 11, 16, 34, 47, 52, 58, 67, 88, 126, 148, 194, 214, 218–19, 305, 325, 514–15, 519–20, 531, 539, 566–67, 590, 609, 614–15
San Antonio Viejo, Rancho de, 549
San Augustine, Tex., 97, 451, 575
San Bartolo, Rancho de, 40, 57, 93, 96n, 163, 165, 185–86, 208, 214, 217, 225, 323, 385, 511, 521, 531, 548, 561; Andrés Hernández and, 60–63, 70, 71; conflict over, 63–65; Indian attacks on, 187, 209–10; livestock at, 219–20, 230–31, 245, 258–58. *See also* Rincón, El
San Bartolomé, Rancho de. *See* San Bartolo, Rancho de
San Bernardo, Misión de (Coahuila), 25, 27, 106, 139, 141, 439
San Bernardo, Bay of, 522
San Bernardo, Rancho de, 495–96
San Carlos, Presidio de (Nuevo Santander), 361
San Casimiro, Arroyo de, 443
Sánches, Joseph, 133
Sánches, Juachín, 29n
Sánches, Juan José, 493, 496–97
Sánches, Manuel, 497
Sánches, Mariano, 497
Sánches, Martín, 29n
Sánchez, Alejandra, 24
Sánchez, Josef de Jesús, 361n
Sánchez, Manuel, 97n
Sánchez, Tomás, 23, 24, 443
Sánchez Navarro, José Miguel, 261

Index

San Cristóbal, Arroyo de, 578
San Cristóbal de Espanta Perros, Rancho de, 230, 385
San Diego, Tex., 615
San Diego River, 263n
Sandies Creek, 95
San Estéban Tombecbe (Tombigbee), 426
San Fernando de Austria, Villa de (Coahuila), 263n, 266, 303, 305, 458n, 505
San Fernando de las Barrancas, Fort (Memphis), 433
San Fernando de Béxar, Villa de (Tex.), 90, 125, 130, 202, 223–25, 295–96, 385, 474–76, 487–89, 511–16; disputes at, 14–21, 73, 99–105, 107–109, 115, 135–46, 165–71, 184–85, 231–34, 248–49, 261–63, 283, 288–89, 310–11, 317–18, 341–43, 354–55, 359–60, 366, 372, 397–402; founding of, 13–15; revolutionary disturbances at, 525–46, 553–76; visits to, 75–77, 89–94, 146–60. *See also* *ayuntamiento*; cabildo; San Antonio de Béxar, Presidio de
San Fernando Memorial of 1787, 22n, 70n, 285, 290–91, 333–43, 353–54, 364–66. *See also* livestock taxes
San Francisco, Rancho de, 93, 110, 148, 163, 195, 238–39, 260, 264–65, 288, 302–309, 385; livestock at, 189, 218–20, 230–31, 245; Luis Antonio Menchaca and, 63–65; Vicente Micheli and, 477–78. *See also* Menchaca, Luis Antonio; Rincón, El
San Francisco, Rancho de, 494. *See also* Mora, José María
San Francisco Solano, Misión de (Coahuila), 25
San Gerónimo, Rancho de, 616
San José y San Miguel de Aguayo, Misión de (Tex.), 33, 35, 40, 42, 47, 66, 91, 94, 281n, 283, 321, 323, 382n, 412–13, 419, 484, 510, 546. *See also* Atascoso, Rancho del; missions; San Lucas, Rancho de
San Joseph, Rancho de, 89, 90. *See also* Ramírez de la Piscina, Manuel; Señor

San José, Rancho del
San Juan Bautista, Misión de (Coahuila), 25–31, 45, 99, 100, 106, 457n
San Juan Bautista del Río Grande, Presidio de (Coahuila), 13, 15, 17, 24–31, 56, 133, 214, 266, 339, 384, 569. *See also* Río Grande del Norte, Presidio del
San Juan Capistrano, Corral de, 40, 91
San Juan Capistrano, Misión de (Tex.), 33, 40, 46, 61, 64, 72, 89–91, 94, 101, 104, 106, 113, 145, 239, 323–25, 331, 511. *See also* missions
San Juan de Carricitos, Rancho de, 448
San Lucas, Rancho de, 41, 413, 510. *See also* San José y San Miguel de Aguayo, Misión de
San Luis Potosí, 75, 198, 208n, 353n
San Luis Potosí, Intendencia de: formation of, 468; and Texas stock raising, 267n, 386, 396, 469, 517, 551–52, 555
San Marcos de Neve (settlement at), 473, 506–507
San Marcos River, 184, 309, 330, 373–75, 473, 506, 532, 551, 565, 596
San Miguel, Leandro, 552n
San Miguel de Buena Virtud, Rancho de, 519
San Miguel de los Patrie, Rancho de, 501
San Patricio, Rancho de, 451, 495. *See also* Barr, William
San Patricio, Tex., 506
San Patricio County, 615
San Pedro, Arroyo de, 16
San Pedro, Rancho de, 519
San Rafael de Pataguiya, Rancho de, 91, 116, 148, 375, 385, 548; Erasmo Seguín and, 62n; livestock at, 218–20, 228, 230, 245; partition of, 69n; Simón de Arocha and, 71, 237–39. *See also* Arocha, Simón de; Pataguilla, Laguna de; Rincón, El
San Rodrigo River, 139
San Sabá, Presidio de (Tex.), 107, 108, 369, 439
San Salvador del Tule, Rancho de, 446–47
San Simón del Capote, Rancho de, 89, 90, 215, 357
Santa, José de la, 224n, 372n, 397n, 403n
Santa Ana, Manuel de, 27, 29n

Santa Anita, Rancho de, 447
Santa Anna, Antonio López de. *See* López de Santa Anna, Antonio
Santa Clara, Arroyo de, 40, 219
Santa Clara (Calif.), 82
Santa Cruz, Mariano, 496
Santa Cruz, Rancho de la, 447
Santa Cruz, Saragoza de, 498
Santa Fe Expedition of 1841, 464, 604–605
Santa Fe Trail, 594, 604
Santa Gertrudis, Rancho de, 416, 595
Santa Margarita Crossing, 506, 519n
Santa María de Adelaida, Rancho de, 440. *See also* Hormigas, Rancho de las
Santa Petronilla, Rancho de, 98, 99, 108, 416, 443
Santa Rita, Rancho de (near Nacogdoches), 498. *See also* Caro, José
Santa Rita, Rancho de (on Rio Grande), 506, 551. *See also* Portilla, Felipe Roque de la
Santa Rosa María del Sacramento, Presidio de (Coahuila), 27, 180, 216n, 266, 277, 304
Santa Rosa, Valley of, 216n, 263n, 266, 346
Santo Domingo, Arroyo de, 578
Santo Domingo, Rancho de, 183, 497
Santoja, José, 267, 378
Santos, Antonio de los, 561
Santos, Francisco de los, 127n
Santos, Gertrudis de los, 455–59, 501
Santos, Joaquín de los, 179
Santos, José Guadalupe de los, 578, 581
Santos, Joseph de Jesús de los, 457
Santos, María de los, 561
Santos, María Antonia de los, 500
Santos, Pedro de los, 133
Santos, Tadeo, 265
Santos Coy, Francisco de los, 493, 496–97
Santos Coy, José de los, 493, 497
Santos Coy, Manuel de los, 497
Santos Coy, Nicolás de los, 444
San Xavier River, 27
San Ygnacio, Rancho de, 24, 62
Sartuche, Ignacio, 575n
Saucedo, José Antonio, 264, 354, 403n, 437n, 512, 528n, 539, 545, 583

Saucedo, María, 68
Schertz-Cibolo, Tex., 325
Scott, Florence Johnson, 444
Seguín, Bartolomé, 154, 372n, 412
Seguín, José Erasmo, 62n, 412–13n, 496, 515, 528n, 541n, 544, 548, 555–56, 567–68, 576–77, 579, 582, 595
Seguín, Juan Nepomuceno, 68, 598–99, 607–608, 615–16
Seguín, Leonidas, 68
Seguín, Mariano, 88n
Seguín, Nicolás, 520
Seguín, Santiago, 167, 169, 245n, 271n, 312, 323, 330n, 342, 356, 372, 412, 491
Seguin, Tex., 41, 68, 184, 210n, 615
señales. *See* branding; ear marks
Señor San Antonio, Rancho del, 457–58. *See also* Leal, Antonio; Tiquitania, Rancho de la
Señor San José, Rancho del, 126, 208n, 379, 550
Shaler, William, 532
Sheridan, Henry, 491
Sierra, Juana María, 477, 497
Sibley, John, 509
Sidick, Anthony, 520
Sidick, John B., 520
Sierra Gorda, Count of. *See* Escandón, José de; Escandón, Manuel de
Silva, Fr. Manuel, 405–408, 416
Sinaloa, Province of, 301
síndicos: role of, 511–19, 531. *See also juez de campo*
Sinfonía, Encinas de la, 94, 95
slavery: of blacks, 120, 186, 428, 430, 435, 453, 476–77, 516, 595, 604–605, 609; of Indians, 77, 521. *See also* mulattoes
Smith, Luther, 451–52
smuggling: efforts to control, 118, 119, 122, 234, 250–51, 450–51; between Texas and Interior Provinces, 362–63; between Texas and Louisiana, 114, 116–23, 183, 190, 204–205, 388–94, 425–26, 438–39, 452–64, 483–84, 490, 493, 503–504, 518, 544, 572–76; views on, 117, 220–21, 251, 508–10. *See also* livestock trade
soldiers: described, 73, 74, 77, 78, 82–84; as poachers, 231–33, 293–94,

307, 342, 378, 381, 404n, 576–77, 582; racial composition of, 13, 130, 189, 358; and smuggling, 266–70, 438–39, 464, 469–71, 480, 482–84, 493, 575; and stockmen, 17, 109, 125, 142–43, 145, 181, 195, 196, 200, 209, 212–14, 219, 223, 229, 248, 276, 368, 384, 407–408, 439, 489–90, 506–507, 549, 565; as stockmen, 13, 16–20, 54–65, 83, 89, 91–94, 97–99, 116, 117, 126, 167, 189, 202, 287–88, 305–306, 392–94, 413, 443–47, 507–508, 539–40, 551, 558–62, 568–70
Solís, Fr. Gaspar José de, 40, 47, 48, 59, 88–97, 290
Solms-Braunfels, Carl (Prince of), 611
Sonora, Province of, 259, 301, 314, 392
Soto, Marcelo de, 516, 518. *See also* St. Denis, Louis Juchereau de; Bermúdez y de Soto, Antonio Manuel
Soto, Silvestre Joaquín de, 372n
South Carolina: and Texas ranching, 436n, 437n, 590, 593–94, 612–13
Stephenson's Ferry, 575
Sterne, Adolphus, 590
Stocman (Esctozman), Frederico, 590
strays: defined, 9, 10, 75, 96, 184, 191, 336–41; quarrels over, in Louisiana, 428, 430–35; quarrels over, in Texas, 16–20, 25–31, 55, 126–28, 138, 141–46, 152–54, 165–71, 174–80, 197–200, 231–34, 254–55, 266–70, 280–86, 290–95, 298–300, 302–309, 313, 317–18, 326–30, 346–48, 366–69, 381, 479–80, 532, 544, 576–78, 580–82, 592, 595–96, 599–601; regulations concerning, 155–57, 161–62, 178, 200–201, 204, 226, 228, 241–44, 252–53, 259–60, 272–74, 323–25, 344–46, 365, 383–84, 409–10, 417–23, 568–69, 511–14, 559–61, 565–68, 579–80, 583, 597–98, 601n. *See also* roundups; rustling
Sutherland Springs, Tex., 40, 413n
Symes, Richard, 441n, 501

Tabares, Antonio, 23
Tajillo, Arroyo del, 206
tallies, lists of, 220, 230, 245, 259, 350.
See also branding
Tamaulipas, 52, 55. *See also* Nuevo Santander, Province of
Tamiques, 144, 168
Taovayas, 21, 134, 263, 279. *See also* Nations of the North
Tarín, Vizente, 490
Tawakoni Crossing (on Cibolo Creek), 109
Tawakonis, 21, 195, 439, 456, 467n, 472. *See also* Nations of the North
Taylor, Creed, 606–607
Taylor, Paul S., 608–609
Taylor, Virginia H., 239, 441
Tejas, 75, 472
Tenerife (Canary Islands), 216
Tepalcate, Arroyo del, 358–59
Terán, Manuel Mier y. *See* Mier y Terán, Manuel
Terán de los Ríos, Domingo, 54
Terreros, Fr. Alonzo Giraldo de, 27, 29
Tessier, José, 502
Tessier, Pedro, 502
Tetillas, Las, 110, 165, 168, 170, 178, 206, 219, 228, 330
Texas, General Land Office of, 60, 238n, 239, 407, 441, 476, 493–96, 500
Texas, Republic of, 71, 478, 496, 520, 545, 600, 603–606
Texas, Supreme Court of, 608, 616
Texas Almanac, 601
Texas Revolution, 53, 68, 76, 496, 571, 592, 597–99, 600, 607, 616–17
Texas Stock Directory, 614–15
Thonhoff, Robert H., 95, 97, 147, 196, 202n, 304n, 385
Tienda de Cuervo, José, 23, 443
tierras realengas (royal lands): acquisition of, 373–74, 448–49; defined, 60, 127, 340, 419; livestock in, 156, 160, 178, 234, 240, 242–43, 258, 281–82, 285, 307–308, 335, 398. *See also* land grants
Tijerina, Andrew A., 609
Tío Gerónimo, Paso de (on Guadalupe), 210n, 223. *See also* Flores, Gerónimo; San Gerónimo, Rancho de
Tiquitania, Rancho de la, 458n, 500–501. *See also* Señor San Antonio, Rancho del
tithes, 25n, 67, 163, 177n, 196n, 205,

218, 227–28, 261–62, 305, 307–308, 310, 355–56, 363–64, 382, 386, 401–403, 447
Tivoli, Tex., 325, 407
Toledo, José Álvarez, 555
Tombigbee River, 426, 429–30
Tonkawas, 21, 196, 244, 246, 439, 467n, 472, 499. *See also* Nations of the North
Tordillo, Arroyo del, 577
Toro, Joseph Antonio del, 140
Tortuga, Rancho de la, 493, 498. *See also* Flores, José
Tovar, Francisco, 126, 163
trail driving: to frontier presidios, 44, 127, 131, 138–39, 176–80, 205–207, 215–17, 226–29, 240–41, 264–71, 301, 303–305, 308–13, 333, 357–58, 361–63, 371, 402–403, 410; to Louisiana, 5, 192–98, 204, 208–11, 236–37, 250–52, 260, 287–88, 293, 314–15, 354, 580–81, 606–607n. *See also* livestock trade; smuggling
Trammell, Gerrard, 571
Trammell, Nicholas, 571–76
Trammell, Philip, 571
Trammell's Trace, 572–76
Travis, William B., 616
Travieso, Francisca Álvarez, 169
Travieso, Francisco Álvarez, 167, 226n, 245n, 249, 326, 330n, 342, 489, 526–27, 532
Travieso, Juan Andrés Álvarez, 101, 105, 128n, 167, 169, 174–75, 178n, 207n, 216, 224n, 226n, 245n, 342
Travieso, Juan Nepomuceno Álvarez, 133–35, 136n, 139–41, 144, 186, 234
Travieso, Tomás Álvarez, 71n, 131–33, 164, 178n, 200–201, 209, 219, 226n, 229, 231–35, 238, 245n, 249, 385, 387n, 545
Travieso, Vicente Álvarez, 65, 69–71, 93, 101–105, 128n, 131, 133, 141–43, 150, 164n, 167, 169, 178n, 185–88, 248, 332. *See also* Mulas, Rancho de las
Travieso, Vicente Álvarez (grandson), 514–15, 525, 541n, 543, 545, 553
Tres Llanos, Rancho de los, 97, 556
Treviño, Antonio, 268–69, 333
Treviño, Francisco, 531

Trinidad de Salcedo (settlement at), 473, 477, 489, 491, 506–507, 515–16, 532
Trinity River, 97, 115, 116, 120, 129, 177n, 181, 192, 251, 455–58, 473, 477, 484, 489, 503, 516, 532, 537–38, 554, 575n
Tulillo, Arroyo del, 237, 330
Twohig, John, 478

Ugalde, Juan de (commandant general), 301, 365, 369–72, 377, 378n, 379, 389, 508
Ugarte, José Joaquín de, 472–74, 479–80, 483–84, 489–90, 502
Ugarte y Loyola, Jacobo de (commandant general), 301, 310, 344–48, 369, 377, 380–81n
Unionville, Tex., 575
Unzaga y Amézaga, Luis de (governor of Louisiana), 121, 122
Uranga, Francisco Xavier de, 438, 469–71
Ureña, Mariano, 330n
Urrutia, Joaquín de, 71
Urrutia, Joseph de, 16, 55–57, 63, 66, 189n
Urrutia, Juan Antonio de, 484
Urrutia, Manuel de, 57, 189, 232–33
Urrutia, Toribio de, 20, 40, 41n, 56, 57, 64, 70, 189n
Uvalde Canyon, 370

Valcárcel, Domingo, 25–27, 339n
Valdés, Marcelo, 209, 223, 227, 229n
Valdés, Rev. Gavino, 510
Váldez, Rev. José Antonio, 520
Valentine, Andrés, 440
Valero, Misión de San Antonio de (Tex.): founding of, 11, 25, 33; land grant of, 38, 101, 144–45, 152, 208; ranching at, 34–40, 45, 90, 94, 113, 143, 146, 195, 217–20, 230–31, 245, 264, 273, 288, 290, 323–25, 331, 349–53; secularization of, 184–85, 287n, 406–407, 411–13n, 475, 511, 564n, 576. *See also* missions; Mora, Rancho de la
Valle, Dionisio, 482, 499
Vallejo, Fr. Bernardino, 440, 484, 546
Vallesillo, Rancho de, 97, 556

Index 703

Valtemore, David, 590
Valverde, Fr. Asisclos, 104–106
Vancouver, George, 82
vaqueros: casualties among, 153, 187, 209–11, 215, 224, 374, 466, 470, 549–50; described, 73–78, 138–45, 167, 196–201, 204, 213, 216, 231–34, 249–50, 258, 270, 305–309, 315, 330, 347–50, 361–62, 429, 444, 457, 471, 480, 508, 512–16, 521–22, 544, 595, 602; and Indians, 34, 56, 62, 88, 145, 148, 219, 223–27, 263–65, 386, 437, 480, 546–49; Indians as, 5, 57, 348, 350n, 353, 423, 603–604, 606; influence of, on Anglo cowmen, 5, 75n, 80, 81, 463, 503, 585–617; mission Indians as, 18, 29, 34–35, 41–49, 58, 101, 144–46, 169–70, 248, 257, 268–69, 281–82, 291–94, 348, 350, 407–408, 411–12, 415–16, 419; shortage of, 43, 76. *See also* labor
Varela, Mariano, 505–506, 552n
Vasconcelos, Fr. Mariano Antonio, 352, 385
Vásquez, Antonio, 577
Vásquez, Francisco, 267–69
Vásquez, José Encarnación, 578
Vásquez, Manuel, 519
Vásquez Borrego, Anastacio, 543
Vásquez Borrego, José, 23–27, 443, 542
Vásquez Borrego, José Fernando, 24, 542
Vásquez Borrego, Juan José, 24, 542
Vásquez Borrego, Macario, 542–43
Veracruz (city of), 65, 121, 198n, 247, 280, 508
Veramendi, Juan Martín de, 515, 528, 541n, 543, 555–56, 565n, 576
Verazadi, Manuel Gaspar de, 392
Verger, Rafael José, 261–62, 291, 295, 310, 335n, 356, 363–64
Vernam, Glenn R., 75n, 612
Viana, Francisco, 498
Viciente, Miguel, 501
Victoria, Tex., 57, 325, 599
Vidal de García y Villena, Melchor, 361
Vidaurri, Juan Antonio de, 27
Vidaurri, José Fernando de, 24
Vidaurri, José Marjil de, 542–43, 549
Viejo, Rancho, 34, 47, 58

Villalpando, Francisco, 493, 499
Villarreal, Enrique, 550
Villarreal, María Petra, 478
Villaseñor, Ignacio, 515, 565n
Villegra, Fr. Manuel de, 323, 326

Wacos, 439
Walker Ranch, 331
Wallace, James, 440
Washington, Villeta de (Ark.), 574
Webb, Walter Prescott, 3, 4, 589, 593, 610
Weber, David J., 604
Wellman, Paul I., 612
West Florida, Province of, 430–31, 452, 481
Whitaker, Arthur P., 460–61, 586–87
White, James Taylor, 236, 590
Wichitas, 21, 279
Wilkinson, James, 456
Willacy County, 448
Wilson County, 59, 64, 68, 71, 73n, 88n, 218–19, 325, 614–15
Wister, Owen, 612
women: as ranchers, 72, 87, 93, 144, 385, 408, 419, 477, 521; in Royalist counter-revolution, 537, 544–45; in Spanish society, 132, 133–34, 140, 149, 186n, 225, 359–60, 455–59, 477, 481, 486–88
Wooten, Dudley G., 598
Workman, William, 605
Wortham, Louis J., 583, 593

Ximénes, Diego, 29n
Ximénez, Alberto, 196
Ximénez, Melchor, 166

Ybarbo family. *See* Gil Ybarbo
Yermo, Francisco de, 205–207, 227, 266–68
Yndios, Arroyo de los, 237
Yorktown, Tex., 611
Ysurieta, Juan de, 129, 204–205, 215, 250, 355
Yturri, José, 565
Yturri Castillo, Manuel, 576

Zacatecas, Colegio de Nuestra Señora de Guadalupe de, 33, 43, 90n, 104, 106,

112, 113, 247, 266n, 280, 291, 295, 299, 379, 385, 406, 408, 412, 414, 416n. *See also* missions
Zapata County, 24
Zepeda, Marcos de, 127n, 215, 224n, 225, 245n, 372–73, 397

Zerda, Francisco de la, 226n, 305. *See also* Cerda
Zerda, Martínez de la, 105n
Zerda, Salas de la, 127n
Zúñiga, Santiago de, 359–60

www.ingramcontent.com/pod-product-compliance
Lightning Source LLC
Chambersburg PA
CBHW030256080526
44584CB00012B/343